Rebuilding a House Divided

Rebuilding

A Memoir
by the Architect
of Germany's
Reunification

Hans-Dietrich Genscher

a House

Divided

Translated from the German by Thomas Thornton

BROADWAY BOOKS

NEW YORK

BROADWAY

Editing by Agnes Krup
Cotranslated and edited by Ruth Hein

Library of Congress Cataloging-in-Publication Data

Genscher, Hans-Dietrich.
Rebuilding a house divided: a memoir by the architect of Germany's reunification / Hans-Dietrich Genscher.—1st ed.
    p.   cm.
Includes index.
ISBN 0-553-06712-5
1. Genscher, Hans-Dietrich.   2. Foreign ministers—Germany—Biography.
3. Germany—Foreign relations—1945–   4. German reunification question (1949–1990)
5. Germany (West)—Politics and government.   I. Title.
DD260.65.G47A3   1997
943.086—dc21   97-11772
CIP

FIRST EDITION

Designed by Paul Randall Mize

Photo-editing and research, Monica Suder.

All photos are copyright by Helmut R. Schulze, except the following (page numbers refer to insert page numbers): *page 1 (top):* Courtesy Hans-Dietrich Genscher/Siedler Verlag; *page 2 (top):* Bild/Rhowedder (Siedler print); *page 2 (bottom):* Bild/Rohwedder (print courtesy Siedler Verlag); *page 3 (top):* Bundesbildstelle, Bonn; *page 4 (top):* Bundesbildstelle, Bonn; *page 8 (bottom):* Bundesbildstelle, Bonn; *page 10 (bottom):* dpa/Athenstaedt; *page 12 (bottom):* World Wide Photos; *page 13 (top):* Dieter Bauer/Stern; *page 14 (top):* dpa; *page 14 (bottom):* Ullstein Bilderdienst; *page 15 (bottom):* dpa; *page 16 (top):* Beitlich/Bild.

98 99 00 01 02 10 9 8 7 6 5 4 3 2 1

For my parents,
Kurt Genscher and Hilda Genscher, née Kreime

Contents

Contents

Prelude

This is not a work of history, nor is it an attempt to describe and explain every aspect of eighteen years of German foreign policy. Not enough time has passed to undertake such an assessment.

In writing this book I have retraced my life's road. I have lingered over instances that at first appeared to be merely fleeting moments but that, in hindsight, turned out to mark milestones or even forks in the road.

The most important milestone is and always will be—as I realized even at the time—May 8, 1945. What I personally experienced as the gift of a new life with the end of the war proved to be for Germany the beginning of a new era, one that does not let us forget the years before that fateful moment.

My memory recalls many events as much more simple and less problematic than they actually were. What had been annoying pales in retrospect, old wounds have long since healed. In looking back, reading what I have written, and reliving it once more, much that I thought I had forgotten came back to life. Many a bitter experience hurt me more deeply in retrospect than when it first occurred.

In looking back—but at no point and at no time in anger—all events are bathed in a softer light. This phenomenon is good, for it preserves us from cynicism. We should look on this softening as a gift. I myself have never run the danger of bitterness. From the bottom of my heart I am grateful for what life has given me—

personally and professionally. Discontent was never in my vocabulary, envy and resentment are emotions with which I have never been familiar, and I have never quarreled with my fate, not even when, during my twenties, I was compelled to spend three and a half years in hospitals and sanatoriums, never knowing whether the expectations I had for my life would be fulfilled.

During my life I have encountered many people—great, impressive figures, human beings whose modesty and the matter-of-fact way they traveled through life, deeply impressed me. I have found good and loyal friends. That politics is a necessary evil, as so many claim, is not something I can confirm—quite the contrary. In this sphere especially I have met with dependability and loyalty, decency and humaneness. Politicians are used to unfair treatment and criticism; in their unique case, however, what happens to them, the good as well as the bad, occurs in public. But that is a situation everyone knows about beforehand, and no one is forced to enter politics.

Surely there will be people who have heard me use expletives when this or that did not go the way I wanted. Swearing could be a way of ridding myself of anger. But no one has ever heard me complain about the burdens of my office and my responsibilities. I chose my career, and therefore I gave everything I had to the tasks I took on in my long life as a politician—frequently to the limit, and beyond, of what seemed possible.

The only pain I feel in looking back is the realization that I judged and at times even treated others unfairly. Aware of this flaw, I never took personnel decisions lightly.

I have always considered it my generation's responsibility to prevent a repetition of the events of the period 1933–1945 in Germany, committed by Germans. That task will go on in perpetuity. We must prevent even a relapse into a new nationalism, since it would contain the seeds of every aspect of pathology: condescension and intolerance, contempt for human dignity, xenophobia, and self-centered nationalism at the expense of others.

Only those who assume responsibility for the future accept responsibility for the past. This dimension of responsibility tells us whether we have learned the lessons of the past. That circumstance holds true in every respect: in protecting human dignity, in preserving peace, in safeguarding the basic and natural necessities of life, and in upholding social justice. In other words, taking responsibility is necessary if we want to ensure that in the future humankind—in increasing numbers—can live lives of dignity. Such lives must do justice to each individual's inviolable and inalienable human rights, as Article 1 of our Basic Law dictates.

I have never for one moment doubted that the saying "Political liberalism is the most comprehensive alternative to any form of oppression" has shown us, and still points in, the right direction. I am grateful to all those I have encountered in my life who in many ways—including as critics and opponents—have helped my life run the course it has. I also want to thank all those who helped me with this book, by advice and deed and by remembering along with me, by proofreading and editing. It is a thank you to old comrades in battle as well as to my former and present colleagues.

I feel deeply grateful to have been allowed to contribute to the unification of Germany and to the formation of a new Europe. Why that was so important to me, how I viewed this task, and how I faced it—these elements have determined the content and boundaries of these memoirs.

—H. D. GENSCHER

In Place of
an Introduction:
The Circle Closes

The hours I spent in the German embassy in Prague on September 30, 1989, remain among the most moving of my life. As early as the fall of 1988 in New York I had told Soviet foreign minister Eduard Shevardnadze that I was expecting protest demonstrations to take place in East Germany the following summer unless some reforms were instituted. The ongoing collapse of the Communist political and social order could not be denied, and this development would not stop at the borders of East Germany. On the contrary: It had been accelerating dramatically since early 1989. On May 2, 1989, Hungary began reducing its forces at the Austrian border; this withdrawal made a chink in the Iron Curtain at a crucial location. On June 27, 1989, the foreign ministers of Hungary and Austria, Gyula Horn and Alois Mock, cut through the barbed wire that separated Western and Eastern Europe—a historic event, whose significance was probably recognized by only a few. Along with Czechoslovakia, Hungary was the East Germans' favorite vacation spot. From now on they could freely leave from there to the West, which had previously been barred.

Rebuilding a House Divided

A few months earlier, on January 18, 1989, speaking at the CSCE (Conference on Security and Cooperation in Europe) follow-up conference in Vienna, I had said:

> The Helsinki Final Act encourages the forces that are now pushing for fundamental reforms in several countries. . . . What has happened to peaceful demonstrators in Leipzig and Prague in the last few days must not happen again. . . . [The common house of Europe] must be a house with open doors and windows, in which human rights and human dignity are respected, in which everyone can live without fear. It is a historic fact: even decades of separation, even years of Cold War have not turned one Europe into two, and one German nation into two. Everything that is trying to maintain an artificial separation is increasingly becoming anachronistic—the Wall in Berlin is such a relic. Let us seize the opportunity to fundamentally change the situation in Europe, let us resolutely continue on this road, the European road of peace. . . . When Europe finds itself again, all Europeans will find one another. As it is written in the Letter on German Unity, the Federal Republic of Germany will continue to work toward a state of peace in Europe in which the German people will regain its unity in free self-determination.

As I did every year, in August 1989 I prepared to attend the opening session of the United Nations General Assembly in New York. It was at this time that the situation at the German embassy in Prague became critical. In July about one hundred East Germans had sought refuge in this embassy; in August another 150 joined them. Wolfgang Vogel and Gregor Gysi, two lawyers from East Berlin, were sent to Prague to persuade the refugees to go home; the attorneys assured the dissidents that they would be allowed to leave the country within six months after returning to East Germany. Vogel and Gysi had to go back to East Berlin without having succeeded in their plea.

In the meantime the flood of refugees could no longer be contained. All members of the embassy were busy day and night. Hermann Huber, the West German ambassador, as well as his wife and his entire staff made a superhuman effort, but the regular routines by which refugees were processed were no longer sufficient. We sent more and more members of the Foreign Office and from other embassies into the Czech capital, where they were put up in hotels. The authorities tolerated this process, even though the Central Committee of the Communist Party was still in office. Evidently there was some uncertainty among the party leadership. At the same time the situation of the East German refugees worsened from day to day. More and more East Germans were seeking asylum, and this flood increased even more dramatically after September 11, when the Hungarian government officially opened the border to Austria for all East Germans who wanted to leave the country. By mid-September another 250 refugees had thronged the embassy, and by the end of the month there would be over six thousand more.

On Saturday, September 23, I traveled to New York for the UN General Assembly. I was accompanied by a team of doctors completely equipped in case I suffered a heart attack above the Atlantic. Since I had had a first heart attack on July 20, 1989, the danger of a second one could not be ruled out; they were therefore prepared to perform any necessary intervention on the plane. In the hotel, too, the doctors were put in rooms immediately next to the suite my wife and I occupied.

I addressed the General Assembly on the morning of September 27, 1989. My speech contained a passage about Germany's eastern border, a section I had revised repeatedly on the plane to New York. Given what was happening in East Germany and the other Communist nations, I could not ignore the issue, because if a possibility existed that the Iron Curtain, and therefore the division of Germany, could be eliminated, we needed to state a clear position regarding the eastern border. Both the East and the West would be concerned with the question of the Oder-Neisse Line. If we kept our silence, we would be abdicating to East Germany our role as protector of the western border of Poland. But where would such a course lead? Would it strengthen the division of Germany? Obviously we could not avoid making an unambiguous promise.

Thus, fifty years after the outbreak of the Second World War, I solemnly declared before the world forum, the General Assembly of the United Nations:

> Fifty years ago the Polish people became the victim of a war that was started by Hitler's Germany. It shall know that we Germans will not question its right to live within secure borders, not now or in the future, by making territorial demands. The wheel of history will not

be turned back. We want to work with Poland for a better Europe of the future. The inviolability of borders is the basis for peaceful coexistence in Europe.

This passage was directly addressed to Polish Foreign Minister Krzysztof Skubiszewski who, as I knew, was present in the chamber. The international response to this speech was tremendous—confirming my sense that it was urgently necessary.

After the meeting of the General Assembly, Foreign Minister Shevardnadze had invited us to lunch at the residence of the Soviet ambassador to the United Nations. He expressed appreciation of my speech. Evidently he had understood my message, for I had commented not only on the issue of Germany's eastern border but also on the general stipulations for the two Germanys' rapprochement and probable unification: "In the long run no nation will be able to keep apart from these events," I had said in reference to the reform movement in Eastern Europe.

> Those who are hoping that the reforms will fail will be overtaken by current developments. Nor should anyone in the West underestimate the new possibilities; rather, all should resolutely take advantage of them in the interest of all of Europe. History does not tend to repeat its offers. I am appealing to the nations of Europe not to miss this historic moment. . . . The Federal Republic of Germany views the peaceful European order as a framework for its goal as well, which is contained in the Letter on German Unity—that is to say, for working toward a peace in Europe in which the German people will regain its unity in free self-determination. We want to achieve this goal with total regard to the treaties we have signed. That can happen only with all countries in Europe and not against them. No one in Europe has reason to be afraid of us politically. Our politics is embedded in the fate of the whole Continent. It is a politics for peace in Europe. That, of course, precludes isolated actions.

That was the framework within which we wanted to achieve the goal we had formulated in the Letter on German Unity.

During the course of the conversation I also touched on Shevardnadze's speech to the United Nations of the previous day, in which he had recalled the old coalition of the Second World War and cautioned against the kind of revanchism arising in Germany, which was trying to jeopardize the European postwar order. No one, he had said, may deliberately or involuntarily encourage the forces of revanchism. I had read the speech with great dismay and alarm, for especially at this point we could be hurt by such polemics and all their consequences. After I consulted with my colleagues, I took the bull by the horns.

I began by noting that I wanted to be very frank in responding to his statements of the previous day. The German people had paid close attention, since—considering the quality of our relations—they had believed that such declarations were no longer possible. The Soviet foreign minister replied that his statements had been occasioned by certain elements in the Chancellor's speech at the CDU (Christian Democratic Union) Congress in Bremen, especially the passage on unification. He said that he had deliberately avoided mentioning names in order not to make matters even worse.

I rejected this interpretation of Helmut Kohl's speech in Bremen. I insisted that there were no grounds for such a reading. I also knew the Chancellor's stand on the border issue: He evaluated the situation as I did, and my address earlier that day should have been clear enough. I very firmly spelled out our policies for Shevardnadze: We took seriously the German-Soviet agreement arrived at early in the summer of 1989; it was important not to lose our common gains. In the end Shevardnadze agreed to a joint wording for a press release: We agreed to continue developing relations between the Soviet leadership and the Federal Republic of Germany, and absolute mutual trust was assured.

After this delicate point was settled, I addressed my real concern—the situation in East Germany. I introduced this topic by recalling what I had said in our earlier meetings; I had pointed to the necessity of reform in the GDR (German Democratic Republic) because the causes of the general discontent and reasons for the wave of refugees were not predominantly economic ones. Then I described to the Soviet Foreign Minister the increasingly unbearable conditions in the West German embassy in Prague and the similar predicament in Warsaw. I urgently asked for help in our efforts to solve these problems and in gaining the East German government's permission for these refugees to emigrate.

Shevardnadze, who indicated that he, too, believed that reform in East Germany was necessary, immediately promised to brief General Secretary Mikhail Gorbachev on our conversation. This

5

time he was obviously convinced that my analysis was correct. When, a year earlier—also in New York—I had pointed out to him that unless reforms were introduced, certain events in East Germany would become inevitable, he had expressed grave doubts about my interpretation of the state of affairs. But at that time, too, he had promised to brief Gorbachev.

On the evening of September 27, 1989, I dined with East German Foreign Minister Oskar Fischer at our embassy. Our meetings had become a useful tradition, giving us a chance to discuss general East-West issues, the CSCE process, and current problems. Issues affecting West and East Germany reciprocally were not on our agenda; since the Federal Republic did not consider East Germany a separate nation, the Chancellor's Office handled any such matters. Of course East Germany would have liked nothing better than a discussion between our foreign ministers concerning relations between the Federal Republic and the German Democratic Republic. Such talks would have reinforced the GDR's claim that the two Germanys were foreign nations to each other. However, I consistently addressed humanitarian issues; experience had convinced me that cases discussed on these occasions could be resolved.

I began this meeting by asking Foreign Minister Fischer for a private and confidential conversation. Federal Minister Rudolf Seiters, who was responsible for relations with the GDR, and I had agreed that I would discuss the current situation with Fischer. I therefore described to him the conditions then prevailing in our embassies in Prague and Warsaw, matters in the Czech capital being unquestionably the more serious. Fischer repeatedly nodded his agreement during my presentation; evidently he was well informed on the current situation. I followed up with two suggestions about solving the problem of emigration for the asylum seekers. *First alternative:* We would permit East German officials into our consulate, where they would provide the East Germans who had sought refuge in our embassy with the necessary emigration permits. The refugees would then travel by special West German trains from Prague directly to West Germany; the stamped passports would preserve East Germany's sovereignty. *Second alternative:* Special trains would travel from Prague to West Germany through East German territory; in that case the necessary paperwork could be done on the train.

Just before I presented the alternatives, we had an open, serious exchange. I explained to Fischer that under no circumstances were the East Germans willing to return to their previous homes. "Why couldn't it be done in six hours instead of the typical six months?" I asked, alluding to the second alternative.

My impression was that Fischer realized a solution was essential. That day, by the way, I saw a side of him that was entirely at odds with his behavior when I had first met him about fifteen years earlier. Suddenly I no longer heard the words of a man who merely mouthed the opinions of the Politburo or the Central Committee. Fischer, too, was seeking a way out, and he promised to talk to Erich Honecker immediately upon his return; he could not, he said, conduct this discussion by telephone or letter. In my view, his belief was based not on malice or political blindness, but on the fear that someone—but who?—could argue against this view. Was Fischer certain of Honecker's willingness but worried about other interests? When I asked him when he would return to East Berlin, he replied, "On the weekend." "That's too late," I retorted. He had to act now.

The following morning at nine o'clock I telephoned Fischer. Again I called his attention to the increasingly intolerable situation in the Prague embassy. At my urgent request he finally promised to pass my suggestions on to East Berlin. It was my impression that Oskar Fischer would try to reach a solution by following one of my suggestions.

That same day I spoke personally with Czech Foreign Minister Jaromir Johanes and appealed to him to contribute to a solution. Something had to happen. Johanes agreed only to inform his government of my appeal; he himself, however, did not seem concerned and suggested that the entire matter be worked out between Bonn and East Berlin. His government, he said, had no responsibility for the current situation. "That's not the problem," I replied. The point was to help people. I tried to restrain myself; after all, the Czech government was not interfering with our efforts to supply food, offer medical aid, and send numerous members of the West German Foreign Office to Prague. Though these were routine steps, a few months earlier the situation would have been very different.

Late that night there was a dinner for the G7—the United States, Canada, Great Britain, France, Italy, Japan, and Germany. When I talked about the situation on this occasion as well, James Baker and the French Foreign Minister, Roland Dumas, immediately offered help. The crucial turn of events, however, had apparently resulted from that afternoon's conversation with Shevardnadze in the Soviet Embassy. Through Frank Elbe, a director in the Foreign Office, I had urgently requested a personal meeting. My Soviet colleague had responded promptly, asking me to come immediately. Because meetings with other foreign ministers were already scheduled in my hotel suite for that afternoon, our limousines were not available; Elbe approached a New York squad car. He briefly explained the situation to the policemen, then we got in. With sirens and flashing lights we sped to the Soviet embassy, where this unusual way of arriving understandably created a stir but perhaps also stressed the urgency of the situation.

I explained the whole situation to Shevardnadze with great seriousness. I emphasized that I was asking for help; we needed instant permission for the refugees to leave immediately. We also required safe housing outside the embassy grounds because the number of refugees was increasing by the hour. The Soviet Foreign Minister asked, "Are there children among them? How many?" "Many." "I'll help you." He would speak with Gorbachev as well as the East German and Czech governments, and he expressed the utmost consternation at my description of the situation. This sensitive man was responding as a human being, he did not hide behind an ideology or supposed reasons of state. He probably remembered what I had told him a year earlier at this same location. When I left the embassy, I thanked him. I pressed his right hand between both of mine.

On Friday, September 29, around 5 P.M., when I was just about to leave the hotel to return to Bonn, the telephone rang: A colleague of Foreign Minister Fischer—the GDR's Ambassador Niklas— informed us that the following morning East Germany's permanent representative in Bonn would arrive at the Foreign Office with new instructions. "Mr. Fischer wants Mr. Genscher to know that it is always worthwhile to have a conversation with him." I left word that Fischer was to go not to the Foreign Office, but to the Chancellor's Office, as usual. It was because I especially did not want to blur boundaries during this dramatic phase in East-West German relations that I insisted on proper procedures. The issue here was not one of formal authority but of status. Even before leaving the hotel I briefed the Chancellor and Federal Minister Seiters.

In many respects this week was absolutely symbolic for the changes occurring in Europe and in the world. While I was still struggling to get the East German government's permission for its citizens to leave Prague, Hungary's Foreign Minister Horn presented me with a piece of the barbed wire which had once divided Europe at the Hungarian-Austrian border. I gave this symbol of unity a place of honor in my library, so that I would always be reminded both of the past and of the truth that nothing is impossible—neither the division of Europe nor the peaceful triumph over such a division.

During my conversation with Horn I learned that he had a problem with his return flight to Europe. I invited him to come along in our German army plane, and so I spent the return from New York to Bonn sitting next to the foreign minister of a nation that was still a member of the Warsaw Pact. My colleagues and I openly discussed our plans and concerns for the following day in his presence. We trusted him; he was one of us. He had acted humanely, he had proven that Hungary had firmly set out on a new road.

On the morning of September 30, 1989, we arrived in Bonn. East Germany's permanent representative, Neubauer, explained to Seiters and me in the Chancellor's Office that after weighing the two alternatives I had mentioned, his government had decided in favor of the second one—the passage through East Germany.

I replied, "In the meantime the situation has become even more serious. It is therefore necessary that top West German government officials ride on the trains. Furthermore, I myself will go to Prague, since every observer has noted that the tension has risen to a degree that the refugees are fearful of leaving the embassy. I need to make you understand the situation as it really is. The refugees don't trust you. But I am sure that by giving them some sort of personal guarantee I can persuade them to travel through East Germany. It is going to be important that Herr Seiters and I, as well as top officials, go with the trains as a way of inspiring confidence."

Neubauer returned to his office in Bad Godesberg, telephoned his government, and came back to the Chancellor's Office to give us East Germany's agreement.

The same afternoon Seiters and I flew to Prague. It was important to me that he come along, for the situation was such that I wanted to show the accord between the ruling partner and the coalition partner to the outside world as well. We were accompanied by several top-ranking officials, among them Assistant State Secretary Dieter Kastrup and Frank Elbe from the Foreign Office. Shortly before the plane doors closed, a noncommissioned officer called me to the telephone. I was informed that the situation had changed yet again: Contrary to our agreement of a few hours earlier, East Germany's permanent representative now said that his government did not approve of Seiters and myself traveling on the special trains. As I took in the news, I became extremely worried about our ability to gain the refugees' trust for a journey through East Germany, given the circumstances. There was no question that our presence on the trains would have made things easier. I announced that I would speak with Neubauer again from Prague.

During the flight I thought about what to say to the people gathered at the embassy. This was when I realized that more was at stake than allowing a few thousand East Germans to leave our embassy for the Federal Republic. A historic moment was at hand: East Germany was finished. What was happening was that the GDR was collapsing from the inside and from below; the end of the Wall was becoming a reality. While emigration through Hungary had elicited the East German government's angry protest, the people now at the Prague embassy—only twenty days later—were going to depart with the GDR's consent. The flood of refugees had turned into an avalanche of history. What I had stated over and over again in one speech after another was becoming true: "Even decades of separation cannot turn one people into two."

I also remembered that West Germans at times believed that when we admitted East Germans to our embassies in Central and Eastern Europe, we were unnecessarily interfering with détente. East Germany's demand that we refuse Germans from the GDR entrance into our embassies found willing listeners, but it was a suggestion I had always rejected. We could not let ourselves be turned into agents of the policies of separation; we could not administratively erect another Wall at the gates of our embassies.

In the afternoon I was very formally welcomed at the airport in Prague by the secretary of the Czech Foreign Office. The government thus officially acknowledged our visit. We drove straight to our embassy; outside its gates a huge crowd was anxiously awaiting our arrival. As soon as we entered the building, we could see even from the doorway that the cots were stacked three high. Some of the refugees had to remain lying down because there was not enough standing room for everyone.

Ambassador Huber came with me down the corridor. At first, I realized, no one noticed that the Foreign Minister had arrived. Stepping over sleepers, we went upstairs to the Ambassador's private apartment, where I again telephoned Neubauer to point out to him the possible consequences if Seiters and I were not traveling with the refugees. Neubauer told me that he had no new orders from East Berlin. We would therefore have to try to gain the refugees' confidence in some other way.

We stepped out onto the balcony. "My fellow Germans"—there was an outburst of jubilant cheers. Then I began: "We have come to tell you . . ." Before I could finish the sentence, there was another burst of deafening cheers. Even today, in retrospect, the memory touches me deeply. Then I declared: "The first train is leaving today. I ask that you allow those who are ill and mothers with small children to find seats first." I continued, "I also want to explain the itinerary to you. The trains will cross the border between Czechoslovakia and East Germany."

All at once the atmosphere was fraught with great anxiety. "Please listen carefully," I continued. "The trains will not stop anywhere. You will not have to leave the trains at any time. I know what you are feeling. Many of you are approximately the same age I was when I left East Germany. So I empathize with what you are feeling right now, and I do understand your concerns." Only if these people believed me personally, I felt, could I convince them. "If someone with a history like mine gives you his personal guarantee that the promises are going to be kept, you can believe him." Again there was applause. "Each train will include two of our officials—one from the Chancellor's Office, and one from the Foreign Office. Here they are." I introduced the officials by name. "All of them will be on the trains. You can trust us."

Then I addressed the refugees from my hometown. "Is there anybody here from Halle?" Immediately several people shouted, "Yes, here!" It was an unforgettable moment, for me as well as for those gathered at the embassy. To this day I sometimes run into people who tell me, "We were there that day, in the embassy in Prague!"

The first train heading for East Germany left Prague on the evening of September 30, 1989. The accompanying officials telephoned me the following morning. "You have no idea what we saw," they told me. The demonstrations of camaraderie along the way had been overwhelming. All along the tracks East Germans had waved at them. Quite a few had even hung bedsheets out of their windows.

If anyone had asked me after my conversation with Foreign Minister Fischer in New York which of the two alternatives the East German government would choose, I would have bet on the first one—direct passage into the Federal Republic of Germany. How was it possible that the East German government underestimated the psychological effect of transporting thousands of refugees through the GDR? The outcome was incalculable. Choosing a direct route, such as the one from Hungary to Austria, would hardly have had such serious consequences; now, however, the political avalanche had been set in motion and could not be halted as it rushed through East Germany. The thaw had originated in Prague, the most European of all European cities. But as the stream ran on, it gained force from the people's will to freedom and self-realization. How long I had waited for that moment; how much of my life I had spent struggling for it! For a long time the goal had seemed difficult to reach and far away, then it became a possibility, and finally, in an instant, it was so vivid that I thought I must be dreaming. When I returned from Prague to Bonn, as the foreign minister of the free part of Germany, my thoughts returned to my childhood and youth in Halle: Back then, after the liberation from National Socialism and after the end of the Second World War, what would we have given for the opportunity to start anew together in a united, democratic Germany? Now I was filled with the hope that, more than forty years later, such a possibility would become reality.

Part One

The Early Years as Foreign Minister

1

Stops on the Road to the Foreign Ministry

Crucial Experiences: War and Totalitarianism

I was born on March 21, 1927, in Reideburg near Halle. Both my parents were raised on farms, but my father, Kurt Genscher, attended the university where, at his father's urging, he studied law. In 1933 we moved to Halle, where my father worked as legal advisor to an agricultural organization. In January 1937 he died from the delayed consequences of an injury incurred in the First World War.

I was nine years old at the time, and my father's death was a tremendous blow to me. My memory of him is very vivid; perhaps I inherited my tendency for harmony from him. He was a kind and caring man with artistic inclinations and a rather conservative temperament—shared by almost all members of both sides of my family. As a member of the moderately conservative DNVP (German National People's Party), he was critical of National Socialism. I will never forget what he said over and over again: "Hitler—that means war."

Rebuilding a House Divided

□   □   □   □

All my life I have been proud of Halle, my hometown at the center of Germany, a modern and cosmopolitan industrial metropolis, a cultural center, and a university town. Halle's character was determined both by its educated middle class and its self-confident, highly skilled industrial workers. In the 1930s Halle had a population of 220,000; today that number has risen to approximately 300,000.

I attended secondary school in Halle, and during my first year there, my fifth year of schooling, on Hitler's forty-eighth birthday—April 20, 1937—along with all the boys my age, I was inducted into the Jungvolk (Young Folk). Boys were members of the Jungvolk from ages ten to fourteen, at which time they joined the Hitler Youth.

On February 15, 1943, I was drafted into the antiaircraft service of the air force as a helper, as we were called. This was a great shock to my mother. When war had broken out in 1939—I was twelve years old—she had said, "Thank God you won't have to go. No war lasts that long."

Drafting those born in 1926 and 1927 into the antiaircraft service was a response to the reverses at Stalingrad and the annihilation of the Sixth Army in January 1943. A new Sixth Army was assembled by taking soldiers from units stationed in the Reich. The troops that were taken from the antiaircraft batteries were replaced by us.

We still "went to school" three times a week, five hours each day. Our teachers came from Halle to the antiaircraft installation. One class was taught in the mess hall and another in the village pub. If there had been an air-raid alarm the previous night, we were allowed to sleep late and school was canceled; the success of our teachers' educational endeavors was limited.

Antiaircraft auxiliaries lived in barracks. I was assigned to a radar unit. We were the first ones to know when and from which direction planes were approaching; air defense in this highly industrialized area was very tight.

We learned of the July 20, 1944, assassination attempt on Hitler from the radio. That night I was sitting on my bunk with my friend Friedrich Kräger, my ear pressed to the small speaker to learn more details from Radio London (a station which was offi-

16

cially prohibited). We were hoping for the success of the revolt. Today, more than fifty years later, it is hard to imagine that young people were on the one hand doing their duty as "air-force helpers," while on the other hoping for the abolition of the National Socialist government. Many soldiers in the German armed forces experienced the same conflict. Our feeling was: This government is not our government, but Germany is our fatherland. There was not one among my friends in the antiaircraft service whom I would have called a devout National Socialist, and many were—as we called it then—"in opposition." Hardly anyone believed in the "ultimate victory," which was so fervently invoked by the political propaganda.

In the fall of 1944 we were discharged from the air force so that we could undergo basic training for the army proper. In camp we made few bones about our political beliefs, and we talked openly about the senselessness of the war. One night a fellow soldier with whom I happened to be on barracks duty approached me. We called him Stalin because of his crewcut. We liked each other, and so he said, "I get the feeling you're in opposition, too."

"Sure. And you?"

"You guys don't know what an honor it is for me when you call me Stalin. I'm a Communist."

I blurted out, "But that's no better."

"You have no idea," he replied. "That's so typical. My father was trained in the Soviet Union in the twenties. The Soviet Union means the future. Here everything will come to an end soon. I volunteered for the army. When the time comes, I'm going to desert to the Russians." He had a very clear concept of the future he was looking for, and I too was hoping for a quick end of the war and a new beginning.

"And how do you think matters will turn out here if you don't think much of the Soviet Union?" Stalin asked me.

I replied, "Something like England and the United States." In my mind these two nations represented democracy.

Many years later, reading the newspaper, I came across the name of an applicant for membership in the Politburo, the executive committee of the SED (Socialist Unity Party) in East Germany: Dr. Werner Jarowinsky; it was "Stalin." Subsequently he became a full member of the Politburo. We had met as youngsters during a difficult period. In 1944 we were in agreement in rejecting the Third Reich, but our ideas about the future were diametrically opposed. Each of us pursued the road on which he had set out—Jarowinsky as a Communist in the German Democratic Republic and I, a political liberal who wanted to see Germany become a democracy modeled on the Anglo-Saxon system, in the Federal Republic of Germany.

I joined the regular army on January 6, 1945, and was assigned to an engineering unit in Wittenberg.

We were made to drag heavy steel pontoons and build makeshift bridges across the Elbe. It was during that time, in February 1945, that the air raids on Dresden occurred. Some of the men in our barracks were from Dresden. After the firebombing they were given two days' compassionate leave, from which they returned utterly changed. What they told us about their families, the destruction of Dresden, and the number of dead was a heavy burden—on us as well as on them.

During that time, too, endless streams of refugees from Silesia fled across the Elbe Bridge. Horse-drawn wagons carried older men, women, and children. The miseries of war, which had first struck the Germans in the form of air raids, were now also causing the loss of their homeland, flight, and expulsion. Anxiously, silently, and very sadly we watched the wagons pass. I could not know that around the same time my future wife, Barbara, her mother, and her fifteen-year-old brother were also traveling by horse-drawn wagon from Lower Silesia to Saxony.

We were sent to join the Twelfth Army under General Walter Wenck, which in the spring of 1945 was preparing to march on Berlin. Since the Soviets had launched their Oder offensive on April 16, the situation at the eastern front had drastically worsened; by now Berlin was almost entirely encircled. Because Hitler had chosen to remain in the capital instead of retreating southward, the troops directed against the American forces were recalled so that the units gained in this manner—among them the Twelfth Army—could be used for the defense of Berlin.

My unit began by marching along the Elbe on a reconnaissance mission, to determine whether the Americans, who were approaching from the west, had already reached the river. In one village we came under artillery fire. I was marching next to an older soldier, who foolishly was not wearing his steel helmet. He took a bullet to the head—the first soldier I saw die in action.

At that time the Ninth Army, under General Theodor Busse, was already encircled by the advancing Red Army near Frankfurt-on-the-Oder. General Busse tried to bring his remaining units through to the Twelfth Army. Many of his men were injured.

Those dramatic days taught me a lesson in what today would be called leadership skills. Our unit, which stood south of Berlin, was ordered to form a circle. General Wenck himself had arrived. He addressed us: "Men, I promise to lead you across the Elbe into American captivity. You will not become Soviet prisoners of war, but you must hold out here for three more days. Our comrades from the Ninth Army are trying to get through to us from the area of Frankfurt-on-the-Oder. There are many casualties among them as well as nurses and women auxiliaries serving in communications. We have to take them with us—we owe it to them."

Our unit was the first one to make contact with the Ninth Army. Everyone was on foot, there were no vehicles. The injured were carried by Russian prisoners of war, nurses walking beside them, thousands in a seemingly endless column. They had been able to march only at night, since Soviet planes kept up their merciless bombardment all day long. As long as it was daylight, therefore, they hid in the forests. After they joined us, we continued our westward march.

Another occurrence was characteristic of Wenck's way of thinking and his attitude: his Order of the Day on the occasion of Hitler's death on April 30, 1945. To understand its significance, it is important to remember that after the failed assassination attempt on Hitler on July 20, 1944, the Hitler salute was made mandatory for the army. This regulation, which until then had applied only to the Waffen-SS (armed SS) while all other units had employed the customary military salute, was intended to humiliate the armed forces, since top-ranking officers were among the would-be assassins. Wenck's Order of the Day on April 30 read: "To all members of the Twelfth Army! The Führer is dead. As of today the official military salute will again consist of placing your right hand against your cap. Wenck, General of the Tank Corps." Many years later, when I met Wenck at a dinner party, I told him, "In two sentences you said more than countless editorial writers ever manage to express."

During this time the soldiers in our unit had only one goal: to survive. We were also concerned about our families and what was happening to them. The officers were no longer exhorting us to hold out; nor would such orders have been obeyed. We were terrified of falling into Soviet hands. Later we learned how well-founded our fears had been.

Wenck had planned ahead. We reached the eastern bank of the Elbe on May 5, two days before the German surrender. When I spent one night in a barn in Schönhausen, Bismarck's native village, I was still ignorant of the painful symbolism of such places. It would be almost fifty years before we Germans could again live as one nation, and a long stretch of the Elbe would mark the border between the two parts of Germany.

A footbridge had been built across the ruins of the Elbe bridges, which the Americans opened every day from 8 A.M. to 6 P.M. During these hours the remnants of the Ninth and Twelfth Armies, tens of thousands of men, could cross the river, a process that took three days in all. I crossed the makeshift bridge in the late afternoon of May 7, shortly before the Red Army—pushing on toward the increasingly shrinking German bridgehead from the north, the east, and the south—reached the Elbe at the same spot. While crossing the river, I saw the Americans on the other side, while the Soviet soldiers were 3,000 to 6,000 feet to the east. Thus I was among the few German soldiers who at this moment in history were able to choose. Americans or Soviets—the choice was not difficult. Considering the present situation, it was a weightier decision than we could have realized at the time.

Fate had been kind to me. I had been in actual combat for only a brief period—a circumstance I felt as divine mercy. Nevertheless, the horrors of the war would mark my thinking for the rest of my life. I could never romanticize military life. Often I had felt fear and worry; now, with the war over, I thought, Somehow life will go on. I lived through this. I was just eighteen years old, and when with thousands of my fellow soldiers I became an American prisoner of war, we were thinking of life and of the future.

I was able to return home to Halle as early as July 1945. The city was now in the Soviet zone of occupation. My main concern—and the question that plagued all the young people—was the political future of Germany. We believed that the partition into occupied zones was temporary. We could not imagine that Germany would be cut in two. I vividly recall how startled I was to hear my grandfather in Reideburg say, "My boy, don't deceive yourself, they'll divide Germany up for fifty years." He turned out to be right. I, on the other hand, had high hopes of the Americans; surely they would make their idea of democracy prevail throughout Germany and Europe.

Political life in the Soviet-occupied zone began in the summer of 1945 with the establishment of political parties. The KPD (Communist Party), the SPD (Social Democratic Party), the CDU (Christian Democratic Union), and the LDPD (Liberal Democratic Party of Germany), all ran membership campaigns. I was eager to be politically active, since like most Germans I was determined that what had happened would never happen again. But what was the best way for me to make my contribution? I could not even consider the Communist Party. As for the SPD, I could not accept the idea of socialism. The ideas of the Christian Democrats appealed to me; my parents were Protestants and had raised me in that faith. Politics based on the tenets of Christian responsibility impressed me. But the party was calling for "Christian socialism"—could those terms be reconciled? The doubts I had when I was eighteen were later confirmed again and again.

One day I attended a meeting of the LDPD addressed by Harold W. Esche, the editor in chief of Halle's *Liberaldemokratische Zeitung,* the organ of the LDPD. This mesmerizing speaker won me over with the following sentence: "Liberalism is the most comprehensive alternative to all forms of oppression." That statement persuaded me. And indeed, the LDPD in Halle was the party that used the clearest language against the Communists' claims to power. On January 30, 1946, I joined the Liberal Democratic Party of Germany.

Yet in 1946 it was already becoming clear that true democracy was utterly impossible in the Soviet-occupied zone. The SED, the Socialist Unity Party of Germany, which supported Soviet ideology and which had the Soviet Union's absolute support, increasingly hampered the development of all other parties by resorting to undemocratic means—interrupting meetings, exercising censorship, and invalidating the outcomes of democratically conducted elections. I quickly realized that my hopes for life in a democracy would not be fulfilled. Since, in my opinion, the LDPD adapted too easily to the prevailing state of affairs, my political activities came to a halt before the end of 1946. At the same time I had my first serious outbreak of tuberculosis, a disease that would afflict me repeatedly for long periods of time and force me into extended stays in hospitals and sanatoriums.

On October 15, 1950, I voted for the first time in my life, in the elections for the Volkskammer, the East German parliament. Since the result was predetermined, I invalidated my ballot in this sham election.

I had resumed my schooling as early as December 1945. When I finished my interrupted secondary school education, I began to study law and passed the first state boards on October 5, 1949—two days before the establishment of the German Democratic Republic. About six weeks later my candidacy for the higher civil service was approved. On November 22, 1949, I began a clerkship at the Halle municipal court.

The narrow world we clerks inhabited was marked by countless contradictions. Using commentaries and textbooks—the same ones that were used in West Germany—we drafted opinions in civil cases as well as in criminal proceedings as they pertained to the penal code. At the same time political trials were going on in Halle, as elsewhere in East Germany, but we were carefully kept away from these. The infamous Article Six of the East German constitution, "Boycott Agitation," became grounds for convicting persons who were out of favor. More and more people tried to evade the insecurity under the law and the ideological patronage by fleeing to the West. More and more I came to reject the GDR both as a state and a legal system, and in conversations with others I made no bones about my feelings. I had no wish to hide my political views; such behavior seemed hypocritical. But then, I told myself, I must act accordingly and leave East Germany.

Finally, there were more and more indications that inquiries were being made about me—I had come to the attention of the authorities frequently enough. It was time to act. On August 20, 1952, pretending to set out on a vacation, I and two friends met at the principal railroad station in Halle. In order not to arouse suspicion during passport controls, we traveled in different train cars. Furthermore, I had bought a ticket to Stralsund, a town far beyond Berlin, so that I would remain inconspicuous when tickets were being checked. I had packed my suitcase as if for a vacation. We got off the train in Berlin; in 1952 it was still possible to travel from one sector of the city to another. In Marienfelde, which was part of West Berlin, my friends and I were granted provisional entry and were given the status of political refugees from the GDR.

On October 6 I became a clerk at the court in the northern German seaport of Bremen. My mother had received a letter addressed to me dated September 19, 1952, in which I was informed that, since I had left East Germany, I had been dismissed from the court system. In 1953 my mother also arrived in Bremen, carrying no more than one suitcase.

There was a world of difference between the two German states. I was sorry to leave Halle. Yet I had no other choice if I was to live in a political environment with which I could be at peace. Soon after settling in Bremen I joined the FDP (Free Democratic Party), the Federal Republic's party of political liberals. I wanted to become politically active in the German state I had chosen for my personal future, even though the West Germans' lack of interest in a possible unification disturbed me. As I saw it, they were much too satisfied with themselves and their economic miracle.

Beginning of a Political Career

On September 1, 1954, I was admitted to the West German bar. Unfortunately, another outbreak of tuberculosis forced me to interrupt my career for more than twelve months. Finally, in November 1955, I was able to resume work.

I had never considered a career in politics. But in December I was asked by the local heads of the FDP whether I would be interested in becoming the research director of the FDP caucus in the Bundestag, the West German parliament. Just after my twenty-ninth birthday, I moved to Bonn.

The FDP was and still remains the smallest of the leading West German political parties. Its convictions and goals place it somewhere between the SPD, which is further to the left, and the conservative CDU (Christian Democratic Union) and its sister party CSU (Christian Social Union), which exists only in Bavaria. The FDP is therefore the crucial coalition partner, wooed by both the SPD and the CDU/CSU, since only rarely does one of the larger parties gain an absolute majority of seats in the Bundestag. The relatively small FDP can therefore assert its liberal political positions rather forcefully, but this role also has its dangerous side. What is at issue is the FDP's identity: Does it view itself as an independent party or merely as a vehicle for providing a majority? Repeatedly I stated at party congresses, "First and foremost we are Germany's Liberal party; we are a coalition party only secondarily."

German unity has always been one of the FDP's core issues. No other party in West Germany can boast of a large number of members who had come from East Germany. Many of them had, like myself, made the move from the LDPD to the FDP, and these members were tremendously influential in shaping the party's position on relations between the two Germanys. When it became increasingly clear that the partitioned German states would not be reunited for a long time—and unification was not a priority for the CDU/CSU, which ruled through most of the 1950s and 1960s, nor for the SPD, for that matter—the FDP at least promoted ameliorations in travel within Germany and to and from Berlin. At the same time, under the influence of Walter Scheel, who served as federal president from 1974 to 1979, the FDP became a party of European unity as it was being developed in the European Community. Scheel, from 1958 until 1969 a delegate to the European Parliament, also advocated close cooperation between West Germany and France. The global political outlook changed after the Berlin and Cuba crises: The two superpowers, the United States and the Soviet Union, began to practice détente. We political liberals welcomed any cautious steps in this direction, and we called for diplomatic relations between West Germany and the countries of central and southeastern Europe. At the same time I remained firmly convinced that West Germany's ties with the West were an absolute prerequisite for carrying out effective policies in the East.

In 1965 I was elected for the first time to the Bundestag as an FDP delegate. Now I could give much more time and energy to issues of policies between the two Germanys. After the national elections of October 1969 the SPD and the FDP formed their first coalition. In this administration I held the office of minister of the interior, which included wide responsibilities. I oversaw domestic security as well as environmental issues, sports, culture, and all matters pertaining to government employees.

The Hostage Crisis During the 1972 Olympics in Munich

The most frightful time in my entire tenure as a member of the federal government came with the killing of the Israeli athletes during the attack on the Israeli Olympic team in Munich in 1972. When I became minister of the interior, I also automatically became one of the vice presidents of the organizing committee for the upcoming Olympic Games. Under the chairmanship of Willi Daume, its president, the National Olympic Committee included three governments: the city of Munich, as the host; Bavaria, as the sponsoring state; and the Federal Republic of Germany. Munich was represented by its mayor, Dr. Hans-Jochen Vogel and Bavaria by Dr. Ludwig Huber, the state minister for culture. I represented the republic in my capacity as minister of the interior and therefore also as minister for sports. Cooperation in this organizing committee, whose press relations were handled by Hans Klein, who would become the government spokesman and a federal minister, proved to be excellent; there was no antagonism whatever among the three member bodies. Their staffs worked well together and with great mutual trust, and Willi Daume and the organization's vice presidents also enjoyed a harmonious relationship. I was impressed by Vogel's comprehensive knowledge when presenting all the problems and details that needed to be considered if we were to accomplish our common task. I had no sense of Vogel's pedantic side, so often mentioned in the press. His familiarity with all the details of his job was impressive, and if—and it may certainly have happened—some thought him pedantic, it may have been because they were simply unwilling to tackle the problems of our task as vigorously as Jochen Vogel did. At any rate, I came to appreciate Dr. Vogel then—an admiration continued later in the cabinet and in the Bundestag. He was always thoroughly knowledgable, he was a fair-minded colleague, and I found him a stimulating conversationalist. Dr. Huber's tremendous factual knowledge also impressed me deeply.

If we are to judge the security plans for the Olympic Games, we must understand that the German Constitution gives the individual states jurisdiction over the police. At the time Bavaria also had a municipal police force in its capital of Munich, headed by Police

25

Chief Manfred Schreiber. He was well known throughout Germany as one of the most experienced and prudent police officers. For that reason alone Schreiber—who, after years of successful collaboration, has become a personal friend—was the right man when the organizing committee was looking for someone to head security. As of May 1, 1970, therefore, the committee's head of security and the Munich official responsible for overseeing the police were one and the same. At the same time the Bavarian government created the office of security commissioner, which was conferred on Dr. Heinrich Martin. It was his job to advise, inform, and aid the Bavarian state and municipal police departments that shared the responsibility for the preparation and execution of the Olympics. Manfred Schreiber was given the responsibility of designing a security plan for the Olympics. The organizations at the top—the National Olympics Committee and the International Olympics Committee—wanted the Games to be lighthearted and relaxed. We approved in principle the plan he ultimately submitted to the committee.

Detailed documentation subsequently issued by the federal government and the state of Bavaria, entitled "The Attack on the Israeli Olympic Team," clearly demonstrates that, though the Games were to appear lighthearted and relaxed, stringent security measures were taken. More than two thousand officers from every police department in the country were employed in the security force; they wore the uniform of the organizing service and carried no weapons. In addition to the police in Munich and the district of Upper Bavaria, a significant number of federal and state troops were employed as well: 2 units of the border police, 6 police squads, a helicopter outfit—to be precise, 20 helicopters belonging to the federal border police and 4 belonging to the Bavarian police—for a combined force of 4,905 men. In addition, there were 1,618 security police officers and 973 plainclothesmen, among them 37 officers from the federal department of investigation and 123 officers from the technical service as well as drivers. There were also 24 police officers who served as interpreters.

There were no specific indications that Israeli athletes and institutions were in danger; in any case, the organizing committee was not made aware of any. On August 9, 1972, the Israeli government itself sent a security attaché to police headquarters in Munich, where he inquired about the security measures taken for

Israeli guests of honor and the Olympic team. On that occasion he was given a thorough explanation of the structure and organization of the Olympic Village as well as an explanation of the primary responsibility of the Organizing Committee's security police force. At the time Israel also confirmed that no concrete indications of pending disturbances, let alone assassination plans, existed. In fact, Israel found no fault whatever with our specific arrangements and our overall concept concerning security.

The Olympic Games opened with good cheer and high spirits. Our country showed itself to the world in a way that was impressive in its lightheartedness. The contrast with the Nazi Germany of the 1936 Olympics was pronounced. Then, abruptly, we were jolted out of our high spirits. On September 2, 1972, shortly after six o'clock in the morning, I received a telephone call. There had been an attack on the housing of the Israeli athletes in the Olympic Village, at 31 Connolly Strasse; hostages were taken.

While the Games were going on, my wife and I were staying at the Hotel Conti. I immediately leaped out of bed. I woke up drivers and security guards, dressed, and arrived at the Olympic Village around seven; the security squads were already in place. The Bavarian minister of the interior, Dr. Bruno Merk, arrived soon after me, as did Avery Brundage, President of the International Olympic Committee, and Willi Daume, followed shortly by Dr. Hans-Jochen Vogel. The police immediately assembled a special task force; its responsibilities have been extensively documented in the report jointly issued by the federal, state, and local authorities. At the same time we formed a preliminary emergency staff, consisting of the Bavarian minister of the interior, the representative of the city of Munich, myself as the federal minister of the interior, and the president of the National Olympic Committee. NOC President Daume was in touch with the International Olympic Committee. Police Chief Schreiber was also part of the staff.

My first step was to telephone Chancellor Willy Brandt and Walter Scheel, the foreign minister. Brandt called a cabinet meeting for 11:30; he also authorized me, working cooperatively with the Bavarian government, to do everything necessary to save the hostages. At the same time the top levels of the government tried to effect the release of the hostages through diplomatic channels— by contacting Arab governments.

A high degree of responsibility and seriousness marked the discussions within the Munich task force. To this day I have the greatest respect for this group. At no time did any of those involved try to evade responsibility, not even after we failed to free the hostages. It was a matter of course for me, as federal minister of the interior, to be a fully responsible member of the emergency staff, even though the federal government had no authority over police actions in the case. All I could do, therefore, was to support the agencies of Munich and Bavaria. The coordination of diplomatic activities, on the other hand, was in the hands of Undersecretary von Braun from the foreign office. Brandt and Scheel also became involved in our efforts to free the hostages; Brandt carried on a number of talks with leading figures in the Arab world.

It was important to learn how many Israeli athletes were still alive and how many had died during the attack. One athelete for whom medical assistance had been summoned was dead by the time the doctors got to him. We kept in close touch with the Israeli ambassador, who late that morning had been brought to Munich in an army plane: We made no move without first informing and consulting him, especially since Israel had decidedly more experience in such situations. We also wanted him to tell us how his government was planning to respond to the terrorists' demands that two hundred Palestinians be released from Israeli jails. The ambassador was given a room with a telephone so that he could be in constant touch with his government.

From the very beginning the Israeli government left no doubt about its position: Releasing all, or even some, of the prisoners was out of the question. Around noon the Israeli ambassador announced that an Israeli security officer would be coming to Munich; he was a high-ranking expert, and he was bringing a deputy. They arrived around seven o'clock in the evening. I talked with the officer several times; when I asked if Israel were going to deploy its own forces to liberate the hostages, he assured me that such was not the plan. When we spoke together, he never expressed any criticism of the measures our police detail had planned and begun to put into action.

It had been possible to move very quickly to set aside rooms for the various police and political initiatives and for the Arab representatives to the Olympics. The political crisis team was on tap around the clock. With the approval of the Israeli representative we were trying to gain time: The Israelis shared our experts' opinion that if the ultimatum were to expire without results, the terrorists would kill hostages. By constantly talking with them— initially the talks were conducted by Police Chief Schreiber—we were able to persuade the terrorists to extend the ultimatum several times. It was first pushed back from nine to noon; then, at 11:54, they agreed to wait until 1 P.M. The Palestinians refused another extension. They voiced their suspicions that we were simply trying to buy time so that we might eventually overtake them by surprise. Already, early that morning, they had rescinded a previous written ultimatum handed to the police chief and declared that from then on, there would be only verbal demands: Two hundred Arab political prisoners held in Israel—named individually—were to be released. They further demanded that after this release, whose successful completion was to be reported by an authorized person through the use of a code word in Arabic, they be allowed to leave unmolested, along with the hostages, who would subsequently be released. Finally the police chief no longer saw a chance for extending the ultimatum again; he even feared that two hostages would be killed before the one o'clock deadline.

Simultaneously the federal government engaged in diplomatic approaches, and the police made preparations to use force in freeing the hostages. Bruno Merk, the Bavarian minister of the interior, and I decided to speak directly with the ringleader of the terrorists. At least we were able to effect several further postponements of the ultimatum—first from 1 P.M. to 3, then to 5, to 7, and finally to 9 P.M. We explained that we were in touch with the Israeli government, which was true, and that the German government also needed to make a decision on how to proceed; after all, the Israelis had to check the list of names.

We were hoping to find a way out by playing for time. The ringleader of the terrorists was wearing the white suit that has since become notorious from many photographs of the event. He carried a hand grenade in each breast pocket, the firing pins dangling over the edges. He was holding a third grenade, ready to pull the pin. Though his look was calm, his features expressed firm resolve.

I made every effort to convince him that killing innocent people, who were in no way politically involved, could not be in the interest of the prisoners in Israel. I appealed to his conscience and

29

sense of personal responsibility, hoping to dissuade him from carrying out his threats. He shook his head; he could not engage in such talk. His precise words were: "I am a soldier. I act only on orders. I must carry out my orders, and I will." What did he really feel and think? Did he know what it meant to us, as Germans, that here of all places Jews were once more in mortal danger? The murder of Jews in Germany—in 1972! The very thought made me choke. At the same time I was more and more convinced that no argument, no appeal could dissuade him from insisting on his demands.

To Dr. Merk, Dr. Schreiber, and me, these talks corroborated the police's assessment: We needed to take the threat of the ultimatum very seriously. Though the time had been extended, the deadline had been established over and over again. We were not even sure if any of the Israeli hostages were still alive, and if any were, how many of them survived. During one of our first talks I said as much to the ringleader.

During the afternoon the ringleader let one of the hostages, his hands tied, step to the window. However, he was not allowed to tell us how many Israelis were still alive. He was only permitted to say that all hostages who had survived the night were still alive. Near 5 P.M. the ringleader brought a second athlete to the window. This one said that he hoped the Israeli government would meet the terrorists' demands. Furthermore, the hostages were willing to fly to Cairo with the terrorists.

At about the same time the terrorists first demanded to leave unhindered along with the hostages, linking the demand to the threat of immediately killing their prisoners in Cairo unless the two hundred Palestinians awaited them on their arrival at 8 A.M. At this moment I had firmly resolved that under the given circumstances the terrorists and their hostages must by no means be permitted to leave; if we had agreed, we would have violated our trust obligation as hosts of the Olympic Games—a position everybody involved shared, without exception. The president of the International Olympic Committee also believed it impossible for Germany to escape responsibility if it allowed the terrorists to leave the country. The Israeli government, speaking through its ambassador, asked whether it was true that we were negotiating the hostages' flight to Cairo, and if so, whether the government had made sure that the Egyptian government would let the hostages leave Cairo for Israel, whether the exit would be made on a German plane, and whether the hostages were to be accompanied by a high-ranking German official. At the same time Israel affirmed its rejection of the demand for releasing the imprisoned Palestinians. Von Braun informed the Chancellor of the Israelis' inquiries, and Brandt, in turn, kept all lines of communication with Israel open.

What would be the consequences if, during this terrorist act on German soil, more Israelis were to die? At the time I felt a very special responsibility. Concerned about the anxiety-filled, frightened, and hopeful hostages in the hands of the terrorists, I was conscious more strongly than ever before of the full burden of our history in relation to Israel and the Jewish people. Twenty-seven years had passed since 1945, and once more it seemed that Jews would be murdered in Germany. We had wondered so often how it had been possible for a movement to arise in Germany that led to the Nuremberg Laws, to the so-called Crystal Night of November 9, 1938, to the wearing of the Star of David, to the Wannsee Conference, and to Auschwitz. Since September 2, 1972, I have felt that burden even more strongly. When the killings in Auschwitz were going on, I was already a young man, even though at the time we were unaware of that death camp. I was ready to risk my life if I could save the captive Israelis. I knew what I had to do.

During the talk that led to the extension of the five o'clock ultimatum I offered myself as a substitute for the Israeli hostages. I had not discussed this decision with anyone. Shortly before, I had called my home. My wife was with me in Munich—she was waiting at the hotel. At home my mother answered the phone. The events had rattled her. I tried to reassure her with the promise that we were doing everything possible. Then I asked if my daughter, who was eleven at the time, was home. She was outside, in our garden. I asked my mother to call her to the phone. I wanted to talk to her one more time, hear her voice, before taking a step I was firmly resolved to take though there was no way to predict what its results would be. I could not have lived with myself had I not tried everything possible, and I cannot now remember how many times I prayed on that day. I asked Martina what she was doing and told her I was hoping to be back in Bonn soon.

After the telephone call I went to the appointed meeting with the ringleader. I reminded him that Germany was hosting these

Olympics and that Germany had a special responsibility to the Jewish people. I was therefore asking him to free the hostages in exchange for me. I was at the terrorists' disposal as a hostage until the Israeli government met their demands. He replied that he was not authorized to make such a decision. He was not interested in German hostages, however, only in Israelis.

All attempts to change his mind were in vain. I urged him to consider the relationship between his people and Germany—to no avail. Then I made a last attempt: If he was not in a position to decide, why not get in touch with his superiors? Again he declined. Next I inquired about the Israeli hostages—how were they faring, how many were still alive. I asked that, at the very least, I be allowed to enter the house where they were held. First he rejected this suggestion. Finally, however, I persuaded him.

We went into the house together and went upstairs. The hallway of the upper floor offered the sight of Palestinians holding machine guns. The door at the end of the hall opened: In a small room the hostages sat huddled on two cots, one each along the room's right and left sides. On the floor between them, covered with a sheet, lay a body.

I introduced myself as the German minister of the interior and told them that we were trying to find a solution by talking to the Arab and Israeli governments. We would do everything we could to achieve their release. The hostages asked me to inform their government that they were expecting the Arab prisoners to be released.

I will never forget the sight of the people sitting on their beds, their eyes filled with hope. Their voices expressed both expectation and seriousness; they seemed composed. During our conversation two of the terrorists stood behind me with their machine guns.

The windows of the room that held the nine surviving Israelis were covered; the light was dim. The arms and feet of the athletes were bound in such a way that they were able to move their hands. They gave me their names and repeated their request that their government meet the terrorists' demands. Under those circumstances they were willing to accompany the Palestinians to Cairo. The Israeli ambassador was immediately informed about this exchange.

After just a few minutes the Palestinians indicated that the visit was over. I went back downstairs and repeated to the ringleader my offer to remain as a hostage. Again he refused, repeating that he had no authorization for such a move and that he would not even try to obtain it.

After seven o'clock Merk and I went back to meet with the spokesman for the terrorists. We told him that an Israeli government representative had arrived who wanted to talk to him on the telephone. The man declined, saying this was just another Israeli attempt at dragging out negotiations; he had nothing more to say. He wanted the German authorities, as well as the Israelis, to understand very clearly that he and his comrades could no longer put off their departure—for physical reasons if for no others. If they were prevented from leaving the house within the next few minutes, they would carry out their threat and shoot two hostages to begin with. He told us to inform the Israeli government that his original statement remained in force: All the hostages would be killed the following morning in Cairo if the Arab prisoners had not arrived there by that time.

Meanwhile Chancellor Brandt had made the following appeal to the heads of state and governments of the Arab nations: "It is with great distress that the German Federal Government acknowledges that the peace of the Olympic Games has been disrupted by an assault that has cost human lives and is putting still more in jeopardy. At this time I appeal to you to do everything within your power to regain the freedom and safety of the hostages now in the hands of the assassins. The whole world is looking to you to make your influence felt."

After von Braun had informed the Chancellor of the Israeli government's position with regard to the terrorists' leaving with the hostages, Brandt tried to speak with the president of Egypt by telephone. He did not succeed. At 8:40 P.M., however, he managed to talk with the Egyptian prime minister. Brandt argued that it would be in Egypt's interest as well if a German airplane could safely continue on to Israel with the hostages after the terrorists had deplaned. The prime minister rejected the offer: Egypt did not wish to become involved in the matter. Thereupon the Chancellor telephoned me shortly before nine, and in the course of our conversation—during which I informed him about the discussions among the crisis team in Munich—we came to the conclusion that all diplomatic efforts must be considered to have failed; the only chance the hostages had to survive was through an attempt to free them by force.

We were unable to gain an extension beyond nine o'clock. The ringleader explained that he and his men had not slept for a long time. They feared their physical and psychological strength would give out, a situation that would put them in greater danger of being overtaken by the German police. Therefore he was forced to reject our request for an extension of the deadline, even though we were ready to assure him that the police would not act even after it had expired.

During all my conversations with him I gained the impression that the ringleader alone had the power to make decisions. The other members of the crisis team in Munich were equally willing to offer themselves as substitute hostages. Since that day I have felt connected to Dr. Bruno Merk, Dr. Hans-Jochen Vogel, and Dr. Manfred Schreiber, by the shared experience of a trial by fire.

After the terrorists had been granted permission to leave by bus for the helicopter landing pad and to continue from there to Fürstenfeldbruck airport, I flew there as well. I was already in the helicopter and the door was just about closed, when I spied Franz Josef Strauss, then chairman of the CSU, among the bystanders. I asked if he would like to come with me to the airport, an invitation he accepted. Once there, we waited in the tower building for the police—who were under the command of the police crisis team—to act. We were taken through a side door into a small room. In speaking with Strauss, I again realized that everyone was aware of all the possible consequences implicit in any decisions regarding the police action. The sense of shared responsibility overcame any political and personal animosities. Only a few years later, when terrorist activities were at their height, we—members of the crisis team—experienced a similar sense both of resolve to accept responsibility and powerlessness in several circumstances. I recall especially the abduction of Peter Lorenz, the head of the Berlin CDU, in 1975 by the members of the Red Army Faction; the kidnapping of Hanns-Martin Schleyer, president of the Employers' Association in the fall of 1977; and the hijacking of a Lufthansa plane, with its successful rescue in Mogadishu by the special antiterrorist squad known as *Grenzschutzgruppe 9*.

All preparations and the execution of the liberation attempt in Fürstenfeldbruck were masterminded by the police crisis team.

Accordingly, in the three-part report subsequently issued by the federal and the Bavarian governments, the third part, which deals with the police action in Munich and Fürstenfeldbruck, was composed by the Bavarian government alone.

Even the site had been determined by the police, after they had weighed and dismissed the idea of attempting the rescue of the Israeli athletes in the house where they were held captive; the police had also rejected the plan of a raid on the route from the house to the buses or to the airport. I believed at the time, and I still believe, that both the state and the municipal authorities exhausted every possible opportunity that knowledge and experience suggested at the time. There could have been no better choice than Dr. Schreiber as security commissioner and Munich police chief.

When the police raid began, the terrorist commandos turned their weapons not only against the police but also against the hostages, and several deaths resulted. After the failed attempt we returned to the Olympic Village, where there was a general air of joy because an incorrect broadcast had spread the belief that the rescue attempt had been successful—a spokesman for the government had announced as much. The news that the raid had misfired was therefore all the more shocking. We decided to hold an international press conference to explain the sequence of events. Merk, Schreiber, and I also promised to issue a detailed official report.

I did not return to the hotel until the early hours of the morning. My wife welcomed me back almost wordlessly; she gave me a questioning look but asked no questions. She listened while, hesitantly at first, everything I felt at this moment of despair and disappointment, of pain and grief, burst out.

After this, I decided to fly to Bonn to attend the cabinet meeting. I participated only briefly and delivered a short report. Helmut Schmidt (the defense minister at the time) spoke next, followed by Georg Leber, the minister of transportation. Both expressed their personal respect and appreciation for me. Their words touched me deeply at this difficult time, and I will never forget them. Much later—between 1980 and 1982, when our government coalition fell apart—they continued to be important to me. I never felt anything but respect for Helmut Schmidt as a person, even though, unfortunately, we never forged a close friendship.

After the meeting I returned to Munich. Those of us who had formed the crisis team met to assemble all the known facts and begin the preparation of the report that was later issued by the federal government, the Bavarian state government, and the city of Munich. The origin of this report, the thoroughness with which it presented the facts, and the absolute candor with which all those who had been involved in the events described what had happened, all prove that they tried their best, did their utmost, and acted to the best of their knowledge and belief.

The international response to the taking of the hostages and its tragic outcome could not be predicted. Given the press coverage, however, I had no doubts that the Federal Republic's reputation abroad could be seriously compromised. I discussed this eventuality with my wife, who was as upset by events as I was. I told her that after the decision had been made to continue the Games, and after the federal president, the federal chancellor, and the foreign minister had arrived, I would meet with the chancellor. I planned to render my resignation, for that act—or so I thought—could improve the government's position.

I told Willy Brandt about the report we were compiling, and then I added, "None of us can predict how the world will judge these events in the future. Therefore I wish to offer you my resignation."

Brandt looked at me intently and rejected my offer immediately and categorically. "Under no circumstances will I accept your resignation. No one can level the least charges against you. You did everything that could be done." He would not even mention, he said, the fact that the federal government had no authority over the police, which was controlled by the states.

I urged him to remember my offer and reconsider if the events of following days should indicate that it would be in the interest of West Germany and its government's standing to free the cabinet of one of its members. I would not withdraw my offer, I assured him. He could act on it at any time. Brandt rejected that suggestion as well, but he promised to reconsider his decision and to consult with me if such a necessity should arise. In the event, he never mentioned my offer again. Walter Scheel supported him in this position.

During this time the view that we had done everything conceivable and possible became generally accepted both at home and abroad. That I had offered myself personally as a hostage and that I had visited the hostages and thus put myself in the hands of the terrorists played a part in this judgment. Many letters from all over the world assured me that my personal conduct was more important to the writers than were matters of legality or tactical police decisions. The president of the German Red Cross even planned to confer the golden pin of honor on me for offering myself in exchange for the hostages. I assured him that what I had done was nothing out of the ordinary and I did not deserve to be honored; rather, the award should be bestowed on the injured pilot of the border police.

In analyzing the tragedy with my colleagues in Bonn, I came to the conclusion that a new stage of violent conflict had set in—and now on German soil as well. New forms of police response were required. I therefore proposed the creation of an antiterrorism unit within the border police. Such a unit should be optimally equipped and trained, have maximum mobility, and be available to the states. If it should prove necessary, and with the authorization of the appropriate departments, the unit might even be deployed abroad if German citizens were in danger. Thus the GSG-9 *(Grenzschutzgruppe 9)* was created as a unit of the federal border police; the squad which proved itself most notably in Mogadishu during the liberation of the airplane that was hijacked by the Red Army Faction, but at many other opportunities as well.

The Guillaume Affair and Its Aftermath

During Brandt's second term, his popularity declined rapidly. Brandt had always kept the administration on a long leash; he left people alone, to use their own judgment. He saw his role as that of a gardener, not a lion tamer. When the disputes over foreign policy became less heated, what had been a positive character trait was suddenly judged a lack of leadership. It is characteristic of Brandt that in an interview of September 1972 with the magazine *Spiegel* he said, "When it comes to his basic manner of dealing with others, you can't change Willy Brandt now—he's too old for that." It was strange: Earlier when Brandt was in jeopardy and in danger of being put out of office, he appeared strong. Nevertheless, what the public increasingly perceived was a loss of power and control. The SPD contributed to this impression as well. And yet it was not a fair assessment: Brandt's first term as chancellor was characterized by significant events, by domestic reforms and increased openness toward the East, as well as by the political momentum of the first years of his chancellorship. When Herbert Wehner, a colleague in the SPD leadership, described Brandt to journalists as limp and removed, it is interesting that he chose to make his remarks in Moscow.

After Wehner's remarks in Moscow, I telephoned Walter Scheel. "Walter, you must call on Brandt and suggest that he demand that the SPD Bundestag delegates choose—Wehner or Brandt. After all, Brandt is the chancellor. If he sits still for this kind of undermining and doesn't put Wehner in his place, his authority will continue to decline. As of this moment Brandt still carries enough weight. But soon he won't." It is likely that in retrospect Brandt never forgave himself for failing to discipline Wehner in front of the SPD delegates.

The attacks from within his own ranks hurt Brandt tremendously. Though he had calmly warded off the CDU/CSU's attacks on his foreign policy, he was not able to deal with the antagonists within his own party. He never would have treated his political allies the way Wehner treated him.

On May 15, 1974, Walter Scheel was elected federal president, the fourth man to serve in that office. That act ended his tenure as minister, a change that had been indicated as early as the summer of 1973, when Scheel had declared that he wanted to visit me during my vacation; in other words, he was going to come to Berchtesgaden from his vacation home in Austria. During a walk he shared his secret: He intended to run for the office of president. At the same time he thought it would make perfect sense for me to succeed him as party chairman; he added, "It's too late for anyone to make a name for himself in foreign affairs. Whatever could be accomplished there has been done. I'd therefore recommend that you keep the position of minister of the interior."

But the suggestion that everything possible in foreign affairs had already been completed reminded me of a story that happened a long time ago. After graduating from his secondary school, Max Planck entered the university and was told by a physics professor, "You want to major in physics? I'd advise against it, young man. In that field all the major discoveries have already been made."

As much sense as it made for Walter Scheel to aim for the highest national office—and I was sure he would be an excellent president—his plans did not coincide with mine. I told him that I had a different view of my own future. I intended to give up the ministry of the interior in 1976; I would try for the chairmanship of the finance committee and return to the practice of law. In my opinion we needed younger, active politicians to voluntarily give up their posts as ministers and use their experience to strengthen the legislature against the executive branch. When I had worked for the party as a young man, I had come to realize the weight important committee chairmen carried: If Hans Wellhausen or Herbert Wehner, Erwin Schoettle, Willy Max Rademacher, or Kurt Georg Kiesinger took the floor, they spoke for the entire chamber. And, in a positive sense, they often rose in opposition to the ruling coalition.

And now Walter Scheel's carefully thought-out decision had confounded my plans. I told him, "The ministry of the interior is very complicated, there are a lot of mines buried there. I would never advise combining the ministry of the interior with the party chairmanship. But if the party wishes me to become chairman, I want to be foreign minister as well." Scheel accepted my proposal at once. It was only during this conversation and in this connection that I saw the foreign ministry as a possible objective in my political future.

In February 1974 I had a conversation with Chancellor Willy Brandt in his house on Venusberg, assuming that I would soon become his deputy and foreign minister. By this time Walter Scheel had made a public announcement of his candidacy. The SPD put no obstacles in his path, a position in line with the SPD's general attitude toward its coalition partner: It was eager to work with a strong FDP. Brandt was helpful to us, both personally and politically. Because he realized that a successful FDP would be a much less troublesome partner than a party that must continually fear falling below the 5 percent of votes needed to remain in the Bundestag, the Free Democrats' success was important to him. When Brandt spoke of my appointment to the offices of foreign minister and vice chancellor, he was unfailingly amiable. The whole interview ran a very personal and harmonious course. I talked about the road I had taken in life and about my goals; our encounter was colored by the certainty that in a few months we would be working together on a new and different footing. And so it came about—but in quite different ways than Brandt or I had imagined.

Problems arose only during the brief transition period from Willy Brandt to Helmut Schmidt. After his election to the chancellorship Schmidt wanted a free hand in naming his cabinet. He believed that he was not yet in a position to settle all personnel issues, and therefore he needed to begin by putting together a core cabinet. If I remember correctly, this administration consisted of only a few "key ministers": Walter Arendt (labor), Georg Leber (defense), and Hans Friderichs (commerce). I was not included.

When Schmidt presented his ideas to Walter Scheel, the latter was taken aback. "Do you have any idea of the situation on the leadership level of the FDP? Hans-Dietrich Genscher will be my successor as chairman. I would suggest that you try to work with him as closely as possible. Besides, we do not think highly of a core government, the full cabinet should be named immediately."

Schmidt listened and dropped the idea of a core cabinet. Thus I became foreign minister and deputy chancellor in the Schmidt administration. At the national party convention in Hamburg in early October I succeeded Walter Scheel as party chairman. As one of three deputy chairmen, I was acting chairman of the FDP until that time. Scheel and the two other deputies, Wolfgang Mischnick and Hildegard Hamm-Brücher, were satisfied with this outcome.

Before the changeover in the Foreign Office could take place, something happened that came to be known as the Guillaume Affair. For me this course of events began in 1973. On Monday, May 28, 1973, I was told that the head of the internal security agency wanted to see me. It was important for Günter Nollau—as it was for Horst Herold, head of the federal office of criminal investigation—to have the right of "immediate access." Neither one ever exercised this right without good reason. Therefore I always agreed to see them without delay, even when my time was completely booked. In all matters of internal security I had to assume that the occasion was an urgent one.

And such was the case this time as well. In the presence of the head of the political staff in the Foreign Office, Dr. Klaus Kinkel, I met with Nollau on May 29. He announced that his visit was due to an embarrassing matter. There was some reason to suspect one of Chancellor Brandt's personal aides in the chancellery, Günther Guillaume. It was not beyond the realm of possibility that he was a spy for East Germany. For one thing, some technical proceedings, with which I was familiar, pointed in Guillaume's direction. For another, the final five months of Guillaume's life before he came to live in West Germany were unaccounted for. The technical proceedings, however, had not always been reliable, and at that particular time there was the case of a high-ranking official in the federal government who had unjustly come under suspicion.

At the time of our meeting I did not know that Nollau had a number of other substantial clues—for example, a tip from the BND (Bundesnachrichtendienst, federal intelligence office), and another one from the investigative committee of Liberal Jurists, as well as reports on problems connected with Guillaume's hiring.

I had not been aware of an aide to the chancellor by the name of Guillaume, though because the name is so unusual, I would certainly have remembered if I had ever met him. The matter was not really surprising, because, as Nollau explained, Guillaume was responsible for party matters, and thus there were no professional occasions where he and the minister of the interior, who was a member of the FDP would encounter each other.

Nollau told me he had not learned of the suspicions until the previous day, and he asked me to keep the information to myself. He explained that he was speaking to me at this stage only because I had asked him to notify me immediately in cases that might have crucial political significance. I ordered Nollau to keep me up-to-date and to treat the matter with the utmost urgency. I could not, however, honor his wish to keep the information secret: The Chancellor had a right to be told at once. After first steadfastly defending his position, Nollau eventually seemed to realize that my position was correct. He expressly asked that the Chancellor make no changes in any of Guillaume's responsibilities; the man must on no account realize that he was being investigated. Nollau's news electrified me—not on account of the weight of the evidence but because Guillaume was so close to the Chancellor. Furthermore, Willy Brandt needed to know that the investigation of Guillaume would of necessity put him under the microscope as well.

That very same day the opportunity presented itself for me to speak with the Chancellor. We met in his study in Schaumburg Palace. I asked Brandt to describe Guillaume's responsibilities; his account confirmed Nollau's. I then pointed out that in light of his position, an investigation of Guillaume might well involve him. To my surprise, the possibility did not trouble him. Finally I told him that at first Nollau had expressed doubts about passing on his information. Brandt thanked me for apprising him so quickly and for telling him everything I knew. Then he mentioned that Guillaume had already been delegated to go with him on his vacation in Norway. Should the arrangements remain in force? I replied that, in my opinion, matters should go on unchanged, even in this aspect. But I needed to consult Nollau first, then I would get back to him. The office responsible for counterintelligence should have the last word.

My position was consistent with my principles. I firmly believed that those responsible for security must also remain responsible for procedures. As a rule, managing such operations from a higher level of authority resulted in less, rather than more specificity. The distance from the problem at hand increased and the so-called bottleneck effect caused decisions to be delayed. Furthermore, the particular departments were more knowledgeable in matters relating to their fields.

When I briefed Nollau the following day—on May 30—he was decidedly in favor of Guillaume's traveling to Norway. The Chancellor so informed State Secretary Horst Grabert, and his colleague Dr. Wilke, the head of the chancellery. In the weeks and months that followed I repeatedly asked Nollau, both in person and through Klaus Kinkel, whether there were any new developments that would justify turning the matter over to the attorney general. Klaus Kinkel had long risen from my colleague to my adviser and confidant.

In early 1974 (when more than seven months had passed since my first talk with Nollau) my patience reached its limits. Such a critical matter could no longer be put off. I therefore demanded that Nollau submit a final evaluation; then we would decide whether to place the case with the attorney general. However, since Nollau had obtained no new information, I also considered the consequences if the allegations could not be proven. In that case the security services—and I along with them—would be vulnerable, holding ungrounded suspicions about one of the Chancellor's confidential aides.

My pressure on Nollau paid off. On March 1, 1974, he informed me, and then repeated his report to the Chancellor in my presence, that the general attorney's office could now legitimately be involved. In the meantime I had repeatedly spoken with Undersecretary Grabert about the matter. Like me, Grabert wanted to see the affair cleared up as soon as possible.

Even after the attorney general received the final report, no immediate action was taken—that is, Guillaume was not taken into custody. He was finally arrested on April 24, 1974, almost eight weeks later. I was told what would happen the day before. We could only hope that the evidence we had was sufficient to indict; otherwise the whole affair could too easily be interpreted as an intrigue against the Chancellor hatched by various departments. At that time I could not possibly know—as I was later told—that Guillaume himself would provide the proof of his guilt. The words he uttered at his arrest, according to the report—"I am an officer of the National People's Army"—provided the necessary evidence. Thus a custom that had been introduced to give spiritual support and moral uplift to East German agents—that is, the possibility of raising them to the level of officers and bestowing medals on these agents (who were called "scouts for peace")— had an effect not originally intended.

I immediately informed the parliamentary opposition, to be precise, CDU Parliamentary Chairman Karl Carstens, of the events. The SPD had been kept apprised by Nollau through Herbert Wehner.

On the morning of April 24 a cabinet meeting was held. Willy Brandt was not present. He was on his way back from a trip that had taken him to Algeria and then to Egypt. The Director of the Chancellor's Office, State Secretary Grabert, and I went to the military section of the Cologne airport, where government planes take off and land. Near one o'clock in the afternoon the Chancellor deplaned. Grabert and I informed him of Guillaume's arrest. Since Nollau had already advised him that the case had been handed over to the attorney general's office, he did not seem surprised. He displayed the equanimity that I frequently observed and admired in him in difficult situations. With Willy Brandt it was difficult to tell how deeply something affected him.

Once Guillaume's arrest became public, matters ran their course. On the whole all sides of the coalition withstood the temptation to make accusations and counteraccusations and to engage in mutual blaming. Nollau was an exception. His subsequent claims about the amount of information passed on to me was untrue, nor was there any rhyme or reason to his attempt to absolve himself of the responsibility for allowing Guillaume to remain unobserved during the trip to Norway. His behavior confirmed many of the prejudices raised against him previously.

On May 1, 1974, I received a telephone call from Horst Herold to tell me that he was sending a messenger with a letter of far-reaching consequences. The letter alarmed me deeply. Herold reported on interviews with members of his office's security unit who had been conducting investigations of the Chancellor's private life. The interviews were held in order to determine whether Guillaume—whose principal job had been to travel with Brandt on vacation trips—could have learned any compromising facts. I was particularly alarmed by Herold's statement that he had already shared this information with Nollau.

I took the letter to Walter Scheel, who saw me at his home on Venusburg, Schleichstrasse. He took the matter as seriously as I did and encouraged me to carry out my intention of transmitting the letter to Brandt at once. Since Brandt was in Hamburg at the time, I planned to send it by a confidential agent. I called the Chancellor, asking him to expect my closest colleague, Klaus Kinkel, who would hand him an important document. Willy Brandt agreed; Klaus Kinkel started out for Hamburg.

Walter Scheel and I realized that any misuse of these records could have an electrifying effect on the public. But we saw no reason to believe that any negative consequences would ensue. We would, in any case, do all we could to avoid such an outcome. This attitude was shared by the various FDP committees, especially by Wolfgang Mischnick, who took exactly the same view we did.

As minister of the interior, I was troubled by the question of why Willy Brandt's security guards had been questioned. The inquiries were being conducted by the attorney general's office. Did these include interviews with the guards? Both the federal office of investigation and the attorney general's office were run by men I held in high regard, personally and professionally: Horst

Herold and Siegfried Buback. (The latter was later murdered by terrorists when he was federal prosecutor.) Not only was it unthinkable that either would authorize activities that went beyond the boundaries of the matter under investigation, their characters guaranteed that no untoward measures would occur. But that did not change the fact that I believed the inquiries to be inappropriate and, for the purposes of the investigation, unnecessary. Not even after I moved to the foreign office did I learn the real reason for these inquiries. Now events ran their inexorable course.

More than once in those days I deliberated the question of whether I should resign. An argument against resigning was the problems the FDP and the government might have to face as a result. I realized that difficult times lay ahead of me, but it seemed to me that I had no right to augment these problems by resigning. Nevertheless, the party's and the coalition government's needs could not be the deciding factor. The crucial question was whether I had violated the responsibilities of my office or was responsible for the mistakes of others, mainly Nollau's. But I could see no reason for answering that last question in the affirmative. After all, I had repeatedly urged Nollau to bring the counterintelligence investigation to a conclusion, and I had no authority to intervene in investigative procedures. Besides, closing the investigation too soon might have impeded the gathering of evidence. The case was certainly not clear-cut, and in the end it was Guillaume's statement alone—"I am an officer of the National People's Army"—that convicted him. If I had insisted on handing the case over to the attorney general's office earlier, thus interfering with the specialists, I could have been blamed for preventing proof of Guillaume's guilt from being discovered.

In the end the only question that remained was whether I was responsible for Nollau's appointment to head the internal security agency. When I first encountered him, he held the post of vice president, a high-ranking position, and no objective reasons arose to prevent his promotion. The only problem that remained for me, therefore, was whether I had assessed his character correctly. This was a concern that troubled me only after Guillaume was unmasked, when Nollau tried all sorts of maneuvers to evade his responsibilities.

I saw no reason for Willy Brandt to resign. However, what did worry me was that Nollau had kept Wehner informed of the investigation. What would Wehner do with this knowledge, since as everyone knew, he was increasingly critical of Willy Brandt's chancellorship? No one in the FDP leadership was asking Brandt to resign—quite the contrary. Walter Scheel, Wolfgang Mischnick, and I, all told the SPD that we were eager to continue a government under Chancellor Willy Brandt; this remained our position even after the events in Bad Münstereifel, where the SPD leadership convened. We communicated our decision to the Chancellor and the SPD leadership on Monday, May 6. Walter Scheel had already informed Brandt of our position, after the Chancellor had shown him his letter of resignation.

Much has been said and written, and even more surmised, about exactly what happened in Bad Münstereifel. I have no observations of my own to add. Only those who were present can shed light on these events. Willy Brandt's resignation was a severe blow, both to the country and to me personally; I regretted it deeply. In those days I realized that I felt a great closeness to this otherwise reserved and distant man.

Later, when I served as foreign minister as well as chairman of the FDP, for eleven years, Brandt and I met frequently during the customary discussions among coalition members but much more often just the two of us, even after 1982, when the FDP formed a government coalition with the CDU/CSU. He gave me a copy of his book, *People and Politics: The Years 1960–1975,* which appeared in Germany in 1976, with a handwritten inscription that read, "To Federal Minister Hans-Dietrich Genscher, in memory of years of fruitful cooperation, Willy Brandt." After his resignation we never mentioned the Guillaume case again.

In retrospect I believe the true reasons for Willy Brandt's resignation go further back, and are more complex than the events connected with the Guillaume incident. Wehner's public statement in Moscow had been a major provocation, a fundamental challenge to Brandt's position of power. I realized as much at the time. The Guillaume Affair may have furnished the immediate motive for his resignation, but it was hardly the principle cause.

I had imagined a different beginning to my tenure as foreign minister, and I had wanted it to be so, just as I had hoped that my departure from the ministry of the interior would be different. In 1974 Walter Scheel could leave office a satisfied man. He had held the foreign ministry during a historic phase, and after initial problems of cooperation with the Chancellor's office he enjoyed great success. He was Willy Brandt's respected partner and an important member of the government. His relationship with Willy Brandt facilitated cooperation within the coalition. As party chairman he exerted great authority. Clear-thinking, purposeful, and highly skilled, Scheel was not at all as his opponents tried to represent him. To me he was more than a valued colleague: More and more he became a cherished friend.

Not until I left office did I realize how close I felt to the ministry of the interior. When I left on May 16, 1974, it was hard to say good-bye. The many and very different assignments I had had to carry out had become dear to me. The same was true for the many highly qualified coworkers, both in the ministry and in the subdepartments. I had reason to feel appreciation and gratitude to all of them for the way we had worked together, which cannot always have been easy for them. We had accomplished a great deal, and had initiated a great many projects.

Saying good-bye to Herbert Schmülling was particularly difficult. He had been my spokesman during my entire tenure; not only that, he had also become an adviser and friend. I did not ask him to come with me because I wanted a spokesman in the Foreign Office who was thoroughly familiar with that area from the start. Succeeding Josef M. Gerwald, Herbert Schmülling later became the FDP's spokesman during my time as party chairman. I owe much to both these men.

On May 18 the Federal Border Police gave me a good-bye party at its Hangelar quarters, complete with taps. They let me pick the serenade, and I chose the "Great Elector's Troopers' March." When I arrived in Hangelar with my mother and my wife, the difference between previous role as the acting and my new role as the former minister of the interior became immediately clear: Whereas the commander used to report to the minister upon his arrival, now he was welcoming me.

During the playing of taps the weather turned rainy, furnishing one more reason for my mood to be bleak as I left the Border Police quarters. An important chapter of my life was over, a new chapter lay ahead. At the time I would not have expected it to last eighteen years.

2

Difficult Beginnings

Continuities and Breaks

When I took over the office of foreign minister on May 17, 1974, German foreign policy had already gone far toward overcoming the division of Europe. Its bold policy of concluding treaties resulted in agreements with Moscow, Warsaw, Prague, and East Berlin. These had significantly enhanced West Germany's ability to accomplish its aims in the area of foreign policy, not only concerning the nations of Central and Eastern Europe but in all international relations. Furthermore, this German policy had established the prerequisites for the Four Power Agreement of 1971, which was intended to improve, and did, in fact, improve the situation in Berlin.

Until the end of the 1960s East-West relations were characterized by confrontation and by increasing inflexibility and repression within the Soviet sphere of power. As late as 1968, a year before the SPD and the FDP came to power, the Soviet Union had militarily intervened in Czechoslovakia, a Warsaw Pact nation. It was an infamous continuation of Moscow's history of forcible interference: the bloody suppression of the revolution in East Germany on June 17, 1953, and the invasion of Hungary in 1956.

The recent treaties enabled West Germany to deal with Moscow in new ways. It further opened avenues to the other nations of Central and Southeastern Europe, with which—except Romania—Bonn had not yet established diplomatic relations. Politically, West Germany had ceded this part of Europe largely to East Germany, though economic contacts with these countries were well developed at the time.

Furthermore, the Federal Republic, and East Germany as well, had joined the United Nations. Bonn thus had a forum in which to enunciate its political beliefs and goals. By expressing to the UN General Assembly recognition of the Palestinians' right to self-determination, the Federal Republic made an important foreign policy statement as early as 1974; the other Western nations soon followed the new member. The two Germanys' membership in the United Nations Security Council proved that an imaginative, future-oriented policy is capable of effecting new initiatives.

The Brandt-Scheel government's final balance sheet thus provided an excellent opening balance for its successor, the Schmidt-Genscher administration. At this point it should also be noted that it was surely one of Willy Brandt's greatest achievements that, when he was foreign minister in the mid-1960s, he had a major role in crafting the so-called Harmel Report. With this report the Western Alliance in 1967 devised a political program to deal with the division of Europe; the policy was based on secure defense capabilities and trusting cooperation with the East, as much and wherever possible. The Alliance's ultimate goal was the creation of a lasting and just peace in all of Europe, a goal that subsequently had to be recalled to Germany (as well as the allies) on numerous occasions. According to the Harmel Report, overcoming the division of Germany was of paramount importance for overcoming the division of Europe. For West Germany, the Alliance's political program thus furnished the framework for achieving both German and European unity.

In his inaugural address on May 17, 1977, the new chancellor, Helmut Schmidt, recognized Willy Brandt and Walter Scheel's statesmanship, and he stressed his government's determination to assure continuity. However, he placed new emphasis on the issue of international economic problems.

Almost at the same time Valéry Giscard d'Estaing was elected president of France, succeeding Georges Pompidou. This outcome set the course French policy would pursue for at least seven years.

I welcomed the French election results because I knew Giscard to be pro-European, and such an attitude was important in a Europe that was developing ever closer ties. Further, his political views were more in line with those of the FDP than were the politics of his rival for the office, François Mitterand, who at that time was largely unknown to me.

Giscard's election also pleased me in regard to German-French cooperation and the increasingly problematic international economic situation, particularly as I knew that since the time when both had served as ministers of finance, Giscard and Schmidt were united not merely by political ties but also by personal friendship.

As head of the Foreign Office what was most important to me was that the new French president appointed an experienced career diplomat to the post of foreign minister. Jean Sauvagnargues had most recently been the French ambassador to Bonn and had played a pivotal role in the negotiations leading to the Four Power Agreement. He had a superb understanding of policies concerning East-West relations as well as relations between the two Germanys. I knew him well and held him in high esteem. His vast knowledge in these areas and about Berlin built a solid foundation for our future cooperation.

Jean Sauvagnargues was the first of six French foreign ministers with whom I was to deal in my eighteen years in office. All were impressive figures, and all were deeply aware of the importance of German-French cooperation. Eminent among them was Jean François Poncet, who was thoroughly familiar with Germany through his father's many years in the diplomatic corps and whose German was fluent. His political mind-set, his great analytical talents, the way he conducted conversations—always with remarkable logic and brilliance—made him a valuable partner in any discussion, and one from whom I gained useful insights. We became friends, and that friendship has survived to this day.

Claude Cheysson, foreign minister after François Mitterand was elected president of France, was a political thinker with a great

50

commitment to North-South cooperation. He had come to know Germany as a young officer right after the Second World War. For years the two of us have also shared a friendship based on mutual esteem and trust.

Claude Cheysson was succeeded by Roland Dumas, a traditional French lawyer, Mitterand's highly educated and superbly competent personal and political confidant. We developed between us a political consensus, a personal trust, and finally a friendship that I would call unique. With him I carried on a dialogue about the past and the future that was longer and franker than any talks I had with my colleagues. It was not unusual for us to telephone each other several times a week. Even when he left government during France's first *co-habitation* (France's government coalition), our political contact continued, and our personal ties certainly remained. My conversations with this man, the son of a Frenchman who had been shot to death as a hostage by the German occupation forces, allowed me an even deeper understanding of our French neighbor and of German-French cooperation.

But all these events occurred much later. When I took over the Foreign Office on May 17, 1974, the attendant circumstances were by no means encouraging. I was often attacked for my lack of experience in foreign policy and my insufficient knowledge of foreign languages. The high public-approval rating I had received during the difficult years as minister of the interior seemed to have lost its validity. But this change of attitude did not particularly bother me at the time; I had met with similar criticism when I was appointed minister of the interior. Back then, however, the issue, to my astonishment, had been whether it was proper for a Free Democrat to serve as minister of the interior. Now, in 1974, when I was criticized for my lack of knowledge of foreign languages, I brushed these misgivings aside by remarking that I had no intention of working in the Foreign Office as an interpreter. Furthermore, as far as I knew, none of the Western foreign ministers spoke Russian, Arabic, Chinese, or Japanese, although the importance of those countries to international relations was not in question.

The Acrobat Under the Big Top: Henry Kissinger

My first important meeting with a foreign colleague was with Henry Kissinger. We had agreed to meet informally at the Hotel Axelmannstein in Bad Reichenhall. When our American guest arrived by car from Salzburg, which was less than four miles away, a large crowd had gathered to give him an extremely warm welcome. His car could hardly make its way through the pedestrian zone. Kissinger was coming directly from an international press conference in Salzburg, where he had replied to charges leveled against him in connection with Watergate. First the two of us talked alone. Kissinger, agitated and upset by the events, began the conversation with a detailed explanation of his motives for holding the press conference. Quite clearly he felt deeply wounded by the accusations. He considered them totally unjustified, and in fact later events would confirm their lack of foundation. He had decided to hold this press conference, he said, in order to do justice to the significance of his office and to his capacity to act in his office as foreign minister. It was impossible, he added, to pursue foreign policy when not only your president was weakened but you yourself were forced to defend yourself in every direction.

It seems to me that during this difficult transition period before President Gerald Ford's inauguration in August 1974 Kissinger accomplished a feat of historic importance: Specifically, he signaled to the Soviet Union that it would be a mistake to try to take advantage of this seemingly vulnerable period in American politics. But Kissinger's impact went far beyond foreign policy. Whenever I tried to explain as much at the time, I would use the image of a circus tent, where Kissinger accomplished the most audacious feats, high up under the big top. Mesmerized, the audience stares at the daring artist on the flying trapeze and fails to notice that the president down in the ring is completely fettered by his struggle for political survival.

After two hours, which we used to get to know each other and to exchange basic views, we joined our delegations in Bad Reichenhall. Since January 1, 1974, the Federal Republic of Germany had held the presidency of the European Community.* As a new president was elected every six months, I held that office only briefly, from May 17 to June 30. During my first meeting with Kissinger I therefore met with him in that capacity as well. It was especially important to me to convince Kissinger, and through him the United States, that the EC's decision to open a dialogue between Europe and the Arab countries was both proper and practical. At the time we had set ourselves the goal of developing relations between the European Community and the Arab countries by establishing institutionalized talks on a broad range of topics in order to contribute to the stability of the region. Incidentally, this multinational offer for holding a dialogue was one of the EC's first steps in a joint foreign policy. It was important to us to start this initiative in agreement with the United States, because we were eager to avoid any strain in European-American relations—after all, we were well aware that the Middle East was very important to the United States.

In principle Kissinger had no objections to close political collaboration with the EC. However, he did have misgivings about the EC's turning its attention to the Middle East. He left me in no doubt that he considered the Middle East within the United States' sphere. The discussion went back and forth for a long time, and although the tone was friendly, the marked difference in our opinions was evident. Finally Kissinger withdrew his objections for the time being. It was my impression that one reason for his courtesy was his consideration for a colleague, whose prestige within the circle of EC foreign ministers depended heavily on the success of his first talk with the American Secretary of State.

On a personal level I found the conversation exceedingly pleasant. I appreciated the fact that Kissinger, the star of international politics and the media, never tried to use his standing or that of his country against me. In our talk he treated me as an equal, and not for a moment was he preachy or condescending. On the contrary: It was my impression from the beginning that he was intent on establishing a relationship with me based on personal respect and trust. Quite clearly he hoped that working closely with me would

---

* In 1974, the European Community consisted of the following members: Federal Republic of Germany, France, United Kingdom, Italy, the Netherlands, Belgium, Luxembourg, Ireland, and Denmark.

be one way to secure German-American cooperation and collaboration within the Alliance. My colleagues had the same experience with their counterparts in the United States delegation. I became particularly aware of Helmut Sonnenfeldt, who hailed from the Altmark region and had emigrated to America with his parents to escape persecution by the Nazis. I pricked up my ears when he told me his life story because the Altmark was part of my native region; after the war it became part of Saxony-Anhalt.

Kissinger and Sonnenfeldt were men who had every reason to feel bitter toward Germany. Yet they above all others brought a deeper understanding for postwar Germany, its problems and interests. In the United States they were among those who sought to awaken stronger sensitivity in people less familiar with events in Europe. I frequently commented in conversations that it was above all émigrés who after the war became advocates for the new democratic Germany in the United States, as did those Americans who had spent time in Germany when they were in the armed forces or had held responsible administrative positions during the occupation. In such discussions I would frequently mention such outstanding personalities as Lucius Clay and John McCloy.

In all likelihood Kissinger was also willing to agree with my proposals because he believed that nothing would come of any European-Arab dialogue, so that the United States' accord would do no real harm. In hindsight it can be said that both sides assessed the situation correctly. The dialogue opened a new era of European-Arab relations and established the basis for new mutual trust. Nevertheless, the talks did not have the intended effect, and meetings among ministers were problematic in part because (and from their point of view this is understandable) the Arab League made participation of PLO (Palestine Liberation Organization) representatives a prerequisite. But at least European-Arab relations were set in motion, leading eventually to an active European–Middle East policy.

The Middle East and the CSCE were the first areas in which the EC acted jointly. The Middle East Resolution, issued in Venice, defined the principles for a future Middle East solution and was the visible result of this common action. At first Israel resisted the resolution vigorously, and the United States was critical as well. It demonstrated to the Arab states, however, that the West included governments that, while leaving not the least doubt of their support of Israel's right to exist, were also sympathetic to the Arab cause. The Venice resolution, incidentally, was forged with the close collaboration between François Poncet and myself.

Germany's Middle East policy also established new priorities. As early as 1974 Rüdiger von Wechmar, West Germany's first ambassador to the United Nations, announced at the General Assembly session that the Federal Republic was ready to acknowledge the Palestinians' right to self-determination. With this speech Germany became the first nation to consider the Palestinian question not as a problem of refugees but as an issue of national self-determination. Given the historical burden on German-Israeli relations, this step was not taken lightly; even though I was convinced that I was doing the right thing, some political boldness was involved. At the time I therefore did everything I could to reassure Israel that this necessary and proper move implied no change whatsoever in West Germany's attitude toward Israel and its right to exist.

Israel's foreign minister, Yigal Allon, turned out to be an impressive, even ideal, counterpart to me. I assured him that we were aware of our historical responsibility. Allon was one of Israel's great political figures whose thinking went beyond the boundaries of the many taboos that determine Israel's policies and who concerned himself with ways to establish a lasting peace in the region. Unfortunately, he died prematurely of cancer.

Allon's successor, Moshe Dayan, and I also enjoyed a harmonious relationship. He appeared energetic and combative in photographs, but in personal encounters he seemed rather frail and cautious. In political dialogues he proceeded less openly and directly than Allon, perhaps in part because he lacked the full support Allon had enjoyed in Israel. Allon could count on the backing of the kibbutz movement, an important faction of the Labor Party; Dayan, on the other hand, after switching parties, did not have sufficient political support.

My working relationship with Dayan's successor, Foreign Minister Shimon Peres, evolved in a very constructive and friendly way, particularly since I liked and valued him tremendously. I met Yitzhak Rabin when he was prime minister and defense minister.

Discussions with Menachem Begin were tough but fair. Begin used to explain his position first and then listen to my views. In our talks I frequently stressed the fact that Israel could prosper only in an atmosphere of trust. Trust and détente, I would say, guaranteed the nation's security. I referred to the situation in Germany, especially in West Berlin; would not a similar approach— cooperation and measures to strengthen mutual understanding— be an equally correct direction for Israel, leading to a point where Israel and its Arab neighbors arrived at shared interests and, on some issues, even agreement?

Many of my colleagues had described Foreign Minister, and later Prime Minister, Yitzhak Shamir as tough and difficult as well. However, to me he seemed a man who listened to arguments, a good listener in general. He held clear positions, but that was an advantage and not a disadvantage, particularly since he was honestly trying to understand and reach agreement.

Almost the same was true for Foreign Minister Moshe Arens, though I had been told that he was inflexible as well. And I have always found the current president, Ezer Weizman, to be independent and unconventional in his actions.

But back to my first meeting with Henry Kissinger. In my capacity as EC president, we discussed not only Europe's Middle East policies but also the Resolution on Atlantic Relations, which had been issued at the conference of NATO foreign ministers on June 19, 1974, in Ottawa and was to be signed by the heads of government on June 26 in Brussels. This resolution was designed to strengthen the North Atlantic Treaty as the basis for Western security and thus to strengthen conditions for future international initiatives, for example, in the areas of détente and disarmament. These aims were to be achieved through increased cooperation between the United States and Western Europe.

Kissinger and I soon developed personal points of contact. We grew closer beginning with the first ministerial session of the North Atlantic Council of Ministers. Since both of us enjoyed soccer very much and Kissinger always inquired about the German teams, I invited him to a World Cup game in Dortmund on July 3, 1974. One of my mother's friends, Frau Husemeier from Soest, had knit a sweater for the American Secretary of State just for this occasion, and I handed it to him in the stadium. The press covered that moment with almost as much fanfare as they did the fact that we were there at all. This gesture by a German woman, however, meant a great deal to Henry; it is not always the statesman's handshake that makes a difference.

On July 6, 1974, I again met with Secretary Kissinger, this time in Miesbach, where he had come at my invitation. He was returning from Moscow and I was particularly interested in his report on the talks regarding the Helsinki Final Act that he had conducted there. At the time of our first encounter in Bad Reichenhall I had already gone out of my way to impress on Kissinger that I placed great importance on measures to establish mutual trust within the framework of the CSCE; at the same time, I felt strongly that the renunciation of force made sense only if peaceful and mutually agreed upon shifts of frontiers remained an option. Now Kissinger told me that he had informed Andrei Gromyko that we wanted the term *peaceful change* mentioned in the declaration of principle concerning the inviolability of frontiers. Though initially Gromyko had rejected that wording as unacceptable, he nevertheless stated that he was prepared to accept an equivalent term in the first declaration of principle concerning sovereign equality. In that case, Kissinger countered, the temporary wording agreed to in Geneva would need to be changed. When Gromyko asked if he could suggest new wording, Kissinger had handed the Soviet foreign minister the text we had composed: "In accordance with international law, the participating states consider that their frontiers can be changed through peaceful means and by agreement." Gromyko promised to have the text examined, but in the course of the talks he had not returned to the issue. When Kissinger had handed him the text, he had emphasized that it represented a provisional suggestion by the United States. He would first have to discuss the precise wording with the Western allies—above all, with the Germans.

This was a classic case of skillful negotiation. Since Kissinger would have to expect the Soviets to suggest another compromise derived from this compromise, he characterized the proposal as an American suggestion that required further discussion, particularly with us. In fact, he was telling the truth. If, therefore, Gromyko suggested various cuts, new demands, in the name of Germany, could always be added to keep the proposed changes in balance.

We also turned to other issues involved in the Final Act. Of particular concern was the area where confidence-building measures would be applicable. One of the important questions was whether they would apply to the Soviet Union. Kissinger agreed with me that it would not be acceptable if confidence-building measures were applied to all European countries while the Soviet Union refused to be subject to them. Although not all of the Soviet Union's European territory need be included, it was essential that the principle apply to a boundary strip. Kissinger suggested that we continue to ask for 300 miles, even if we were to agree on 200 miles in the end. To us, the precept that Soviet territory was not exempt from confidence-building acts was crucial. We also agreed that we would make our willingness to participate in a final conference at the highest level, in which the Soviet Union was particularly interested, contingent on our demand for further concessions.

During our meeting in Miesbach Kissinger took the opportunity of a long walk to explain to me his philosophy of foreign policy, his image of the Soviet Union, and the consequences that followed for American foreign policy. He believed that direct talks with the Soviet leadership were particularly important. He had therefore granted a privileged position to the Soviet ambassador in Washington, Anatoli Dobrynin, since Dobrynin had direct access both to Leonid Brezhnev and to Andrei Gromyko. This device gave Kissinger another chance for a direct exchange of opinions with the Soviet leadership through its ambassador.

Altogether our meeting in Miesbach was successful in three aspects: the personal relations developing between Kissinger myself; the working relationship we had created; and finally the CSCE, which was so important for German foreign policy. After all, we had agreed on three important issues: on the possibility of a peaceful change of frontiers, on confidence-building measures in a part of Soviet territory, and in our joint assessment that it was also in the West's interest to hold a conference on the highest level of government once the second phase had been successfully completed, that is, after agreement on the Final Act had been reached.

All these points were important to me, not least because I looked to the CSCE—if it should indeed come about—as a new operational sphere for German foreign policy. The CSCE would give us an opportunity to play an active, even an influential, role in West-East relations without restriction of the Four Power rules. We would bring our concerns to the West's shared political platforms—the EC and NATO—and by introducing new ideas, making broad contacts, and taking advantage of our Eastern treaties, we could gradually develop our relations with the Warsaw Pact nations within a multilateral framework. Furthermore, the Helsinki Final Act offered possibilities for improving relations between the two Germanys as well.

I was soon able to continue my talks with Kissinger. I traveled to Washington as early as July to meet with the Secretary of State. The final days of the Nixon administration were approaching, and the political climate in Washington was dominated by Watergate.

Impressed by Kissinger's vigorous pursuit of foreign policy measures despite the enormous domestic upheaval, I resolved that as long as I was in office, I would carefully protect my freedom to act in foreign affairs. Foreign and security policies must never be made subservient to domestic policy or partisan politics. My resolve would frequently be put to the test: during the realization of the NATO double-track resolution, in my persistence in struggling for German unity, in successfully fighting for the zero-zero option, and in rejecting the upgrading of the Lance in early 1989 (in other words, at a time when the façade of the Eastern nations was already showing cracks), and in the struggle to make a reality of the historic chance promised by Gorbachev and his policies.

A Departing President and New Challenges

My visit to the United States also included a meeting with President Richard Nixon, who was vacationing in San Clemente on the West Coast. At that time I could not know that I would be Nixon's last foreign guest, just as my predecessor, Walter Scheel, had been the last foreign visitor to the White House whose talk with Nixon had been taped. After his meeting with Scheel, Nixon had gone by helicopter to Walter Reed Hospital. While he was still there, Watergate had begun.

Kissinger offered to take me on his plane from Washington to San Clemente; however, I would have to agree to a stopover in the Midwest. Kissinger was offering his support to a senator running for reelection whose vote in the Senate was very important to Kissinger. The stop also gave us an opportunity to inspect the installations of the U.S. intercontinental missiles. Kissinger showed me missile silos and the workrooms for the technical staff. I was given a detailed explanation of the precautions as they applied to the staff and the technical provisions that would prevent the unauthorized launching of a missile in case of human failure. It was the first time that such a demonstration had ever been given.

The following morning, during a walk on Nixon's beautiful estate in San Clemente from his home to his offices, we talked about American policies during and after the Second World War. I mentioned to Kissinger that I had never understood why the United States had abandoned Central and Eastern Europe to the Soviet Union. Though the Soviet Union, which had carried the main burden of the war against Hitler's Germany, had every right to an occupation zone in Germany, I did not understand why the West allowed the two nations that had been Hitler's first victims—Czechoslovakia and Poland—to come under Soviet influence. Kissinger believed that during the crucial talks President Franklin D. Roosevelt, who was already very ill, had been influenced by "Moscow-minded" advisers.

After our walk we met our delegations on the terrace of the building compound that had been built specifically so that the President could attend to his daily business while on vacation. Suddenly there was a call from Washington: Traffic had been stopped on the autobahn leading from West Germany through East Germany to West Berlin. The traffic lights on that route had been switched to red by the GDR authorities. What was to be done? What had apparently triggered this action was West Germany's decision to situate the newly established Federal Environment Office in Berlin, though that city was not, according to the Four Power Agreement, part of West Germany. Now I had a chance to see the determination and decisiveness with which Kissinger threw the full weight of the United States into protecting our common interests in Berlin. He directed Helmut Sonnenfeldt to break off the talks being held in Washington with a GDR delegation on the subject of entering into diplomatic relations. Until the autobahn was reopened, these discussions would not resume. He communicated to Soviet Ambassador Dobrynin through an aide, Frederick Hartmann, that Washington considered the interruption of traffic an issue between the United States and the Soviet Union. Kissinger made all these decisions and issued his orders while the two of us remained seated on the sunlit terrace. Our jackets were off, because until the news came in, we had been chatting over cool drinks more about personal topics than about matters of foreign policy.

Then it was time for my meeting with Nixon. The president was quite composed during our talk, a fact that impressed me, since his mood could easily be imagined. His presidency was just about to end, and he could not be certain whether he would actually be impeached. Along with Kissinger, others present at this meeting were Martin Hillenbrand, the United States ambassador to West Germany; Berndt von Staden, West Germany's ambassador to the United States; and West Germany's Deputy Foreign Minister Günther van Well. Nixon was focused and extremely well prepared, the mark of the true foreign policy expert, and as the conversation went on, he visibly relaxed. Time and again he exclaimed that we took the same view on relations between Europe and the United States, on NATO, on economic and currency policy, on the situation in the Mediterranean, on détente, on CSCE, and—obviously—on Berlin. The President welcomed the accord on issues of economic policy that existed between West Germany and the United States. It was particularly in this respect that Chancellor Schmidt had impressed him at the NATO conference in Brussels on June 26, 1974; after all, we all recognized that fighting inflation was of preeminent importance.

During the NATO debate Helmut Schmidt's arguments had indeed been very convincing. Contrary to almost all the other representatives, who had restricted their support to matters regarding the Alliance's defense policies, he had pointed out that political stability was achieved by economic and social stability.

Finally I reported to Nixon my conversations on détente with United States senators. Since, for our part, we could see no alternative, it was not so much a matter of whether to accept or reject détente but whether to pursue it in a realistic or delusional way. The policy could be successful only if it was based on an adequate defense; as long as the Soviet Union sought military superiority, détente must not lead to the illusion of security. And only the North Atlantic Alliance offered security. Rather, it was the purpose of détente to avoid conflicts and to change the situation in a positive way—this was its role in bringing about political change.

Next the President brought up the subject of the CSCE. He fully understood our desire to secure the possibility of peaceful change, he said, and he pointed out that the United States had supported this point in negotiations with the Soviet Union, which had not been easy. I confirmed that, as far as the CSCE was concerned, considerable progress had been made. If the outcome justified such a move, a summit conference should be the next goal. Even at this stage a discussion of peaceful transformation could be put on the agenda. Incidentally, I added, *peaceful change* did not refer merely to Germany but to all of Europe as well, since the division of Germany was an expression of the separation of Europe, and one could not be healed without bridging the other.

Nixon agreed with me. Peaceful change, he said, was important especially for a Europe split in two: The Soviet Union could not simply draw a frontier through the center of Europe and dictate that there would be no changes on either side. However, he was still uncertain how the concept could be introduced. It was obvious, he said, that the Eastern European countries were interested in gaining their independence. For that reason, too, the Iron Curtain must not be ratified forever, though that was the Soviet Union's intention. Kissinger, myself, and the other Western foreign ministers—all of us would have to use all our skills to work out a plan for peaceful change.

The President further asked me to take a message to my eight fellow ministers in Europe: Unity between Western Europe and the United States was the top priority. Particularly, the larger European nations must work together to prevent instability on the Southern rim. We must not allow economic, currency, and political issues to create rifts among us. Any unilateral actions must be avoided. The new French president (he meant Giscard d'Estaing) clearly understood economic and foreign policy issues; while pursuing a larger agenda he was forced to respond to criticism within his own country. He must not be put under too much pressure, since for the time being he needed to put his administration on a firm footing. Nixon was convinced that under Giscard, France would to play a constructive part in Europe; furthermore, German-French relations would have a key role in European policy.

To me Nixon's statements sounded like the political musings of a president who knew that his time in office had come to an end. How right he was.

□   □   □   □

The first time I saw Nixon after he left office was in October 1981, when we met in Cairo on the occasion of President Anwar as-Sadat's funeral. He had come with two other ex-presidents, Gerald Ford and Jimmy Carter, to pay his final respects to Egypt's head of state. When we had a chance to speak, Nixon brought up our meeting in San Clemente. Apparently he remembered his last talk with the representative of a friendly government as well as I did.

My final meeting with Richard Nixon (with whom I had met twice more in the United States) took place in Bonn on March 18, 1994, just a few weeks before his death. Nixon was returning from a visit to Moscow. The American ambassador in Bonn, Richard Holbrooke, was hosting a luncheon at his residence. Again I was impressed by the clarity with which Nixon, now eighty-one years old, described the events of his trip to Moscow and discussed their consequences for American and Western policies. After lunch I had the opportunity to have a confidential chat with him. He was quite clear in his request that Russia be included as much as possible in international cooperation, including as a participant at G7 summits, which should be turned into G8 summits. As for West-East relations, he considered German foreign policy crucial.

There can be no doubt that with regard to foreign affairs, Richard Nixon was an outstanding president. Realism, clearly defined goals, and a great sense of responsibility marked his presidency. By turning the United States in new directions for its policies toward the Soviet Union and the People's Republic of China, he left a lasting imprint on the future of international relations. I was also impressed by Henry Kissinger's personal loyalty to Nixon after his resignation; this loyalty extended both to Nixon as a person and to the policies the two of them had forged.

It was remarkable how quickly Kissinger and I came to trust each other during my first months as foreign minister; eventually we became good friends. Since then we have seized every opportunity to meet. Whenever I went to New York to attend the United Nations General Assembly, we tried to have a talk; whenever he came to Germany, he visited me in the Foreign Office or at my home. Trust and friendship are not limited to government posts, as long as the terms are used with care. I always shied away from calling a new colleague *my friend* after only one meeting, or pretending that being on a first-name basis, which is customary in the English-speaking world, was a sign of special mutual trust. Being old-fashioned, as a foreign minister I always used the term *friend* as carefully as I do in my personal life.

I particularly remember one of my last meetings with Henry Kissinger during my tenure as foreign minister. It was on January 7, 1992. I had participated in a meeting at the government's guest house on Petersberg. When I left, I ran into James Callaghan, the former British foreign secretary and prime minister, in the large reception room. While we chatted and he was asking me if we could see each other that evening (he did not want to attend a boring reception), Henry Kissinger joined us. The three of us agreed to go out that night, and I invited them to Ria Alzen's restaurant, Maternus, with its large selection of choice wines. Ria and her restaurant have long been familiar to my foreign visitors in Bonn: It is her natural style to apply great discretion with all her customers. We were accorded no special treatment; Ria refuses to use high-ranking guests as publicity for her restaurant. She has long been an institution, and not merely locally.

That night we were placed at the table off the main entrance, in the left-hand corner. Though the table affords a view of the entire restaurant, it remains inconspicuous. "Retirees" Henry and Jim took the opportunity to grill their old, still active, colleague for news and opinions. After this part of the conversation was finished, I took the role of listener. They talked of their lives "afterward," about writing memoirs and handling speaking engagements. I found these anecdotes particularly amusing because only a few days earlier I had informed the Chancellor of my intention to resign the post of foreign minister in May 1992. When the three of us spent the evening together, therefore, I had already made up my mind. But between themselves and toward me, the two of them acted as if retirement had no relevance to me at this time. I would have liked to tell them that they were giving me some very useful advice, since I was obviously thinking about "afterward." But I had promised the Chancellor that, in the interest of leaving the government free to act in foreign policy matters, I would not make my decision public, and therefore I was forced to keep these two old friends in the dark, much as it pained me.

□   □   □   □

But back to 1974. After a few months spent familiarizing myself with the tasks of the German foreign minister, I began to concern myself with the question of how Germany's voice could make itself heard within the Western Alliance. As far as West-East relations were concerned, we would have such an opportunity after the completion of the treaties with the Eastern-bloc nations and within the CSCE process. For the sake of the consistency of Western policy, however, it was important that we wait until opinions within the Alliance and the EC were determined, so that we could then work in unison for improving East-West relations. These thoughts corresponded to a question Henry Kissinger raised at about the same time: In what small circle could sensitive issues of West-East relations be confidentially discussed?

I suggested to Kissinger that we make use of the talks among the foreign ministers of the United States, the United Kingdom, France, and the Federal Republic, which were originally intended to deal with Germany and Berlin as a whole. This way other basic issues of Western policies could also be raised within a small circle. Thus these talks, which always took place before the conferences of the NATO Council of Ministers, took on a new structure.

It had been our custom that the team that dealt with Berlin and Germany opened the meeting by delivering a report; this was followed by a report from the West German foreign minister on the state of relations between the two Germanys. Finally, after a discussion, a brief statement was issued on the Berlin and Germany policies, which the other NATO ministers included verbatim in the NATO communiqué.

Now Kissinger and I proposed adding a second part to the sessions in which to discuss other issues. This proposal eventually resulted in the following procedure: The sessions rotated among the embassies of the four participating countries. We would meet around seven o'clock in the evening. First we discussed issues concerning Germany and Berlin and, as usual, ended the debate by agreeing on a statement for the communiqué. Then a smaller group—the four ministers plus two aides apiece—met over dinner and confidentially discussed sensitive issues related to the Alliance and West-East relations.

These meetings of foreign ministers enabled the four nations to develop a uniform political strategy. Confidentiality was strictly maintained. Not once was I disappointed—the basic substance of these talks and the outcomes always contributed to the Alliance's cohesion. In the difficult times of the Cold War and of East-West tensions, as well as during the transition to new relations between the former blocs these talks were of great value.

Nevertheless, the procedure was not without problems for the cohesiveness of the Alliance, since the four nations naturally represented a privileged group. How was such a distinction compatible with West Germany's position in NATO and in the European Community? Our counterparts suspected, of course, that during these meetings, which officially dealt only with Berlin and Germany as a whole, we also discussed other issues. Our absolute discretion made it easier for them to accept the situation. If there had been open speculation about our discussions, the response would have been quite different, because we would have been seen as belittling the other governments. One foreign minister, a personal friend, told me in private, "As long as you don't talk about it, it's all right. If it becomes public, we owe it to our self-respect to be critical."

These meetings were particularly important for the Germans. The Federal Republic made the largest contribution to Western security by furnishing our own armed forces, our compulsory military service, and all the territory on which Allied forces were stationed. Our contribution was, of course, in the interests of our own security; but it also served to protect the security of the powers who kept forces on German soil.

In the 1970s the divided Germany—or rather, the Federal Republic of Germany—gained a powerful voice in formulating and enforcing Western policies. It did so through participation in the CSCE process, support of the new discussion format of the Four Powers, membership in the United Nations, and finally, participation in the international economic summits. The CSCE was largely the result of German efforts: The structure of the Four Powers originated in a German-American initiative, and the world economic summit grew out of a German-French suggestion. All things considered, we could manage without a permanent seat on the Security Council; the omission created no serious problems.

First Talks with Moscow

When I assumed office, most nations adopted a wait-and-see attitude. Only the countries east of the Iron Curtain, especially the
Soviet Union, reacted strongly. Subsequently the foreign ministers
of some of the smaller Communist nations told me that Moscow
had painted an ugly picture of the new foreign minister: "émigré"
from East Germany, minister of the interior for four and a half
years—these were negatives of the first order. Two colleagues
from that circle later confessed to me that they had anticipated
their first meetings with me with serious misgivings.

One of my first visitors was the Soviet Union's foreign minister,
Andrei Gromyko. Before I met with Gromyko for the first time on
September 15, 1974, I prepared very carefully. Gromyko was said
to have a superb memory, and that reputation was not exaggerated: During Brezhnev's final visit to Germany in November
1981, Helmut Schmidt invited him, along with Gromyko and me,
to his home in Hamburg. At lunch Brezhnev complained about
our alleged violations of the status of Berlin. He accused us of
straining bilateral relations by trying to extend our rights over
Berlin. "I'm afraid I must tell you that you are barking up the
wrong tree," I replied. "Much to my dismay, my own party, along
with the SPD, of which the Chancellor is a member, Adenauer's
CDU and Strauss's CSU, all anticipated your problems with Berlin
and decided against it as our capital, while the Communist Party
was for it. That was probably the only time the Communists and I
agreed on an issue. At a session of the first parliament the West
German KPD (German Communist Party) made a motion to
move all federal government offices to Berlin. The other parties
defeated the proposal." Brezhnev looked at Gromyko, incredu-
lous. "Yes, Comrade Leonid," Gromyko acknowledged. "Herr
Genscher is telling the truth. Of course that was before the
remilitarization of West Germany." A classic Gromyko reply.

It was my general impression that neither Gromyko nor Brezhnev harbored anti-German sentiments. The inflexibility shown by
this generation of rulers in the Kremlin toward the German question and Berlin was much more the result of what they took to be
the rights of the stronger or of the victor. At the same time this
older generation of ideological-orthodox Soviet politicians had

considerable respect for the new Germany that had evolved in the Federal Republic. Gromyko himself, however, seemed to focus mainly on the United States. He believed it crucial for the Soviet Union to be recognized as on a par with the other superpower. His feelings may have been colored by his time as ambassador in Washington during the Second World War. Gromyko realistically assessed the United States' immense resources when that nation felt provoked. While he was ambassador, he had witnessed the United States waging war in the Pacific and later in Europe, lending support to the Soviet Union, and still not suffering any economic hardships. Brezhnev, on the other hand, seemed emotionally more interested in Germany.

Yet whatever the various priorities may have been, one thing was clear: The Kremlin leaders viewed their West German opponents—the chancellor and the foreign minister—as important in the dialogue between East and West. The weight our divided country carried in the international arena undoubtedly was to our advantage, but we had gained this significance not by a whim of fate or as an undeserved gift from God. Rather, it was the result of a clear policy West Germany had pursued from the first. The reputation we enjoyed in the Western alliances (in NATO and in the European Community), our economic skills, and our political stability also had a bearing on the degree of Moscow's respect. But to exploit this limelight and to gain acceptance of Germany's interests required more: a clearly drafted, constructive policy toward the East, marked by our responsibility for peace, a policy carried out not by unilateral actions but in harmony with an overall Western strategy. This was a goal toward which we had to strive again and again. Especially in the years from 1986 to 1989 I learned what this struggle involved. I need merely repeat the key words: CSCE, response to Gorbachev, zero-zero option, and the controversy surrounding the upgrading of the Lance.

The West's utter helplessness during the suppression of the East German rebellion on June 17, 1953; the suppression of the uprising in Hungary in 1956; the erection of the Berlin Wall on August 13, 1961; and the Warsaw Pact's intervention in Czechoslovakia in 1968—all these had been traumatic experiences for me. We simply could not allow such helplessness to recur. We needed a policy that allowed for peaceful transformations. The fact that West German foreign policy assumed a leadership role in developing such a program increased the country's clout, even in Moscow. Europe could not be changed in opposition to Moscow, but only in concert with the Soviet Union.

In the period from October 28 to 31, 1974, Chancellor Schmidt and I visited the Soviet Union. Before we left, I again publicly pointed out that Berlin was the touchstone of détente. In Moscow the two heads of government quickly relegated this topic to Gromyko and myself. The Soviets tried to distance themselves from the problem; they did not consider Berlin the center of international events. Moscow's point of view was understandable, but Berlin's status and situation remained a central issue for Germany.

At the time of our visit bilateral relations were strained, to say the least. In July the Soviet Union had given its approval when East Germany blocked through traffic to Berlin to prevent West Germany's situating the Federal Environmental Office in West Berlin. The Soviet government considered the establishment of West German offices in West Berlin inconsistent with the Four Power Agreement. Berlin was and remained a delicate issue. Treaties that were all but signed had to be set aside because we could not arrive at an agreement on how they applied to West Berlin. These same treaties were not concluded even at the German-Soviet summit in May 1978. In my opinion the formula concerning strict adherence to the Four Power Agreement required a dynamic interpretation; any other attitude would have increasingly drained and weakened Berlin's ties to West Germany. What was at stake was no more and no less than Berlin's survival. For this reason, all we achieved in Moscow was an official agreement between our two governments "on the further development of economic cooperation"; at least the document contained a stipulation regarding Berlin, which had been our goal.

Brezhnev was fascinated by large-scale projects and was hoping for German aid in exploiting Russia's huge reserves of raw materials. And, on a pragmatic level, reciprocal economic interests furnished the stable basis for German-Soviet relations. At no time, however, did our economic interrelationship reach the degree that would have made us dependent on Moscow. For example, West German foreign trade with Austria and Switzerland was always greater than with the Soviet Union; the Federal Republic of Germany was therefore never vulnerable to pressure, either through trade policies or through any other avenue.

While we would never have yielded to the pressure of internal economic interests, we maintained a supportive partnership with German trade. Otto Wolff von Amerongen, who headed the commerce committee dealing with the Eastern bloc, always respected policy. He frequently consulted me before meeting with representatives from the Soviet Union. Thanks to his great personal authority and experience not only did he not cause difficulties for German foreign policy but, on the contrary, supported it vigorously.

On the whole our Moscow visit of October 1974 was successful: We had been eager to get to know the Soviet leaders better in order better to understand their political thinking. Conversely, we had also wanted to make sure that the Soviets understood the foreign policy of the Schmidt-Genscher administration. The Soviet leaders needed to know that we were planning on continuing and building on the Brandt-Scheel administration's policy toward the Eastern bloc. At the same time we made it very clear that for our part Berlin was going to prove the seriousness of détente and that we were not going to pursue détente at the cost of giving up our security.

During the closing press conference in Moscow on October 30, 1974, Helmut Schmidt announced regular yearly consultations between the two countries' foreign ministers. "In these talks," he declared, "both sides have expressed their determination to further expand contractual relations." Moderate progress seemed to reenter German-Soviet relations.

3

The East Is More
Than Moscow

Stages in a Difficult Approach: Prague, Sofia, Budapest, and Bucharest

On July 10, 1974, less than two months after I had taken office, the Bundestag ratified the treaty with Czechoslovakia. This was one in a series of treaties regulating our new relationships with our Eastern neighbors. The process had started with the Moscow Treaty and continued with the Warsaw Treaty and the Berlin Agreement.

The treaty of July 1974 paved the way for improved relations with Czechoslovakia. In the cases of Poland and Czechoslovakia the crimes of the Third Reich added a special moral and historical dimension to bilateral relations. Czechoslovakia had been the first victim of Hitler's expansionism, and the attack on Poland had triggered the Second World War. Both countries were crushed; Czechoslovakia, termed a German protectorate, and occupied Poland—the so-called Generalgouvernment—were turned into European colonies. The National Socialists planned to turn the people of Poland into slave laborers and to eradicate the Polish intelligentsia. Our relationships with Hungary, Romania, and Bulgaria carried less historical baggage, and any foreign policy aiming for change in Europe obviously had to nourish and develop contacts with these other nations as well.

Whenever I visited Prague, I made it a point to call on the Archbishop of Prague, Cardinal František Tomášek. I always insisted that the media be granted access to these encounters, because German and Austrian television penetrated to the areas just within the Czech border. The position of the Catholic Church was infinitely more tenuous in Czechoslovakia than it was in Poland; public documentation of the respect paid to its highest representative by a foreign visitor could therefore be helpful. At my first visit with the Cardinal I asked, after the press had left, "Can we speak freely here?" He replied instantly, "Of course, Minister," but even as he spoke, he was shaking his head. In the car I later said to the West German ambassador, "He is assuming the presence of microphones but not of cameras."

I also thought it important to talk with representatives of Charter 77. Therefore I invited former Foreign Minister Jiři Hájek from Alexander Dubček's administration to talks in the German Embassy. I had met Hájek the first time I had visited Prague, during the "Prague Spring" in August 1968, when I had traveled with Walter Scheel. In Czechoslovakia's capital, which at that time was full of activity and excitement, this sensitive scholar spoke calmly of his fears for the future. German ambassadors in Prague were always instructed to keep in touch with Hájek and other representatives of Charter 77.

Czech foreign minister Bohuslav Chňoupek was fluent in German—he had spent his childhood in Bratislava—the former Austrian Pressburg. He appeared thoroughly cosmopolitan. I used our talks to explain to him again and again the principles of our Eastern policy and to caution him not to misjudge German policies. For example, on a subsequent occasion I told him, "The NATO double-track resolution will be enacted, and you can be sure that we will adhere to it." At other times I strongly impressed upon him that when West Germany discussed the right to self-determination, we were not engaging in mere rhetoric. I also let him know in no uncertain terms that we were taking Gorbachev's attempts at reform seriously and that we would make certain that the West would respond appropriately. Our determination to cooperate with the new leadership to arrive at basic improvements in East-West relations was not to be left in any doubt whatever. I wanted Prague to be very sure that our Eastern policy could be relied upon.

I also held extensive talks with President Gustav Husak and Prime Minister Lubomir Strougal. These discussions always centered on the same basic topics: promoting change and humanitarian improvement in the spirit of the Helsinki Final Act. We also talked about the possibility of arms control and disarmament, and ways and means to increase mutual trust and intensify cooperation in all areas.

All our talks with our neighbor to the east aimed at détente, arms control, and disarmament in a period of confrontation. Of course we took the usual path in diplomatic relations by dealing with the government, but our real efforts were directed at the people themselves. We wanted them to realize that for us the Iron Curtain did not mark the end of Europe; we took great care to avoid giving the impression that in foreign policy we were going to cede the Eastern countries to the German Democratic Republic. A West German policy for Eastern Europe directed toward the fundamental transformation of the current situation in Europe must turn, not merely to the Soviet Union, but to the other Warsaw Pact nations as well.

I repeatedly requested of my Western counterparts that they contribute to the diversification of relations with these countries through discussions and visits. Such a course of action could, naturally, be carried out only within the narrow limits of the "bloc discipline" Moscow expected. Nevertheless, some leeway remained, as became obvious time and again whenever multilateral issues such as CSCE and the Conference on CSBMs (Confidence- and Security-Building Measures) in Europe were on the docket. While this maneuverability was generally unofficial, it was quite noticeable. The Warsaw Pact countries, it became clear, had long since ceased to be a monolithic entity, and we had to act vigorously to prevent their retreat into unanimity. Further, we had to keep focused on the signals our own actions sent to the peoples living within the Soviet sphere of influence. We thought it essential to impart the message that we would never forget the part of Europe on the other side of the Iron Curtain. Again and again I opposed the thoughtless use of the phrase *Eastern Europe.* The Cold War had increasingly imposed an ideological meaning on the terms *West* and *East,* so that now even Poland and Czechoslovakia had become Eastern European countries. I therefore repeatedly stated, "Poland is a Central European nation. Beyond the Polish eastern border lies Eastern Europe, not Western Asia."

Talks with the governments in Central and Southeastern Europe offered me the opportunity to become aware of changes in the Soviet sphere of influence as happened during a visit to Prague on February 1 and 2, 1983, when I held a reception in the German Embassy. At the time no one could foresee the importance the embassy would acquire in 1989, only six years later. During the reception Prime Minister Strougal and Foreign Minister Chňoupek asked for a private interview. Strougal reported on the steps that had culminated in the decision to impose martial law in Poland. There had been a meeting of the Warsaw Pact members in which the Communist Party heads, as well as the prime ministers had participated. That was why he, Strougal, had also been present. The principal topic had been that of military intervention in Poland. For the first time members of the Soviet delegation had offered differing opinions. Mikhail Suslov and Dmitri Ustinov had pleaded for prompt intervention, while Brezhnev and Gromyko had shown conspicuous restraint. "It was our neighbors, yours and ours," Strougal added, "who advocated intervention"—by which he meant the East German delegation. Todor Zhivkov, the Bulgarian head of state, had been the first to argue against military intervention. "I'm sure you think that Prime Minister Janos Kadar of Hungary was next to speak," Strougal continued, "but that is not what happened: We did. President Husak was the first one to support Zhivkov." Only then, Strougal explained, did Kadar join them. "Your neighbors and ours"—again he was referring to the East Germans—"were in favor of intervention." Romania, incidentally, had not been present at the session; Nikolae Ceauşescu had refused to participate. Finally Brezhnev had said, "Since most of our allies object to intervention, it is not possible for us to intervene. We must look to our Polish comrades to solve their own problems." The truth of this version is corroborated by a conversation I had during a visit in Sofia some time later. Without referring to my conversation in Prague, I asked President Zhivkov how the Warsaw Pact's position on Poland had been arrived at.

Zhivkov replied, "I was against intervention, and the Czechs supported me." He added that when he stated his position, he had been uncertain of the reaction it would provoke, since there had been no prior discussions or arrangements. This conversation, too, is a good example of how important it was for us to develop a relationship that allowed talks with individual nations and their representatives, to the extent that this was possible given our ideological and political differences.

Germany and Poland: A Complicated Relationship of Neighbors

On the whole, our Eastern policy in the mid-1970s, after the treaties were completed, was mostly a matter of slogging uphill. We made only very slow progress, particularly in our relations with Poland.

As soon as I took office, I tried to assess our relationship accurately. I came to the conclusion that since the signing of the Warsaw Treaty in 1970, German-Polish relations had not moved ahead in ways we had hoped. Though both sides stressed the necessity of normalizing the relationship, each held an entirely different idea of the meaning of normalization. To the Poles, it meant prompt economic aid from West Germany; we, however, defined it as greater civil freedoms, the open exchange of information and opinions, and a satisfactory solution to the problem of people of German descent living in Poland. After the Warsaw Treaty was signed, between 100,000 and 300,000 Germans had applied for exit permits and were awaiting government approval. Our clashing positions on resettlement and keeping families together, as well as the Polish leaders' attempt to exert pressure by threatening the future of these people, were straining the political climate in dealings between the Federal Republic of Germany and the People's Republic of Poland.

In early 1975 Poland still had not received the loan the West German government had approved back in October 1973; even the amount and particulars of the loan had not yet been resolved. Edward Gierek, first secretary of the Polish Central Committee, urgently needed the loan to carry out his ambitious economic program. We, on the other hand, were disappointed by Poland's attitude toward the Germans who wanted to move to West Germany, particularly since during negotiations for the Warsaw

Treaty, Poland had assured us of flexibility on the issue of resettlement. The reverse proved to be true: While in 1971, 25,243 people had been allowed to leave Poland for the Federal Republic, in 1974 the number was only 7,827.

Poland had suffered hardships in the Second World War from the beginning. The advances of German troops in the western parts of Poland were followed by the oppressive measures of the SS, which turned the independent republic into the Generalgouvernment, in effect, a German colony. The deliberate eradication of the intelligentsia and the genocide of European Jews was promptly instituted. Beginning on June 22, 1941, the German war machine also crushed the eastern part of Poland, which the nefarious 1939 pact between Hitler and Stalin had allocated to the Soviet Union. With the exception of Europe's Jews, no other group suffered for as long and as hideously in the war as did the Poles. Even though the entire country was occupied, no other nation fought with so many soldiers on all fronts—on the side of the Allies as well as within its own borders. The exclusion of Poland from the victorious powers, its displacement from the West without consulting the Polish people, and finally, ceding the nation to Stalin and accepting its incorporation in the Soviet sphere of influence must, I believe, be included in the list of the Western Allies' incomprehensible decisions during the final phase of the Second World War and in the immediate postwar period.

The more I studied domestic and foreign policy after the Second World War, the more I came to the conclusion that Germany's eastern borders could no longer be changed; Germany would have to accept the Oder-Neisse Line. Those Germans who had been driven from the former eastern regions of Germany had, in a charter, early on committed themselves to German responsibility for peace and had rejected any further injustice. Recognizing the Oder-Neisse Line was an issue of deep moral and historic significance. The question was whether the vicious circle of injustice and more injustice could be broken once and for all. But perhaps Germany's responsibility consisted specifically in taking this historic step, Poland having been the first and most severely damaged victim of the war triggered by Hitler.

As early as the summer of 1975 the new climate of détente was felt positively at the CSCE summit conference in Helsinki. When Poland's Central Committee's First Secretary Edward Gierek,

Prime Minister Piotr Jaroszewicz, and Foreign Minister Stephan Olszowski met with Chancellor Schmidt and me, both sides were honestly in search of solutions.

Bonn held intensive talks to prepare for the meeting. Chancellor Schmidt and Minister of Finance Hans Apel were reluctant to incur additional financial burdens. I pointed out the moral and historic dimensions of the relationship between Germany and Poland, as well as the large number of Germans—in fact, hundreds of thousands—who wished to leave Poland. I added that anyone aware of the predicament of these Germans, and anyone who realized the significance of a better future in the relationship between Germans and Poles, could not accept the current state of affairs. When Helmut Schmidt and I met with the Polish leaders in the Polish Embassy in Helsinki for a business dinner, our concern was with the steady improvement in relations between our two nations. We had to build new confidence. One thing all Poles agreed on: They wanted at last to live within secure rather than disputed borders.

After negotiations that at times took on dramatic proportions and continued for more than seven hours, ending only in the small hours of the morning, we agreed on a joint declaration. The agreements contained regulations concerning pensions, loans, and the unification of families. To satisfy Poland's demands for pensions, we agreed to pay a lump sum of 1.3 billion deutsche marks in three equal installments, the first to be handed over in 1976. We further agreed to a loan of 1 billion deutsche marks on generous terms, also payable in three installments beginning in 1976. For its part, Poland undertook to allow the departure of approximately 120,000 to 125,000 persons for West Germany within four years. In addition, an open-ended clause was intended to guarantee that applications for exit permits could be submitted even beyond the four-year period.

The meeting in Helsinki was enormously effective. One night Helmut Schmidt had a long conversation with Edward Gierek, in the course of which the two men came to trust each other. Schmidt never concealed his appreciation of Gierek, not even when Gierek had fallen from grace—an attitude which I believe deserves respect. Olszowski and I carried the burden of the negotiations during that night, and Olszowski was not an easy man to deal with. We had retreated to a bungalow on the grounds of the

Polish residence; the delegations were seated in the living room. We were surrounded by countless shopping bags: Olszowski's wife had taken advantage of the CSCE conference to go on an intense shopping spree, presumably providing for friends and family as well. Olszowski seemed annoyed at the presence of the bags, but by the time we arrived, it was too late to move them.

The parliamentary opposition in West Germany vehemently attacked the agreements we concluded. Franz Josef Strauss, the CSU party chairman, spoke of "endless Communist demands for money." Almost ten years later, faced with requests for loans from the East Germany, he took a different view. That time he was right.

On October 9, 1975, I left for my first official visit to Warsaw in my capacity as foreign minister. Olszowski and I were to finalize the understanding between West Germany and Poland that provided for the payment of pensions. We would also sign the agreement concerning loans and a long-term program for the development of economic, industrial, and technical cooperation between the two nations as well as on arrangements for resettlement of the Germans now living in Poland.

In the speech I delivered on November 7, 1975, to the Bundesrat (the states' parliament) on the occasion of the first reading of the treaties, I expounded in detail on the government's position on these contracts. The particulars of the resettlement were our top priority. I ended with a plea for the Germans living in Poland. Growing up in the part of Germany that later became East Germany, I had decided in 1952 to resettle in the other part of my homeland, the part where I would find freedom and democracy. I therefore felt a particular obligation toward those Germans in Poland who found themselves living in areas that had been split off from Germany after the Second World War. If they wanted to live in West Germany, I had an obligation to ease the way.

I did not ignore the shortcomings in the agreements, which I regretted as well. I freely admitted that "the government would have preferred reaching a final agreement on all resettlement applications within a specified period. The arrangements for resettlement indicate what is possible today; more could not be achieved at this time. The government has decided not to risk what is possible now by keeping an all-or-nothing stance." Such was precisely the decision the delegates of the West German Bundestag and, in the Bundesrat, the various German state governments were facing.

At the turn of the year the public took an active part in the debate on German-Polish relations. Early in November 1975 the synod of the EKD (the German Protestant Church) called on those who held "political responsibility . . . to keep this reconciliation—in full appreciation of all the objections raised against the agreements—from failure." The executive committee of the Central Committee of German Catholics issued similar statements, as did other organizations.

In my speech to the Bundestag, the states' senate, during the final debate on the German-Polish agreements on February 19, 1976, I again appealed to the opposition parties—the CDU and the CSU. (In the Bundesrat, the states' chamber, these parties held the majority of seats, and therefore they could nullify any treaty.) I said, "If we really want to arrive at an understanding, we must be willing to do what it is possible to do today, to keep the door open for what is still required, and to pave the way for what remains to be done in the future. Never believe that in German-Polish relations a willingness to compromise is asked only from Germany and only for our concerns."

The Bundestag vote resulted in 276 votes for the Polish treaties, including 13 from CDU delegates and 1 from a CSU delegate, and 191 against. However, the CDU/CSU made its approval in the Bundesrat contingent on a guarantee, to be obtained by some objective procedure yet to be determined, that all Germans in Poland would be allowed to leave within four to six years.

Ratification was in serious jeopardy. In the end I tried to settle the issue under debate between Poland and West Germany by suggesting new language: "The government of the Federal Republic of Germany attaches great importance to the renewed assurance that in the course of four years approximately 120,000 to 125,000 persons will be granted approval of their application for permission to leave Poland on the basis of the information obtained and in accord with the criteria and procedures contained therein, and that furthermore no time limits will be set for the expedited processing of applications by people who meet the necessary criteria, which means that in these cases permission to leave may also be granted according to said procedures." After renewed contact, Poland finally agreed on March 11 to accept my written language and to meet our final demand: to eliminate the word *may*.

Securing the Bundesrat's ratification was principally accomplished by two men: Franz-Josef Röder, at that time prime minister of Saarland, and Ernst Albrecht, prime minister of Lower Saxony, both members of the CDU. It is because of their efforts that the Bundesrat adopted a constructive attitude, which advanced our national interests. Thus what had begun as a test of strength between the administration and the opposition became an exemplary case of cooperation. Of course this outcome was possible only because the administration and the opposition had, or at least agreed on, a common goal. The administration must be ready to listen to and use the opposition's arguments without ill-conceived self-importance. The actual historic significance of softening the CDU and CSU heads of the various states in the Bundesrat, a feat that Röder and Albrecht accomplished, lay in the implied decision on West Germany's future relations with Poland. It was important to have the two Christian Union parties on board in this matter, especially since there could be no doubt that Röder and Albrecht had acted with the backing of Helmut Kohl, at that time chairman of the CDU. The full importance of this incident, however, became clear only after Kohl assumed the chancellorship.

In the years that followed, the Polish government honored the agreements. Between 1976 and 1979, 134,000 Germans arrived in West Germany, and by 1982 the number had reached almost a quarter of a million.

Glancing Ahead: Changes in Poland and the Policies of the Kohl-Genscher Administration

The policy we pursued in the 1970s was to prove fruitful in later years. On March 19 and 20, 1981, I again visited Poland. At that time we were deeply concerned with the possibility of intervention by the Warsaw Pact. In Warsaw I held talks with President Wojciech Jaruzelski, with Secretary Stanislaw Kania, and with Foreign Minister Jósef Czyrek.

During my after-dinner speech I had already called for a policy of nonintervention in the internal affairs of foreign nations. My statement was directed at those members of the Warsaw Pact who were critical of the rise of Solidarity in Poland. In my conversation with Jaruzelski I became more explicit. "If a foreign power were to intervene by military force in the internal affairs of Poland, the consequences would be incalculable. Intervention would produce a fundamental change in Europe." During this talk, as during other exchanges, I left no doubt that intervention on the part of other Warsaw Pact members would evoke a Western response that differed markedly from Western reaction to analagous actions in the 1940s, 1950s, and 1960s.

Martial law, which was imposed on December 13, 1981, also called for an unambiguous response. I spelled out our position to Deputy Prime Minister Mieczyslaw Rakowski when he came to Bonn in late December to explain the situation in Poland.

I stated that under no circumstances could West Germany accept martial law, and I referred to the Helsinki agreements, to which Poland was also a signatory. Current events, I said, were in fundamental opposition to both the content and the spirit of the Helsinki Final Act. In our country, just as within our government, the union known as Solidarity and its leader, Lech Walesa, were profoundly respected. I therefore demanded that martial law be lifted immediately, that those who had been arrested be released, and that a dialogue be initiated with the leading representatives of Solidarity as well as with the Catholic Church. Later, at the CSCE review conference in Madrid, I again appealed to the Polish government: "Abolish martial law. Release the prisoners. Resume the dialogue with Solidarity. Allow the scholars and scientists to resume their work. Take seriously the wishes of the nations of the European Community and the Western Alliance to pave the way once again for a continuation and deepening of the CSCE process and to keep the door open to expansion of political and economic relations. We are aware of the hardships of the Polish people. It is our wish to see a Poland whose government, now and in the future, resolutely walks the path of renewal and once again takes up the road to reform, just as the Polish government promised its own people and the governments of Europe. Such a Poland can count on our active support." I added, "I appeal to the government of the Soviet Union: Let the People's Republic of Poland determine freely and without outside influence its road to renewal and reform, in accordance with the principles of the Helsinki Final Act."

West Germany's attitude to Poland did not change after Helmut Kohl's election to the chancellorship in 1982. Clarity and continuity were still the dominant elements. The SPD, which was now the parliamentary opposition, gave my policy in regard to Poland its unconditional support.

I had planned an official visit to Warsaw to begin on November 21, 1984. The night before my departure, only a few hours before my plane was scheduled to take off, I canceled the visit because all attempts to settle three items of great political importance had failed. The first matter concerned the journalist Carl-Gustav Ströhm of *Die Welt,* a conservative newspaper, who, as usual, wanted to report on my visit from Warsaw. Known for his biting critical commentary on my foreign policy and events in Poland, he was refused the necessary entry visa, a form of censorship I found absolutely unacceptable. A basic principle was at stake.

The second point turned on the fact that I planned to lay a wreath at the grave of a German soldier. It was a custom I had exercised in Czechoslovakia and other nations, even in the Soviet Union; in spite of the past, therefore, I thought the gesture should be appropriate in Poland as well. During a previous visit I had planned on placing a bouquet of flowers on a German soldier's grave that had been unearthed at a building site in Warsaw. My schedule had not, after all, permitted me to carry out my intention, but I had a member of our delegation put the flowers on the grave. Now I hoped to make up for the earlier omission, though I was well aware that my action would touch a particularly sensitive nerve in Poland, and above all in Warsaw.

But graves are the ground on which peace must begin. Our war cemeteries are not shrines intended for hero worship. Each grave is an admonition that peace is precious and one must risk everything to preserve it. When we stand at these gravesides where each cross bears the dates that mark the lifespan—usually so short—of the dead, we become aware of what the war Hitler unleashed did even to our own people and how far the torch of war was flung throughout Europe and beyond. So many hopes that mothers and fathers bestowed upon their children in their early years, so much love felt by wives, girlfriends, children, brothers, and sisters for the dead—all buried here with these soldiers. No one ever asked them whether they approved of the war, or whether they were willing to fight in it. Most of them were children when Hitler came to power. Such a soldier's grave might have been dug for me as well—not in these foreign fields, but somewhere in Germany, where, before the war was over, I was sent to what had become the front. Whenever I visited German military cemeteries with my delegation, we felt even more strongly what it meant to work in the service of peace. It is a fact: Peace must begin at the graves, not only for the dead but also for the spirit of peace among the living. Graves are the place where our desire for peace must draw its strength.

But perhaps refusing to grant a visa to a journalist and forbidding my visit to the soldier's grave were mere pretexts. I had also—and this was the third and probably most serious bone of contention, openly criticized by the Polish government's press officer—intended to visit the grave of Father Jerzy Popieluszku, who had been murdered by the police. I meant to express my sympathy and solidarity with the women and men of the Polish liberation movement by placing a wreath at the graveside.

Whatever the underlying reason, Poland's government felt unable to grant my request on any of these three issues. When, late the night before my departure, Warsaw still had not given in, I canceled my visit. It was not an easy decision, but to this day I believe it was the right one. German-Polish relations remain historically difficult and need special nurturing. However, at the time we could not accept censorship of the German press, nor was I willing to accept being barred from the graves of the German soldier and Popieluszku. Surely it should be possible to quietly honor German soldiers fallen on Polish soil. And surely we owed it to the Polish opposition and its representatives, as well as to the Polish Church, to honor Popieluszku, the victim of political murder.

The cancellation of my visit attracted considerable notice. Reaction in Poland told me that my decision evoked a great deal of understanding, though each of the three issues received a very different response. There was great sympathy both for my insistence on visiting Popieluszku's grave and my support of the controversial reporter; opinions were divided, however, on my wish to lay a wreath on a German soldier's grave. The latter was to play an important role when, during a stopover in Warsaw in 1985, I had a meeting with Jaruzelski.

On March 6, 1985, I accompanied West German President Karl

Carstens on an official visit to Helsinki. From there I intended to fly to Sofia by way of Warsaw. At this time Communism was losing its grip on Eastern Europe. On March 10, 1985, the Soviet head of state and party chairman Konstantin Chernenko died, and with him died the rule of the old men, Brezhnev among them. Mikhail Gorbachev was a member of the Politburo at the time; his statements during his earlier trip to England had provided a reason to pay attention.

I wanted to use my stopover in Warsaw, which would last several hours and, because it was informal, was not restricted by protocol, to continue talks with the Polish leaders that had been broken off the previous winter. I met with Jaruzelski and Olszowski, as well as with Primate Josef Cardinal Glemp. Jaruzelski, who seemed genuinely interested in improving relations, had taken the opportunity of my brief stopover to arrange a dinner for me, at which Deputy Prime Minister Rakowski was also present, along with the foreign minister and Party Chairman Kowalczik. During the talk I made it clear that an official visit could not be considered until the three reasons for the cancellation of my previous scheduled visit were resolved.

Cardinal Glemp, on whom I also called, expressed his pleasure at my visit; I replied that my trip entailed great difficulties. Today, I said, I could make an informal stopover, which could not take the place of an arranged official visit. I meant my words to indicate that the conditions I had set down earlier would hold for my coming visit as well. Nothing could be retracted, and in fact, I later fulfilled all my plans: I laid the wreath, I visited with the Church, and paid my respects at Popieluszku's grave. Furthermore, the makeup of the German press delegation was as I had proposed.

In the course of our conversation Cardinal Glemp mentioned that he was very optimistic about the future; from the Church's point of view, it was important to support the cause of peace and to see to it that Poland took its natural, appropriate place within the family of nations.

I told Cardinal Glemp that in Germany we had focused intently on events in Poland since the murder of Popieluszku and that I hoped the Polish people could sense how deeply this crime touched West Germans. "What consequences," I finally asked, "will the trial against the assassins have on relations between church and state and on the Polish domestic situation?"

Glemp replied that the murder and the trial marked crucial stages; a new era was about to begin. The Polish government was willing to expose evil within its own official apparatus and to create respect for the law. This intention, he thought, was commendable.

In response to my question about the ways West Germany could contribute to an understanding between Germans and Poles, ways that would win favor with the Polish people as well, Glemp pointed out that it was a complicated problem. Germans and Poles were very familiar with each other, they had been living cheek by jowl for a long time. Yet the patriotic organizations of the Germans whose territories had been assigned to Poland, both Silesians and Pomeranians, exerted an unfortunate influence. Of course there was a right to a place to call home, but the search for Germans and for Germany here in Poland of all places seemed somewhat artificial.

All human beings should have the right to embrace the nation they chose, I replied. We were therefore hoping that our efforts on behalf of those who wanted to leave Poland would be successful, since this was one way to ease tensions. And as for the border issue—that is, the Oder-Neisse Line—the Chancellor and I had explained our position often enough. There was no cause for anyone in Poland to be troubled on this score. Nor should the problem be seen as a tool; it was not a suitable weapon with which to attack the Germans politically. Those Germans exiled from their home in what was now Poland were supporting our Eastern policy just like any other citizens, but no one could take their past from them. Besides, looking back was only part of our job; it was time to work together to forge the future.

I continued by telling Cardinal Glemp that when speaking with Olszowski, I had expressed the hope that the Polish government would not prevent the Church from holding services in German. Olszowski had merely replied that this decision was up to the Church. Glemp acknowledged that if the priest could speak some German, confessions could be heard in German but that there was no interest in German-language masses. Perhaps we could join in organizing a mass in German, I rejoined, to show him the lively interest in such a service and the number of the faithful eager to confess in German.

Relations with the People's Republic of Poland continued to unfold at a snail's pace. On January 10, 1988, I was finally able to set out on my official visit, which had been postponed for more than three years. I wanted to give new impetus to stagnant German-Polish relations. Of course diplomatic contacts had been maintained, but until my visit, no further agreements had been negotiated to a final stage.

In his speech the Polish foreign minister picked up my phrase *moral dimension,* as an aspect of our relations. Part of this dimension, he noted, was the fate of Germans who had lost their homes. I pricked up my ears. It seemed that the Polish government realized for the first time what expulsion meant to us.

The heart of all the meetings was my talk with Jaruzelski. He complained about our lack of aid, our lack of trust, and the West's interference in the internal affairs of his country. He argued that the situation in Europe would have worsened drastically if the Polish government had not imposed martial law in 1981. Perhaps the very building in which we were meeting would no longer be standing. The decision, in December 1981, had been dramatic for Poland. He respected, he said, the way I had handled the "private" part of my current visit—an allusion to my visits to the military cemetery, to Popieluszku's grave, and to Glemp the previous day. These three visits, and the cordial reception we had received from crowds waiting for us, were impressive proof to me of the Polish people's will to freedom. On the other hand Jaruzelski was harshly critical of my contacts with groups he called "mercenaries in the pay of a foreign superpower," referring to my meeting with Lech Walesa, the leader of Solidarity.

I realized that, politically speaking, Jaruzelski had his back to the wall at the time. It seemed to me that he was striking out in every direction. I replied, "Open up every opportunity for freedom of opinion, freedom of the press, and political pluralism. Our opposition to martial law was not because we want to harm Poland but because we want to help the Polish people." I added that when the Polish foreign minister visited West Germany, he was free to meet with whomever he chose. I was reserving the same

right for myself during my visits to Poland, and I was not prepared to have this right curtailed.

Toward the end of our talk Jaruzelski apparently realized that
he had gone too far, and he tried to soften his stand. He ended by
saying, in a conciliatory tone, that he would be happy to see the
Chancellor in Poland before long.

My talk with Jaruzelski in 1988 proved to me that the Communist leaders in Poland were increasingly removed from the realities
of their own country. Though they stopped making direct attempts to prevent my meeting with Walesa, they did try to cast
doubt on Walesa's probity. I have often speculated on the place
history will assign Jaruzelski. After the Second World War figures
of historical significance emerged among the enslaved and op-
pressed Polish people. For a time Stefan Cardinal Wyszynski embodied the Poles' hope and faith in the future, as the Catholic
Church and its prominent representatives had often done during
the country's fluctuating and tragic history. Pope John Paul II is
another native of Poland who gave the people strength and faith
in the Catholic Church from its highest seat of power. And, of
course, there is Lech Walesa, a man of extraordinary courage,
which is rooted in his Catholic belief and his Polish identity. Even
during the Brezhnev regime Walesa initiated the course of events
that led to freedom in the Soviet sphere of power. The Polish
people, who had been the first victims of the Second World War,
thus became the pioneers of the liberation movements in the Warsaw Pact nations in the 1980s. This is what constitutes Lech
Walesa's historic and European importance.

Given this background, what place remains for Jaruzelski? Was
he the Polish patriot who imposed martial law in order to prevent
war and civil war and thus the intervention of the Red Army and
the other Warsaw Pact forces? Or was he the willing agent of the
Soviet claim to power? It is the Polish people who will have to
render a verdict on him. It seemed to me that Jaruzelski was a Pole
first and a Communist second, and that if he had been completely
free to make his own decisions, he would have set out on the path
to democratization more speedily and more resolutely. Preventing
outside military intervention seems to have been his highest priority. What would intervention have meant for Poland, for Europe,
and for the further course of history?

Perhaps Poland needed both men, Walesa and Jaruzelski, before the nation could become the pioneer in the European strike for freedom. History knows such examples. Gorbachev has a high opinion of Jaruzelski. How much does Gorbachev really know about Jaruzelski's role? The peoples of Europe should never forget that early, very early, freedom-loving Poland, represented by Walesa and Solidarity, kindled the flame of hope and not only for its own people. Time will tell what role the Polish people ultimately assign to Jaruzelski. Yet Lech Walesa and his courageous fellow fighters have already found their place: in Polish history, as symbols of the will to independence and freedom and of the steadfast faith typical of their countrymen; and in European history as pioneers of liberty.

I fully understood how wrong Jaruzelski's assessment of Solidarity's influence was when I received Lech Walesa on the early afternoon of January 12, 1988, for a talk at the West German embassy. He was accompanied by Professor Bronislaw Geremek; by Tadeusz Mazowiecki, who later became prime minister; and by Dr. Olyskjevic. I opened the conversation by remarking that a long time before, I had wanted to meet with representatives of Solidarity and visit Father Popieluszku's grave; back then, these actions had been prohibited, but I had persisted in pursuing my goals. Today I had finally succeeded. Walesa thanked me for my insistence as well as for providing an opportunity to have this meeting. As to what was customary in foreign policy and diplomacy, he urged me to understand why, during this phase of the struggle, Solidarity could not always act according to the rules of diplomacy and forge ties with whomever it chose. I broke in to note that until 1952 I had lived in East Germany and therefore had personal experience of many of the difficulties he was facing.

Walesa then explained his views of the political, social, and economic problems of his country. I was impressed both by his person and by what he had to say. His principal concern was economic reform; Poland, he insisted, must no longer be Europe's beggar. He therefore gave primary importance to relations with West Germany. He hoped that mutual cooperation could be further advanced. I replied that we would gladly increase economic cooperation; decentralization and a decrease in bureaucracy were important. Walesa emphasized that aid from a nation as powerful as West Germany was significant to Poland's progress.

I learned that in order to meet with me, Walesa had been forced to bow to conditions that were unacceptable. He told me that the shipyard management had turned down his application for a vacation, which he had submitted in order to meet with me; he had therefore permitted himself to take a leave of absence. Though he was smiling, he added that he was afraid he might lose his job.

Walesa described the system's oppressive nature and the people's lack of faith in the future and their lack of hope. Jaruzelski was headed in the right direction, he agreed, but he was moving much too slowly. At the current rate, another two or three hundred years would have to pass before the country would see any change; since there was not that much time, he and Solidarity had deliberately decided to speed up the course of events. I noted that not only was Poland at the top of our Eastern policy's priority list, but it also had the most famous Catholic cleric and the most famous union leader in the world. Lech Walesa was visibly pleased to be mentioned in the same breath with the Pope.

He looked utterly determined as he calmly noted that the second phase of Solidarity's struggle was about to begin. I declared that Solidarity was evidence of the power of freedom in Poland, and without Solidarity, Poland would be a different country. I told Walesa that I was hoping we could talk again soon, not only in Warsaw, and above all, under more favorable circumstances.

My meeting with Walesa reinforced my impression that the reform movement Walesa and Solidarity represented had gained a great deal of ground in the Soviet sphere of power. Yet just as in the early 1980s, most observers in the West were not able to recognize that with the emergence of this movement the first step on the road to freedom and independence had been made. At that time, however, no one could know with absolute certainty whether this evolution was truly irreversible and most importantly, whether the use of Warsaw Pact forces to quash the movement could definitely be ruled out.

In the course of the past forty years the West had become accustomed to thinking of the Soviet sphere of power in a way that consistently overestimated the Communist camp's internal stability and unanimity. What the West tended to regard as firm and solid had in reality long since become rotten, hollow, and rigid. Such misinterpretations were among the main reasons for the numerous arguments among the Western allies in 1988 and 1989— well before short-range missiles became the issue.

Relations with the Vatican: United in the Desire to Decrease Confrontation in Europe

When Pope John Paul II ascended the papal throne, a new era of the greatest significance began for the Vatican's foreign policy, and my private audiences with him therefore mattered a great deal to me. Serious and thoughtful, the Pope made a lasting impression. He spoke flawless German, and his slow and heavy speech lent his words great depth. Every time we met, we discussed the situation in Poland and in East Germany, our relationship with the latter, and events in the Soviet Union. We agreed that among the Warsaw Pact nations the Church fared best in Poland and East Germany. As regarded our policy of cooperation with the Warsaw Pact nations, our encounters encouraged me greatly.

The Pope always received me in the same room. He sat at the long side of a heavy desk with a large, empty surface; I had a seat along the narrow side. Listening intently, he rested his chin on his right hand. I tried to convey to him my conviction that the CSCE's policy of détente and the sincere struggle for disarmament would eventually lead to success. These were the methods, I would argue, that would ultimately heal the rift in Europe, so that a unified Germany and Poland would enjoy an entirely new kind of relationship.

Repeatedly I stressed my favorable judgment of Gorbachev's policies. The Pope seemed particularly focused on the questions of what Gorbachev wanted and what he was setting in motion.

During our conversations the Pope spoke not only in his capacity as head of the Catholic Church (his evaluations showed clearly that he received superb intelligence from the Catholic Church in the Soviet sphere of power). He also spoke as a Pole. He understood very well why I preferred cooperation between West and East to confrontation. Referring to some previous remark, I once suggested that despite all discrepancies in questions of faith and social policies, we probably understood each other so well because we had both lived in the Soviet sphere of power, without either of us entertaining thoughts of revenge or becoming trapped in the blind mentality of crusaders. Quite the opposite: Neither of us could see a justifiable alternative to the policy of détente and cooperation, and to the CSCE process, in which the Vatican was a participant.

It was to turn out that we were in agreement on yet another issue: in our assessment of events in Yugoslavia in 1991. More clearly than many Western governments, the Vatican recognized the dangers bound to arise from the Serbs' claim to hegemony, a claim that was becoming more and more clearly expressed, threatening the peaceful coexistence of the peoples of Yugoslavia. When it came to recognizing Croatia and Slovenia, the Vatican displayed extreme reluctance. During my visit in the Vatican on November 29, 1991, this attempt to remain aloof was particularly apparent. I understood that attitude; the accusation that on this issue the Vatican and West Germany formed a "conspiracy" is therefore very wide of the mark. No one outside of Yugoslavia was interested in the least in the dissolution of Yugoslavia; it was only the pan-Serbian strife for hegemony that set the country's dissolution in motion. It was the Serbian heirs of the nation's founder, Tito, that destroyed the Federal Republic of Yugoslavia.

During that visit to the Vatican I first met the Vatican's "foreign minister," Angelo Sodano. I explained to him that in regard to the issue of recognition, Bonn was not going to act unilaterally. Rather, the EC and the CSCE needed to arrive at a joint position, and care must be taken to make sure that the old fronts of 1914 and 1941 were not reactivated. For historic reasons, I argued, Poland's attitude was going to be particularly important. Like us, the Vatican Secretary of State was disappointed about the conference in The Hague.

Subsequently I spoke with the Pope for an hour, as always, in private. He, too, was concerned with events in the collapsing Yugoslavia. As a Central European, familiar with the significance of nationalism for Central and Southeastern Europe, he was well aware of the suffering the issue had caused time and again throughout history—a knowledge that explained the Vatican's cautious and dispassionate responses. We also discussed Poland and events in the Soviet Union since the coup of August 1991.

We parted on a note of shared pessimism. This was my last meeting with the Pope in my capacity as foreign minister. I had come to know him as a pope who in a historic era used his authority and whatever was in his power to help abolish the division of Europe by peaceful means and who, supported by the gospels, opposed the spirit of confrontation in order to pave the way for mutual understanding through cooperation and détente.

Part Two

---

*Three Pillars
of Germany's Policy
of Responsibility*

4

The CSCE Process

Multilateral Eastern Policy on the Road to German Unity

The Helsinki Final Act

By issuing the draft of the Harmel Report in 1967, NATO confirmed that the German question continued to be crucially important to peace in Europe. At the same time the Western Alliance agreed on a new two-track strategy toward the Eastern bloc: on the one hand, strengthening defenses; on the other, building on the first, a willingness to enter into a dialogue and to cooperate with the East. The original aim of this strategy was the healing of the division of Germany and of Europe; instead, the Alliance's "highest goal" became the creation of a permanent and just peace in Europe.

The West began to give more open-minded consideration to the Soviet and Warsaw Pact plan for a pan-European security conference. But the proposal was not seriously pursued until, after 1969, the socialist-liberal Brandt-Scheel administration, with its novel Eastern policy, set out on the road of cooperation with the Soviet Union and its allies, in particular with East Germany. The treaties with Moscow and Warsaw, the Basic Treaty with the GDR, and the treaty with Czechoslovakia were an expression and a result of this policy.

The Four Power Agreement on Berlin of September 3, 1971, was an integral part of the treaty policy of the new West German government, which dared to break away from the rigidity of the 1960s, just as the Letter on German Unity was linked with the treaties with the Soviet Union and East Germany.

When the time came to lay down specifics for a conference, the Europeans insisted on the participation of the United States and Canada, contrary to Moscow's wishes. The West also refused to limit the conference to the topic of military security; it was firm about including in the agenda the human dimension—especially human rights and humanitarian issues. In November 1972 negotiations for the CSCE (Conference on Security and Cooperation in Europe) began with a conference of foreign ministers in Helsinki. Both German nations were represented by their foreign ministers, Walter Scheel and Otto Winzer. On July 3, 1973, the CSCE was launched in Helsinki; the foreign ministers of thirty-three European nations, Canada, and the United States participated.

Negotiations on the Helsinki Final Act were fully under way when I became foreign minister in May 1974. During the first days of my tenure—before my first meeting with Henry Kissinger in early June—Günther van Well called my attention to the issue of peaceful change; this disputed, but for us absolutely crucial, clause centered on the necessity of keeping alive not only the German question but also of taking further steps toward unification within the EC by including the specific wording in the Helsinki Final Act. It was intended to assure a peaceful change of borders and to secure for us the German as well as the European option for such transformation.

Initially even our Western partners had no real comprehension of our reason for insisting on the clause about peaceful change. It was my impression that not only the Soviet Union but also some of our Western friends were worried that we might use the clause to question the Oder-Neisse Line—the post–Second World War border between East Germany and Poland.

During a confidential meeting with Gromyko in 1974 I took the bull by the horns, and told him that I would never agree to the Final Act if it did not appropriately and unequivocally allow for the possibility of peaceful change of frontiers. "You will never get us to ultimately approve the status quo on the basis of two German nations," I clarified my point.

"Do you want to raise the issue of borders in Europe again?" he asked.

"If you wish," I replied, "we can specifically link the 'peaceful change' clause with removing the border between the two Germanys and thus with abolishing the division of Germany and with its integration into the EC."

I was aware that Gromyko would consider that solution to be the less acceptable alternative. He rejected it wordlessly, with a mere gesture. I told my Western counterparts about this conversation. It seemed a way to allay their secret fear about Germany's eastern border without my having to address the topic explicitly.

In the end the diplomatic triangle of Kissinger, Genscher, and Gromyko settled the issue of peaceful change satisfactorily. Even Kissinger, who otherwise maintained a healthy skepticism toward the CSCE, backed our vested interest on this issue. Gromyko assumed that Kissinger's proposals—which we always agreed on beforehand, word for word—reflected the United States' attitude and respected them as such, and we accepted the result without qualifications. During my close collaboration with Secretary of State James Baker in the course of the Two-Plus-Four talks in 1990, I remembered my "peaceful change cooperation" with Kissinger fifteen years earlier. In 1990 the same close collaboration with the United States was what ultimately worked in winning Moscow's agreement.

Principle I of the Helsinki Final Act includes the Hamlet Wording, according to which each nation has the right "to be or not to be" party to treaties of alliance. Subsequently, during the Two-Plus-Four meetings, we could allude to this clause to affirm our right to belong to NATO even as a unified Germany. Conversely, Hungary later based itself on the same clause when it chose to withdraw from the Warsaw Pact. The Final Act contains other fluid principles that take cognizance of the future, particularly the principle of human rights and the right to self-determination. These principles also supported our endeavor to unite the two Germanys. For us Germans, who lived in two states, the Final Act's so-called Basket III, which dealt with humanitarian concerns, the "human dimension," was also of particular importance.

□   □   □   □

All these reasons enabled me, in the government's declaration of July 25, 1975, to the Bundestag, to recommend unqualified approval of the Final Act and conclusion of negotiations at the summit level in Helsinki on August 1. To the best of my knowledge, the Bundestag was thus the only parliament of the Western nations that became involved with the CSCE process in detail, an illustration of the important role foreign policy played in the divided Germany. The Final Act required neither the West nor Germany to change its policies or principles; but in order to fulfill its commitment, the East was obligated to gradually soften, both domestically and toward the rest of the world. The train had been put back on track; now it was starting to move, driven by the people within the Soviet sphere of power, who could now refer to the Final Act, but also kept in motion by the Communist nations' growing interest in expanding cooperation within the CSCE. The West, on the other hand, had the responsibility of overseeing adherence to the Final Act; it made use of the CSCE review conferences, which were held every other year, as well as all the other numerous CSCE forums to this end. The CSCE's underlying purpose, that all participants be able to use the agreement to their advantage, was thus corroborated. The policy of all or nothing, which until 1969—the beginning of the new Eastern policy—had suffered one defeat after another, was terminated. The new policies gradually changed the overall European situation.

Nevertheless, it was not easy for me to persuade all my Western colleagues that the broadest possible CSCE process was the surest means of fulfilling the obligations agreed to in the Final Act. Again and again disputes arose as to whether interrupting the CSCE process might work to move the Soviet Union in one direction or another. I adamantly opposed such considerations, which Washington raised regularly; if the CSCE was furthering the development of Western values, an interruption of the process could not be a suitable means of "punishing" the Soviet Union. I never tired of pointing out that "the West will not be the first to leave the negotiating table." Preserving the momentum of the CSCE process meant maintaining the dynamics of change, at first almost imperceptibly, but then more and more overtly.

Though it was not made explicit, the controversy about peaceful change had turned the German question into a central point in the debate on the Final Act. Even more significantly, the debate led to the programmatic result we had desired. The way the Soviet Union dealt with the problem points to the core of our negotiating strategy in foreign policy: Had Moscow accepted the term *peaceful change* without objection, the term would not have been closely related to the German question. Yet by attempting to attain the seemingly unattainable, we arrived at a fundamental breakthrough in the problem that was central to our foreign policy: abolishing the division of Germany and of Europe, in a document that was signed by thirty-five nations, among them the four countries responsible for Germany as a whole. That element was especially important to us.

At the time I wondered what had made a man as experienced in negotiations as Gromyko maneuver himself into a position that left him no option other than total retreat. Then as now I believed that the Soviet foreign minister was firmly convinced that he would be able to assert himself. His remark at the beginning of the talks—that he and the three great Western powers (the United States, the United Kingdom, and France) were of one mind—proved how sure he was of himself. I have often thought back on those disputes; they became a constant reminder never to make an impossible demand that would land me in a situation bound to end in a deterioration of the status quo.

The Helsinki Final Act obligated the Soviet Union and the other Warsaw Pact nations to adapt their domestic situations to the protection of human rights and freedoms in accordance with Basket III. Such adherence could not be accomplished overnight but could come about only gradually, in a frequently painful process that demanded patience, judgment, and perseverance and did not preclude relapses. An understanding of the CSCE as a *process* thus became its core. The Final Act finalized nothing, nor did it create a new situation; but it opened the door to fundamental changes in Europe and to a new relationship between West and East.

The signing of the Final Act successfully ended the largest international conference in Europe since the 1815 Congress of Vienna. In West Germany the CDU and the CSU voted against ratification. The only other country in which a minority party rejected it was Italy, and Albania was the lone European nation that did not join the CSCE. The signing of the Final Act was an unprecedented step in postwar history: For the first time since the United Nations Charter of 1945 the West and the Communist nations committed themselves to rules of conduct in their relations. They were further able to agree on questions of values, even if, for the time being, such agreement was only a formality.

One of the positive experiences in the negotiations on the Final Act and the CSCE program was cooperation with the neutral and uncommitted countries—Sweden, Finland, Austria, Yugoslavia, and Switzerland. Though we were not linked with them through the Western Alliance or the European Community, our shared values connected us nevertheless. The Swiss, otherwise rather reluctant in matters of multilateral development, assumed a particularly active role in the CSCE process; Edouard Brunner, their longtime United Nations representative, is closely identified with these efforts, which opened a new dimension in Swiss foreign policy.

Helsinki 1975: A Time and Place for the Birth of a New Europe

On August 1, 1975, Chancellor Helmut Schmidt and I traveled to Helsinki for the signing of the Final Act. All participants in the CSCE summit in Helsinki sensed that Brezhnev was in very poor health. His condition became glaringly obvious during the state dinner Finland's President Urho Kekkonen hosted the evening of the opening day; after the first course Brezhnev left the table, and his seat remained empty. None of those present turned the event into a public incident.

The German-Soviet meeting was scheduled for the second evening. It was preceded by Finland's farewell reception for the delegations, with Brezhnev and Gromyko also attending. We left the function at about the same time, since the meeting had been scheduled for six o'clock in the Soviet Embassy—one of those Soviet buildings, by the way, whose sheer size was meant to symbolize Moscow's supremacy over the host nation. Its massiveness reminded me of the Soviet Embassy in East Berlin, which resembled an embassy less than it did a ruler's residence. It is one of Finland's great political achievements that the Soviet Union never managed to influence it to such an extent. Finland's policies were always characterized by good judgment, realism, and a national consensus to prevent the Soviet Union from directly interfering with its freedom to make its own decisions about its political and social system and to preserve enough elbow room to keep the country from having to join the Warsaw Pact. In exchange, Finland gave up joining NATO and the EC.

For the German-Soviet meeting in Helsinki, the plan was to follow an initial talk with a joint dinner. Chancellor Schmidt and I had also prepared a subsequent meeting with the German press at our hotel. In scheduling the meeting, we had assumed that the entire event—the talk as well as the dinner—would, as usual, take about three hours. But the conversation progressed very slowly. Brezhnev was apparently having serious health problems, and it was difficult for him to talk. After about an hour Gromyko gave me a sign that he wanted to speak with me. He led me into an adjoining room, where a huge table had been set. "You can see that we really intended to offer you dinner, but I must ask you to suggest to the Chancellor that our meeting end. You will have noticed how difficult it is for the Secretary General to continue." We returned to the negotiating chamber, and in a whisper, I passed Gromyko's request on to Schmidt. Finishing his thought, Schmidt deftly found a formulation leading to a concluding remark: Since everything had gone so well, we could be pleased with the outcome of our talk. Then we left with adequate ceremony.

Leaving was not easy, however. The press had assumed that the meeting would go on for some hours so we had to consider what to do. Of course we would not reveal the true reason for the evening's early end. Nor did we want the press and public to learn how short the meeting had been, as it was commonly acknowledged that the Soviets chose to indicate the importance it assigned to its counterparts by the length of time it spent with them. In Germany as well as the rest of the world it would be assumed that our meeting had been cut so drastically short because a serious difference of opinion, if not a crisis in German-Soviet relations, had arisen—and such a belief would not be in our best interest. We therefore decided to conceal the actual extent of the meeting; we directed our fleet of cars to go by a roundabout route, and finally, without arousing too much attention, we arrived at our hotel. Later we held the press conference without going into details of the talk, which never became known during the Secretary General's lifetime. I am convinced that our discretion regarding

101

Brezhnev's physical condition contributed to the Soviets' increased trust in us, a feeling that could only be in the interest of German-Soviet relations.

I behaved in a similar fashion on a subsequent occasion when Gromyko felt faint while addressing the United Nations. He had to cut his speech short and was led from the speaker's platform by two Soviet diplomats. He nevertheless insisted on attending the scheduled luncheon at the West German embassy. When he arrived, I led him to the library on the pretext of conversation. I offered to let him rest on the sofa while I read quietly in a corner and told him no one would ever learn what had gone on in the room. He was content to rest in an armchair for half an hour. We never revealed the truth of this encounter either.

The presence of two German delegations at the first CSCE summit could not help but draw considerable attention from all sides. I was not present at the first meeting between Helmut Schmidt and Erich Honecker, but I did have a meeting with East Germany's deputy foreign minister, Oskar Fischer, representing Otto Winzer, who was already seriously ill and whom he subsequently succeeded in office. Our meeting was cool and formal; only gradually did a relationship develop that allowed us to talk freely with each other.

Fischer seemed to see me first and foremost as an emigrant from East Germany—he clearly had great reservations about me. I, too, was unable and unwilling to suppress my feelings. Later on, however, I came to appreciate Fischer as a person. He appeared to be a true believer, but he was not a fanatic. And in instances that required the cooperation of both German states for securing peace in Europe I sensed his absolute agreement, even though it was clear that he could operate only within strict limits. I believe that his efforts to help solve humanitarian problems were sincere, particularly in September 1989, when we were faced with the dilemma of the overcrowded Prague embassy.

A Process Gets Under Way:
The CSCE Review Conferences and Forums

In my opinion two basic principles had to remain central to the CSCE process: first, linkage between political and military security, and second, the demand that détente benefit people directly and be supported by them.

After the Helsinki summit, however, the CSCE struggled along only with some difficulty. As we had predicted, the Soviet Union and other Warsaw Pact nations did not immediately fulfill the high expectations in the area of human rights (which were especially high in the United States). Nevertheless, as we had hoped, citizens of the Soviet Union and other Communist countries now began to invoke the Final Act; this was true for many well-known dissidents, such as Yuri Orlov, Andrei Sakharov, and Václav Havel, as well as many others who were less well known. It was especially these unknown protesters who must not be forgotten, as I repeatedly emphasized.

The first CSCE follow-up meeting took place in Belgrade in 1977–1978. Discussion centered on the Soviet Union's practices in the area of human rights; criticism was raised primarily by the United States. By comparison the remaining CSCE topics were not of great significance. Yet this exclusive focus on one theme, however central, was not in accordance with the European CSCE philosophy, for the "genius of the Final Act" lay precisely in the concept of the so-called baskets—Basket I: principles, security; Basket II: economic cooperation; Basket III: the human dimension. In our view the further development of the process and its own dynamics could best be served if everyone, including the Eastern nations, profited from the CSCE. Since 1975 I have not ceased to advocate this view.

The Belgrade meeting ended without substantial agreement and in a spirit of controversy. The only achievement was that agreement was reached on organizing future review conferences on a regular basis. This project assured the continuity of the process that we had wished for. The United States, however, remained skeptical, and during the following CSCE conferences I repeatedly and intensively had to try to sell our program to the secretaries of state of the changing United States administrations.

The Madrid follow-up meeting, which dragged on from 1980 to 1983, was long overshadowed by complex West-East crises. Even before the conference opened, the Soviet Union had invaded Afghanistan, and martial law was declared in Poland in December 1981. Both these events represented severe and blatant violations

103

of the Final Act. Could détente continue under these circumstances? The United States, and in particular Secretary of State Alexander Haig, spoke out strongly for breaking off the Madrid conference. After several intense contacts, however, I succeeded in the spring of 1982 in persuading him to keep the review conference going. My basic argument was that the CSCE process was clearly in the West's interest, since we could use the CSCE forum even in the future to effectively advocate the preservation of human rights, continue the dialogue with the smaller Eastern countries, and insist on enhanced human rights across the borders between blocs. But since we had such an overwhelming interest in maintaining the CSCE, we would not be "punishing" the Soviet Union by breaking off the Madrid conference—such an action would harm only ourselves. The CSCE, after all, was the vehicle that enabled us to push for disarmament and arms control. We were dealing with a specifically European security interest; when disarmament negotiations between the two superpowers frequently came to a halt, it was Europeans who felt seriously threatened by the Soviets' superiority in conventional weapons.

In Max Kampelman, head of the American delegation to the CSCE—without a doubt one of the outstanding figures at the Madrid follow-up meeting—we found a counterpart who was open to German and European CSCE concerns, and in the end we managed to convince him and win his support. During a long conversation about basic ideals, which took place at my invitation in the garden of our residence, I won Kampelman over to our CSCE philosophy. Subsequently he defended it in Washington with such vigor that eventually Secretary of State George Shultz became more and more supportive of our program.

One of the unforgettable events of the Madrid follow-up meeting was the encounter between Shultz and Gromyko after a Soviet plane shot down a Korean jet over Soviet territory. Shultz refused to shake hands with Gromyko when they met, and the two of them had a sharp confrontation. Afterward Gromyko arrived at the headquarters of the West German delegation for a talk with me. His account of the dispute agreed word for word with the report Shultz had given me over the phone while Gromyko was on his way.

In Madrid Shultz and I continued to work closely—and, more important, successfully—together. It was necessary for the Western nations to respond to the entirely unjustifiable downing of the Korean plane not only with verbal protests but also with strictures against Soviet air traffic. The Europeans were right in rejecting a complete shutdown of air traffic—such a curtailment would have contradicted all our attempts to promote traffic across the frontiers between the blocs. It took great efforts on my part to persuade both Europeans and Americans to engage in a joint strategy that avoided such a drastic solution but was nevertheless unambiguous. The joint Western stand laid the groundwork that allowed the Americans to return to the negotiations on nuclear missiles, which, since this was just before the decision was made concerning the deployment of American medium-range missiles, was of paramount importance for West Germany.

After harsh criticism of events in Poland, the Madrid meeting could finally conclude in September 1983 with a substantive document. The implementation of human rights was one of the areas that showed progress. We succeeded, for example, in increasing the number of German-born citizens who were allowed to leave the Soviet Union and in promoting travel between the two Germanys: In 1985, 1.5 million Germans traveled from East Germany to West Germany and 6.7 million West Germans were able to travel to East Germany.

The creation of the CSCE process was one of the Western democracies' great achievements because it introduced respect for human rights and the human dimension in West-East relations. As late as 1972 Nixon and Brezhnev had failed to consider human rights in their important declaration on basic principles of relations between the United States and the Soviet Union. The Helsinki Final Act was the first international document to set human rights next to the traditional rules of international relations as a principle of equal importance. I myself considered the Final Act the preliminary blueprint of the foundations for the lasting peace in Europe toward which the Western Alliance was striving and which we Germans hoped to use as a framework for regaining our unity. These purposes required both sides to agree on issues of shared values; it was precisely such agreement that was recorded in the Helsinki Final Act and later, even more comprehensively, in the Charter of Paris.

To preserve equilibrium among the various Baskets during the continuation of the CSCE process, in the early summer of 1985 human-rights experts met in Ottawa. This conference was the last occasion for a confrontation on human rights between East and West. Though the conference on communication across the borders held in Bern in the early spring of 1986 moved matters along considerably, the United States could not agree to the final document, and the meeting therefore came to an end without the paper that all other participants accepted. I particularly regretted this outcome because from our point of view the document contained several clear improvements, one being in the area of reuniting families, one of our major concerns. I was deeply concerned about the United States' position because it violated the idea of codifying the elements of progress that were possible and working toward a solution of the remaining problems.

One result of the events in the CSCE process whose significance has been underestimated was the Budapest cultural forum held in the fall of 1985. Artists and other outstanding cultural figures from all the European states participated as nonvoting members of the various governmental delegations. This forum collected a "treasure trove of ideas" relative to cultural projects and contacts that transcended all frontiers. I was glad that Budapest had been chosen as the place for the forum, because even at that time old political structures were clearly beginning to crumble in Hungary.

Mainly at Germany's instigation the CSCE's foreign ministers met in Helsinki from July 30 to August 1, 1985, to commemorate the tenth anniversary of the CSCE. It was Shevardnadze's first appearance on the international stage. His speech still alluded to Lenin, who had, Shevardnadze noted, predicted "the objective necessity for peaceful coexistence" that had given its impetus to the Final Act's vitality.

There was no ignoring the fact that as Shevardnadze assumed office, Moscow's foreign policy was changing, and not merely in its outward form. Even my meeting with him on August 1, 1985, was a sign that the content of Soviet foreign policy was being altered. Shevardnadze conveyed Gromyko's respects and expressed his hope that relations between the two of us would be as good as those his predecessor and I had enjoyed. In fact, the relationship would be much better and quite different from the interchanges between Gromyko and myself. Shevardnadze's explanation that because he had just assumed his office, he preferred to listen rather than expound foreign-policy ideas was impressive. I came to attention: His statement could mean only that Soviet foreign policy was being carefully scrutinized so that the government could subsequently decide whether to implement any changes and if so, which ones. The times, my new Soviet counterpart remarked, called for a greater sense of responsibility—we needed to search out and destroy the roots of the tensions between us. That sentiment sounded promising as well; and even more, it sounded sincere. For my part, I stressed the significance of German-Soviet relations for West-East relations, and I pleaded for cooperation and confidence building within the framework of the CSCE process. In his reply Shevardnadze—and this, too, was new—not only alluded to the sacrifices made by the people of the Soviet Union during the Second World War but also added, "I am aware of the sacrifices the German people made." On such an occasion a remark of this sort was unheard of. I therefore left Helsinki feeling hopeful. Shevardnadze had impressed me; I sensed that I would be able to find a common language with him, though not literally, of course. Later he told me that his reaction had been similar.

In good time before the third CSCE follow-up meeting, held in Vienna in November 1986, the Stockholm Conference on Confidence- and Security-Building Measures was successfully concluded. It had reached a breakthrough: On-site monitoring, which Gromyko had rejected as "legalized espionage," had been agreed to. At the opening of the conference in January 1984 Gromyko had accused me, "You're trying to drill a peephole in our fence." "No, I'm not," I countered. "I'm trying to get rid of the fence altogether."

The Vienna CSCE follow-up meeting, which lasted from November 4, 1986, to January 19, 1989, was in harmony with the transformation in West-East relations; the conference even expedited it. Ultimately it smoothed the passage to end the era of confrontation between the two blocs. In 1986 I declared in Vienna, "The CSCE makes it possible for my people—which has a legitimate desire for a state of peace in Europe in which it can regain its unity in unhampered self-determination—to act in cooperation with all of its neighbors peacefully and full of mutual confidence." A statement that at the time sounded to many like an illusion or a vision at best became reality only three years later.

In the military sphere, the NATO alliance and the Warsaw Pact nations managed to agree on deliberations for actual disarmament of conventional weapons at the CCSE (Conference on Conventional Security in Europe), held in Vienna from March 1989 to November 1990. In time for the Paris CSCE summit of November 1990, the CCSE reached agreement on an unparalleled reduction of heavy conventional weapons, with particular emphasis on offensive operations; because the Soviet Union's stocks were so much larger, it was obligated to relinquish a far greater number of weapons than the West.

A line from Hölderlin may serve to characterize the period 1989–1990: "There never was so much beginning." No doubt the CSCE—"that common voice of all Europeans," as Václav Havel once called the organization—contributed its share of beginnings. In the summer of 1989 Hungary explicitly referred to the Vienna resolutions on exit permits when, in violation of the 1969 bilateral agreement between Hungary and East Germany, it allowed East German citizens to cross the border to the West. The CSCE also substantially influenced negotiations on German unification and greatly facilitated the Two-Plus-Four meetings. The CCSE forum in Vienna furnished the occasion, in late August 1990, for Lothar de Maizière and me to announce the joint declaration of the two Germanys concerning our binding commitment that a unified Germany would reduce armed forces to 370,000 troops. By the winter of 1990 the time was ripe: On November 19 the treaty on conventional disarmament was signed in Paris, where the heads of state and government and all CSCE foreign ministers had convened. In addition, the 1990 Vienna concluding document was accepted. Thus a big step toward conventional disarmament in Europe had been taken, and the limitations on German armed forces became an integral part of pan-European disarmament procedures.

The vision that had played such a large role in the Two-Plus-Four talks became a reality in Paris on November 21: The Charter of Paris for a new Europe was signed. With this German idea, supported equally by Gorbachev and Mitterand and strongly backed by Bush and Baker, we had created one of the keys that would open the door to German unity. After the signing, Gorbachev and I shared a heartfelt handshake. He knew that I had had to work hard to persuade the Western allies to accept the proposal. Now the Charter of Paris created a foundation for all the basic values and principles of a free social order. As Gorbachev was appending his signature, I murmured to Kohl, "With this signature we are witnessing the Secretary General's endorsement of a free-market economy."

The various mechanisms to promote the human dimension ratified in Vienna were applied at subsequent conferences in Paris (summer of 1989), Copenhagen (summer of 1990), and Moscow (September 1991) to further the concrete implementation of human rights on the basis of the West's understanding. At the beginning of the Vienna follow-up meeting in 1986, directly after Shevardnadze's pertinent suggestion, I was the first Western foreign minister to agree to a human-rights conference in Moscow, provided certain prerequisites were met. The other Western nations, above all the United States and the United Kingdom, did not give their consent until the final days of the "Vienna end game." For my part I believed that an open human-rights conference in Moscow would positively affect human rights within the Soviet Union even before the fact.

During this Moscow conference, a few weeks after the Moscow putsch in the summer of 1991, the Soviet Union joined my proposal to include nonacceptance of any unconstitutional change of power within the codified CSCE regulations. The Soviets were equally willing to affirm that enforcing regard for human rights was not subject to the prohibition against interference in the internal affairs of other nations.

Berlin 1991: A New Chapter in the History of the CSCE

In late June 1991 I presided at the first CSCE council of foreign ministers to be held in the Berlin Reichstag. To hold this first council in the reunited Germany, and at a site with so much historical significance, was certainly an acknowledgment of our efforts on behalf of the CSCE. Among the council's resolutions was the so-called urgency mechanism for crisis situations. A separate resolution expressly affirmed the rights of the Yugoslavian people to freely determine their own future. This document was to carry weight subsequently as it affected the EC resolution of December 1991, in that it called for international recognition of Croatia's and Slovenia's independence—a resolution approved unanimously.

I have always been an advocate of a strengthened CSCE. Its current membership of fifty-three nations makes the decision process based on consensus extremely difficult. Therefore at an early stage I took the initiative for introducing the principle of consensus minus one. This rule would prevent a single member nation from denying resolutions agreed upon by *all other* member nations. The principle was adopted by the Prague CSCE council in January 1992 and was applied for the first time in the decision regarding the suspension of CSCE membership for the former Yugoslavia.

The CSCE proved to be the appropriate mechanism for abolishing the West-East conflict and creating a free Europe. The program of incorporating Germany in the West before using our bilateral Eastern policy and the CSCE to link East and West in an increasingly intricate network substantially contributed to the peaceful evolution of our continent. It was this same process that ultimately made unification possible. From the beginning it was crucial that the Final Act be recognized as a process that marked every outcome if the CSCE were to be properly understood. The results in turn set in motion a course of events that by tightening the links among *nations* allowed inviolable human rights to achieve recognition. At the same time, since all the participants were interested in the continuation of the CSCE process, a relapse into Cold War was prevented. In addition, the CSCE process ultimately created such stable conditions in Europe that neither the revolutionary events in Poland in the 1980s nor those in the Soviet Union and the countries in its sphere of power at the end of the decade ended in military confrontation within the Warsaw Pact or between East and West.

The CSCE could be successful only because the member nations did not seek individual advantage but weighed the competing interests of all the participants. Its beneficial effect on the situation within the Communist countries and on improvements in East-West relations proves the CSCE's ability both to bring about change and to stabilize events.

For West Germany, the CSCE offered the chance to participate on equal terms in West-East relations. The process also offered us the opportunity to assume a leading role both in formulating political and strategic programs and in carrying them out. My repeated call for both German states to do their utmost to meet the obligations outlined in the Final Act (to grant themselves a kind of most-favored nation status, as it were) was in the interest of the people of the two Germanys as well as all of Europe. Thus, despite all antagonisms, despite the Wall and violence at the frontier, despite repression within East Germany, the framework of the CSCE enabled the two Germanys to establish a relationship that under any other circumstances would have raised questions in both West and East.

The German policy of treaties with the Eastern nations and the creation of the CSCE initiated a new chapter that concluded with abolition of the divisions within Europe and Germany. Cooperation, events proved, was more effective than submitting to confrontation.

5

West Germany and the United Nations

Worldwide Interdependence: The Web of International Cooperation Thickens

In 1977 and 1978, while the Federal Republic of Germany was a member of the United Nations Security Council, the United Nations became a central forum for German foreign policy. We acted on the basis of our conviction that, given our history in the twentieth century, Germany had special reasons to do its utmost to support the United Nation's goals and principles. In 1976 the world consisted of more than 150 sovereign states, all of which wanted to see their own ideas and claims prevail in international politics. International policy was no longer an exclusive affair of the major powers, nor could it remain a closed event produced by a club of the rich and powerful. A responsible foreign policy needed to respect the great variety of national interests, including those of the smallest countries.

In my view this mutual interdependence of diverse nations constituted a new situation that required a revolutionary approach to foreign policy. The traditional logic of power politics, with the ultimate aim of seeking gain for one's own country without considering the consequent loss to others, had to be abolished. In light of growing global interdependence all nations could win only if they held together, or none could win at all. During crises over oil and raw materials and in times of economic recession all nations must understand that their goals will best be realized by pulling together.

The old competition for power, including the East-West conflict, was gradually replaced by the new reality of global interdependence. It remained the first priority of West Germany's foreign policy to secure peace by contributing to the domestic and outward stability of the Western democracies, to unite Europe in the European Community, and, within the CSCE, to seek détente with the East.

Because it was becoming harder and harder to achieve stability through military efforts alone, the United Nations had to do all it could to discover solid and reliable forms and structures of cooperation in which all nations would voluntarily join, impelled by the realization that these mechanisms were just and would serve the nations' individual interests. Indispensable prerequisites for this end were the universal right to self-determination; respect for human rights and the rights of minorities; equal rights for all nations; a willingness to solve conflicts without force, by way of negotiating and of balancing interests; and, not least, tolerance and respect for the diversity of the world's nations.

Economically developing the Third World; lessening the discrepancy between poor and rich nations; providing the rapidly growing global population with food, energy, and raw materials; limiting worldwide armaments; effectively fighting international terrorism; and preserving the ecological balance on our planet, all these goals made global cooperation a necessity. The United Nations was needed as a central forum, to include as many nations as possible in this process of cooperation. Therefore a strong and efficient structure was of crucial importance to the international community while it would also serve our own national interest.

More than ever we were convinced that we had made the correct choice when we joined the United Nations in 1972, though at the time the decision was controversial. Had we done otherwise, West Germany would have been deprived of essential opportunities to contribute to the shaping of international politics and this distancing would have served neither our own interests nor those of the rest of the world. Germany had joined the League of Nations in 1926, only six years after its founding. The United Nations, on the other hand, had been in existence for twenty-eight years by the time West Germany became a member.

In the years from 1974 to 1991 I flew to New York in the second half of September to attend the United Nations General Assembly. As the years went by, the trip became increasingly routine, so that by the end almost every minute of my stay was planned ahead.

My main concern was the preparation of my own address to the assembly, since it physically was impossible to listen to all the speeches in the plenary sessions. Choosing which speeches to attend was a political decision. In addition, each year there were more and more meetings among the foreign ministers of different groups, so that ultimately even all my meals turned into scheduled appointments: lunches and dinners with foreign ministers from the EC and my American counterpart, gatherings of the G7 foreign ministers, and meetings with regional groups. I also sought out representatives of the Third World, such as the foreign ministers of ASEAN (Association of Southeast Asian Nations) and the group of African front nations; in later years I also met with the foreign ministers of Central America.

During its first week the United Nations General Assembly always addresses technical issues. The political aspect of the gathering begins only in the second week, with the United States president addressing the assembly on Monday morning. As the head of the host nation, it is his privilege to be the first speaker. He thus enjoys the opportunity of presenting the United States' policy regarding the United Nations and its activities.

I always occupied the same suite in the United Nations Plaza Hotel, where I was also able to hold meetings. If my presence was needed at the United Nations, I had only to cross the street, and since most of my Western colleagues stayed at the same hotel, any one of them who wanted to speak with me could reach me quickly and easily. I generally used the Sunday after my arrival to polish my address to the General Assembly since my diplomatic activities, starting on Monday, would leave no spare time. Most bilateral meetings took place in my hotel suite. Unfortunately I was never able to satisfy all the requests for private meetings from my fellow foreign ministers.

Talks in New York required meticulous preparation if they were to be fruitful. Such preparation involved a tremendous amount of work, as did the follow-up analyses and evaluations. Some observers have been pleased to make fun of these New York marathon meetings, but they offer a singular opportunity for face-to-face discussions with a number of colleagues. They are a way to initiate negotiations or to unblock stalled ones, to smooth over misunderstandings, and to circumvent time-consuming travel.

One of that week's most important but also most difficult tasks was to get a real feel for the interests and mentalities of the various personalities. Among those I met with regularly were the foreign ministers and the most prominent Arabs of Israel, many of the Africans, and all my counterparts from Central and Southeastern Europe. I also had regular meetings with the Latin Americans and the foreign ministers of China, Japan, India, and Pakistan. In all these talks it was vital that I be attuned to each individual and keep as open a mind as possible.

In later years, in addition to the bilateral and multilateral meetings, we held meetings of the EC foreign ministers in order to reach agreement on our foreign policies. The increasing dovetailing of the EC nations' foreign policies was shown by the fact that each president of the European Community first spoke in the name of the EC and only after addressed his own nation's interests. In addition, it had been agreed that no member would speak before the president. Thus the country that held the presidency could explain the concept of the EC's foreign policy before his colleagues took the rostrum.

When I spoke to the United Nations General Assembly, it was important that I reflected fundamentals and the overall program; at the same time, however, I needed to place emphasis on current issues. Preparations for the speech were therefore very time-consuming, especially since late-breaking events forced me continually to alter my text, eliminating references and here and there shifting my emphasis. My address was the public high point of my stay in New York. Had I put my key ideas across? How were our principal allies and the Communist camp responding? What would the reaction be in the Third World? Where was further work needed? And would the speech succeed in Germany? Such thoughts went through my head as I finished and left the rostrum.

Even though I have often been charged with spending too much time away from Bonn, I actually traveled less than most of my colleagues. In New York I had the unique opportunity of speaking with numerous ministers and diplomats from all over the world without investing too much time. As the years went by, I structured a set of regular encounters, among them the meeting of the four foreign ministers of the Western powers—the United States, the United Kingdom, France, and the Federal Republic of Germany. Since these particular meetings lacked the formal structure of, say, the "talks of the four" before a NATO conference, we kept these gatherings very private; since all four of us stayed at the United Nations Plaza Hotel and could easily meet in one or another of our suites, keeping out the press presented no problem. I simply went to another floor and met with my colleagues to discuss crucial issues.

My encounters also included a regular meeting with the Soviet foreign minister. The Soviets cleverly used protocol to manipulate foreign policy; they established distinct rankings by the length of time allotted to each meeting. The Soviet foreign minister always met at the greatest length with the American secretary of state; the second-longest talk went to the West German foreign minister. These lasted significantly longer than, for example, meetings with the French and British foreign ministers. The meeting site alternated between the German and the Soviet UN residence. There was always a formal dinner, lending these meetings additional weight.

I vividly remember one encounter I had with Gromyko. The West German national elections of October 1976 returned the coalition government of the SPD and the FDP. At the height of the campaign, on September 27, 1976, I left to attend the United Nations General Assembly in New York, but in order to limit my absence, I planned to spend only two days in the United States. On the first day I lunched with Andrei Gromyko. Our talk, during which Gromyko spoke quite harshly, lasted two and a half hours. He criticized not only West Germany's attitude toward détente, disarmament, and the Four Power Agreement on Berlin, but also our policy toward East Germany.

In my response I did not shrug off his attack. Regarding the situation at the frontier between West and East Germany, I noted that the Federal Republic of Germany had many borders with allied, neutral, and Communist countries, but at none of these other borders were people killed, as they were at the East German border.

Gromyko next turned to my upcoming address, scheduled for the following morning, before the General Assembly. He alluded to rumors about certain issues I intended to raise before the international audience. The term *rumors* was not correct, since I had previously informed the Soviet ambassador in Bonn and, by way of our embassy in Moscow, the Soviet foreign ministry of my intentions; in particular I was going to propose the creation of an international court for human rights. Of course I realized that the suggestion would cause great uneasiness among the Soviets. But that consideration must not keep us from going ahead. My meeting with Gromyko therefore offered me the opportunity to explain the motives behind our initiative and to assure him that in our opinion working more closely with the Soviet Union, East Germany, and other Communist countries would be in the spirit of our existing treaties and of the Helsinki Final Act. I wanted Moscow and its allies to understand clearly where they stood with regard to us—both where we agreed and where we, at least for the time being, disagreed.

A man such as Gromyko respected such directness more than he did glibness, public pleasantries, and unpredictability. After I had explained our intentions, Gromyko retorted that if there were any attempt to come too close to East Germany, the Soviet Union, or any group of countries (by which he meant the Communist nations) such behavior would not be tolerated meekly. He did not believe, he stated, that there was any point in creating a tribunal that "would not allow human rights stocks to go up."

I calmly countered that the Soviet Union and the Communist countries had signed the United Nations' human rights agreements as well as the Helsinki Final Act and that it was therefore perfectly legitimate to call for their realization. The human rights issue, I noted, was crucial to us. We intended to raise the issue objectively; no one acting in goodwill could possibly be offended. However, I was careful to add, we would note all responses minutely. If someone was eager to quarrel with us on this matter, we would oblige him. But for our part, we were not looking for trouble.

For me to advocate a human rights court was not simple. Not only the Soviet Union opposed the proposal—many Third World nations, concerned that the West might meddle in their internal affairs, expressed qualms or worse. Some members of the West German government coalition, though not among the top levels of the SPD, frowned at or expressed criticism of the proposal. Nor was it clear how other Western nations would respond. They too had been given advance notice, but so far supportive reactions were limited. Just as it had with the Helsinki Final Act, West Germany took the initiative at the United Nations for the protection of human rights.

In his address to the General Assembly on the following day, September 28, the Soviet Foreign Minister, somewhat polemically, took up the issue of human rights—without mentioning me by name. "There are also attempts to represent détente almost as if it were something like a license to interfere in the internal affairs of other nations. How else to interpret the hypocritical concern of one or another government with the rights of citizens in other countries?" Evidently this highly intelligent man feared that a public debate on human rights and humanitarian concerns would result in systemic changes within the Communist sphere of power. He thus proved to be more clear-sighted than the timid opponents of our policy of détente in the West. At a later time the German delegation to the United Nations introduced an initiative against capital punishment; we also supported the antitorture convention. Insisting on these initiatives in the deliberations of the United Nations required infinite patience and tenacity; but what was important was that this forum develop concrete steps toward the protection of human rights in the first place. And it was equally important that such proposals be initiated, or at least supported, by Germany. We refused to be deterred in such matters of principle, even when important friends, partners, and allies took divergent stands as, for example, when the United States opposed our effort to abolish capital punishment.

An Example of a Foreign Policy of Responsibility:
The Namibia Conflict

From the moment West Germany joined the United Nations, Bonn was given the opportunity to keep the promise Walter Scheel had made in his speech on September 29, 1973, on the occasion of Germany's acceptance into the international body: "I assure you: Wherever a battle is being waged to liberate humankind from physical affliction and to guarantee the right to live in dignity, you will find the Federal Republic of Germany in the forefront."

The election of the Federal Republic of Germany into the Security Council from 1976 to 1978 provided a special opportunity for us to increase our active international commitment. Particularly in view of the escalating problems in southern Africa, we were prepared to accept greater responsibility, in concert with others. We closed the German consulate in Windhoek, the capital of Namibia, which was run by our embassy in Pretoria, so as to send a signal that we would not recognize South Africa's rule over Namibia. Further, we decided that the cultural agreement with South Africa would not apply to Namibia.

Because Namibia was at one time a German colony and a rich German cultural life continued to flourish there, and as the area still held so many resident Germans, we were interested in actively supporting the process of decolonialization. Almost half of Namibia's population was of German origin. After the Second World War the Republic of South Africa was unwilling to acknowledge United Nations jurisdiction over the mandate of Namibia; in 1966 the United Nations therefore revoked the mandate and placed the territory under the direct jurisdiction of the international body. South Africa, for its part, was unwilling to honor this resolution. The so-called gymnasium conference, which opened in Windhoek in 1975, included all of Namibia's ethnic groups with the exception of the most important—the liberation movement SWAPO (South West African People's Organization), even though this was the group the United Nations had recognized as the legitimate representative of Namibia. South Africa committed itself to holding free elections, but the purpose of the conference was to identify an internal solution for Namibia that excluded SWAPO. In the early and mid-1970s SWAPO repeatedly

119

tried to gain Western support. When that failed, SWAPO increasingly looked to the Communist nations for support. In the meantime South Africa intervened militarily in Angola so as to destroy SWAPO's ground for armed warfare.

The Marxists' assumption of power in Angola and Mozambique in 1976 raised serious fears in the Western world. On September 28, 1976, I spoke to the thirty-first General Assembly of the United Nations in New York. I noted, "We can expect peaceful development in southern Africa and can take peace for granted only when there are no attempts to block a historically necessary change. Let everyone, including the peoples of southern Africa, understand: There is no room for racism and colonialism in this world. Those days are over."

During the years that followed, I repeatedly made it clear as I addressed the United Nations that we endorsed the liberation movement's goals but that we lent political and economic support only to those who renounced force. By this decision we balanced our belief in the peoples' right to self-determination with the renunciation of violence as a way to solve political problems.

The five members of the United Nations Security Council formed a contact group to negotiate a generally acceptable solution with all the parties to the conflict. The group created a model for a constitution, for election laws, and for political transition in Namibia. In April 1978—after complex negotiations with South Africa and SWAPO, and in excellent cooperation with the front nations, including Nigeria, which were eager to arrive at a compromise—we formulated a settlement proposal that provided for free elections in all of Namibia under the supervision and control of the United Nations according to the principle, and this was the core of the proposal, of one man, one vote.

The meetings of the contact group took place in the American embassy to the United Nations in New York; they were attended by representatives of Namibia, by the gymnasium alliance under Dirk Mudge, by SWAPO President Sam Nujoma, and by Foreign Minister Pik Botha, representing South Africa. We made notable progress. Pik Botha (not to be confused with South Africa's President Pieter Willem Botha) was a man of unusually strong feelings, straightforward in voicing his opinions, and despite all our differences, quite likable. These traits made working together much easier.

In October 1978 the contact group's foreign ministers—Cyrus Vance for the United States, Mark McGuigan for Canada, David Owen from Great Britain, a high official representing the French foreign minister, and I—visited first Namibia and then the Republic of South Africa.

On the occasion of a dinner hosted by President Botha in Pretoria, which was attended by Pik Botha and the five delegation heads, an unpleasant incident occurred: South Africa's president criticized the attitude displayed by the five nations constituting the contact group; his behavior was outrageous. Addressing each one of the delegation heads individually, he declared that—thank God!—all would be sure to lose in the next national elections. He first insulted Vance, then Owen, our Canadian colleague McGuigan, and finally the French official. When he was about to turn to me, I interrupted him and banged on the table. "Before you address me in the same manner," I said, "I must inform you that in the nations represented here, there could be no change of government if—as in your country—three-fifths of the population were barred from voting. Do not get your hopes up: My administration will remain in office, and so will I."

I should add that Botha's predictions did, in fact, turn out to be true for the four other nations. In any event, that evening President Botha cut short his speech, I rose and left the room, and the President and his foreign minister rushed after me, imploring, "Let's have coffee in the adjoining room." We took our seats. The two of them placed me between them and continued the conversation, chatting most pleasantly with me, as if nothing had happened. My unusual gesture of banging on the table hard enough to rattle the glasses and my pointed remarks were like a thunderstorm that had a purifying effect on the atmosphere of the meeting.

The contact group worked closely primarily with the American administration, for one, because Andrew Young, the American ambassador to the United Nations, strongly and positively influenced Jimmy Carter's policy on Africa. The situation changed in 1981, when Ronald Reagan assumed the presidency. His administration made an effort to link pacification in Angola with a solution to the problem of Namibia. The Europeans in our group were skeptical; we feared the linkage would jeopardize, or at least considerably slow, the peace process in Namibia. We believed that the proper way to proceed was in exactly the opposite direction: First pacifying Namibia and then using the now peaceful country as a basis for tackling the Angola issue. The black Africans, in particular the representatives of the front states, rejected the idea of linkage.

The policy of linkage led to increased tensions, especially between Washington and Paris. I nevertheless tried to prevent our five-nation group's initiative from becoming paralyzed. What aided my effort were two circumstances: One, Secretary of State Alexander Haig and I worked together well and amicably; second, the new United States administration retained the concept of the five-nation group as an indispensable initiative. Such a position was not a foregone conclusion, since the contact group in particular had been a prominent foreign-policy project of the Carter administration, specifically, of Andrew Young.

The process of finding a solution for Namibia thus dragged on until the end of confrontation in Angola in 1988, partly as a consequence of the change in East-West relations. Once again I received confirmation of my belief that the only way to put an end to imposing the East-West conflict on the Third World was not from the periphery but from the center. Détente between the superpowers and détente in Europe relaxed the situation on the periphery of the conflict as well.

The more Undersecretary of State Chester Crocker studied the matter, the more he struggled for continuity and sought to work closely with the contact group. Secretary of State George Shultz, who had taken over from Al Haig in 1982, was also sympathetic to our basic thinking. Ultimately, therefore, we managed, together with Shultz and Crocker, to develop a program for a forceful, harmonious negotiation policy. In the end I even succeeded in removing some of the Americans' doubts and to persuade Crocker to meet personally with Sam Nujoma, the chairman of SWAPO. It turned out to be a productive meeting, and during his trip through southern African capitals in the fall of 1982 Vice President George Bush withdrew the linkage concept from the discussion. Again George Shultz proved to be a pragmatic conservative with firm principles. In general he always sought to collaborate productively with his European partners, not least with the Germans.

In the 1980s the other Western nations followed West Germany's lead. A solution was pushed for on two levels: For his part, Crocker tried to negotiate a way to secure Namibia's independence in talks above all with Angola and Cuba—in many rounds that took place in London, Cairo, Geneva, New York, and Brazzaville—even as he worked for the withdrawal of the approximately 50,000 Cuban troops stationed in Angola. In a parallel effort we worked to advance the negotiation process within our contact group. When Crocker presented new ideas concerning policies in southern Africa at a meeting in Paris, I explained to Secretary Shultz that the United States' Namibia policy and our own ideas were almost identical.

In late December 1988 South Africa, Cuba, and Angola, meeting in New York, reached an accord whose substance our contact group supported without qualifications: Resolution 435 stipulated that the process leading to Namibia's independence would begin on April 1, 1989; it further established that the 50,000 Cuban troops would be withdrawn by mid-1991. The end of the East-West conflict, which was becoming more and more discernible, made possible a joint solution of the Namibia and Angola problems.

Between November 7 and 11, 1989, while the Wall was coming down in Berlin, Namibia held free elections, supervised by 1,400 international observers. With 57.5 percent of the votes, SWAPO became the strongest party, and in the end it was also SWAPO that, all pessimistic predictions to the contrary, drafted a democratic constitution for Namibia. I had been right: SWAPO was not a Communist fellow traveler, it had serious intentions about Namibia's beginning as a democracy. One of the misunderstandings circulating in the West, including Germany, and prevalent mainly in conservative circles was the belief that the racist regime in South Africa and its colonial rule over Namibia were an outpost of the Free World against increasing Communist influence in Africa.

It was precisely this attitude and the policies derived from it that drove the African liberation movements into the arms of the Communist nations, though they never allied themselves with the Soviet Union. Democracy, the value system of the Free World, could not gain a foothold in South Africa and Namibia until the old racist order was abolished. Democracy began with free elections and ended both racist oppression within South Africa and South Africa's colonialism in Namibia.

On March 21, 1990, Namibia celebrated its independence, with many representatives of foreign powers in attendance. Finally the goal was reached. On this occasion I first met Nelson Mandela, the man who had long been a symbol of freedom and democracy in Africa; we had repeatedly tried to effect his release from prison. The meeting confirmed my belief that a great man had suffered for his country and through his suffering had paved the road to freedom. I felt enormous satisfaction when events in South Africa led to the end of apartheid in 1994. After the first free elections in the Republic of South Africa on April 28, 1994, the system of apartheid was abolished, and in May 1994 Nelson Mandela was elected the first president of a South Africa without apartheid. In this, too, I had been right: It was not the white regime of oppression and apartheid that had been the outpost of the Western world; the real outpost of freedom in those times was to be found on Robben Island, where Nelson Mandela had been jailed for twenty-eight years. In April 1994 the black majority's horrible lot finally ended, and white minority rule was abolished. It was a day of liberation when 23 million South Africans were free to elect four hundred delegates to the National Assembly.

In retrospect I am highly gratified that as early as the 1970s German foreign policy unambiguously supported the abolishment of the apartheid regime in South Africa and Namibia's independence; I truly believe that our clear, dependable, and unaltering position on this issue served the causes of peace, progress, and the realization of human rights, as well as our own interests in southern Africa. Not least, its unswerving rejection of apartheid won West Germany greater prestige in the United Nations.

I also attempted to introduce our ideas of human rights directly into South Africa; in this effort I raised the initiative of a Code of Conduct in the councils of the European Community. With this code, to apply to companies with subsidiaries, branches, and agencies in South Africa, the nations of the European Community contributed to the acquisition of equal rights by black workers. Soon after the code was implemented, we became aware that significant changes were taking place in the workplace. Thus we also gave indirect support to the role of trade unions in South Africa.

West Germany's Global Responsibility

West Germany's United Nations policy took its direction from the following principles: Both West and East Germany having joined, it was our mission to make use of the opportunities furnished by the United Nations to expound our policies. If every time I addressed the United Nations, I called for the realization of German unity, I was not simply uttering an obligatory platitude; I was giving expression to what had been the central issue in West Germany since 1949. My speeches thus made certain that the German question remained on the agenda of the top international forum day after day, year after year. The world's people and their governments were to know that we would never become resigned to a divided Germany. When now and then some German politicians announced that unifying Germany was not currently on the agenda, I never understood what they were talking about.

Firmly convinced that the program of realistic détente in which the German question was embedded could be seriously pursued only within a European framework, I advocated increasing integration of the Federal Republic into the Western community, intensification of relations with Eastern Europe, and an extension of détente. The catchword could not be confrontation but must be cooperation, including relations with East Germany. At times our allies failed to remember that the Harmel Report had identified the ultimate goal of a mutual policy to be the abolition of division in Germany and Europe and the creation of a permanent, just foundation for peace in all of Europe.

After delivering my credo in regard to the German question in my addresses to the General Assembly, I had a further concern: to emphasize before this international body Germany's active commitment to peace and harmony in the world. Special attention was given to our strategy that recommended regional cooperation of the European Community with other groups of nations. The Euro-Arab dialogue, cooperation between EC and ASEAN countries, our contacts with the Gulf Cooperation Council, the European Community's work with the countries of Central America, the agreements with the Maghreb and Mashrek nations, the Lomé treaties—all these were new forms of foreign policy based on co-operation. In these efforts Germany played a growing role, at times a central one; and most important, Germany led in the introduction of innovative programs. The fact that from the outset we recognized that the nonaligned nations were striving for independence and the development of national identities allowed our foreign policy greater flexibility. The concept of insisting that Third World nations side with the West or the East carried the danger of bringing the West-East conflict to the Third World. In addition, Helmut Schmidt and French president Giscard d'Estaing, by their deep involvement in international economic policy, had contributed to the Third World's continuously growing interest in German and French foreign policy.

It can therefore be truthfully said that during the 1970s and 1980s Germany became more and more influential in international politics. Of course such a position carried with it an enormous responsibility. NATO relied equally on West Germany's participation and on the United States' presence in Europe. The larger our contribution to NATO, the greater Bonn's influence on Western security policy. The West's Eastern policy was also largely defined in Germany. By our global policy of responsibility West Germany's reputation in the United Nations rose significantly; consequently, when the Federal Republic's term in the Security Council ended, many nations requested that it continue as a member of the contact group that was instrumental in settling the Namibia issue. Germany played an extremely important role not only in Europe but globally, and particularly in the Third World, ever since the 1970s, well before unification. Germany acted to stabilize and to resolve conflicts, all by nonmilitary means.

The North-South dialogue became a crucial focus relating to foreign policy and international economics. It was our goal to change international economic conditions in such a way that over time the developing nations might enjoy equal opportunities within the framework of the market. The Communist industrialized nations offered little material aid; they remained onlookers, supporting the developing nations' requests with words but not backing these with the corresponding deeds. Nor did the COMECON nations open their markets to Third World products. The Western industrial nations absorbed 75 percent of the developing nations' exports, but the Communist industrial nations accepted less than 4 percent. In other words, the Communist world as a whole expended less than half of West Germany's contribution to aid the developing countries. Speaking at the United Nations and in talks with representatives of the Third World, I frequently pointed out this discrepancy. I also pilloried the Communist nations' arms exports to the Third World, which only helped fan the flames of conflict without filling empty stomachs. For the sake of greater clarity, I initiated a proposal for a weapons-export registry in the United Nations.

The Schmidt-Genscher administration's Third World policy in the United Nations was characterized by respect for these nations' independence. We made no effort at any time to export our political, social, or economic order, much less force them on others or make economic aid dependent on the acceptance of our principles. Nations were free to decide whether to adopt our political and economic model in whole or in part. Failure to adopt our methods did not lead us to conclude that they were rejecting the West. The only element on which we insisted without fail was that human rights be respected.

We saw the principle of nonalignment not as a threat but as an opportunity. Nations that were uncommitted were first and foremost sovereign states, which we respected and with whom we sought friendly, cooperative relations. I therefore insistently warned against thoughtlessly exporting the antagonism between East and West to the Third World, against rashly labeling the developing countries and assigning them to one or the other camp. I absolutely refused to divide them into pro-Western and pro-Eastern nations.

In order to support their struggle for independence, I proposed a North-South cultural dialogue. Many Third World nations were quite justified in fearing a loss of identity; after having been intellectually and culturally dominated by colonial powers, often for centuries, the same oppression seemed to be happening again, this time by way of Western movies, radio and television programs, and records and tapes. Frequently the reaction was religious fundamentalism, events in Iran being one extreme. And it seemed an irony of fate that it was an Islamic "tape revolution"—the wide distribution of tapes carrying the words of Khomeini—that laid the groundwork for the Ayatollah's return to Iran. Success in persuading all societies to engage in a cultural exchange that could lead to political peace would not be won by the triumphal march of Western ideas. On the contrary, it required respect and care for all cultures.

We placed great importance on cultural policy as a force for identity and peace. The independence of the Goethe Institutes is one of the great liberal achievements of postwar Germany: These federally funded institutes (which spread and deepen understanding of German culture by offering language courses and organizing and sponsoring cultural events) do not reflect the views of administrations and government majorities; instead, they are established to present an image of German society with all its problems and tensions, conveying its preoccupations and discourses, just as these are reflected in all areas of German culture.

A crucial concern of West Germany's United Nations policy was the Federal Republic's participation in the United Nations' struggle for disarmament and arms control. Our experiences within the CSCE proved helpful in this effort. We introduced the same program to United Nations negotiations worldwide, though adjusting for local differences. On June 8, 1978, West Germany proposed the creation of regions of confidence-building measures. Our proposal contained a catalogue of specific measures, and during the coming years these would prove to be eminently farsighted:

- disclosure of defense budgets, in order to achieve limitations or cuts;
- disclosure of the size and structures of all armed forces;
- prior notification of any changes in these structures;
- exchange of military personnel, including visits by military delegations;
- prior notification of military maneuvers including smaller exercises;
- exchange of observers at military maneuvers;
- notification of military movements;
- establishment of internationally staffed observation posts and stations for electronic supervision in areas of crisis and demilitarized zones.

The German proposals were warmly received. The General Assembly passed resolutions that reflected our ideas, though in diluted form. Such changes illustrated that the antagonism of national and political interests within the United Nations made it extremely difficult to reach agreement on concrete measures that were to be applied globally. Several Third World countries voiced grave reservations about the provision for electronic supervision; they feared intervention in their domestic affairs. The Warsaw Pact nations, above all the Soviet Union, were averse to disclosing their defense budgets.

Undaunted, in the early 1980s we introduced further initiatives. West Germany chaired a fourteen-nation working group, which introduced an additional list of confidence-building measures. At the same time, following a German suggestion, the United Nations established a standardized reporting system for defense expenditures: At long last defense budgets would be intelligible and capable of being compared. However, apart from our nation, in the end only eleven other Western and six nonaligned nations disclosed their annual defense budgets using this system.

Finally, in 1990, German unification also became a fact in the United Nations, where two separate German states had had seats and votes for eighteen years. It was a big day for me when, on September 25, 1990, I could announce to the forty-fifth General Assembly, "Since the Federal Republic of Germany joined the United Nations, we have demanded before this forum the unification of our indivisible nation. Beginning in 1974, I myself spoke yearly to the General Assembly of the United Nations and expressed our desire to work toward a state of peace in Europe in which the German people would regain its unity in free self-determination. When I gave this speech, I always thought of the Germans in my native country—East Germany—of those who lived where I was born and grew up. I knew that they were longing for German unification as much as we did in West Germany. But they were not free to express their feelings and opinions. Now they have declared their allegiance to freedom and unity. Together with them, we are now looking forward to a unified Germany. We know that this unification will bring unity to Europe as well."

In 1990, just a few days before German unification, I had spoken at the United Nations as the representative of the old Federal Republic of Germany; on September 25, 1991, I first appeared as the foreign minister of a united Germany. I said, "Since 1974 I have spoken here in the name of the Federal Republic of Germany. Each year I again expressed our desire to work toward a state of peace in Europe in which the German people would regain its unity in free self-determination. On October 3, 1990, this desire became reality. At this moment I want to remember all those who gave their lives and yielded their freedom at the Wall and its barbed wire, in prisons and in camps, for their desire to live in a European Germany of freedom, of democracy, and of human rights. We are full of respect for all those in the former German Democratic Republic who, just as those in Central and Eastern Europe, took to the streets in order to peacefully gain freedom, democracy, and unity. Today I am speaking for the first time as foreign minister of a united Germany. Germany is taking its place in the family of the United Nations on the basis of our League of Nations charter. As a European country we are committed to the Charter of Paris. We interpret the increased importance of our people, which is united in one nation, to be a call to assume increased responsibility for freedom, democracy, and human dignity in a European Germany, which has left behind the nationalist thinking of the past. Just as the division of Germany symbolized the division of Europe, German unification today contributes to the unity of Europe. Europe stands at a turning point in its history. We Germans want this Europe to develop with ever closer transatlantic ties. These are manifested by the North Atlantic Alliance and the United States' and Canada's participation in the CSCE process. The European Community's Transatlantic Declaration underscores its desire for ever-increasing cooperation between Europe and North America."

This was my maiden speech as foreign minister of the unified Germany; it was my farewell speech before the United Nations as foreign minister.

6

European Unification

The Road to Maastricht

Beginning with the 1972 EC Summit in Paris, the European Community's goal was a unified Europe. At the time the heads of state and government had declared that they looked first and foremost to transform the totality of relations among the members into a European Union before the end of the century. Given the time this decision was taken, it was an historic one. Internationally during the 1970s the EC had made agreements with the Maghreb and Mashrek nations and with Israel and had initiated a Euro-Arab dialogue that deserved its name: Responding to West German suggestions, more and more regions had been included in this drive toward cooperation. We were convinced that in the long run small and medium-sized nations would be able to serve their own interests, politically as well as economically, better than before through regional cooperation. Regional cooperation could also become an important element of the new stable world order.

The first initiative of this kind I introduced in the EC was the cooperation treaty of March 7, 1980, with the ASEAN nations—

Indonesia, Malaysia, the Philippines, Singapore, Thailand, and Brunei, which joined later.

The San José dialogue also came about as a result of our efforts. I had prepared the event in conjunction with Luis Alberto Monge, the president of Costa Rica at the time, and in 1984 the first round of talks took place in San José, Costa Rica's capital. After years of noncommunication among themselves, Central American foreign ministers with a great diversity of political positions met; they represented Costa Rica, Guatemala, Honduras, Nicaragua, El Salvador, and Panama. Personal contact alone had a calming effect. In addition, the EC tried to help our Central American partners in furthering regional identity and the diversification of political and economic relations in individual nations.

The EC also supported regional peace initiatives. Mention should be made above all of efforts by the Contadora Group, consisting of Mexico, Venezuela, Colombia, and Panama; the Esquipulas Peace Plan developed by President Oscar Arias of Costa Rica, for which he was later awarded the Nobel Peace Prize, is equally worth noting. We believed that political solutions, in combination with economic cooperation and the advancement of regional collaboration, would gradually counter the spread of the East-West conflict to other parts of the world.

In addition, there was growing fellowship with the Andes Pact nations—Ecuador, Colombia, Peru, and Bolivia—and with the Contadora group. Regional alignment can make significant contributions to regional and global stability. The European Union in particular, as the most advanced association, holds great promise in this respect, especially since it is the only regional cooperative represented in the G7, where it can work toward promoting regional concordance. At the same time, the G7 nations must do everything possible to use the emergence of increasingly important regions to heighten awareness of the necessity of interdependence and cooperation. Just as renewed nationalization in Europe must be fought, the concept of collaboration must be made to prevail globally. The various regions of the world need to understand that they are the building blocks of a new cooperative world structure. Otherwise, all the mistakes of the era of European nation-states will be repeated globally on a grander level.

Among the European Community's most impressive efforts toward cooperation with Third World countries is the Lomé Convention—a series of agreements with the countries of Africa, the Caribbean, and the Pacific, which hardly would have come about without the tireless efforts of Hans-Jürgen Wischnewski, federal minister in the Foreign Office at the time.

In the early 1980s the gradual transformation of the European Community into the European Union was chiefly the work of Emilio Colombo, my Italian colleague at the time, and me. Colombo is one of the eminent figures of postwar Italian politics; he has served his country as foreign minister, minister of finance, and prime minister. We introduced into the EC a concept for a joint foreign policy for all members. Our suggestions were grounded in the concepts of democratization and respect for human rights; we also sought to advance close cooperation in the areas of cultural policy and law, and the development of an economic and currency union. We named our draft the European Document; it aimed at a network of treaties, and these were subsequently realized in the Maastricht accords.

In the midst of this debate came a change of government in Germany: In the election of 1982, the combined CDU and CSU won out over the SPD, and Helmut Kohl was elected chancellor. The FDP supported the change and formed a coalition with the ruling parties. The Free Democrats' continuation in the administration guaranteed continuity in foreign policy.

The Genscher-Colombo initiative for the European Union profited from Germany's change of administration; Helmut Kohl in particular had made strong statements on this point while he led the opposition. I saw this as a good sign. While opinions certainly differed between the FDP and CDU/CSU in some areas of foreign policy—on the German-Polish border, for example, and on policy regarding Africa, particularly in regard to Namibia and South Africa—European policy became a connecting link within the coalition. Helmut Kohl's commitment became a significant constant for the further development of the European Community.

François Mitterrand, too, was interested in further emphasizing European policy and giving it greater momentum. In late December 1983 he therefore appointed Roland Dumas as Minister for External Relations in the French Foreign Office. Claude Cheysson remained foreign minister. The West German Embassy in Paris considered the appointment of Dumas—whom I had not met at that time—of great importance for European policy. I was told that Mitterand and Dumas were friends.

I took the opportunity of my next visit with Cheysson to call on the new European minister in his office in a side wing of the Quai d'Orsay. I brushed aside objections to the effect that as European minister, Dumas was not on the level of a foreign minister, and that it was therefore up to him to pay the first call. Such matters of prestige and protocol do play an important role, but they can be used in two directions. This time I was the one to take the initiative with the new man. As it turned out, I would gain a reliable partner and a good personal friend.

Mitterand's decision to imbue European politics with a new dynamic became significant especially against the backdrop of the general course of events in Europe at the time. In November 1983 West Germany had made a critical decision by opting for the deployment of American Pershing II and cruise missiles, sending the Soviet Union a clear signal. In January 1983 President Mitterand had spoken before the German Bundestag and pleaded in favor of the double-track resolution, even though France, which was not part of NATO, was not involved in the decision.

We were sending a twofold message: The ties among the European democracies were strengthened, and the Western Alliance would not hesitate to engage in every necessary move for its defense, even as it kept up the process of cooperation and détente on the basis and in the spirit of the Helsinki Final Act and the German Eastern treaties.

I therefore found it highly encouraging that President Mitterand, by appointing Roland Dumas, placed the unification of Europe at the top of his agenda; I felt especially hopeful because my first visit with the new European minister was utterly harmonious. The meeting was cordial, marked by mutual curiosity and the wish to get to know each other. Dumas was a lawyer by profession, knew what he wanted, and appeared self-confident; his was a strong personality. I never felt the need to correct any of these first impressions. There was no rivalry whatever between Dumas and Cheysson.

Trying to open up the EC to include Spain and Portugal also turned into a successful venture. Germany and France had been among the proponents of expedited negotiations for admitting the two countries. On June 10, 1985, we signed the requisite treaties—in the morning in Lisbon, and in the afternoon in Madrid—allowing both countries to become members of the EC on the same day. I felt gratified at this outcome. Even a few years back, at the time Greece joined the EC, I had strongly supported opening the door to the EC to Spain and Portugal once their dictatorships had been abolished. It was my belief that the EC was obligated to extend its stabilizing functions—political, economical, and social—to all new democracies as soon as these expressed an interest in membership. During the campaign for the admission of democratic Spain I never ceased reminding the others that we could hardly welcome a nation into NATO while barring the door to the EC, following the principle, "We want your soldiers but not your produce."

In February 1986, after tough infighting within the EC, the European Council finally signed the treaty on the Unified European Act. Now European integration could progress. The European Parliament became more powerful, the European Council was transformed into an organ of the EC, and European Political Cooperation obtained a legal foundation. The requirement for a qualified majority within the EC was extended to additional areas, and policies regarding the environment and technological progress were institutionally strengthened. In addition, particular importance was attached to the decision to achieve a common European internal market by the end of 1992 and our focus—once more—on working toward a European Economic and Monetary Union.

After Spain and Portugal joined, membership in the new European Community consisted of twelve nations. The Unified European Act defined the level of consensus that was possible between the member nations at that point. But what was possible was accomplished at the right moment: In March 1985 Mikhail Gorbachev had become secretary general of the CPSU (Communist Party of the Soviet Union). A new era was beginning, not only in the Soviet Union but also in West-East relations.

Once the Unified European Act took effect, European integration gained momentum, but its continued vigor was still not secured. Now all efforts had to be directed toward the political, economic, and monetary union; here too, German-French cooperation would have to be the driving engine.

The ensuing steps seemed to me to have even greater urgency. It was necessary for Germany to resolutely advance West-East relations; this effort would include the CSCE and bilateral relations with Moscow. My appeal—voiced in Davos on February 1, 1987—to take Gorbachev seriously served this end. At the same time the process of European integration had to be firmly supported.

Whenever I spoke in public or private, I called attention to the two phenomena that had sprung up in Europe and were gaining their own powerful dynamic: enhanced East-West relations and European integration within the framework of the EC. The European Community must not be allowed to lag behind if balance in Europe was to be maintained. In my view healing the division of Europe and of Germany became increasingly important. If, as I put it in my speech of February 1, 1987, at first unification was an "historic opportunity that must not be missed," during the course of 1988 it became a certainty that 1989 would see dramatic events in East Germany as well. In September 1988 this certainty persuaded me to appeal to Shevardnadze not to send in the Red Army to intervene in confrontations within East Germany. Late in 1988 and early in 1989 this same feeling was the reason why I fought with all the means at my disposal against the modernization of nuclear short-range missiles. In such an uncertain situation members of the European Community had an obligation to do their utmost to promote actions leading to the establishment of the European Union.

The question that caused most of our neighbors considerable worry, of what the unification of Germany would mean for Europe, for its stability, and for its balance, would arise much sooner and on a deeper level than many expected. The issue of balance was a political and economic one and not primarily a military one, since the integration of the Bundeswehr (the West German armed forces) into NATO had a stabilizing effect. Besides, our troops had won the trust of our allies to such an extent that they were not considered to be a potential danger—the Bundeswehr was and is, after all, NATO's strongest European army—but were seen as a guarantee of our allies' security as well. However, politically and economically, cooperation needed improving in order to achieve a balance and thus achieve the stabilizing effect the EC was seeking.

During that time the German-French partnership proved to be particularly fruitful. Chancellor Kohl and President Mitterand had long since formed a friendship that went beyond the political limits and that was sustained by an awareness of their shared responsibility. As a result they made every effort to proceed collaboratively on all important issues and to use their agreement to profit European integration.

My close professional collaboration with Dumas, who had become foreign minister in December 1984, grew quickly into a deep and lasting friendship; how special our relationship was can probably be appreciated fully only with the knowledge that initially Roland Dumas had the strongest reservations against Germany and the Germans. The history of the Dumas family—Roland's father was murdered, a hostage of the German occupation force; and Roland was a member of the French Résistance—explained his coolness. As I was convinced of the historic necessity of German-French reconciliation and German-French cooperation, I was particularly sensitive to my colleague's, and eventually friend's, feelings. The friendship with Roland Dumas is one of the most valuable gifts from my time as foreign minister.

I vividly remember a particular visit by Foreign Minister Cheysson, before Dumas took office. My French colleague asked for a private talk, and I received him at my official residence on Venusberg. "How will West Germany respond if Moscow plays its trump card and offers you unification?" he asked out of the blue. "Would you pull out of the EC and NATO?"

I never made any attempt to find out if he had been asked to approach me or if he had taken the initiative on this point. The answer I gave reflected my position and actions up to the time of unification: "Moscow has no 'German card.' Only our three Western friends Paris, London, and Washington can deal Moscow the 'German card.' And they can only do so when Moscow offers unification and the West rejects the offer, in violation of the assurances given in the Basic Treaty. We do not view our membership in NATO and the European Community as allegiances that allow qualifications. When we chose to join these organizations, we took a position in favor of a democratic Germany. Our memberships are irrevocable. On the day of German unification they will become binding on all Germans."

Seven years later, in the months after German unification, German-French cooperation was once again a pioneer in the matter of

European integration. It is true that negotiations during the government conferences that led to the Maastricht accords were excruciating, but in retrospect success is the only thing that counts.

The Maastricht accords opened the door to a European future that would have been unthinkable at the end of the Second World War. They allowed for a common currency and economic policy as well as for a united stand by all EC member nations on issues of foreign and security policy. Nor did it seem to me a disadvantage that the EC's members conducted heated debates on the significance and necessity of the European Union. On the contrary: The debate itself revealed the historic significance of Europe's unification policy. Nevertheless, many of its advocates seemed to me too much on the defensive, while its opponents' argument that the end of East-West confrontation had abolished the essential reasons for an integrationist policy fails to recognize the motives underlying the European process of integration.

The founders of the European Community had not intended the Community to respond to the East-West conflict—that idea had given rise to NATO. Rather, the men who initiated the EC were reacting to the errors of European history, to centuries-old regional wars, and above all to the two world wars of the twentieth century. The nations of the continent should never again turn on each other but should join forces for a new culture of cohabitation. This idea continues in effect, and given the tendencies to renewed nationalism, it is more salient than ever. The possibility of a new nationalism is the essential danger confronting Europe after the great changes of the early 1990s. The ideological and intellectual struggle, the conflict between value systems, must therefore be replaced by a new European culture of living peacefully together, a culture based not on power politics but on responsibility. Is it really true that in the new Europe nations will lose their identity? Is it not rather the case that only now can they fully realize their true identity, without the smaller nations fearing the more powerful, and the powerful fearing one another?

There is one aspect that should never be forgotten in Germany: By opting to belong to the Western associations—the European Council, the European Community, and NATO—the Federal Republic also defined its own spiritual and political position; this position is irreversible, even inviolable, if insecurity and instability are not to return to the heart of Europe. Richard von Weizsäcker was absolutely correct when he reminded us that "Our history has never belonged only to ourselves." The same holds true for our future. We are inextricably intertwined with the fate of Europe, for better or worse. It is for this reason that we take such a deep interest in seeing that events in Europe proceed in a positive direction.

To me it seems almost a miracle that today the representatives of the European Union's member nations confer together and arrive at joint decisions, impelled only by their desire for common progress, never by any intention to dominate others. The concept of a directorate of the powerful would destroy such a union, and—I want to be very clear on this point—it is not something German-French cooperation was ever meant to be, its intention being to serve as a driving force. Germany's friends among the other founding nations always realized that our cooperation with France would result in a gain for all and never in a loss to others. We ourselves have never lost sight of this principle. Frequently my talks with Dumas focused on this responsibility, which the French and the Germans share. In particular we discussed German responsibility, and I am certain that the memory of Thomas Mann professing to belong to a "European Germany," rejecting a "German Europe," makes the point abundantly clear. For this reason my work frequently placed the emphasis on cooperation with the smaller nations of the European Community in particular.

I feel that the EC's bigger members owe it to the smaller ones to contribute more to the search for a road to the future that can be traveled together. In this endeavor I encountered outstanding European statesmen among Germany's immediate neighbors—Luxembourg, Belgium, the Netherlands, and Denmark; in some cases these colleagues became good friends. The representatives of the EC's smaller nations are eminent Europeans and as such are true patriots. Their European mentality and sense of responsibility led them to seek and facilitate friendship with Germany. In my commitment to European unification I never forgot what our neighbors suffered at the hands of Germans and in the name of Germany in those terrible twelve years. Making certain once and for all that such a situation can never recur is the most difficult task as well as the greatest responsibility of my generation.

If Europe is to accept its responsibility and face its global challenges—victory over hunger and misery in the Third World; securing the basic necessities of life; the struggle against a population explosion, the spread of weapons of mass destruction, and international crime—it must find a way to act as one. All these considerations must be kept in mind in casting the vote for or against Europe, for or against renewed nationalism.

The road we traveled from the Genscher-Colombo initiative of 1981 to Maastricht was leading in the right direction and was also necessary. The outcome of Maastricht remains a positive one: The process of European unification was given a considerable impetus, it became impossible to turn back, as Maastricht proved. This situation was of the utmost importance to Germany in this era of challenges and risky transitions. Defying all skeptics, Maastricht made history as the summit at which accord was reached on a European Economic and Monetary Union and on a comprehensive European Union in legally binding terms, after decades of preparation. Germany's contribution to this outcome is beyond question.

The Maastricht accords were concluded on December 10, 1991. Given the complicated nature of such accords, it is not surprising that immediately after the political settlement, the legal experts and the translators took over. On February 7, 1992, after weeks of fine-tuning, the accords were finally signed by the finance and foreign ministers; for the sake of symbolism, the ceremony took place in the hall where the European Council had convened. To me this signing symbolized the fulfillment of the promises I had made during the German unification process that a unified Germany would resolutely and with undiminished commitment continue the policy of European integration. After the ceremony we were given the fountain pens we had signed our names with. There are only three pens from my years as foreign minister that I keep: one is from Maastricht, the second is the one I used to sign the Two-Plus-Four agreements in Moscow, and the third was used in New York when the Four Power privileges were abrogated.

It was a stroke of luck that during this historic period Jacques Delors was president of the European Commission. With an iron will this president did his utmost to keep the European ship on course and under steam. François Mitterrand and Helmut Kohl became the partners with whom he made sure that progress toward European unity could no longer be halted or reversed.

Today the European Union is faced with the task of unifying all of Europe. The European treaties we initiated are already linking us with Poland, the Czech Republic, Slovakia, Hungary, Bulgaria, and Romania. Similar treaties are in the works for the Baltic nations, for Albania, and for those successor states of the former Yugoslavia that are committed to human rights, minority rights, and democracy and that also meet the economic requirements.

The time has come to establish a timetable for negotiations on joining the European Union. Furthermore, political, economic, and ecological cooperation treaties with Russia and the rest of the successor states of the former Soviet Union are needed to fix the pan-European perspective firmly in sight. The establishment of a pan-European infrastructure—including traffic and telecommunications as well as joint efforts dedicated to questions of energy production and conservation—are required in order to realize the great potential of the pan-European economic area. The accusation that vision and perspectives are lacking will become groundless the moment Europe discovers its mission to bring about unity. Herein lie the European Union's tasks, potential, and responsibility.

Part Three

*New Challenges
and Crises*

7

Bonn and the Intransigence of the Superpowers

The Neutron Bomb and Its Second-Class Funeral

After the election of Jimmy Carter as president of the United States, it became necessary to develop relationships with a new administration of new people and ideas. The situation was made easier by the fact that Cyrus Vance, who was highly experienced in American-European relations, was appointed secretary of state. Carter's security adviser, Zbigniew Brzezinski, was also an experienced diplomat. Yet problems arose even before Carter's inauguration. As is common practice, a transition team was set up immediately after the election. We were told through our embassy that the Carter administration could not agree to the German-Brazilian accord on the sale of nuclear reactors, since Brazil was not a signatory to the Nuclear Nonproliferation Treaty. The problem was that Brazil viewed this treaty as limiting its sovereignty and, even more crucial, an expression of United States hegemony in Latin America. Serious considerations, therefore, kept Brazil's leaders from accepting the nonproliferation act. Our accord with

Brazil therefore contained stipulations that extended the principles of the nonproliferation treaty to Brazil as well, by imposing such strict regulations for nuclear reactors that everything we shipped to Brazil more than met the requirements of the international nuclear agency.

And so we found this announcement from Washington alarming. It angered Helmut Schmidt. Peter Hermes, an experienced diplomat known as a tough negotiator, was the person in the Foreign Ministry responsible for the agreement with Brazil; he contacted Warren Christopher, the Carter administration's deputy secretary of state.

As early as March 12, 1977, I flew to Washington myself to discuss the issue with President Carter. We had a long talk, not in the Oval Office, but in the cabinet room, where Carter seemed to prefer holding meetings. Clearly interested in friendly cooperation, he nevertheless tried to persuade us to cancel our agreement with Brazil on the shipment of nuclear reactors, even though we were demonstrating strict adherence to the policy of nonproliferation. At least I managed to convince Carter that Germany could in no way be in breach of contract. I told him that neither his predecessor nor the other nuclear powers had raised any objections to this agreement, and I added, "Mr. President, we are your most important ally in Europe. You cannot want Germany, a nation that holds a preeminent position in Europe, to breach a contract— today with Brazil, tomorrow with you or with one of our other partners. Such a position is impossible, especially if you consider the events in German history brought about by broken contracts." I noticed that this moral-ethical argument made a deep impression on Carter. Had I pursued a formal legal or political line, he might have been less attentive. Whatever the case, at the end of the conversation I thought I could detect a chink in the United States' position.

Nor were subsequent encounters with the Carter administration without their problems. On the one hand, the President sincerely aimed at a good relationship with the Chancellor as well as myself, and Vance's personality made constructive collaboration a certainty. Brzezinski was similarly predisposed. On the other hand, the Carter administration repeatedly engaged in abrupt policy changes that resulted in problems arising between the European allies and the United States. An example were the negotiations on the development of the neutron bomb, which met with tremendous opposition in Germany. Schmidt and I, however, were anxious to establish a consensus on the matter within NATO. In the end we agreed with the other allies on a resolution according to which NATO acknowledged that the United States would produce neutron bombs. Only if arms control negotiations should fail, however, would these new weapons be deployed. Schmidt and I had our own problems with this decision. Not only among Germans in general but also within the political parties—though more seriously within the SPD than the FDP—were objections voiced. I had to overcome scruples of my own.

In 1978, shortly before Easter, NATO was to announce its position in favor of producing the weapon. It was agreed that the head of the United States delegation would argue for the introduction of the neutron bomb into the alliance, after sending a copy of this statement to the West German delegation. According to this plan, our delegate would take the floor next to support the proposal. Subsequently, in a so-called silent procedure, in which consensus is implied if there are no objections, approval was to be granted.

After this procedure had been voted on and the German government had reluctantly decided to endorse it, I received a surprising telephone call from Cyrus Vance, informing me that the previously scheduled session of the permanent representatives to the NATO Council need not take place, because the President did not want to arrive at a decision on manufacturing the neutron bomb at this time. He would be sending Warren Christopher to Germany to explain the details to the Chancellor and to me.

I received Christopher in the Foreign Office that same afternoon. He explained that the President now had grave doubts about the introduction of the neutron bomb and therefore wished to refrain from production. I replied that at this time I could merely take note of the information but wished to point out that West Germany had not been at all eager to accept the American proposal. Rather, we had overcome considerable difficulties within our parties in order to give the green light to the NATO resolution. We had done so only in the interest of unity among the allies. The Chancellor and I would be facing great unpleasantness domestically, I went on, if the proposal we had fought so hard for was suddenly withdrawn.

After this conversation I telephoned the Chancellor, who was

147

planning to receive Warren Christopher in Hamburg the next day. I suggested that he fly to Washington afterward to consult with the American government on the best way to proceed. On Monday, April 3, a few of us—the secretary of defense, the Chancellor, and I, as well as two close associates—met in Helmut Schmidt's study to decide on the steps we should take during the subsequent meeting of West Germany's security council. We agreed that in view of all the preparations, the United States would be wrong to announce that it was definitely abandoning plans for the production of the neutron bomb; for the moment the statement should merely declare that a final decision was being deferred. With this strategy the option of producing the weapons might be productive in the arms control negotiations. All of us were greatly relieved at Carter's decision, though it cost us a political headache.

On April 4 I flew to Washington, where I first met with Vance for a private talk, which took place in the Secretary of State's small study behind the large conference room in the State Department. Vance explained that he himself had been taken completely by surprise at the President's decision; he wished to let me know expressly that, aside from himself, Secretary of Defense Harold Brown and Vice President Walter Mondale had also raised objections to this about-face. I announced to him that keeping in mind the aim of disarmament, we thought it best that the option of producing a neutron bomb be retained. He agreed. He also considered this solution a way of avoiding tension within the alliance, since the other European governments had finally given their approval, or at least dropped their objections, under difficulties similar to those we encountered at home.

Berndt von Staden, our ambassador in Washington, one of the outstanding figures in the foreign service after the Second World War, came with me to the subsequent talk with President Carter, in which the Secretary of State and the Security Adviser also participated. Together with his wife, who had been employed in the Foreign Office herself, von Staden—whose distinguished conduct gained him respect wherever he went—made the German Embassy in Washington not only a social center but a superbly informed and influential meeting place.

After a brief preliminary talk with Brzezinski, von Staden and I were warmly welcomed by President Carter in the Oval Office.

Clearly determined to take the offensive in defending his view, Carter voiced his irritation at the European allies' "volatile stand," as he put it. He was no longer willing, he noted, to accept unrelenting criticism of his defense plans. If the Europeans were unwilling to deploy the neutron bomb, it was simple enough to keep it out of NATO. Only a few days earlier, the head of an allied nation had told him that he was opposed to the neutron bomb.

At this point I interrupted. I told him that recently it had been my impression that the European allies, including those who had only reluctantly agreed to the weapon, stood firmly behind the NATO resolution. When I asked him to whom he was referring, Carter replied, "Chancellor Kreisky."

At this, Vance leaned over to the President and said, "But Austria isn't a member of NATO." Carter, exasperated, replied, "Maybe not. In any case, he's a Social Democrat."

We then tried to continue the discussion dispassionately. After Brown, Vance, and Brzezinski had all weighed in, we ended by formulating a statement to the effect that the decision on developing and producing the neutron bomb would be deferred. This move, in effect a second-class funeral for the neutron bomb, enabled us to save face at home, and we hoped it might prove advantageous in the upcoming arms control negotiations.

As we left the meeting, I said to von Staden, "Ambassador, you know that you have an obligation to render a truthful report. But perhaps you might leave the President's remark about the 'Social Democrat' Kreisky out of your telegram. We want to avoid Chancellor Schmidt's feeling hurt—and this remark would give him ample reason."

In the end German-American relations survived these battles intact, and when in July 1978 the heads of state and government of the United States, Canada, France, England, Italy, Japan, and West Germany met for the fourth world economic summit in Bonn, harmony reigned supreme. On July 14 President Carter addressed the German public in front of the city hall. He acknowledged that the Federal Republic of Germany and the United States share an enormous responsibility and that they had similar concerns. He recognized Bonn as the capital of one of the United States' most important allies. "Our security," he said, "is your security, and your security is ours." He spoke of Americans and

Germans as creative cosmopolitans, who joined forces to try to help other regions in the world toward economic prosperity and economic stability. Both nations, he stated, were united by a fundamental belief in the same values: the values of human liberty and the conviction that everyone has the right to live his life fully, without intervention through external oppression or internal disorder.

Humiliation of a Superpower: Hostages in Iran

In July 1979 Iran underwent a revolutionary change: Accompanied by 50 associates and some 150 journalists, the Ayatollah Khomeini returned to Tehran in an Air France jet, formed a government, and appointed Mehdi Bazargan prime minister.

These events came as no surprise to me. I had long been convinced that the days of the Shah's regime were numbered. In view of its fragility I had exercised the greatest caution in dealing with the Shah's administration. West Germany kept up normal diplomatic relations with Iran, but in the five years of my tenure as foreign minister before the Islamic revolution began, I had not once visited the country. This was to play a significant political role later on.

After Khomeini's return and the Shah's fall, Iranian delegations kept coming to West Germany, obviously charged with promoting a favorable response to the Islamic revolution and to an independent course for Iran. These delegations typically consisted of younger men who had studied abroad and spoke German or English so well that they could explain the meaning and aims of the Islamic revolution without the use of interpreters. They stressed their deep interest in good relations with the nations of the European Community, including Germany. Under no circumstances, they said, did they intend to become dependent on or come under the influence of the Soviet Union and, as they put it, its "atheist" system. Nor did they try to hide their rejection of, and even animosity toward, the United States.

I explained to them that a crucial aspect in our dealings was whether the Islamic revolution would indeed take an independent course. For the rest, Tehran must understand that the United States was our closest ally and that it was therefore unrealistic to think that good relations with Bonn would serve as a sort of counterweight to Washington. Furthermore, my attitude toward the Shah's regime had been determined mainly by his violation of human rights; hence the issue of human rights would also be a critical factor in our judgment of Iran's new leaders.

In September 1980 one Sadegh Tabatabai, an Iranian citizen who happened to be in Bonn, asked to meet with me for a confidential talk. I had met him before—he was a member of one of the Iranian delegations. I was aware that he was part of the Ayatollah Khomeini's innermost circle; his sister was married to Khomeini's son, Ahmad. When we met, he requested that I put him in touch with the United States government concerning the hostage crisis. When I asked why he had come to me and who had authorized him, he replied that only Khomeini and two other members of the Iranian government knew about his initiative; it had been decided to approach me because I could be trusted to think favorably about Iran—after all, I had never paid an official visit to Tehran during the Shah's regime. Tabatabai assured me that he was authorized to negotiate the release of the American hostages with an official agent of the President of the United States; the sooner such an agent could come to Bonn, the better. Negotiations could be conducted here but must be kept in the strictest confidence. It was mandatory, Tabatabai noted, that I chair the meeting, and in case an agreement could be reached between Iran and the United States, I would have to vouchsafe that the United States would keep its end of the bargain.

After Tabatabai left, I informed Helmut Schmidt of the Iranian leaders' strange request. Like myself, the Chancellor thought we were obligated to pass the proposal on to the United States government and if it agreed, to arrange for the stipulated talks as well. Later that day I telephoned Ed Muskie, at this time secretary of state, to inform him and to ask if the United States government would agree to such a meeting. Muskie promised to let me know. Not much later President Carter personally telephoned and expressed the greatest interest in arranging such a meeting. His eagerness was understandable, since in the United States the humiliation of the hostage crisis was at the forefront of public debate; it was probable that the outcome of the forthcoming elections would be critically affected by developments in the hostage crisis. Carter declared that he was ready to send an agent to Bonn immediately and to give him full authority; he had Deputy Secretary of

State Warren Christopher in mind. Christopher seemed an excellent choice to me; the talks with Khomeini's agents were likely to be extraordinarily difficult. Christopher would bring a phalanx of legal experts, since in return for the release of the hostages the Iranians would surely insist on the release of Iranian accounts and assets frozen in the United States. On Monday, September 15, the American Deputy Secretary and his staff arrived in Bonn.

Only very few employees in the Foreign Office were told about the operation. My personal adviser took care of organizing the meeting, he even saw to it that drinks were provided. The interpreter for the Foreign Office assisted at the meeting as Tabatabai spoke no English, only German. Norbert Montfort, our deputy secretary for Middle Eastern and Far Eastern affairs, also attended. During the meeting, which took place on Tuesday, September 16, in the Foreign Office on Bonn's Venusberg, Iran was represented only by Tabatabai and the United States by Christopher and an associate.

I chaired the meeting, though I largely confined myself to listening. I spoke up only occasionally, especially when it was a matter of getting the Iranian to understand the difficulties that can arise in open, democratic societies when certain agreements need to be put into practice. Tabatabai repeated his claim that the Iranian government had insisted the discussion take place in my presence. Christopher declared that the President had given him the power to negotiate with great flexibility, and that the United States welcomed my presence as well. Tabatabai emphasized that Iran wanted me to be more than a witness to the negotiation; I was also to be guarantor that any potential agreements would be observed. As expected, the talks focused principally on the release of Iranian accounts in the United States and on Iran's assets frozen by other Western nations. The Shah's personal property formed a part of these assets.

Gerhardt Ritzel, our ambassador in Tehran, had laid the basis for the trust the new Iranian government placed in West Germany and in me personally. Ritzel employed great sensitivity in creating a climate of discussion with the new Iranian leaders that had been extraordinarily helpful even before the Iranian-American negotiations. I had brought Ritzel from Tehran to meet with Secretary of State Muskie, who happened to be in Europe on the occasion of the twenty-fifth anniversary of the Austrian State Treaty. Ritzel was able to give Muskie and his Middle East advisers a realistic assessment of the situation in Tehran and of the chances of obtaining a release of the hostages. Once again Vienna served as the locus of international politics.

The negotiations on the Venusberg lasted late into the evening. Along with Deputy Secretary Christopher, I spoke with the Chancellor on the morning of September 17; that afternoon I had another meeting with Christopher and one with Tabatabai, to prepare for the second round of talks, scheduled for Thursday.

The second discussion went on for some two and a half hours. Tabatabai informed us that he would be returning to Tehran on Monday, September 22, to consult at once with the decision makers. I made sure he understood that he could reach us at any time through Ambassador Ritzel. From September 22 to September 24 I would be in New York for the United Nations General Assembly, at which time I would also be meeting with Secretary of State Muskie.

Further contacts eventually led to a plan for releasing the American hostages on Thursday, October 2. A German plane was to pick them up in Tehran and fly them to Frankfurt where a United States aircraft was to pick them up and fly them home.

A few days before the arranged date, on September 27, we were informed that at this time it was impossible to resolve the hostage problem. Our immediate assumption was that this sudden reversal had something to do with developments between Iran and Iraq. It was later bruited about in Tehran that President Carter was the instigator of the Iraqi war against Iran. To this day I cannot say with certainty what the true reason was; in any case, Iranian sources soon announced that under no circumstances would the hostages be released before the United States elections in November. Iran had no intention of lending aid and comfort to Carter's campaign.

Subsequent contact between the United States and Iran occurred by way of Algeria. On one visit to Algiers I encountered Warren Christopher again. The newly elected president Ronald Reagan, would ultimately allow his predecessor to welcome the hostages at the Frankfurt airport, and on that occasion Carter once more expressed his thanks for our efforts on behalf of and our part in the release of the American hostages.

NATO's Double-Track Resolution

The NATO double-track resolution tested the Schmidt-Genscher administration most severely. At an early stage the Chancellor had been the first to point out, during an address in London in October 1977, that the Soviet Union, with its SS-20 intermediate-range missiles, was building up an arsenal that posed a threat to all neighboring countries—in particular, of course, the United States' European NATO allies. It seemed to us regrettable that the SALT II discussions on strategic weapons had failed to include a safeguard against circumventing the agreements; the introduction of intermediate-range missiles, which could be to added to the current arsenals, had not been explicitly banned. The heads of government of the United States, France, the United Kingdom, and the Federal Republic of Germany—Jimmy Carter, Valéry Giscard d'Estaing, James Callaghan, and Helmut Schmidt—met in Guadeloupe to discuss the problem. They agreed to accept the Soviet challenge, which was clearly designed to rupture the policy on security shared by the European allies and the United States. West Germany and more precisely, almost exclusively the FDP, worked out a plan eventually termed the double-track resolution. It included a decision to allow deployment of American intermediate-range missiles (Pershing II and cruise missiles) while it proposed negotiations on the gradual or total elimination of nuclear intermediate-range missiles—the so-called zero option.

In 1978 a German-Soviet declaration was signed during a visit to West Germany by Brezhnev and Gromyko, which contained wording we considered crucial. It articulated the fundamental principle that no nation would strive for military superiority and that approximate balance and parity would guarantee a sufficient defense. This guiding principle would govern military relations between East and West.

In July 1979, on his way to the world economic summit in Tokyo, Helmut Schmidt stopped over in Moscow, where he met with Prime Minister Alexei Kosygin and Foreign Minister Andrei Gromyko. Once again he emphasized our worries about the potential danger of Soviet intermediate-range missiles. When I spoke with Gromyko in New York in September of that same year, I pointed out once more that we were interested in negotiating the intermediate-range missiles but that we would not hesitate to resort to rearming if the Soviet Union proved unwilling to agree to negotiations with the aim of totally eliminating Soviet prearmament, the term I coined for Moscow's quantitative lead.

On November 21, 1979, Gromyko arrived in Bonn for a three-day visit. In my speech during the official dinner in La Redouté in nearby Bad Godesberg, I elaborated on the situation that pertained to security policy; the current position, I explained, worried us a great deal. I then addressed Gromyko directly. "We do not look on a realistic policy of détente as a mere episode, a transitory phenomenon; we define it as a constant striving for peace, understanding, security, and mutual confidence." Reminding him of the declaration of 1978, I added, "Now is the time for the promises of that moment to prove themselves."

Gromyko's response was disappointing. "We and West Germany do not speak the same language here. The Soviet Union believes that sustaining parity is sufficient to guarantee security." During a press conference at the conclusion of his visit he reiterated the fact that Bonn and Moscow held widely diverging views. His exact words were: "Unfortunately we must realize that, as our negotiations here in Bonn have shown, the government of the Federal Republic of Germany is favorably inclined toward NATO's plans to deploy missiles. Such a plan is a way of heating up the arms race. It marks the beginning of a new stage, a new round in the arms race." I could not help thinking that Gromyko spoke so harshly because he felt that it was too late to change the Western Alliance's mind.

Chancellor Schmidt, Minister of Defense Hans Apel, and I were fully aware that the Alliance was faced with an historic decision. We were convinced that the Soviet Union's willingness to enter into negotiations now or even at a later date depended on whether the Alliance stood firm. When it was time for NATO to decide on December 12, 1979, all voting members were aware that deployment of United States intermediate-range missiles in Europe was still three or four years off. The West German government was eager to see this grace period used for arms control negotiations with the Soviet Union. Precisely because we were a divided country, we were especially concerned with the continuance of détente and cooperation.

Smoothing the way for the NATO double-track resolution was a major achievement by our representatives to NATO and to the Special Consultations Group established for that particular purpose. These consultants and negotiators managed to secure a great deal of influence on the execution of both tracks of the resolution for the members of the alliance—in particular such nations as West Germany, where missiles would be deployed. West Germany was particularly concerned that the number of intermediate-range missiles to be deployed be precisely defined. We refused to be the only nation where they were to be stationed. Understandably, we had no desire to be singled out. In the end we had to accept the decision that the Pershing IIs, with their more limited range, were deployed only in West Germany, while the cruise missiles were placed in Italy, the Netherlands, Belgium, and England as well.

Until shortly before the crucial NATO meeting on December 12 we remained in constant touch with our United States partner. Secretary and Mrs. Vance arrived in Bonn on the afternoon of December 11, where the Secretary met with both the Chancellor and me. That night the couple came to dinner at my home in Wachtberg-Pech. It was clear once again how much sympathy this excellent secretary of state had for what troubled us. Our working relationship, which had been good from the beginning, was increasingly characterized by mutual respect, trust, and the closeness of friends.

The Positions Harden: Afghanistan and the Boycott of the Olympic Games in Moscow

No sooner had NATO's double-track resolution been voted in, than—that very evening—the "Western Four" had reason to debate the next difficult issue: the situation in Afghanistan. Peter Lord Carrington, the British foreign secretary, expressed his concern with recent events. When he asked whether any indications existed of an imminent Soviet action, Vance replied in the negative. To this day I do not know whether the Carter administration actually had more information than it admitted to, as some have claimed. We, too, worried that Moscow might involve itself directly in Afghanistan. Carrington and I therefore asked to have our concerns made part of the public communiqué on the meeting of the NATO Council of Ministers.

On December 21 I received Soviet Ambassador Vladimir Semyonov to apprise him of our position in regard to the NATO double-track resolution. I also asked him about the situation in Afghanistan, but I received no reply. Three days later, on Christmas Eve, Soviet troops marched into Afghanistan. For the first time since the Second World War the Soviet Union invaded a neighboring nation that was not a member of the Warsaw Pact.

On January 17, 1980, the Bundestag addressed the Afghanistan problem. I ended my speech by noting, "Germans want peace not only at home but all over the world. We want stability. And we are eager to export aid—not conflicts, and not ideologies. We want to work together. We want understanding. We want, not tension but détente. As someone whose heart still beats in and for his home in central Germany, I am saying: I cannot imagine that there is anyone more interested in being allowed to continue working for détente and balance in Europe than the German people, who are forced to live in two states."

As I finished and the prolonged applause from every side was dying down, a unique event occurred: Willy Brandt rose from his seat, walked toward the government bench, and congratulated me with a firm handshake. We looked at each other—this moment united us in shared worry that once again, as West and East drifted apart, Germany would be hit the hardest.

In response to the invasion of Afghanistan, President Carter—without first consulting his allies—proposed a boycott of the 1980 Olympic Games that were to be held in Moscow. He thought he was taking an important step that would impress the Kremlin leaders. Though we had serious doubts about the efficacy of such a measure, we did our utmost to display solidarity with our ally. Overcoming their reservations and well aware of their civic responsibility, the German sports organizations announced that they were willing to support the decision to boycott the Olympics. As for myself, I had rarely found a political move as difficult as this one: It was a great disappointment to our athletes, who had practiced rigorously for the Games.

Prime Minister Margaret Thatcher's conduct irritated us. While we informed our sports organizations first and asked them to join in a show of solidarity among the Western nations, Prime Minister Thatcher immediately announced that she wholeheartedly endorsed President Carter's call for a boycott. And yet, when the

157

time came, the British athletes went to Moscow after all. By way of explanation, London commented tersely that British sports organizations were independent. Thus the only NATO nations that observed the boycott were those we sometimes jokingly referred to as "frontline states" because they were immediate neighbors of the Warsaw Pact nations: Norway, West Germany, and Turkey. Remarking on London's attitude, I observed that firmness was good, iron firmness even better, but cast-iron firmness no good at all in response to serious provocation—it was mere lip service.

At the threshold of the new decade a complex world had emerged that consisted of more than 150 nations, in which hegemony and military force was bound to lead to only one outcome: chaos, economic regress—in short, a decline of political power for those who staked their future on such anachronistic behavior. I therefore believed that the Soviet incursion into Afghanistan had gained only superficial and temporary extension of that power's influence. Of course we needed to be very clear about our willingness to join with our allies in deterring the Soviet Union from further extending its power, but I also asked myself whether Soviet prearmament and its military invasion in Afghanistan might not also point to the beginning of an historical reversal that in the long run would diminish Soviet influence.

Given the global political situation, intermediate-range weapons played a key role as the new decade was about to dawn. The crucial question was whether balance could be achieved on a lower level, through disarmament, or whether we would continue to be forced to reach parity on a higher plane, by continuing the arms race. In this phase the zero option seemed to me to be of utmost importance, which is why I publicly declared: "Should agreement ever be reached successfully on abolishing—and I mean abolishing globally and totally—even a single weapons category, such an agreement will send a definitive signal in favor of nuclear disarmament." Many people—including a number who supported my policies on principle—rejected my call; they argued that it was too radical. I responded to their objections with my willingness to accept temporary solutions as well.

Let Us Negotiate

On May 16, 1980, I had met with Foreign Minister Gromyko in Vienna in anticipation of a visit to Moscow that Chancellor Schmidt and I had planned for June 30 and July 1. I wanted to prepare Gromyko for our positions and concerns. Schmidt had announced that he would like to talk not only with Brezhnev and Gromyko but also with Dmitri Ustinov, the minister of defense. He also wanted to meet with other members of the Politburo; the Soviet leaders promised that such encounters would be arranged.

During the Moscow meeting we engaged in the usual exchange of opinions that at heart was not a genuine exchange at all. As always, Schmidt made his case strongly and convincingly, but Brezhnev—as had been his habit for some time—read in a monotone from a paper. In 1980 he was already seriously ill. Only once, at the end of the morning meeting, did he come to attention, jolted by one of Schmidt's remarks. The Chancellor had said, "In addition, I want to thank you sincerely for letting us meet with Marshals Ustinov and Nikolai Ogarkov this afternoon, before our next meeting." Hardly had he uttered these words than Brezhnev replied vehemently, "But only Ustinov is a member of the Politburo." Here the importance of political rank became evident. He simply could not accept the same treatment being accorded to two marshals of whom only one was a member of the Politburo.

The meeting with Ustinov took place in the Soviet Ministry of Defense, a building we had not visited before. Ustinov was with numerous generals, all wearing many medals. Ogarkov was present as well. The dialogue that developed between Schmidt and Ustinov was conducted with great skill on both sides, though Schmidt tried repeatedly and with great deftness to include Ogarkov. I cannot claim that the meeting brought about any miracles, but it can have done no harm for the military leaders of the Soviet Union to hear and take in the political reasoning of one of the West's most important and best-informed heads of government. Encouraged by this discussion, subsequently Schmidt and I, in talks with representatives of smaller Warsaw Pact nations, took every opportunity to elicit information about their relative military strength and to bring forward new reasons in support of our criticism of Soviet positions.

159

Almost the entire membership of the Politburo attended the dinner. Never had I seen so many of its members in one place. For the first and only time I also had an opportunity to chat with the Party's chief ideologue, Mikhail Suslov.

In his after-dinner remarks Schmidt clearly expressed his disapproval of the Soviet invasion of Afghanistan. "I am sure that you, Mr. Secretary General, would significantly contribute to defusing this dangerous crisis if you could declare that the promised withdrawal of some Soviet units from Afghanistan is the beginning of an action that will continue until the moment of complete withdrawal."

Of course we had no power to compel the Soviets to withdraw from Afghanistan. But we were able to persuade them to agree to negotiate with the United States on intermediate-range missiles. They dropped their demand that the NATO double-track resolution be abandoned before such negotiations could be considered.

As had been arranged beforehand, immediately after our return I flew to Washington to brief the American leaders on our Moscow meetings. Of course I also had a hidden agenda: to persuade the United States government to initiate negotiations. My visit was brief; on the morning of Thursday, July 3, I landed in Bonn again, the United States having agreed to these tactics.

If it is to Helmut Schmidt's credit that he was the first to focus attention on the problem of Soviet prearmament, the effort of bringing about the double-track resolution and the subsequent negotiations on intermediate-range missiles were our joint achievements. We worked incessantly toward this end, in Moscow, as well as in Washington. During the final days of our collaboration, in the fall of 1982, we were told about the "walk in the woods" in Geneva by the two chief negotiators Paul Nitze (United States) and Yuli Kvitsinsky (Soviet Union). Helmut Schmidt and I never had an opportunity to discuss its results—our government coalition had fallen apart, partly as a consequence of the NATO double-track resolution.

By the beginning of the 1980s it was increasingly clear that the coalition of SPD and FDP was no longer viable, especially when it came to economic and monetary policy as well as to matters of security. It seemed evident that the SPD would no longer back Chancellor Schmidt and NATO's double-track resolution, while the vast majority of the FDP supported the double-track resolution. The end came in September 1982; we had drifted too far apart on crucial issues of foreign and security policy and on matters concerning the Western Alliance. The SPD had ceased to pursue policies based on the government program to which we all had agreed; Helmut Schmidt was unable to win majority support for his positions within his own party.

Leaving the coalition was difficult for me; the social-liberal administration had taken important decisions and solved significant concrete issues. Yet the present course of events was unstoppable, partly because Helmut Schmidt seemed often to have been reluctant to be open with me, the deputy chancellor and chairman of the FDP, the minor coalition partner. He had not judged it fit to discuss with me problems he had within his own party. Matters might have turned out better if we had talked openly about these issues, especially since at times I had the distinct impression that Chancellor Schmidt was siding with his party even though at heart he agreed with me.

In September 1982 I adamantly supported negotiations that would lead to a coalition with the CDU/CSU, although the switch in coalitions was vehemently debated within the FDP. The new shared program of FDP and CDU/CSU clearly bore liberal marks. During the switch of coalitions I made it a priority to safeguard the continuity of German foreign policy.

But back to the events of the autumn of 1981. In November Brezhnev and Gromyko flew to Bonn. When we met for the first talk among the delegations on Monday, November 23, I was amazed at Brezhnev's apparent frailty. A shift in power had also clearly occurred—Andrei Gromyko seemed to be gaining more and more influence and every now and then he found it necessary to intervene. When, for example, Chancellor Schmidt expressed his regret at the fact that the Soviet Union had not participated in the North-South summit in Cancún, we could hear Brezhnev asking Gromyko what Schmidt was referring to; the foreign minister did no more than reply tersely that the subject was the meeting they had recently discussed. Schmidt explained to the Soviets that unless negotiations between Washington and Moscow led to an agreement, United States intermediate-range missiles would be deployed in West Germany and elsewhere in Europe in late 1983. He emphasized that there was no change in our support of the zero

161

option, since it represented the best solution. It was still in the Soviet Union's power to prevent deployment by reversing its arms buildup.

All in all, little was accomplished at this meeting. I came away with the distinct impression that Moscow was not convinced the West would be able to deploy the missiles in the first place. And indeed, positions within the SPD gave the Soviet leaders enough reason to hope that the West German government would not be strong enough to enforce deployment in Germany; under those circumstances, the NATO double-track resolution would not be realized in its entirety.

In conversations with Gromyko I again made certain that he understood deployment was not an empty threat; I said, "Take the zero option seriously. It is a serious proposal. It is our idea, not an American invention. We developed it in Bonn, within our government coalition, especially within my own party." Even though this meeting ultimately ended without any tangible results, Chancellor Schmidt and I had done all we could to convince the leaders in the Kremlin that the West would respond seriously to Soviet missile buildup and that we would also do whatever was necessary, through arms control and disarmament, to prevent a renewed arms race.

More than a year later the situation had not materially changed. In the early afternoon of January 16, 1983, a Sunday, I welcomed Foreign Minister Gromyko and his wife at Cologne-Wahn airport. That evening they came to dinner at my home in Wachtberg-Pech; since it was a private occasion, the conversation dealt chiefly with family matters. Gromyko was rapturous when he talked about his grandchildren; he immensely enjoyed the part of the doting grandfather. After dinner I had a talk with my Soviet colleague about the situation in Germany and the crucial topic of the NATO double-track resolution. I began by praising him for his initiative in making this visit: It was a good and necessary thing he was doing, for the Soviet government would be dealing with the new West German government coalition of Christian Democrats and Free Democrats, formed in late 1982 after the collapse of the SPD-FDP coalition, for a long time to come. The administration would certainly be reelected in the upcoming election. The economy would continue its upward curve, and the NATO double-track resolution would be voted in. Gromyko responded with an explanation of Moscow's stand. I reiterated our desire for good relations over the long term. All in all our talk made it clear that a relationship of mutual and professional respect had developed between the two of us. I was nevertheless certain that Moscow would do its utmost to prevent deployment of the intermediate-range missiles.

What was truly unusual, however, was that after our official negotiations were concluded, Gromyko used a press conference to stage a propaganda event that could not be interpreted in any way other than as an attempt to interfere in West Germany's internal affairs. I was in my office and watched his appearance on television. Of course I had assumed that his statements would be biased. For the sake of an immediate response, I myself issued a public commentary on arms-control policy right after Gromyko's press conference. I noted that we were proceeding on the premise that the Soviet Union would grant us the same degree of security it demanded for itself and that any decrease in security, such as was caused by the unilateral deployment of the SS-20s, remained unacceptable to us. Once again I called for the zero option.

It now became clear that Gromyko had misjudged the psychological climate in Germany. While there was an element that was impressed by the heavy artillery rhetorics he had used, the shot nevertheless backfired: The West German government remained adamant, and our stance never altered during the election campaign. The television debate between the party chairmen, Helmut Kohl, Franz Josef Strauss of the CSU, and me left no doubt that if the government coalition was reelected, we would proceed with deployment unless the negotiations led to an agreement. The SPD's leading candidate, Hans-Jochen Vogel, who was in trouble from the outset by representing his party's position, was hardly helped by Gromyko's performance in Bonn.

Another visit in January 1983 was of crucial importance to Germany's role in enacting NATO's double-track resolution. On the occasion of the twentieth anniversary of the signing of the Elysée Treaty, President Mitterand came to Bonn and addressed the Bundestag. In an impressive speech the French President endorsed the NATO double-track resolution, even though, as a nonaligned member, France did not vote on the Western Alliance's resolution. His words highlighted the West's cohesiveness and determination. They further supported the West German government coalition, while dealing a blow to the opposition party. The SPD now found itself cut off from its most important partner in the socialist international movement on an issue of strategic dimensions. My colleagues in the SPD looked stupefied as they listened to the words of the French President—an unforgettable sight. On this occasion, as on others as well, Mitterand proved to be a politician of European stature, not merely a party politician concerned with aiding his German fellow socialists.

Contrary to our custom, and to mark the special occasion, I had met the French President at the Cologne airport and driven in to Bonn with him. In the car, however, he confessed that he still had to work on his speech and apologized for not being able to talk to me. Then he totally revised the draft he had brought. At the Chancellor's Office, he also asked the Chancellor's permission for time to work on his address. The resulting vignette may symbolize the trust that characterizes German-French relations: the French President seated in the West German Chancellor's Office, quietly working on his speech.

Mitterand's core message—approval of and support for a deployment of American missiles in Germany and Western Europe—carried great weight, precisely because France was not among the aligned members of NATO. In particular, his warning that Europe must not be allowed to separate from the United States aroused attention: Despite its independence and self-sufficiency, France did not hesitate for a moment to explicitly affirm the alliance with the United States at a time of high tension.

These visits by Gromyko and Mitterand marked a turning point in the discussion on the deployment of intermediate-range missiles. Both the Soviet foreign minister and the French head of state had made their positions unmistakably clear. Their stands provoked widespread international attention, and because their declarations were made in Bonn, West Germany's importance to the future of West-East relations and to the security of Europe was underscored once again.

This was the period when it was determined whether the Soviet Union would gain political power in Western Europe through military superiority, and whether it would succeed in separating Western Europe from the United States. Later events proved that it was precisely the firmness of the Kohl-Genscher administration, coupled with its willingness to negotiate, that had paved the way for new West-East relations. When Mikhail Gorbachev was asked, in 1993, whether it had been the NATO double-track resolution or SDI (Strategic Defense Initiative) that had brought about the reversal in the Soviet Union's attitude, and most particularly had caused the Kremlin to rethink West-East relations, he replied, "It was the NATO double-track resolution and not SDI, about which we felt exactly as Hans-Dietrich Genscher did."

Once the Kohl-Genscher administration was firmly established after the 1983 election, we did everything in our power to reach a solution by way of negotiation to prevent the actual deployment of United States intermediate-range missiles, which was scheduled for the end of that year. Ultimately another important event would help persuade Moscow to yield: the world economic summit of the seven leading industrial nations, which took place in Williamsburg, Virginia, on May 28 through May 30, 1983. For the first time this body took a stand on issues of East-West relations and disarmament—specifically, on the intermediate-range missiles.

The summit statement on issues of foreign and security policy was noteworthy for two reasons. The fact that it was issued at all was remarkable. But that France and Japan—both of which had, until then, been determined to keep the summit restricted to issues of the international economy—also signed the statement marked a turning point. For Helmut Kohl, participating in a world economic summit for the first time, and for me this turn of events implied support of our trip to Moscow, which was planned for July 4–6.

In our talks with Secretary General Yuri Andropov, Prime Minister Nikolai Tikhonov, and Foreign Minister Andrei Gromyko we explained the policies of the new administration, which were characterized by continuity based on the existing treaties. Addressing the factual situation in Europe, Kohl called the Germans' will to unite the two Germanys one of these facts. We left no doubt that we were serious about both parts of NATO's double-track resolution, emphasizing that our interest lay in achieving agreement through negotiation. If agreement were not reached by the end of the year, deployment, in the prearranged numbers, was inevitable; Kohl reiterated that we would prefer to see both sides relinquish intermediate-range missiles—that is, we were in favor of the zero-zero option.

When I met Gromyko in September that same year at the United Nations, our positions were once again irreconcilable. It was increasingly clear that Moscow was hoping the West German government would be unable to carry out its plans in the face of public opposition; such a hope was not entirely unfounded, though I believed it to be illusory. An opinion poll taken in August showed two-thirds of the population opposed to deployment. One SPD party organization after an other openly attacked the NATO double-track resolution.

The vote in the Bundestag was scheduled for November 21 and 22. Before the parliamentary debate could take place, I decided to take a dramatic step: I proposed to Gromyko that we meet in a neutral setting, so that I could have one last try at persuading him of West Germany's determination. Gromyko accepted immediately and suggested Sofia as a meeting place. I found that suggestion unacceptable—after all, Bulgaria was a member of the Warsaw Pact, and thus not politically neutral. Besides, immediately after our proposed encounter, a Warsaw Pact meeting was scheduled to take place in Sofia. I therefore rejected his suggestion. I really hoped to meet in Vienna. But so as to give Gromyko an opportunity to reject my suggestion as well, and then be all the more sure that we would indeed agree on Vienna, I proposed Belgrade, the capital of Yugoslavia, which we considered a nonaligned nation but which the Soviet Union viewed as a country that had seceded from the Soviet sphere. Not surprisingly, Gromyko refused. He himself then proposed Vienna, after I had already dropped a hint.

On October 15 I traveled to Vienna. The sessions took place alternately in the Soviet and the German embassies, which are very near each other. We began with a luncheon in the Soviet embassy. Gromyko was eager to create a friendly climate. During the luncheon we talked about our childhood and life in the country, since we had both been raised on a farm. We even discussed agricultural issues. Because Gromyko expressed an interest in a thoroughgoing exchange of opinions, we scheduled an additional evening meeting. I used the talks to reexplain our basic thoughts on foreign and security policy, on détente, and on the double-track resolution. I impressed on my Soviet colleague how extremely important it was that Moscow understand the situation correctly: We were firmly resolved to deploy the missiles unless negotiations led to a last-minute agreement. Since we were interested in markedly improving relations with the Soviet Union, I continued, we wanted to make certain that Moscow harbored no illusions about our intentions. Then I addressed a basic tenet of our foreign policy: Nothing was more dangerous than misjudging the intentions, motives, and determination of others. Such false conclusions led only to disaster. German foreign policy was therefore designed to be absolutely lucid and open—a philosophy to which I had always felt obligated to adhere. I am convinced that our openness made our policies understandable and thus predictable, and it was this trait in particular that was our essential contribution to stability in the Alliance, in the European Community, and in West-East relations. I assured Gromyko that this openness in foreign policy could be depended on in future as well.

During our Vienna sessions we met for more than eleven hours altogether. We talked late into the night. Our discussions were extremely serious and our arguments were supported by facts, as was appropriate for the gravity of the international situation. Even when Gromyko expressed harsh criticism of American policies, he never attempted to drive a wedge between West Germany and the United States. He was too well aware of the history that had led to the double-track resolution and of my part in it. And repeatedly it seemed to me that, despite the harshness of the talks, I detected signs of resignation. Did Gromyko feel that Moscow had set the stakes too high and had misjudged the situation?

In my view our Vienna meeting remains the classic attempt at damage control in a difficult situation—and it was successful. If Moscow had miscalculated, West Germany was in no way to blame for this mistake. We had always been entirely straightforward. Perhaps this behavior also holds the key to explaining why we did not experience another ice age, as the SPD had feared and predicted. On the contrary: The firmness of the Kohl-Genscher administration on the NATO double-track resolution enhanced our reputation in the Alliance as well as in NATO. The years that followed were to prove how urgently this kind of credibility was required if we were to make the necessary impact on East-West relations.

When I left Vienna, I had made certain that Moscow could no

longer harbor any illusions. If no last-minute reversal of Moscow's attempt at superiority occurred, it would be because the Soviet leaders were not ready or were unable to bring about change. However, I had the distinct impression that Moscow would continue to be interested in a good relationship with us, and I predicted a short, rather than a prolonged, period of turmoil. In any case, the respect and trust between Gromyko and me had increased, precisely because our talks had been so open.

The parliamentary debate on the double-track resolution turned into a fundamental debate on détente, security, and foreign policy. In the end the Bundestag approved the resolution.

8

Heralds of Change in German and International Policy

A New Actor on the Global Stage: Ronald Reagan in Cancún

On July 19 through 22, 1981, the seventh world economic summit took place in Canada, this time with an almost entirely new cast of characters: the United States was represented for the first time by Ronald Reagan; François Mitterand had been president of France only since May; and Prime Minister Zenko Suzuki had just taken office in Japan. Italy sent its prime minister, Giovanni Spadolini, while the European Commission was represented by the eminent Luxembourg liberal Gaston Thorn, the Commission's president. Helmut Schmidt—who was chancellor until 1982—and I were the senior members of the group, as it were. It quickly turned out that not only in foreign policy but also in economic policy the new United States administration had changed course. It was precisely for that reason that this economic summit was so important.

What had not changed, however, was the United States position on a North-South summit, which Mexico and Austria had initiated and which was to take place in Cancún on October 22 and 23. It was the purpose of this conference to bring together representatives from eight industrial and fourteen developing nations for a dialogue.

Since Helmut Schmidt was unable to participate in the Cancún summit because of an unexpected coronary problem, I chaired the West German delegation. From an early stage I had been in total agreement with the Chancellor in support of the Cancún summit.

Algeria, Austria, Canada, France, India, Mexico, Nigeria, Sweden, Tanzania, and Yugoslavia had participated in the planning meetings held in Austria in November 1980 and March 1981. Astonishingly, the People's Republic of China was a participant in the summit proper, while the Soviet Union, after long deliberation, finally decided against attending.

I had tried to persuade Gromyko twice to change his mind. Either he was unable to be decisive or there were clashes of opinion in the Politburo—such, at least, was my impression. And then again, perhaps the Soviet Union was reluctant to compel Brezhnev to travel to such an exhausting climate, since he was already in failing health. Whatever the reason, the Soviets cannot have been happy about China's participation, especially since the other superpower, the United States, was represented by its president. It may be that the Soviet leaders feared criticism at this conference for the meager aid the Soviet Union and the other Communist nations rendered the developing countries. In any case, the North-South dialogue went off without a Soviet voice.

Though there were no concrete results, the conference marked an important step, if only because it was a dialogue conducted with civility and a large degree of mutual understanding. In addition, the contributions of the leading representatives of the Third World, particularly when their statements were buttressed with moral arguments, made a profound impression on Ronald Reagan. This was especially evident when Indira Gandhi and Tanzania's President Julius Nyerere spoke; the latter turned out to be exceptionally well-versed in Scripture and cleverly larded his remarks with quotations from the New Testament. As always at such events, a concluding communiqué was issued; when we considered its wording, Margaret Thatcher sought my support in preserving the principles of a free-market economy and free world trade. She was apparently afraid that Reagan was overly captivated by the representatives from the Third World.

A similar worry—but in the area of security—was voiced very much later, when some statesmen in the United States and in Europe (including West Germany), thought that Reagan was listening too closely to Gorbachev's arguments in Reykjavík. Neither in Cancún nor in Reykjavík were such concerns warranted. In reality both events were meant for the benefits of face-to-face meetings and their impact on dissolving prejudices. Reagan, who was frequently criticized in Europe, proved more flexible and open than were many of his younger critics.

Quite aside from the topics under discussion, the Cancún conference was profitable for me because I was able to meet with all the delegations; conference protocol arranged that Reagan and I were seated together at two official dinners. Since the king of Saudi Arabia was sitting to my left and the president of Venezuela to Reagan's right, with no room for interpreters at the table, we were destined to talk to one another. The result was an intense exchange of opinions. For example, I explained to the President of the United States how European citizens felt about the security of their borders. In the United States, I said, a country of continental proportions, only a tiny percentage of citizens along the Mexican and Canadian borders considered themselves a border population, and even these did not consider their neighbors a threat. How different the situation must have been in the past for such countries as Luxembourg, which unlike the United States, had not two neighbors but three—Belgium, France, and Germany. We, the largest country in the European Community, or at least the one with the largest population, were living in such a confined area that any point in Germany was no more than two hours away by car from a border, including the border between West and East Germany. This fact alone was reason enough for us to wish for good and trusting relationships with our neighbors. Stability in Europe demanded no less. This was the reason, I went on, Europeans worked so hard to render frontiers meaningless and to arrive at a new culture of coexistence, such as was realized in the EC. The EC was more than an economic community, and the East's policy of demarcation contradicted the historical tendency to abolish separation.

Given Reagan's and my penchant for trading jokes, we could

171

not let the occasion pass without providing each other with a new supply. Later I would hear jokes that were ascribed to Reagan but which I recognized as having originated in our chat in Cancún.

James Baker, who would become secretary of state, came to Cancún in his capacity as White House chief of staff. We soon developed a good relationship, and used the rest periods in the negotiations to talk. Subsequently, whenever I was in Washington and time allowed, I called on him at the Treasury, until he finally moved to the State Department. During one of these visits I found a dollar bill on the stairs in the Treasury Department. Arriving at Baker's office, I waved it at him, remarking that you could tell the United States was a rich country: The road to the Treasury Secretary was paved with dollar bills. Baker examined the bill closely and figured out that it was part of the first series that bore his name. He promptly signed the bill alongside the printed signature.

I was very sorry that Cancún was not followed by another summit of the same kind. With new heads of state and government taking office in Mexico and Austria, the initiators of the first summit lacked the necessary impetus, and the general course of international events reduced interest in a North-South dialogue conducted so responsibly. All efforts to organize a subsequent conference failed. In my opinion a follow-up could have contributed greatly to mutual understanding and confidence building between North and South. The G7 are purely North-North summits, even if now Russia is invited. During these conferences the issues under discussion are of existential significance to the Third World nations as well.

The program for regional cooperation, initiated by Bonn and increasingly gaining support, is an important element of global responsibility. And yet it fails to meet the specific requirements that are essential to global dialogue at the highest level. Considering what it meant for Latin America, the Arabic world, and Africa to have been represented in Cancún on a level with India and the People's Republic of China, I feel strongly that the idea of the Cancún initiative should be revived, possibly even with different participants. Such an informal North-South summit need not, succumbing to the pitfalls of routine, convene every year. Whatever the structure, it might lend renewed momentum to the efforts to ensure a heightened institutional awareness of North-South issues and the preservation of basic necessities of life—always, of course, within the context of United Nations reform. In any case, in 1981, West Germany's crucial role in bringing about the Cancún conference won worldwide recognition as an expression of our country's North-South policy—dialogue and cooperation. We thus made an important contribution to global stability.

A policy of global stability can be successful only if African, Latin American, and Asian nations are included. Since bilateral relations with Japan, one of the participants in the world economic summit, were of particular importance to us, I suggested that annual foreign ministers' consultations be instituted. West Germany also supported Japan's request for observer status at CSCE meetings. This request emphasized the importance Japan assigned to the stabilizing influence the conference had over the vast area from Vancouver to Vladivostok.

Our relations with mainland China also reflect our recognition of the political and economic importance of this huge country and of its permanent membership on the United Nations Security Council. Such relations are required by our foreign policy, which is aimed at stability.

Our Chinese counterparts took an open and realistic position—though always mindful of the Soviets' attitudes as well—in regard to the German question and our goals. This was particularly true for Zhou Enlai, whom I met in 1973 while I served as minister of the interior, but it also applied to Deng Xiaoping, with whom I repeatedly discussed whether it would be the Chinese or the Germans who would be united first. He agreed with me that the Germans would be the first to experience unification until our last meeting, when he was almost euphoric because of new contacts between Beijing and Taiwan. "Now I think we'll get there before you!" I contradicted him vehemently: Gorbachev was already on the scene.

Because we cared greatly about harmonious relations with India and Pakistan, we attached great importance to the selection of ambassadors to these nations. Today P. V. Narasimha Rao, the former Prime Minister of India, with whom I had worked when I was foreign minister, and I are good friends. I hold the former Pakistani prime minister, Benazir Bhutto, in particularly high esteem; she took on a great responsibility with tremendous astuteness and energy. Until the very end I did all I could to support clemency for her father.

A New Man and New Policies in the Kremlin

In late February 1985 I resigned as chairman of the FDP. My resignation was an expression neither of defeatism nor of alienation from my own party; after all, I had led the party for eleven years. Nevertheless, I could pass on the chairmanship secure in the knowledge that the problems that arose when the FDP switched its coalition partner from the SPD to the CDU/CSU had been dealt with. A sound foundation had been established for clear-cut liberal policies in the new administration, especially since I was firmly resolved to carry on a liberal foreign policy as foreign minister. I was not mistaken: The FDP was increasingly identified with this foreign policy—a situation confirmed by the fact that my continuation in office was one of the decisive issues in the election of 1983 as well as that of 1987.

By relinquishing the chairmanship I cleared the way for a new generation within the FDP leadership. I firmly believe that in a democracy responsible leadership includes making room for new leaders. I therefore always paved the way for younger people in the FDP. Similarly, my resignation as foreign minister seven years later cleared the way for a new generation.

On Sunday, February 24, I returned from the FDP convention to Bonn, for the first time aware that I could devote all my efforts to my work as foreign minister. Only a few days later (the following Sunday) I flew to Moscow and from there to Helsinki, Warsaw, and finally Sofia. Foreign policy now had my complete attention.

On March 12, 1985, Mikhail Gorbachev became general secretary of the CPSU. That date was to take on historic significance.

At that time I was on a tour of South America. I was in Montevideo when I learned of Konstantin Chernenko's death on March 10. To cut my visit short because of this news seemed inappropriate. My hosts in Uruguay and in Brazil, my next stop, would have had every reason to feel slighted.

In the meantime Chancellor Helmut Kohl had flown to Moscow for the funeral. The "funerary diplomacy" that had been established when Brezhnev died and been carried on with Andropov's funeral was thus continued. It was as useful as it was necessary: It gave the Chancellor the opportunity to meet the new head of the Soviet Union as early as March 14, 1985.

Kohl also met with the head of East Germany, Erich Honecker—another valuable encounter; the meeting, secondary to the funeral ceremonies, allowed the two leaders to discuss the problematic relationship of the two Germanys and to do so face to face, without much fanfare and without the complications of protocol. Such an informal encounter could do no harm; in fact, the meeting could essentially be called a success. Relations between the two Germanys were imbued with a new urgency, and this dynamic proved advantageous not only to the people of East Germany but also to the cohesion of our nation and stability in Europe.

Some time passed before I had my first meeting with the new general secretary. After meeting Eduard Shevardnadze for the first time in Helsinki at the end of July on the occasion of the tenth anniversary of the Helsinki Final Act, and then again at the United Nations in September 1985, I prepared for a trip to Moscow in 1986. I assigned great weight to this visit, planned for July 20 through 22. At long last I would have the opportunity to talk personally with Gorbachev and to compare my impression of him and his ideas with the declarations and speeches I was already familiar with. I prepared thoroughly. I met repeatedly with the Foreign Office experts on the Soviet Union and Eastern Europe to discuss all aspects of the policies of the new leadership.

Further, I held meetings with Otto Wolff von Amerongen, a leading industrialist, and Wilhelm Christians, a banker. Wolff had excellent contacts in Moscow and he was a superb judge of people; he was able to give an impartial assessment of the economic situation in the Soviet Union. As chairman of the Eastern Committee of the German Economic Association he heartily supported our foreign policy. His independence as well as his absolute loyalty to the West German government's policies—even in areas where he might not have been in full agreement—were exemplary. Wilhelm Christians of the Deutsche Bank was experienced in dealings with the Eastern-bloc nations and thoroughly knowledgeable about the Soviet Union; he too always represented the position of the West German government.

Speaking with foreign visitors who happened to be in Bonn, I also tried to learn as much as possible about Gorbachev and his politics. Among the people I questioned were the Hungarian foreign minister, Peter Varkonyi; United Nations General Secretary Javier Pérez de Cuéllar; and President Hosni Mubarak of Egypt, who had been my good friend for a long time. Mubarak had been trained as a military pilot in the Soviet Union, and now he took a special interest in that nation. His factual knowledge about Soviet matters was encyclopedic; in addition, he had a huge stock of general knowledge, and his judgment was absolutely reliable. Everyone I talked to painted a similar picture: Gorbachev was at the very least a man with new ideas. As further preparation for my trip to Moscow, I spoke with Ambassador Yuli Kvitsinsky of the Soviet Union; the British ambassador, Julian Bullard; the United States chargé d'affaires, James Dobbins; Ambassador Yitzak Ben-Ari of Israel; and Ambassador Ronald Lehman, the United States negotiator for START (Strategic Arms Reduction Talks).

I was particularly interested in the opinion of President Mitterand of France. He had visited the Soviet Union from July 7 to 10, 1986, and had called Gorbachev's proposals for disarmament "truly spectacular." Evidently the SALT I (Strategic Arms Limitation Talks) agreement and President Reagan's SDI program had influenced his thinking significantly. I traveled to Paris on July 18, after Dumas had arranged an appointment with the President. I immediately went to the Elysée Palace. Mitterand described in minute detail his talks with Gorbachev, which had gone on for hours. In total, according to the President, they had spent almost three days together. He characterized Gorbachev as a Soviet leader of an entirely new type, similar perhaps to top Western politicians, both in his demeanor and the way he conducted talks. While the new general secretary considered the United States his principal Western partner, he was attempting to arrive at an understanding with Washington by way of the European nations as well. He had a marked preference for France, probably because of that nation's prominent role in Europe. However, Mitterand cautioned, the possibility that even today Gorbachev would try to take advantage of past German-French discord should not be disregarded. Mitterand had therefore impressed on Gorbachev the nature of our current relationship. His sense was that the new Soviet leader's attitude toward West Germany was marked by a peculiar dialectic: On the one hand the Soviet Union felt an attraction to Bonn, while on the other, West Germany seemed too closely tied to the United States. And then there were always the problems of the two Germanys.

In Mitterand's judgment, the "Star Wars" issue was of crucial importance to Gorbachev—and that might be the reason why France seemed so attractive. Unless there could be some compromise on this issue, everything else would also be doomed to failure. Nor should we think that the entire Soviet Union would collapse tomorrow—some day, perhaps, but not tomorrow. The Mitterand-Gorbachev talks had also covered intermediate-range missiles and, of course, the French strategic systems, with Mitterand explaining France's now-familiar point of view. In connection with intermediate-range missiles Gorbachev had mentioned a zero option for Europe that should include both the Pershing II and the SS-20 missiles. Altogether Gorbachev had been noticeably frank, making no effort to conceal internal Soviet problems. Furthermore, he had repeatedly referred to himself as a European.

When I left Paris, my need for information was satisfied. Thanks to my talk with Mitterand, my image of Gorbachev was becoming increasingly three-dimensional. I doubted whether the Soviets really assigned a privileged position to France; it was more likely that the new general secretary regarded Mitterand as a potential ally against SDI. But I was quite certain that Gorbachev kept a close eye on West Germany as an important member of NATO and the European Community and relations between the two German states were bound to continue being an issue for Moscow. We could hardly object to being seen as a close ally of the United States, as Mitterand had implied; such a characterization only increased our significance.

In view of what I had heard in Paris, I was glad that I had agreed to Secretary Shultz's request that I spend a few hours in Washington immediately upon my return from Moscow, so that I could brief him on my impressions. I was further encouraged by Mitterand's report that Gorbachev had mentioned the possibility of a zero option for the Pershing II and SS-20 force in Europe, since that was essentially the aim of the NATO double-track resolution. Of course in view of the range and mobility of the SS-20s we insisted on a global zero option rather than one that was limited to Europe, but the breakthrough in planning was already showing.

177

□   □   □   □

A meeting with Shevardnadze was planned for my first morning in Moscow. The prearranged sequence of talks—first with the Foreign Minister, then with the General Secretary—followed the traditional order. Events were to run a different course, however. I was asked first to call on Gorbachev in the Kremlin. The Foreign Minister; Kvitsinsky, the Soviet ambassador to Bonn; and the General Secretary's personal adviser, Anatoly Chernyayev, were with Gorbachev. My party included the West German ambassador to Moscow, Jörg Kastl, and Gerold von Braunmühl, who headed the political division in the Foreign Office.

Gorbachev opened the meeting by remarking that my visit was more than an ordinary occasion; after all, we were both eager to deepen bilateral relations between our countries. The current international situation necessitated political dialogue and cooperation to a particularly high degree. He therefore offered me a frank exchange; I could indulge in diplomacy with Foreign Minister Shevardnadze. This remark revealed that he had already adopted the habit of other heads of state, government, or parties—presenting himself as the sole negotiator of hard-core foreign policy. I responded with a somewhat indulgent smile, at the same time giving a friendly nod to Shevardnadze to remove all doubt. There was a solidarity among foreign ministers, even beyond political systems.

Gorbachev began by asking how the present West German government viewed the current world and about any worries and problems in my nation. To the Soviet leadership, frankly speaking, our policies did not always make sense; above all, there seemed to be a sharp discrepancy between declarations of a desire for peace and actual deeds. But if this view was mistaken, he begged me to enlighten him.

I would be only too happy to try, I replied. Of necessity we would have to talk about what united us as well as about the differences we had to overcome. We, too, considered this visit an important event, as shown by the very fact that I was bringing a message from the Chancellor. Emphasizing the importance of talking face to face—a method the General Secretary also seemed to prefer—I advocated a personal meeting, at the earliest possible opportunity, between the Chancellor and the General Secretary.

Therefore, I said, I wanted to underscore the Chancellor's invitation once again.

Next I raised the topic of the international situation. What connected us, I said, among many other things, was geographical location or—to use Gorbachev's term—the European house. It was precisely the relations between our people that had always deeply influenced the situation in this house. Recent times had furnished both negative and positive examples: on the one hand, the Second World War, on the other, the Moscow Treaty, which could be called a key document. After all, the treaty had enabled us all to sign the Helsinki Final Act which, even ten years later, in August 1985, had been confirmed by the participating nations as a step in the right direction. However, realism was also called for; inarguably, many hopes and expectations of the 1970s had not come to fruition. Now it was time to consider ways to create positive prospects for the future. The key concept of the Final Act, I argued, was the term *cooperation,* which applied to politics, economy, culture, and humanitarian concerns as well as to human rights.

Areas in which progress was lagging behind, I noted, were arms control and disarmament. There was a need to build cooperative structures—the real point was to build the European house in such a way that its nations could feel secure, and its people might live free of fear. So it was a matter of structuring an order of peace in Europe such as had been laid down in the Helsinki Final Act. We Germans, I assured Gorbachev, had learned our historic lesson: As a great people at the center of Europe, we were interested in good relations with our neighbors to the east and the west. All inhabitants of the European house must be aware that they shared a common fate and that only cooperation could guarantee their common survival.

To the General Secretary's objection that though he could fully endorse these basic beliefs, he failed to see any German contribution to their realization, I replied that an incorrect assessment of our policies might be to blame here; that at times it was difficult to understand the policies of another country when an understanding of its basic thinking was missing. For example, our contribution to the inception and continuation of the CSCE process had to be seen correctly; West Germany was clearly taking a leading role in keeping it active. I was convinced, I added, that an intensified

179

exchange of views between West Germany and the Soviet Union could not only enhance bilateral relations but would also deepen an understanding between the two alliances. The Soviet-American declaration of January 8, 1985, reaffirmed at the Geneva summit of November 1985, also formed a solid basis for negotiations between the two superpowers. In that declaration Secretary Shultz and Foreign Minister Gromyko had called for an end to the arms race on earth and the prevention of its relocation in space.

Now Gorbachev moved to what was clearly a central issue: It was impossible, he said, to abandon the impression that our policies were inconsistent. The West German government had been the most fervent proponent of the deployment of missiles; further, it had tried to dictate to the Soviet Union and to impose ultimatums. And yet the process of negotiations and the submitted proposals demonstrated that the Federal Republic was actively seeking solutions. Gorbachev noted that while he understood the United States' interest in deploying missiles in Europe, he was puzzled by Germany's advocacy of that plan.

Since this argument echoed the old way of reasoning, I was very familiar with it. The General Secretary, I replied, had asked that we leave the past aside; but now he was focusing on our decision to support the deployment of intermediate-range missiles. Ex-Chancellor Schmidt and I had always pleaded with the Soviet Union to discontinue development of the SS-20s. He, Gorbachev, must believe me when I said that the call for rearmament had been one of the most difficult decisions Schmidt and I had to make during our administration. I emphasized that we had not posed ultimatums but had asked for some understanding of our situation, especially since we had never left any doubt that we would react responsibly and efficiently to Soviet SS-20 prearmament. Gorbachev interjected that, after all, the SS-4s and SS-5s had already been in place and had merely needed modernization. I continued by mentioning that one of his predecessors, Brezhnev, had told me the SS-20s posed no threat to the United States. And that, I had replied, was precisely the problem. "We Germans live in Europe."

As for his objection, I argued that when the SS-20s were compared with the older missiles, we were dealing with a whole new level of weapon. The earlier missiles were relics from a time when the United States had possessed strategic superiority; by now, however, parity was solidly established in this area, and the SALT treaties were aiming for balance. Now a solution had to be found for the missiles of intermediate range. We therefore welcomed the General Secretary's words about removing all nuclear weapons, especially since the result of this approach promised the world-wide elimination of intermediate-range weapons. We certainly also acknowledged the Soviet leaders' statements concerning problems in the eastern section of its nation. Since we were real-ists, the Chancellor had also raised the possibility of interim solu-tions, as long as these were not confined to Europe.

When it came to strategic weapons, I noted, the Soviet Union had also suggested gradualism. In response I could only say that we considered any reduction a progressive step—the bigger, the better. Since Gorbachev had been critical of our rejection of a chemical weapon–free zone in Central Europe, I pointed out that Moscow had good reasons to negotiate a global prohibition with us: The problem of verification, difficult at the best of times, be-came even more complex when agreements covered only a limited area.

Gorbachev parried. He could not help wondering whether Ger-many was still pursuing the objectives of the Moscow Treaty. The Eastern treaties in general could be interpreted in highly problem-atic ways as well—apparently an allusion to a renewed debate over the Oder-Neisse Line. I replied tersely that our attitude toward the treaties had not changed.

Concluding discussion on the subject, Gorbachev reassured me that Moscow was making no attempt to drive a wedge between West Germany and the United States. He did not consider such a tactic to be sound politics. It was important that the Federal Re-public never be placed in a situation in which it felt its security was threatened. Such a position would not be acceptable either to Bonn or to Moscow, especially since in such a case we would reach out to those allies that would guarantee our security. Never-theless, it was highly desirable to achieve absolute clarity on the basic principles of the Moscow Treaty as well as the follow-up agreements.

He felt, Gorbachev continued, that our approach to some issues was still too strongly influenced by the past. He must have meant to refer to our experiences with former Soviet policies and the Cold War. He recounted an anecdote: Some old partisans had been tracked down who were still busy blowing up trains in those parts of the Soviet Union that had been occupied by the Germans, even though the war had been over for so long.

"We do not blow up trains; we are laying new tracks," I responded, trying to steer the conversation into another direction. But clearly a terminal was needed, so that the trains could arrive at a destination. Alternately, I added, it was just as possible to disable some tracks by insufficient understanding for the other side, and I very much feared that the words of the General Secretary were demonstrating precisely such a lack. And that, I said, was why I was eager to underline three times, if necessary, that the present talks were essential. Since his ideas about West Germany were apparently based on misconceptions, I continued, they were bound to lead to false conclusions. Nevertheless, I assured him, I could also glimpse an encouraging element in the words of the General Secretary: If I understood him correctly, he was granting all nations, large, medium-size, or small, the same right to security. Germany considered herself to be medium-size. A second encouraging point, I noted, was his statement that the Soviet Union did not intend to drive a wedge between us and the United States. Alliance and cooperation with the United States were, I declared, an inviolable condition, and any attempt to separate us would be to no avail. Besides, any such effort would also run counter to Soviet interests.

Chaos would indeed ensue, Gorbachev commented, if either of us tried to separate the other from any ally. No doubt this remark referred to Moscow's relations with East Berlin—an aspect that would continue to be an important element in the new Soviet leadership's policies toward the West and Germany.

The General Secretary remarked that history had shown that much depended on the kind of cooperation that existed between the Federal Republic and the Soviet Union. I responded by suggesting that we be bold enough to institute a new beginning in West-East relations. Instead of focusing the spotlight on every detail that kept us apart and perhaps even denying the other side's goodwill, it would be more helpful to acknowledge constructive contributions. Both of us, I argued, needed the other.

I was emphatic about the fact that we were not unduly sensitive; we did not expect the Soviet Union to agree with all our actions. After all, we belonged to two different alliances and lived in different societies. Nevertheless, I argued, it would be unjust to doubt our goodwill. But if the General Secretary could endorse our basic thinking on international policies—as he had implied he could—we were already operating on a sound basis. I had, I said, devoted many years of my life to working for new policies in Europe, and I was determined to continue on that course; I was, after all, a member of a generation that was only too familiar with war. Moreover, I added, personal experience had taught me what it meant to force one people to live in two separate states; I was pointedly referring to my origins in the GDR, as I always did in conversation with representatives of both the West and the East.

Europeans must never forget that they are Europeans, I continued. The Moscow Treaty and the Helsinki Final Act were not part of the past, they were guidelines for the future. Surmounting the differences between the administration and the opposition as well as the various attitudes of the parties, the West German Bundestag expressed consensus on shared essentials: German-French friendship, membership in the Western Alliance and the European Community, and the will to continue our policies toward our Eastern neighbors as laid down in the existing treaties and within the framework of CSCE.

What then, the General Secretary asked, were the Soviets to make of President Reagan's most recent statements that, despite Yalta and Potsdam, both of which were far in the past, Europe must become united?

Our position regarding the inviolability of borders was clear, I replied. However, I could hardly believe that when he used the term *European house,* the General Secretary had in mind a house divided. President Reagan had merely attempted to clarify that situation. Especially because our nation was divided, we Germans were obviously thinking along the same lines. The German question was on the table—now as always when the agenda dealt with German and European policies.

The General Secretary told of an experience he had when traveling through West Germany in 1975. He had stopped for gas on the autobahn near Frankfurt. The gas station attendant, who recognized him as a Russian, had reminded the traveler of Stalin's saying, "The Hitlers come and go, but the German people remain," and asked why the Soviet Union had divided Germany into two states. He, Gorbachev, had asked the man's age in return. The attendant was born in 1926. In that case, Gorbachev instructed him, he was old enough to know that it had been Churchill who had wanted to divide Germany. Besides, the Federal Republic had been founded before the GDR had been established.

I smiled as I responded. Gorbachev had been lucky that the gas station attendant had not been a historian, or he would have offered the exact Stalin quote, which included an important addition: "The Hitlers come and go, but the German people and the German nation will remain." Gorbachev agreed. "Would you still endorse one unified German nation today?" I asked, and then I went on, "History will answer that question, as will *all* Germans, just as the Letter on German Unity provides." All of us, I argued, would have to work toward the goal of robbing European borders of their significance and of changing the current situation in Europe by cooperating with each other.

When I declared that all Germans would have to decide on German unity, I had two reasons for the language I used. For one, it was inappropriate for responsible German politicians to "transfer" the decision on unification to history alone—such an approach was too passive and failed to demonstrate any German effort. It was clearly our responsibility to move events in a direction that would end up in unification. But the phrase *all Germans* also implied that the residents of both states were called upon to make a decision; the point was not to impose a situation on the Germans living in the GDR, particularly since I had no doubt about the East Germans' choice of a unified country, if only they were free to decide.

Especially after the exceptionally pointed discussion of intermediate-range missiles, Gorbachev had left the impression that he wanted to put a quick end to the conversation. The more West-East cooperation and the German question came to the fore, however, the more our talk took a different turn. Now he seemed to want to discuss the future, bilateral questions, and the opportunity for Germans to emigrate from the Soviet Union.

Concluding our exchange on this day, he finally said the Soviet leadership would give some thought to ways of making our mutual relations more active, positive, and dynamic; of course the Soviet Union expected the Federal Republic to take certain steps as well. "Let us turn over a new leaf in our relations." That was the crucial sentence—now there were no ambiguities between us. We could start discussing the future.

Gorbachev turned the talk to the Party convention in Moscow from February 25 to March 6, 1986, where the program for the future had been outlined. If the West thought that the Soviet Union would give up its position and capitulate, the West was in error. But if both sides were willing to compromise, the Soviet Union would cooperate. Until now, Gorbachev noted, Soviet initiatives had not been met with an adequate response. It seemed that the West was expecting further promises from Moscow, believing that the Soviet Union was prepared to make still more concessions; it appeared that only at such a point would the West be willing to respond. To wait for that moment, however, he warned, would be a waste of time. Gorbachev intimated what would become even more explicit at the end of 1989 and in 1990: He was ready to initiate a fundamental change of direction in Soviet policies, but he insisted on personally controlling the speed and amount of the changes. They must not appear to have been forced on him from the outside.

Abruptly Gorbachev asked himself a question: How was it that the Soviet Union could keep up with the Americans militarily and in space but was finding it so difficult to provide for its own people? The answer to this conundrum, he said, still escaped him.

I was astonished. I had never witnessed such an admission from a leader of the Soviet Union. President Mitterand had certainly been right: Gorbachev was a new type of Soviet leader.

And yet, the image of the Soviet Union in the German media, the General Secretary complained, was too critical. Our media were independent, I replied. They were not always uncritical of West German leaders either. On the contrary: There were some of us who would be happy to be dealt with as gently by the press as was the General Secretary.

Gorbachev countered that the Federal Republic also limited freedom, pointing to the law that bars "radicals"—individuals pursuing goals hostile to the constitution—from working in the West German civil service. When I replied that I had never seen a staunch liberal in the Soviet services, either, Gorbachev responded with friendly laughter and immediately turned back to the domestic situation in the Soviet Union. He talked about the right to work, to housing, to food, to medical care, and to education—a cluster of rights that unfortunately led too many to believe that it was possible to live well without making much of an effort. That, he said, was the genuine problem inherent in Socialism.

Given all the impressions and experiences I had gained in previous conversations with Soviet leaders, I found this last a truly surprising, even sensational, statement coming from a General Secretary of the CPSU. Laughing, I argued that he had just given a liberal definition of the problems of Socialism. But I continued in a serious vein: The differences must not be glossed over. Gorbachev was a Communist, I was a liberal; yet we had to tackle common tasks. In our country, I could assure him, there was no animosity toward the Soviet Union.

Again Gorbachev returned to his presentation of the Soviet Union's internal problems. An entirely new course had been taken, in domestic as well as in foreign policy. The people were now expecting him to establish order at home, to raise the standard of living, and to bring about world peace. Should West Germany decide to participate actively in such a process, it would be welcome. The point was, Gorbachev argued, that new ways of cooperation must be developed; Moscow was also interested in global stability. There were 280 million people living in the Soviet Union. He had a sense, he said, that internal criticism of the situation in the Soviet Union was already sharper than the scrutiny experienced by other nations. The closed society of the old Soviet Union had suddenly opened up. It seemed, however, that the United States was still clinging to mistaken preconceptions about the Soviet Union.

That was precisely why, I insisted, it was so important for the General Secretary to continue his talks with the president of the United States. Gorbachev stressed his desire to meet with Reagan in any place of the President's choosing; what was important was to come to agreements that could lead to further decisions. He had written to Reagan in that vein. He added that he was not interested in a meeting staged for no better purpose than to provide a television opportunity. In this context he expressed his appreciation for the realistic statements issued by former President Richard Nixon. He considered West Germany a serious participant in any political dialogue and believed that a sincere exchange of views that could improve the situation.

I nodded in agreement: He had expressed our goal as well.

Much of what Gorbachev had said about common interests, about building stability and trust, was in line with the thinking of the Chancellor and myself. In the area of economics, too, there were a number of possibilities, as leading representatives of German business had told me before my departure. Germany, I said, supported an American-Soviet summit, which should have a tangible result—the same thing we hoped to see coming from the German-Soviet dialogue. And since our people expected us to discuss the crucial issues, I mentioned the Chancellor's invitation one more time. I pointed out that Kohl was interested in substance, not in a television appearance with Gorbachev. Laughing, Gorbachev advised me that he himself would not be entirely satisfied if television was completely absent.

Like him, I said, West Germany believed that the past must not be forgotten; but I could agree without qualification to his suggestion that we turn over a new leaf. Germany would have to think of a way to improve our relations through cooperation. Such a move would be in the interests not only of both our countries but of all of Europe as well—we might even say, of *our* Europe.

The conversation, which had started out on such a sharp note, had taken a more conciliatory turn. What mattered were the new venues for domestic and foreign policies Gorbachev had opened, the realization that there was an internal connection between the two, and the acknowledgment of international interdependence.

Concerning the outcome of my visit, the Soviet Politburo remarked that the exchange of views had a "positive significance," even though in many respects the policies of the West German government were still shaped by the past; the talks had nevertheless revealed concrete possibilities for a political dialogue and for cooperation between our two countries in several areas. According to the Politburo, West Germany could play an important role in improving the global situation, solving problems regarding disarmament, and guaranteeing security in Europe; the Soviet Union was therefore willing to cooperate with Bonn without the two nations' infringing on each other's obligations toward the alliances to which they belonged. This declaration represented an objective assessment and a correct evaluation of our obligations to our alliances. The underlying message was the reference to new prospects. I publicly commented on the meeting with similar factualness, never denying that there were problems to be solved.

□   □   □   □

My first, very promising, impressions of Gorbachev were corroborated in the subsequent exchange with Foreign Minister
Shevardnadze. We discussed the entire list of outstanding arms-
control issues; in this connection, referring to Gorbachev's remark
that the Soviet Union did not wish to separate West Germany
from the United States, I briefed Shevardnadze on the ongoing and
close consultation mechanism within NATO.

Shevardnadze seemed impressed by this kind of cooperation.
He listened attentively when I explained that the weight we carried in the disarmament talks was due to the fact that we contributed the largest amount for defense within NATO, thus providing
for Western security. A true believer in realpolitik, he understood
this equation. Completely in the same vein as the talk with
Gorbachev, Shevardnadze approved of our consultations in form,
spirit, and content: They had made it clear, he thought, that the
Federal Republic of Germany had a great potential for active participation in international negotiations.

At the conclusion of my visit, on July 22, I made a public statement to the effect that Moscow and Bonn had begun to establish a
new foundation for the shape their relations would take. One
element of this new dynamic was a plan for regular meetings
between Shevardnadze and me. In addition, I announced that intensive consultations by the two governments' disarmament negotiators would occur.

Afterward, I recapped the details of the visit with Gerold von
Braunmühl, the political Director of the Foreign Ministry, who
had participated in the talks. Both of us believed that these meetings would have a crucial effect on further events. What we did
not know was that at that time Gerold von Braunmühl's death
sentence had already been pronounced by a group of terrorists full
of blind rage and contempt for human life: He had less than three
months to live. On October 10, 1986, he was assassinated, when
the seeds he had sown with such energy and commitment were
about to begin to bloom.

As for the relative weight given to the NATO double-track resolution, it seemed to us that Gorbachev assigned greater significance to the Pershing II missiles than to SDI. Seven years later, in
December 1993, in a conversation after the Menden Forum organized by Ulrich Bettermann, a businessman, Gorbachev confirmed

that the NATO double-track resolution had been the real cause for the new direction in Soviet foreign policy. "SDI, on the other hand," he declared, turning to me, "that's something we took no more seriously than you did."

The points of view that emerged during our 1986 talk left Gorbachev well informed on what was happening in Europe and clarified the importance of Germany for him. Mitterand had been quite correct when he told me that Gorbachev had ambivalent feelings about West Germany. Admiration for its economic capability was mixed with worry about its strength when combined with that of the United States. This concern became particularly clear when Gorbachev expounded on our technical assistance to SDI, which he overestimated every bit as much as did the German SDI enthusiasts. The realization that Germany was the cornerstone in the creation, the establishment, and the permanence of the NATO double-track resolution increased our importance on the one hand, but on the other it also raised the potential for friction. In both areas, France had an easier time of it: It had not entered into any agreement for technical participation in SDI, and it was not a participant in the NATO double-track resolution.

Regarding the German question, Gorbachev had opened a door: He agreed when I amended the quotation from Stalin, nor did he contradict me when I said that history and, according to the Letter on German Unity, *all* Germans should make the decision—hardly an inadvertent omission. I could not, however, ignore his pointing out the importance of East Germany to the Soviet Union. Here much "new thinking" was required.

We were at any rate firmly convinced that Gorbachev was serious about reform; he had already crossed the Rubicon. Democratization and economic reform, the two central items, of necessity brought about a revised foreign policy. It was by no means a tactical variable, which could change at any time; it became a measurable constant, which was also influenced by the Soviet Union's domestic situation.

Democratization of nations and societies and subsequent greater transparency are the crucial prerequisites for building trust and predictability—a truism that applies to foreign policy as well. I had a theory, which I had frequently explained to Gromyko: that if nothing else, it was the openness of the Western societies that allowed them to make a significant contribution to constructive

West-East relations. My feeling was that this theory would find confirmation in the interdependence of Gorbachev's domestic reform policy and his "new thinking" in foreign policy. The West's initial deep distrust of the General Secretary's true intentions had its roots in a lack of appreciation of this internal connection as well as in a failure to realize how profoundly the reforms and the "new thinking" influenced foreign policy and Soviet society. The think tanks in Europe and the United States at first also failed to perceive the interdependence of Gorbachev's domestic and foreign policy reforms.

Only two months later I would be able to continue my talk with Shevardnadze. We met in the New York residence of Hans Werner Lautenschlager, West Germany's ambassador to the United Nations. The Soviet Foreign Minister remarked favorably on our earlier meeting in Moscow. Gorbachev, he said, shared his opinion. He also approved of my address to the General Assembly. On the whole, our assessment of the meeting in Moscow had not been exaggerated.

Back from Moscow, I stayed in Bonn only briefly to take part in a cabinet meeting on July 23. Before the meeting came to order, I briefed the Chancellor on the Moscow talks. We were dealing with an entirely new Soviet leadership, I announced; Gorbachev was not only talking about a new foreign policy but was also endeavoring to change the Soviet Union from the ground up and from inside. His determination guaranteed that the new course would be steady and earnest.

That afternoon I flew to Washington to meet with Shultz. The Secretary of State, who was clearly intent on making the visit enjoyable and informal, described the United States media reaction to my visit to the Soviet capital as decidedly favorable.

My stay in the Soviet capital, I explained, had to be seen in the context of President Mitterand's visit to Moscow and Foreign Minister Shevardnadze's visit to London; the Soviet Union was making it clear that it was interested in continuing talks not only with the United States but with European nations as well.

Compared to his predecessors, I said, the leader of the Soviet Union certainly had a new way of carrying on a conversation. My experience confirmed what President Reagan had told NATO after their encounter in Geneva and what President Mitterand had reported as well: Gorbachev spoke off the cuff, felt free to interrupt, but let himself be interrupted as well. Thus a real conversation had occurred, contra in distinction to the monologues we had come to expect in the Brezhnev era. I described Gorbachev's objections to the NATO double-track resolution and my qualms about a zone free of chemical weapons limited to Central Europe, which I had justified by pointing to verification—a problem even harder to solve. Part of our conversation, I informed Shultz, had dealt with the German question; when it came to relations between the two Germanys, Gorbachev was evidently very sensitive.

Shultz was curious to know what the term *sensitive* meant in this context. I replied that the General Secretary seemed deeply concerned that these relations not cause problems for the Soviet Union. I gave a blow-by-blow account of our discussion following the quotation from Stalin; I related that Gorbachev had not objected when I ended the debate by pointing out that no matter what the final decision on the question of German unity, it was important that it would be made by *all* Germans. This would prove to have been the key sentence—only three years later, events would bear me out: In January 1990 Gorbachev respected the decision Germans would arrive at in their two separate states.

It was my impression, I continued, that Gorbachev, apparently aware of the stabilizing influence of the Western Alliance, had no intention of driving a wedge between the United States and its European allies. He also seemed to count on the present West German ruling coalition's continuing in power, at least he had made no move to differentiate between the governing parties. He was also accepting European unification as a reality.

On the whole there were sure signs that we were dealing with a genuinely new set of policies, not only in form but also in substance. Now it was my suggestion that, in line with NATO's Harmel Report, we concentrate on examining the possibilities for progress in Europe arising from the changes in the Soviet Union.

Two days later, in Bischofsgrün near Bayreuth, at the opening of the festival, I met with my friend Roland Dumas, a Wagnerite who attended every year. At a breakfast I briefed him—President Mitterand's close confidant—thoroughly on my visit to Moscow. I also made certain that every ambassador and bureau chief of all members of the European Community were fully briefed.

On October 2, 1986, I delivered a government report on the

Stockholm Conference on CSBM in Europe to the Bundestag. I pronounced the conference a major leap forward. There was confirmation of what we had hoped for from the new Soviet leadership. My joint appearance with French Foreign Minister Roland Dumas had not only strengthened German-French cooperation but had also revived a conference that was threatening to ebb away. The fact that Dumas and I hosted a joint reception, that we even jointly invited the delegations to talks, made clear to many, especially to Eastern diplomats, the degree to which German-French cooperation had already become a reality.

My report to the Bundestag gave me the opportunity to draw a positive interim conclusion about our East-West and arms control policies. I myself, however, was in poor health and was forced into the hospital for a few days. Though I had not suffered a heart attack, my physical limitations had become much clearer.

On Friday, October 10, we were confronted with limitations of an entirely different sort. Since my release from the hospital I had recuperated at home; the following week promised to be taxing. At about nine o'clock that night the telephone rang. Frau von Braunmühl was calling: "My husband has been shot and killed right outside our house." Gerold von Braunmühl, one of the leading officials of the Foreign Office, who had accompanied me on my recent visit to Moscow, was among my closest and most valued colleagues. His wife, obviously in shock, talked about the horrible crime in a voice both calm and toneless. "I'll come at once," I responded. "Where is your husband now?" "He's still lying in the street."

I will never forget the picture of Gerold von Braunmühl as he lay in the street before me, next to him the briefcases he had just taken from the trunk of the taxi when he was gunned down. Devastated, we stood beside him, until at last we went into the house to be with Hilde von Braunmühl and her children. The same feelings stirred us all: profound sorrow, horror, helplessness.

That afternoon Gerold von Braunmühl had met with French Ambassador Serge Boidevaix. When I read the minutes of this meeting the following day, they vividly reminded me of Gerold von Braunmühl's great analytical faculties and his capacity to plan and project. The way he conducted the talk on aspects and prospects of German-French relations was brilliant.

The Red Army Faction took responsibility for the assassination. Its first generation had committed vicious murders and terrorist acts against leading figures in politics and industry in the 1970s, while I was minister of the interior. Their crimes included the attack on the German embassy in Stockholm and the hijacking of a Lufthansa passenger plane to Mogadishu. Police investigation subsequently revealed that Gerold von Braunmühl had been shot with the same handgun that had killed the president of the West German Employers Association, Hanns-Martin Schleyer, in October 1977, after he had been held hostage for several weeks. In their ideological fanaticism and their contemptuous mental set the terrorists considered politicians to be robots, tools guided by remote control. Von Braunmühl had been assassinated because the terrorists interpreted newspaper stories as indicating that the Political Committee of the European Community was a sort of steering committee for our common foreign policy, the nameless war room of an imperialist conspiracy. Their letter claiming responsibility made absurd statements: that West Germany, as a member of the European Community, supported the imperialist policies of the United States. Even as the first cracks in the Communist view of the world were coming to light in Central and Eastern Europe, delusional fanatics in our country were repeating the absurd theory of the anonymous power of the political machinery, of the function of big capital, and of imperialism. That von Braunmühl had been guided by the directives of the foreign minister and had helped create policies aimed at securing peace, establishing disarmament, and promoting realistic rapprochement—these facts did not fit into the terrorists' view. They had fallen victim to the illusion that when they aimed at Gerold von Braunmühl, their target would be the spider at the center of the web.

When the Foreign Office department heads met the following Monday morning, one chair remained empty. A vase of flowers was placed on the table at Gerold von Braunmühl's seat.

That same Monday, after the American-Soviet summit in Reykjavík, as we tried to summarize the consequences of the summit, von Braunmühl's absence was particularly noticeable. Some of the last documents he had helped draft were devoted to this summit: the Chancellor's letter to President Reagan (I had discussed it with von Braunmühl during my hospital stay) as well as the statement I delivered the night before Reykjavík. We had spent a long time polishing the text: "Good judgment and a feeling for what is possible must now prove their mettle," it read in part. "No one is more interested in finally reversing the arms race than the Germans, who live at the center of the divided continent. We hope that the future of West-East relations will be defined by a balance of interests and meaningful cooperation with a view to common tasks for the future."

Giving a eulogy for my friend, I said, "Some may think that the terrorists who murdered von Braunmühl viciously and cowardly did so by mistake. The horrible truth is that they did not. They hate peace; domestic and external peace, they want violence, their way of thinking is contemptuous of human beings." I had begun by describing von Braunmühl's extraordinary nature as a man and a thinker. Several times I repeated, "And that is the man who was murdered," in order to point out the criminality and senselessness of their act. I used this rhetorical device not in the mistaken belief that I could make the murderers feel guilty but in the hope that I could persuade some who sympathized with the terrorists to think, perhaps even to change course. Bohuslav Chňoupek, the foreign minister of Czechoslovakia, told me at a later time that he had circulated the text of my eulogy in his ministry.

My speech also honored von Braunmühl's many coworkers whose service to the freest and most humanitarian state in German history had brought about their violent deaths: Freiherr Rüdt von Collenberg, killed on May 5, 1968, while serving as West German envoy in Saigon; Ambassador Karl Graf von Spreti, assassinated on April 5, 1970, in Guatemala; and Heinz Hillegaart and Lieutenant Colonel von Mirbach, both attached to our embassy in Stockholm, victims of an attack by German terrorists on that residence. I also mentioned Suhair Daou, chauffeur to the German ambassador, who had been fatally machinegunned down in Beirut on August 16, 1985.

Deeply shaken, I ordered the names of all these dead affixed to a wall in the ministry's large antechamber, which was suffused with light and easily accessible from the stairs. On the opposite wall a plaque commemorates the names of those members of the Foreign Office who lost their lives because of their participation in the attempted assassination of Hitler on July 20, 1944. "They gave their lives for the honor of the German people," is inscribed below these names. Even though these Germans failed to free their country of fascism, their attempt deserves our gratitude and deep respect. They acted for all of us—those who were alive at the time and those who were born thereafter.

An Interview and Its Aftermath

After my visit to Moscow the Foreign Office avidly followed the further evolution of Soviet policies; we also scrutinized Soviet public statements. More and more I was convinced that my first impression of Gorbachev and his new policies had been correct and that cooperating with this Soviet leader in a new way would prove to be worthwhile. Motivated by a strong wish that the world public, and more especially Western statesmen, seize the opportunity offered by the "new thinking," I planned to take a public stand on the basic changes taking place in the Soviet Union.

My opportunity came at the world economic summit, scheduled to take place in Davos on February 1, 1987; for the first time a Soviet delegation was expected to take part. This addition gave the gathering a whole new character; it must be remembered that at the time the world economic summits had not yet attained the importance that was attached to them in the 1990s.

Even before the Davos World Economic Forum, on November 4, 1986, I met with the Soviet foreign minister in Vienna, where the third CSCE follow-up meeting (after Belgrade and Madrid) was scheduled to begin. On November 7 I addressed the meeting; essentially I demanded that a peaceful order be established for all of Europe and that the promises made during the CSCE process be fulfilled. I remarked critically on cases in which, violating the right to freedom of movement and settlement, borders had seen the use of brute force. Freedom of speech and religion, protection of minorities, fair trials, and freedom of the press, I said, were inviolable elements of the CSCE process. "We will not stop speaking up whenever citizens suffer harm only because they base their actions on the Final Act." As the only Western foreign minister in attendance at that point, I also supported the Soviet suggestion that a CSCE conference on human rights be held in Moscow. I could not understand why many of my Western colleagues hesitated or rejected the proposal. A CSCE conference on human rights in Moscow could only expand the potential of our human-rights policy; I expressed this thought openly in my support of the Soviet suggestion. If we chose Moscow as the site for the conference, we would have an opportunity "to state our demands for the realization of basic freedoms and human rights in the Soviet capital." Perhaps the new men in the Kremlin had had the same idea?

The meeting on November 4, 1986, ranks among my most impressive encounters with Foreign Minister Shevardnadze. We had planned the usual bilateral exchange on the periphery of a CSCE follow-up meeting. During Gromyko's term as foreign minister it had become our custom to use international conferences for detailed discussions. The choice of date as well as the time allotted to these talks revealed that Gromyko—and subsequently Shevardnadze—considered these meetings with the West German foreign minister to be on a par with his meetings with the American secretary of state. The importance of the discussions was not due merely to the volume of material to be covered; the Soviet leaders made political use of protocol procedures as well. Therefore the length and regularity of these meetings clearly demonstrated Moscow's consideration of the United States—on a global scale—and the Federal Republic of Germany—on a European scale—as their principal counterparts. In the Gorbachev-Shevardnadze era this attitude became even clearer after my visit to Moscow in January 1986.

The West German Foreign Office had carefully prepared for my meeting with my Soviet counterpart. The plan was that we would go into detail on German-Soviet relations in particular and West-East relations in general and explore their future implications. I was eager to continue along the lines begun in Moscow. But matters would turn out quite differently.

Before the meeting, the Chancellor had given an interview to *Newsweek;* it had caused a stir in Germany and internationally. Newspaper reports had given the impression that the Chancellor had compared Gorbachev to Josef Goebbels.

At the time our embassy in Vienna was only a few steps away from the Soviet Embassy. The German Embassy, an unimaginative postwar building (certainly no showpiece of our public buildings) is markedly modest next to the beautiful old palace that housed the Soviet (now Russian) embassy. Unlike Gromyko, Shevardnadze met me at the embassy entrance, with the press in attendance. His greeting was ostentatiously friendly. When we gathered on the first floor in the familiar conference room, an oblong, tastefully decorated room in which the two delegations faced each other across a long table, he maintained his cordial tone; the whole reception took place within eyesight and earshot of the reporters. Shevardnadze inquired after my health. He was glad to hear from me in person that I was feeling well.

Because we already knew—since the Soviet delegation had announced as much—that Shevardnadze would mention the *Newsweek* interview, I took the bull by the horns and raised the subject myself. I began by explaining that I was speaking not only for myself but also for the Chancellor, and that I would like to read a statement expressly authorized by the Chancellor. Since it was important for the Soviets to understand the statement correctly, I had brought along a Russian translation, which I handed to the Foreign Minister. Then I began to read:

> In an interview with [the daily newspaper] *Die Welt* on November 2, 1986, the Chancellor stated that his conversation with *Newsweek* had not been reported correctly. He deeply regrets the erroneous impression that he compared the General Secretary of the Central Committee of the CPSU, Mikhail S. Gorbachev, with Goebbels. He unequivocally dissociated himself from any such statement. He has declared that it was not his intention to insult the General Secretary and that he is taking seriously the General Secretary's efforts to improve West-East relations. The Chancellor has always acknowledged these efforts. The Federal Government is pursuing a policy of communication and cooperation. In so doing, it is fully aware how severely millions of victims among the people of the Soviet Union suffered at Hitler's hands. The Federal Government wishes for—and the Chancellor asserted as much in his *Welt* interview—normal and good relations with the Soviet Union, our most important neighbor to the East. Therefore it also wishes to contribute to peace in Europe and the world. It is of the opinion that the Soviet leaders', and especially General Secretary Gorbachev's, approach to disarmament and cooperation serve the same goal.

I concluded by noting that it was important for Gorbachev and the other Soviet leaders to assess the sincerity and the meaning of this declaration correctly. Moreover, the Chancellor would repeat his position on this topic in the Bundestag this same week.

Now began a discussion that, although—or perhaps because—the situation was such a difficult one for Shevardnadze and myself, impressed me deeply; it even made me feel closer to Shevardnadze the man. I felt that I was facing someone who was personally affected by the consequences of the interview and yet was trying to get beyond it by thoroughly honorable means. Clearly he was reluctant to see the Soviets' strategic goals obstructed by this episode.

Considering the significance of the occurrence, the Soviet foreign minister replied, it was appropriate for me to have initiated the topic with my statement; the incident had no precedent in German-Soviet relations. When word of the interview first reached Moscow, there had been initial disbelief. It was thought that it was an unfounded rumor, floated to make trouble. A check with *Newsweek* and its tape recordings revealed that the Chancellor's remark had been reported correctly. After the Chancellor, through his spokesman, had denied the statement, Moscow contacted *Newsweek*'s editor in chief, Maynard Parker; he repudiated the Germans' claim that the Chancellor was misquoted, and he pointed out that the interview was on record. Of course the editor did not endorse the Chancellor's remarks and had never cited them as the magazine's views, but the magazine believed that it should not keep from its readers what was recorded as the Chancellor's opinion.

The Chancellor, I objected, had never seen a transcript of the interview. I had not spoken idly when I said that it was important to us that the General Secretary correctly gauge the sincerity of the statement I had just read. Of one thing I could assure him: I had known the Chancellor for many years, not only in a close working relationship, but also personally. His attitude toward the Soviet Union, to its leaders, and to the General Secretary, I said, was certainly not the same as that expressed in the interview in question.

The interview had placed the Soviet leadership in a very difficult position, Shevardnadze replied. It was a well-known fact that the course of German-Soviet relations had been extremely difficult at the end of the war; it had not been at all easy to persuade the people of the Soviet Union to adopt a positive attitude toward Germany, particularly West Germany. Nevertheless, great progress had been made. He was further asking us to keep in mind that to date not a word had appeared in the Soviet press about the interview. Foreign broadcasters, such as the Voice of America and the German Wave Channel, had not observed the same restraint, so that by now the Soviet leadership was in receipt of many letters asking for an explanation. The unfortunate comparison affected the feelings not only of the General Secretary, it must be remembered, but those of numerous other families. We must remember that 20 million had died in the war, and the inquiries must be seen in that context. Gorbachev's name, Shevardnadze continued, meant profound and serious changes to the people in the Soviet Union: economic reforms, efforts to raise the standard of living, the modernization of industry, and the broadening of democratic rights. The Soviet leaders could not help but consider the people's feelings. It just so happened, he warned us, that the Soviet Union was dealing with problems of infinitely greater complexity than those that faced the West German chancellor.

Since I had not the slightest doubt that Shevardnadze was looking for a solution in earnest, I did not believe he was posing a rhetorical question when he continued, "What shall we do, how shall we respond?" He repeated the question, and despite the many delegates on both sides (there were perhaps some twenty people in the room) I felt that the conversation was going on between the two of us alone. I was facing a man who had no wish to aggravate the situation but who was also aware of the degree of maliciousness Gorbachev had to endure from his own who confronted him with news reports and editorials in the Western media commenting on this incident in light of his efforts toward improved relations with us. Only rarely have I felt such regret at not speaking the same language as the person with whom I was exchanging views. I could have told him with even greater intensity that we, the Chancellor and I, were utterly serious in our desire to keep this episode from wreaking any harm.

I found myself in a difficult situation. It was easy to understand that the reports of the interview created problems for the Soviet Union. Nor was I entirely pleased with the way the subject was treated in the West German media. At the same time, however, I knew with certainty that Helmut Kohl, like myself, was trying for good relations with the Soviet Union; of course he had never meant to equate Gorbachev with Goebbels. Once again I appealed to Shevardnadze not to doubt the sincerity of Kohl's statement. I pointed out the great weight attached to the Chancellor's making a statement on the matter to the Bundestag, since this forum was reserved for pronouncements of particular importance. Further, the Chancellor had publicly dissociated himself from the printed version of the interview.

The Soviet leadership, Shevardnadze countered, had found itself compelled, in reaction to this affair, to cancel important visits. Of course these were merely cosmetic measures. Moscow was not interested in letting the matter escalate into a full-blown crisis in German-Soviet relations; nevertheless, the Chancellor did not seem to be taking into consideration the full history of German-Soviet relations, a history filled with suffering, which laid a particular responsibility on Moscow. Shevardnadze reported that he had held conversations with Geoffrey Howe, the British foreign secretary, discussing among other topics international terrorism and Muammar al-Qaddafi. President Reagan had once compared Qaddafi to Hitler, and Qaddafi himself subsequently equated Reagan to Hitler; that move marked the end of that incident. But since a government as responsible as the Soviet Union's could not afford such shenanigans, how were the leaders to explain this incident to the Soviet people? With great earnestness I asked him if he could recall any other incident in international relations in which a nation's leader had made such an unequivocal statement as the one by the Chancellor I had just read.

Again I announced that we wanted to hand out this pronouncement to the press, a plan to which Shevardnadze did not object. I deeply regretted that an opportunity I had hoped to use to discuss the central questions of German foreign policy now had to be devoted to an attempt to eradicate any misunderstandings about the *Newsweek* interview. And yet, the meeting with Shevardnadze served a good purpose after all: It increased my conviction that the new leaders in the Soviet Union were genuinely planning closer cooperation with West Germany. My initial impression of Eduard Shevardnadze was also confirmed and reinforced. I sensed that I was dealing with an honest, serious, and responsible man, someone I could trust.

When I left the embassy I ran into a phalanx of reporters in the street such as I had rarely seen. All these people were interested only in comments on the *Newsweek* interview. I referred them to our official statement, which was being released at that very moment.

Back in the German Embassy, I telephoned Kohl to brief him on the talk. I advised Kohl to take seriously Shevardnadze's obvious attempts to cool the situation and to openly acknowledge the Soviet foreign minister's efforts in the Bundestag. It was my impression that I had succeeded in convincing Shevardnadze—and Gorbachev—of the Chancellor's true thinking, as well as of my desire for constructive cooperation.

The Work of Persuasion

I chose to focus my Davos address of February 2, 1987, on one central theme: that the West take Gorbachev at his word so as not to pass up a historic opportunity. I articulated the alternatives open to the West, and I depicted the consequences.

> Mankind is faced with the decision of whether to die by confrontation or to survive by cooperation. Survival means cooperating in securing the necessities of life, development in every area, and creating cooperative security structures. If we are going to believe Gorbachev, we must be ready to cooperate. If we refuse to cooperate, we act against our own interests. The West has no reason to fear cooperation. We can have only one guiding principle: Take Gorbachev seriously, take him at his word!
>
> If, after forty years of confrontation in West-East relations, we might now have an opportunity to arrive at a turning point, it would be a mistake of historic proportions for the West to pass on that opportunity only because we cannot rid ourselves of a mentality that always assumes the worst in regard to the Soviet Union.
>
> Let us not sit still with folded arms, waiting for what Gorbachev may bring. Let us instead try to influence events, to push matters forward, and to shape the situation.
>
> It would be dangerous if, rather than feeling emboldened to do our part in shaping events, we succumbed to the mistaken belief that the Soviet Union is acting out of weakness, a situation to be exploited or exacerbated by us. Firmness is called for—but any policies of power, of striving for superiority, of excessive rearmament are ways of thinking that belong squarely in the past, in the West as well. Such an attitude would of necessity lead to catastrophe.

The response evoked by this speech held no surprises. One side voiced enthusiastic agreement while the other exhibited extraordinary skepticism, even rejection. The term *Genscherism*—never meant as a compliment—was heard once more. Even though originally coined by the German left as a criticism of my realistic policy of rapprochement, the term now came from the United States and England, though with an entirely new meaning. Now it expressed the reproach that I harboured overly large illusions with regard to the Soviet Union. In Germany too there was both open and implicit criticism, even within the government. But none of these attacks could make me waver, for by now I was absolutely convinced of Gorbachev's and Shevardnadze's true intentions. The Vienna talk had only reinforced my views.

The core question was no longer what amount of trust to place in Gorbachev, but the ways in which the West could best take advantage of the vistas he had opened in order to realize the goal of a just and lasting peace in a unified Europe, including the goal of the Harmel Report, German unity. The West, including German West-East policy, must be prodded to move forward. Germans passionately cared about abolishing the division of Europe and solving the German question in the spirit of the Letter on German Unity. Stable conditions were required to accommodate the predictably dramatic changes that would result from the democratization of the Soviet Union and the rest of the Warsaw Pact nations. And anything that could jeopardize this process had to be avoided: Even given Gorbachev's and Shevardnadze's sincere intentions, it was hardly realistic to assume that no other powerful forces in the Soviet Union would prefer to keep the old policies in place. It seemed hardly likely that everyone aware of the probable consequences of the "new thinking" would be ready and willing to abandon the solid position of power and influence the Soviet Union had gained in the postwar political order in Europe. During our talk in Moscow I had seen that it was difficult even for Gorbachev to accept this realization, when he had reacted critically to President Reagan's suggestion that the results of Yalta be laid aside.

Western policies must now be directed toward securing positive responses to Gorbachev and the forces supporting him. It was essential, especially for us, to keep from furnishing Gorbachev's opponents with political ammunition, particularly since there was as yet no guarantee that Gorbachev was firmly entrenched. He was entirely different from the unpredictable Khrushchev, but if he continued with his revolutionary changes, even the power-conscious and persistent Gorbachev could be in jeopardy from the orthodox forces among the Soviet Union's leaders.

At that time United States policies were inconsistent, I thought. Quite obviously President Reagan wanted to end the division of Europe and of Germany, an attitude entirely in line with the ideas of our own nation, since we were a member of NATO, committed to the Harmel Report. The United States' proposals on disarmament were also in our interest, even though I held a different view from that of some conservatives in Europe and the United States, who, as is well known, accused Reagan of being too soft.

I did, however, have problems with two planks in Reagan's platform. One was the SDI program, which was more likely to cause insecurity and destabilization, even different degrees of security for the United States and European allies. And given the circumstances, I deplored Reagan's moral condemnation of nuclear weapons, a stance that gave support to those forces in Germany that opposed the NATO double-track resolution. Until West-East relations changed fundamentally, the security of Western Europe depended on nuclear deterrence. The Alliance understood, and had reconfirmed as much in 1981, that the strategy of deterrence was aimed solely at the deterrence of war—that is, the prevention of war. And yet during this delicate phase Reagan's approach to the disarmament of strategic weapons and intermediate-range missiles was fully in accord with my own judgment and expectations. It was only his subsequent intention to modernize nuclear short-range missiles that we could not support because it was oddly in conflict with his moral rejection of nuclear weapons. The potential victims of these missiles, with their limited range, would be the people of Central Europe.

Thus Gorbachev's entrance on the international stage was a vivid illustration of the theory of personality in history. "With your new thinking," I told him at a later time, albeit when he was still in office, "you corroborate the view of philosophical idealism, which believes that history is determined by predominant figures. You are therefore also a contradiction to philosophical materialism, which denies this role of personality."

Gorbachev and Shevardnadze made history. This fact will eventually determine how history judges them. History must also record, however, that the West's initial reaction was not uniformly farsighted; Western responses were frequently timid, determined by old ways of thinking. The controversy concerning the new thinking in Moscow—that is, the attitude toward Gorbachev and Shevardnadze—was in reality a struggle over an historic direction. Even at that early stage it was a question of riding the coattails of history.

The degree to which Gorbachev's and Shevardnadze's policies affected the lives of people in the countries of the Eastern bloc was becoming increasingly clear. An example from my own family illustrated the change. In March 1987 my East German relatives visited me. The entire family was able to cross the border, for as long as ten days, so that on March 21 we could jointly celebrate my sixtieth birthday. I noticed that my relatives behaved more freely than in former years. Their more relaxed manner was strikingly illustrated the night before my birthday, when we hosted a large party at our house for friends and family. Since a television station wanted to report on the party for a few minutes outside the house, I cautioned my relatives from East Germany, so that they might be spared difficulties on their return. "Be careful," I said, "the television people are coming." But the younger ones replied, "We don't care, let them see us." This was a wholly new outlook. Later they told me that people at home had stopped them on the street because they had seen them on television. For me their unexpected assurance was a further unmistakable sign that things were beginning to change in East Germany as well.

On May 4, 1987, I accompanied the federal president on an official visit to Switzerland. While there, I had an encounter that touched me deeply. The German contribution to the agenda of the trip included a concert of the Berlin Philharmonic. During the intermission the President and I went to call on the conductor, Herbert von Karajan, in his dressing room. After the President had thanked the conductor, von Karajan turned to me. This was not our first meeting, but it was the first in relative privacy. Von Karajan approached me, held my hand in both of his, looked into my eyes for a long time, and thanked me in moving words for my foreign policy. I could have no idea, he said, how much my policies meant to him, he only hoped that I would continue on the same course. Especially at this time of political controversy, his gesture heartened me.

204

In May 1987 I was again at the center of the controversy around the intermediate-range missiles. On the evening of May 10 I flew to Washington for discussions on this topic. The following morning Secretary Shultz and I held our first meeting at the early hour of quarter past seven; at ten o'clock I was at the White House. Over the lunch that followed I met with leading figures from both parties in Congress, and in the afternoon, I had a meeting with Secretary of Defense Caspar Weinberger. After further talks with various senators I flew back to Bonn the same night.

I had made it a habit to keep my visits in Washington as busy as possible. When I arrived, our ambassador and our delegation would pick me up at the airport; the car ride to the hotel gave me an opportunity to hear the ambassador's analysis of the current situation.

My travels taught me that a short visit also reduced jet lag; the effect was similar to staying up too late one night. By now I was almost as familiar with the confines of the State Department as the spaces of my own ministry. How often had the main gate admitted me to the office of various secretaries of state. Here I had called on Secretaries Rogers (while I was Minister of the Interior), Kissinger, Vance, Muskie, Haig, Shultz, and Baker. While Jim Baker was in office we forged a new custom: After our discussions we went to the large entrance hall and, standing behind a high desk, we issued a press statement. Thus both host and visitor had a chance to give the public a thorough idea of their exchange.

George Shultz was a somewhat stolid, serious, and utterly dependable conversational partner. We developed a good relationship; in the end we even became friendly. On May 10, 1987, we discussed current issues of arms control and disarmament. Back at my hotel I held a press conference at 9:15 in the morning; because of editorial deadlines in Germany, such matters had to be attended to as early as possible. As a rule the press conference was followed by a meeting at the White House that ended in a television appearance. Whenever I left the President's residence, the White House press corps as well as reporters for German television stations were waiting outside. Well aware of the influence of congressional representatives, I also made sure to pay several calls in the Capitol. My visits usually ended with a summary and evaluation of my talks, which I composed with the ambassador as we drove back to the airport.

Rebuilding a House Divided

I boarded the plane around six in the evening, and after I had some supper, I made myself available to the reporters who had made the trip with me. They expected a summary review of my visit. Finally I discussed with my coworkers the results of the visit.

More and more, those years revealed, the West German government was in worldwide demand when conferences and discussions were held on significant matters. By this time I had long remodeled my office, a room next to mine served as a parlor where I had installed a table that seated eight people. I used this room for "small dinners" and luncheons, which I hosted for guests from abroad. The limited number of seats ensured that the occasions were truly working suppers or lunches. Later, as an additional way to "rationalize" my time, I introduced the working breakfast—an innovation that did not please everyone. Lord Carrington, for example, once remarked that he found business lunches bad enough, but for me now to have introduced business breakfasts as well. . . . At any rate, he noted, he was anticipating fearfully the time when I would suggest the business nap. I interrupted: "You haven't thought of business funerals!" For funerals too, not only in Moscow, were increasingly used for meetings.

The Beginning of Rapprochement Between East and West

On June 8 to 10, 1987, Helmut Kohl, the minister of finance, the minister of economy, and I attended the world economic summit in Venice, which brought together the seven leading Western industrial nations. Rarely have economic concerns been so heavily overshadowed by foreign and security policy as at this summit.

Primarily we discussed ongoing events in the Soviet Union. At our instigation, the final pronouncement on East-West relations ultimately read, "Since our last meeting new opportunities for progress in East-West relations have come about. We feel encouraged by these events. We follow with great interest the latest development in the Soviet Union's domestic and foreign policies. We trust that these will prove highly significant for improving relations between the nations of the East and the West politically, economically, and for security."

The summit witnessed a skirmish between President Mitterand and Margaret Thatcher on the topic of short-range missiles. During an intense discussion Prime Minister Thatcher asked the French president, "Are you sure you won't use your short-range missiles once the Russians have conquered Cologne?" Whereupon President Mitterand unequivocally declared, "Cologne is an allied city. We would not do so." This remark exemplified the spirit of German-French cooperation during the complex disarmament negotiations taking place at this time.

NATO's subsequent spring conference was held from June 10 to June 12 in Reykjavík, at a time when progress in arms control seemed possible. I emphatically advocated that we use the encouraging signs of Soviet domestic and foreign policies to try to achieve breakthroughs in the American-Soviet disarmament negotiations in Geneva. However, I pointed out in Reykjavík, a 50 percent reduction in strategic arsenals was not enough. Intermediate- and short-range missiles must also be cut down significantly, just as progress must be made in banning chemical weapons. I further advocated a comprehensive, stable, and verifiable conventional balance of power at a lower level. We appealed to the Soviet Union to scrap its SS-20 arms entirely.

It was exceedingly difficult in these negotiations to arrive at a common position within NATO. Nor was it simple to come to an agreement on the disarmament of conventional weapons. The United States wanted negotiations between the alliances, while the French, who did not participate in the integration of NATO, preferred to negotiate within the CSCE framework. Since our own interests dictated simply that *any* negotiations come about I tried for agreement between Washington and Paris. George Shultz was willing, but the French delegation hesitated. Finally I called my old friend Roland Dumas, who during that time of *co-habitation* was not in office. He spoke with the President. Shortly thereafter Paris gave the green light, and the French delegation no longer insisted on its proposal.

That year Berlin celebrated the 750th anniversary of its founding. Next to Ronald Reagan's speech of June 12, 1987, in which he made his historic call for tearing down the Wall, the outstanding event was the beginning of the Tour de France, which started off from the Brandenburg Gate—a political statement. Prime Minister Jacques Chirac of France came to Berlin for the event. Together we saw the bikers on their way. I had run into Chirac the night before, in a restaurant on the Kurfürstendamm. I asked him what he had had for dinner, and he replied, "Well, of course, pickled pigs' feet and sauerkraut." I was not sure whether that was meant as a compliment or if he assumed this was the only food Germans liked.

The following day my wife and I left early in the morning for the Handel Festival in my hometown, Halle. Change was in the air; we immediately felt a greater openness. When on that Sunday morning we took part in the outdoor opening ceremonies in the marketplace, we were greeted in the friendliest manner and frequently addressed directly. Formerly the people had been reserved, if they had dared to take any notice of us at all. That evening we were assigned seats in the upper tiers so that we were out of sight of the audience below. Nevertheless, word of our presence spread quickly. The theater manager invited us to a small reception during intermission. After the reception, when we tried to leave the restaurant, we had trouble opening the door because so many people were pushing against it. My wife and I were applauded heartily. Again and again people shook my hand, and others called out, "It's good to see you here. Great that you came. Hi, Herr Genscher. It's important for us to have you here!" These encounters in my hometown always moved me, I realized how grateful people were for my visit. With even greater urgency I asked myself: Where will this lead?

From July 6 to July 11 I accompanied President von Weizsäcker on his trip to the Soviet Union. His official visit was remarkable in several respects and of great significance because the *Newsweek* interview was still not entirely forgotten.

It was the President's purpose during this visit to give renewed impetus to German-Soviet relations. He accomplished his mission successfully, with his characteristic dignity and with great sensitivity. Again it was clear how important a federal president of the stature of a Richard von Weizsäcker was to our country's reputation and influence abroad. Gorbachev proved eager to settle our differences; he was seeking rapprochement. He was most attentive to the President personally, who devoted himself responsibly to improving German-Soviet relations, but Gorbachev also emphasized the significance of German-Soviet relations themselves. During his conversation with the President the General Secretary recalled that I had been the last high-level West German official with whom he had held discussions; a year had already passed since our meeting.

The discussion between President von Weizsäcker and General Secretary Gorbachev was sometimes rather blunt, at times even harsh. To Shevardnadze I voiced my surprise that *Pravda* had published only a censored account of the President's speech. The published version lacked all his remarks on German-born Soviet citizens' freedom to choose to emigrate and all statements on German unity.

After the talks the Tass news agency declared that Gorbachev had made it clear the German question was no longer to be considered an open one. I believed the opposite to be the case. While President von Weizsäcker seemed disappointed at the General Secretary's remark that it was impossible to predict what things would look like in a hundred years, I argued differently during our follow-up discussion. I pointed out that though Gorbachev's statement covered a long period of time, he had basically been saying that the German question was open indeed. That had been his real message.

I was certain that we would not have to wait a hundred years— quite the contrary. Long before 1987 I had answered the question of whether I believed that German unification would take place in my lifetime with: "If God grants me an average lifespan, yes." The fact that Tass interpreted Gorbachev's remarks in the old sense merely proved that there were conservative counterforces who were not happy with Gorbachev's statement. That fact corroborated my interpretation that Gorbachev had left the German question open.

That East Germany also never considered the German question to have been answered definitively I learned from an unimpeachable source during the memorial service for Indira Gandhi on November 3, 1984, in Delhi. During the long outdoor ceremony Horst Sindermann, the president of the Volkskammer, East Germany's parliament, stood next to me. I talked with him (he had once been party secretary in Halle) about energy supplies in East Germany and lignite mining. In that context Sindermann said, "You must have noticed that we didn't tear down the house where you were born. One day it might become a historic site; but how it is going to be managed—that depends on whether you'll do it or we will!" Back in Bonn, I told Kohl about this exchange, adding,

"That is the open German question—in the Politburo!" By the way, Sindermann was wrong about the house. He must have confused it with the house where my father was born. There actually was supposed to be a lignite bed under that building.

How much glasnost and perestroika had changed in the Soviet Union in two years became clear to the President and me when we—Herr and Frau von Weizsäcker, my wife, and I—met with Andrei Sakharov and Yelena Bonner in the library of the West German embassy. The encounter was as riveting as it was encouraging. Though Sakharov made critical remarks about Gorbachev—especially regarding his willingness to carry out domestic reforms—he nevertheless suggested that we support Gorbachev, and not only for reasons of foreign policy. While he spoke with some reserve, Bonner expressed herself much more clearly and urgently. "The prophet and the lioness," I commented to my wife after our conversation.

My encounters with Gromyko during this visit had a certain melancholy quality. What were his thoughts on Sakharov's freedom? This was our first meeting after he became president, though, of course, I knew him well from his time as foreign minister. His way of moving about as he hosted official functions and led the talks indicated that he was not entirely at ease in his new role. I realized that he did not feel his election to the presidency was a promotion. As the official host at dinner, he seized every opportunity to address me directly across the table and to ask about the current state of our foreign policy and to inquire into a number of details. Was he trying to let me know that he was no longer kept fully briefed on foreign policy? It seemed as if he were reminiscing about his years as foreign minister—as well as our former relationship, which had certainly not been without its problems—with a certain rosy nostalgia. There had been other signs as well. For example, in 1985 Gromyko had sent Ambassador Semyonov to me. The diplomat, who had been employed in Soviet foreign policy for almost a half-century, was holding a small package. "My errand today makes a first in my entire diplomatic career. Andrei Gromyko has asked me to hand you a copy of his memoirs; he has never done that before." The volume consisted, not of memoirs but of speeches and articles. The inscription read, TO MY COLLEAGUE OF MANY YEARS, HANS-DIETRICH GENSCHER, AS A MEMENTO AND WITH GOOD WISHES. A. GROMYKO, 20 MAY 1985.

I have somewhat mixed feelings when I think back on the times we worked together. Often I had felt bitter about the methods Gromyko used to get his way, particularly when the discussions concerned Berlin. Beyond all political controversies, however, on a human level we had many things in common. Eventually we even came to like each other. There had been mutual personal and professional respect. Even remembering that for decades he had repeatedly obstructed progress in foreign policy, rapprochement, and disarmament, during this visit I was very sympathetic to the personal feelings of my former counterpart. My wife and I also fondly remember the conversations with Gromyko's wife, who had always impressed us with her great personal dignity and her maternal manner.

My sense that Gromyko nostalgically idealized his years as foreign minister was later confirmed when I met with my fellow foreign ministers from Central and Eastern Europe during the CSCE conference in Vienna. They told me that during the last Warsaw Pact summit they had talked about me with Gromyko. Even as president he had immediately and quite naturally gravitated to the cluster of foreign ministers. That was the group in which he felt most at ease.

From September 7 to 11, 1987, the general secretary of the Central Committee of the SED and chairman of the East German Council of State, Erich Honecker, visited West Germany. I fully approved of the invitation extended by the West German government. The visit could only help relations between us, because every rapprochement between the two Germanys could only bring relief to the people in East Germany. East-West relations in their totality were also aided when difficulties between the two Germanys were kept to a minimum; the "community of responsibility" of West and East Germany could, and in my opinion must, contribute to positive developments in West-East relations. That theory was the core of and motivation behind my efforts at improved mutual understanding and for cooperation in disarmament and arms control wherever possible. The term "community of responsibility" strengthened the sense of all Germans that they belonged together, for such a community exists only here, not in any other

211

nation. I did not share others' worries that Honecker's visit to the Federal Republic might exacerbate the partition of Germany. On the contrary: I was convinced that it could only heighten the awareness of our nation's unity. The image of West Germany as the enemy would begin to pale, and the awareness of our common past would grow stronger. Of course the outcome of such a visit also depended on what advantages could be taken of the specific circumstances and what was said in the official speeches.

Somewhat earlier, the Chancellor had asked me for my ideas regarding the program for the visit; he himself found the event troublesome. I understood, I replied; but the visit had to happen. We owed it to the people of East Germany to use such opportunities to improve their situation; further, I suggested, the visit was an important and valuable event for West-East relations as well. Especially in view of the opportunities Gorbachev's policies were offering, we had to reduce—or, better still, avoid—problems in the relationship between the two Germanys.

It was obvious that Honecker considered his visit to Bonn and West Germany the pinnacle of his political career. Only an invitation to Washington might have been a greater event for him. On the other hand, the visit to West Germany, particularly to the state of Saarland, where his family had lived, was more emotionally charged than any visit in the United States could ever be.

I met with Honecker during the dinners the President and the Chancellor held for him in the Villa Hammerschmidt and at La Redouté. On these occasions the Chancellor spoke plainly about our attitude toward German unity, as did the President. On Tuesday, October 8, at the Hotel Bristol, Honecker hosted a dinner, where we found time for a brief chat.

What was new was that I received Foreign Minister Oskar Fischer in the Foreign Office on Tuesday morning. This was the first time we spoke on German soil; since we did not treat the GDR as a foreign country, it did not fall into the category of foreign relations. Relations with East Germany were solely the responsibility of the Chancellery. This time, however, Fischer was traveling as a member of Honecker's delegation.

On October 23, 1987, I visited Tirana for the first time. The occasion was West Germany's opening diplomatic relations with Albania. Over the past few decades Albania, as a result of its self-imposed isolation, had become a sort of European terra incognita; its mystery was deepened because it was the only European nation not to participate in the CSCE. Shortly before my plane landed in Tirana, I saw something peculiar—rises in the ground that looked like molehills. During our trip from the airport into town I noticed that these hummocks were small concrete bunkers that had been built throughout the country to protect against paratroopers. They were especially prevalent around the capital and the airport.

By the time of my visit the old Communist dictator, Enver Hoxha, was no longer alive. It had been his policies that had isolated Albania so completely and cut the country off from all diplomatic relations. Initial contacts between Bonn and Tirana in 1975 and in the early 1980s had come to nothing because Albania had insisted on making diplomatic relations dependent on reparations for damages caused by the German army during the Second World War. We had rejected that demand. In the spring of 1984 new exploratory talks were initiated, and in March 1987 Albania finally withdrew its demands. Now the inclusion of West Berlin in the planned bilateral agreements was possible, and Tirana went beyond the stipulations of the Four Power Agreement—a decision that may be considered an expression of the country's independent foreign policy.

Enver Hoxha's regime had resulted in the most severe oppression and economic hardship for the people. His successor, Ramiz Alia, promised greater political openness and flexibility. In a serious conversation with him I predicted critical upheavals for Albania unless the government initiated reforms promptly.

When I visited Albania a second time in 1991—we were preparing for Albania's admission into the CSCE—Alia smiled at me: "You can see that we've done everything you told us to during your first visit. We are now heading toward democracy." Though that boast was somewhat exaggerated, I did indeed come to a country that had fundamentally changed. Having been allowed to meet with representatives from various opposition parties and groups, I made the invitation to an Albanian delegation to the first CSCE conference of foreign ministers in Berlin dependent on representatives of these opposition parties' being included in the delegation; only on that condition, I declared, could I, as chairman of the conference, support Albania's admission into CSCE. During my talks in Tirana I had been particularly impressed with Dr. Sali

Berisha, a physician who described the goals of his party and the situation in his country. At my request Chancellor Kohl—who gave the opening address at the CSCE conference of foreign ministers—received Berisha in his office in the Reichstag. At the time we could not know that Berisha would be the first freely elected president of Albania.

The Double-Zero Option

Politically 1987 became the year of the double-zero option—a triumph of German security policy, particularly the security policy of the FDP. The zero option originated in Europe, and more specifically in Germany, since it had been the Schmidt-Genscher administration that proposed the zero option as the most important goal of negotiations. On November 18, 1981, President Reagan had made an offer to the Soviet Union: The United States would desist from deploying intermediate-range missiles if the Soviet Union agreed to dismantle its SS-4 and SS-5 weapons and, most important, their SS-20 missiles. Before Mikhail Gorbachev became General Secretary in 1985, Moscow had refused the offer. It was not until the Geneva meeting in November 1985 that this attitude changed, and even if no direct progress was made in INF negotiations, the Soviets for the first time expressed their serious interest in major arms control agreements.

In 1979 as in 1983, in military terms but even more so politically, the West had responded appropriately to the Soviet threat; the essence of this policy had been created by the West German government. Only our firmness led to fundamental reevaluation of Soviet interests; this reevaluation in turn instigated Gorbachev's foreign policy reforms, combined with Soviet rethinking of disarmament policies and the policies toward Europe and Germany. The NATO double-track resolution of 1979 and the deployment of missiles in 1983 were the point of departure for the comprehensive changes of 1989.

In late 1983, after the NATO double-track resolution had been established, I made the following assessment of the political situation. After rearmament had begun, the time was ripe for a new attempt toward a broad, long-term basis for rapprochement, arms control, and disarmament. Since the Soviet Union was taking advantage of its new status as an equal among world powers by advancing into the Third World, with intervention and increased armament, the results of the policy of rapprochement had been only partially successful. Further, the Soviet policies of rearmament and disengagement had infringed on Western Europe's vested security interest, severely encumbering rapprochement. In the face of the West's resoluteness, demonstrated by its rearmament, the Soviet leadership was now forced to choose among three foreign-policy alternatives: one, resuming increased confrontation; two, return to a partial policy of rapprochement; or three, a new, comprehensive kind of cooperation on a long-term basis of equal rights.

Reagan and Gorbachev held a summit in Reykjavík from October 10 to October 12, 1986. On the topic of intermediate-range missiles, both sides were considering a global limit of 100 warheads each, with the removal of all American and Soviet long-range theater nuclear forces (LRTNF) in Europe. In actual numbers, this would have meant that the Soviets would destroy 408 SS-20 missiles, 1,224 warheads altogether, while the United States would have had to remove 216 missiles with as many warheads— an outcome Germans along with all Europeans in the West and the East would have accepted with great relief. However, the difference of opinion on space weapons precluded any agreement.

Nevertheless, the Reykjavík summit proved the seriousness of both American and Soviet leaders in finding new avenues. Reykjavík was only a beginning, preliminary to a new phase in West-East relations. All observers felt that the climate between West and East had become warmer; in Germany in particular, the hope that European rapprochement and disarmament would receive a new stimulus was expressed. More than a year earlier, in a statement on January 8, 1985, Secretary Shultz and Foreign Minister Gromyko had declared that the arms race must be prevented in space and ended on earth.

Comparing the two initial positions of 1981, it was doubtless the Soviet Union that made the critical concessions. But for Germans and other Europeans the essential problem—the short-range intermediate nuclear forces (SRINF)—was not removed by Reykjavík. Gorbachev did hint at possible limitations even of SRINF. After all, in Reykjavík both the United States and the Soviet Union had agreed on negotiating further reductions. On

215

October 16, 1986, Secretary Shultz hinted at the possibility of agreeing on total elimination.

If Reagan and Gorbachev could have come to terms on SDI and the ABM treaty, the meeting in Reykjavík would have achieved historic significance. However, the prospect of a world free of nuclear weapons, reflected in the visions of both powers, elicited different reactions, sometimes even shock, in the West and the East. What mattered was that after Reykjavík the center of the dialogue on arms control shifted; the spotlight moved from American-Soviet negotiations on strategic weapons to talks on about intermediate-range missiles.

In Reykjavík Reagan and Gorbachev had far outdistanced the Alliance's previous discussions. In Western Europe and the United States, therefore, opinion on events in the Icelandic capital was divided. As for myself, I was delighted that the old patterns of thinking had been shattered; I publicly welcomed the results and defended them against objections that both the left and the right raised in Western Europe. For some, Reagan and Gorbachev had gone too far; others thought they had not gone far enough. I felt confirmed in the impressions I had formed during my talk with Gorbachev.

In February 1986, after Gorbachev proposed the zero option for Europe, we urged President Reagan to insist on our original proposal of a global zero option. In a letter to Mikhail Gorbachev of February 22, 1986, Reagan again explained this option, which eliminated all intermediate-range weapons of both the Soviet Union and the United States wherever they were stationed. Worldwide removal—that was the option that had to prevail. At that time Gorbachev decided absolutely that he would not consider the French and British systems while working toward agreement.

A fierce debate broke out within NATO. Gradually two political opinions evolved; some voices within the Alliance welcomed a zero option or even a double-zero option. Others espoused the view that the risk of denuclearization was real. I did not waver in my advocacy of our goal of global and complete elimination of intermediate-range missiles.

February 28, 1987, marked another important event: It was the day Gorbachev stopped insisting on linking negotiations on intermediate-range missiles with SDI and the ABM treaty—a concession I had requested repeatedly in the Moscow talks. Thus Gorbachev cleared the way for a separate intermediate-range nuclear forces (INF) treaty. I found this turn of events encouraging; the zero option that had been developed with the crucial aid of the FDP and West Germany's Foreign Office had been adopted by the Atlantic Alliance, and in 1981 it had been introduced into United States-Soviet negotiations. "In practical terms," I declared on May 7, 1987, in the Bundestag, "the zero option means the destruction of a great number of Soviet launching mechanisms and missiles, with a total of one thousand three hundred and thirty-five nuclear warheads, while at the current state of affairs, Western missiles and projectiles with two hundred and sixteen nuclear warheads would be removed and destroyed."

When it came to intermediate missiles (with a range of between 300 and 600 miles), the West was confronted with the Soviet Union's overwhelming superiority because no American missiles were stationed within that area, while worldwide the Soviets had 130 to 160 missiles with multiple booster capacity in their launching mechanism. The American disarmament proposal of March 3, 1987, therefore included limitations for intermediate missiles with a 300- to 600-mile range.

We had been able to persuade Washington at least to stipulate in the INF Treaty that follow-up negotiations be held for SRINF with a range of 100 to 300 miles. Several statements by Secretary Shultz reassured me that, as a statement of September 30, 1986, had implied, the United States would stipulate the same ceiling for SRINF with a 300- to 600-mile range and would agree to further obligations for follow-up negotiations on SRINF with a 100- to 300-mile range. What had happened during the SALT negotiations, when the Carter administration failed to prevent a new wave of armament on a level below strategic weapons (that is, in the intermediate range) must not happen again. Matters moved ahead dramatically: The Soviet Union indicated that it was ready to agree on a zero option for SRINF in the 300- to 600-mile range.

When the double-zero option (the complete dismantling of intermediate short- and long-range missiles) was on the table, hardly anyone believed that it could be realized on a global scale. The opponents of rearmament from the left never believed that the Soviet Union would agree to a zero option. They were prepared to accept a moratorium, thus ceding to the Soviet Union a significant superiority, now and well into the future. Conservative supporters of the NATO double-track resolution, for their part, accepted that section only in the certain expectation that Moscow would not agree to a zero option. It was not the first time that the left and the right succumbed to their own misconceptions.

I remained an unswerving supporter of the double-zero option. A breakthrough in disarmament could only contribute to basic changes in all West-East relations; at any rate, it was hard to imagine that, given the conflict-ridden history of the NATO double-track resolution, such a sweeping agreement would not affect relations between West and East. Both Gorbachev and the President of the United States considered curbing the nuclear danger as a political calling that at times preoccupied them to a greater extent than their advisers liked. Such proved to be the case during the American-Soviet summit in Reykjavík of October 1986.

The term *denuclearization* was now haunting the Western Alliance. In view of the large number of nuclear weapons remaining on German soil alone, the word was contrary to the facts, it was a remnant of the old thinking. The West's nuclear artillery, with an unknowable number of nuclear warheads, each equipped with the destructive power of the Hiroshima bomb; the West's short-range missiles; the forward-based systems (FBS) or air-launched nuclear weapons; sea-based nuclear weapons held by the Sixth United States Fleet in the Adriatic; the Soviet short-range missiles on German soil; the other Soviet nuclear weapons; and finally, the strategic weapons of both superpowers—all these arms guaranteed that, even after an accord on intermediate-range missiles, an overkill capacity for Europe and the world remained.

Because Germany bore the chief burden of conventional defense, it was of particular importance to us that conventional disarmament be made a topic for the whole alliance. Since I had become foreign minister in 1974, my objections to mutually balanced force reductions (MBFR) negotiations had focused on the Soviet Union's transparent but dangerous intention of using the MBFR negotiations to reduce the only truly significant European army—the West German Bundeswehr. While all other armies could have evaded their obligation to disarm by relocating their forces in areas outside the Central European disarmament control zone, the Bundeswehr would have had to reduce. My second objection dealt with the fact that, while Soviet forces would merely need to be relocated outside of Central Europe, United States forces would be driven across the Atlantic, since, with the exception of West Germany, other European nations were not prepared to accommodate them. Such an uneven reduction, in terms of force as well as distance, would have driven a psychopolitical wedge between North America and Western Europe. MBFR would have handed Moscow a great triumph. The Bundeswehr—the heart of NATO—would have been seriously weakened in its function as a conventional defense of Western Europe; and the geographic disparity—distance from the United States on the one hand and from the Soviet Union on the other—would have intensified the effect. A consistent disarmament policy within the Alliance was therefore of crucial importance.

Thus MBFR did not focus on immediate disarmament, its purpose was reduction of forces in Central Europe. Actual disarmament was the consequence only for the Bundeswehr. The conflict about whether the ceiling for armed forces in Central Europe on both sides of the Iron Curtain should be set for the alliances in their entirety or for the member nations individually also indicated the direction in which the Soviet Union was pushing. The Soviets wanted national ceilings; they had the Bundeswehr in mind. Over and over I therefore told my coworkers in the disarmament section, "No agreement is better than a bad one." And yet the years of MBFR negotiations were important as a kind of training for talks on genuine conventional disarmament—and that was on the table now.

The day before his meeting with Foreign Minister Shevardnadze in Vienna on November 6, 1986, Secretary Shultz sent me a letter laying out his objectives: 50 percent reduction of tactical-weapons potential within the framework of the START negotiations. As for long- and short-range intermediate missiles, the United States hoped to keep the total to 100 warheads on both sides, stationed entirely within the Soviet Union and the United States. Regarding SRINF, Shultz suggested a ceiling of the Soviet Union's present number. Subsequent negotiations to deal with the reduction of missiles with a range of less than 600 miles should begin immediately.

Basically we were in full agreement with Washington. My only worry was that the floor for SRINF was not established at a range of 90 miles, which Germany wanted, while the Reagan Administration tended toward a floor of 300 miles.

On January 29, 1987, I received Ambassador Richard Burt. Discussing the situation in Moscow, I gave him my assessment of Gorbachev. I emphasized the significance of foreign policy and domestic reforms in the Soviet Union. Now concrete conclusions would have to be drawn at the negotiating table.

As mentioned above, we were unwilling to have the intermediate-range negotiations make the same mistakes as the SALT treaty. SALT should have safeguarded against the possibility of undermining the agreement with new intermediate-range missiles. Now an agreement on renegotiating short-range intermediate nuclear forces had to be formulated in such a way that a zero option for long-range missiles would not be undermined by an arms race in short-range missiles. On February 28, 1987, when Gorbachev severed the problem of intermediate-range missiles from the SDI complex and suggested a special agreement on INF, prospects for an INF treaty abruptly improved. I immediately welcomed the statement from Moscow; it satisfied German demands as well as European security interests.

After an intense talk among Chancellor Kohl, Defense Secretary Manfred Wörner, and me, the West German government publicly declared on April 2 that it would continue to seek a zero option for intermediate-range missiles and to hope, above all, for follow-up negotiations on short-range intermediate nuclear forces.

On April 29 I held another conversation with the United States ambassador. Burt pointed out that his country's position had changed; during Shultz's visit to Moscow, he said, Gorbachev had talked about the global zero option and short-range intermediate missiles. The Russians' demand that the Pershing IA be removed surprised him, even though he, Burt, considered it only logical. He nevertheless still hoped that the Soviets would eventually back down. In response to my question as to why the Soviets were now requesting the removal of the Pershing IA, Burt referred to the fallout from the public outcry in Europe. I objected that it had not been West Germany who had introduced the Pershing IA into the talks. He agreed, but added that Ambassador Kvitsinsky had told him just a few days earlier that elimination of the Pershing IA had been hinted at as early as the walk in the woods in July 1982. This information was new to me. Burt told me that he had also talked to Kvitsinsky about the role of the German weapons systems (that is, the Pershing IA) separately from the discussion of the United States launcher systems. These would keep the Germans close to the alliance—in fact, they were not weapons held by Germans. I found it interesting that in this connection Burt again returned to the second zero option, contending that he did not understand at all why there was opposition to it in Germany.

Within the West German government opinions on the double-zero option diverged widely. In the end, however, the coalition arrived at a compromise, agreeing that, should the Soviets propose a zero option for a 300- to 600-mile range while Shultz was in Moscow, he should neither accept nor reject the offer, instead only ask questions of clarification.

I could subscribe to that agreement, since I felt certain that if this double-zero option indeed became possible, we—the FDP—would be able to impose our belief on the government coalition. As for the United States, the West German government could count on its understanding if we refused to take a position in Moscow; Shultz himself had suggested that posture in a letter to me of April 6. Washington clearly hinted that the United States was supportive of the double-zero option, but it would concur only if West Germany agreed.

Our coalition partner, the CDU/CSU, worried that the second zero option could be succeeded by a third, which would seriously obstruct nuclear deterrence. In view of the Warsaw Pact's conventional superiority, while the Christian Democratic Defense Minister Wörner and others warned against the "denuclearization" of Europe, I took a favorable view of the double-zero option—as did the United States. It opened the possibility of not only demolishing the vast Soviet nuclear superiority but also of stopping, even reducing to zero, the vicious circle of armament, counterarmament, and rearmament. An entire class of destructive weapons might be eliminated—an historic opportunity. Further, the political consequences of such a breakthrough had to be borne in mind.

At that time the public at large was not paying much attention to the problem of the Pershing IA. The Soviet Union had already hinted at including the Pershing IA in the disarmament agreements, since it was the only land-based nuclear weapon with a 300- to 600-mile range. I was convinced that relinquishing this missile would not damage our security interests, unless it was treated as a status symbol. I nevertheless dismissed the suggestion that the Pershing IA be included in the agreements between the two superpowers, because an autonomous German decision was required on this issue. In this way the West German government took its place among the actors and decision makers.

I was certain that Reagan and Shultz were firmly resolved to enforce the double-zero option in the Western Alliance, as I had hoped they would. But Chancellor Kohl spoke out publicly against this option because, he claimed, it endangered the security interests of the German Federal Republic. Open disagreement broke out between the CDU/CSU and the FDP. In this extremely difficult situation—domestically as well as in terms of foreign policy—I flew to Washington on May 11, 1987. Two days earlier I had met with Charles Clark, my Canadian counterpart, in the Southwest German town of Baden-Baden. He also endorsed the double-zero option. His concurrent visit to the Canadian forces stationed in the state of Baden at that time was a significant indication that Canadians would continue to have a presence in West Germany.

In Washington I again held intense discussions with President Ronald Reagan, Secretary of State George Shultz, Chief of Staff James Baker, and Security Adviser Frank Carlucci. They confirmed that the United States were acting very responsibly in their attempt to come to an agreement with the Soviet Union on the expanded zero option, a goal I supported both in private and in public.

However, the crux emerged with increasing clarity: Any agreement between the United States and the Soviet Union depended on West Germany's giving up the Pershing IA. Under no circumstances did the Americans want to finalize an agreement without the approval their European allies, above all Germany. London also accepted the double-zero option. In France it was the time of the first *co-habitation* during François Mitterand's presidency. Previously the French Foreign Minister had publicly expressed doubts about the double-zero option, but I knew from conversations with Roland Dumas that President Mitterand was now favorably inclined to a double-zero option.

□   □   □   □

In May 1987 "travel diplomacy" of a special sort caused unexpected problems in German-Soviet relations. A nineteen-year-old amateur pilot, Mathias Rust, had landed his plane smack in the middle of Red Square in Moscow. The stunt, as rakish as it was thoughtless, caused a sensation. How could a young man with a simple, tiny airplane escape the sophisticated air shield of the Soviet Union? His flight and the safe landing in Red Square in Moscow humiliated the Red Army, and the Soviet air force in particular; the event resulted in the immediate firing of the top military personnel.

In Moscow the situation grew even more problematic. Rust had been arrested and stood trial quickly. On September 4 he was sentenced to four years at hard labor. We had a significant investment in seeing Rust released as soon as possible: The last thing West Germany needed at this point in time was a disturbance in the political atmosphere. The Foreign Office therefore became enmeshed in the affair as well. I spoke to Shevardnadze about the case and told him that I thought the sentence too harsh—even though, for reasons of foreign policy, I saw no advantage in letting the affair upset German-Soviet relations. I therefore personally appealed to Gorbachev and Shevardnadze for a pardon for Rust. Months later I learned that Rust would be released on August 3, 1988, after fourteen months in a labor camp. A few days earlier—on July 30 and 31—I was in Moscow. "We're releasing him as a personal favor to you," Shevardnadze told me, an admission I forbore exploiting in public. I knew that the gesture was good for Rust and above all for German-Soviet relations, and that was good enough for me. With the new openness to the leadership in Moscow, I did not want to see a wedge driven between the Chancellor and the Foreign Minister.

In the summer of 1987 it became increasingly clear that the United States were eager to respond favorably to Gorbachev's proposal for a double-zero option. I also saw it as a crucial breakthrough, which began with the simple zero option. There was no good reason to prevent the negotiations from extending to the shorter ranges of the intermediate missiles.

After weeks of exceedingly harsh wrangling, the West German government voted in favor of the double-zero option on June 1.

In the context of the establishment of a conventional balance and the global elimination of chemical weapons, the German Federal Government endorses the gradual, distinct, and verifiable reduction, through negotiations, of American and Soviet land-based nuclear systems with a range of between 100 and 1,000 kilometers stationed in Europe. A first step would be a globally binding agreement between the United States and the Soviet Union that in the future they will eliminate all short-range [500 to 1,000 kilometers] intermediate missiles. . . . The Federal Government continues to insist that, as before, the 72 missiles of the type Pershing IA are not, and cannot become, the subject of current negotiations. Thus the Federal Government is in agreement with the United States of America and its allies.

I had only reluctantly agreed to the communiqué. My eventual capitulation was based on approval of the double-zero option; negotiations could continue. The note that the Pershing IA was not a subject of current negotiations was factually correct; the claim could nevertheless lead to wrong conclusions if it was interpreted as meaning that we intended to hang on to these missiles, come what may.

The NATO foreign ministers conference in Reykjavík on July 11 and 12, 1987, went well. The fact that the communiqué mentioned neither the seventy-two Pershing IA missiles nor the French and British nuclear forces reflected the consensus that these systems could not be the subject of negotiations between the superpowers. The concluding communiqué's provision for negotiations on nuclear arms with a range of under 300 miles also met West German expectations. Now it was decided that, after the realization of the double-zero option, NATO would not construct a fire wall, as some—most vociferously Prime Minister Thatcher—had demanded. Nuclear weapons of this sort, a threat especially to Germany, would not be excluded from further disarmament negotiations.

On June 24 Moscow charged the United States with wanting to exclude the seventy-two Pershing IA missiles—or rather, their nuclear warheads—from disarmament agreements. When I spoke with Foreign Minister Shevardnadze during the West German President's official visit to Moscow from July 6 to 10, the Pershing IA missiles therefore played a significant role. Shevardnadze left no doubt that there would be no double-zero option unless we relinquished the Pershing IA. According to Shevardnadze, the Soviet Union had already made great concessions to the West with the first global zero option and especially by giving up its superiority with the second zero option. The continued presence of the Pershing IA missiles, however, was unacceptable.

We agreed to keep in touch regarding this question. In case the negotiations threatened to fail, we wanted to start a new set of negotiations. Because this agreement was important to me, I continued to endorse the American position, which supported relinquishing the Pershing IA. And in a speech of August 6, during the Geneva conference on disarmament, Shevardnadze made his position absolutely clear once again. President von Weizsäcker, whom I briefed in Moscow on the state of the discussion on the Pershing IA, supported my position. Before I left for my summer vacation, I had a meeting with the Chancellor at which I spoke in favor of an autonomous West German statement declaring that we had no intention of modernizing the Pershing IA. Such a claim, I argued, would be factually correct, and if we continued to procrastinate, we could be held responsible for a delay in, or even the failure of, the INF negotiations.

In mid-August my wife and I spent a few days near Nice in the south of France. There I received a telephone message that the Soviet ambassador to Bonn, Yuli Kvitsinsky, urgently needed to speak with me, on orders from the Soviet Foreign Minister. The orders he had been given permitted no delay.

I offered to meet with him on August 18 or 19, and Kvitsinsky left for France. He flew to Marseilles, where a car from the local Soviet General Consulate met him and drove him to Théoule. His trip was made possible only with our assistance because— in a sense as a countermove to the limited movement imposed on Western diplomats in the Soviet Union—corresponding limitations were placed on Soviet diplomats in the Western nations. Thus the Soviet ambassador to Germany could not receive an immediate visa for France, where he was not accredited. The Soviet Embassy asked the West German Foreign Minister to intervene on their behalf, and my colleagues telephoned the French Foreign Ministry. Finally arriving in Théoule, Kvitsinsky told me the reason for his visit. Shevardnadze, he said, wanted to remind me of our conversation in Moscow and his promise to get in touch with me immediately if the INF negotiations seemed to be stalled, which was the current situation. The accord on the West's removal of short- and long-range intermediate nuclear forces could be finalized immediately—in other words, the double-zero option was on the verge of acceptance. But what was still missing was a positive statement by Bonn giving up the Pershing IA.

After adapting so extensively to the West's position, the Soviet Union could not now sign an agreement that did not include the Pershing IA. The United States saw the matter in exactly the same way; only Bonn was obstructive. Therefore Shevardnadze appealed to me to do all I could to allow this important step in disarmament to be finalized.

No one knew the history of our negotiations better than Yuli Kvitsinsky. What he had "considered" at the time of his legendary walk in the woods of 1982 with Paul Nitze was only a fraction of what was now on the table. Kvitsinsky did not seem happy with his government's present stand.

I would have liked to inform Shevardnadze immediately that we would comply. But I felt that I was not entitled to take that step, even though I was firmly resolved to bring about the double-zero option by relinquishing the Pershing IA missiles. The fixation on the Pershing IA placed the German attitude in a bad light, particularly since these missiles were of no strategic significance. We were overcoming Soviet superiority in the area of intermediate missiles, the political landscape was changing, and the new dynamic was accelerating—these were facts. The opportunities these facts offered could not and would not be missed. Still, I feared that it would not be easy to turn Bonn around.

After my conversation with the Soviet Ambassador in Théoule and my return to Bonn I immediately contacted the Chancellor. I briefed Kohl on what Kvitsinsky had said and offered him my analysis of the situation; as the minister responsible for disarmament and arms control, I also expressed my view. I pointed out very clearly that relinquishing the Pershing IA was in the spirit of the NATO double-zero option and was a necessity in the interest of both our country and West-East relations. For us to take the initiative rather than being forced by others to relinquish the Pershing IA seemed to me especially important. I argued that the agreement must not be allowed to fail because of West Germany's veto.

It appeared to me that those members of the CDU/CSU who were in favor of hanging on to the Pershing IA did not realize the consequences of their position. Under no conditions was I ready to jeopardize the double-zero option; in 1982 I had switched government coalitions in order to enforce both parts of the NATO double-track resolution. Now, only five years later, we could harvest the fruits of our determination and steadfastness. And all that should come to nought over this one issue? I was single-mindedly determined not to give in.

Helmut Kohl knew exactly where I stood. How would we look if the world learned that the Soviet Union was ready to dismantle all of its army's intermediate missiles but we were preventing an agreement between the superpowers, and only because of the Pershing IA, an outmoded military model without a future? In such a case, I impressed upon the Chancellor, Germany would have to take responsibility for the failure of arms policy, and whatever might hinder the policies of rapprochement in the future. I was, I declared, not prepared for such an outcome.

I found this conversation anything but easy. For weeks I had refrained from publicly addressing this issue because I did not want to put pressure on the Chancellor. Now, as I felt the closeness of Helmut Kohl to me as a human being and as a friend, I found the conversation both harder and easier.

Kohl did not agree with me, but he did not reject my view out of hand. Our talk ended without a clear outcome. Kohl only asked me not to make any public statements. I understood—or at least I hoped—that the Chancellor wanted to make such a statement himself, of his own free will. The impression that I had pressured him into the change of heart was to be avoided.

The following morning I was informed that the Chancellor would agree to the removal of the Pershing IA missiles. I was immensely relieved. I told Kohl that I considered it necessary to inform the Soviet Foreign Minister simultaneously with the public and that therefore I wanted to ask Ambassador Kvitsinsky to come to my office when the Chancellor announced his decision. He did so on August 26, 1987.

In terms of security policy, it seemed to me of the greatest significance that Western Europe be relieved from the threat of intermediate-range missiles and that our program for the NATO double-track resolution be carried out. At any rate, I could never be persuaded of the purely military point of view—for example, that without the Pershing IA missiles a rung on the military ladder would be missing.

The double-zero option also made sense because we had to consider it, as well as the INF Treaty, as an opportunity for fundamental political change in West-East relations; in a further step, it also served to demolish the Warsaw Pact's superiority in conventional weapons. To reject such an unusually far-reaching offer from the Soviet Union might have led to a massive backlash in West-East relations and a tremendous loss of confidence in West Germany.

On August 26 Helmut Kohl announced that under the right conditions he would be willing to relinquish the Pershing IA missiles. He told the press that the West German government had always made it clear that it desired successful INF negotiations between the United States and the Soviet Union; that it could take credit for maintaining a strong, reliable, and firm stand from the beginning of the discussions and thus making a significant contribution to the success in the Geneva negotiations that now seemed so close. He continued:

> As for the German Pershing IA missile systems with their nuclear warheads, which are under the sole control of the United States, they never were, or can be, subject to negotiations in Geneva. From the beginning the Soviet Union has known that negotiations in Geneva are solely about Soviet and American ground-launched nuclear systems. The Soviet demand for inclusion of the Pershing IA in the Geneva negotiations is therefore unfounded and an attempt to erect an artificial obstacle for reaching an INF agreement. . . . The Federal Government has further resolved constructively to contribute to the global dismantling of all intermediate nuclear systems with a range of between 500 and 5,000 kilometers.

If all Soviet and United States intermediate-range missiles were relinquished, Kohl announced, the Pershing IA would be not modernized but dismantled. At the same time he asked Moscow to refrain from modernizing its missiles with a range of less than 300 miles. He urgently insisted on negotiations on the short-range nuclear systems in Europe because, he said, the Federal Republic found it difficult to accept the present imbalance in systems with a range of between 60 and 300 miles.

I was extremely happy with the Chancellor's statement. The press was told that he had come to this decision entirely on his own—and that was important.

According to our agreement I invited Kvitskinsky to the Foreign Office, where I told him about the Chancellor's statement: "Even as we sit here, the following statement is being issued by the government." Then I read him the text the Chancellor was releasing at that moment.

Hindsight tells us that this century has rarely known a situation in which points of view and concerns changed so dramatically in a relatively short time as they did in regard to disarmament toward the end of the 1980s. The INF treaty not only increased the security of West Germany, it also acted as a catalyst for overcoming the East-West conflict. It reinforced Gorbachev's reform policies, and it eased political tension. Thus the political consequences of the disarmament agreement cannot be overestimated. At the same time we strengthened the ties between the United States and Europe and thus made a significant contribution to realistic policies of rapprochement with the East.

Still, after the INF treaty the West did not relinquish all options: The agreement did not ban cruise missiles and conventional launcher systems. The West could therefore continue to make use of its technological capabilities—if that should become necessary. In case of a return to the Cold War, or if for domestic reasons Gorbachev was unable to continue on his course, the West would still have the means to respond even within the terms of the treaties. Surprisingly there was little talk about short-range missiles or nuclear artillery ammunition within the discussion on peace in Germany, even though it was exactly the Germans who were threatened by these weapons. Nuclear warheads with a range no farther than the next city, among them nuclear artillery ammunition with the destructive power of the Hiroshima bomb, became more and more unacceptable to me in light of the changing situation in Central Europe, the result of Gorbachev's policies.

It is the goal of deterrence to prevent war, not to let it seem feasible or winnable. Deterrence was the only way to accomplish peace. Again and again I stated, "The point is not to win wars but to win peace." To me the discussion on a limited nuclear war that had started in the United States seemed extremely problematic as far as Europe was concerned. It was apt to unite opponents of the Alliance from the left and the right. Realizing the danger early on, Helmut Schmidt had returned to this issue time and again in conversations with our American friends. He also rejected the term *theater nuclear weapons*. The term alone implied that war was a stage with nuclear weapons as actors—which was unacceptable.

On December 7, 1987, the INF Treaty with its double-zero option was signed in Washington. It was a treaty of historic dimensions; precisely for that reason it must not be allowed to remain an isolated event. The momentum of the agreement had to be utilized; it must be made a springboard for a comprehensive disarmament process, showing the way. Within the framework of this general concept, the Federal Republic had specific concerns:

1. Standing at the frontier dividing West and East, West Germany in particular advocated the prompt beginning of negotiations on conventional stability in Europe.
2. The Federal Republic of Germany not only bore the principal burden of the West's conventional defense, it would also be the first victim of a conventional war in Europe.
3. The mandate to negotiate on conventional arms control must be made part of a balanced final document of the Vienna CSCE follow-up conference.
4. For the Federal Republic, the prompt global ban of chemical weapons was a foremost priority. As I mentioned time and again, in reality these were not weapons but "means to destroy humans and nature, which themselves needed to be destroyed." Within the Western Alliance's war-prevention strategy there should therefore be no room for chemical weapons.
5. Negotiations on the United States' and the Soviet Union's short-range nuclear weapons must lead to reductions to the same ceilings for both countries. That also served the demolition of Soviet superiority.

At the turn of 1987–1988 I outlined the agenda needed before a cooperative security policy could be attained:

1. Steps toward disarmament that would decrease superiorities and establish parity on a lower level in all sectors of the military balance of power.
2. Qualitative change in the structure of armed forces.
3. Efficient mechanisms for global political crisis management.
4. A network of confidence-building measures.
5. Multilateral global arms control agreements.
6. Abolition of preconceived notions of the enemy and demands for peaceful ways of thinking.
7. Cooperation in mutual aid.

For me December 7, 1987, was a day of deep satisfaction: Now the objectives of the NATO double-track resolution could be realized as they concerned arms control. Short- and long-range intermediate missiles were destroyed throughout the world. The treaty held political significance far beyond disarmament policy. It confirmed my earlier impression of Gorbachev, and it accelerated political developments. To reject this treaty would have been irresponsible, and not only in regard to security policy. It would also have put an abrupt halt to the dynamics of West-East relations, to the point where they might never be resumed.

9

The Struggle Against Modernizing Nuclear Short-Range Missiles

The Controversy Surrounding the Lance

It was not long before the new dynamics in international relations were again put to the test. The Lance, a short-range nuclear missile that was deployed in Germany, was to be modernized. This situation was more complicated for me than the double-zero option had been, since that was a solution the United States itself had advocated for a long time. When it came to modernization of the Lance, however, Washington and the CDU/CSU, our government coalition partner, acted as one.

In 1988 the question of when the Lance would be modernized became the center of discussions within NATO. At the same time there was a universal effort to handle the controversy discreetly and to avoid major disputes. For me personally the conflict escalated in two ways: One, the Alliance was split; and two, it seemed that I differed in certain respects not only with the CDU/CSU but also with the Chancellor. I repeatedly voiced my objections to the modernization plans and cautioned against straining disarmament negotiations by an ill-timed modernization of short-range nuclear weapons and by closing the door on long-term policies of disarmament and détente. On December 7, 1988, I declared to the Bundestag that the government did not intend to make hasty, individual decisions on the modernization of weapons systems. Signals of this kind, I added, were not now on the agenda. "At this time there is no need for us to take any action with regard to the modernization of such systems as the Lance, which retain their currency until 1995."

The year 1988 was defined by this second, utterly superfluous discussion about modernization. I demanded an overall plan even as I requested follow-up conferences for shorter-range missiles. In addition, I tried to delay any decision on modernizing the Lance. On November 17, 1988, the Chancellor stated to NATO conference: "We cannot consider a zero option for short-range nuclear weapons, since such a choice would mark a crucial step toward the denuclearization of Europe, which in my opinion would not advance peace but would pose a threat to the future."

The North Atlantic Alliance's concern about denuclearization increased fears that West Germany would politically drift Eastward. The West exploited possibility of a neutralized West Germany to paint a fearful image that could be erased by such measures as Prime Minister Thatcher's "fire wall." I and my political allies saw no sense in such arguments. Was the modernization of the Lance really to become the litmus test for West Germany's loyalty to the alliance?

There was no real need to discuss the Lance at all at that time, since it was already established that the missile would remain serviceable well into the 1990s, no decision on modernization on the part of the Alliance was called for. The decision to go ahead with the production of the Pershing II had been made unilaterally by the United States as well; NATO entered on this decision only at a much later time. Lance could have been handled in the same way. To decide on the introduction of a successor model in the early 1990s would have been quite adequate.

And, I firmly believed that by then the political situation would have changed so drastically that modernization would be an anachronism. Even now modernization was not appropriate to the political climate—all the more reason, I thought, why matters should be allowed to run their normal course. At the beginning of

233

the 1990s we would know if our expectations of détente would come to fruition. Thatcher, however, insisted that a decision on modernization be made at once.

In the summer of 1988 I had already concluded that dramatic changes were on the horizon in Eastern Europe, though it was impossible to predict the precise form they would take. It was clear to me that the process of democratization in the Soviet Union, Poland, and Hungary would expand and intensify. Sooner or later it would touch East Germany and Czechoslovakia as well. I assumed that mass demonstrations would begin in East Germany, where West German television (and with it news from the West), could be received almost everywhere, so that its citizens were better informed about what was happening elsewhere than were the inhabitants of Czechoslovakia, for example.

In 1988 solutions to long-smoldering conflicts gradually emerged, not only in Europe but globally—in the Persian Gulf as in Afghanistan, in Cambodia no less than in South Africa. East-West détente, which would soon put an end to the Cold War and lead to the collapse of Communism, visibly began to bear fruit. This promising development was the reason for my decision at this time to say no, without ifs, ands, or buts, to the question of modernizing the Lance. New armament decisions must not be allowed to dash all our hopes.

In June 1988 I made my first public appearance in East Germany—public, that is, only in the sense of a performance before the press, since no one else was admitted. In Potsdam, the old garrison town outside Berlin, I spoke to an international congress organized by an American institute. Addressing basic political principles, I began by noting that, "I am deeply moved to be allowed to speak at an international event—thirty-six years after leaving the GDR—as a member of the Federal Government. The GDR is the part of Germany where, in Halle on the Saale, stands the house where I was born, where I was raised. Here is my home."

I made a kind of public avowal of my values. "In 1952," I continued, "I made a decision in favor of the Federal Republic of Germany and thus for its political and social order. The Letter on German Unity, written for the Federal Republic, rooted in the Basic Law and attached to the Basic Treaty, expresses our vision for the future of the German nation." In Potsdam, on East German soil, I reiterated my belief in German unity. This unity, however, could be achieved only by way of Europe: "What is needed is a bold plan that secures peace in Europe. Our membership in the community of Western democracies, the European Community, and the Western Alliance, has allowed West Germans to make responsible use of the freedom we regained on May 8, 1945. Thus we have entered the closest possible connection among nations; we are connected by shared values." I linked the community of values with new avenues in foreign policy: "What is needed is the unfolding, democratization, and humanization of societies, the realization of the United Nations' Human Rights Act and other guarantees like those made by the signatories to the Helsinki Final Act. Each nation must agree to be measured by its actions toward other nations and toward its own citizens." I then appealed to East Germany's leadership to introduce movement in a democratic direction, and alluding to a vision voiced by Gorbachev, I said, "We want a house with wide-open doors, a house of unfettered communication, a Europe of freedom and self-determination."

The Potsdam visit of June 1988 touched me deeply. I also took the opportunity to visit the Nikolai Church, which stands at a right angle to the old city hall. After the turning point of 1989–1990, one of the church's ministers approached me and reminded me of my 1988 visit. And in 1990 a woman told me that she had waved to me in 1988, and only a few minutes later a policeman had requested her identification and written down the particulars. Subsequently, she was given a warning at her workplace: If she was ever caught in a similar situation again, she would be fired. And a reporter told me that he had been barred from attending my speech, but with the help of a technician, he had been able to listen from backstage. Even looking back now, I am still deeply moved: For the first time I spoke in the GDR in my capacity as foreign minister, if not absolutely out in the open, at least to an audience of international journalists. In the summer of 1988 I became more than ever absorbed in the German and European situation. What could we expect? What was going to happen?

In September 1988, at another meeting with Foreign Minister Shevardnadze, I raised for the first time the issue of what would happen in case of riots and mass demonstrations in East Germany. I told Shevardnadze that I foresaw highly dramatic events, and I added, "This time, we in the West will respond differently to the use of Soviet tanks than we did on June 17, 1953." I wanted my Soviet counterpart to understand that the use of military force in East Germany would fundamentally alter the equation.

In this climate of drastic political changes, modernizing the Lance missile would have been the most inappropriate action possible. Fortunately, by now I had found more and more allies, even within the alliance, who shared my feelings. The governments of Italy, Belgium, Denmark, and Greece were skeptical as well; again it was the "frontline nations" that spoke out for prompt short-range nuclear force (SNF) negotiations and against modernizing the Lance missile. At this time there was a need for a comprehensive security program, and such a program had to be realized and supported in the West by bold, congruent security decisions. Just as, at the end of the 1960s, the Harmel Report had revolutionized NATO's definition of what an alliance is, so its security program needed to be in line with the latest state of affairs, now that we were on the threshold of political changes in Europe.

A foundation for a lasting peaceful order in Europe, such as the Harmel Report called for, must be established in cooperation with the Soviet Union and the nations of Central and Eastern Europe. A modernization of missile systems, however, would obstruct the imperative modernization of political thinking in East and West. In order to head off objections, especially in France and the United States, I always emphasized that West Germany rejected unilateral political moves, repeatedly stressing that Germany belonged to the community of Western democracies and was a staunch member of the Western Alliance. I was convinced that this rejection of a policy of neutrality was crucial: Neutrality would have made Germany a factor of uncertainty in Europe and subject to political power struggle between the West and the East. Yet especially at a time when we had every reason for feeling genuine hope, even hope that the division of Europe and of Germany could be overcome, there simply was no room for neutrality and nationalism. It is true that in 1988 I did not foresee that the revolutionary changes of 1989–1990 would be followed by a new wave of nationalism everywhere in Europe.

At NATO's foreign ministers' conference in June 1988 in

Reykjavík, important approaches to a coherent, comprehensive program of arms control and disarmament had been elaborated. The program took into account the opportunities for profound transformations in West-East relations that had ensued both from the new thinking in Soviet foreign policy and from new actions: The Soviets had removed their intermediate missiles—an area where they had superiority—and introduced preliminary inspections, engaged in unilateral disarmament, and retreated from Afghanistan. These moves had historic significance.

I considered the winter of 1988–1989 the most difficult period to date of my foreign ministry. On the one hand I was hoping that the political climate in Moscow and Eastern Europe would warm up. Perhaps we would be granted an opportunity not only to advance arms control and détente but finally also to overcome the division of Europe and of Germany. On the other hand I was extremely concerned with the desire in Washington and London to modernize the Lance missiles. A decision in favor of modernization would have hobbled West-East relations in general and the reform movements in Central and Eastern Europe in particular. But disagreement persisted within the Alliance. With the exception of Hans van den Broek, the foreign minister of the Netherlands, Continental Europeans shared my opinion that this was not the time to decide on modernization. Yet we were reasonable enough not to demand the opposite—absolute refusal to modernize. All we asked was that the issue be left off the agenda of the NATO summit scheduled for the following May.

The course of international events confirmed my assessment of the possibilities and consequences of Gorbachev's policies. My admonition not to allow this historic opportunity to pass us by, to take Gorbachev seriously and at his word, had been quickly followed up—an historic rarity. My Davos speech of February 1, 1987, was not yet two years in the past.

For me personally, 1988 was a sad and difficult year. In March 1987, when my mother had joined us in celebrating my sixtieth birthday, she had been her old, lively self. But during the course of 1988 we saw her energy ebbing away. It was hard to recognize the active, happy woman of old. Only occasionally could we glimpse a spark of life, and at such moments we hoped that her vitality would prevail.

On the morning of Thursday, October 13, 1988, I was in a meeting with Laurent Fabius, president of the National Assembly of France, when we were interrupted by the dreaded telephone call. My wife said: "Your mother has passed away." Fifteen minutes later I stood at the foot of her bed. People speak of the dignity of death; it was mirrored in her face.

As a young man I would not have believed that a man more than sixty years old would feel so much grief at his mother's death. This loss marked a major break in my life, it touched me more deeply than my father's death when I was only nine. I had not realized the full meaning of my father's death until years later. Now I had lost my mother, the person who—apart from brief periods—had walked with me along my life's way. Many memories surfaced on that day, above all the worry and fear my mother had had to endure because of me. Much had been asked of her: There were the war years, when she was afraid for her son; then my illness (which lingered for a decade), and later my heart attack; and until I left Halle, the additional fear that I might voice my political opinion too freely. "Be a little more careful, my boy!"

"Boy," is what she called me all my life. And to the end of her life she experienced and endured all the highs and lows of a politician's life. I still remember vividly a reception I hosted in New York in the mid-1970s in connection with the United Nations General Assembly, where she exchanged anecdotes with Henry Kissinger's parents on how to cope with public criticism of your son.

Only a day after her death I resumed the ordinary daily routine of a foreign minister's life—there was no time for reflection. My mother's funeral on Tuesday, October 18, 1988, was attended by family and many old and new friends, the same people who had come to celebrate her major birthdays, the last had been her eighty-fifth birthday. On this day they came to pay their last respects.

In late 1988 I had firmly resolved to vote against modernization at the present time. I did so in good conscience; I had always advocated that the objective of negotiations be ceilings, not a zero option in the area of short-range missiles. I wanted to bring about negotiations on conditions acceptable to all members of the alliance, for the sake of our common goal—eliminating the Soviets' massive superiority in that area. During the holidays and early in 1989 I was deeply troubled by the question of where my own government would stand on this issue. The direction the discussion would take within the governing coalition was just as uncertain as future arguments within the Western Alliance, since both Washington and London argued in favor of a vote on modernization.

When the Soviet foreign minister and I discussed the political situation at length near the end of the third CSCE follow-up conference on January 18, 1989, in Vienna, I was handed a major surprise: Shevardnadze mentioned that abolishing weapons was a less burning issue than was overcoming the division of Europe. This was a new, even a revolutionary signal. I was not certain, however, whether all of our partners realized the revolutionary nature of the Soviets' attitude. At least Shevardnadze was placing his country's foreign policy in direct opposition to the isolationist policy that Gromyko had always represented in our talks. Against this background the demand for a decision on modernizing the Lance appeared all the more anachronistic. On the other hand, I failed to understand how Shevardnadze could claim that the Soviet Union had made use of all available information resources in East Germany—and I might imagine that these were numerous—and come to the conclusion that the situation in that country was stable. He could not, he told me firmly, see anything whatever to substantiate my prediction of mass demonstrations in the summer of 1989.

I pointed out to Shevardnadze the East's massive superiority in short-range missiles: a ratio of no less than 1,365 to 88. I urgently appealed to the Soviet Union at least to take a first unilateral step.

In order to make this request, I took every opportunity to talk to representatives of the Warsaw Pact, including East Germany. It was my impression that Shevardnadze sympathized with us, yet I was hardly comforted by his remark that the East had already completed the work of modernization.

In my Vienna speech I criticized police brutality against activists in East Germany and Czechoslovakia. Since Shevardnadze had already mentioned the apparent corrosion of the Iron Curtain, I now called for the Berlin Wall to be demolished. It was, I said, an anachronism, no longer appropriate to the times.

While gathered in the capital of Austria we—NATO's foreign ministers—also said good-bye to our colleague George Shultz, who had won our full respect and was liked by all. I had come to appreciate this serious, trustworthy statesman; I still do.

Two days before the new American secretary of state, James Baker, arrived for his first official visit to Bonn on February 12, 1989, Kohl, in an interview with the *Financial Times,* suggested that the vote on modernization be tabled; since the Lance would be serviceable until 1995, no decision was needed until 1991–1992. In the same article Kohl also deplored various attempts by other members to make German agreement to modernization a loyalty test. These were necessary statements, and they were clear enough; I was relieved.

It was politically important for the West German government to take a united and unambiguous stand, since, as I had publicly pointed out time and again, Europe was facing crucial transformations. NATO must not go against the tide of history to obstruct, halt, or reverse a process that was putting events within reach for which the West had been waiting for decades. This may have been the real political breaking point between proponents and opponents of modernizing the Lance. As so frequently, it was the old opposition of traditionalists and evolutionists.

Talks Between Washington and Bonn

Immediately upon his arrival James Baker, the new United States secretary of state, and I retired to the guest residence for a confidential talk. I had already come to know James Baker well during years of collaboration in other functions. During this conversation I emphasized the special nature of German-American relations. For us, I said, this relationship was of vital importance, and it was with this in mind that I would like us to work together. I continued by stating that I was completely opposed to attacks on one another conducted in the press—an allusion to critical remarks in American and German newspapers that had clearly come from American government sources. Baker, who understood the reference, agreed with me and surprised me with a very cordial offer: We were being so formal, addressing one another as "Minister" and "Secretary"—would it not be better to use first names? He was looking forward to close personal relations with me so that he could pick up the telephone whenever he felt such a need. He hoped I would feel free to call him as well. I was pleased at the gesture; though shifting into a more familiar mode would not solve our problems (both of us would remain obligated to our own countries' interests), a more casual interaction between two people can also facilitate dealing with problems.

Next we focused on the issue of an overall program for NATO, which we believed was to be issued at the NATO summit in May. We ended the conversation on a relaxed and cordial note. I drove home feeling that I had gauged Baker correctly from the start. I had never made a secret of the fact that I liked him. Evidently he, too, was eager to bring about a harmonious collaboration.

The official talks began the following day. Baker again spoke to the subject of the NATO summit scheduled for May: If Gorbachev were really to visit Bonn in June, President George Bush would prefer the NATO summit take place in Brussels during the last two weeks of May. This change was agreeable to Prime Minister Thatcher, even if it meant relocating the NATO foreign ministers' spring conference in London. I replied that we also believed that it was extremely important for the NATO summit to occur before Secretary General Gorbachev's visit, since we were on the verge of reaching major agreements with the Soviet Union, and we were reluctant to commit ourselves to anything unless it was based in a joint allied policy. Baker concurred but again addressed the topic of a general program. This issue presented a problem for his administration's relationship with Congress: At this time, before the NATO summit, we needed to arrive at appropriate wording to cover modernization of short-range missiles. Because he believed that modernization should not be a basic issue, he hoped that after our talks he and the Chancellor could issue a joint statement to the effect that West Germany had not changed its position on this matter.

I did not conceal my astonishment; had it not been a faction in Washington and London that had treated the modernization of short-range missiles as a loyalty test? The East's massive superiority in short-range missiles, I replied, was an anachronism, and I wanted to see negotiations dealing with this imbalance at the earliest possible moment. I had found it disconcerting that our allies had passively accepted this situation for years.

That Jim Baker explicitly refused to turn the issue of modernization into a test of our loyalty was a sign of progress, and I welcomed it. His predecessor, George Shultz, had never taken that tack, either. My American counterpart assured me that he would like to help us solve the problem. I mentioned that the modernization of nuclear artillery was just beginning: That effort, too, was not an easy matter for Germans to swallow.

Furthermore, I continued, negotiations on short-range missiles had been voted on in Reykjavík. Especially now, I said, this resolution was particularly important to us, because Soviet short-range missiles were a threat to Germany more than to any other country. I pointed out that NATO had only 88 systems with 700 missiles, which were matched by a far greater number of Soviet missiles. Therefore we were pushing for arms control negotiations with the goal outlined in Reykjavík: to reduce the unequal arsenals to the same ceiling.

The idea that had originated in London—to erect a "fire wall" against negotiations—had come out of thin air, I noted. At its 1988 summit NATO had agreed to keep armed forces at their present strength wherever necessary. I was certain that Baker would remember that during his talks in Washington the new chairman of the FDP, Count Otto Lambsdorff, had pointed out that a decision on modernizing the Lance was not necessary until 1991–1992; the West German government was still committed to that date. The Chancellor, I added, had just confirmed the deadline of 1991–1992 in the *Financial Times*.

I then touched on the issue of our reliability and steadfastness, which were unquestionable. I told Baker that I had repeatedly demonstrated these virtues in the course of my political life; others still had to prove themselves. I was referring not only to my active support of the NATO double-track resolution but also to my decision to leave East Germany in 1952. I tried to explain to Baker that my decision had not been easy: "I do not need any tutoring in steadfastness."

Again Baker turned the focus on the overall program. "We must put in a lot of work in order to show some results at the summit in May." I agreed and suggested that we solve these questions in close contact between our administrations. What mattered was that both sides were interested in the overall program. During our conversation Baker also gained greater understanding for the case I was advocating.

□   □   □   □

Baker and I met again early in March, on the occasion of a CSCE conference in Vienna. I noticed that in our talk he did not address the issue of short-range missiles. Was it no longer important? Perhaps Washington—mindful of the many advocates of modernization in the CDU/CSU and of the position of NATO's current secretary general, the German Manfred Wörner, who also supported modernization—simply assumed that we would arrive at the outcome it was wishing for. I thought the latter more likely.

In my speech on the morning of March 7 I called for a transition from power politics to a politics of responsibility in Europe. I endorsed Shevardnadze's view that the present negotiations were really about overcoming the division of Europe, and that, I said, was the real issue. Entirely in the spirit of the Western Alliance's Harmel Report I said, "We are at the start of a new leg on the road to a peaceful order in Europe, or—as we could put it just as well—on the road to a common European house." I reminded the audience of the values on which this peaceful order must be built; it was critical that freedom of speech and freedom of travel be realized.

Turning to the United States government, I welcomed the announcement that the chemical weapons deployed in West Germany would be withdrawn; this significant step completed the shift away from a pattern of thinking which could only have originated in the occupation period. Did anyone in the West really intend to use chemical weapons in defiance of international law? Hardly. Why, then, keep these weapons in Germany? The answer given again and again—that if the East were to use chemical weapons, we would need to have a response capability—presupposed a mechanism incompatible with our tactics of deterrence.

It was much more essential to protect our troops against chemical weapons as much as possible by giving them equipment and training, and by providing medical and technical aid. No one in the West could seriously consider using chemical weapons on home soil in case of an attack. The strength of Western defense lay precisely in the fact that, thanks to the tactics of deterrence, various options were available in response to an attack. That strategy was the opposite of a "reaction mechanism": conventional response to conventional attack, chemical response to chemical attack, and so forth.

□　□　□　□

The debate on short-range nuclear missiles continued throughout the spring of 1989. France was willing to postpone a vote on modernization until 1992, so as to have time to arrive at a more accurate assessment of the situation regarding East-West relations. Europe was changing dramatically. Civil-rights activists in East Germany were becoming more and more outspoken; the same held true for Czechoslovakia; Hungary had long had a reformist leadership, which stressed the term *reform* and dampened *socialism;* in Poland the situation had changed much more drastically. It seemed as if overcoming the division of Europe had become a specific goal of the Soviet leaders' policies.

The West was simply waiting; but there must be no misreading of this wait-and-see attitude. I would fight adamantly to prevent such an error, both in the administration and in the coalition. And it was no less important for us to avoid unnecessary tension in the Western Alliance.

Of course, the key to solving these problems lay in Washington. If we could persuade the United States to be on our side, London and The Hague would follow. We had long since won over the other European nations. Foreign Minister Giulio Andreotti of Italy made no secret of where his sympathies lay, any more than did my friends Uffe Ellemann-Jensen of Denmark or Thorvald Stoltenberg of Norway. Further, Spain, the United Kingdom, Greece, Brussels, and Luxembourg also sent me encouraging signals. Of course officially some of these nations still held back because they were not certain of Bonn's ultimate decision—or the United States', for that matter.

The question of what position Washington would ultimately take weighed heavily on me. I thought that the closest possible tie to the United States and an unambiguous joint stand of the Western Alliance was the indispensable basis of a successful Eastern policy. Especially now, in the most promising phase of West-East relations, we must not introduce further West-West tension. I had to find a way to persuade Bush and Baker.

First, however, I succeeded in persuading my own administration of my view. On April 18, after weeks of hard struggle the leaders of the government coalition agreed to a German position concerning NATO's overall program for security policy:

- The development of a new short-range missile is and remains a concern solely of the United States.
- The obligation, detailed in the NATO resolution of Reykjavík, to modernize weapons systems wherever necessary, remains in force.
- Should it ever become necessary, a vote on the Lance missile will not be imminent before 1991–1992.
- Until that time the West shall negotiate with the East, while also continuing talks in Vienna on conventional stability in Europe, on equal ceilings for systems up to 500 kilometers.

I had prevailed in another important phase of disarmament.

Certain groups in the CDU/CSU were now demanding that we relinquish the third zero option for short-range missiles. Harsh debates broke out within the coalition; in the end my position was essentially accepted, after I too had shown flexibility in the SNF negotiations: On the Reykjavík agreement and negotiations, I agreed to change *parallel and soonest* to *soon* in the coalition agreement. This rephrasing extended the time frame somewhat. We immediately informed our allies: Helmut Kohl telephoned the American President and agreed that Defense Minister Gerhard Stoltenberg and I would fly to Washington on Monday, April 24, to explain the Federal Government's position. I was not happy about this trip.

The United States did not reverse its stand on modernization until later; in any case, by April 24 the reversal had not yet occurred. I therefore considered our trip to Washington a tactical and psychological mistake. As matters stood, I cautioned the Chancellor, our visit could not, at this time, be of any use.

As expected, we were received coolly and with some reserve. President Bush was away. As we conferred with Secretary of State James Baker and Secretary of Defense Richard Cheney, the latter left abruptly to deliver a speech at the National Defense University. As I learned later, he made these statements, among others: "We must not fall into this dangerous trap [he meant the SNF negotiations]. One of the Kremlin's primary goals remains the denuclearization of Europe. Given this goal, the Alliance must maintain the will to resist the call for a third zero." In our talks Baker also informed us through his speaker that at this time disarmament talks on short-range missiles were a mistake. The Bush administration was obviously not willing to accede to our requests.

During a break in negotiations, which we spent on the State Department's terrace, I took the bull by the horns, suggesting that we should talk matters over calmly and objectively right here and now. I explained that such ways of mutual dealings within the Alliance and West German–American relations were unacceptable; that Stoltenberg and I were two ministers in a government formed out of the desire to enforce the NATO double-track resolution; I had even risked my political career to this end. West Germany, I remarked, also knew the meaning of security. I believe that this conversation on the terrace affected our American colleagues to some extent.

But as predicted, our visit had no concrete results. That Secretary Cheney left in the middle of a conversation to deliver a speech, and that he announced his intention to do so beforehand, remains an unpleasant memory.

In retrospect, however, it can still be said that, as disagreeable as this trip was, it forged an indispensable link in the chain of our meetings, which ultimately led to the accord at the NATO summit in Brussels. At the time I nevertheless considered it a mistake, and I would certainly consider it a mistake again if the same situation were to arise.

The paradox of the situation in April 1989 was that nearly all areas of military power had become the topic of disarmament negotiations: intercontinental strategic missiles, chemical weapons, conventional arms, and intermediate-range missiles—only short-range missiles were excluded. Yet it was precisely the Soviet short-range missiles that posed such an enormous threat to West Germany. Or, to put it more bluntly, the other allies were not within range of these missiles and were not threatened by them.

President von Weizsäcker, whom I regularly briefed on my views and my plans in matters of foreign and security policy, took a stand on the issue of short-range missiles during an official visit to Denmark in April 1989. The Danes were good friends, and the timing was crucial, since the Danish government—like most other nations in Continental Europe, including West Germany—was critical of the modernization of the Lance. In Copenhagen von Weizsäcker openly stated:

The Struggle Against Modernizing Nuclear Missiles

After speaking with the appropriate members of the Danish government, I am pleased to find that we agree on the problems to be tackled at the next NATO summit in Brussels and within the Atlantic Alliance as a whole. The German position is in accord with the resolutions NATO passed in 1987 in Reykjavík by the foreign ministers and reaffirmed in 1988 by the heads of government. There are good reasons for casting out the myth of German isolation when it comes to taking a stand on issues. For the rest, it is good when these Continental European members express their views on the position that is the predominant one in Continental Europe; that is, if NATO's Continental European members themselves voice them rather than letting representatives who have no power of representation speak for them. In these matters we have reached an agreement I find satisfactory.

Responding to a relevant question during the ensuing press conference, Von Weizsäcker stated clearly, "I spoke, not about modernization, but about the German position at the upcoming summit in general. The distinction is an important one, since the summit will deal not only with modernization but with the total program—in other words, with the question of how NATO will remain true to its own principle that defines two inseparable elements in NATO's security policy: defense and détente. I merely commented on the fact that here and there an impression was created that the German position was unique. Such is not the case. The German position is in accord not only with the specific NATO resolutions but also with the expressed opinions we find among most of our partners here on the Continent, including the nation that is playing host to me right now."

The German press paid great attention to this statement. WEIZ-SÄCKER'S COURAGE, one headline proclaimed; another one read, IS HE ALLOWED TO DO THAT?; yet another talked of PLAYING WITH THE TRUMP CARD; a fourth newspaper's comment read, "Strong, with uncommon clarity." "Is he allowed to do that?"—that was the crucial question. With his statement Richard von Weizsäcker, whose office, according to the German Basic Law, is mostly ceremonial, had staked his international reputation on our disarmament policy, and yet he did not overstep the bounds of his office; even those who accused him of just such a transgression at the time subsequently realized that his assessment had been correct.

Once again it was the President who had found the right word at the right time and in the right place.

I was witnessing a president who acted because he considered it his duty and responsibility to stand by those who were unwilling to risk all the accomplishments of German treaty policy and the Western policy of détente for the sake of the issue of modernization—especially at a point in time at which the opportunity to overcome the division of Europe was tangibly close. The signal von Weizsäcker sent in Copenhagen was a significant step on the road to further détente between West and East and to German unity.

In the National Interest

After the government coalition had adopted my position on the modernization of the Lance missiles, however, the conflict within the Alliance remained. Therefore I left no doubt that the German position in this matter was firm. In a statement of April 27, 1989, to the Bundestag I thought it best to summon up my full personal responsibility: "Members of the federal government swear an oath that they will dedicate their full powers to the welfare of the German people. The obligation resulting from this oath does not end at the border that cuts through Germany. The responsibility thus incurred does not exclude the region, the town where I was born, or the people of East Germany—no, my responsibility includes these people. It is not Sunday-morning sermons that disclose our serious intentions for the German nation, it is the daily struggle to strengthen peace and stability and human rights in Europe, the struggle for cooperation and disarmament. The requirement of peace embodied in our Basic Law applies to all the people of Europe."

This reference made the rejection of the modernization of short-range missiles an issue of national interest. It was my aim to convince our friends in Washington and London that not only I was right, but most important, that Foreign Minister Hans-Dietrich Genscher would under no circumstances submit to a vote for modernization at this time. As with the double-zero option, a majority of the Bundestag now backed me on this topic as well.

In the same address I noted that West Germans, situated as we were at the border between West and East, did not lightly decide on preventing the deployment of new short-range nuclear missiles: "Nowhere is the East's superiority as great as in short-range missiles. Therefore it is in the West's vital security interest to overcome this superiority."

At the same I was eager to reassure friends in the United States, to whom we owed so much, whose Berlin airlift of 1948–1949 had never been forgotten, and whose contribution to European security was irreplaceable: "Americans have no need to be concerned if we pause to reflect anew. Fear would only be warranted if we did not reflect. To reflect and ponder a decision on new nuclear weapons is an expression of responsibility. It is anything but a sign of weakness, and it should not be criticized as such. It has conferred honor on our country's citizens, and it confers honor on all those who bear political responsibility.

"This century has seen German political aims quite different from the goal of friendship with all of Europe," I concluded. "After two murderous world wars and decades of confrontation between West and East, today Europe has the historic opportunity of creating the foundation for lasting peace on the whole Continent. We, as Germans, bear a special responsibility in this effort. In 1945 the French diplomat and poet Paul Claudel wrote, 'Germany does exist not to divide peoples but to make the different nations surrounding it realize that they cannot live without one another.'" I also reminded my listeners that these new missiles were directed not only against the Germans in the GDR but also against the Poles and the Czechs and the Slovaks, who had once been the victims of German aggression.

I wanted us to fulfill our mission for peace when it came to modernization as well. To repeat: In the spring of 1989 we had to be careful not to destroy any positive outlook, though without relinquishing our political options regarding arms control. Since at this time it was impossible to predict reliably what the political and security situation would be in the early and middle 1990s, it made no sense to settle on a successor weapons system as early as 1989 if a vote could wait until 1992 or even until 1996 without creating a security problem.

The day after the foreign-policy debate in the Bundestag I received the new American ambassador, Vernon Walters, whom I already knew well, on his inaugural visit. He seized the opportunity to try to make me change my mind about modernization.

Especially since I held him in high regard, I was sorry that I could not agree with him on this issue. He presupposed that the two alliances were in continuing opposition, making an immediate vote on modernization necessary, whereas I was expecting a new popular uprising that very same year. Only rarely does history decide so promptly who is right and who is wrong.

On April 30 the Chancellor met with the British Prime Minister in the Palatinate. Insisting that the short-range nuclear missiles were "absolutely and vitally important" to current NATO strategy, Thatcher claimed that relinquishing these weapons would be devastating for the Alliance. She strongly rejected all suggestions aimed at removing the short-range weapons. These proposals, she argued, would be acceptable neither to the military nor to the public.

Alfred Dregger, the majority leader of the CDU/CSU, supported my position in the current debate—"Mrs. Thatcher and her country are in the fortunate position of never being the target of nuclear weapons with a range of less than three hundred miles." In an interview he stated that he hoped for a reduction of short-range missiles "on both sides to an equal minimum of less than NATO's current level." Dregger noted that he found it astonishing that the German attitude was viewed as a sign of weakness, of "Gorbimania," or an attempt to gain electoral votes, and he added that he was disconcerted to notice how reluctant some of the Western allies were to acknowledge the strategic situation of a people "which in Europe is the only one that is divided and through which the military border between East and West runs."

The Political Background of the Lance Debate

A few weeks before the NATO summit in May 1989 the United States and the United Kingdom were still pleading for an immediate modernization of the Lance missiles. At the same time it became ever more obvious that the great majority of member nations agreed with our call for immediate SNF negotiations. Most members were opposed to a rash and ill-timed vote for modernization.

On May 12 Secretary of State James Baker attended a foreign

ministers' meeting in Brussels to report to the Allies on his visit to Moscow, where short-range missiles had been discussed. Afterward we spoke in private in one of the large conference rooms on the ground floor of NATO headquarters, sitting next to each other at the corner of a table large enough to hold forty. I firmly explained my views to Baker.

My arguments, I felt, made an impression on him: A vote on modernization was not necessary at this time. I insisted that the Alliance should, therefore, not decide in the negative but simply table any vote. Instead we should ask ourselves who the potential aggressor would be. Certainly not East Germany, Poland, or Czechoslovakia, which were within the range of these missiles. If anyone, the Soviet Union was the potential aggressor—even though I was convinced, I said, that such an attack was no longer likely. Be that as it may; the Soviet Union, which might emerge as the aggressor, was beyond the range of the short-range missiles; yet these weapons systems were not even to be deployed in Turkey, the territory from which the Soviet Union could be targeted. The plan made no sense at all.

Baker was visibly impressed. Nevertheless, he countered, "The Alliance, particularly the British, is exerting great pressure to vote for modernization." My reply was dispassionate but straightforward: "NATO is like a public corporation. At the stockholders' meeting the majority of shares decides. May I remind you that England has only few more heavy tanks than does the Netherlands. Germany, on the other hand, has several times as many heavy tanks. If you want me to, I can show you Germany's contribution to NATO in heavy tanks, compared to other nations. All we are insisting on is that an option not be eliminated."

I explained that, until we came to a definitive decision, we could make better use of our resources by promoting détente, while we could do what was necessary for security later but still in good time—unless by then the situation had changed altogether. In other words, even if events in the Soviet Union had gone worse than we expected, we would still have had an opportunity to modernize the Lance. I did not, therefore, ask that the plan of modernization be abandoned altogether; I merely pleaded for time before making a decision.

The will to independence and democracy in Europe had developed such momentum that it could not be stopped, provided that the West responded appropriately. There was no way to foretell what the East German leaders and their National People's Army would do if confronted with mass demonstrations. Would Soviet units be ordered into action? Would East Germany mobilize the National People's Army, and if they did, what would be the Soviet Union's reaction? If we wanted to prevent a violent escalation of events, the situation must not be exacerbated.

In all fairness it must be said that, as far as East-West cooperation and multilateral arms control and disarmament policy were concerned, the GDR, within the options available to it, acted responsibly. In those years the country did not behave like an agitator—or at least no longer did so. Of course the Wall, the barbed wire, and the repression of its own people, made its politics unacceptable. But the more East Germany was drawn into a responsible West-East policy, the less cause there was to fear that it would become an obstacle to Gorbachev's foreign policy—provided we did not hand its hard-liners a reason to tighten the domestic reins, using outside and security pretexts as an excuse.

The transition of power in the Soviet Union, which became increasingly apparent, could occur only in a climate of trust and West-East détente. This was another reason why I considered the preparations for Gorbachev's visit early in the summer of 1989 of such tremendous importance. Foreign Minister Shevardnadze obviously took a similar view. For this reason alone the call for modernization was a mistake: Events in the Communist countries needed to draw their stimulus and momentum from their own people. It was up to the West to provide stable conditions for these unfolding events; tension and confrontation would only increase repression.

Immediately after my talk with Baker I returned to Bonn to welcome Foreign Minister Shevardnadze. The following morning, May 13, the delegations met for first discussions at the Venusberg, the site of the Foreign Office.

As always, all the participants were seated in the comfortable armchairs of the Great Salon, constituting a fairly large discussion group. Shevardnadze suggested that he and I have a brief preliminary talk. I agreed and led him into the adjoining room, the library, formerly the private study of Willy Brandt, who occupied it when his office was at the Venusberg, first when he was foreign minister, then when he was chancellor. Shevardnadze immediately turned to the core problem: "In New York you mentioned possible developments in East Germany. I told you then that we took a different view from yours. In the meantime we've arrived at a new assessment of the situation in East Germany and are trying to be of help there." This statement was of the utmost importance. Now the context of the conference on the German-Soviet communiqué became clear: The Soviet leadership had realized that dramatic events were unfolding in East Germany.

During the discussions that followed, Shevardnadze brushed aside the skepticism of his staff and was amenable to our suggestions regarding the wording of the communiqué. Thus the impressive German-Soviet Declaration, issued in June on the occasion of Gorbachev's visit to Bonn, became a reality. It served to demonstrate Moscow's changed attitude regarding a new political order in Europe and made it clear that the Soviet Union regarded the Federal Republic of Germany as its most important European partner.

I seized the occasion offered by the FDP's party convention in Cologne, which took place on the eve of the NATO summit, to express once more my objections to modernization of the Lance. It was my last opportunity to speak in public before the crucial conference.

The unanimous and resolute way my party supported their country's foreign minister at this convention was impressive. Their position also served as a signal to the upcoming NATO summit conference. At home and abroad the FDP thus made it clear that under no circumstances must a return to the old arms race be permitted; this also indicated that in West Germany there would be no parliamentary majority for such a policy.

Decision at the Brussels NATO Summit:
Washington and Bonn Join Forces

Thus invigorated, on May 29 I went to Brussels for the NATO summit. At the great plenary session the Chancellor suggested that the issue of modernization be dealt with by the foreign ministers; from his perspective this was a clever and correct move, since it allowed him to reserve ultimate choices for himself. First, however, he left to me—the man who, as foreign minister, had most vigorously advocated this position—the task of pushing it through the Alliance.

Those who knew me and the degree of my commitment to this issue realized that I would not yield one inch in regard to short-range weapons, especially since any other stand would have lost my government its majority, both in the Bundestag and among the electorate.

It was important that my resolute stand against a rash decision in favor of modernization send a signal to the Alliance; that trick was more difficult then than it seems in retrospect. For at that time the speed as well as the direction of the dramatic course of events in Eastern Europe were still uncertain, and even though my resolve was based on a careful analysis, on experience, and on intuition, at this point it was not at all clear that history would ultimately prove me right.

As soon as I arrived in Brussels I felt the tension among the group of NATO colleagues; we were all under considerable pressure to arrive at some agreement. During this fortieth-anniversary summit the Alliance was determined to display unity and finally issue an overall program. Instead, attention was focused on the controversy surrounding the issue of modernization, and the important and necessary comprehensive plan was pushed into the background.

Meanwhile in Washington, Paul Nitze, who had been Ronald Reagan's personal adviser for arms control and disarmament, and Sam Nunn, the director of the Armed Services Committee, had expressed their empathy with the German position. Nitze had cautioned Baker against insisting on modernizing American short-range missiles in Europe and against simultaneously rejecting the negotiations with Moscow that we were hoping for: Such a position, Nunn noted, would not be supported by NATO and would plunge West Germany into a crisis. I was grateful to Nitze for his insight, especially since he endorsed prompt negotiations with Moscow. Senator Nunn, too, had plainly asked Bush to pursue our wish for negotiations.

On the other side the Soviet leadership repeatedly warned NATO against modernizing short-range nuclear weapons. Marshal Sergei Akhromeyev, for example, had declared on May 8 that the deployment in Europe of an efficient successor system for the

Lance missiles would inevitably result in a revival of the arms race. Such a deployment, he stated, would create an "absolutely unacceptable situation for Moscow" because the successor system would consist of an entirely new type of weapon, with a longer range, greater accuracy, and heightened destructive power. In passing, Akhromeyev specified Soviet superiority in short-range weapons at twelve to one—a candid admission, such as we had not heard before Gorbachev took office. Conversely, Akhromeyev pointed at the West's superiority in bombers equipped to deliver nuclear bombs: 2,783 Warsaw Pact aircraft as opposed to 4,075 NATO machines.

Shevardnadze, for his part, stressed that in the dispute about modernizing the Lance, the Soviet Union did not intend to drive a wedge between the NATO allies. Instead, it wished to support efforts to negotiate about these weapons: "We need to start negotiations on the reduction and possible elimination of tactical nuclear missiles. In future we must pursue this goal even more aggressively, since it is in the interest of all European nations, of the Soviet Union, and of the United States of America."

In Bonn on May 13 the Soviet Foreign Minister had also cautioned against a vote in favor of modernization, since it would only be interpreted as an attempt to circumvent the agreements on intermediate- and short-range missiles. Such a move, however, placed the INF treaty in jeopardy. "Why must we destroy our SS-23 missiles," Shevardnadze asked, hinting at Soviet concessions, "while the other side is developing and deploying missiles similar to the Lance?"

I firmly believed that the NATO summit should prove that the Atlantic Alliance, based on a sound security policy entirely within the terms of the Harmel Report, was advocating greater détente with the East. This, after all, was the main reason why the summit participants wanted to present a comprehensive program of a security policy for the future. By now, however, there was the danger that the Alliance would be unable to come to an agreement either on an overall program or on the SNF controversy.

Ultimately the crucial discussion in Brussels took place chiefly among the American, British, and German foreign ministers. Our other colleagues held themselves in check; when they did speak out on occasion, they tended to support my position. That was especially true for my Italian colleague, Giulio Andreotti, the liberal Dane Ellemann-Jensen, and the Spanish foreign minister, Francisco Fernandez Ordóñez. All three felt that not only the military, but also the political arguments were absolutely essential.

Jim Baker avoided any harshness in the confrontation. Our previous conversations had convinced me that he was eager to maintain a good relationship with me. President Bush had also come to Brussels with the strong desire to bring the NATO summit to a successful conclusion. His proposal for conventional disarmament was certainly in our interest as well, particularly since his appearance in Brussels was closely connected to his subsequent visit to West Germany. Speaking in Koblenz, the United States President pleaded for "partnership in leadership." From the perspective of the United States, West Germany had strengthened and expanded its central political position in Europe. Forty years after the founding of the Federal Republic, the United States, our ally and friend, viewed us as an indispensable and in fact, as its most important partner in Europe. Since the Soviet Union had also long since made a strategic decision in favor of Germany, we had moved into a key position in East-West relations.

On Monday, May 29, 1989, at four o'clock in the afternoon, the foreign ministers met for their rather unconventional, and by now legendary, evening meeting. Outward conditions were not exactly perfect: The sixteen ministers were convening in a room without windows, seated around a large, round table with room for only two members of each delegation, one for each country's NATO representative and one for its foreign minister. Other officials were seated in the back. It had been important to me that the Defense Ministry and Chancellor's Office were represented.

Each foreign minister was accompanied by as many as five associates. Including NATO staff members, about a hundred people were crowded into the room. Because NATO's secretary general— who usually chairs these meetings—was performing the same duty at the conference of the heads of state and government, we voted to give the chair to the Dutch foreign minister, Hans van den Broek, an experienced negotiator. I welcomed this outcome. Even though van den Broek was more supportive of the British position, during the preliminaries for the NATO summit he had displayed a great deal of goodwill in trying to mediate between the British and German points of view.

Because we were seated in alphabetical order, the German and

French foreign ministers were facing the American and British foreign secretaries. I knew that my French colleague supported me, but since France, as a nonaligned nation, was not involved, he took no part in the discussion.

The debate dragged on; arguments were tossed back and forth like tennis balls, without interruption or breaks. Sandwiches and cookies were served, as were coffee and mineral water, later augmented with whisky and wine. I stayed with my old rule: not a drop of alcohol during negotiations.

In the course of the discussions (which with few exceptions, were held in English so that we could speak with each other directly), I had repeatedly attempted to be alone with Jim Baker for a brief conversation, a wish he shared. We did not leave the room; we retired to a corner in plain sight. Especially during these talks I increasingly gained the impression that Baker sought mutual understanding and gradually came closer to my view of the matter. Finally he left the room, returned after a while, and asked me to step outside with him. The tension among the others increased. Outside, Baker told me that he had just spoken with President Bush and believed that we could arrive at an agreement. Then he showed me a written proposal, which he could accept.

In the course of the conference there had been a controversy, especially with British Foreign Minister Geoffrey Howe, concerning the third zero option: I had expressly refused to exclude that possibility, but I did not insist on it as a necessary goal of our negotiations. Baker therefore proposed to paraphrase the goal of SNF negotiations as "partial reductions" and to underline the word *partial* for greater emphasis. With this wording, he said, the Alliance would express its conclusion that during these negotiations it did not intend to go below a minimum in SNF—a move that theoretically canceled out the third zero option. It seemed that the British would be able to accept this solution. And if a vote for modernization should not come about—an eventuality of which I was convinced—the consequent obsolescence of the old Lance would automatically result in a zero option. And this was, in fact, what happened.

I could live with the word *partial,* which referred to the negotiations on existing short-range missiles. I was solely concerned with preventing a decision on modernization at this time. Baker told the other participants that he had spoken with me and that we were advocating special emphasis on the term *partial*. Everyone was relieved. But Howe, whom Baker and I valued equally and to whom we felt a personal closeness, now announced that he was unable to agree to the wording at this time. He had to consult his prime minister before England could give its definitive answer, which would not be until the following morning. This remark caused surprise and irritation among our colleagues; some of them urged Howe to agree at once, so that the entire matter could finally be removed from the agenda. In this tense situation I asked to speak. "We do understand," I said, "that the British Foreign Secretary wants to discuss this matter with his prime minister. Therefore I'd like to suggest that we discontinue the debate now, end the session, and go to bed."

It was long after midnight. The battle had been won. Modernization was put on ice. Indeed, prospects for negotiations were rosy now—we had carried the day. This anniversary summit was sending out a signal for further West-East détente. The threat of a relapse had been beaten back.

Given the American–West German agreement, I did not believe it possible that the solution we had found could be called into question again the following day. Since Baker had told me that he had discussed the wording with President Bush, I was also convinced that even the overnight opposition of Margaret Thatcher would not change the American leader's mind.

It was now May 1989, and we were only a few weeks away from the first major eruptions in Central and Eastern Europe. Less than six months later the Berlin Wall would crumble; the Warsaw Pact and the German Democratic Republic were about to collapse. Against this backdrop the Brussels debate on modernizing the Lance missiles seems eerily unreal in retrospect. To me, it seemed so even then.

The following morning everyone at the plenary session waited anxiously for the British Prime Minister to speak. When she finally did so, she stated only that of course she agreed to the decision arrived at the previous evening. She had achieved her goal—to prevent a third zero option. History would prove that she had merely postponed it.

After the session the Chancellor and I were walking on air as we went to meet the press. On our way people congratulated us repeatedly: As always when sessions dragged on interminably, the end result had leaked out early, and word had spread. The United States had speculated correctly: Overcoming confrontation paved the way for Bush's suggestions. Further, the West German coalition government gained support as a result of the Brussels agreement, especially since our alliance with the United States was made clear. At home and abroad the federal government's reputation had improved.

I also had a great personal gain from that night: Jim Baker and I had grown closer during this difficult meeting, and our respect for each other had evolved into friendship. In 1990, during the Two-Plus-Four talks, when the unification of Germany was at issue, the basic mutual trust we had won in Brussels proved advantageous for Germany's concerns.

The response to the outcome of the NATO summit was positive, both at home and abroad. It was German-American cooperation that had brought about the change and made NATO's anniversary summit a smashing success. Despite all naysayers, the Alliance had not fallen apart; on the contrary, it had solved controversial issues amicably. The United States, too, had seen the opportunity for historic changes in the East and had put aside purely military considerations. Further, NATO declared its intention of working toward a lasting peace in Europe, from the Atlantic to the Urals, in order to fully utilize the potential of this historic event for Europe.

Looking back at what we had achieved, I was satisfied: Our allies had generally followed Germany's suggestions. "An obligation toward modernization without simultaneous negotiations has turned into an obligation toward negotiations without simultaneous modernization"—in those words I summarized the outcome of the summit.

I had been imploring everyone to pay greater attention to the dramatic changes taking place on the Continent. My belief was confirmed only a few days after the NATO summit: On June 4 Poland held its first free elections. With Tadeusz Mazowiecki as prime minister, the first noncommunist government among the Warsaw Pact nations was elected.

Part Four

---

*Beginning of a
New Era*

10

The Winds of Change
Blow Harder

The Victory of the Liberation
Revolutions in Europe

Bonn as the Two Superpowers' Most Important Partner

After the Brussels NATO summit of May 30 and 31, 1989, President Bush and Secretary Baker visited the Federal Republic. The controversy concerning the modernization of short-range nuclear missiles had been brought to a successful resolution; consequently closer ties formed between Bonn and Washington, as the whole world noted. The West German government's unswerving, self-confident, and insistent stance had not weakened but had strengthened German-American relations; the two leaders of American foreign policy, Bush and Baker, valued West Germany's unswerving posture more than they would some form of rashness unsuited to the importance and concerns of its strongest European ally. Immediately after their arrival in Bonn they met with President von Weizsäcker, followed by a session with Chancellor Kohl and me.

On the morning of May 31 Baker and I had a private thirty-minute talk in the Foreign Office. We discussed ongoing events in

West-East relations. At his request I gave my appraisal of the situation in the Warsaw Pact countries. "East Germany," I said, "is the most complicated of all of them because it lacks any national identity. If truth be told, its people identify with the public figures, decisions, and values of West Germany. Though East Germany is a Communist country—with all the customary limitations on freedom of the press—it has two diametrically opposite media worlds. On the one hand there are the state-controlled television, state-controlled radio, and the state-controlled press. On the other hand eighty-five percent of the population can regularly receive television broadcasts from the West. The economy is similarly divided: Officially the planned economy establishes the rules, but in reality there are two parallel economies. One is based on the plan and the distribution mechanism. But East German citizens also use West German currency; for many of them it is a clandestine second currency, which can be used to buy Western goods in special state stores. Increasingly, however, workers demand payment in deutsche marks for expert work in service industries. The leading politicians try to curry political favor by arranging for more generous visiting regulations with West Germany, and taking credit for the fact that East Germany has the highest standard of living of all Warsaw Pact countries. But they do not win over the people as expected. East Germans compare their living conditions not with those of other Warsaw Pact countries, but with the standard here in West Germany. I am convinced that at this time the German Democratic Republic is the most unstable member of the Warsaw Pact; that instability also explains why its leaders are at a total loss right now. They worry about Gorbachev's reforms because they are losing more and more control over the political, economic, and social processes. If Honecker refuses further reforms, he will be faced with even greater problems. If he opens the door to democratization, he will be in an equally difficult position."

In the Rheingoldhalle in Mainz, President Bush delivered his memorable speech "For an Undivided Europe" before public and political figures. He called for strengthening the CSCE process, for free elections, and for pluralism in the Soviet sphere of power. "More political freedom in the East, a Berlin without the Wall, a clean environment, a less militarized Europe—each one of these is an honorable goal." He continued, "Together, they are the marks of a comprehensive vision—a Europe that is free and lives in peace with itself. Let the Soviet Union understand that it is not our goal to undermine its legitimate security concerns. . . . The foundation for a lasting security does not derive from tanks, troops, or barbed wire. It is based on shared values and on agreements that link free peoples together." All these goals coincided with our own aims and approaches. The discussion within the Alliance of the last few months had not only prevented a dangerous and untimely decision on rearmament, it had also reunited the Alliance on the basis of the 1967 Harmel Report, its philosophy and its goals. Representatives of the "old thinking" must be feeling the new wind blowing from Washington as well.

Especially important was the President's remark that in this era, which was defined by negotiations, the United States was aware that the Federal Republic was carrying a special burden. Though in the atomic age every nation was on the front lines, not all free nations were routinely made to bear the tensions brought about by unfounded activity and the permanent presence of foreign military forces. I had pointed out this circumstance repeatedly during our discussions of recent months whenever I elaborated on Germany's share in preserving our common security, and I always stressed the strength of the Bundeswehr and the presence of Allied forces.

Political events in the historically crucial years 1989 and 1990 were particularly affected by President Bush's invitation to the Federal Republic into a "partnership in leadership." The meaning of this partnership came clear to us most clearly and thoroughly during the Two-Plus-Four talks.

In mid-June 1989, only two weeks later, the president and the foreign minister of the other world power, Mikhail Gorbachev and Eduard Shevardnadze, arrived in Bonn. Alexander Yakovlev, a member of the Politburo, who assisted in shaping Gorbachev's reform policies and vigorously supported them, was also part of the Soviet delegation. Because of his many years as Soviet ambassador to Canada, he was thoroughly familiar with the Western way of thinking and with the constitutionality of American politics.

On June 13, 1989, the Chancellor and the Soviet President signed the Joint Declaration, which had been drafted during intense negotiations between the Foreign Office and the Soviet foreign ministry and during Shevardnadze's visit on May 12 and 13. It read, in part: "The center of politics must be held by human beings, with their dignity and their rights, as well as concern for the survival of humanity. . . . The right of all peoples and nations to shape their destiny must be secured. The precedence of international law in domestic and international policies must be guaranteed."

We defined our joint goal as overcoming the division of Europe. We committed ourselves, each using our own terms, to establishing peace in Europe or to the common European house, "in which the United States and Canada will also find room"; the CSCE was to be the basis for all these efforts. We named the integral elements of a Europe dedicated to peace and of cooperation: Unqualified respect for the integrity and security of each nation; each country's right freely to choose its own political and social systems; unqualified respect for the fundamental principles and norms of international law; the realization of human rights; and the call for furthering contact and exchanging ideas among people. We rejected striving for military superiority.

The following statement, however, was the most important in the Joint Declaration: "In view of the weight the two countries carry in their respective alliances, the Federal Republic of Germany and the Soviet Union realize that the positive development of their relations is of crucial significance to the situation in Europe and to East-West relations as a whole." Thus the Federal Republic not only saw its importance confirmed in the speech of its most significant ally, the United States, in the phrase "partnership in leadership" in President Bush's speech; the Joint Declaration also stressed mutual relations between Moscow and Bonn as eminently important. While the first few months of 1989 still resonated with the risk that the most positive evolution in West-East relations since 1945 would be stopped short by the modernization of short-range missiles, our position having prevailed, we now found ourselves in a unique position with respect to both our allied superpower, the United States, and to the other superpower, the Soviet Union—without this situation being self-contradictory.

In retrospect, therefore, it can safely be said that immediately before the most dramatic phase in our postwar history began, the international impact of German foreign policy reached its peak.

Both superpowers had affirmed Bonn's important position, which was enhanced by our close ties to France. During these months Paris placed particular emphasis on the continuous commitment to European unity it had pledged. The imminent revolutionary changes in the Soviet sphere of power could occur within a stable European and international framework, which we had been instrumental in creating by our activities in the EC as well as in NATO and the CSCE. Our situation could not possibly have been more favorable. And that position had not come about as a whim of history; it was simply the result of goal-oriented policies.

During the Soviet leaders' official visit to Germany I expressed my appreciation for the significant Joint Declaration and thanked Shevardnadze for his contribution to the construction of this document. I went on to give my view of the NATO summit as well as of President Bush's visit to Germany. I emphasized that the Federal Republic and the United States intended working toward a new relationship between West and East. Above all I stressed the new German-American ties. Shevardnadze and I focused in particular on disarmament efforts, especially in the area of short-range nuclear missiles.

I was curious about the long-range political goals that had occasioned this Soviet visit. The rate at which events were unfolding throughout Europe seemed to be causing an ever-increasing tremor. "It is probable that a major discussion on the European Continent's future will take place shortly," Shevardnadze responded. He reassured me that the Soviet Union had no intention of destroying existing structures, since any such plan would be unrealistic and deadly. What was important, he said, were the negotiations in Vienna between the twenty-three NATO countries and the Warsaw Pact nations, as well as the negotiations among the thirty-five CSCE nations on confidence-building measures. Further, it was significant that President Mitterand and I had called for a CSCE summit on security policy; the same was true for the creation of a center for the prevention of war. I stressed again the crucial fact that the Joint Declaration was based on existing structures while presenting a program for the future. Referring to my earlier call, at the United Nations, for an international human-rights court—which was harshly criticized at the time, principally by Moscow and East Berlin—I welcomed the fact that Gorbachev was now voicing the same request.

Then we approached the crucial issue. My Soviet counterpart remarked that all the achievements resulting from the CSCE process could be called truly revolutionary. A bold approach was needed, he noted, as well as a certain degree of tolerance and respect for our partners. At this point I interrupted, asking Shevardnadze to tell me frankly if his remark had been meant as a criticism of the Federal Republic of Germany. He agreed to be straightforward; he had no objections, he said, to President Bush's visiting Bonn, Moscow valued him as a serious partner. But why was Bush fanning the flames against East Germany? Such appeals, Shevardnadze noted, could not alter the course of events. During his recent visit to East Berlin he, Shevardnadze, had not become aware of any reaction except irritation. We should respond with sensitivity: The present changes in human rights policies in the Soviet Union were not the result of President Reagan's statements, either. Then Shevardnadze made a pronouncement that confirmed my assessment of the Soviet leaders: The Berlin Wall would come down when the time was right, but before that event could occur, a certain atmosphere of trust and a respectful attitude must be established.

During the months that followed, I was to notice repeatedly that Moscow had long since recognized the signs of the times. But in its relations with its allies—such as, in this case, East Germany—the Soviet Union was concerned that its decisions and efforts not appear as responses to pressure from the West. It was therefore searching for a European ambiance that inspired trust and did not interpret the new Eastern policies as capitulation to the West.

In replying to Shevardnadze, I said that I was sure he could understand that, like President Bush, I considered the Wall an anachronistic evil, which had become an even more horrible calamity than it had been in the past. I believed that the East German leaders were faced with the problem of being unable to make their state more attractive to its people; unlike Moscow, they would not allow the winds of change to blow in their country.

Addressing the economic situation in East Germany, Shevardnadze noted that it was better than in the other Communist countries. I pointed out in reply that East German workers compared their standard of living, not with conditions in the Communist nations, but with life in West Germany. Principally, however, they looked for democratization, such as was beginning to occur in the Soviet Union. I reminded Shevardnadze how creditable it had been when, early in the year, addressing the CSCE conference in Vienna, he had spoken of the "rusting Iron Curtain." Now matters had developed further; the Iron Curtain was falling apart. Though the Soviet foreign minister did not contradict me, he grew very grave. He thanked me for remembering his speech in Vienna. Looking firmly into my eyes, he said, "I am convinced that all the Communist nations will arrive at democracy." It appeared that the die had been cast in Moscow, but the changes must not appear to have occurred as a result of the West's admonitions.

The full impact of Shevardnadze's commitment to democracy becomes evident if we recall the date of our conversation: June 12, 1989—eight days after the bloodbath in Tiananmen Square in Beijing. The Warsaw Pact nations had responded in a variety of ways to that event. Hungary harshly condemned it, with the state television channel commenting, "They killed in the name of order at a time when history has already passed them by." Moscow made no public comment on the events in Beijing, indicating that the Soviet Union was distancing itself from the Chinese leaders' decisions. The GDR's Volkskammer, for its part, unanimously endorsed the actions of the Chinese government; that vote came on June 8, 1989, four days before my talk with Shevardnadze. The statement declared that the "people's power" had been compelled to establish law and order by the use of arms.

On the morning of June 13, 1989, Gorbachev received me in the Soviet embassy. He tried to make the conversation as cordial as possible, acknowledging the significance of the Joint Declaration and my share in bringing it about. He particularly emphasized that it was in accordance with the United States' international aims—a necessity to which I had alluded as many as three years earlier, during our first meeting in Moscow. To my thinking, the agreement could not have been better for the relationship between Bonn and Moscow. Regarding our operative goal, I explained that the European nations must be brought together, a process that would also include Germany. The current situation was of no advantage to anyone; it did not reflect any European's—or German's—understanding of themselves. But there were no prospects for a better future if one of the two sides tended to regard future events as a personal triumph. I had hit the bull's eye—Gorbachev said, "Very true."

His agreement indicated two facts. One, Moscow harbored no illusions about coming events, either in Europe or in Germany, which—as I had repeatedly explained to Gorbachev and Shevardnadze—was deeply embedded in the Continent. Two, Moscow was eager that this realization appear as anything but an admitted defeat on the part of the Soviet Union, and clearly Gorbachev and Shevardnadze did not see it as a defeat. Their support of democratization meant overcoming the split in Europe.

June 14, 1989, presented my wife and I with an adventure fit for a work of fiction. It was a beautiful summer's day. Because the Chancellor had invited the Gorbachevs to his home for the evening, we invited Shevardnadze, who had come to Bonn alone, to our house. The meal was being catered by the Foreign Office kitchen—soup, asparagus salad, a fish course, and dessert. While my wife and I were waiting for our guest in the garden, twenty minutes before Shevardnadze's expected arrival—the Foreign Office chef suddenly came running from the kitchen looking pale: "The fish has disappeared." "The fish?" "The fish for dinner. I brought it in this silver container. Now the container is empty." "Perhaps you brought the wrong container?" To this day I believe that I had the correct solution to the mystery. However, the chef insisted, "There is only this one. I'll go back to the Ministry at once to get the fish from the kitchen; it must still be there."

The chef left in his car but returned ten minutes later, even paler than before. "That was quick, from here to the Foreign Office and back," I offered. "No," he replied, "I never even got there. I can't. The street is sealed off for Shevardnadze; he's arriving any minute now." "Then we can't escape our fate," I replied. "We'll have to start dinner without the fish."

Shevardnadze arrived shortly. After we had the soup, the asparagus salad was served. I rose for a speech, though it had long been our custom during these informal meetings to do without toasts or speeches. "My esteemed colleague," I began, "you were meant to be served a fish course at this time. But the fish has disappeared. The catering staff do not know where it is, so we are not having fish. As you can see, even in Germany everything is not perfect." Then I suggested that we adjourn to a restaurant, along with my wife and the two interpreters. Shevardnadze agreed at once and laughed; he found the incident quite amusing.

My wife telephoned Maternus, a restaurant extremely popular among politicians and diplomats, and we took off in two cars. The rest of the limousines had left because they did not expect the visit to end so soon. Ria, Maternus' owner, showed us to a table in the beautiful back garden, encircled by ivy-covered walls. Other diners also were seated in the garden, which altogether held no more than ten tables. At one of the larger tables at the back sat a party of men, and I noticed among them State Secretary Waldemar Schreckenberger, who had been the long-time coordinator of the German secret services, working out of the Chancellor's Office. Others in the party were the president of the Federal Intelligence Service, the president of the Federal Office for the Protection of the Constitution, the president of the Federal Criminal Investigation Office, the president of the Military Protection Office, and a few others employed in the Chancellor's Office. They nodded cordially to us.

We ordered the fish we had not been able to eat at home. In her inimitable way, Ria joined us and Shevardnadze quickly warmed to her open manner. She announced that she would like to treat him to a special delicacy and send over an exquisite strawberry punch. Shevardnadze indulged in it with increasing pleasure. Suddenly State Secretary Schreckenberger rose and approached our table. "Sir, would you please introduce me to the Foreign Minister?" "This is Professor Schreckenberger, who until recently was employed in the Chancellor's Office," I said to Shevardnadze, describing Schreckenberger's activities as diplomatically as possible. But my description did not seem to satisfy Schreckenberger. He went into detail, mentioned that it had been his job to coordinate the secret services, and that the various directors of the secret services—he turned his head in the direction of his table—were dining with him. The men raised their glasses to Shevardnadze. The president of the Federal Intelligence Office, who had been ambassador in Moscow for many years, shouted, *"Nasdorovye."*

The Soviet interpreter grew pale as he translated all these titles and functions. For a moment I worried that Shevardnadze might come to believe that the missing fish had been a ruse to get him to

271

the restaurant. I bridged the not altogether relaxed situation by saying, "When you get back to Moscow, you can tell the head of the KGB that you've actually met all those people he knows only from the photographs and résumés in his files."

Shevardnadze laughed heartily. We looked at each other. Both of us knew: Here are two men who trust one another to the point where they can surmount a ticklish situation. Schreckenberger took his leave; but we stayed until well after midnight, chatting with Ria, drinking punch, not content with only one bowl. It turned out to be a cheerful evening, even though all of us realized that we were in the middle of a crucial historic turning point.

The following morning Shevardnadze told me he had had a wonderful time. And then he made a statement that we, who live in the Western democracies, may find startling. Shevardnadze said that the previous evening had marked the first time in many years that he had spent time unselfconsciously in a public restaurant with friends, in complete privacy and enjoying a meal that had not been planned weeks ahead. That, too, is politics—the human element in politics. And it, too, builds confidence, a trust on which one can build when one needs to.

Moscow Rethinks the Situation

Early in July 1989 my staff furnished me with a remarkable paper they had compiled. Describing possible new approaches in the Soviet Union's policy toward Germany, the study analyzed Soviet policy statements made below the official government level. To what degree did these statements imply approaches to a more realistic and less ideologically tainted view? The study concluded that perestroika's internal logic was linked with a new way of thinking in foreign policy, that the Soviet Union was forced to redefine its national interests in Central and Eastern Europe, and that in the future it must inevitably pay greater consideration to the dynamics and realities of the two parts of Europe. The paper mentioned in particular the attraction that the European Community held for the Communist nations.

The study further emphasized the seriousness with which the internal discussions in the Soviet Union addressed the dynamics of the German question. It correctly noted that while Brezhnev and Gromyko had categorically assumed that history had already settled the problem of Germany, Gorbachev had repeatedly implied that this issue could not be considered to have come to an end. The study referred to one statement, among others, from the Secretary General to the Federal President in 1987, to the effect that it was impossible to predict the situation a hundred years from now—a remark I had interpreted favorably even at the time, while reactions in Germany tended to be rather negative. In 1987 I argued that the only important factor was that Gorbachev considered the German question to be open; by comparison, how long it would take to solve it was not really an issue. The paper also recalled a statement Shevardnadze had made in January 1988; alluding to Germany's question, he had remarked that history had not pledged allegiance to any constitution. His words could be taken one of two ways, depending on whether they were applied to West Germany's constitution, and its mandate for unity or to East Germany's constitution, with its insistence on division. Subsequently I summarized the conclusion of this analysis in the phrase that the unification of Europe could not occur *around* Germany.

The staff paper also confirmed what I had told my Soviet counterpart in the fall of 1988 and had discussed with him several times since then. Once again my mind replayed Shevardnadze's behavior during the negotiations on the joint German-Soviet declaration we had prepared in June 1989 before Gorbachev's visit. We had come very near overcoming the division of Germany and of Europe. Now it became ever more important to make certain that the process, which was well under way, was kept free of impediments.

This stricture applied to both West and East and meant that the policy of open communication with the Soviet Union must continue, as must our attempt to cooperate with the other Warsaw Pact nations—not only with Poland and Hungary, the nations where reform was a fact, but also with East Germany and Czechoslovakia, whose leaders seemed paralyzed in the face of events. They must become involved in the West-East dialogue at this time above all. Moreover, we had to make clear to Warsaw that the continued existence of East Germany, and thus the division of Germany, was not a prerequisite to accepting the Oder-Neisse Line as Poland's final western border. Clarification on this point was important for all Poles, whether they were followers of the old or of the new system; it was of equal importance to all of our allies and partners in the West and the East.

We needed to impress upon the West, on the other hand, that the changed situation in Europe would not alter the Federal Republic's position within the Alliance and the European Community. No doubt must be allowed to linger that whatever the circumstances—that is, even as a united Germany—we would retain our membership in NATO and the European Community. German neutralism, a special status for Germany, or any other isolated action must be unequivocally precluded.

The following week made clear to me the full contradictoriness of the ongoing events in Europe. On July 12, 1989, I flew to Prague, where I had a rather fruitless talk with Foreign Minister Johanes. I also met with the chairman of the Council of Ministers. Subsequently I had a meeting with Cardinal Tomášek, an admirable man, who stood up for his convictions, and finally, in the West German embassy I met with Václav Havel. His uncompromising stand, the clarity of his thinking, and his reserved manner impressed me deeply. I had heard a lot about him, and I had frequently talked about him with Jiří Hájek, foreign minister in the 1968 Dubček administration. I told Havel that I would insist to Secretary General Milos Jakeš that Havel be allowed to come to Frankfurt to accept the Peace Prize of the German Book Trade this coming fall. It was no surprise to me that Johanes, who had succeeded Chňoupek, was hewing to the party line. It was nevertheless interesting to note, the following morning, Secretary General Jakeš's insistence on explaining to me his view of democracy in Czechoslovakia. He refused to commit himself in any way to an exit visa for Havel. Just before this meeting, I had breakfasted with Professor Hájek, as I always did, in the German embassy. He painted a realistic image of the progressive, prerevolutionary developments in his country. His description confirmed my belief that here, just as in East Germany, revolutionary change was on the horizon.

My overall impression was that the Czech leaders failed to realize the extent of the changes occurring in Europe and that they refused to acknowledge the current situation in their own country. Before leaving Prague I also had a meeting in the German embassy with former foreign minister Chňoupek, whom I had encountered frequently in the past fifteen years. We often engaged in harsh disputes, but invariably our talks also arrived at a dispassionate and open exchange, beyond the areas of dispute between us, so that over time—despite all our differences—we developed a warm personal relationship. Chňoupek had excellent contacts in Moscow. Without violating his political principles, he always gave me a vivid picture of the state of debate in the Soviet camp, an important source of information, even though he phrased matters in such a way as to avoid any imputation of disloyalty. Conversely, these talks offered me an opportunity to assuage any doubts, both in Prague and in Moscow, about the seriousness of our official positions. On other topics, too, Chňoupek was more open than other Easterners I spoke with. On this particular occasion I could not fail to notice that he had a more accurate view of recent events than did the officeholders. Perhaps he felt free to voice his opinions more openly; whatever the case, I thought that he seemed relieved now that the burden of being foreign minister was lifted from him.

For me those weeks were an emotional roller coaster, days of great optimism and hope and times when I was brought low by the realization of the problems and obstacles yet to be overcome. On the very day I left Prague, July 13, 1989, I went to the world economic summit in Paris, which, as always, had been masterfully organized by President Mitterand and that turned out to be a great success. In the meetings of foreign ministers we talked about the situation in the Soviet sphere of power. I expressed my view that East Germany was the next country in which the will to change would take over. Since the East German leadership gave no indication of any desire to institute reforms, I said, the people had lost all hope, and it was obvious what—lacking national identity—the demand for change meant. I also passed on the impressions I had gained in my talks with Gorbachev and Shevardnadze.

A Tiny Nation Opens the Iron Curtain: The Hungarians' Courage

On August 8, 1989, East Germany closed the Federal Republic's headquarters of its permanent representative in East Berlin because it was serving as a refuge for East Germans trying to leave. The GDR urged the Chancellor's Office to ask me to shut down

275

our embassies in Warsaw, Prague, and Budapest as well. These were Germany's Communist neighbors, countries always open to East German travel. At this time East Germans were taking advantage of this circumstance to place themselves under the protection of the Federal Republic in its various embassies as a way to circumvent the prohibition on emigrating from East Germany.

I refused East Germany's request not only for humane and constitutional reasons but also on political grounds: It could not be our intention to extend the Wall to Budapest, Prague, and Warsaw. On the contrary, it was our responsibility to pave the East Germans' road to freedom. The reasons for the mass exodus lay in East Germany, and that was the only place where they could be eliminated. By August we no longer considered it necessary to accommodate all asylum seekers in our Budapest embassy, since the Hungarian government had assured us that no one would be sent back to East Germany. Indeed, the border opening between Hungary and Austria grew wider and wider. On August 22, 200 people crossed at one site alone. The number of refugees flooding into Hungary was enormous. In September 1989, 21,000 people left the GDR for West Germany, compared to 8,000 in August; by October the number would increase to more than 26,000. Routines to enable them to come to West Germany needed to be developed with the utmost speed.

Events in Central Europe—in particular East Germany, Czechoslovakia, and Hungary—took no account of my health. Though I was still recovering from the heart attack I had suffered at the end of July, I was in constant contact with Gyula Horn, the foreign minister of Hungary. By now Hungary was establishing large refugee camps because our embassy in Budapest could no longer deal with the flood of East German refugees; at the same time the Hungarian government was under enormous pressure from East Berlin. We wanted to facilitate Hungary's exit procedure for the refugees from East Germany to the West as much as possible and were prepared to involve the United Nations' High Commissioner for Refugees. Several times associates from my ministry traveled to Budapest as I could not make the trip myself so soon after my heart attack.

I remained in constant telephone contact with the Hungarian Foreign Office and with Gyula Horn. What could we do to help Budapest withstand the pressure from East Berlin? My assumption that Foreign Minister Horn would be successful in obtaining exit visas for the East German refugees turned out to be correct: He was acting with Prime Minister Miklos Németh's approval. Hungary displayed great steadfastness and admirable courage, turning it into a beacon of humanity during those weeks. Hungary—that meant its small, courageous population and its reform-Communist leaders, who had emerged from the old cadres. Eminent figures had assumed responsibility for supporting democracy and humanity; it will always remain Gyula Horn's historic merit that he took this road with his friends and many likeminded others.

In order to figure out the practicalities of the East German citizens' exodus from Hungary (by bus or by train) Horn and I were eager to meet as soon as possible. Horn let me know that he, along with Németh, was willing to come to Bonn to speak with the Chancellor and me.

On August 25, 1989, the meeting took place in the strictest secrecy. Rarely had I been so filled with anticipation before a meeting. What suggestions would Németh and Horn bring? Németh was a pragmatic economic reformer, easy to envisage as a member of a corporate board of directors; Horn, whom I had encountered numerous times, ever since his time as an undersecretary, was a superb career diplomat. From talking with him, and hearing about him from the Hungarian ambassador to Bonn, Dr. István Horváth, I knew Horn to be a committed reformer who was principally concerned with Hungary's welfare. A short, stocky man, he had the reputation of being courageous, and he was aware of his responsibility. Though I had not entirely recuperated, I flew to Bonn from Berchtesgaden, where I was resting up, to welcome the two.

Horn reported on depressing talks he had held in East Berlin; they had been among the most disagreeable in all his experience. The East German leaders had accused him of treaty violations, since an existing treaty obligated both parties to the extradition of refugees. With its refusal to shutter the Iron Curtain and to send the refugees back, Hungary had definitely crossed the Rubicon of "Communist solidarity."

The Hungarian statesmen also told us that at the Warsaw Pact summit in Bucharest they had called for a revision of the document regulating mutual relations that would grant each member nation the right to its own evolution, and the freedom to choose its own social and political system. Originally the proposal had found no support, and only when Gorbachev solidly endorsed it did the other participants accept it. Each nation was to remain a member of the Warsaw Pact, independent of its particular domestic developments. Gorbachev's attitude proved that he was steadfast in adhering to the spirit of the German-Soviet Declaration; he thus initiated a reversal of the front lines. For the past few decades the Soviet Union had suppressed all attempts at increased independence on the part of Warsaw Pact nations.

At the conclusion of the visit Helmut Kohl and I were certain: Hungary would regulate our fellow Germans' exit from East Germany along the lines we wished. We detailed our policy of closer cooperation with all those Warsaw Pact nations that had decided on reforms. Our Hungarian visitors did not ask for financial aid.

Early in September I received the Hungarian ambassador, István Horváth; he reiterated three important assurances by Hungary:

1. The East German refugees in Hungary constituted a problem between the two German states.
2. The Hungarian government was working toward a humanitarian solution.
3. The Hungarian government was not going to extradite the refugees to East Germany.

I asked that the refugees be allowed to leave quickly by way of Austria, and I promised all possible help in transporting them. The following morning, on September 6, the Hungarian ambassador informed my associate Frank Elbe that by September 10, 1990, a way of handling the problem would be found.

On September 6, 1989, I also received the United States deputy secretary of state Lawrence Eagleburger. I explained to him my belief of what could be expected to happen in the various Warsaw Pact countries, particularly pointing to the precarious situation in East Germany.

In order to support the reform policies in Poland, I suggested that the United States, France, England, and West Germany should send leading figures and experts to Warsaw, where they could serve as advisers. I had discussed these issues with Walesa in

Paris as early as December 1988, though at the time the circumstances were entirely different.

I mentioned to Eagleburger that I took a favorable view of the situation in Hungary, in particular the plans of the Németh-Horn administration. It was not merely from gratitude but also from conviction that I was an advocate for Hungary, which expected greater support from the United States. Then I handed Eagleburger a Hungarian paper that explained Budapest's views. I further seized the opportunity to express my particular appreciation of Németh's and Horn's conduct with regard to the East Germans. I informed Eagleburger that I had told my colleagues at the world economic summit that the next country unable to master its own internal developments would be East Germany.

On September 8, after Eagleburger had left, Lech Walesa brought a delegation to Bonn. On that beautiful fall day we met in the Foreign Office's guest house to discuss recent events in Poland, especially the question of possible opportunities for West Germany and the other Western countries to support the Warsaw government. The fresh wind of change became increasingly noticeable, and where it was ignored—as it had been in Prague and East Berlin—it could quickly turn into a storm. Again Walesa impressed me with his charisma and strength of will. Associates who had never met him before were fascinated by the personality of this man who, coming from the Gdansk shipyards, had entered the annals of the twentieth century. I assured him that we would support a democratic Poland. Regarding the border issue, I declared, "Take with you the certainty that the Federal Republic of Germany, the democratic Germany, will not allow East Germany and the Soviet Union to set the terms for Poland's western border."

The more I thought back on my encounter with Walesa and on events in Europe, the more seriously I considered a "border guarantee" for Poland, to be announced in my speech to the United Nations in late September.

From New York to Prague

On September 7 Dieter Kastrup, of my Foreign Office, telephoned to tell me of an increasing influx of people seeking refuge in our

Czech embassy. He had gone to Prague, but to no avail. The only way the Czech leaders were cooperating with us was by allowing access of food to the embassy.

Later that night there was good, even redeeming news after all from Budapest. We learned, informally, that emigration of the East Germans would begin at once. I was overjoyed.

The following day 117 East German citizens left the Federal Republic's representational offices in East Berlin, where they had camped for almost six weeks. Earlier, they had been promised immunity, the right to return to their workplace, and legal aid in applying for exit visas.

On the afternoon of September 10 we received official confirmation from Budapest that the East Germans could leave. Michael Jansen, a longtime close associate, whom I had sent to Budapest, made the announcement himself in one of the camps; he told me later that he would never forget that moment.

By this time a few representatives of East Germany in Budapest attempted once last time to change the refugees' minds by promising them immunity if they returned voluntarily. At that point, however, their inducements could not persuade anyone to turn back. Moreover, many East Germans then in Hungary had by then already received West German passports, and others were in possession of Red Cross papers that were recognized as valid passports. Now they even had the choice of using their East German passports to depart.

East Germany responded to Hungary's decision with harsh criticism, though the words merely concealed helplessness. We— Chancellor Kohl and I—thanked the Hungarian government, fully aware of how far-reaching the decision was: It was a declaration of humaneness, of European solidarity. The Iron Curtain was torn forever. Thus I meant every word of the message I sent to Hungary: "We, who during the past few weeks shared the fear of the [East] Germans in the camps, will not forget Hungary's decision, which it made by taking full responsibility. Our thanks are due to the Hungarian people and to the nation's government for their understanding and readiness to help the Germans from the German Democratic Republic."

And then a new, unforeseen difficulty arose: Czechoslovakia closed its border with Hungary. The escape route from East Germany, which had just begun to beckon, was blocked again. Desperate, those who wanted to emigrate turned to our embassies in Prague and Warsaw. In Hungary we were dealing with an understanding government, one that was engaged in reforms, but in Prague the same old leaders still held sway, and they were unwilling to allow any reforms. It was not beyond the realm of possibility that the overflow of refugees who could not be contained in our Prague embassy would be sent back to East Germany. I therefore ordered the embassy personnel to accept, accommodate, and take care of an unlimited number of refugees.

Deciding to leave for the Federal Republic, the East Germans had made a difficult choice. People do not lightly abandon their homes and familiar surroundings. When I had left East Germany in 1952, my experiences had been of a similar kind, and for that reason alone I considered it a mistake to cite mainly material reasons to explain the refugees' decision. In fact, the crucial factor was the lack of human, social, and political perspective. I therefore appealed to the leaders in East Berlin finally to abolish the causes that lay at the bottom of the refugees' choice.

In the meantime the Hungarian ambassador, Horváth, came to see me again. Overwhelmed by the expressions of gratitude and friendship so abundantly heaped on his embassy, he reported that no reproaches from Moscow had been received. The tone of Soviet communiqués hinted at malicious glee toward the GDR.

On September 13 some sixty East Germans were quartered in the West German embassy in Warsaw. Dieter Kastrup conferred with Krzysztof Skubiszewski, the foreign minister of Poland, about a solution to the refugee problem, and pointing to the example of Hungary, he asked that Poland find a humane solution.

A day later, on September 14, 1989, I received the American special envoy Paul Nitze, whom I had known and valued for many years. We had had many discussions on issues of disarmament, in particular on the problems of the intermediate-range missiles. Now I told him, "All the events in the Soviet Union make us realize how criminally the Kremlin neglected the question of nationalities in the past. Basically Lenin and Stalin understood the gravity of the problem, but they did not solve it. In a way Gorbachev is now using the dynamics of the issue of nationalities to break up old political structures."

Gorbachev accepted both Hungary's and Poland's choices of direction; for the same reason he rejected Ceausescu's call for a new summit meeting in response to events in Poland. I suggested to Nitze that the United States government take another close look at the declaration issued at the last Warsaw Pact summit in Sofia, since it expressed the member nations' right to self-determination. "That is a true revolution," Nitze agreed.

I continued by noting that Gorbachev had long since realized that stabilizing Central and Southeastern Europe was possible only through reform. The leaders who insisted on clinging to old programs would be overtaken by events, and in East Germany the situation was especially drastic.

"The West," I said, "must support the European Union with as much unity as possible. To the people of Central and Southeastern Europe the West remains as strong a magnet as before, an attractive model for building a lasting peace in Europe." Emphatically I added, "We must always keep in mind that whatever separates Europe also separates Germany, and whatever unites Europe also brings the Germans in the East and in the West closer. Our fate is therefore linked more closely to all of Europe's fate than with that of other nations. That is why I oppose nationalistic tendencies, and that is why I reject the de-Europization of German politics."

Nitze asked whether the European Union might be jeopardized by a renewed debate on unification. "Such would be the case only if we considered and pursued it merely as a national matter. Yet all West German administrations have envisioned German unification only within the framework of a European solution," I replied, reminding Nitze that even in 1967, in the Harmel Report, the North Atlantic Alliance had called, not only for the foundation of a lasting peace in Europe, but also for German unification.

When I spoke to Nitze, I did not know that I would soon have the opportunity to give a European answer to a question by the EC Commission's president, Jacques Delors. He telephoned to ask what kind of relations the European Community should develop with East Berlin. Would East Germany ultimately join the European Community as its thirteenth member? My answer to Delors was in the negative: "The aim is not to make East Germany another member of the European Community but to augment the Federal Republic of Germany with the German Democratic Republic, thus making the GDR, as part of the unified Germany, a direct member of the European Community." Delors agreed.

On September 14 Soviet Ambassador Kvitsinsky asked to see me immediately, he had a message from Foreign Minister Shevardnadze. I was curious: Were we to expect critical and concerned remarks regarding events in Hungary? Not at all; Moscow reacted in the way I had expected. The message dealt with issues of arms control in the area of chemical weapons. A coincidence? No. Moscow was eager to stress its interest in continuing multilateral cooperation. Kvitsinsky's conduct of the conversation reinforced my impression. He never mentioned East Germany but talked instead about his vacation. I broached the subject of East Germany, remarking that given the citizenry's mood, I did not understand the East German leaders' attitude. Drastic changes were unavoidable, I said, since at the moment East Germany was lagging far behind developments in the Soviet Union. Where, I wanted to know, was the slogan we had heard in East Berlin for so many years, "Learning from the Soviet Union means learning to win"?

The refugees' condition in the Prague embassy was becoming unbearable. Bunk beds had been stacked high in offices and conference rooms, and there were not nearly enough bathrooms. In Warsaw some of the frightened refugees could be accommodated in a Catholic church, after German and Polish diplomats had assured them that they would not be sent back to East Germany.

On September 18, 1989, I telephoned Skubiszewski. He had already been briefed by Dieter Kastrup, and he promised to come to a practical and humane decision. I pointed out the increasing number of asylum seekers: The German embassy in Warsaw would soon be overflowing. But we could refer the refugees to accommodations provided by Polish humanitarian organizations only if we could be sure that they would not be extradited. Skubiszewski was sympathetic to our request and confirmed what I had already come to believe—that there would be no extraditions. And in fact there were none. I could always trust Krzystof Skubiszewski.

I was therefore confident about the situation in Warsaw and on September 23 I reconfirmed that, in the spirit of the great European traditions, the new democratic Poland would find a solution for all East Germans within its borders. When it came to Prague, however, I expressed myself more cautiously, because of the political situation that still prevailed: "We hope that a humane solution can be found for the people in our embassy in Prague."

As I did every year, I left for New York to attend the United Nations general assembly. My wife accompanied me, along with the heart specialists in whose care I was; they were equipped with a number of medical devices and medications, prepared to treat another heart attack. This trip to New York—it was my sixteenth to the general assembly—seemed different from all previous ones. The revolutionary changes in Europe and their consequences endowed the upcoming meetings and talks with a new quality. I also needed to capitalize on my stay by finding a way out of our Prague embassy for the East German refugees.

After my talks with Shevardnadze in the summer of 1989 on potential developments in East Germany, neither the flood of refugees nor the mounting and increasingly pointed protests in the German Democratic Republic had come as a surprise. No doubt the call for democratization would grow louder still. I had never doubted that, given greater freedom, the East Germans would also demand German unity—but it was a demand that must originate with them. In a situation as sensitive as ours, the West German government could not appear as an "instigator." Shevardnadze's remarks during our talks in Bonn in May and June of 1989 must be understood to reflect this same understanding. But it was up to us to create opportunities that would allow people in East Germany to express their desires, including their will to unification. For this reason it was important that the right to self-determination was firmly established in the German-Soviet declaration of 1989. I pointed this out in every talk I gave.

The exciting, even cataclysmic days, first in New York, then in Prague, that followed were described at the beginning of this book.

The Wall Is Breached

On October 3 I attended two emergency meetings in the Chancellor's Office with Rudolf Seiters, the minister of the interior at the time. The Federal Republic's offices in East Berlin were his responsibility, as we did not have an embassy proper in East Berlin because the Federal Republic did not acknowledge the GDR as a foreign country. Seiters and I worked extremely well together; we got along well both on a personal and on a professional level.

Our talks concerned the refugees who were already in Prague and those who were still arriving. On October 2, 1989, Representative Neubauer, from East Germany, called at the Chancellor's Office to complain about the West German government's conduct, which, he claimed, broke our agreements. East Germany urgently demanded that the East German citizens who were now housed in the embassies in Prague and Warsaw be expelled so that they could return to East Germany, where they could take care of their affairs in collaboration with the prominent emigration lawyer Wolfgang Vogel.

This intervention was indeed astonishing. It was a last attempt at defiance. For years I had refused to prevent East Germans from going to the embassies that were under my jurisdiction—that is, all West German embassies with the exception of the offices in East Berlin—or to expel them, and it could hardly be expected that I would change my position at this time. Quite obviously, East Germany was trying to close the gate that had been opened in Prague.

On the evening of October 4 I received a telephone call from Secretary Baker. He asked for my advice and assistance regarding eighteen East Germans who were seeking refuge in the American embassy in East Berlin; he indicated that the matter should be approached cautiously and confidentially since, as a matter of principle, in the past the United States had never allowed an overnight stay. He was wondering whether there was a possibility of transferring these eighteen people from the American Embassy to the Federal Republic's Permanent Representation in East Berlin. I thought that such a move was out of the question, since it was impossible to guarantee the refugee's safety during the move. Therefore I urged Baker to let the eighteen Germans stay in the American Embassy, telling him that we had already assigned the problem to Dr. Vogel. I also pointed out that Germany would be at a complete loss if the United States expelled the refugees from the embassy. Baker reassured me. "Such a thing will most certainly not happen. I'm worried about the next few days, though. Our embassy is small, and we do not have the resources to offer refuge to any more people." I promised to speak with Minister

Seiters, as the person responsible for our East Berlin offices and all relations with East Germany. "Time is working in your and the United States' favor," I remarked. "The government in East Berlin is trying to find a solution before Gorbachev's visit on the celebrating of the fortieth anniversary of East Germany's founding. A conflict with the United States is the last thing they need right now."

It was my impression that Gorbachev's conduct during the events celebrating East Germany's fortieth anniversary did indeed clearly indicate that the rift between the Soviet and the present East German leaders was widening.

On October 18 Honecker was forced to resign as head of state and as party chairman. Egon Krenz succeeded him as secretary general of the SED. But even after this change in leadership there were no radical reforms, particularly since Krenz, after a conference with Gorbachev in Moscow on November 1, declared that German unification was not on the agenda, that there was nothing to unite because both German states belonged to different military alliances and were therefore part of stability in Europe. He added that the Berlin Wall did not limit an individual's freedom of movement; instead, it formed a kind of moat between two social systems and military blocs. He still talked the talk of the past and in terms of the "old thinking."

An official visit by Chancellor Kohl and myself to Warsaw had long been planned for November 9. On November 8, the Bundestag held its annual debate on the government's report on the state of the nation. Anyone taking a realistic view of the effects of the border opening in Hungary, of the granting of exit visas on September 30 to the Germans in the Prague Embassy, and of the constant protest rallies in many East German cities must understand that this would be the last report on the state of the nation in a divided Germany.

On November 8 I had risen very early to go over the draft of my speech for the debate one last time. From my desk I looked out into the night. What would it be like when tomorrow, in a week, in a month, in three months the Wall opened and Germans from the West and the East could meet unimpeded? Would the revolutionary changes affect only the East or would they touch the Western part of Germany as well? Occupied with these and similar thoughts, I polished the sentences I was to speak in the Bundestag a few hours later: "Nothing will be the way it used to be—not in the East nor in the West." Addressing those holding political responsibility, I continued, "Even today we must prepare the Germans here, in the Federal Republic, for great sacrifices they will have to make for the unity of the nation." I admonished the powers that be in East Berlin that it was no longer enough merely to enable their citizens to travel more freely; the Wall itself must come down. I could not have guessed that this very act would occur a mere twelve hours later.

Our upcoming visit to Poland was another topic of discussion in the Bundestag debate. My statements at the United Nations in New York, which had received a tremendous response by the public at large, and in particular in Poland, were incorporated verbatim in a resolution the Bundestag passed with 4 votes against and 33 abstentions. I stated to the Bundestag, as I had stated in New York in September, "Fifty years ago the Polish people became the first victims of the war that Hitler's Germany unleashed. It shall know that Germany does not question its right to live within secure borders, either now or in the future, by making territorial demands. The wheel of history will not be turned back. We want to work with Poland toward a better Europe of the future. The inviolability of borders is the basis for peaceful coexistence in Europe." Thus, at a crucial moment in history our intention of recognizing Poland's western border became proof of West Germany's policy of responsibility, but not a favor in return for Germany's unification. East Germany's function as the guarantor of Poland's western border was therefore eliminated—and that was an important factor at this point. My statement therefore also created one of the requisites for German unity, which, after all, was one of the reasons I had spoken as I did at the United Nations.

The following morning the Chancellor led the delegation to Warsaw. Many talks had been scheduled for the afternoon. First I held an intense discussion with Foreign Minister of State Skubiszewski on the current situation; subsequently we signed a German-Polish consultation protocol. Next I conferred with Minister of State Jósef Czyrek, whom I had known for many years. We had first met when he was deputy foreign minister of the Polish People's Republic. In 1976, when we were working hard to reach an accord on the second treaty with Poland—arguing mainly about the so-called exit protocol—he had been helpful and constructive during the discussions. After serving as Poland's foreign minister, President Jaruzelski, whose confidant he had long been, appointed him minister in his presidential office. The same evening the new Polish prime minister, Mazowiecki, hosted a dinner at the Palace of the Council of Ministers. It was there the news reached us: East Germany had opened the Wall. We were electrified. What would happen now?

As we learned later, the news about the opening of the border reached the Bundestag delegates in the middle of their debate. The debate was suspended; events in East Berlin were given precedence on the agenda.

After the German delegation in Warsaw returned to its quarters, the Chancellor and I were still discussing the next step when we learned that a large rally was planned outside the City Hall of Berlin-Schöneberg for the following day—the same location where John F. Kennedy had delivered his famous Berlin speech. After brief deliberations the Chancellor and I decided that on such an historic day for Germany our place was in Berlin. Our Polish hosts understood immediately.

On the morning of November 10 I breakfasted with Walesa and Geremek; the opening of the Wall obviously dominated our conversation. Walesa seemed worried, even frightened. The opening of the Wall caused him anxiety. Geremek noticed that Walesa's reaction disconcerted me. I was grateful to him for saying that this was a good turn of events for Germany, Europe, and Poland. This experienced and courageous man had realized that unification would make all of Germany part of the West and that the situation in Poland would change for the better as well. After all, the nation would no longer be positioned between the Soviet Union and a country in which 300,000 Soviet soldiers were stationed; instead, it would abut directly on the Western communities. Later I expanded on this argument as I held meetings in Poland and Czechoslovakia: "What is new is that we are now neighbors of an entirely different kind than we were in the past. We Germans are facing you for the first time in history not only as a neighboring German state but also as a member of the European Community and of the Western Alliance." Such a change, it could be said, was an historical quantum leap.

Subsequent to this noteworthy conversation I held another meeting with Foreign Minister Skubiszewski to discuss events in Germany. I noted, in part, "To our people ongoing events in East Germany are overwhelming and moving. Germans from the Federal Republic and the German Democratic Republic met last night. Their encounter testifies to the unity of the nation, which never ceased to exist. You, and through you the Polish people, and all of our neighbors, shall know that we are witnessing a pledge by all Germans to commit themselves to freedom. Free Germans have never constituted a threat. That is important for all the peoples of Europe and throughout the world. The unchanging truth is: The Federal Republic of Germany has an undisputed place in the community of Western democracies, in the European Community on the road to political union, and in the Western Alliance. The Federal Republic of Germany honors every treaty it has concluded and all the obligations it has assumed. Among them are the Moscow Treaty, the Warsaw Treaty, the treaty with Czechoslovakia, the Basic Treaty with East Germany, and the Helsinki Final Act."

In this historic moment, Skubiszewski understood my clear rejection of separate national actions; he correctly understood my allegiance to the Western democracies and our treaties, and he expressed his sympathy for my pledge to the unity of our nation. Nevertheless, he noted, the full complexity of the situation did not concern the two German states alone. At the conclusion of our talks the spokeswoman for the Polish government, Niezabitowska, summed up Poland's standpoint on unification: "The Polish government acknowledges all peoples' right to self-determination, including the Germans'. But before unification can occur, a number of conditions must be met. The first is that the desires of Germans in both states be expressed and respected equally. Second, that the Four Powers, which continue to be entitled to participate in the decision on Germany as a whole, must give their consent. Subsequently the issue—formal unification of the two Germanys—must be considered within the context of all of Europe, and guarantees must be given that the new, unified Germany, most certainly a powerful state, will not threaten security and cooperation in Europe. All these factors naturally go along with a fundamental issue concerning Poland: The permanence of the Oder-Neisse Line. Two separate issues must not be comingled:

the issue of unification and the issue of borders. The German states can unite only and exclusively within their present borders. No other options are available."

I sympathized with Poland's concerns. Given predictable developments in East Germany, I had therefore clearly expressed my position on the issue of borders in my speech to the United Nations on September 27 as well as in my address to the Bundestag on November 8.

Our departure did not mean that we abruptly cut our visit short; we merely interrupted it—at least Helmut Kohl did. As agreed, he would return to Warsaw. As for myself, an early departure had been planned anyway, and I returned directly to Bonn after stopping in Berlin. Despite events before and during our stay, the visit to Poland turned into a success, even into a milestone on the road toward a new relationship between Germans and Poles.

Arranging the trip from Warsaw to Berlin had not been easy. The German military plane in which we had arrived was not allowed to fly directly from Warsaw to Berlin, because the legal situation at the time did not allow German military planes to land in West Berlin. Therefore we decided to fly from Warsaw to Hamburg; the Chancellor's Office asked the United States for a plane from Hamburg to West Berlin, where we landed around four o'clock in the afternoon.

During the two flights I drafted the speech I would deliver at the Schöneberg City Hall. I realized that close international attention would be paid to our words. The whole world was looking at us: How would the West German government, how would the West German people respond to the razing of the Wall? I wanted to set forth to the international public the motives, intentions, and interests of West German policy. I would, however, be speaking directly to all Germans.

After we landed, we proceeded at once to the Schöneberg City Hall, where tens of thousands were waiting.

It would have been only natural to let my present emotional state dictate the words I was to say to the people at the rally. Yet as foreign minister I had to keep Germany's future concerns in mind. The whole world would be listening to what members of the federal government had to say in Berlin on this day. The representatives of the three traditional parties—CDU Chairman

Helmut Kohl, SPD Honorary Chairman Willy Brandt, and I as foreign minister and representative of the FDP—undertook a clear positioning of Germany. It felt good to speak with these two men in particular here in East Berlin. I described our position at this historic moment: "Our decision remains in force. We have decided in favor of the community of Western democracies." That position must remain our basic foreign-policy principle beyond November 9. The whole world must understand where our allegiance lay. No doubts must be allowed to arise about our membership in the European Community and the Western Alliance.

I also talked about my good fortune at being able at this moment to greet the people in my native land who in the past weeks and months had exemplified the Germans' will to freedom: "The Germans in the Democratic Republic are shaping the German and European history of freedom." Were we not witnesses to a revolution from below, a revolution whose driving force was the people? Two hundred years after the French revolution an *ancien régime* that was historically exhausted was toppled by a *levée en masse*. The will of the people prevailed over the old rule. Yet this revolution was taking place without violence, without bloodshed. This phenomenon is specifically what remains the accomplishment of the people in East Germany. They have enriched all Germans.

If the change happened peacefully, this is also thanks to those East German leaders who actively opposed the use of force. This stance must also be borne in mind if we wish to do historical justice to the men who were in power at that time. The outcome might have been quite different, as is shown by the events of June 17, 1953, when the East German people's uprising was suppressed by violence. First and foremost, the East Germans' reluctance to use force was due to the Soviet leaders, Gorbachev and Shevardnadze in particular. My talk with Eduard Shevardnadze kept going through my mind on this day in particular.

In my speech outside the Schöneberg City Hall on November 10 I also stated, "Events that began in Budapest and continued in Warsaw and Moscow are now also occurring in East Germany. Germans participate whenever freedom is at stake. The dignity, the prudence, and the maturity with which the people of the German Democratic Republic demand their right to freedom honors the whole nation. All these qualities must be a model for our own conduct at this time. We are asked to exhibit the same dignity, the same respect, and the same prudence. We do not intend to replace state control in East Germany with unwanted advice from us."

Thus I established the guidelines for our actions in the months ahead. The East Germans must not again be controlled, we must avoid any sense that they were being manipulated to satisfy the West's political aims. Our goal of German unity—constantly reiterated, grounded in our constitution, and formulated in the Letter on German Unity—was an offer to the people of the German Democratic Republic. This offer needed to be accepted, and I never doubted that it would be indeed. Yet my certainty was no substitute for the East Germans' explicitly accepting our offer. It was necessary for them to do so for the unification of our nation and its security against the world. No one at home or abroad was to have reason to denounce unification as a development compelled by the West. And unification was indeed not an imposed event: In reality the idea of unity was more firmly embedded in many East Germans than it was in a number of West German citizens. The right to self-determination was a right of *all* Germans. That was the reason why, in 1986, during my first meeting with Gorbachev, I had stated that the German question was going to be answered by history and by *all* Germans. That statement needed to remain valid now.

Outside the Schöneberg City Hall I expressed my opinion as a private citizen as well as my stand as foreign minister. "At this time it is becoming clear that forty years of separation have not split one German nation into two. There is neither a capitalist nor a Communist Germany but only *one* German nation, committed to peace and liberty. My fellow citizens, today the world is looking at our nation and at this city. Our fellow citizens in East Germany have placed Germany's destiny at the very top of the international political agenda. First and foremost, Germans want to live in peace with all their neighbors, and they want to live their lives in freedom. No people in this world, no people in Europe needs to have fears because the gates between West and East have been opened and freedom and democracy are being realized in East Germany. Germans in a free and democratic country have never posed a threat to other nations."

Then I recommitted myself to the policies we had pursued until this time. For me, the Federal Republic's political road set the guidelines for future events as well: "We have made a decision in

Hans-Dietrich Genscher in 1944 as a 17-year-old Wehrmacht soldier.

During the Olympic games in Munich in September 1972, Palestinian terrorist commandos took the Israeli team hostage. HDG (second from left), in his function as minister of the interior, negotiates with the leader of the commandos (right, with hat).

Henry Kissinger, HDG, Helmut Schmidt, and Gerald Ford in the White House. During Genscher's eighteen years in office, he met with five American presidents and six secretaries of state.

The professional relationship between HDG and Henry Kissinger soon developed into a personal friendship. On the occasion of a soccer game they attended in Dortmund in the summer of 1974, both sported vests handknitted by a friend of Genscher's mother.

With Cyrus Vance, Helmut Schmidt, and Jimmy Carter.

HDG and Ronald Reagan exchanging jokes during the North-South summit in Cancun in the fall of 1981.

HDG and George Schulz in Bonn, 1990.

With George Bush.

With James Baker, in Bonn, 1990.

With Anwar as-Sadat in Abukir in 1981. Their long and trusting relationship ended abruptly with Sadat's assassination later that year.

With Queen Noor and King Hussein in Amman.

With Shimon Peres during Peres's time as foreign minister.

Menachem Begin (second from left) and HDG (right).

HDG visited Israel immediately after the Iraqi attacks during the Gulf War to underline Germany's solidarity with and support for the Israeli people.

Returning from a trip with Chancellor Helmut Kohl (1989).

With Margaret Thatcher in 1991. Not all of their conversations were conducted in such an amicable manner.

With Winnie and Nelson Mandela in 1990.

With Indira Gandhi.

Ever since their first meetings in the mid-eighties, HDG had thought Mikhail Gorbachev to be a serious, trustworthy partner. Here they are in Genscher's private home in Bonn in the early 1990s.

HDG put special emphasis on improving the relationship between Germany and Poland. While paying his respects for the murdered priest Jerzy Popieluszku in early 1988, Genscher was greeted by the still illegal labor union Solidarnösc.

Walesa came to meet with the West German foreign minister in early September 1989, at a time when the pressure on the Communist governments in the Warsaw Pact countries was rising virtually by the hour.

Even though West Germany never recognized the GDR as a nation, HDG always met with his East German counterpart at the UN conference in New York. In 1989, HDG met Oskar Fischer, the last foreign minister of a Communist government in East Germany, for a final time. Their only topic: the situation of the East German refugees in Prague and Warsaw.

As foreign minister, HDG addressed the United Nations every September. When he did so in 1989, he again repeated the quest for the unity of the German people.

In September 1989, from the balcony of the West German embassy in Prague, HDG announces to thousands of East German refugees that they are free to start a new life in the West.

It was a moving experience for HDG to give a speech at the historic Market Church in Halle in December 1989. As a child, he had attended services here with his parents. Now, for the first time, he spoke as the foreign minister of West Germany in his East German hometown.

December 22, 1989: The Brandenburg Gate, barred for decades, is finally open again, and the two German governments meet. Present are Hans Modrow, prime minister of the GDR (front row, second from left); Walter Momper, mayor of West Berlin (at the microphone); and to his left, Helmut Kohl and Hans-Dietrich Genscher.

Just one day after the opening of the Brandenburg Gate, another symbolic act took place: On December 23, 1989, HDG and his Czechoslovakian counterpart Jiri Dienstbier cut through the barbed wire along the Bavarian-Czech border. Genscher and Dienstbier had met for the first time in August 1968 in Prague, where Dienstbier was a young journalist and actively involved in the Prague Spring movement.

The first official meeting of the Two-Plus-Four took place in Bonn on May 5, 1990. From left to right: James Baker, Eduard Shevardnadze, HDG, Roland Dumas, Markus Meckel (foreign minister of the first East German government in office through free and democratic elections), and Douglas Hurd.

The deed is done: On September 12, 1990, the representatives of the
Two-Plus-Four nations toast the signing of the treaty in Moscow.

By the fall of 1990, counterparts and partners of past years had long become
friends. HDG made it a point to take some of his closest friends to visit his
Saxonian hometown Halle as a personal demonstration of what the
reunification meant for the Germans. In November 1990, he attended class
at his old high school with Eduard Shevardnadze.

Barbara and Hans-Dietrich Genscher after his resignation, June 1991.

favor of the community of Western democracies. It was a long road that has led us to this point. Steps along the way were the treaties of Moscow and Warsaw, the treaty with Czechoslovakia, the Basic Treaty with East Germany, and the Helsinki Final Act. It was a patient struggle for peace, for human rights, and for freedom. We are continuing along that road. We stand by the treaties we have concluded. Today we came from Warsaw, where we told our Polish neighbors: Our European neighbors can feel safe in the future because the Polish people know that never again will Germans question the border between Germany and Poland."

Directing my words to Moscow, I continued, "To the nations of the Warsaw Pact in which the transformation to democracy is already taking place, and to those who will walk that road in the future, we want to express our determination never unilaterally to use to our advantage the problems that may arise there, never to take advantage of any difficulty that will spring up on the road of transformation. We do not want unilateral advantages; we do want reform, freedom, and democracy to be possible in those nations as well. We want such developments to occur within a stable framework." The final sentence expressed an important principle of our policies: The stable framework must not be jeopardized by demanding too much of Moscow's leaders. I went on, "What we are witnessing in these weeks is a Europe that is remembering its noblest virtues and its great culture, to which all European peoples have contributed greatly. To these peoples we say: Today Germans cherish the great aim of acting everywhere in Europe in such a way that our neighbors will experience our happiness as their own and as a guarantee for a secure future. A long road has brought us to an important way station. We will now continue along this road with the same good sense, responsibility, and prudence."

I expressed my own feeling of happiness: "My fellow citizens, when the hour of freedom strikes all over Europe, we can say that Germans have contributed their share and that we were there. My greetings to all of our fellow citizens, to all Europeans, to all those who have made this moment possible." What I had said in the Bundestag only two days earlier had now become a vivid reality: "Even today, we want to tell the citizens of the Federal Republic of Germany: Our determination will require a great deal from us. But I am not talking about sacrifice, I am talking about investments in a free and peaceful future for Germans and Europeans there and here. What will be continuing day by day proves that the section of our nation that, since 1945, has had to carry the heavier burden of our history, has not been destroyed by that burden. The East Germans' will to freedom is not broken; it is strong. The East Germans know what the freedom means that they are fighting for. Forty years of separation have not turned one Europe into two or one German nation into two. Nations are not founded on ideologies. The Germans in the GDR are writing a new chapter of German and European history. They alone have the right to decide the kind of relationship they want with us and how and where they want to take their place in the common house of Europe. It is our responsibility to see to it that the door between us is not locked but remains open. Removing the Wall and the barbed wire, along with holding free elections, will test our credibility." By mentioning the East Germans' freedom to decide, I was anticipating and defusing any possible criticism that we were appropriating East Germany.

On November 8, in the Bundestag, I had also noted, "There would be cause for worry only if our nation were to take unilateral actions. That would be a cause of concern not only for our neighbors but for us as well." During the past years I had repeatedly warned against neutralist unilateral actions, which would constitute a return to the past. They would create new instabilities in Europe, would seriously jeopardize West-East rapprochement, and would therefore also damage Germany's national interests, which had come to be identical with Europe's interests. Germany's international position must still be valid the day after the demolition of Wall. Never again must Germans let themselves be seduced by nationalistic pied pipers.

After the Wall fell, the Soviet ambassador to Bonn, Kvitsinsky, sent a telegram to his administration noting that a new mass exodus had started which would probably cause East Germany to bleed to death. No belated reform of any kind, neither democracy nor glasnost, would persuade the East Germans to continue to live and work in the GDR. Anyone not leaving for the West must truly love and believe in Communism.

After the Iron Curtain had been drawn aside in Hungary, and the embassy in Prague had been opened, the breaching of the Wall on November 9 was the major political event of 1989, a year that

294

events in Central and Eastern Europe made the revolutionary turning point of the century. What effects would all these events have on the Federal Republic's foreign and Germany policies? And, even more important, how could our policies have an impact on events and influence them to our liking?

The Four and Unification: Talks in Washington

The day after the Wall came down and I returned from Warsaw, I telephoned my colleagues and friends in Paris, London, and Washington—Roland Dumas, Douglas Hurd, and James Baker—to thank them for all their help and solidarity in difficult times and to reconfirm our political course. The Foreign Office's telephone operator placed the calls for me; when she had Baker on the line, she said, "Mr. Baker, God bless America!" Baker was deeply moved, as he told me immediately when she had connected us. I replied, "She merely expressed the sentiments of all Germans."

On November 11, 1989, a Saturday, I telephoned Eduard Shevardnadze. I wanted to thank the Soviet leaders for acting so responsibly during the past few weeks. In addition, with a particular emphasis on the importance of the German-Soviet Declaration, I reassured my counterpart that we were upholding all our contracts and commitments.

In view of the dramatic changes going on in Europe, particularly in East Germany, President Mitterand in his capacity as chairman of the European Council, called for a special summit in Paris on November 18. It was obvious: Mitterand looked to advance two situations. One was the reform movements in Central Europe, in particular in Poland and Hungary, where the most progress had been made; the reform nations were to be entitled to become members of the European Council and GATT. Second, a bank was to be established for supporting changes in the reform nations. Thus the European Bank for Reconstruction and Development came into being. At the same time Mitterand wanted to continue the European unification process, with the goal of the European Union.

At no point did I have cause to doubt France's support of German unification. My friend Roland Dumas had made his position crystal clear in a television interview on November 10. To the remark, "François Mitterand once said, 'If the Federal Republic and the German Democratic Republic unite, we have reason to tremble,' " he had replied, "We have no reason to tremble, for matters are progressing peacefully; but we do have to assume political responsibility, we have a duty to reflect."

On the evening of November 20 I flew to Washington. Thus began my round of visits to the capitals of the four nations that, according to the Four Power Agreement, were responsible for Germany as a whole: Washington, Moscow, Paris, and London. Moscow would be my last stop. My goal was to elaborate on the changes occurring in Germany and in Europe, to present our position, and to determine the reactions to German unification, which was on the horizon.

The mood in Washington was extremely cordial, genuinely congenial, even warm and deeply friendly. President Bush received me in the Oval Office. I was accompanied by Ambassador Jürgen Ruhfus, Deputy Undersecretary of State Dieter Kastrup, and the director of the disarmament division, Deputy Undersecretary Josef Holik. The President had asked Vice President Dan Quayle, Secretary of State Baker, Chief of Staff John Sununu, and Security Adviser Brent Scowcroft, as well as his associates Robert Gates and Robert Blackwill and Ambassador Vernon Walters to join him. As a symbol of our gratitude I presented the President with a brick from the Berlin Wall, explaining that tearing down the Wall symbolized the will to freedom and democracy and that we wanted to express our thanks for the support and steadfastness with which the United States had helped us during the difficult years. I continued by noting that we must now realize reforms in Eastern Europe and the German people's right to self-determination; basing ourselves on the CSCE process, we needed to create the foundation for a lasting peace in all of Europe. The President thanked me and paid moving homage to the events in Berlin.

Next he touched on a subject with which we had still been preoccupied through all of 1989—the short-range missiles. Some American newspapers alleged that we were trying to renege on agreed points. I replied that the issue should not be discussed until 1992, just as we had agreed upon. I could say as much in good conscience, since at this point, in November 1989, no one could seriously believe that three years from now we would have to vote *in favor* of deployment.

President Bush then turned to more pressing issues. He told us that he had been criticized for failing to make stronger statements and "not jumping on the Wall." But, he argued, events were moving toward freedom, and circumspection was required to deal with the multitude of problems. I affirmed the President's judicious stand. Now, I remarked, it turned out that the resolutions taken at last summer's NATO summit had constituted worthy guidelines. We should remain calm and maintain our policies, which were directed at stability and at overall cooperation. Bush referred to the American saying "Never change a winning team" and added that "Never change winning guidelines" would be equally apt. I expressly welcomed the upcoming summit between Bush and Gorbachev; I noted that we were interested in further improved relations between the United States and the Soviet Union, since such a move would lead to greater flexibility in Central and Eastern Europe, where impressive changes leading to freedom and democracy were under way. I added that the fate of all of Germany was embedded in these developments. In working for all Germans' right to self-determination, we should avoid isolating ourselves. We were loyal to the Alliance and to our commitments, and by extension we would advance the integration process of the European Community. This path should be further pursued at the Strasbourg summit.

By speaking of our insistence on the right to self-determination, I had brought up the subject of German unity, and George Bush immediately mentioned Gorbachev. He said that the Secretary General was worried about the German question. The dynamics of change in Poland, Hungary, and East Germany—and probably in Czechoslovakia before long—made it likely that in the near future German unity would be called for. The United States, he said, supported Germany's concern for self-determination, unity, peace, and liberty, and yet it was possible that the process was happening more quickly than we had expected. I replied that precisely because of the effect it would have on Moscow, it was the East Germans' business to make a statement on the issue of unity. Our constitution already stated the will to unity; we were in favor of it, as I had emphasized on September 28 before the United Nations. At this point demands in East Germany predominantly concerned reforms, democracy, and free elections, but during rallies—for example, in Leipzig—the demand for unity could be heard as well. There were frequent references to the East German national anthem, "Deutschland, einig Vaterland" (Germany, United Fatherland). If the East Germans achieved freedom and democracy, such a change could not really be disadvantageous to Europe. Yet one factor must be made absolutely clear in this context: We had no intention of taking unilateral actions, we stood with NATO and the European Community. While in the past, I remarked, there was frequent open concern about Germany's playing a special role, today Germans must not be forced into a special role by excluding them from the pan-European course of events. Such a position would be just as unacceptable.

I continued by stating that it was important to send signals to the Soviet Union indicating that in regard to security concerns, the West would not unilaterally try to take advantage of the events, and therefore the issue of borders was of crucial importance. The Bundestag had issued a resolution, approved by a large majority, confirming the declaration on Germany's eastern border I had delivered at the United Nations the previous September. In my opinion this vote proved that Germans acted responsibly when emerging developments called for a response.

To my question regarding the upcoming American-Soviet conference in Malta, President Bush replied that he hoped to seize the opportunity to get to know Gorbachev better on a personal level. Above all, he wanted to learn the limits of Gorbachev's sphere of action and what he had meant when he said that the idea of German unification called for caution. He thought it important to get a sense of how the economic situation and the problem of diverse nationalities were unfolding in the Soviet Union. If there were going to be negotiations on disarmament, Bush would defer to the Alliance.

Then the President, addressing me in very personal terms, returned to events in Germany. He remarked that he was well aware what the current development in East Germany meant to me, who had been born there. He understood me, and not only on that day; clearly he also understood the motives that had led me to reject the modernization of the short-range missiles in the early months of this historic year of 1989.

I left the White House knowing that I had been with friends, who supported our desire for German unity, who helped us and who, along with us, thought about methods by which we could realize our goal in such a way as to make certain that all of Europe would gain something, and win the Soviet Union's approval.

After talking with the President, I met separately with Scowcroft. Again alluding to my statements to Bush, I reiterated that it was crucially important to grant the German people the opportunity to exercise the right to self-determination. It was unlikely that many in the West would scent danger in the fact that East Germany was taking the road of democracy and that East Germans were seizing their chance to exercise their right to self-determination. I noted that I had always been convinced that as soon as East Germans could express their will democratically, they would lay a claim to unity.

Scowcroft was wondering whether, when we talked about exercising the right to self-determination, we were thinking of a peace treaty or of a Four Power conference. I rejected the idea of a treaty, arguing that we had long since left that option behind, since we were partners and friends of three of the Four Powers, as well as of most of those nations that had been involved in the Second World War. We also had a good relationship with the Soviet Union. On the other hand, under the present circumstances, a Four Power conference would also mean a step backward, nor was it wise to assign the Germans a minor and separate role in negotiations on the German question, as had been done in Geneva during the 1950s: All six participants must sit down together at *one* table. The six were the two Germanys—the Federal Republic and the GDR—and the Four—the United States, the Soviet Union, France, and the United Kingdom. This was already the basic concept for the negotiations to come.

Scowcroft also displayed an interest in the economic conditions in East Germany. I informed him about the Paris EC summit of November 18, where we had agreed to establish a bank for European cooperation. It was important that we convince the Soviet Union in the immediate future that we would not take unilateral advantage of any difficulties arising during the transition period.

I also met with Jim Baker in the State Department for a private talk. We delved more deeply into the topics the President had touched on. The mood was fairly relaxed. Within a few months the climate had changed drastically. The reserved and cold reception Secretary Baker and Secretary Cheney had given Defense

Minister Stoltenberg and myself in this same room in the spring was almost forgotten. Now our identical appraisal of the situation and the opportunities resulting from it was uniting us. Our personal rapport had been forged a long time ago.

The fact that from the beginning we had discussed our different positions with the openness and clarity called for by friendship now paid off. Neither President Bush nor Secretary Baker cared to have the United States' most important European partner obsequiously applaud every turn of American public opinion. The discussion on short-range nuclear missiles—which we had conducted with clarity and self-confidence—had had the effect of a purifying thunderstorm. Our unequivocal support of the concerns of the indivisible German nation and our policies of responsibility toward our Eastern neighbor, Poland, had had a positive political effect, as had the decision on modernizing short-range missiles.

On my flight back from Washington I let the events of this visit unfold yet again before my mind's eye. My view had been confirmed: Whatever happened now, if we tackled the process of German unity responsibly and rationally, the United States would stand by us.

On Friday—two days later—I flew to Budapest to confer once again with Foreign Minister Horn and Prime Minister Németh. Hungary needed to be assured that we did not intend to dismiss it now that the nation had been useful to our ends. Germany would continue to support reform policies in Central Europe, and it would never forget what Hungary had done for Europe's and Germany's future.

The Chancellor's Ten Points

November 28, 1989, was to become a crucial date in the relationship between the Federal Republic and the GDR. On that day the second debate on the 1990 budget was held, starting with the departments of the chancellor and the Chancellor's Office and the federal ministers for inter-German relations and the Foreign Office. During the preceding days rumor had it that the Chancellor wanted to use the debate for presenting his own ideas on the German question. Since, according to the rumor, he wanted his statements to be understood as his personal opinion, he did not intend to discuss them within his department or the coalition; the

CDU had to reassert its lead on the German question. There was also talk of a response to my appearance in Prague.

Even at the time I had sensed that my efforts on behalf of the asylum seekers in the embassy, as well as my trip to Prague in general, had not caused unalloyed joy in the government coalition. Yet before and during my trip to New York I was in constant telephone contact with the Chancellor and Minister Seiters. The Chancellor's Office was kept informed on all my actions and had given me the green light.

There had been no alternative to my decision to go to Prague to convince the refugees in the embassy that they could safely pass through East German territory. But I had asked Minister Seiters to accompany me, even though any activity in the embassy was part of my office and my responsibility alone: It was important to me to prevent any possible jealousy, such as had arisen on previous occasions. Nevertheless in the days that followed I was told repeatedly, by journalists as well as by Christian-Democratic politicians close to me, that the CDU/CSU had responded to my activities with skepticism, even with displeasure, because my behavior might be advantageous for the FDP. I found it difficult to believe these reports.

I also found it very hard to understand the critical reactions within the CDU, and they annoyed me; but I had not the slightest interest in letting intracoalition frictions debilitate me during this crucial phase in German politics and history. We would need all our strength and to be as near to unanimity as possible within the coalition.

What did seem important to me in this phase was to explain the German position with absolute clarity to the West and the East, even under conditions that changed day by day. For this reason I had decided to go to Washington, London, Paris, and Moscow. It was clear to me that in future a united Germany would need to remain a member of the European Community and of NATO. We must find ways to make this decision acceptable to the Soviet Union as well.

How did the Soviet Union appraise the situation on November 8, 1989, the day on which we debated the state of the nation in a divided Germany? What expectations did it have at this point in time, when there still was an East Germany that was in need of reforms but, according to Moscow, also able to institute them?

After all, on November 8, 1989, the Wall was still in place. Addressing this issue, I had therefore told the Bundestag, that increased freedom to travel alone would not suffice; the Wall must come down. In August 1989, before the CSCE conference in Vienna, I had called it a relic that needed to be removed. I had decided to focus my statements on unification of the nation, the consequences of such a change, and the fact that German policies must be grounded in European policies. I also spoke about the ways our policies could lead to positive changes within a larger European context.

That Helmut Kohl's ten-point declaration had not been discussed with the FDP was the coalition's affair. But it had not been discussed with our most important allies either, and yet we would urgently need their support in the coming weeks. Instead, officials from the Chancellor's Office telephoned several embassies to suggest that their countries pay close attention to the Chancellor's Bundestag declaration because it contained statements of the utmost importance.

On November 28 Helmut Kohl presented his ten-point plan to the Bundestag. It was composed of many elements, among them a long-range program for cooperation with East Germany. The Chancellor also addressed the "treaty community" suggested by East Germany's prime minister, Hans Modrow, in his government declaration, stressing that we were ready to work with this idea. That statement seemed good and necessary to me, since it could serve to diminish the expected opposition from the Soviet Union. Pointing out both states' common institutions and confederate structures, on the other hand, might lead to confusion and insecurity. At the end of his statement Kohl emphasized our desire to reestablish German unity. I, too, had made that same declaration, year after year, at the United Nations, and I had reiterated it as recently as September 28, 1989. Just prior to that time, to my great satisfaction, the Chancellor had called the CSCE process the core of the pan-European structure. For the CDU/CSU this statement was an about-face on CSCE policy, and for the FDP and for myself, a reason to feel particular satisfaction.

It was necessary to think carefully about our response to both the form and content of the Chancellor's plan. I had reservations about the model of a confederation of two Germanys; I thought such an alliance was not viable and ultimately had no future. How could the partners in confederate structures belong to two different alliances? Such an eventuality could have led to the dangerous road of special status. The division of Germany was the result of an ideological confrontation, the conflict between West and East, and problems of that nature could not be overcome within the structures of constitutional law. It was the underlying policies that must be changed. Only such an alteration would allow a solution to the problems.

After the lunch recess I took the floor. During the break I had formulated our party's position and discussed it with the other leaders of the FDP. They, too, were vexed that a declaration of such impact had not been discussed ahead of time either in the coalition or within the administration. It was clear to me that foreign reactions to the Chancellor's speech would lead to problems between West and East that could have been avoided. Factually the declaration lagged far behind our actual stage in the unification process.

The course of events had long since gone beyond the stage of confederate cooperation. Unification from below was already fully in motion, and the fact that the process had started from below was beneficial. Abroad, both in the West and in the East, the situation would be looked on much more favorably than would a process imposed from the top. What remained important was to allow national unification to lead to an inner unification of Germany. As I had said when I spoke at the Schöneberg City Hall, East Germans must not again perceive their situation determined from outside and above. It was up to them to decide and to express their decision on whether or not they chose to accept the offer of unification codified in the Basic Law.

It was obvious that there would not be enough time to create confederative structures. The unification of Germany must be completed as quickly as possible, and that process required the approval of all those directly concerned—specifically, the four powers responsible for Germany as a whole. For the sake of the issue at stake I decided that in speaking in the Bundestag I would not criticize the coalition's and administration's approach. At this historically crucial phase we must not stage a spectacle that showed a government at loggerheads over procedural and, as regards confederate structures, fundamental issues. For the same reason I forbore pointing out weaknesses in the declaration; for example, the Chancellor's plan had not taken a position on the issue of Germany's eastern border. In this latest phase of German politics, national concerns had absolute priority.

In my speech I referred to the declaration by the FDP's executive committee of the previous day. This declaration stated in part, "The FDP calls on the new East German leaders to revoke the SED's constitutional right to sole leadership, to allow additional parties, and to prepare for general, free, and secret elections in the near future by establishing an election law that grants parity to all parties." The FDP had already stated that the old goal of a policy that would codify Liberal principles in Germany, the effort to work toward a state of peace in which the German people would again be unified by free self-determination, as stated in the Letter on German Unity, was closer to realization than ever. At the same time we pledged our unqualified commitment to the European Community and the continuation of the process of European unification, to NATO, and to the meaning of the CSCE.

In my speech to the Bundestag I addressed the issue of Germany's eastern border, pointing out that jointly we had made an important decision on the border with Poland. I intended to reaffirm my statement on Germany's Eastern border to the United Nations in September, referring to the impending unification of Germany. I then turned to unification itself, addressing my East German fellow citizens: "You will not have to pay; we will make certain that you get the same opportunities—forty years later—that we, through a lucky turn of historical events, have enjoyed in the Federal Republic of Germany." Those who knew the true situation in East Germany realized the massive problems ahead of us in connection with unification.

Finally I reiterated my assertion that the Germans' desire in both German states to unify was a prerequisite. As soon as free elections had been held, I said, we would know where our fellow citizens in East Germany wanted to go and how they wanted to shape their own domestic order.

Six weeks later, on December 20, 1989, when I had occasion to make a public appearance in Halle, my hometown, for the first time, I returned to that idea: "We have made our decision in favor of the unity of our nation," I said. "Now it is up to you to decide which path you want to take, whether you want to live with us." I was aware that, particularly with regard to the Soviet Union but elsewhere as well, it was important that the Germans in the East also express their will to unification. West Germany must never allow the false impression to arise that it was eager to absorb the East Germans and place them under Western control, as it were. A great deal depended on our taking these steps in full agreement with our Western partners as well as with a display of absolute candor and trust toward Gorbachev and Shevardnadze.

We had established a solid basis for this process, our latest effort being the German-Soviet Declaration of the summer of 1989, which Shevardnadze and I had elaborated and polished for a long time. Together with my associates I had witnessed my Soviet colleague's dismissing many of his advisers' doubts. Repeatedly they tried to persuade him and give him contrary advice. He had become impatient, because he realized that the Federal Republic and the Soviet Union were forging a declaration that would set the course for the future, a declaration that literally constituted New Thinking and established it as the subject of actual policies.

The Four and Unification II: Talks in London, Paris, and Moscow

On November 29 I flew to London. First I met with Prime Minister Thatcher for a talk in which Foreign Secretary Hurd also participated; later she and I continued the conversation in private. Thatcher addressed the issue of the evolution of the West's Eastern policy. She argued, using the term "containment," that initially the policy had been entirely defensive; but with the CSCE, the West had become more courageous, taking the offensive, particularly by demanding freedom and democracy. Nevertheless, only President Reagan had truly challenged the East and pushed through a strong defense strategy; under his leadership the Soviet SS-20 missiles could finally be counterbalanced by the NATO double-track resolution and the subsequent deployment of the Pershing II. I was happy to hear her appraising the CSCE so favorably. I politely mentioned, however, that it had been the Schmidt-Genscher administration that had given the decisive impetus to the double-track resolution, and the Kohl-Genscher administration that was responsible for its enactment.

I addressed the different ways reforms were being realized in the Warsaw Pact nations. In East Germany and Czechoslovakia, I said, the reform movement had orginated at the bottom, but in the Soviet Union it arose at the top; in Hungary the political leaders had initiated the transformation, and in the process had themselves undergone a transformation.

Thatcher recalled the Paris EC summit of November 18, 1989. She remarked that she had believed a consensus had been reached that had resulted in a program. Now she realized that everything was in flux. She was obviously alluding to the Chancellor's ten-point plan, which I then explained in greater detail, without discussing its inception or my reservations. I also expounded on the general conditions for future developments, pointing out that we must resolutely continue our disarmament and arms-control policy. I particularly emphasized our firm position within NATO and the European Community. When at this point Secretary Hurd interjected, arguing that the Chancellor had not given a timetable for unification, I explained how much our policies were integrated into European policies; at the same time I contended that the unification of Europe must not occur without Germany.

It was my impression that Thatcher had reservations about German unification. Her repeated warnings not to alter the status quo also indicated that she could accept current events only reluctantly. But I left London convinced that if Washington and Paris would agree, we could reach an accord with London as well. In any case I could count on Douglas Hurd. If we maintained a clear stand on NATO, the European Community, and the Oder-Neisse Line, we would be able to move events along.

I also took the opportunity of my meeting with Margaret Thatcher to advocate supporting Gorbachev politically and economically. Without such support the conflict between West and East could hinder German unification.

From London I continued on to Paris, where I met with Roland Dumas and subsequently with former president Giscard d'Estaing and Alain Poher, the president of the French senate. Dumas was concerned that during the Paris EC summit nothing had been said about what was now summed up in the Chancellor's ten points. Further, he said, Bonn was increasingly expressing reservations about the economic and currency union. Dumas also mentioned that there was some ill feeling about the way the Western allies had been briefed on the ten-point plan.

That day I was invited to attend a session of the French Senate.

Before going on to the agenda, President Poher extended me a warm welcome, and the senators gave me a standing ovation—a great distinction for German foreign policy and the German foreign minister himself. In all my meetings I delivered the same message: I emphasized that Europe could not unify without Germany. We wanted unification to be fully integrated in Europe; our membership in NATO and the European Community was not open to discussion. I also pointed out that it was particularly important to accelerate the economic and currency union. The European Community's internal dynamics must not lag behind the dynamic that was determining the reshaping of West-East relations.

President Mitterrand received me in the late afternoon. After he asked me to speak first, I stated that we were living in rapidly changing times and that the ongoing events in East Germany were rocking the foundations of our nation. I noted that, because of my origins and my current position, I was especially shaken, and I did not want to conceal my pride in my fellow countrymen in East Germany, who had peacefully promoted freedom and democracy. In my opinion, I continued, it was absurd to wish to deny the two German states the effects of the process of rapprochement between Western and Eastern Europe. It was important that we determine our joint position now, a task that should be accomplished at the upcoming Strasbourg summit. These words brought me to the issue of the general conditions that had to be resolved if German unification was to be obtained. Strasbourg must send a twofold signal: A firm intention of enhancing integration in the EC on the one hand and a readiness to cooperate with the East on the other. I argued that in Europe we were now entering a competition of sorts between two dynamic processes. One was the West's integration in the European Community, and the other was developing reforms in the East; in addition and resulting from these reforms, there was West-East rapprochement. Unification within the European Community was therefore important not only economically or financially, but also politically. For future stability, I continued, it was important that we pledge our unquestionable allegiance to NATO and to a continued United States military presence in Europe. The Alliance, I argued, would be more political in the future, and it must become more actively involved in the disarmament process. Further, another condition for stability in Europe was the Federal Republic's unequivocal stand on Poland's western border. I reminded Mitterand that I had already made a statement to that effect at the United Nations in September, which the Bundestag had affirmed by an overwhelming majority on November 8.

It was necessary that the NATO conference in Brussels on December 4—where President Bush was going to report to us on the Malta summit with Gorbachev—and the European Council meeting in Strasbourg send out the message that we were eager to contribute to the success of the Eastern reform movement and that we did not intend to take unilateral advantage of problems. We were interested in a long-term, permanent European framework.

Mitterand replied that events had unfolded with incredible rapidity. He agreed with me that if we wanted to advance West-East relations without taking risks, progress on European integration was necessary on two levels simultaneously. If integration in the West stood still, it would soon lag behind; in such a case, however, Europe would undergo fundamental change, and new, privileged alliances would be formed. It was not impossible that Europe would regress to the political ideas prevailing before the First World War. If German unification was to occur in a Europe that ultimately had made no real progress, then the European partners, who in the future were going to face 80 million Germans, would probably be looking for a counterweight. I responded by noting that those counterweights would not be necessary if European integration was progressing along the lines we hoped for.

Mitterand agreed. And as he went on to remark that the problems that needed to be cleared up at the European Council in Strasbourg should be seen from this perspective. He also mentioned his impression that the Federal Republic—which so far always had been the engine of the European unification process—was no longer interested in hurrying the process along; it was, in fact, slowing it down. Others, he argued—evidently alluding to London—who at heart supported neither the advancement of European unification nor German unification, would take advantage of that circumstance.

Mitterand emphasized that, as far as he was concerned, unification was an unstoppable "matter." Caution demanded that as this course developed, conflict with the Soviet Union must be avoided. German unification, however, was historically necessary: "We will support you in this, but where will a unified Germany stand in regard to European unification?" In each phase of this change, he noted, Germany and France must advance in concert. West Germany must not lay itself open to attack. Of course much could be explained by Germany's domestic state of affairs, but this situation was secondary compared to the historic decisions that needed to be taken in Strasbourg.

Over the years I had had a number of conversations with President Mitterand. This one, however, was the most important. At this moment in time, as always, President Mitterand proved to be a statesman of European stature and Germany's reliable friend, intent, not on erecting obstacles to German unification, but on creating a general environment in which German unification would be a gain for Europe. This attitude coincided with my own thoughts and strategy, and I replied, "We have made our choice"—a sentence I could utter in good conscience. While I was expressing my personal opinion, it was also true that within the West German government we were in agreement on our European commitment; this was particularly true for Helmut Kohl. Nevertheless, the Christian Union parties were reluctant to name a date for starting the government conference, since it might overlap with the national elections, scheduled for late 1990.

I had no use for such hesitations. In fact, given the circumstances, I considered them problematic. They must never be allowed to create mistrust in Paris and thus also affect German-French relations and France's position on German unity.

Mitterand admitted that, if Germany helped to build up Europe, there were unlimited possibilities on the German question. One day even the Soviet Union would be able to live with German unification within the EC, while it would most certainly oppose an autonomous unification process. "Enlarged by the German Democratic Republic and active in the larger European association, Germany will have friends in the European Community; otherwise, Germany will merely have partners with individual reflexes." Thus, he said, Germans were indeed confronted with a far-reaching decision.

I replied firmly, "In Strasbourg we will be able to make the decision in favor of the government conference and decide on when it will begin. Our future lies with the European Community. It does not lie between East and West; if it did, forty years of creating policies would have been in vain." I continued by noting that we were perfectly aware that Gorbachev would also prefer us to be in the EC rather than isolated. Further, West Germany's governmental policy was supported by the opposition SPD. East Germany and the Soviet Union had a role in deciding on the schedule for German unification, but the dates coincided more closely than many had expected. However, I remarked, European unification could be determined by the EC member nations themselves, and that was why a decision was going to be made in Strasbourg—and it would be the right one. The events in the East had merely strengthened the arguments for unification further.

I wanted to thank the President of France for supporting German unification. For us, his position was of historic significance. And so was our answer to European unity.

I left the Elysée Palace and Paris in a sanguine frame of mind. I had learned that we could count not only on France's sympathy but also on its support. The latter was particularly important. Here, too, my old rule of thumb held: Nothing is possible without France; with France, almost anything can happen.

It was characteristic for Mitterand's concept of history that he did not make his stand on German unity dependent on our stand on European unification; he was correct in considering it unavoidable. In believing that if Germany hesitated on European unification, this reluctance could set in motion new developments in Europe, he was also correct; that situation must not be allowed to arise. The Europeanization of the German question had brought about the revolutionary changes on the whole Continent that were opening up an historic chance for Germany right now, and for that reason alone any de-Europeanization in the direction of the West was out of the question. Being—or even merely seeming to be—hesitant about European unification might have such an effect, and that was the last thing we wanted.

At the time—in 1988, 1989, and 1990, as well as later, in looking back at those years—some people smiled knowingly when I kept emphasizing that the German question must be part and parcel of European developments, and when I repeatedly pointed out that we were a member of the European Community and of NATO. For me these were basic elements of Europe's future development, including German unification. I was convinced that for our Western partners, the issue of Germany's eastern border, and our attitude toward the EC and NATO would be the crucial issue.

In an effort not to allow mistrust to develop as a result of the American-Soviet summit meeting on December 2 and 3, 1989, in Malta, President Bush and Secretary of State Baker went from Malta to Brussels to inform their European allies on Monday, December 4. Chancellor Kohl and I received a special briefing. The President met with the Chancellor and I met with Secretary Baker, who gave me a comprehensive synopsis.

Public statements to this time had made it clear that the German question had played a crucial role in Malta. As President Bush said, he had affirmed "NATO's traditional position"—in other words, a commitment to German unification. At the same time he had committed himself to the inviolability of borders, and in this connection he spoke of the concept of "permanent borders"—a reference to the unalterability of the Polish border. Besides, Bush told the press, he had declared "that for our part we do not want to do anything unrealistic that could lead to regress in any country or that could draw our own people into a conflict. In my opinion we have tried to act the way President Gorbachev has indicated: With great consideration."

I was extremely grateful to Jim Baker for keeping me fully abreast of the latest public statements, giving me more information than was revealed at the NATO Council the following day, and for adding his personal comments on these statements. Because of my imminent trip to Moscow, the information was important to me.

Apparently Gorbachev had indicated in Malta—as he would when he spoke with me in Moscow—that he did not intend to relinquish control of events. However, as regards the German question, he seemed to have been rather inflexible in Malta.

On the morning of December 5, 1989, President Bush officially informed the heads of state and government as well as the foreign ministers about his encounter with Gorbachev in Malta. I subsequently went to Moscow, where I arrived at eight o'clock that night. The visit had been thoroughly prepared. After my talks with the American, French, and British leaders I now wanted to discuss with the Soviet representative the most recent developments in Europe and German unification.

After the talks in Washington of November 1989 we could be confident about the United States' support. The same was true for France. In light of United States support, I did not expect serious obstacles from Margaret Thatcher; I was certain that Douglas Hurd understood our concern. Now I needed to convince Moscow that with German unification, a pan-European policy would be possible that, provided there were new European structures and a new relationship between the alliances, would be more advantageous to the Soviet Union than were the partition of Europe and the existence of two German states.

When I arrived at the Moscow airport, I was not met by Eduard Shevardnadze, who was attending a Moscow conference of the Warsaw Pact's party leaders and heads of state. Deputy Foreign Minister Anatoly Adamishin came in his stead. We left the government section of the airport, driving in huge SIS limousines along a wide avenue, heading for the city. It was dark out and visibility was low because of snow flurries. We were a little more than a half-mile past the airport when we saw a long fleet of cars on the opposite lane, which had stopped on its way to the airport. Adamshin explained that these cars were transporting the East German leaders—Secretary General Krenz, Prime Minister Modrow, and other top members of the East German government; they had been in Moscow for the conference. Apparently the fleet of cars had stopped so as to avoid an airport encounter with me.

After our arrival in Moscow I talked first with Shevardnadze in the Foreign Ministry's guest house, which was familiar to me from previous visits. Speaking privately, with only the interpreters present, I sensed the Soviet leaders' exasperation at the Chancellor's ten-point plan. Shevardnadze pointed out that the German-Soviet Declaration, which we had compiled early in the summer after arduous negotiations, had laid down our agreement to consult with each other on important issues. And now the ten-point plan, which touched on crucial issues of Soviet policies and on German-Soviet relations, had been put forward without preliminary discussions.

Apparently the East German leaders who had just left had also complained about the declaration. Shevardnadze seemed depressed. He seemed to understand the inevitability with which events were unfolding, and he did not seem to regret the way matters were moving—quite the contrary. However, he was aware of the problems and upheavals the changes would cause his country and in particular for Gorbachev and himself. From earlier conversations with me he was bound to realize that our goal had always been German unification. After all, over the years of working together we had developed a truly cordial relationship, we had even become friends, and his help in opening the Prague Embassy had brought us still closer. Now he admitted how dumfounded Gorbachev was by the content of the ten-point declaration. My visit with the Secretary General would therefore hardly be easy. It scarcely need be said that I had hoped for a different reception, particularly since the time had come for constructive talks about the immediate future, especially pan-European perspectives, the situation in East Germany, and the requirements for unification of the two German states.

It was to be my most unpleasant meeting with Gorbachev, whom I had been the first to recognize as a man whose policies would change the world. I was particularly sorry that the chance to speak with Gorbachev about the really important topics was lost for the moment. I was thinking back to my unpleasant meeting with Shevardnadze in Vienna after the *Newsweek* interview. Now, too, there must be no disturbance between Bonn and Moscow, since we needed to win Moscow over for German unification; that approval was the key. Nothing must happen that might darken the atmosphere; instead, Gorbachev's disappointment and vexation must be overcome as quickly as possible. During our talk I advocated Helmut Kohl's position, but I avoided anything that could have escalated the conflict. Never before or since have I seen Gorbachev so agitated and so bitter.

At this conference with Gorbachev the Soviets were also represented by Foreign Minister Shevardnadze and by Vadim Zagladin, and the Germans by Ambassador Klaus Blech and by Undersecretary Dieter Kastrup. In 1974–1975 Blech had played a crucial part in the concluding sessions on the Helsinki Final Act. He is one of the brilliant minds of German diplomacy and supremely knowledgeable in West-East relations, in particular ongoing events in the Soviet Union. His appointment as ambassador in Moscow thus underscored the significance we placed on our relations with the Soviet Union.

Even as he welcomed me, Gorbachev remarked that current

circumstances had placed a special twist on my visit and that even though he was considering me a privileged visitor, he felt compelled to add that, compared to previous meetings, we found ourselves in a difficult situation.

I transmitted the Federal President's and the Chancellor's regards and emphasized how good it was to be talking at this moment. I told Gorbachev that I considered this meeting an important one because I was eager to exchange thoughts in the spirit of our various agreements, quite openly, sincerely, and clearly. Gorbachev understood. He asked for my appraisal of the situation.

By way of introduction I noted that both sides needed to display a considerable degree of responsibility, farsightedness, caution, and prudence. The Secretary General, I continued, knew very well that our policies were based on the Moscow Treaty, the Warsaw Treaty, the treaty with Czechoslovakia, the Basic Treaty with East Germany, and the significant Joint German-Soviet Declaration, which, as was well known, had tremendous impact, not only on bilateral relations, but also on West-East relations in general. The Federal Republic of Germany was firmly integrated into the Western Alliance and the European Community. We were, I proceeded, staunch supporters of the CSCE process and had never left any doubt that we would not consider or support unilateral national actions. Increasingly Europe was coalescing; no nation must be excluded from this development. However, I also wanted to emphasize that the two German states' coalescing must be made to fit into European structures and developments. I reminded Gorbachev that, in connection with the Moscow Treaty, the West German government had sent the Soviet government the Letter on German Unity, in which our stand on the German question was unequivocally laid down—to work toward a state of peace in Europe in which the German people could regain its unity through self-determination. Moscow, I noted, had always been aware of this goal.

The Secretary General replied that political philosophy was one thing but concrete steps were another. He wished to tell me quite frankly that some of the events occurring in Germany were worrying him. He noted that he could not comprehend how the Chancellor, in his ten points, could give ultimatums to East Germany; such actions challenged everyone concerned. He would have expected that the ten points would be formulated only after they had been discussed. Or did the Chancellor believe that discussion was no longer necessary? He spoke harshly to say that such behavior was not acceptable by any standards; it was not the way to make progress in European policies. The West German government's concrete actions must adhere to our agreements. We needed to trust each other. Gorbachev emphatically pointed out that the events in East Germany had been possible only because of the Soviet Union's new policy. The Chancellor had promised him by telephone that he would act prudently. The previous day, Gorbachev continued, Chancellor Kohl had said that President Bush supported the idea of a confederation of the two German states. He, the Secretary General, could not help but ask what, in that case, would happen with NATO? What would happen to the German-Soviet agreements?

I could not just let Gorbachev's criticism pass. Not only its form but also its content were unjustified. I therefore objected that in his ten-point program the Chancellor had declared that we were willing to give aid and to cooperate; that he had presented possibilities of rapprochement between the two German states, nothing more. The plan was an offer, not an ultimatum or an order. I remarked that I had personally spoken with Kohl before my departure and that he had assured me that he had intended his program to present a perspective, to offer East Germany the option of acceptance or refusal. The ten points must be kept strictly separate from East Germany's domestic problems, for which the West German government was not responsible.

The Secretary General remarked that I was trying to act as the Chancellor's advocate, but that my efforts were in vain. His statements, he said, were likely to destroy everything that we had established by our joint policy. Our conversation turned into a harsh argument, during which I rejected Gorbachev's criticism of the Chancellor.

Gorbachev continued by saying that he respected me personally but that we were talking about adding fuel to the flame. The plan was part of an election campaign—a remark I categorically rejected by saying that we could certainly disagree on concrete matters, but when it came to intentions and goals, it was essential that we trust each other. We were not adventurers, I said: "We know our responsibility." The East Germans must decide on what to do with their freedom. There was no need to take back anything of what we had jointly stated in the German-Soviet Declaration.

In the end Gorbachev remarked that he considered our talk useful, an open discussion at a crucial point in time. He noted that he had no intention of casting doubt on our previously concluded agreements but that he was extremely worried and was eager to state how dangerous unpremeditated actions generally were. His request for cooperation, which he was extending to West Germany, was being tendered at a decisive phase in international politics. The world must experience no more surprises.

I was concerned that details of our conversation might leak out and confuse and trouble the East Germans. Such an eventuality might have aggravated the situation, since new prospects would be placed in jeopardy. Further, especially at this point, the West German chancellor's freedom of action must not be limited by public criticism in this area. I therefore noted that if the Secretary General called for cooperation without surprises, I could only agree. That objective was exactly what we wanted as well, and ultimately it was the reason for my visit. My call for caution and responsibility, however, also extended to today's conversation; I therefore wanted to ask, in all frankness, about the public face both sides should put on our conversation.

Gorbachev understood immediately. Apparently he was just as eager to avoid a public escalation of the situation. He suggested that it was not yet time to make our appraisals public, a situation that would not change for the time being. But—and Bonn must be fully aware of this—the Kremlin would be paying close attention to the actions of the West German government. We should take the Soviet government's worries seriously; no rash actions should be taken. Nor would he play the Chancellor off against his deputy. He said that while I had defended the Chancellor's ten points, it must surely also be true that I had learned about them only during the Bundestag debate. My response was unequivocal: "That is an internal issue, it should not be discussed here."

Gorbachev continued by noting that our public statements should point out that we had held extensive talks about European issues in connection with the changes currently taking place; that the Soviet Union had explained its basic stand on the German question, while I had pointed out that Bonn stood by the Eastern treaties and the Helsinki Final Act; that Germany desired a stable situation in Europe; and that the Soviet Union and the West German government had agreed that the times demanded responsible politics. However, Gorbachev added, if West Germany was going to continue along the lines the Chancellor had laid down in his program, the Soviet position would change at once. I concluded the conversation by remarking that we were going to continue our policies of responsibility.

When we said good-bye a little later, a remark by the Secretary General caught my attention: "If the pan-European process and relations between the Soviet Union and the federal government develop positively, new developments will be possible in the German question as well." The message was clear. Thus this visit to Moscow proved once again that the door to German unity was already open. Now the future would depend on our shaping the process toward that goal as an element of pan-European developments.

My appraisal of the conversation was as follows: On the one hand, Gorbachev clearly did not want to leave the impression that he was overwhelmed by current events. He wanted to remain a mover and shaker, to keep a firm grip on events, and to avoid being put on the defensive. On the other hand, he realized that after everything that had happened in East Germany, the German question required a response. His parting remark was in the nature of a strategic message: The Soviet leaders had accepted that German unification was inevitable. The question now was how and when.

And so, despite some irritation about the course of the discussions, I left Moscow in the welcome certainty that at bottom the Soviet leaders were taking German unification for granted, though they wanted some input on determining the way to that end. The message was a significant one. Putting it into practice called for responsibility and clarity on our part.

During my talk with Shevardnadze we had once again closely examined German policies. Confidence-building measures were a crucial factor, since we would need the Soviet Union if we were successfully to tackle the tasks ahead of us. I therefore emphatically reminded the Soviet foreign minister that when West Germany had signed the Moscow Treaty, it had attached the Letter on German Unity, which provided that the German question would be embedded in the context of Europe. Even back then it had been clear that we could reach this goal only if a qualitatively new state of affairs were established for all of Europe. In response to my explanations, Shevardnadze used the term *public defender*—a judgment Gorbachev, using different words, had already made. I pointed out to Shevardnadze, as I had done to Gorbachev, that we were not responsible for events in East Germany. As late as the spring and early summer of 1989 I had told Shevardnadze that I thought that East Germany was failing in instituting comprehensive reforms. I pointed out that we felt no sense of triumph whatever, but that the problems could not be solved by us. I explicitly reminded Shevardnadze that the East German citizens were acting with extraordinary responsibility. They had avoided anything that might become a cause for concern. No force of any kind had been used.

In a talk I had held the previous spring with a confidant of Honecker, I had told him that East Germany could not exclude itself from a process that had started in the Soviet Union and was carried on in Poland and Hungary. Even at the time there had been much hopelessness in East Germany. In June, during another meeting, I therefore had asked what on earth the leading East German politicians had been thinking when they held local elections by the old rules—as if nothing had changed, even though shortly before, the Soviet Union had held elections with a choice of several candidates.

My visit to Moscow proved how important it was to us to assure ourselves, during every step on the way to German unification, of the trust of our Western allies as well as of the Soviet Union and our Eastern neighbors.

Control Council or Partner?

On the evening of December 7, 1989, I went to Strasbourg to present to Roland Dumas a communiqué that held particular importance for us in respect to German unification. This time it was essential for us to avoid tensions such as those that had occurred during the special meeting of the European Council in November in Paris, and indeed the atmosphere at the European Council meeting in Strasbourg was fundamentally different from the one at the Paris meeting. We had thoroughly prepared the political part of the conference during an intense meeting of foreign ministers. However, even though we were in basic agreement, working on the draft the political directors had produced turned out to be rather difficult. In this area—as well as later, during the Two-Plus-Four talks—Undersecretary Kastrup proved to be the ideal man. An impressive figure, well versed in conducting discussions and negotiations and equipped with the ability to envision concepts and structures, Kastrup was able to assert and clearly express himself.

The European Council was intended to encourage the nations of Central and Eastern Europe to continue on their way toward democracy, pluralism, and constitutional law. Above all, German unity needed to be turned into a concern of all EC countries; that objective would be a clear signal to the East German leaders and to the Soviet Union. It would let them know that we were not alone on this issue because we could count on the support of our partners in the European Community.

Our concern was supported by the joint final declaration. The discussions about details went deeper than issues of wording; now we could see how beneficial it had been to include the forging of German unity as the alliance's joint goal in the final declaration on the occasion of NATO's fortieth anniversary conference, which had concerned itself mainly with concluding the discussion on short-range nuclear missiles. Except for Ireland, which was not a member of NATO, all EC nations had already drawn from the Letter on German Unity seven months earlier. Nevertheless, at the time, in May 1989, the difference in the positions within the alliance was noticeable. On the one hand the arguments focused on short-range missiles that could reach East Germany, Poland, and Czechoslovakia; on the other there was our own conviction—which most of our partners shared—that Europe had already stepped across the threshold of overcoming its separation. In Strasbourg several representatives thought that the NATO declaration on the European Community was essentially too specific, perhaps even went too far. It was, however, accepted in connection with the issue of borders, an issue where the aftereffect of the EC Paris summit meeting could still be felt. We could agree to this overall plan, which was, in any case, inevitable. The European Community had realized that events were irrevocably headed toward German unity. At the same time, however, the importance of clarity on the issue of German borders became obvious.

As the foreign minister of the country that held the chair in the European Community, France's Roland Dumas reported on the European Council on December 12, 1989. Speaking in the European Parliament, Dumas explicitly referred to my statements to the United Nations. He commented on the conclusions regarding German unity, noting that the part that dealt with this issue was unusually direct and that it had been the subject of thorough debate among the political leaders, the foreign ministers, and the heads of state. The issue had been carefully examined, since it would play an immensely important part in the years to come—a part on which the European Community's branches would have to take a stand in every declaration of the member nations. Dumas continued, "Today it is clear that this"—he meant changes to come—"can occur only under certain circumstances. It is necessary for all of us to realize as much." Regarding the inviolability of borders, he argued that reference to the Helsinki Final Act was sufficient. Further, anyone who needed to do so could refer to the declaration Foreign Minister Genscher had delivered to the General Assembly of the United Nations in September 1989. In regard to the Oder-Neisse Line he had declared, in the name of the West German government and before the entire international community, that Germany was not now making any territorial demands whatever on Poland nor would it do so in future.

Indeed, I had long since considered the linkage of the right to self-determination and the inviolability of borders a necessary requirement for solving the German question.

For West Germany the Strasbourg declaration was a great success. All twelve nations had now formally adopted the wording of the Letter on German Unity, which also stated that the "process of unification must take place peacefully and democratically, in accordance with the agreements and treaties as well as with all principles set forth in the Helsinki Final Act in the context of dialogue and East-West cooperation. It must also be part and parcel of the perspective of European integration." This perspective was accomplished through the agreement to follow the road of the European Union, to create a common domestic market, and to call for a government conference intended to convene as early as 1990 at the invitation of the Italian government, which would be the next member to hold the chair.

Again it became clear that any German attempt to work toward German unification unilaterally would have landed us in the greatest difficulties, and any attempt to renationalize German foreign policy would throw us into total isolation.

Thus the European Council meeting's outcome was an essential step in obtaining international approval of German unity. Our approval of the declaration affirmed what I had told President Mitterand during the talk we had at Elysée Palace that had been so important to me and had encouraged me: A unified Germany will continue on its European course. The confusion that had come about weeks before in Paris and other capitals regarding the unanswered question as to whether the West German government would agree to a government conference on the economic and currency union before the end of 1990 had been resolved. And it was true that at this time such doubts would have been more troublesome than ever before. Mitterand's and Dumas's strategy of connecting German unification with our integration in the European Community coincided with our own view and plans. That was the only move that could assure German unification as a gain for Europe rather than a European problem. From this time on we knew that, regarding the German question, our partners in the European Community were on our side.

Yet Strasbourg also made clear Mitterand's and Thatcher's fundamentally different positions on German unification. It seemed that the British prime minister had political and emotional doubts, while Mitterand wanted to prevent a repetition of the old feuds on both sides of the Rhine through the Europeanization of German unification. He viewed the issue of Germany's eastern border similarly. His demand that the Oder-Neisse Line be acknowledged as the border was intended not to set up an obstacle to German unification, but to lend it a pacifying effect for all of Europe. Mitterand realized more clearly than many German politicians the general historical conditions that were essential to German unification.

I sensed that the British prime minister, on the other hand, was reluctant to accept the idea that German unification was inevitable. But her insistence in Paris had had only a meager response; support for our policy had become too strong within the European Community. In this connection the debate in the British House of Commons on December 12, 1989, was extremely informative. In her report on the European Council meeting in Strasbourg Thatcher appeared to believe that the statement on ongoing events in Eastern Europe and above all German unification was not very important. However, unlike previous occasions, she did not attempt to prevent a government conference on European unification policy. She evidently sensed the interest our partners took in making progress on the road to European unification—a desire enhanced by the pending German unification. Thus it was left to opposition leader Neil Kinnock to comment on the German question: "In our opinion the summit was smart enough to accept the communiqué that underscores the German people's right to gain its unity in free self-determination." This, he noted, was a matter not only for the German people but for all Germany's neighbors in West and East. Kinnock also posed a question: "Does the Prime Minister realize that these positive decisions were basically made in Strasbourg despite, and not because of, her attitude?" Margaret Thatcher replied rather gruffly. She hoped everyone realized that the opposition leader had not been in Strasbourg and therefore could not know what had actually taken place. But she did not respond to Kinnock's words about the German question. Once again the topic of Germany was broached; it was the Labour delegate Ted Rowlands who asked, "Isn't it anachronistic to talk about German questions without Germans being present?" He was alluding to the meeting of the ambassadors representing the Four Powers in the Federal Republic, which had taken place in the Control Council Building in Berlin the previous day. He was right.

The meeting had taken place on December 11, 1989, at the Soviets' instigation and had received a great deal of attention. The ambassadors considered it appropriate to gather for a photograph. What was the purpose of this exhibition? A reminder to the Germans? The United States ambassador, Vernon Walters, chaired the meeting. Why was the picture taken? Was this, given the present circumstances and the site (the Control Council Building), the Four Powers' response to the peaceful revolution for freedom in East Germany and to the Germans' will to freedom, democracy, and unification? I knew President Bush's and Secretary of State

Baker's position well enough to know that such a display could not be what they wanted. The same was true for President Mitterand and Roland Dumas. When I saw the pictures, I was very upset.

The Western Three took advantage of the meeting to place their Berlin initiative, which they had submitted some time ago, at the center of the discussion. The initiative was intended to improve West Berlin's situation. Dealing with this initiative on December 11, 1989—in other words, more than a month after the Wall collapsed—was not therefore entirely timely. Speaking for the three Western nations, Ambassador Walters read a statement that sounded as if we were still living in the period before the Wall opened. Nevertheless, we would not have objected to a text that could have been discussed by all of us. What was crucial to us was that the Four Powers—especially in this committee—not discuss the German question without us. On this point three of the ambassadors adhered strictly to the agreement that the respective three powers had made with us.

At the meeting in the Control Council Building Soviet ambassador Vjacheslav Kochemassov presented Moscow's interpretation of the status quo; since at the time Soviet diplomacy was still holding on to the existence of East Germany, unimpeded unification was by no means guaranteed. "We are in an historical phase," Kochemassov said, only to continue in an admonishing tone, with reference to the democratic process in all of Europe and in East Germany, "We welcome the changes in the German Democratic Republic. They are accompanied by internal and international difficulties. Certain people in the Federal Republic apparently cannot help but influence events in East Germany. We repeat what Secretary General Gorbachev said in his speech of December 9: That we will not allow East Germany to be downgraded. It is our strategic ally and a member of the Warsaw Pact. We must accept the realities of the postwar era—that is, the reality of two independent, sovereign German states that are members of the United Nations. And we cannot allow the realities of the postwar to be questioned again; such an action jeopardizes stability in Europe. That does not mean that relations between East and West Germany cannot be changed. Peaceful cooperation between both German states can and must be developed further. Its future will be determined by history within the framework of comprehensive

323

Rebuilding a House Divided

processes occurring in Europe." He concluded by referring to the Soviet Union's position as a victorious power, to the necessity of respecting territorial realities, and to the process and the results of Helsinki. He stated: "As far as the European Continent is concerned, it is the prerequisite to peaceful development that we remove the existing difficulties, acknowledge territorial realities, and exercise caution, and also respect the process and the results of the Helsinki conference. That is the only way to shoulder the responsibility resulting from the agreements made during and after the war. It seems to us that the statements by the governments of the three [Western] powers more or less express our own view. At the meeting in Malta there was substantial agreement on this matter, in particular concerning the necessity of balanced changes in Europe. The same is true for problems in East Germany. It is important that both sides look at them in the context of the general European process. The meeting between Gorbachev and Mitterand proved the same fact. Mitterand's view of the situation in Europe comes very close to our own, and we have noticed that Prime Minister Thatcher takes a similar view." In conclusion, he stated, "Strengthening stability in Europe is an important task in the historical phase in which we live."

The French ambassador was the first to respond to Kochemassov's statements. He urged everyone to talk only about Berlin. France, he said, wanted to emphasize the importance of the Four Power Agreement on Berlin. Both points were important: That Germany not be discussed without the Germans and that the Four Power Agreement remain the framework for such a discussion. British ambassador Christopher Mallaby's position was similar, but he added some statements on the outcome of the European Council in Strasbourg, noting that it proved that there was agreement with the Soviets' ideas about stability. Ambassador Walters, the chairman, remarked that the United States, like all others, was concerned about stability, and that President Bush had therefore welcomed the outcome of Strasbourg. The emphasis on this remark expressed the United States' solidarity with the European Community and sent a clear signal to Moscow.

There was a rather lengthy discussion among the four ambassadors about the statement to be published after the session. Again the importance of stability in Europe was emphasized. Ambassador Boidevaix of France immediately briefed us on the meeting and its results—an act for which we were extremely grateful.

Yet what was the point of the manner in which the meeting was conducted? Was it really appropriate with respect to our relations with the three Western powers? The world reacted with sympathy, compassion, and respect to the peaceful revolution for freedom in East Germany. Never before in their history had the Germans been so in accord with the feelings and beliefs of the other European nations as they were in those turbulent months. During the Cold War, of all the European allies, Germany, with its Bundeswehr, had made the greatest contribution to Europe's joint security. We were in an alliance with the United States, France, and the United Kingdom; with two of these we were also joined in the European Community as partners with equal rights. Or did this conference do justice to the relationship we had developed with the Soviet Union? It could perhaps be explained most readily on the part of Moscow, though it still was not understandable. Apparently the anger about the ten-point plan still had not been entirely assuaged.

To prevent further Four Power meetings, I was determined not to overlook the manner of the meeting or the fact that it had taken place in the Control Council Building. I decided to make this meeting the subject of a talk with my three Western counterparts. The spectacular form of the meeting in particular had clearly come between us, all the more so since I had cultivated close, even personal, contact with all three ambassadors during their tenure in Bonn.

On December 13 I had an opportunity to take up the matter during the NATO conference in Brussels, where the four foreign ministers had convened. It was the traditional meeting of the four—the United States, France, Britain, and the Federal Republic of Germany. I declared that the four ambassadors' conduct had cast a blemish on the dignity of the German people. We were proud of the peaceful revolution for freedom in East Germany; the East Germans were acting with extreme responsibility. Such a dramatic meeting in the Control Council Building was therefore entirely inappropriate to our mutual relationship. Germany, I remarked, was a member of NATO, and of all European partners it carried the principal burden of European security. We had never let ourselves be enticed into swapping our responsibilities and obligations in the Western Alliance for neutralization; we were a member of the EC, and within that community we were among those who were advancing European unification. I stated, "You must decide between cooperation with us in NATO and the European Community or with the Soviets in the Control Council." I spoke these words in English and in a harsh tone, unlike my customary delivery. I wanted my friends—I could say of all three that they were indeed my friends—to know that a revival of the Four Power mechanism was not acceptable to us. The three realized very well that they were being addressed, not about some momentary irritation, but on a fundamental issue concerning our mutual relationship, and that in the face of the dramatic events occurring in Germany we must decide how to act in comparable future situations. It was Jim Baker who at that moment took my hand and said, "Hans-Dietrich, we get your point." The faces of Roland Dumas and Douglas Hurd, too, reflected their understanding not only of my words but also of the underlying cause.

Thus, the meeting of the four in the Control Council Building had an important and positive effect after all. My reaction had made our partners realize that the issues concerning Germany and Berlin were no longer a matter that the allies could discuss with the Soviet Union and without us in their Circle of Four. There was no longer a way around the inclusion of Germany as a partner with equal rights. I had made that point. My appreciation for the three ambassadors was not diminished by their meeting, but that fact did not keep me from being absolutely clear on this point.

On February 10, 1990, during a conversation with Shevardnadze in Moscow, I had an opportunity to discuss the ambassadors' meeting in Berlin, when I explained to the Soviet foreign minister my ideas about the Two-Plus-Four mechanism regarding the negotiations on German unification. "We will not agree to any negotiations," I stated, "in which the Four sit in judgment over us. Each nation has its dignity. We want to talk *with* the Four. We were not pleased about the meeting of the four ambassadors in Berlin early in December. I will not attend a conference such as the one in Geneva in the 1950s, where the German delegation was seated at a side table."

At the End of an Historic Year

In mid-December 1989 my wife and I took a trip through several cities in East Germany, among them my hometown of Halle. I had some memorable encounters with the leading minds of the East German reform movement, the so-called Round Table and the churches, who were always conscious of their special responsibility and political role.

I was touched in particular by the service in the Halle Market Church, mentioned earlier. All the seats in the church were taken. It had been announced that I would speak after the service. When the service was over, there was a short break. Meanwhile visitors from other parishes joined us, so that the Market Church was almost literally bursting.

I was deeply moved to find myself in the church I had frequently attended as a child with my parents and—after my father passed away—with my mother. For the first time I could speak in my hometown of Halle as the West German foreign minister. I recognized some of my former classmates and their wives in the first pews of the nave. My wife had taken a seat there as well.

I spoke about my emotions, but above all about German unity. In the Federal Republic we had made our decision, I said, and now the question of where they stood on German unity was posed to the East Germans. Here, too, I thought it important—with regard to other nations, particularly the Soviet Union—to avoid giving the impression that German unity was something to be forced on the East Germans. Saying yes to freedom had to be their own decision. As to how they would decide, however, there was no question in my mind. Nevertheless, the answer must be heard with absolute clarity throughout the world.

But I was not merely interested in the international audience; most important were, first and foremost, the people sitting before me. They must not be told once again what to do, this time by politicians from the West. The revolution for freedom was their own affair. It was their irreplaceable contribution to the German history of freedom and democracy and to German and European unity. The decision on what to do with this newly won freedom needed to be their own affair as well.

That same day I met in Leipzig for the first time with the conductor of the Gewandhaus Orchestra, Kurt Masur, who had played a responsible role during the Monday demonstrations in Leipzig, trying for agreement between the citizens' movement and the state's representatives. We spoke about the events of the last few months and about unifying the two German states. We now had a chance at German unification, I stated, if the people in East Germany wanted it. As far as I was concerned, the shouts of "We are *one* people," heard at rallies, had only confirmed what I had always believed: If Germans had a chance to express themselves freely, they would call for *one* nation. Masur had asked the organist Michael Schönheit to play the organ of the Gewandhaus. While I was listening to the music, my thoughts went back to the years 1948–1949, when toward the end of law school and during final exams, I took the train from Halle to Leipzig and back almost every day. And now I was being given this beautiful concert in the city that had become the symbol for the Germans' will to freedom and unity. After my wife and I had taken leave of Masur, we walked to the Nikolai Church, which had been a crucial center for the Leipzig Monday rallies. A pre-Christmas service was under way. The church was full, many congregants were standing, and we too remained near the entrance until the service was over. Together with the people of Leipzig we experienced the Christmas spirit.

The following day I lunched with Roland Dumas in Brussels. We prepared for the afternoon session of the EC foreign ministers' conference. I told him what I had experienced in Halle and Leipzig; I wanted to convey an impression of the real mood among the East Germans.

The evening brought a high point and a premiere. For the first time a Soviet foreign minister was the guest of the twelve foreign ministers of the European Community. We gathered in the room where we usually lunched, around an oval table at which there was room for the foreign ministers as well as the members of the European Commission. On this special occasion enough interpreters staffed the booths to allow everyone to speak in his native tongue. Roland Dumas welcomed Foreign Minister Shevardnadze, who had taken the seat next to him.

Shevardnadze emphasized how special this meeting was and that it was a first. Then he gave his appraisal of the dramatic events in Europe and in Germany. For me this meeting was especially significant because Eduard Shevardnadze referred to the conversation he and I had held in New York in September 1988. He said, "My friend Hans-Dietrich was the first, and the only one, who early on—more than a year ago—pointed out to us what was happening in East Germany. I must say in all frankness that initially we did not believe him, but we finally realized that his interpretation of the situation and of events in East Germany was correct."

The Portuguese foreign minister, João de Deus Pinheiro, who was seated next to me, pushed a slip of paper in my direction. The note stated how important Shevardnadze's remark was to him. During an informal meeting of the EC foreign ministers in 1988 I had also voiced my predictions for future events in the Warsaw Pact countries. On that occasion I had remarked that in 1989 we could expect dramatic changes both in East Germany and in Czechoslovakia. For Pinheiro, a good personal and political friend, it was important that I had spoken with equal clarity to Shevardnadze as I had to our colleagues in the European Community. This kind of clarity and openness had always been important to me. One could gain trust only by speaking unabashedly.

On that day Eduard Shevardnadze had already delivered a speech before the political committee of the European Parliament, in which he had cautioned against acting rashly. He had spoken out against immediate unification and had raised the issue of the status of a unified Germany. He was now asking about West Germany's stand on the border issue, which once again affirmed my conviction that vagueness on this problem would create additional difficulties for German unification.

I was the only one who had a private conversation with Shevardnadze that evening. Once again he cautioned me against any rash actions. Then I told him what my personal impressions suggested to me about future events in East Germany. The Soviet Union, I remarked, would be well advised to forego any obstruction of the will to unity. During this conversation, too, I became convinced that Moscow had every intention of remaining in control of events but was fully aware of the speed and force of events. I became more and more certain that the Soviet Union would accept change in East Germany as long as it would occur in an orderly fashion and without animus against the Soviet Union or behind its back. This sense was basically the message underlying Gorbachev's concluding remark in Moscow. Referring to the speech I had given in Halle the previous day, I told Shevardnadze how much approval I had received in response to my statements in the Market Church expressing my belief that the Germans both in the Democratic Republic and in the Federal Republic had no other goal than unification. I added that, as they strove for this goal, all Germans were aware of their responsibility to Europe and to their neighbors.

I came away from the meetings in Brussels with the conviction that we could obtain the Soviet leaders' approval more easily if we did not confront Moscow with *faits accomplis*. German unification must be the outcome of serious discussions. It must never appear to be a humiliation of the Soviet Union.

François Mitterand visited East Germany from December 20 to 22. Dumas had advised me of the planned visit some time earlier. My response had been that it was up to France to decide if such a visit was necessary. It was necessary to realize that Prime Minister Hans Modrow and Chairman of the State Council Manfred Gerlach represented a provisional government: "Possibly President Mitterand will be the first and last state visitor this government receives." Again, I said, it was important for Mitterand to clearly embrace German unity; I also noted that one of his stops was Leipzig, the center of the peaceful revolution for freedom. I suggested that he meet with Kurt Masur.

Mitterand conducted himself just as I had expected. Speaking to students at Leipzig University, he remarked that German unity was above all a concern of the Germans; only free and democratic elections would prove what Germans on both sides wanted. France would respect such a decision. In his after-dinner speech he made similar statements to his host, the new chairman of the Council of State, Gerlach, and he added that the inviolability of borders must be in agreement with the CSCE accords—he was referring to Germany's eastern border. Further, he supported, just as I had, a CSCE summit conference, and he proposed that it be held in Paris. Thus Mitterand advocated two general conditions that we, too, considered necessary.

□   □   □   □

On December 22, 1989, the Brandenburg Gate in Berlin was opened. We—the representatives of West Germany—met at the Reichstag building and proceeded to walk toward the gate with the Chancellor. The East German delegation was walking toward us. For the first time I met the East German prime minister, Hans Modrow.

December 23 brought another one of the high points in a year that had been so rich in peaks. I took a helicopter to Waidhaus at the German-Czech border, where the new Czech foreign minister Jiři Dienstbier and I were to cut through the fence separating the Federal Republic of Germany and Czechoslovakia. I was facing a man whom I had first met in 1968. At the time Walter Scheel and I were paying a visit to the leaders of the Prague Spring. In one of the back rooms of a small restaurant in the old part of town we had met with young Czech journalists who supported Alexander Dubček and his reforms. Among them was Jiři Dienstbier, whom I now faced as Czechoslovakia's new foreign minister.

Holding huge wire cutters, we approached the border fence from both sides and made a cut. Thus we symbolically expressed the fact that the Iron Curtain had fallen here as well. Particularly at the German-Czech border our act had a special meaning. We were recalling the moving events that had taken place in the German embassy in Prague only a few months earlier. During our flight I could not help but think of Czechoslovakia's being the first country Hitler had occupied, shattered, and partly annexed to Germany. The massacre of Lidice had become a horrible symbol of this occupation. After the war the Sudeten Germans had been expelled from Czechoslovakia, and there had been serious offenses in Prague as well as in the areas occupied by the Sudeten Germans. I knew that many an historic debt would still have to be repaid, but now this task would be up to democratic governments.

11

Two Plus Four

Positioning the Unified Germany: We Belong in the EC and NATO

During the Christmas season that year I was even more preoccupied with politics and work than my family had become accustomed to. How were we to organize the negotiations concerning German unity?

The course we had decided on in Washington in November 1989 was the correct way to proceed. A peace conference was out of the question just as much as was a peace treaty as no treaty had been officially signed after the Second World War. Our membership in the United Nations, NATO, and the European Community, as well as the treaties we had signed with the Soviet Union and our neighbors in Central and Eastern Europe, the German-Soviet Declaration of the early summer of 1989, and our activities in the CSCE had rendered such a treaty obsolete. A peace treaty would have made the delicate matter of German unification even more difficult, if only because of the incalculable number of participants. Negotiations would have been hopelessly mired in the issue of reparations. And perhaps a treaty ran the risk of repeating all the mistakes made after the First World War in regard to a defeated Germany. The same was true for negotiations within the CSCE. They, too, would have resulted in a European peace treaty, with consequences similar to a worldwide treaty. Thus only one option remained: All issues of foreign and security policy concerning the future status of a unified Germany must be resolved in talks with the Four Powers. It was necessary to find a way that we, the two German states, could conduct such negotiations *with* the Four Powers, on the same level, and with equal rights.

I could not even consider the option that German unification could be accomplished by neutralizing Germany. No third way between West and East existed. Or, as I put it in speeches, "We are not wanderers who move between two worlds." We had decided in favor of the community of Western democracies once and for all.

As early as 1946 I was fascinated by Winston Churchill's Zurich speech, in which he called on the European democracies to create a united Europe, assigning—and that element, as I fully appreciated only much later, was the truly outstanding point—special roles to Germany and France. At the time I had written a letter of support to Churchill, addressing it to the House of Commons, London. Did he ever receive it? Whatever the case, I never received a reply.

The more I pondered these questions during the 1989 Christmas season, the more urgent it seemed to me to make a clear public commitment to the unified Germany's membership in NATO and the EC. In the meantime President George Bush and Secretary of State James Baker had also publicly stated that they were working with the assumption that the united Germany would be a member of NATO. Their declaration also prompted me to say in public what I had long since stated in private: Even a unified Germany will remain a member of NATO and the EC. In my talks with representatives of our allies in 1989 I had repeatedly expressed my position, for instance in November 1989, when I held meetings with President Bush, Prime Minister Thatcher, and President Mitterand. Early in January 1990 my belief in the need to make a clear statement on our position was reconfirmed. I noted with concern as I held numerous conversations that the merits of unity *or* NATO were being debated in Germany; many people considered it unlikely that the Soviet Union would agree to a unified Germany's membership in NATO. It was therefore essential to make certain from the outset that any special status for the unified Germany be avoided. Limiting our choice of alliance, even in the form of neutralization, was out of the question—not only for our benefit, but for the sake of European stability. In my discussions with my associates we came to the conclusion that a unified Germany that remained a member of the Western Alliance would probably be more acceptable to the Soviet Union if a different relationship between the alliances could be created and West-East relations could be improved in other respects.

Using the framework of the CSCE, we had already made significant progress in East-West relations. The German-Soviet Declaration of 1989 established a relationship with the Soviet Union that would have been unthinkable only a few years earlier. When Shevardnadze and I talked about this declaration in May 1989, we noted the many objections expressed by his associates that my Soviet counterpart was forced to allay before we could open the door to this New Thinking. Yet relations between the alliances were still antagonistic, as was vividly demonstrated by the language of both NATO and Warsaw Pact communiqués.

Further, we recalled very clearly the harshness of the struggle within NATO a year earlier when I had objected to modernizing short-range nuclear missiles. The turn of events confirmed the anachronistic nature of the arguments put forward by the proponents of modernization; they had not felt the fresh air of history. Now that the underlying political antagonisms were gradually dissipating, we needed to search out opportunities to use cooperative security structures to diminish the chance of military confrontation as well. It was important to work resolutely toward a foundation of peace for all of Europe—identified in the Harmel Report as the Alliance's primary goal.

Each year the FDP holds a so-called Twelfth Night Meeting on January 6, at which current political issues are discussed and perspectives for liberal politics are developed. On January 6, 1990, I announced in Stuttgart, "As regards the process of building a foundation for lasting peace in Europe, NATO and the Warsaw Pact have a special function of political leadership. The first step must be to strengthen the security the alliances grant the nations of Europe; cooperative security structures are the way to achieve this end. The next step must transform these cooperatively structured alliances into an organization of joint and collective security; that is, structures *between* the alliances must be established that gradually overcome the antagonism between the alliances." The words "between the alliances" implied that while I wanted NATO to continue to exist I also desired new forms of cooperation with the Warsaw Pact countries. These new forms developed with increasing rapidity. Who among my audience in the Stuttgart State Theater could have guessed that less than two years later I, along with Jim Baker, would propose a North Atlantic Cooperation Council? Ultimately all NATO members would be part of it, as well as the members of the Warsaw Pact and, in time, all the Soviet Union's successor states. I believed that the idea of cooperative security was the only possible way to create structures through which the unified Germany's NATO membership could be accepted in Moscow. Early in 1990 I therefore requested that Soviet security concerns be considered, for only if such concerns were acknowledged and treated as legitimate could we trust that the Soviet Union would not obstruct the transformations about to take place in Europe but actively support them.

On January 31, 1990, I spoke to the Protestant Academy in Tutzing, fulfilling an earlier commitment. I used the opportunity to clarify our stand on our membership in NATO—words that had become urgent because more than the German debate on our nation's future status was on the agenda. We were being bombarded with questions from Western capitals in response to an interview Chancellor Kohl had given to the *Washington Post*. Published on January 18, 1990, it read in part: "He appeared to take issue with the Bush administration's insistence that unification be achieved 'in the context of Germany's continued commitment to the North Atlantic Treaty Organization.'" Helmut Kohl was quoted as saying, "I don't think it would be wise to give vent to such thoughts at the present point of the discussion."

The Associated Press gave a variation of the statement: "On the subject of reunification, the Chancellor said that developments in Eastern Europe had overtaken the American position that German unity could be achieved only in connection with Germany's membership in NATO. Kohl said that on this issue there were differences of opinion with Washington. He thought, however, that the

American position could change if the relationship between NATO and the Warsaw Pact changed."

It was not what was said in the interview that disconcerted me, for I knew Kohl's position on NATO only too well. With regard to the international—as well as the German—public, however, it seemed to me that our intention to remain a member of NATO needed urgent clarification. Such a step was necessary for my credibility's sake as well, since I had assured our allies of our position all through 1989.

My speech in Tutzing was intended to affect the German public and to send an unmistakable signal to the countries of the world. Primarily, I stressed our objective: "To serve worldwide peace, to become an equal member of a united Europe, and to preserve Germany's national and political unity—these are the missions of our Basic Law." Thus our constitution places our national goal in a European context and subordinates it to our obligation to peace. I placed crucial importance on the elections to the Volkskammer—the first democratic parliamentary elections in East Germany—to be held on March 18, 1990. "By the end of March 18, 1990," I said, "the world will know more precisely which road the East German people chose." We needed to utilize the time remaining as "it would be wrong to assume that until the election date nothing or only little can occur." I pointed out the necessity of pan-German solidarity: "German unity cannot be obtained without a price—not economically, not financially, not politically." In addition I called for a treaty between the Federal Republic of Germany and the Democratic Republic as a "framework for German-German unification." That suggestion subsequently resulted in the treaty of union between the two Germanys.

Touching on the external aspects—that is, positioning the united Germany in the Europe of the future—my speech noted in part, "The question Germans must answer is: What is it that is to be united? The answer is clear: The two German states, including Berlin. No more and no less. . . . The first joint declaration of intent of the two German parliaments and administrations must guarantee our borders with all our neighbors." Then I moved on to the core of the issue of our political position; I emphasized that the Federal Republic must "answer the question of how it will treat its membership in the European Community and the Western Alliance in case of German unification. The answer is clear:

Should we unite, our membership in the European Community is irrevocable, and so is our will to advance further integration until we achieve political union." These words were meant primarily for François Mitterand, but I meant them to be heard by all other Europeans and allies as well. I was saying yes not only to our membership in the EC, but also to advancing the EC—as, almost two years later, the Maastricht Treaty did in fact succeed in doing. Regarding the issue of NATO, I declared, "The same is true for our membership in the Western Alliance. We do not want a neutral united Germany." I deliberately used the phrase *united Germany* in order to avoid any misunderstanding that East German territory might possibly be excluded from membership in NATO and therefore kept neutral.

There were many different ways to do justice to the Soviet Union's concerns regarding security, but all of Germany should have membership in NATO. Nevertheless, I accounted for the possibility that East German territory might be accorded a different status. "Creating the necessary conditions for such an eventuality," I therefore said, "will require a large degree of European statecraft. Any idea of integrating the part of Germany now known as the German Democratic Republic in the military structures of NATO would be an obstacle to German-German rapprochement." On the eve of the signing of the Two-Plus-Four Treaty in Moscow on September 12, 1990, I learned how appropriate my warning had been. Further, the Two-Plus-Four talks brought us to the conclusion that the NATO structures that were valid for West Germany should not be extended to the territory of the former East Germany. In order to change external conditions, I called for the alliances to change from confrontation to cooperation; I again emphasized the necessity for a CSCE summit. This speech thus laid the foundation for the unified Germany's position within the overall European architecture.

My speech created quite a stir in Tutzing. Some members of the audience felt I had gone too far; they considered my demand that all of Germany hold membership in NATO a threat to German unification. My effort, however, was to enunciate our fundamental views without any equivocation. The Soviet leaders must be made to understand that we were considerate of their security concerns as well and were seriously trying to "de-enemize" the relations between the alliances.

The NATO declarations of Turnberry and London in the spring of 1990 confirmed my predictions. My suggested approach was the only possibility we had to pave the way for Moscow to reconsider its position. Strong German statements about NATO membership—without reference to the necessary political or security policy changes—displayed as little insight into the complexity of the matter we needed to negotiate as had the SNF debate of a year earlier, which misjudged the situation just as gravely. It was this complexity to which Helmut Kohl, in his nuanced statements to the *Washington Post,* had apparently wanted to do justice.

Accord in Washington

On February 2, 1990, I set out on what was probably my shortest but also my most important visit to Washington.

During the flight I prepared for my meeting with Baker; I wanted to reach an understanding with him that from the perspective of foreign policy, German unification was secure; the matter could not be settled with dispatch unless it had the United States' unqualified support. Even at that time I was convinced that the Soviet Union had already made a strategic decision to stake its fortune on the United States in regard to global relations and on Germany in the matter of European relations. For that same reason Washington and Bonn must be in harmony with regard to German unification; we must be in agreement on the best way to proceed to negotiations and on the general framework for these.

The Open Skies Conference, which was scheduled to begin on Monday, February 12, in Ottawa, would offer the opportunity for these matters to be discussed among the Six—East Germany, West Germany, the United States, the Soviet Union, France, and the United Kingdom. Since the conference would include every NATO member, and all Warsaw Pact nations, all representatives from the West and the East would be present. It was essential that we avoid another scene such as the one at the Control Council Building in Berlin, nor did we want a repetition of the arrangement that had sidelined the German delegations at the negotiations of the Big Four in Geneva in the 1950s. The treatment Germany's first democracy had experienced at the Versailles Peace Treaty was another type of humiliation to be avoided—even a debate on a peace treaty was unacceptable. A unified Germany must be able to walk into the future unimpeded by unresolved questions and discriminatory conditions. Germany's democratic stability must not be jeopardized a second time. A radical right-wing opposition must not be allowed another opportunity to rise.

At the airport in Washington I was met by Frank Elbe, who had arrived earlier for preliminary meetings. Dieter Kastrup was with me. Elbe told us that the stand I had taken in Tutzing, insisting on NATO membership, had been favorably received. The United States was in favor of talks that would include the Four and the two German states—a decision I had expected after our November meeting. It was important to me that the two German states, the ones most concerned with unification, discuss foreign-policy aspects with the Four, rather than the other way around. Any appearance of the Four negotiating *about* Germany must not be allowed to arise. This consideration dictated the order in the name given the conference: Two plus four, not four plus two. After my talk with Elbe, I was sanguine about the imminent meeting with Jim Baker.

My first meeting with Baker was a private one. When he asked me for my ideas, I came straight to the point: The precondition for the upcoming negotiations with the Soviet Union must, as I had always told him and his predecessors, be Germany's refusal to be drawn into any discussion about its membership in the Western associations, NATO and the European Community. We saw the future unified Germany as a member of NATO and the EC. As for the territory of the still-existing German Democratic Republic, we would probably have to define a special status for its membership in NATO, the particulars of which could be worked out at some later time. Even so, there had to be assurance that that part of Germany would not be turned into a territory with diminished security in Europe. Baker agreed with my suggestion, thus officially confirming the earlier talks Elbe had had with Baker's close associates Robert B. Zoellick and Claude Ross.

Next Jim Baker and I discussed Moscow's possible reactions. I remarked that the Soviet Union would have to be offered something. We should think of a different relationship between the alliances, of an affirmation and strengthening of the CSCE process and a CSCE summit, and of developing security-building measures and a cooperative security policy. In short, we would have to build a situation in Europe that offered advantages to the Soviet Union as well. There was no other way to win over the Soviet leaders. It was necessary to put Gorbachev and Shevardnadze in a position to defend their stand in Moscow against those forces among the country's leaders who opposed German unification and, to an even greater extent, a unified Germany's membership in NATO and the European Community.

Later I introduced an idea that went far beyond what we had previously discussed: In view of the continuing negotiations on arms reductions in Vienna, we should also consider a reduction of forces in the unified Germany; perhaps there might even might be fewer troops than there had been in the Federal Republic of Germany. That thought was consistent with the way West-East relations were already evolving. If the Soviet Union were prepared to agree to both German unification and the country's membership in NATO, if a new relationship between the alliances were to develop as well as other, corresponding, changes, a reduction in forces would occur everywhere in any case. A unilateral German step would merely anticipate what everyone else would ultimately enact. However, I noted that I would prefer such an agreement to be made within the framework of the Vienna disarmament negotiations so as to preclude any possibility that Germany be singled out and discriminated against.

Finally I explained why, for psychological as well as political reasons, it was important that the negotiations be called "two plus four" and not "four plus two." Baker kept the conversation lively, particularly by interjecting questions; he asked whether I really believed that the Soviet Union would agree to Germany's membership in NATO. I replied in the affirmative, listing the general pan-European conditions I considered necessary to that end. By and large this comprehensive all-encompassing program coincided with the ideas Baker had apparently already discussed with his staff. After speaking in private for some time, we asked our associates to join us. Baker gave them a brief summary of our conversation and confirmed what we had agreed upon.

Subsequently, when President Bush received me at the White House, he gave his blessing, as it were, to everything Baker and I had discussed. I was impressed by the easy way and the personal concern with which Bush and Baker promised their support. When I briefed the German journalists, I felt jubilant. However, I concealed my satisfaction, since I was determined to do nothing to irritate the three other powers—London, Paris, and Moscow—by rash reports of the "mission accomplished" type.

After all, we must still convince Moscow of our plan. My American counterpart promised to talk with Shevardnadze and Gorbachev the following week about the arrangement we had discussed. In particular, he would mention that we wanted to reach an agreement in Ottawa on content, general arrangements, and a start-up date for the talks. Baker made his remarks with his customary precision and thoroughness. In response to my request that I be kept informed about the Soviets' reaction—the Chancellor and I were going to be in Moscow immediately after Baker— he left a letter in Moscow that filled us with optimism. Helmut Kohl and I could be sure that Washington supported us and had laid some of the groundwork for our talks with the Soviet leaders.

At the meeting in Washington on February 2 the issue of Germany's eastern border also had been important to Baker. I referred him to a statement I had read at the United Nations and that had since been adopted by the Bundestag.

Opening in Moscow

On Saturday, February 10, 1990, the Chancellor and I left for Moscow. Jim Baker's efforts in the Soviet Union had been successful: Its leaders now knew that Germany and the United States shared a common purpose. In addition Baker had obtained Foreign Secretary Hurd's and Foreign Minister Dumas's support for the "two-plus-four" formulation. Conversations with my American counterpart had made clear the many reservations, doubts, and opposition in Moscow concerning Germany's membership in NATO. Security concerns played a major part in the Soviet Union's thinking. Much remained to be done before we could present Moscow with a different European situation. It was crucial to create a Western position that would protect future Soviet security interests better than did the Soviet attempt to preserve the partition of Europe and the partition of Germany by force—if need be even by military force.

The Soviet leaders could not have overlooked what had been occurring in the other Warsaw Pact nations. Changes in Germany had been even more glaring. Jim Baker had urgently impressed upon Mikhail Gorbachev that it would be unrealistic for Germany, with all the weight it carried, to remain neutral, simultaneously pointing out the dangers a neutral Germany might pose to the Soviet Union. I agreed with Baker's view: I was firmly convinced that the solution we proposed was better, not only for us, also for our neighbors, including the Soviet Union.

As events unrolled, it turned out that the method of proceeding cautiously, by signaling to the Soviet Union that we wanted to be full members of NATO but were also taking Soviet security concerns into consideration, was more promising than the proper but unadorned demand that Germany must be a member of NATO. All the rights and obligations resulting from the united Germany's membership in NATO, including the guarantee of protection and defense pursuant to Articles Five and Six of the NATO Treaty, had to be secured. Such an arrangement required the creation of new general conditions for our membership in NATO that would make it easier for Moscow to agree—for example, reducing Germany's armed forces; Germany's renunciation of atomic, biological, and chemical weapons; the promise that no allied troops would be stationed in the territory of the former East Germany; and "de-enemization" of the alliances.

My fundamental experience of resolving issues that seem to be unsolvable by changing their environment—that is, the conditions surrounding them—would have to prove itself once again. During the Two-Plus-Four process my fear that undifferentiated statements would only exacerbate Moscow's reservations was confirmed again and again.

During my talk with Eduard Shevardnadze I dealt at length with preparations for the Ottawa conference and with the Two-Plus-Four talks we had planned. Above all I needed to convince Shevardnadze that the general conditions for negotiations should be laid down in Ottawa. I emphasized that it was important for us to limit ourselves to the group of the two plus the four and to accept the formulation in that order.

Simultaneously with our discussions, the Chancellor was conferring with Gorbachev. Subsequently we met all together, and Kohl told Shevardnadze and me that they had arrived at an agreement: Unification was the concern of the Germans. Obviously Gorbachev and Shevardnadze had already discussed this point, otherwise my Soviet counterpart could not have spoken with me in such detail about the foreign-policy aspects of German unification.

While we were seated around the table, I was thinking back to my conversation with Gorbachev in 1986, which had filled me with so much hope; now we had come a giant step closer to fulfilling these expectations. But I also remembered the West German president's visit to Moscow when the issue of German unity had been broached. At the time Gorbachev had replied that history would decide the German question—perhaps in a hundred years. This reply had disappointed me less than it had others. To me the words meant simply that Gorbachev did not regard the German problem as settled by our country's division. To him it remained an open question, even if he thought in terms of longer time spans than we did. And was his estimate really so different from that of most Germans? Perhaps many—even most of us thought in similarly long periods of time as did the Secretary General.

At the same time I recalled the rather unpleasant conversation I had with Mikhail Gorbachev and Eduard Shevardnadze on December 5, 1989—only two months earlier. When we ended that discussion, there was already a hint that the Soviet position was beginning to soften. Our new talks in Moscow confirmed that by now the Soviet leaders had come to terms with the idea of German unity. Now their concern was not to give the appearance of being acted upon but to take the stage as participants in actions and decision making.

Our visit resulted in a joint statement to the effect that the Soviet Union, the Federal Republic of Germany, and the German Democratic Republic shared the belief that the Germans alone must settle the issue of the unity of the German nation and must make their own choice as to the form of such a government, the time, the speed, and under what conditions unification would be realized.

I can still see the incredulity in the faces of the reporters when they learned of this outcome at the international press conference held in Moscow. It signified an historical break in a wall of thinking. Helmut Kohl summarized the event in a sentence that was both simple and clear: "Tonight I have a single message for all Germans: Secretary General Gorbachev and I agree that only the

German people have the right to decide whether they want to live together in one state."

Ottawa, Birthplace of "Two Plus Four"

Around noon on Sunday Helmut Kohl and I returned from Moscow, and I continued on to Ottawa at once, arriving in the afternoon.

The Open Skies Conference became the next crucial step on the road to German unity. I addressed the plenary session. Once again I emphatically reminded my listeners of my remarks at the United Nations in September 1989, when I had expressed my position on the border issue. My words left a deep impression on all those present, paving the way for the agreement on the Two-Plus-Four talks. I added an historic dimension to the imminent unification of the two German states, quoting Thomas Mann's dictum, "We want a European Germany, not a German Europe."

That was also my goal during my talks with the foreign ministers of our eastern neighbors. The previous day I had talked with Jiri Dienstbier; with the Romanian foreign minister, Sergin Celac; with Gyula Horn of Hungary; and with Bulgaria's foreign minister Philip Dimitrov. On Monday evening I also met with Jim Baker. Continuing the talks we had started in Washington, we exchanged impressions of Moscow.

The following morning saw a meeting of the Western Four—the United States of America, France, the United Kingdom, and the Federal Republic of Germany—at the quarters of the German embassy. The session was intended to prepare for our meetings with the Soviet Union and the German Democratic Republic on the implementation of Two-Plus-Four talks. Speaking from our ambassador's residence, I telephoned the Chancellor in Bonn, before our breakfast meeting, which was scheduled to start at 7:30 A.M. I briefed him on the current status of my various meetings, particularly my meeting with Jim Baker. I wanted to start on serious discussions with the three Western powers, I added, before talking to Shevardnadze about these issues. Kohl agreed with all my suggestions. At breakfast Baker, Dumas, Hurd, and I agreed on a unified Western position regarding the upcoming negotiations on German unification and on the Two-Plus-Four structure.

A meeting of NATO foreign ministers was scheduled for the

afternoon. The talks with the Soviet foreign minister, which were always conducted separately, mainly by Jim Baker and me, began in the morning. I met with Shevardnadze several times; he and I had grown even closer in the last few months. I liked him a great deal, and my Western colleagues responded to him in the same way. It was easy to sense the difficulties these talks posed for him. Baker's and my visits to Moscow had prepared him for the events about to occur, and his demeanor indicated that he understood the full impact of the imminent negotiations and the beginning of the Two-Plus-Four talks. How hard these discussions were on him personally, in the truest sense of the word, is also made clear in his memoirs (*The Future Belongs to Freedom,* 1991). Referring to his talks with me, he wrote that we argued constantly.

I was firmly resolved not to leave Ottawa without an agreement on the implementation and contents of the Two-Plus-Four talks. It was impossible to know when all the relevant ministers would have an opportunity to meet again. And if I could not create unanimity among them, the opposing forces had too many opportunities to at least delay negotiations.

I accused the Soviet foreign minister—as he recalled correctly in his book—of having a "heart of stone." Again and again he examined my proposed text for the implementation of negotiations. In the end we arrived at a resolution that stated, in part, that we "would meet and discuss the external aspects of creating German unification, including the security of its neighboring countries." Periodically Shevardnadze would leave the conference room. Was he seeking counsel from Moscow? I did not ask.

When at long last everything seemed perfect, a sudden unexpected obstacle arose. Jim Baker told me that, according to a White House memo, there was reason to doubt whether Chancellor Kohl agreed to the implementation of the Two-Plus-Four talks. After sixteen years as foreign minister, this was a new experience for me; it was to remain the only one of its kind. Baker was visibly uncomfortable, but he acted correctly in seizing the bull by the horns. I swallowed my anger—not at Baker or President Bush, but at the source of the misinformation from Bonn.

I did not understand his question, I replied. After our talks the night before, and even before the meeting with the three Western colleagues, I had briefed the Chancellor and assured myself of his complete approval. To my question, "Where does this come from?" Baker replied, "I don't know, but the issue was raised by the security adviser." I responded, "In that case I can imagine where precisely in Bonn it originated." Baker nodded. Whatever may have happened, at that moment I did not really care—most certainly not after the breakthrough in Ottawa. It was only important that we clear the matter up immediately.

From Baker's room I had someone connect me with Helmut Kohl's office. Juliane Weber, his personal assistant, told me that the Chancellor was in conference elsewhere in the Chancellor's Office. But she immediately understood the urgency of my call, and the Chancellor called back a few minutes later. After I had informed him about my conversation with Baker, I urged him to clear up the misunderstanding with President Bush. I pointed out that irreparable damage could be done, and he agreed without hesitation. We could not accept any attempt to set traps for us on an issue that was so crucial for Germany, I added. The Chancellor promised to get in touch with President Bush as quickly as possible. No doubt he was as surprised as I had been. Shortly after my conversation with Kohl, Baker received clearance to proceed from the White House. Once again the consensus between Helmut Kohl—who obviously perceived the situation just as I did—and myself prevailed.

Later I learned that the Secretary of State had been made extremely uncomfortable by having to ask me for reconfirmation of the Chancellor's approval—a feeling I could well understand. For the rest, and in view of the major changes in the offing, we both considered the trick someone had played fairly insignificant.

During my last conversation with Shevardnadze, in which we reached agreement on every detail, he noted that there was a sixth person with whom he had not consulted: East Germany's foreign minister, Oskar Fischer. Shevardnadze asked me to wait in his room while he spoke to Fischer and obtained his approval. Fifteen minutes later he returned, satisfied that Fischer was in agreement. Would I have any objections to a photograph of all the foreign ministers including Fischer? I told him that I would not have it otherwise: "We are talking about Two-Plus-Four meetings." I noticed that, with regard to Poland's western border, Shevardnadze was eager to gain the approval of Poland's foreign minister, Krzysztof Skubiszewski, for the title Two-Plus-Four meetings agreed on in Ottawa. That wish accounted for the phrase "including the security of its neighboring nations" which we inserted.

I met with Foreign Minister Fischer that same evening after a session with Foreign Minister Skubiszewski. Overcoming an initial coolness, over the years Fischer and I had found a way to talk in a neutral way, and in quite a number of cases when humanitarian aid was called for, Fischer had met me halfway. Discussing political issues of détente or disarmament, at times we even agreed. More and more I came to appreciate him as someone who was straightforward in his own way, though he clearly was not given much leeway in discussions. In the end we arrived at a closer personal relationship.

Now we were confronting each other in Ottawa. He knew as well as I did that negotiations on the Two-Plus-Four talks implied negotiations on the end of East Germany. Much too experienced to overlook this element, Fischer told me that he wanted to leave politics and retire. He retired decently and honorably, and the manner in which he reacted to events—during our encounter to Ottawa as well—compelled my respect. It was typical of his attitude that on October 3, 1990, he wrote me a letter on the occasion of Germany's unification.

The Ottawa photograph was taken. Early in the afternoon Jim Baker, Eduard Shevardnadze, Roland Dumas, Douglas Hurd, Oskar Fischer, and I gathered for the picture. Afterward I went to meet with the German press to announce the outcome of our discussions. Did all the reporters realize what an historical decision regarding the unification process had been taken at that moment? I told them that we had deliberately chosen the term *creation of German unity*. It differed from such terms as *contractual community* or *confederation*. Once again I emphasized that a unified Germany must absolutely be part of NATO, but I left open the possibility of different arrangements for the NATO structure on East Germany territory.

After the press conference I went to the conference room where all my NATO counterparts were meeting. Baker, leaving the room, approached me. "Things are wild in there," he said. "Our colleagues are angry because we made the agreement with the Soviet Union on the Two-Plus-Four meetings without consulting them. They demand that the talks be reopened. We've held the fort; now it's your turn. Roland Dumas has already left. Of the four of us only Douglas Hurd is still inside." When I entered the room, the Dutch and Italian foreign ministers were raising their hands to speak. Both noted that negotiations on the external aspects of German unification were a matter that concerned all NATO members. The Dutch foreign minister added that the Netherlands were also neighbors of Germany, and that the meeting with Shevardnadze must be reopened.

I was deeply alarmed. What was the purpose of reopening negotiations? I felt that Shevardnadze had made all the concessions in his power (subsequently we heard from colleagues in Moscow that he had gone even further). Reopening negotiations could therefore only worsen our situation—not to mention the time factor. Further, we could not have concluded such new talks in Ottawa because everyone was already getting ready to leave. Roland Dumas, for one, had already gone. And what would be the result of such a new debate? There was little doubt that matters would have escaped our control. Overcoming my otherwise somewhat conciliatory nature, I now needed to make absolutely certain that the talks would on no account be resumed.

Turning to my Dutch and Italian colleagues, I asked, "Are you among the Four Powers responsible for Germany? Are you one of the two German states? You are neither." After a few brief additional remarks, I concluded my drastic intervention by noting, "You are not part of the game!"

It was not easy for me to speak so bluntly, but I had no choice. At that moment it became clear to all my colleagues that the request for the resumption of negotiations had gone too far. The debate was over quickly; some of my colleagues came to my aid. The chairman—Canada's foreign minister, Charles Clark—noted that, at least for the day, the matter was closed. That statement reassured me, since anything else would have had disastrous consequences for the negotiations and for our timetable. Yet I also realized that it would take a great effort to avoid discord with some of our European partners.

On the other hand, any other procedure would have been totally unacceptable. If we had been forced to solicit approval from every NATO member for every single phrase in our discussions with Shevardnadze, negotiations would have dragged on for an unjustifiable period. It would have meant doing precisely what we were trying to avoid by adopting the Two-Plus-Four procedure. Besides, we were pursuing a goal all NATO partners had repeatedly supported: Creating German unity. Consequently there were no objective reasons for anger at our methods. Our colleagues could rest assured that the West German government, as well as the United States, French, and British representatives, would safeguard NATO's concerns.

Before my departure I called on the Canadian prime minister to report on the negotiations with Shevardnadze and on the content and consequences of our agreement. Prime Minister Brian Mulroney indicated that he appreciated the gesture of my visit, which had not been scheduled. He expressed his great concern for the process of German unification, congratulated me on the result we had reached, and assured us of Canada's support. It made sense to him that the four acting NATO members—the United States, the United Kingdom, France, and Germany—had had no other choice. We had to seize this historic opportunity and conduct the negotiations as tightly and confidentially as possible.

It was obvious that enlarging the group of negotiators—even if only to allow for consultation—would result in a loss of confidentiality. Such publicity might have unleashed many antagonistic forces and made it more difficult for us to reach our goal in Ottawa: Creating the foundation and the general conditions for negotiations on German unity.

As early as February 19, 1990, I sent personal messages to the foreign ministers of the United States, France, the United Kingdom, and the Soviet Union, thanking them for the breakthrough in Ottawa.

The following day I received the Israeli foreign minister, Moshe Arens, at the Foreign Office. I briefed him on the meetings in Ottawa, and we discussed the situation in the Middle East and German-Israeli relations. How would Israel respond to German unification? Arens did not voice any misgivings. After all that had happened, I certainly had not anticipated his reaction as a matter of course. But I decided that I would make a public statement remembering the fate of the Jewish people at the opening of the Two-Plus-Four meetings.

The dynamics of the events went beyond what many could have imagined, even in the West. While we did all we could to bring the

Two-Plus-Four process to a conclusion by the fall of 1990, we heard that in Berlin, when envoys of the three Western allies met, some presumed that the two German states would continue to exist separately for a long time. Perhaps it was merely their privileged position in Berlin these representatives had come to value. But then, why should the envoys take a more realistic view of the situation than did many Germans?

Rally Under the Five Towers

February 16, 1990, is a date I will never forget. In the morning I called on the West German president to brief him on the state of negotiations on German unification, at least its foreign policy aspects. Subsequently I took a helicopter to Herleshausen, and from there I drove to Halle.

Around five o'clock in the afternoon, after I had held several meetings, a police escort drove my wife and me to Halle's marketplace, where a rally was scheduled to take place. We drove until we were near the square, through streets I had known since childhood but most especially from the time I had been a schoolboy in Halle and, later still, when I had served time at the court and worked with Fritz Herzfeld, a lawyer. It was almost impossible to get out of the car. The street was thronged with countless people who were trying to get to the market. Our own security officers— as well, it seemed, as some East German officers—cleared the way for my wife and me to reach the raised dais by the back stairs.

I had written a speech for this occasion, but I already knew that I would not deliver my prepared text. I had a need to speak to the people from my heart. A banner outside the city hall welcomed me as the architect of German unity. An immense crowd had gathered, approximately eighty thousand people, some carrying banners demanding German unification. Others were holding signs naming the many towns around Halle, where these spectators came from, and quite close to me I saw a group holding a sign reading KLITSCHMAR. They were friends of my cousin Achim Scharf, who had been living in Bochum since the early 1950s, greeting me. When I was a child my parents and I had often visited Klitschmar, where Achim's family owned a farm.

Listening to the first speakers, my thoughts went back to my childhood, to our parents, and to another cousin, Günter Michel.

The three of us—I was the youngest—had spent many wonderful days together.

The crowd cheered when I took my place at the speaker's podium. Representatives of the liberal parties with whom we collaborated—the Liberal-Democratic Party and the East FDP—were gathered around me. Former schoolmates were also present; here and there, near the podium, I spotted a few who drew attention to themselves. When it was my turn to speak, I addressed the people of Halle, my hometown.

My state of mind and my feelings can probably be understood only by those who themselves have had to leave their homes, those who, like me, have been able to visit relatives only under restricted circumstances and finally had a reunion, a return, like this one.

How often I had wished—and during the memorial service for Tito I had told Honecker as much—that I could speak in Halle during an election campaign. Obviously this event was part of the Liberals' campaign for the 1990 election to the Volkskammer, but to me it represented my official return to Halle. I was moved in an entirely different way than I had been moved a few weeks earlier, when I had spoken to the people of Halle at the Market Church on the Sunday before Christmas of 1989. I had to work hard not to let raw emotion carry me away. This was the moment when so much came together for me. I did not think of myself as the foreign minister of West Germany, but as a citizen of Halle. And the townspeople may have thought of me as one of them. As I was speaking, my gaze kept returning to the towers that had become the symbol of Halle—the four steeples of the Market Church and the Red Tower.

After the rally it was difficult for me to descend from the dais. Many people approached me, reminding me of encounters we had had in the past. Some of them I remembered, others I did not. Only with a great effort did we reach our car, which inched up the street in the direction of the Hansaring. From there we returned to Herleshausen and, by helicopter, back to Bonn.

The second half of February and March 1990 in the Ministry consisted mainly of intense preparations for the Two-Plus-Four talks. In addition I was in touch with numerous friendly governments. On March 2 I met with Spain's Foreign Minister Ordóñez and Prime Minister Felipe Gonzáles Marquez to discuss the unification process with them. Both were pleased at the prospect of German unification. I also went to Copenhagen. The Danish foreign minister, Uffe Ellemann-Jensen, had always, and without reservation, supported German unification—something that could not, unfortunately, be said of all members of Denmark's administration at that time.

There was another official visit I remember very fondly. I accompanied the West German president to Prague, where I spoke with President Havel and Foreign Minister Dienstbier. Since that unforgettable day, September 30, 1989, this city meant even more to me than it had before. I had always found Prague to be the most European of European cities, but how different it was now— and how different my encounter with Václav Havel, the republic's new president.

On the Road to Two Plus Four: With Baker and Shevardnadze in Windhoek

On the morning of March 20, 1990, we traveled to Windhoek, the capital of Namibia, which would officially gain its independence on March 21 and become the one hundred sixtieth member of the United Nations. Jim Baker, Eduard Shevardnadze, and I, together with many other colleagues, attended the ceremonies arranged for the occasion. This trip gave me great satisfaction, since I had actively fought for Namibia's independence since the late 1970s. The United States, France, the United Kingdom, Canada, and West Germany had worked toward that end in the United Nations Security Council's contact group. I was vehemently criticized in Germany for this effort; the criticism concerned my meetings with Sam Nujoma, the president of the SWAPO, whom I met with repeatedly in Bonn and abroad. German foreign policy was among the most resolute pioneers in advocating Namibia's independence and the forging of a stable democracy; the value system embedded in our constitution had to prove its validity in overcoming apartheid in the Republic of South Africa and in ending South African colonial rule over Namibia as well. I remembered the confrontations I was exposed to after our consulate in Windhoek was closed: A law office assumed the consulate's responsibilities, so that no one suffered from our action. But in shutting down our consulate we expressed our rejection of South Africa's continuing rule over Namibia. This policy, however, met with criticism in some quarters of the CDU and—even more—the CSU. When on March 21, 1990, Sam Nujoma—branded for a long time by many, in Germany as well, as a terrorist—became president, neither the West German government nor the German foreign service had cause to apologize for past conduct.

Around eleven o'clock at night the independence-day ceremonies opened in the stadium; we witnessed great enthusiasm and great dignity—and these feelings alone proved wrong those who never ceased to criticize me, with racist condescension, for my support of the liberation movements SWAPO and ANC. "One man, one vote"—that principle, my critics claimed, was not feasible in countries in which whites and blacks lived together, for blacks were not ready for democracy. Coming from Germans, after everything that had happened between 1933 and 1945, such sentiments sounded particularly self-righteous and arrogant.

Windhoek gave me another opportunity for a talk with Jim Baker as well as with Eduard Shevardnadze. My Soviet counterpart and I met under a garden umbrella in the garden of the West German residence. Each of us was accompanied by only one associate—in my case Frank Elbe—and the interpreters. We went over the many problems that required solutions before German unification could be achieved. I noted that Shevardnadze was intent on making his country's approval dependent on the Potsdam Agreement and our meeting all its stipulations. His suggestion that "We must carefully go over the Potsdam Agreement point by point," led us to the expropriations carried out in the Soviet-occupied zone, including so-called land reform. Apparently these were to appear not as initiatives for creating a Socialist social and economic order, but as measures in the struggle against fascism and militarism, thus adhering to the Potsdam Agreement. It was therefore not possible to annul them, as having violated the law, after the fact. That issue was to play a significant part during the course of the subsequent negotiations. But even in Windhoek I began to gain the impression that it would be possible for us to keep the door open to regulations concerning reparations for those who had been hurt by these measures. Only later did it turn out that dealing with expropriations also involved a problem between the two Germanys and that the issue of reparations also made for a problem within the coalition.

According to Shevardnadze, the Soviet people and Soviet policy had always relied heavily on the Potsdam Agreement, and still did so. And since the agreement was based on the assumption that eventually a peace treaty would be signed, Shevardnadze also intended to raise that issue at the Two-Plus-Four meetings. Negotiations on the agenda for the meetings had already started among public officials; the Soviet foreign minister expressed his appreciation of the fact that the department heads had already been in touch with one another. Theirs was the level where the agenda should be set, so that in future the foreign ministers would not have to have that kind of discussion.

These procedural remarks were a sign that progress had been made. Most past conferences that had dealt with Germany had failed because there was dissent on the agenda. If Shevardnadze was willing to leave these details to the career diplomats, Moscow no longer considered these issues worth political controversy. Nor were they apparently to be exploited to block the negotiations—a promise that filled me with hope. However, I could not accept the idea of a peace treaty as a principal agenda item. Shevardnadze's remark that "everything must be finalized in the peace treaty" had become anachronistic, nor was it acceptable in principle. I therefore protested: "The peace treaty is a concept of the past. After the Second World War, history took a different course; two German states were created, but we have remained one people. The Federal Republic of Germany is a member of NATO and the European Community, we have treaties with the Soviet Union, with Poland, with Czechoslovakia, and with East Germany. Ongoing events in Germany and Europe are in full accord with the Helsinki Final Act. We are building a new Europe. In this situation a peace treaty would be a step backward."

I continued, "The Two-Plus-Four talks must not take place in a vacuum; they must articulate a vision, combining those German and European policies that point to the future." I then noted the three general European developments that were important to the talks: One, the CSCE economic conference, which was scheduled to take place in Bonn shortly and whose focus would be economic cooperation; two, the disarmament negotiations in Vienna; and three, a new view of the future of CSCE beyond the East-West conflict.

Shevardnadze saw no difference of opinion between us in this matter, but he did return to the peace treaty. "Surely such a treaty would not interfere with the pan-European process?" he asked.

Should all the Second World War enemies participate—even Namibia, although it was only a day old? I retorted. It was impossible to tell from the foreign minister's expression whether he was smiling or feeling attacked. But he must have understood me correctly, because he continued, "I understand that Germany cannot leave NATO."

I sat up. His message, though encoded, was sufficiently clear: He was speaking of a united Germany's NATO membership.

Shevardnadze added, "On the other hand, the Soviet Union cannot allow the Warsaw Pact to disperse. Such an eventuality would alter the balance between West and East."

Thus three elements were emerging: One, as far as my Soviet counterpart was concerned, the German question had basically been settled. Two, he feared—and even expected—the dissolution of the Warsaw Pact. Three, he acknowledged that Germany could not and would not leave NATO, though this membership would result in a problem of imbalance for which we had to work together to find a solution.

At the same time his tone and the way he spoke made me realize that he feared certain political forces in the Soviet Union. Again and again he and Gorbachev were accused of being well on their way to unnecessarily surrendering foreign-policy positions. There were no longer any security guarantees, as there had been throughout the Communist system's existence, and though Soviet troops were still stationed in East Germany, even Shevardnadze no longer considered such deployment appropriate. No doubt he feared anti-Soviet demonstrations, even acts of violence against the Red Army. No people, the foreign minister noted, could tolerate the presence of foreign troops in the long run. I agreed with him on that point, although I did not think anti-Soviet rallies were imminent.

During our talk I also tried to point out to my Soviet counterpart the advantages to his country that would result from a unified Germany. "Despite horrible wars, there has never been any sworn enmity between our peoples. That is an important basis for future developments; therefore we should discuss all aspects of this issue calmly. The unification of Germany will be advantageous to the Soviet Union as well," I said, and I continued, "Our countries have many similar concerns. The economic potential for future cooperation is essentially unlimited." Shevardnadze agreed.

On March 21—my birthday—Jim Baker arrived at the West German residence; he extended warm and personal good wishes. The first free elections for the East German Volkskammer had taken place three days earlier. Baker welcomed the results: The three-party Alliance for Germany (AFD), of which the CDU was the strongest member, received 48 percent of the vote; the SPD, 22 percent; the PDS, consisting of Socialists and former Communists, over 16 percent; and the Association of Free Democrats (BFD, an association of the three liberal parties), more than the 5 percent necessary for parliamentary representation. I remarked to Baker that both the CDU and the Liberals in East Germany supported West Germany's position on the issue of the united Germany's membership in NATO; but that Shevardnadze was encountering increasing criticism in his own country for being too sympathetic to our stand on the German question. Baker replied that our Soviet colleague was made nervous by the speed of developments in Germany—and indeed, it was difficult for him to support the united Germany's NATO membership at home. Therefore he, too, was leaning toward neutrality.

I remarked that according to our information, Czechoslovakia, Hungary, and Poland were opposed to neutrality for the united Germany; my efforts to persuade our Eastern neighbors that their stability would increase if Germany remained in NATO were bearing fruit. I also emphasized the value of the United States' continued presence in Europe and participation in pan-European structures in the spirit of the Harmel Report. As for the future strength of the German forces, I mentioned that reductions were conceivable, but this matter should not be included in the Two-Plus-Four talks. It was essential to avoid creating a special status for Germany. It would be better to discuss the issue of troop strength in Vienna, during the negotiations on conventional security in Europe, as part of the larger context of limitations imposed on all participants. Incidentally, Baker also spent a great deal of time discussing the issue of Poland's border.

As mentioned previously, in Windhoek I met Nelson Mandela for the first time. I had long since had contact with South Africa's liberation movement, the African National Congress. Above all,

356

however, I was preoccupied with Nelson Mandela's fate; I tried to learn everything about him. I believed more and more that he was right when he called himself a political prisoner, that he was not in jail for murder, as South Africa's racist leaders and their sympathizers in Germany claimed. During Mandela's prison term, Oliver Tambo, whom I received in Bonn in 1977, led the exiled ANC.

I had tried repeatedly to obtain Mandela's release. I made representations to the South African government suggesting that it free a man with such responsibility as quickly as possible. He could be a participant in negotiations, I argued, whose authority would make possible arrangements that would also provide fair opportunities for the white minority in the future. Of course such ideas met with general incomprehension both in West Germany and in South Africa in the mid-1970s. Only much later was Mandela released. He became the Republic of South Africa's preeminent leader and the white government's negotiating partner in Pretoria on the matter of leading South Africa out of apartheid. Today he is the elected president, and the one who made peaceful transition possible.

On March 29, 1990, Mandela thanked me as the representative of all those political forces in Germany who for years had so insistently fought on his behalf. He knew that in discussions with the South African government as well as in speeches to the United Nations and the EC I had advocated his release. When we faced each other at last, I felt the presence of an eminent figure. He mentioned South Africa's new president, F. W. de Klerk, with respect; when I met with de Klerk a few hours later, he in turn spoke respectfully of Mandela.

In the case of another black South African leader, Mangosuthu Gatsha Buthelezi, the Zulu chief who headed Inkatha, my impression was less favorable. Again and again conservatives in Germany and South Africa tried to persuade me that he was an important person to talk to. I did, of course, receive Buthelezi in Bonn, just as I received Dirk Mudge of the Democratic Turnhalle Alliance in Namibia and Joshua Nkomo of Zimbabwe. But Buthelezi was thinking in tribal terms; he feared the democratic and nationalistic competitor he correctly saw in Mandela. Nor did I ever figure out exactly what to make of the rumors that Buthelezi's contacts with the white minority government were closer than they seemed.

□   □   □   □

After my return from Namibia I rushed to Lisbon to attend the March 23–24 special conference of the European Council's foreign ministers, which discussed changes in Central and Eastern Europe. The European Council encompasses European democracies that are members neither of NATO nor the European Community. I wanted to have detailed discussions on the German question with these colleagues; good neighborly relations dictated as much. All participants were open-minded, so that at the conclusion of the conference I could genuinely call it a happy day for Europe. My suggestion that we hold regular foreign ministers' meetings under the umbrella of the CSCE and create one central organization for settling contentious issues and another one for disarmament control, as well as an environmental agency, were well received. As we worked on the new European architecture, the European Council also came to play a rather important part in protecting human and minority rights, in furthering cultural cooperation, and in organizing a joint legal territory.

The discussions within the Western Alliance of future security structures in all of Europe made clear once again the distinction between traditionalist and evolutionary thinking. It was obvious that overcoming the political and ideological antagonism between East and West would have an impact on the alliances. As Marxism-Leninism lost ground as a political doctrine and thus as the ideological foundation of the Soviet Union's predominance over large parts of Central and Southeastern Europe, the rug was pulled out from under the Warsaw Pact: It was disbanding. For NATO, on the other hand, as the West's community of shared values, yesterday's enemies were becoming today's and tomorrow's partners. The first response to the new situation was the 1991 Baker-Genscher initiative for the North Atlantic Cooperation Council, which was followed by the offer of a Partnership for Peace. And yet the latter was no more than a first response. It prevented a vacuum from forming around security policy, it represented an offer of cooperative security policies, and it contributed to the creation of new pan-European security structures. It had, and still has, the advantage of being very flexible, an offer that in individual cases keeps open the option for a differentiated partnership, including special relations with Russia—the superpower that, while not a member of the Western Alliance, is tied, appropriately, with the United States, NATO's superpower—in a strategic partnership.

It will be crucial to NATO's future that the organization not lose sight of its "highest goal": Building the foundation of a lasting and just peace in Europe that is called for in the Harmel Report of 1967. Now that NATO's other goal—peacefully overcoming the division of Germany—has been achieved, a concept for a pan-European foundation of peace in the spirit of the Harmel Report must be developed. We therefore need something like a Harmel Report II, assisted, if possible, by a transatlantic partnership such as was first called for in the Baker-Genscher initiative. In order to meet their global responsibility, North Americans and Europeans require both broader and closer cooperation in all areas—in other words, even beyond NATO. Such cooperation will be indispensable even in the future. Now that the Cold War is over, the Atlantic must not be allowed to grow wider.

On March 26 the West German president and I left on an official visit to Portugal. Foreign Minister Deus Pinheiro genuinely shared our pleasure at the course of European and German unification, as did Prime Minister Anibal Cavaco Silva, whom I received in the afternoon for a cordial conversation.

On March 27 Alois Mock, the foreign minister of Austria, arrived in Bonn, and the following day Prime Minister Charles James Haughey of Ireland came on a visit. On March 30, 1990, the Chancellor and I flew to London for talks with Prime Minister Thatcher and Secretary Hurd.

From April 3 to 6 I visited the United States and Canada to discuss details of the Two-Plus-Four process. Once again President Bush and Secretary Baker assured me of their support in the effort to forge German unity. I pointed out that the West German government had a vital interest in seeing the Two-Plus-Four talks concluded before the CSCE summit in November, if at all possible. Otherwise, I noted, the CSCE meeting would turn into some sort of conference on Germany, and it was important to avoid any impression that the thirty-five CSCE countries were deciding the fate of Germany—a misinterpretation we had been eager to thwart from the outset.

I also strongly advocated a larger role for the United States in forming the future structures of all of Europe. Asked during the press conference if we had discussed modernization of the Lance missile as well, I replied in the negative: "We only talked about the future," while modernizing of the Lance was an issue of the past.

In less than twelve months history had confirmed my objections to SNF modernization. A responsible foreign policy requires the ability to analyze and, on the basis of a sound analysis, properly to assess future events. It spoke in favor of President Bush's and Secretary of State Baker's great professionalism in foreign policy that in 1989, only a few months after they took office, they allowed themselves be persuaded that the development of West-East relations had long since overtaken these issues.

In Washington I advocated turning the CSCE process into an ongoing institutionalized organization, so that complicated security issues arising in connection with German unification could be settled at once.

In connection with this suggestion I also emphasized in Ottawa the necessity for a presence of Canadian NATO forces in West Germany. Canada's ties to Europe must continue to be visible, avoiding troop clusters consisting solely of the former occupation powers. Finally I thanked the Canadian government for its support of German unification.

In Ottawa and Washington I called on the North American democracies and all EC members to issue a joint declaration in favor of a new transatlantic partnership. The document should address all political, economic, technical, and cultural aspects of our various relationships. The construction of the common European house could succeed only with the cooperation of the United States. If new CSCE institutions were created, our Eastern neighbors, including the Soviet Union, must also be involved in the construction of the common house. It was important that we open peoples' eyes as soon as possible to the prospects of future transatlantic relations, since all discussions were still entirely focused on German unification. After the end of two horrible wars, in 1918 and in 1945, the United States had taken two different tacks. In 1918 it had turned away from Europe and left the Continent to its own devices; in 1945 it had stayed. What would it do now that the Cold War was over? Ever closer cooperation, beyond the alliance, between Washington and Europe would be one of the missions we had to accomplish.

What impelled my intense "information exchange and meeting

marathon" with our close and distant neighbors was the realization that neither German history nor Germany's future (to borrow Richard von Weizsäcker's words) belongs to us alone. Constant communication with our neighbors was intended to express our awareness of the fact that the Germans' and the Europeans' fates are inextricably intertwined. The German unification process, too, was supposed to evolve through its foundation in NATO, by and through further integration in the European Community, through the CSCE process, through a stable partnership between West and East, through building the common European house, and through the establishment of the pan-European peace that was called for by the Western Alliance. Everyone must know: The Germans do not want to go their own special, isolated way—the Germans want to walk the European road.

On April 11 the CSCE economic summit, which had started on March 19, ended in Bonn with the acceptance of a concluding document. The conference had hardly been spectacular; nevertheless it illustrated the dramatic manner in which events were developing. For a long time the Western camp had discussed whether to hold the conference at all, and we repeatedly had to struggle to obtain the United States' consent. Washington feared that the export restrictions for the East that had been established in the COCOM (Coordinating Committee on Multilateral Export Controls) list would be relaxed. Even at the concluding CSCE foreign ministers' meeting in Vienna in January 1989 the idea of an economic conference was as controversial within NATO as was the human rights conference in Moscow. West Germany, on the other hand, regarded an economic conference in Bonn as encouraging Gorbachev's policy of reform, and it recognized a human rights conference held in Moscow as an opportunity to demand respect for human rights in the Soviet sphere of power itself. The Moscow leaders were expected to commit themselves to including in the conference various civil rights groups from their own country as well as from other Communist nations. Thus, if the conference were to pose a threat at all, it was not to the West but to the Soviet leadership unless the Soviets were willing to further reform in the spirit of Gorbachev and Shevardnadze's policies—and I was convinced that the Soviets did indeed want such changes. I increasingly gained the impression that the Secretary General's and the

Foreign Minister's expectations for this conference were similar to ours: They too intended to use it to strengthen and accelerate the liberalization process against the dogmatic forces in their country. In the end our view regarding both projects won out, signifying a breakthrough in two important areas of our comprehensive CSCE strategy—human rights and the economy.

As so frequently in the past, two diametrically opposed views had struggled against each other on this issue. The traditionalists remained mired in status-quo thinking: They believed change to be impossible, or they thought that the methods leading to change were too risky. A principal skeptic had been the British prime minister, who initially had exerted great influence on Washington. She was opposed by the evolutionists, represented above all by German foreign policy, which staked its future on the power of freedom. "Nothing is as powerful as an idea whose time has come"—I used this saying more frequently than ever before during the second half of the 1980s. I never had greater reason to do so. I staked Germany's fortune on changes based on our value system. These would bring about changes in the general political, security, and economic conditions and help to resolve issues that heretofore had resisted solution.

CSCE in Bonn

As early as November 1986 Foreign Minister Shevardnadze had suggested that the CSCE human-rights conference be held in Moscow. My response was favorable on the whole. Two days after Shevardnadze I spoke at the CSCE conference in Vienna, which had just opened, emphasizing that such a conference in Moscow would give us an opportunity to demand the observance of human rights in the appropriate site. I continued: "If, by way of such a conference, implementation of what has already been resolved is not delayed, if this conference can take place under the appropriate conditions, and if we succeed in formulating a mandate for it that is sufficiently specific and advances our cause, then such a conference can serve the needs of all humanity." Mine was a point of view that allowed us to define the West's goals with the necessary precision.

Finally a three-part conference was agreed upon. From May 30 to June 23, 1989, two hundred years after the French Revolution, a preliminary meeting was held in Paris to deal with the human dimension. From June 5 to 29, 1990, a second meeting was scheduled to take place in Copenhagen, and from September 10 to October 4 we would convene in Moscow. It would be the first international conference after the coup d'état in Moscow.

The Paris conference established the criteria for the future meetings, including Moscow. In Copenhagen significant progress was made with regard to the Two-Plus-Four talks. In Moscow, under the influence of the putsch against Gorbachev, it became possible to place the CSCE nations' domestic democratic order under the protection of the Final Act.

The CSCE economic conference in Bonn gained historic significance for the CSCE process in that it did justice to the new prospects opened up by the upheaval in Central and Eastern Europe. With the help of the new political leaders, who believed in a market economy, it was expected that changes would be made that would overcome the economic division of Europe. The Bonn Final Document therefore obligated all thirty-five CSCE members to adhere to the elementary building blocks of the Western political and social order: An open social system, based on pluralism, democracy, and constitutionality, was to become the absolute prerequisite for economic efficiency in all of Europe.

In that respect the document represents a benchmark of economic policy. For the first time all CSCE nations pledged themselves to support a market economy. I therefore noted in my speech of April 11, "It [the document] is one of the key statements to the effect that respect for human rights, nondiscrimination, political pluralism, free elections, democracy, the supremacy of law, and a market economy that is based on private initiative are inextricably intertwined. This market economy has a social and environmental dimension, it is a social and ecological market economy."

In that context I noted the possible long-term prospects of this development: At the 1992 CSCE summit in Helsinki, I remarked, a sort of Magna Carta of European security and cooperation could be sealed. Further, I believed a series of new procedures and institutions for all of Europe was necessary to advance CSCE—for example, regular foreign ministers' meetings and a European center for the early recognition and political settling of conflicts. These would, in a manner of speaking, institutionalize a new form of crisis management. In future the European Council's jurisdiction, including the Human Rights Court and the Human Rights Commission, should be extended to all of Europe. In addition, the right to free elections should be firmly established in CSCE, a European environmental agency should be created, and EURECA cooperation should be made accessible to all Europeans. It was evident that these activities, which affected all of Europe, would be able to support the German unification process politically even outside of the Two-Plus-Four process; changes in surrounding areas were intended to facilitate progress in the key areas.

Two German Foreign Ministers

On April 17, 1990, the new East German foreign minister, Markus Meckel, was invited to my home for dinner. Each of us was accompanied by two associates. During the meal and afterward we discussed our cooperation and preparations for the Two-Plus-Four meetings. Meckel impressed me with his modesty as well as his self-confidence. This was the first meeting between the first freely elected East German foreign minister and a West German foreign minister who had left East Germany in 1952 in favor of West Germany. Among Meckel's closest associates, some of whom had come from the Federal Republic, was a younger brother of Gerold von Braunmühl, my associate who had been assassinated. If he had not been killed, I thought, two brothers would have met here to discuss ways for the two German states to unite.

I described our point of view and our plans for the Two-Plus-Four talks, explaining my impression of the attitude of the Four Powers. I also suggested to Meckel that we engage in close political and personal collaboration, since it was important for me to take no action without his cooperation.

During his next visit, on April 24, 1990, in the Foreign Office, Meckel remarked that in view of the speedy unification we were facing, East Germany's foreign policy had a special, formative task. "We could contribute extremely close relations with Poland," he explained by way of an example, still caught up in the notion that East Berlin's relationship with Poland was better than Bonn's. And yet it was precisely Poland that had always placed special emphasis on its contacts with the Federal Republic of Ger-

many, even at a time when Warsaw's foreign policy was still entirely determined by the Communist United Polish Workers'
Party. Nevertheless, by openly recognizing Poland's western border, in Poland's view—and this was true for the entire spectrum of
political opinions in Poland—East Germany had ultimately secured for itself the role of guarantor.

Meckel was eager for a foreign policy that was not solely focused on giving East Germany a fitting burial. He explained that
his principal objective was the unification of Germany without
jeopardizing European stability. That goal coincided absolutely
with my own intention. Speaking of his visit to Warsaw, he told
me that Poland was adhering to Skubiszewski's proposal to initial
the border treaty now and to have it signed and ratified subsequently by the government of the unified Germany. He had also
gained the impression that President Jaruzelski found it harder to
accept Germany's membership in NATO than did Foreign Minister Skubiszewski. I could only agree with Meckel's interpretation.

Then, repeatedly referring to my United Nations speech of September 1989, I clearly explained my position on the Oder-Neisse
Line. Markus Meckel listened attentively, clearly very much in
agreement.

On April 25 and 26, 1990, the fifty-fifth German-French consultations took place in Paris. I conferred with Roland Dumas on the
further preparations for the Two-Plus-Four talks, as well as on
developments in East Germany. I pointed out that any delay in
creating the German economic, currency, and social union would
only exacerbate all problems. Domestic policy—or, more precisely, the continuing flood of refugees from East to West—also
demanded speedy unification. Since January 1990, an additional
200,000 people had moved from East Germany to West Germany.

This summit once again demonstrated the harmony and con-
cord between Germany and France. During the joint press conference after the talks, President Mitterand and Chancellor Kohl
stressed their unconditional support of Germany's membership in
NATO. They also emphasized the significance of the German-
French initiative for the European Union; they were alluding to
the initiative Helmut Kohl and Francois Mitterand had presented
to the Irish prime minister, then chairman of the European Council, in a joint message on April 19, 1990. Of particular importance

was the Chancellor's statement that Germany was making no territorial demands: Psychologically speaking, his message that the unification of both German states signified the removal of a source of conflict in Europe came at the right time and in the right place.

At the special EC summit in Dublin on April 28 a discussion took place of the consequences of German unification for the European Community and its future relationship with those countries in Central and Eastern Europe that were willing to institute reforms. During previous German-French consultations both sides had agreed to use this summit to set the course for a speedy realization of the Political Union in Europe. Since we were aware of the dynamics the German unification process was assuming at this time, Helmut Kohl and I made special efforts to emphasize our firm resolve regarding the Western European integration process. In their final statement the members of the EC welcomed the unification of the two Germanys: The EC, the statement read, "is looking forward to the fruitful contribution the entire German people can make after the imminent integration of East German national territory into the Community. We are confident that the unification of Germany will be a positive factor in the development of Europe in general and the Community in particular."

The next day, while delivering a speech at an important event of my party, the FDP, I began to feel increasingly weak, so much so that I was forced to step down. My arrhythmia was striking again.

The news agencies immediately reported my attack, so my appearance that same afternoon on a live German TV broadcast of a discussion about Europe's road to political union was a great surprise. We had to go on with our work; wherever and whenever I could, I wanted to recommend our policy to our people. Further, I was eager to demonstrate that I really had suffered no more than a passing weakness. The accusation—frequently made and not always without foundation—that politicians always want to present themselves to their constituents as strong and virile was beside the point in this case. Several incidents had made it widely known that I was not in the best of health, and my years-long struggle with pulmonary tuberculosis as a young man was no secret. Nor had I concealed my heart trouble. On the contrary: At my instigation the Foreign Office officially announced that I had suffered a heart attack on July 20, 1989.

This time, however, foreign policy reasons made me eager to preclude any public doubt about my well-being. During this most intricate, and most promising, phase of German foreign policy efforts after the war a great deal depended on the personal trust placed in the Federal Republic of Germany's representatives—the President, the Chancellor, and the Foreign Minister. Under no circumstances must any suspicion arise about my personal capabilities—a conviction Shevardnadze personally confirmed on September 12, 1990. Before then, however, I would still have to overcome a number of health problems.

On May 2 I accompanied President von Weizsäcker on his official visit to Warsaw. I held a confidential conversation with Foreign Minister Skubiszewski about Polish concerns regarding the unification process of the two Germanys before participating in the discussions between the President, Prime Minister Mazowiecki, and President Jaruzelski.

In comparison to the Chancellor's and my official visit of November 8, 1989, this visit was clearly set in a changed atmosphere. German unification was now accepted as a fait accompli, and Germany's membership in NATO and the European Community was recognized as advantageous to Poland. My repeated assertions that German unification would allow Germans and Poles to approach each other in a new way—especially since Poland's Western neighbor was not Germany alone but also the European Community and NATO—had been properly understood. Only the particulars and the date for signing the German-Polish border treaty had not yet been decided. Skubiszewski declared that if the President was speaking for the majority of Germans, the future of German-Polish relations was looming brightly. Once more the tremendous amount of confidence Richard von Weizsäcker enjoyed worldwide was evident.

That same evening I flew from Warsaw to Brussels to participate in the NATO foreign ministers' conference scheduled for the following day. In Brussels Secretary Baker briefed us on his conversations with the Soviet Union.

I again seized the opportunity to gauge the various positions of my Western colleagues regarding the first Two-Plus-Four conference, which would open in Bonn two days later. Next I reported on my conversations with Victor Karpov in Bonn and passed on what I had learned about the Soviets' attitude. Moscow, it seemed, feared that the introduction of the deutsche mark, planned for July 1, 1990, would have negative consequences for the Soviet troops stationed in East Germany. For that reason I was asked how the united Germany foresaw its relations with the Soviet Union; this key question was also significant in regard to Moscow's interests in further institutionalization of the CSCE process. Apparently the Soviet government was apprehensive that it might be pushed out of Europe. In Moscow this worry is ever present, independent of political systems and leading figures. It is a reality the West must never overlook.

Above all, however, we discussed the question of a united Germany's alliances. On this issue there were encouraging signs from the Soviets; my impression was confirmed that our efforts toward a change in attitude between the two alliances was gradually leading to a "de-demonization" of NATO in Moscow.

I then briefed my colleagues on the status of the border issue. Both German parliaments, the Bundestag as well as the Volkskammer, agreed to issue identical statements in this matter; these statements were then to be formally communicated to the Polish government. This procedure would achieve a high degree of commitment. As I knew from conversations with Prime Minister Mazowiecki and Foreign Minister Skubiszewski, this solution, which I had supported in Bonn and in Moscow, was acceptable to Poland.

Once again I stressed the importance of speedy Two-Plus-Four conferences. The momentum—the favorable time and dynamics of the present—must not be lost; we had to take full advantage of it. I could not rid myself of the fear that unexpected events, either internationally or in the Soviet Union, could make the German unification process more difficult or even block it altogether. The attempted putsch in Moscow in August 1991 confirmed my fears, but fortunately it happened at a time when the unification process as well as the ratification of the Two-Plus-Four Treaty were already "in the bag." What would have happened if events in Moscow had occurred a few months earlier, or—an even more threatening eventuality—if they had led to more dramatic consequences? Similar questions arose in connection with the Gulf War.

First Two-Plus-Four Meeting in Bonn

The following day I prepared for the first Two-Plus-Four meeting, which was scheduled for May 5. Shortly after eleven in the morning I received Jim Baker at the Villa Venusberg, the guest house of the Foreign Office, to discuss the most pressing details. Foreign Minister Meckel was expected to arrive in the afternoon and Foreign Minister Shevardnadze in the early evening. After their arrival I hosted a dinner attended also by Douglas Hurd and Roland Dumas.

On May 5 the conference began. I received the arriving delegations in alphabetical order, according to the German spelling of their names: The German Democratic Republic, France, the Soviet Union, the United States, and the United Kingdom. At that moment all must have felt the significance of this first conference on German unification. We had placed a large round table in the so-called World Room. I sat with my back to the global map, and Shevardnadze was placed directly opposite me.

Arrangements for the first Two-Plus-Four meeting had been under way since February 28. Afterward the Western representatives—Dieter Kastrup (West Germany), Bertrand Dufourcq (France), John Weston (the United Kingdom), and Raymond Seitz (the United States)—had met in London. In addition, Kastrup held exploratory talks with Anatoly Adamishin, the Soviet assistant foreign minister, on March 2, and on March 9 he had spoken with Deputy Foreign Minister Krabatsch of East Germany in East Berlin. These talks took place before the undersecretaries met for the first time in Bonn on March 14, 1990, and prior to the elections to the Volkskammer. We were thoroughly prepared.

Even though the meeting of May 5, 1990, fell on a Saturday, many members of the Foreign Office managed to obtain special passes to witness for themselves the beginning of the negotiations. Everyone, it was evident, was aware of the moment's historic significance. I had spent a long time polishing my opening speech as chairman and my introduction to the discussion. It was important that wherever it seemed necessary, I place the emphasis on the salient detail.

Forty-five years earlier, almost to the day—on May 7, 1945—I, barely eighteen years old and a soldier in General Wenck's army,

369

had become an American prisoner of war. During the last few weeks of the war I had experienced all the deprivation and all the misery of the criminal war Germany had unleashed. I therefore began my speech in the Foreign Office with the following words: "Forty-five years ago, almost to the day, a war ended in Europe that took countless victims and caused endless pain. We remember the victims of the war and the reign of terror by jointly reaffirming in the first sentence of the Helsinki Final Act our desire to contribute to peace in Europe, to security, to justice, and to cooperation. That is the spirit in which we set out on our talks today. We are eager to establish the basis for a new chapter, for a peaceful and happy period of German and European history. The horrors of the Second World War and the Holocaust are not forgotten. After the war there were more deaths during expulsion and flight. Others lost their lives and their liberty because they called for liberty. An Iron Curtain divided Europe. It divided the German people. We know what emotions and memories the people associate with what was done to them in the name of Germany. President Richard von Weizsäcker spoke for all Germans on May 8, 1985. Since the end of the war it has been possible, despite all tensions and confrontations, to preserve peace. Forty-five years without war— that is a new experience for our continent. All people will be able to look at the unified Germany as a contribution to a better Europe."

I continued by remarking that the unification of the two German states was taking place according to all Germans' wishes, though never implying that territorial demands were being made on any part of the territory. "German unification," I declared, "which is what the people in both German states and their democratically elected governments and parliaments desire, will be the result of a politics of responsibility. The united Germany is coming into being in observance of the right to self-determination, which is firmly rooted in international law and in the principles of the Helsinki Final Act. Self-determination also means that the Germans themselves are choosing their form of government, when, how fast, and under what conditions they want to realize their unity. That is what Secretary General Gorbachev stated in Moscow on February 10, 1990, and I believe that this is the way everyone around this table understands it. The modalities and the time schedule for German unification are becoming clearer. The

Federal Republic of Germany and the German Democratic Republic have equal rights as participants in the unification process. We start out from the existent rights and responsibilities assigned to the Four Powers for Germany as a whole and for Berlin; we are eager now to take charge, in an orderly way. That is essentially what we will be discussing around this table." During this process there must be neither discrimination nor singling out: "The Helsinki Final Act explicitly emphasizes that all principles have a fundamental significance. In this context let me point out the principle of sovereign equality, which grants all member nations the right to be or not be a contractual party to an alliance. Since we know the peace- and security-building effect of the Western Alliance, which has been preparing for the changes in Europe, a unified Germany without an alliance would not be a gain for Europe." I had thus unambiguously expressed two objectives: One, that Germany *would* exercise its right to decide to which alliance it would belong; and two, *how* it was going to arrive at its decision—by being, as a unified country, a member of NATO. The fact that Bonn was where the first conference was set further underscored our equality in discussing with the allies the issues associated with unification—a point Kastrup had had to enforce on his group of colleagues.

Both German states, I continued, viewed national unity not merely as a goal of German policies, but as a contribution to a new Europe. Therefore from the outset we integrated our unification policy in the European frame. German unification was not intended to create new problems for the Continent but was meant to establish permanent stability; that is what I called Germany's European vocation at the end of this century.

However, since Germany's unity concerned not merely our immediate neighbors but all of Europe as well, we had made it our aim to present the result of the Two-Plus-Four talks at the CSCE countries' special summit in Paris in the fall of 1990. Before my colleagues spoke, I announced:

> The process of Germany's unification not only changes European structures, it also touches on the bilateral interests of numerous partners of the Federal Republic of Germany and the German Democratic Republic. We do not intend unification to cause harm to or result in disadvantages for other countries. We are convinced that a united

371

Germany not only would not weaken but would significantly increase the potential of intensive, mutually advantageous cooperation. This is particularly true for the united Germany's relations with the Soviet Union, which will continue to be crucially important to a unified Germany. We realize that we must find answers to a number of difficult questions. Yet we would like to hold these talks without delay, and we must do justice to the expectations of the people of both parts of Germany.

Shevardnadze, whose contribution we were all particularly anxious to hear, declared that he was essentially in agreement with what I had said. How acutely aware he was of his great responsibility and all the problems involved became clear when he remarked in his speech:

> We endorse the Germans' right to self-determination. We believe that a united Germany will join the European family of nations as a democratic and peace-loving country aware of its responsibilities and obligations to world peace and security. Our conviction is strengthened by our recognition of the values of the new generation of Germans, their aspirations, and their views of life. We have neither reason nor cause to doubt their love of peace and their allegiance to universal human and humanistic values. The worst we could do would be to rely on worn-out clichés and ideas. In our opinion discriminating against Germans, legally or psychologically, is out of the question today.

That statement was one I was deeply grateful to hear. Germany's postwar policy toward the Soviet Union, the talks with Shevardnadze and with Gorbachev, had not been in vain. And since one of the aims of these Two-Plus-Four talks was to avoid the mistakes of the past on the part of the victorious powers, the German people must be allowed to decide on its future without being discriminated against. Shevardnadze tried to express the high quality of the personal relationship between the two of us when he said, "Finally, allow me to say—not out of politeness but in all truth—a few kind words to our hosts and above all to my friend, Hans-Dietrich Genscher, about his rare diplomatic qualities of tact, goodwill, and the ability, in the most difficult situations, to create an atmosphere that is conducive to serious and quiet work as well as to the search for solutions and compromises."

"My friend Hans-Dietrich Genscher"—my Soviet counterpart had used that expression for the first time a few months earlier, addressing the European Community's foreign ministers in Brussels in December 1989. The fact that he repeated it here, in Bonn, during the first round of negotiations on German unity, proved to me that the talks had started off well. But it also proved once again that a revolutionary political change had taken place: Only a few years earlier, the words *my friend*, uttered by a Soviet foreign minister about a Western colleague—and especially a German foreign minister—would have been his political undoing.

All of us could feel the change that had taken place in German-Soviet relations and between its protagonists. Because Shevardnadze understood very clearly that we viewed the German question as an issue that was integral to the development of Europe, his speech pointed out that we were trying to address more than merely Germany and its problems. Indeed, that was precisely the crux. But he made no attempt to conceal how difficult the road would be for the Soviet leaders now that Moscow had agreed to back German unity. "Neither this nor any other Soviet leadership can dismiss public opinion. The Soviet people must see to it that the past is left behind with dignity and with fairness. I am speaking with extreme sincerity and frankness. We are describing the situation as it is, as we see and perceive it." No one in the room doubted the honesty of these remarks. Shevardnadze was not displaying tactical tricks. Everyone was aware of the difficulties the Soviet Union's foreign minister and Gorbachev as well were facing back home by trying to accomplish what we expected of them. And I must remind anyone who, in retrospect, believes that the events of 1990 unrolled as a natural given: They did not.

Shevardnadze's address contained an important statement that would carry great weight in the subsequent discussion on Germany: What was the meaning of the Potsdam Agreement in regard to unification? Shevardnadze noted: "Obviously Germany must not revise and cast doubt upon the measures and regulations the Four Powers decreed in the zones of occupation."

The structure of Shevardnadze's speech was psychologically clever, particularly the part that dealt with Germany's commitments and the two alliances' reciprocal position. "In returning to the issue of the military's political status," he remarked, "I must reiterate our negative attitude toward a united Germany's membership in NATO. Such a solution would affect our security interests in an essential area, would imply a severe disturbance of the balance of power in Europe, and would create a military and strategic situation that is dangerous for us." This statement corroborated my view that in future it was essential for us to work for change in the relationship between the two alliances. NATO's foreign ministers' conference in Turnberry would be crucially significant in that respect, as was the subsequent NATO summit in London. At least Shevardnadze had not turned the NATO issue into a fundamental problem. His concerns regarding the Soviet Union's security could be countered.

Shevardnadze continued by addressing the question of the possible reasons for the unified Germany's NATO membership; he attempted to interpret the fact that others besides West Germany wanted to see Germany within NATO as a last remnant of mistrust.

> There are certainly reasons to assume that by making the new country a part of NATO the existence of that military bloc is to be legally perpetuated. Or is the issue really one of mistrust of the Germans, the fear of leaving them out of a bloc and thus losing control over Germany? In that case we should decide the basic question: How far-reaching is our treaty, and will we trust the Germans? If yes, I believe we have to do so completely. Otherwise, from the outset we would cause a dangerous rift in the arrangement for Germany, we would even move toward a new division of Europe, toward renewed conflict and revived confrontation. However, if our goal is different, then we should rely not on blocs but on security structures for all of Europe, which should be created without further delay.

He added,

> Apart from the purely military argument, Germany's membership in NATO is not acceptable for domestic reasons either. Our country's population, which has suffered such horrible losses in the past war, cannot be reconciled to the idea of incorporating a unified Germany in NATO, as an opinion poll showed just recently. Our Supreme Soviet is ruled by the same sentiments. We have to take that circumstance into consideration. Therefore I ask my colleagues not to fall

prey to the illusion that we are playing games, or are bluffing. Rather, I appeal to you to join in looking for solutions that take into consideration not only our concerns but also the overall concern of peace in Europe and of global security.

"To us, NATO remains what it has always been," Shevardnadze added firmly, "an opposing military bloc, with a particular doctrine and ideology and with the capacity of unleashing the first nuclear strike."

Why did Shevardnadze employ these gloomy phrases from the propaganda arsenal of the Cold War? Then as now I believed that he intended to give public expression to the arguments raised by his opponents within the Soviet Union. Like Gorbachev, during the entire negotiations on German unity he was under enormous pressure at home—something the Chancellor and I fully realized, though not every Western observer could sympathize. In confidential talks at a later time I found the Soviet position to be much more flexible. Yet my concern remained: In what way would mistaken actions at the Two-Plus-Four talks, and more particularly the way they would be perceived in the Western media, affect the internal situation of Moscow's pressured leaders? Conversely, if Gorbachev and Shevardnadze were suddenly politically paralyzed or even removed from power, what dangers for the unification process would result? What we could see at the beginning of the Two-Plus-Four process was barely more than the tip of the iceberg. And the Soviet foreign minister expressly warned his partners in the Two-Plus-Four process against voting on the external aspects of German unification without taking the domestic situation in his country into consideration. "We are dealing with an issue of major importance to the people in the Soviet Union, to our whole society," he noted. "If an attempt should be made to drive us into a corner on issues concerning our security, then— and I make no bones about it—a situation will be created in which our political flexibility will be radically limited. Emotions in our country will come to a boil, the specters of the past will come back to haunt us, and the nationalist complexes rooted in the tragic chapters of our history will be revived." These were the same concerns I had already sensed during my visit to Moscow the previous December.

Shevardnadze's question whether a unified Germany's membership in NATO did not reflect the West's mistrust called for a firm answer—from us. It was essential to convince the Soviet Union that membership in NATO was what the Germans wanted. Under no circumstances must our membership appear forced upon us— and in fact, of course, it was not. Moscow must be made to realize that a new relationship between the alliances would contribute to the stability of the Soviet Union as well. That some arrogant remarks—emanating from Germany as well, by the way, consisting of unqualified statements taken out of context, regarding our membership in NATO—disregarded the emotional and psychological position of the Soviet Union was therefore no harmless matter, even if, taken objectively, these remarks were not entirely at odds with our opinion. Those who were critical of our consideration—as they called it—for Gorbachev and Shevardnadze then and those who still hold that belief should understand Moscow's political and psychological problems. Typically, only the previous year, the same critical voices had demanded a NATO resolution in favor of deploying short-range nuclear missiles pointed at East Germany, Poland, and Czechoslovakia. The fact that other Western nations ignored Gorbachev's and Shevardnadze's problems even more carelessly was short-sighted and dangerous but more understandable than in the case of Germany. After all, our concern was German unity, not British or American unity. That Jim Baker and President Bush took the same view of the situation as did West Germany—and Douglas Hurd also agreed—was all the more laudable.

On May 5, 1990, a new problem arose. Shevardnadze went on to note, "To our way of thinking, arrangements for the internal and external aspects of German unity must not necessarily be made at the same time, and unification does not need to take place within one transition period. Even after the establishment of a centralized parliament and government, certain measures will surely remain for a number of years that will regulate the external aspects of the arrangement." That plan was correct insofar as certain restrictions would continue to be in effect, at least for a transition period, since they resulted from the presence of Soviet troops on the territory of the former East Germany for a limited period of time. On the other hand, it was clear that the unified Germany must never be burdened with unresolved issues. For that reason we had to conclude the Two-Plus-Four talks before the unification of the Germanys; in other words, those of the Four Powers' rights that withheld our full sovereignty must be terminated without delay.

After all the other participants had delivered their introductory statements, I took advantage of my position as chairman. First I summarized the six foreign ministers' remarks as I had understood them. I noted with satisfaction that all the ministers' statements had acknowledged the Germans' will to unity. Next I recalled that there was agreement on the idea that the process of unification should occur without delay. Third, I acknowledged the agreement on Poland's participation in the negotiations about its borders. Finally I noted the unanimous agreement on the fact that Poland's current western border would never change.

I continued by saying that I had noticed the remarkable consensus in appraising the CSCE process. All the foreign ministers agreed on extending, deepening, and institutionalizing that process. Finally, I remarked, there was agreement on the crucial importance for us, as Germans, that the rights and responsibilities of the Four Powers would be superseded by an arrangement based on international law.

Shevardnadze was the first to speak. He basically agreed with what I had said, but he wanted us to consider whether we should be clearer about Poland's participation—for example, by including Warsaw in talks at which its security interests would be discussed. I replied, "That issue should be tabled until the issue of Poland's participation has been discussed." To begin with, the agenda prepared by the undersecretaries had to be adopted: First, border issues; second, political and military issues; third, problems concerning Berlin; fourth, final arrangements in accordance with international law and abolition of Four Power rights and responsibilities. Again Shevardnadze asked for the floor; he wanted to remind us that the Soviet Union had suggested that the synchronization of external aspects of German unity with the general European process be included as a separate item on the agenda. These issues could be included as number five on the agenda, or they might be placed in connection with number two, which concerned political and military issues and agreements on the synchronization of German unity with the general European process. This suggestion seemed problematic to me: Though I was convinced that German unification would be conducive to Europe's increasing cohesion, holding it hostage to general developments in Europe would prolong settlement of settling the external aspects indefinitely. Such a situation must not be allowed to arise.

The East German foreign minister raised his hand. Markus Meckel appeared to think much as I did. He remarked that all the ministers had agreed that there was a connection between German unification and the general European process. That idea furnished a guiding principle of sorts for the whole enterprise. Therefore this issue should not be listed as a special agenda item. After all, he noted, we were attempting to deal with the specific situation in Germany—that is, the abolition of the rights and responsibilities of the Four Powers and everything that resulted from this action. Considerations beyond these issues were part of the CSCE process, where other European nations also had an opportunity to speak. Just like me, Meckel apparently had problems with the term *synchronization*, which was to be included in the agenda. To him, synchronization did not mean that everything had to happen at the same speed; rather, he thought it was important to note that the process of German unification was running its course more swiftly than that of European unification.

It was significant that this statement came from East Germany's foreign minister; I endorsed it. Roland Dumas also supported this position, noting that he did not like the suggestion of a special agenda item. German unification was a matter for the Germans, after all, and Shevardnadze himself had joined in the unanimous agreement on this concept. Sychronization would question the Germans' right to determine the tempo of their unification.

Shevardnadze, intent on providing some relief and in an attempt to cool down the atmosphere in the Soviet Union, remarked that it was not necessary that German unification coincide with the abolition of the Four Powers' privileges. After all, the two need not be identical—an insight that was correct, since the two would never be enacted on the same day. In fact, after German unification the Two-Plus-Four Treaty had first to be ratified by the five participants. On October 3, 1990, German unification turned Two-Plus-Four into one plus four.

We were reluctant to delay German unification unnecessarily, once the Economic and Monetary Union had been scheduled for July 1. The freely elected all-German Parliament was supposed to ratify the Two-Plus-Four Treaty, not the parliaments of the two separate German states.

Shevardnadze mentioned another matter: He wanted to synchronize the German question with the development of new security structures for all of Europe. He meant his remark as an encouragement to new security structures; that is, he wanted to quicken the restructuring of the relationship between the two alliances. The Soviet foreign minister stated further, "Nothing is settled until all aspects of the arrangement have been agreed upon, until a complete balance of interests has been established." I nevertheless doubt to this day if my Soviet counterpart, as public debate concluded at the time, was genuinely aiming at a separation of internal from external unification.

Like Baker and myself, Douglas Hurd voiced objections to a sychronized process: He remarked that placing synchronization on the agenda would ultimately postpone Germany's right to self-determination. All the ministers, he noted, had pointed to their obligations to the CSCE process; now we must prevent the CSCE process from obstructing the Germans' right to self-determination.

Shevardnadze, realizing that the Soviet position was untenable, remarked that his suggestions referred only to the external aspects of German unification. He would therefore withdraw his proposal to make sychronization the fifth item on the agenda. However, should it be merely the term *synchronization* that we objected to, he would offer a compromise: "Political and military issues as well as agreements concerning the implementation of measures wherever German unification and the establishment of security structures in Europe are compatible." Finally, after several changes had been deliberated, the phrasing "political and military issues in consideration of implementing suitable security structures in Europe" was adopted.

All participants had acknowledged the Germans' will to unity. There was also agreement that the unification process should take place without delay and that Poland be invited to the negotiations concerning its borders. Altogether the morning had gone well. Replacing the Four Power Agreement by a concluding agreement based on international law was also supported by all participants—which for Germans was of particular importance, since here we were dealing with reestablishing Germany's full sovereignty.

The meeting adjourned for lunch, allowing me an opportunity to brief the Chancellor by phone on my first impressions. At three o'clock we reconvened. Once again Shevardnadze expressed his fear of becoming a political victim of German unification. Dogmatic opponents in the Soviet Union were waiting for another chance to accuse Gorbachev and his foreign minister of some sort of political capitulation; therefore, whatever he conceded to the Germans during the unification process, he noted, would provide a welcome opportunity to his opponents to slander Gorbachev's German policy. Understandably Shevardnadze quoted James Baker's phrase, "We must find a solution where there are neither winners nor losers."

I tried to explain Shevardnadze's motives to the press. Regarding his proposal to separate, if possible, internal and external unification, I noted, "It seems that the Soviet Union wants to entrust to European development—which we all want—the answer to questions that, in its opinion, may not yet be answerable. Since these are complicated questions, the presence of Soviet troops in the territory of today's German Democratic Republic may be conceivable for a certain period." Anyone knowledgeable in this matter knew from the outset that the units of the Red Army stationed in Germany would not be leaving immediately after unification and the enactment of the Two-Plus-Four Treaty anyway. Only deluded observers could believe that Moscow would withdraw from the former East Germany by the end of 1990. The fact that the Two-Plus-Four Treaty was not enacted until much later—March 15, 1991—further illustrates the difficulties the ratification process released in Moscow. Eduard Shevardnadze's resignation in December 1990 underscored the fact that an open power struggle was being waged in the Kremlin at that time, which was connected as well with the Soviet leadership's position on the German question. Whatever the case, the formerly Soviet and by now Russian troops were not withdrawn until the fall of 1994. Events ran their course in the way I had predicted.

I did not assume that Shevardnadze and Gorbachev's proposal was a sign of evil intent. I was trying to shift the Soviet concerns carefully and prudently in the direction of our goal. The question as to how long Soviet troops would continue to be stationed on our soil—without limiting Germany's sovereignty—could not be avoided in any case.

Separation of internal and external aspects of Germany's reunification was eventually established, though it had a different—and, for Germany, advantageous—effect. In the Two-Plus-Four talks the Foreign Office managed to obtain the assurance that the Two-Plus-Four Treaty would, as we had wished, be signed even before German unification. We felt that this precious document must be signed not a second later than absolutely necessary. Further, we managed to obtain from the Four Powers a statement that their rights would be suspended for the period between German unification and enactment of the Treaty. Once again it was demonstrated that it is not the method of "all or nothing" that leads to the desired result, but rather an understanding of the participants' domestic needs and problems. I can still hear Eduard Shevardnadze's entreating words, "Do not make a decision on the external aspects of Germany's unification without considering the domestic situation in my country."

The six foreign ministers decided to meet again in Berlin in June, in Paris in July, and in Moscow in September. In Berlin we planned to deal with political and military topics; in Paris the border issue would be discussed with the Polish foreign minister's participation. Foreign Minister Meckel of East Germany supported Warsaw's proposal of a separate border treaty and declared that he would endorse whatever the Poles thought would promise them the greatest security—a position I understood very well.

Since my East German counterpart and I were in total agreement on the issue of Germany's eastern border, I could declare for both of us, speaking at the press conference in Bonn, "Today the two German governments have expressed their determination to declare Poland's western border—as defined in the treaties of Görlitz and Warsaw and the documents pertaining to them—the unalterable border between Poland and Germany and that this declaration will be the subject of a treaty, based on international law, which the unified Germany will make with the Republic of Poland."

Roland Dumas, with whom I had discussed the issue beforehand, immediately agreed to my suggestion to invite Foreign Minister Skubiszewski to the Two-Plus-Four meeting in Paris. And when, a year later, I suggested to Dumas and Skubiszewski a meeting in Weimar of the foreign ministers of France, Poland, and Germany, I knew the way France viewed the relationship between Germany and Poland. In 1991 Dumas and I made our relationships with Poland a matter of mutual concern for both of our countries—historic progress, after all that had happened in this century. For Skubiszewksi, on the other hand, it was important to realize that Bonn and Paris were serious about building balanced relations. Nonetheless, much ground remained to be covered in German-Polish relations.

In 1993, three years almost to the day after the Two-Plus-Four meeting in Bonn, Shevardnadze and I once again were seated opposite each other in the same conference room in Bonn. Who could have predicted the events that occurred between May 1990 and June 1993? I had resigned from office in May 1992. Facing me (I was now a member of the Bundestag) was not the Soviet foreign minister but the president of the sovereign Republic of Georgia. The Soviet Union had ceased to exist.

I was satisfied with the opening salvo of the Two-Plus-Four talks. Now it was important for the unification process to be supported by signs of cooperation in the area of security policy. Speaking to the Bundestag on May 10, I therefore remarked, "Both alliances— as different from each other as they may be—are called upon to define their roles more and more along political lines and eventually to become instruments of security-building cooperation. For this reason we must also establish a new relationship between our alliance and the Soviet Union. Foreign Minister Shevardnadze's visit to NATO in Brussels proves that the Soviet Union is also governed by this idea. The Secretary General's invitation to NATO to visit Moscow suggests a similar position."

The next few months were extraordinarily difficult for the Soviet Union; we were asking for a fundamental change in its German policy and requested final, definitive arrangements in this matter. I therefore continued my speech to the Bundestag: "We have no wish to burden the unified Germany with open questions, not even on issues for which temporary solutions must be found— for example, the agreement on where Soviet troops on East German soil are to remain for the present. That decision should be a matter of course, really." My purpose was to clarify the issues and to avoid open questions, nothing more.

Cooperation with my East German counterpart had begun well, as I duly mentioned in the same speech: "Markus Meckel, foreign minister of East Germany, was correct in calling May 5, 1990, a great day for Germany and Europe. I agree with him, and I would like to take this opportunity to express my appreciation for the way my colleague Meckel and I worked together."

This initial conference in Bonn sent out a heartening message. The Germans' long-cherished desire to unite peacefully was well on its way to fulfillment. At the conclusion of the meeting I could therefore declare, in agreement with my colleagues in West and East, "All participants have acknowledged the Germans' desire to proceed with the unification process in an orderly manner and without delay. Germany's unity will be a gain for all countries."

All the participants in the Bonn meeting had come to realize the truth of what I had pointed out repeatedly in the past: German unification would not create a problem for Europe; rather, it would alleviate a difficult situation. But when I spoke to the Bundestag, I wanted to send a clear signal to the Soviet camp as well; I was concerned that the Soviets realize that we appreciated their country's complex concerns. Therefore I said:

> It is in our interest that President Gorbachev's domestic and foreign policy succeed. The problems of the Soviet Union must be solved in the Soviet Union, but the West's confidence-building policy and solidarity can create confidence and advance progress in the Soviet Union as well. We are aware of the complex problems the Soviet leadership is facing. This situation demands a large degree of responsibility on our part. Part of this policy of responsibility, which has superseded the policy of force of the past, does not seek unilateral advantages. In view of the Soviet Union's numerous contractual agreements with East Germany, it is of tremendous importance that the unification process do no damage to it. The same holds true for other signatories of treaties with East Germany. We will keep our promise that German unity will not be achieved at others' expense. German-Soviet relations will not be able fully to develop their true significance until after German unification. We are eager to take advantage of German-Soviet relations in all their aspects. Germany and the Soviet Union can and will contribute a great deal to Europe.

The Supreme Question: NATO Membership and the Meeting with Shevardnadze in Geneva

In mid-May of 1990 I gave an interview to the magazine *Der Spiegel*. I was asked whether I was optimistic about the outlook of the Soviet Union's eventually agreeing to NATO membership for the unified Germany; I replied in the affirmative. I explained my reasons: "We will be members of a fundamentally changing Europe, in which our alliance is not only changing but also increasingly turning into a factor of newly developing cooperative security structures, at an historic time when disarmament is increasing." These words were a brief summary of the program contained in the NATO declarations of Turnberry and London.

The new course of events began to emerge during Secretary of State Baker's visit to Moscow on May 15–19. On the basis of plans conceived during the Two-Plus-Four talks held by the undersecretaries, Baker presented the following nine-point program:

1. We are resolved to hold follow-up negotiations on conventional forces in Europe (CFE), which will also have to cover the troops stationed in Central Europe.
2. We are prepared to accelerate the progress of negotiations on short-range nuclear forces (SNF), which are to begin as soon as the CFE Treaty is signed.
3. Germany will reaffirm its obligation to neither produce nor possess nuclear, biological, or chemical weapons.
4. NATO will undertake a comprehensive assessment of its need for armed forces and of the strategy, as to both conventional and nuclear weapons, to adapt them to the changed circumstances.
5. NATO forces will not be extended to the territory of the former East Germany for a transition period.
6. The Germans have agreed to a transition period for Soviet troop withdrawals from East Germany.
7. Germany will make firm commitments as to its borders, clarifying that the territory of a united Germany will comprise only the Federal Republic of Germany, the German Democratic Republic, and Berlin.
8. The CSCE process will be strengthened.

9. Germany has made it clear that it will endeavor to solve economic issues in such a way as to support perestroika.

These nine points had by and large been elaborated by the Western undersecretaries in the weeks before Baker's trip, with Kastrup making the critical contribution. The points were effective because of the way they summarized the issues and because of when and where they were presented to the Soviet Union.

The fact that the United States assumed a new responsibility, along with the Federal Republic, and that it was willing to do so from the outset, not only during preparations for the Washington summit and the summit itself, but during the entire Two-Plus-Four process, was an invaluable contribution. The United States adopted the cause of German unification as well as our freedom to choose the alliance we would join. With its full weight as a superpower, the United States could extend political guarantees to Moscow, and Gorbachev and Shevardnadze could counter their opponents most effectively because of them.

On May 23, 1990, I met with Eduard Shevardnadze in the Soviets' United Nations mission in Geneva; our talk went on for more than three hours. The Foreign Minister opened with some general remarks, once again voicing his country's concerns. During the entire conversation he used the terms *meetings of the six* and *Two-Plus-Four talks* alternately, thus indicating the awkwardness he still felt at the term *Two Plus Four*. Today we know that after his return to Moscow he had been harshly critized for having agreed to that formulation in Ottawa.

It was interesting to note that speed now mattered to Shevardnadze. He remarked that resolutions could be drafted quickly and professionally, since the process of unification was taking on its own momentum; however, the connection between external and internal aspects must be taken into consideration. For that reason the Soviet Union was using the term *synchronization;* it avoided inconsistencies. Further, he believed that the external aspects could be settled much more quickly than could the domestic ones.

It was clear that by now the Soviet Union had come to realize that it might be hurt if internal unification were to proceed faster than external arrangements. We were equally interested in settling the external aspects as quickly as possible: We did not want Germany to be burdened with unresolved questions after unification, nor did we have any desire to leave final decisions regarding arrangements to the uncertain developments in Moscow. Once again Shevardnadze used the term *transition period*. I replied that I had commented on this issue in the Bundestag; in regard to the Soviet troops' temporary presence, such a period was certainly conceivable. On all other fronts, however, the unified Germany should not be encumbered with open questions—that, too, I added, must be made absolutely clear. Since we agreed that all problems must be resolved before the CSCE summit, I asked Shevardnadze to explain the Soviet Union's chief problems. After all, I noted, it was necessary for us to understand each other's difficulties. Such an understanding would make it easier to overcome them.

My Soviet counterpart explained that at the present time his government was drafting some principles concerning a government based on international law in a document dealing with German unification. Only through such a document could the Second World War finally be laid to rest. Only such a document could make certain that only peace rather than military actions against others would ever again originate on German territory and that there would be no military actions by third-party nations with comparable goals. With this remark Shevardnadze touched on a sore spot: Clearly he was hinting at the question of our alliance. I therefore interrupted to ask whether other nations should be allowed such actions. Should commitments such as the ones Germany was accepting—and the commitment to peace was, indeed, entirely in line with our overall stand—not also be made obligatory for all other countries as well? After all, I said, we were working for a Europe in which no nation could initiate military actions directed at other nations, and we were prepared to sign all resolutions that promoted this goal. But what would be the impression in Europe if German soil was mentioned but not that of other countries? Clearly we were not pursuing such intentions, as we, along with East Germany, had stated repeatedly. And these had been voluntary German statements. Furthermore, I said, it should be remembered that Germany had renounced atomic, biologial, and chemical weapons and was one of the signatories to the nonproliferation treaty. Not least, in addition to the joint declarations with East Germany, we were constitutionally prohibited from waging a war of aggression—surely a unique case.

Shevardnadze agreed. The demand on the table, he replied, was already implied in the United Nations Charter. On the other hand, certain German idiosyncracies, including psychological aspects, should not be underestimated—a remark I could not help but agree with. In any event, Shevardnadze remarked, comparable provisions were necessary for the Four Powers as well, so that it would be evident that no discrimination against or restriction of Germany was intended.

The Soviet foreign minister next spoke of the future ceiling for the troop strength of a unified Germany, and he mentioned certain structural changes. It seemed that the Soviets were thinking of a total of between 200,000 and 250,000 soldiers, a ceiling to be achieved within three years. This process, he noted, would run parallel in a way to the negotiations in Vienna; indeed, it fit into the overall context of all issues of troops and armament throughout Europe, but the circle of the six must agree on the ceiling. Finally Shevardnadze remarked on how pleased he was that we were ready publicly to renounce atomic, biological, and chemical weapons.

He again raised an issue that was to become a tremendous problem for us at a later time: a unified Germany's being compelled to accept the legitimacy of measures introduced by the Four Powers. These, he noted, included the nationalization of property—he was referring to expropriation measures taken before 1949. He went on to add that Germany must be ready to contribute to the restitutions made to forced laborers; after all, the Nazi movement and its ideology must not be allowed to rise again. According to Shevardnadze, a particularly sensitive issue in this context was the inviolability of memorial sites, in particular of war graves and monuments. The final important point was that all the treaties and accords entered into by both East and West Germany continue to be binding on the united Germany.

During a transition period, Shevardnadze went on, the basic circumstances must not be altered; in this principle he included East Germany's membership in the Warsaw Pact and the Federal Republic's membership in NATO. These were ideas I had already considered dangerous during the discussions on a confederacy and on confederate structures. Both notions ultimately implied a special form of neutralization while formal membership in the alliances continued.

Shevardnadze pointed out a number of alternatives regarding a solution of the issue of status. One possibility, he noted, was to leave the Warsaw Pact as well as NATO; another was neutrality—but he knew that these would find no support in Germany. Finally, resigning from the alliances might be mitigated by the introduction of security structures for all of Europe. There also was the further possibility of having both the Warsaw Pact and NATO dissolve simultaneously into a restructuring of all of Europe. But, Shevardnadze was quick to add, all these were hypothetical variations. The Soviet Union was looking for a solution. Perhaps it was conceivable that NATO and the Warsaw Pact might conclude an accord on an association, cooperation, or something of the sort. Shevardnadze stressed the fact that he and Gorbachev would not find it tenable, either psychologically or politically, to support NATO membership for a unified Germany. The question of Germany's political-military status remained the chief problem, he argued, the supreme question. Another problem was created by the presence of Allied troops in Germany; these would have to be significantly reduced. Shevardnadze concluded with a few thoughts on the question of how the rights of the Four Powers could be abolished.

What was I to make of these statements? Personally I interpreted them as a sign of resignation. Apparently the Soviet Union considered Germany's membership in NATO to be inevitable, and Shevardnadze had merely repeated the alternatives being discussed in Moscow. "We are looking for solutions"—these words were supposed to mean that no one was committed to any of these alternatives but remained open to new suggestions. Shevardnadze was really searching for new options by voicing old ones. I found the possibility of agreements between NATO and the Warsaw Pact interesting, an idea that touched on precisely the question around which our own thoughts were revolving: Could Germany's membership in NATO be made more attractive to the Soviet Union by "de-enemizing" the relationship between the two alliances? It was necessary to create a new relationship between the alliances in order to bring about an entirely different situation in Europe while simultaneously strengthening the CSCE.

I responded to Shevardnadze by stating that the Soviet Union had much to gain from German unification. The relations between Moscow and a unified Germany would no doubt be more than the sum of its relations with East Germany on the one hand and those with West Germany on the other. I noted that it was important to view the situation realistically. In the past the division of Germany had always placed a barrier between Bonn and Moscow. Aware of our historical responsibility, we had always tried to keep the potential for disturbances at a minimum. That effort, I argued, had been more than merely realpolitik; it had expressed our deep-rooted historical and moral responsibility. It was good that our relationship was being shaped by a generation that had directly experienced war, fascism, and its aftermath. And as far as I was personally concerned, I said, I saw German unification as more than merely the satisfaction of a national desire. Rather, Germans were eager to be an equal member of the community of European people and to contribute to a better Europe.

As for the issue of the border, I continued, there was no doubt what it was that we wanted to unite: The Federal Republic of Germany, the German Democratic Republic, and all of Berlin. There were no differences of opinion with Warsaw on the actual border: The existing frontier was recognized by international law. Both German parliaments and governments endorsed this recognition and would so inform the Polish government; if the latter wished to respond, it was, of course, welcome to do so.

In response Shevardnadze asked what function the unified German parliament would have regarding this issue. I replied, "The parliament of the unified Germany will ratify the border treaty."

As far as the ceiling for our military strength and the structures to be established were concerned, I remarked, I believed that in the area of conventional weapons it was important to stability in Europe that a number of basic steps toward disarmament be introduced. It was my opinion that limiting such regulations to Germany while ignoring other nations was a mistake. We certainly did not intend to procrastinate in this matter. I told Shevardnadze that we regretted that the Viennese negotiations had come to a standstill. If the Soviet Union were interested in obtaining a commitment in Vienna regarding the military strength in Europe or in certain areas in Europe, we should discuss the matter. West Germany, at any rate, was only too willing to contribute to disarmament in Europe and believed that the process of German unification would only accelerate improvements in Europe. We were prepared to negotiate on a reduction of our military strength as part of such an arrangement, which obviously concerned other forces as well. That end could be accomplished by specifying actual numbers, which could be related to the numbers for other countries. I noted that we would have no difficulty in reaching such agreements if others were to react with equal speed. But a special arrangement for Germany should definitely be avoided.

I had been assuming all along that the unified Germany would have less military strength than the two German states combined had had, and I even considered it possible that eventually the unified Germany's troop strength would be insufficient to meet West Germany's needs to protect its own as well as the alliance's interests during the time of West-East confrontation. I was thinking along the lines of 350,000 to 400,000 soldiers—numbers I did not mention at this Geneva meeting, however.

All I said to Shevardnadze was, "Regardless of Germany's willingness to cooperate in the area of reductions, the numbers you quoted are totally unacceptable." I also reminded him that the act of limiting the German army to 100,000 troops had been one of the harsh and permanently damaging consequences of the Versailles Treaty. What he had just suggested, I said, was not much better.

My ultimate concern was to utilize Germany's preparedness to reduce its military strength as a sort of catalyst for reducing Europe's other armies. At this time, therefore, I was not eager to mention the figures I had in mind; I merely wanted to resolutely reject the numbers Shevardnadze had quoted.

If Germany's strength were placed in relation to the strength of other nations or certain European areas, the amount by which German troops were reduced could serve as a lever to bring about more comprehensive military reductions. All the while I never lost sight of the possibility that the Two-Plus-Four Treaty might set a ceiling for German troops—even though I looked at that eventuality as only a last resort. Should, however, this eventuality actually come about, I would do my best to establish a connection with the negotiations in Europe. In fact that is what the two German states did by formally notifying the Vienna conference of the content of the Two-Plus-Four Treaty. Incidentally, we underlined the significance of this additional notification by the fact that Prime Minister Lothar de Maizière, acting as East Germany's foreign minister, and I personally went to Vienna to make our statements to the conference. This act indicated the link between the Two-Plus-Four talks and the negotiations in Vienna. We wanted at all costs to avoid the possibility that a ceiling would be set for German troops forces without considering the European context—if only to avoid any psychological problems and preclude a long-term infringement on our security concerns and thus on the stability in Central Europe. In the improbable, but not entirely inconceivable, case of a new wave of a significant arms build-up, the united Germany must retain its right to increase its own military strength, if need be, by referring to the former state of negotiations and level of military strength. This *clausula rebus sic stantibus,* however, could be preserved only by linking the ceiling with the negotiations in Vienna.

As for the measures taken after the Second World War based on the rights of the Four Powers, I continued, these were of an entirely different nature and should be considered separately and individually. I referred Shevardnadze to the negotiations on the state treaty between West and East Germany, where the method of handling expropriations prior to 1949 had been discussed at length. However, these talks were not under the authority of the Foreign Office but were conducted by the Department of the Interior.

With regard to commemorative sites and monuments, I assured Shevardnadze of our respect of the dead of all nations: We would unreservedly recognize all the monuments erected in commemoration of the most horrible of all wars. We had no wish to suppress or remove any reminders of history, most especially postwar history. And on the topic of international treaties between each of the two Germanys and third countries, I pointed out to my counterpart the variety among those treaties; I also called his attention to the negotiations undertaken by West German Undersecretary Hans Werner Lautenschlager and Deputy Foreign Minister Ernest Obminski of the Soviet Union.

I moved on to another subject. Our security status and the issue of commitment must not be considered static, most certainly not with a view back to the Cold War. Certain principles must be borne in mind, the first question dealing with equal rights for the united Germany. If such rights were granted, Germany could, if it wanted, exercise the right to belong to an alliance, as guaranteed in the Helsinki Final Act—and this right was precisely our principal demand. The second question asked whether the united Germany would contribute to greater or to diminished stability. It was our belief that a united Germany should assure greater stability in Europe; it was therefore important that a shift in the balance of power not occur in future. The precise power relationships, and which nations would be involved, remained open for discussion, of course. Were the terms *West* and *East* still valid? The third question concerned ways of responding to the past. I told Shevardnadze that we understood the Soviet citizens' feelings and realized that these influenced the Soviet leaders. A way must therefore be found to link Germany's right to decide on its affiliation with an alliance, as established in the Helsinki Final Act, with new perspectives on a cooperative security policy. In any event the Soviet Union must understand—honesty alone demanded it—that Germany would exercise its freedom by choosing NATO membership.

Besides, the larger picture, all the complex data concerning the future, must be brought to bear on any discussion. First, we were considering plans for a united Germany; very well, we had made ourselves clear: Germany was eager to promote good relations with its neighbors, including first of all the Soviet Union. Next, the border issue must be resolved; we had already reached agreement on this matter as well. Then there was the question of whether to extend the present NATO structures to East German territory and whether Soviet military forces would remain in today's East Germany for a still unspecified period; unless such a period were to be extended too far, we could agree to this stipulation. Finally, it was important for Germany to reaffirm its renunciation of atomic, biological, and chemical weapons, as well as to confirm its future participation in the nonproliferation treaty. I pointed out that we had not yet discussed future events throughout Europe. But, I noted, Shevardnadze knew very well that the Federal Republic was interested in expanding and institutionalizing the CSCE process. I reminded him that I had participated in the Helsinki process from the beginning and that I believed its greatest wisdom to be contained in the principle that no exceptions be made to any rules. The CSCE process would bring about fundamental change in Europe—not at some indeterminate future time but, if that was what we wanted, in the form of a summit this very year. I was sure Shevardnadze would agree with me on this point.

Touching on NATO, I continued that the organization was in the process of examining its strategy, its identity, and its goals. The NATO summit scheduled for July would begin to unfold positive perspectives. The speed with which events were proceeding in Europe, I remarked, was evident in the issue of modernizing short-range nuclear missiles, which was already completely outdated. And for obvious reasons we very much welcomed the fact that the Soviet Union was in the process of developing a new relationship with the Western Alliance; Shevardnadze's visit to NATO had sent a meaningful signal. I noted that I had no idea of the Soviet Union's vision of the future of the Warsaw Pact, but that alliance would surely also undergo a number of changes. The new situation could also result in cooperative policies between the two alliances—and that was the larger context in which I saw the status of the unified Germany as a member of the Western Alliance.

Arriving at the end of my statement, I was satisfied that I had described the larger program within which the "supreme question," to use Shevardnadze's term, must be solved.

Once again the Soviet foreign minister returned to the idea of a transition period. I referred back to my statement in the Bundestag: If a transition period meant the stationing of Soviet troops for a clearly defined, limited time after ratification of the final document, we would certainly consider such a possibility. However, we could not maintain indefinitely the conditions that had resulted from the war and the postwar period. In other words: The rights of the Four Powers must not be kept up in perpetuity. Shevardnadze concurred. We agreed that our officials should continue their talks. As the need arose, we would meet again.

Before we parted, Shevardnadze suggested that we continue our personal bilateral talks, as a way to resolve a number of issues. I agreed but pointed out that the Soviet Union and West Germany belonged to different alliances: As two of the six participants in the Two-Plus-Four talks, we had to be frank with the others—no actions must be taken behind their backs. At the second Two-Plus-Four conference he and I scheduled another meeting in Berlin. In

393

our confidential talk I confirmed at last—after discussions with the Chancellor—that we were prepared to provide financial support. For Gorbachev and Shevardnadze this prospect meant a great deal.

Our discussion, which went on for hours, served to clarify problems and perspectives. I no longer had any doubt: Shevardnadze was looking for a solution—not to gain time but to seek out new viewpoints and new arguments to support them. Step by step we cautiously approached the resolution to the NATO question, which had moved into a new political context; we needed Moscow for a solution. During this difficult phase Germany's task consisted of developing the program to achieve a different political context, to do so in harmony with our Western partners, and to facilitate Soviet acceptance of our ideas. Should the negotiations be broken off or fail altogether, because Gorbachev and Shevardnadze were either impeded or removed from office, the impact on Germany would be greater than on other nations. Much greater, in fact such an eventuality might conceivably place the prospect that now seemed within reach—the unity of a sovereign Germany—out of our grasp.

I left Geneva full of hope. Shevardnadze, I had learned, was looking for a solution, and he trusted me. I was certain that the road to resolving the problem of the alliance, which seemed the crucial question to Moscow, ran by way of restructured mutual relations between the alliances and the changes in the political context I had alluded to in Geneva. NATO's ministerial conference, to be held in Turnberry in June, and the London NATO summit, scheduled for July, would therefore become crucial. I left Geneva for Paris, where I briefed Roland Dumas on my talk with Shevardnadze.

On the Way to Overcoming the East-West Conflict

The following day Hungary's foreign minister, Gyula Horn, was awarded the highly distinguished Karl Prize in Aachen for a truly European action: Opening the borders. I had happily accepted the offer to deliver the eulogy. The occasion allowed me to express some of my personal thanks, as well as the gratitude of all Germans, to this courageous Hungarian reform politician and staunch European, as well as to his courageous people.

On May 25, 1990, I flew to Washington, where I met with Secretary Baker. I wanted to brief him on my talks with Shevardnadze. Subsequently I also met with Security Adviser Brent Scowcroft.

That same day the president of France was in Moscow. About 70 percent of their discussions, Mitterand and Gorbachev stated later, had centered on German unification. Gorbachev repeated to his visitor his assurance that he welcomed the birth of a unified Germany: "The German people realize their potential under the present historical conditions that have provided this opportunity. But it is a matter for Germany alone." However, foreign policy problems arose when the General Secretary added, "Many are now eager to pin us down to the position that a unified Germany must on all accounts be a member of NATO." This eventuality, Gorbachev argued, would violate the balance of power on a point of strategic importance, because that was where the strongest forces were confronting each other. "Since the unified Germany abuts on the two military-political blocs," he remarked, "we should perhaps look for structures that can develop these connections. Perhaps we should even take advantage of this momentum to demilitarize the blocs." This proposal gave some inkling of our own way of thinking, even if it was couched in the language of the old era.

The American-Soviet summit held from May 30 to June 3 also advanced the process of German unification. No one had expected the question of unification and, above all, of the commitments made by a unified Germany, to be solved in Washington. Yet the statements made by President Bush during the press conference he held jointly with Gorbachev on June 3 clearly indicated that the United States and the Soviet Union had grown significantly closer on this issue. Bush emphasized that a unified Germany needed to be a full member of NATO: "President Gorbachev, frankly, does not hold that view. But we are in full agreement that membership in the alliance is, in accordance with the Helsinki Final Act, a matter for the Germans to decide."

That agreement was a step forward. Gorbachev remarked that it had not been possible to arrive at a compromise on the foreign policy aspects of German unification. Yet that lack of accord "does not mean that our efforts were to no avail."

In Washington, Gorbachev suggested that an agreement be forged between NATO and the Warsaw Pact. Baker commented that some political accord might make it easier for the countries of Central and Eastern Europe to support the idea of full NATO membership for all of Germany, and help the Soviet Union to accept the idea. This suggestion coincided with my own intentions. At the Washington summit the two superpowers stated that one stop on the road to German unity was each nation's right to choose an alliance, as guaranteed in the Helsinki Final Act. And it was this admission that mattered in the long run.

Immediately before the NATO ministerial conference in Turnberry, Scotland, a Warsaw Pact summit was held on June 7, 1990; it differed from all previous Warsaw Pact conferences in the nature of its participants, procedures, and outcome. For the first time East Germany was represented by a prime minister who had been freely elected and was not a member of the Communist national party: Lothar de Maizière, a Christian Democrat. The same applied to József Antall, the prime minister of Hungary. Romania was represented by the recently elected President Ion Iliescu and Bulgaria by Petar Mladenov, the successor to Todor Shivkov, long-time president and the party's secretary general. I had worked with Mladenov for years when he served as foreign minister, and he had made a generally favorable impression on me— given the circumstances.

What marked the conference was the effort to hold the Warsaw Pact together, even in the new and different situation. Soviet sources announced that the united Germany's membership in NATO had found no support. But no objections to that course had been expressed—and that precisely seemed crucial to me.

For the present it was impossible to overcome the differences of opinion on the mission and continued existence of the Warsaw Pact; clearly there was agreement only on tabling the problem. We scrutinized with particular attention the paragraph of the communiqué that dealt with the external aspects of German unification. Stress was laid on the fact that unification must take place within the context of the general European process and on the basis of its principles. The legitimate security concerns of Germany's neighbors and of all other nations was also emphasized; finally, firm guarantees for the inviolability of all borders in Europe was demanded. It was very significant that the unified Germany's commitment to an alliance, which Shevardnadze had termed the "supreme question," was never mentioned. This omission could only mean that the heads of state and government had not been able to arrive at a shared position on this issue. On the contrary, we knew that there was pronounced disagreement on this matter among the Warsaw Pact members, some even sympathizing with our desire to remain in NATO.

In studying the text we noticed the highlighted passages—the prominence given to CSCE, the reference to welcome steps taken by NATO and the Vienna Negotiations on Conventional Forces in Europe. Most notable, however, was the remark that the nations present at the conference considered it necessary to reexamine the nature and function of the Warsaw Pact.

From the smaller Warsaw Pact nations came hints to corroborate our interpretation. Besides, talks with Warsaw, Prague, and Budapest had already referred to the advantages of Germany's continued membership in NATO. Shevardnadze had certainly taken cognizance of this covert support—understandably so. Such statements made his work within the Soviet Union a great deal easier.

The Turnberry Signal

On June 8, 1990, we convened for the NATO spring meeting in Turnberry. Before our sessions began, it was essential to send an unambiguous signal to the Soviet Union to the effect that we were supporting a new relationship between the alliances: NATO's members wished to overcome the West-East adversarial attitude. Here too our close ties to the United States proved invaluable, for Baker, who had come to Turnberry with intentions similar to ours, showed himself eager to add additional weight to our statement, in both form and substance.

Typically, such communiqués were prepared by NATO officials in Brussels. However, when he began to study the prepared text, Kastrup became aware that, although correct and appropriate, it was worded too generally: It did not send a political signal.

Kastrup is a master at formulation as well as at assertion. In the end he submitted his own draft, which with the support of the United States, all NATO partners accepted. I explained to my Western colleagues that Germany's membership in NATO would continue to be a precondition for stability and security in Europe; Germany was intent on exercising its right, established in Helsinki, to choose its own alliance. But since the prospect of a united Germany's membership in NATO was hard for Moscow to swallow, positive political signals were necessary to indicate to the Soviet Union that the Western Alliance was adapting to the new conditions of a post–Cold War world and was ready to work with the Warsaw Pact nations within a new security structure. Regular consultations were to be instituted to this end. In that same spirit the NATO ministers in Turnberry welcomed the Moscow Declaration of June 7 by the Warsaw Pact members. Its encouraging message, which implied a readiness to constructive cooperation, filled us with hope.

In their final communiqué the Council members expressly supported the expansion and deepening of political exchanges of political opinions between NATO and the Warsaw Pact nations. "We look to further such opportunities in the future," the document read. "A Continent divided for four decades is searching for new patterns and structures of cooperation." Accordingly, NATO attributed great significance to finalizing a treaty on conventional forces in Europe. This treaty was to remove destabilizing imbalances as well as the ability to wage surprise attacks and initiate offensives with the intent of winning territory. The NATO negotiators in Vienna were given new instructions; the treaty on short-range ballistic missiles was scheduled to be concluded that year. In addition, NATO proposed a series of new measures, such as a procedure for discussing extraordinary military activities. After finalizing the CFE treaty, follow-up meetings were to be initiated to advance the disarmament processes on an even wider scale. The document aimed at a global prohibition of chemical weapons, with an added ban on the proliferation of nuclear and chemical weapons and the missiles to deliver them. In other words, the Turnberry NATO meeting sent a signal to the Warsaw Pact nations assuring them of accountability, mutual trust, and increased security. The CSCE process was highlighted as the framework for European security. That circumstance was new and would certainly quicken the process of gaining the Warsaw Pact nations', particularly the Soviet Union's, goodwill.

The Turnberry signal inaugurated a new relationship between the alliances. The ministerial communiqué stated, "We, the alliance's Foreign Ministers of the Alliance, express our determination to seize the historic opportunities resulting from the profound changes in Europe to help build a new peaceful order in Europe, based on freedom, justice, and democracy. In this spirit we extend to the Soviet Union and to all other European countries the hand of friendship and cooperation. . . . We are convinced that German unification makes an essential contribution to stability in Europe."

Since renewed harsh confrontations could be expected between Gorbachev and his opponents—a CPSU party convention was about to begin—our appeal was very important for Gorbachev's and Shevardnadze's efforts, and it was yet another step toward the "de-demonization" of NATO. To stand his ground at the CPSU party convention, scheduled to begin on July 1, Shevardnadze needed hard facts with which to take the edge off the staunch dogmatists' arguments and to persuade the majority of delegates that both German unification and overcoming the division of Europe were introducing new and better prospects for the Soviet Union as well.

That night I had one of my very rare instances of insomnia. As I tried to fall asleep, I made an attempt to put myself in the place of the Soviet leaders, especially Shevardnadze, who over the years had increasingly become my friend. I could not stop recalling our talks; frequently quick eye contact was enough for us to reach mutual agreement.

Breakthrough in Brest

The next, and perhaps most important, German-Soviet meeting in the preliminary period leading to unification was the one between Shevardnadze and me on June 11, 1990, in the Belarus city of Brest. He had chosen the site deliberately; at the age of twenty-one his brother had been killed in action and buried there during the early days of the war, in June 1941.

Brest was a symbol of the difficulties presented by our joint history, as Shevardnadze put it. Nevertheless, meeting in that city made clear our determination to learn from the past and build relations that would be marked by a heartfelt neighborly spirit and by fruitful cooperation instead of fear—or at least so I hoped.

Yet I also knew that choosing Brest would awaken Polish sensibilities. In March 1918 the truce between the German empire and revolutionary Russia was signed in Brest (then called Brest-Litovsk). In late September 1939 Brest symbolized the Hitler-Stalin Pact, drafted at the expense of Poland; to further humiliate Poland, German and Soviet military troops had both been conspicuous at the ceremony. But I put my qualms aside, since Shevardnadze wanted to meet there to honor very personal memories. That was all that mattered.

Eduard Shevardnadze, born in early 1928, was too young to have fought in the war himself. But aware that German unification would meet with emotional resistance among many in the Soviet Union who had suffered loss and deprivation because of the war, he was looking for ways to communicate his preparedness for reconciliation, even though his family, too, had sacrificed a great deal during the Great Patriotic War. What gesture could be more convincing than to visit his brother's gravesite in the company of the German foreign minister? My hunch proved correct: The suggestion to meet in Brest was also aimed at his own people.

To make certain, I telephoned the Polish foreign minister to inform him; under the circumstances, I asked, would it not be possible for Poland to accept unreservedly the idea of Brest as the site for a German-Soviet meeting? "Since I believe we all have an interest in the current course—that is, that an easing of the West-East conflict find widespread support in the Soviet Union as well." I said to Skubiszewski, "I would be grateful to you if you would do everything possible to make our motive understood." He grasped my intention and the significance of the meeting at once; I had no need of further persuasion. Skubiszewski was conscious of history even as he looked to the future. He reacted with as much understanding as did the Polish people as a whole.

On June 11, 1990, we took off for Brest shortly after six o'clock in the morning. This meeting would be a particularly important one. The reasons for choosing the site alone indicated Shevardnadze's seriousness about putting, to use his phrase, the Second World War to rest at last. Yet it should not and could not wipe out history. During the subsequent press conference I stated my great appreciation for Shevardnadze's gesture in inviting me to Brest, a city with which his personal feelings and those of his family were so closely intertwined. The willingness to rebuild relations between our two nations was consistent with the desires and feelings of the Germans in both parts of our country.

Our meeting lasted five hours. Shevardnadze welcomed me in great friendship. We met in one of the typical "guest houses" we had become familiar with throughout the Eastern bloc. A long table had been set up in the large hall for the two delegations. We had also been given an apartment where our delegation could retire if necessary. Shevardnadze thanked me for agreeing to Brest as the site of the meeting. He noted that the city had a symbolic meaning because it was reminiscent of the difficult times of our shared history, but the meeting also expressed the desire for mutual understanding. Therefore he was once again eager to emphasize the Soviet government's basic position: It was in favor of unification and the creation of German unity. President Gorbachev had said as much on several occasions, and with this in mind the Soviet Union had agreed to the Two-Plus-Four procedure; it allowed representatives of both German states and the whole German nation to participate in the process. Unification would be an element of stability and peace in Europe.

These words were highly significant. Only six months earlier, at the beginning of December 1989, the Soviet ambassador, speaking to the three Western ambassadors, had elucidated the danger to European stability that could result from German unification. Much had happened since that meeting in East Berlin. Step by step we had succeeded in convincing the Soviet Union that unification would have positive consequences for the entire Continent.

Again I made some basic remarks on the common history of Germany and the Soviet Union, before pointing out that the year 1990 offered opportunities we must not miss on any account. We could take great satisfaction in noting that the process of unification had accelerated events in Europe; Shevardnadze was therefore correct when he stated that unification advanced stability and security in Europe. The interdependence of the German question and European development was becoming evident. No one, I argued, would be deprived in any way at bilateral talks between Germany and the Soviet Union. Because our two nations shared a special responsibility, we could arrive at special achievements.

Shevardnadze suggested that we begin with one of the most complicated issues, one that caused a great deal of concern: Germany's membership in military alliances. The basic problem remained unchanged. He felt a need to remind us that he had proposed a number of different solutions in Geneva, and he would like to repeat them once more. One phrase in particular caught my attention: The question would certainly arise how a united Germany would fulfill its obligations to the Warsaw Pact and to NATO. Shevardnadze noted in this connection that he was eager to stress the fact that the Warsaw Pact had already taken a major step and arrived at a fundamental decision: its transformation into a political alliance. If NATO underwent a similar change, the picture in Europe would be entirely different. An accord between Warsaw Pact and NATO nations was of outstanding importance, since an agreement on the basic shape of the relations between the two alliances during a transition period would have immediate consequences for the realization of agreements made about the external aspects of German unification.

Thus, Shevardnadze considered our NATO membership to be a distinct possibility, provided that a new relationship between the two alliances could be brought about. He went on to brief us on his talks with Secretary Baker, with whom he had already discussed some ideas about relations between two politicized alliances, as he put it. Incidentally, in this connection, my associates pointed out to me that Shevardnadze was talking about "politicized alliances," while the Soviet interpreter consistently translated the word *alliances* as *blocs*.

By now these ideas had been elaborated further, partly as a reflection of the Warsaw Pact conference in Moscow; but they were only tentative thoughts, of course. Quite obviously, the position of some of the Warsaw Pact nations—that a Germany within the Western Alliance was preferable to a neutralized nation—already had an effect. The essential element, my Soviet counterpart continued, was for both sides to affirm that neither the Warsaw Pact nor NATO held an adversarial view of the other. After all, President Gorbachev had stated in Malta that he no longer viewed the United States as an antagonist. Shevardnadze now made some suggestions as to the shape of a new relationship between the two alliances.

I thanked Shevardnadze for elucidating the Soviet leaders' thinking. The future of the alliances and relations among their member nations, I remarked, were issues of principal concern to the twenty-three member nations themselves, and the Federal Republic being one was therefore in a position to comment. Surely the NATO foreign ministers' message in Turnberry had shown that we had interpreted the Warsaw Pact's Moscow Declaration in an extremely favorable light. I read from the Turnberry communiqué, stressing the passage on the order for peace in Europe and the Soviet Union's and all other European countries' willingness to extend their hands in friendship. I noted that Shevardnadze had repeatedly alluded to a relationship between blocs; but the term *bloc* had become obsolete. Shevardnadze was quick to interject here: No, he had meant *alliances*. He remarked that at times Old Thinking left its mark on terminology; apparently new and old ways alternated in the text and in his interpreters' translations.

I continued by remarking that the renunciation of force was of particular importance to the future of Europe. NATO had explicitly stressed that view as early as the Bonn summit of the summer of 1982. Renunciation of force meant renunciation both of the use and the threat of force—a basic principle of all peaceful coexistence. It was therefore necessary, especially now, to consider Europe's unity as a whole, both during the disarmament negotiations and within CSCE; there must be no zones of different degrees of security. The NATO summit set to take place in London in July would explain how our alliance had adapted to the new situation.

A unified Germany, I proceeded, must be neither singled out nor discriminated against. But acknowledging the Soviet Union's justified security concerns included making sure Moscow understood the military force the unified Germany could summon up. Fundamental changes had altered a number of problems, as the results of the Paris CSCE summit would make even more obvious. There would also be a new relationship between the two alliances, though I was still unable to provide him with definitive and complete facts. One thing was already certain: The London NATO summit would establish a positive basis for future developments, similar to the NATO foreign ministers' Turnberry message. After all, what mattered was to conclude the disarmament negotiations successfully, and within this larger context the question regarding a ceiling for the German army would surely be answered. As far as Germany's eastern border was concerned, after unification a binding treaty between Germany and Poland would be enacted.

I had thus presented important elements of the complex facts crucial to Europe's development. In additional remarks I once again addressed the unified Germany's military potential. I tried more and more to use the—probably unavoidable—determination of a ceiling for German military strength as a positive momentum for the efforts on behalf of disarmament in Europe. In order to prevent the imposition of special status on Germany, however, such a ceiling had to be established within a multilateral framework—the Vienna negotiations.

For Germany, I told Shevardnadze, it was important that the Soviet Union was not looking for a discriminatory solution, either in content or in procedure. It would be best to reach an accord in Vienna that we could recognize in the Two-Plus-Four negotiations. What mattered now was not substance but the framework, especially since we were eager to advance the disarmament process in Europe. The unified Germany must on no account be burdened with unresolved questions, and for this reason we must intensify and speed up our work.

The Soviet Foreign Minister raised a number of additional issues but was quick to acknowledge that it would be impossible to solve all of them before the CSCE summit—and the Two-Plus-Four Treaty was scheduled to be signed even earlier. "Which questions cannot be solved now?" I asked. "Many," he replied. I countered that while we were looking for solutions, we could not agree to transition periods, since such a measure would slow down and finally paralyze the overall dynamics of the process. I wanted to be quite clear on this point: The external aspects of unification must not turn the Germans into prisoners of European development. We wanted to be an engine of this development—a positive development—but not become dependent on uncertainties in the European process.

I stressed once more that we must not fail to take advantage of the opportunities this year was offering. If we recognized all that had already been achieved, including the upcoming CSCE summit, we could not help but wonder why the Four Powers should not be able to relinquish their rights and responsibilities by that time within the framework of the Two-Plus-Four document that was our goal. I said that I had already told him in Geneva that we had decided on economic, currency, and social union of the two German states; but this union could be fully effective only if there was stability, not if the unified Germany was burdened by imponderables. It was therefore crucially important to our future role that none of the participants continue the endeavor with full force.

Shevardnadze considered commitment the most important issue. The CSCE agreements, I countered, affected every nation, including a unified Germany. They specified each country's right to join an alliance or remain unaffiliated—an unqualified principle. The Foreign Minister argued that unless a transition period were introduced, the Soviet Union would find itself isolated. The balance would shift, and East Germany would be in NATO through the unified Germany. Furthermore, changes were occurring in Eastern Europe. For the present, the Soviet Union had no guarantees whatsoever for its own security, and it was impossible to foresee where the changes would lead.

This statement clearly showed how seriously Moscow was taking all uncertainties about the new direction for Europe. I understood that Shevardnadze had little faith in the Warsaw Pact's survival—and he was correct. He seemed to assume that we would retain our NATO membership. For us that element meant that the race against time became even more momentous. Shevardnadze pleaded for a transition period partly because of the presence of Soviet troops. When I asked for a more specific explanation, he argued that as long as the Four Powers' rights remained in effect, the Soviet Union had no need to justify the stationing of troops in East Germany. If, however, these rights were abolished, a new basis must be established. We should therefore try for compromise.

Such a compromise should be possible, I replied, particularly since, in the autumn, conditions for a united Europe would be created. I explained that I was thinking of the Paris summit conference and the Charter for Europe; a special status for the Germans would stand in contradiction to them. I assured Shevardnadze that I understood Moscow's desire for certainty about the unified Germany's military strength; it was clearly a legitimate concern. Yet when discussing shifts in the balance of power, we must also discuss the Soviet units in East Germany. Finally Shevardnadze admitted that the Soviet Union trusted no one more than Germany. It was even ready to agree to our neutrality and the removal of all foreign military forces from our soil. However, obviously problems of trusting our allies remained.

To avoid any misunderstanding, I stated, "We do not feel in the least constrained by our NATO partners, we are not *forced* to, we *want* to be members of NATO." And once more I pointed to the freedom of choice. The Western Alliance made an important contribution to European stability, I argued; it was therefore important for us to retain our membership. NATO would be needed in future as well. Besides, I wished to call attention to a factor in European geography that resulted in a disparity of power: The superpower Soviet Union was in Europe, while the superpower United States of America was very distant. That fact provided another reason for the necessity of NATO. Moscow needed to bear this circumstance in mind; the Federal Republic was, after all, the easternmost nation in the Western Alliance. Finally I referred once more to the NATO summit scheduled to take place during the preliminaries of the CSCE summit. In Vienna, I argued, progress could be made if only the participants were willing.

As conversation drew to a close, Shevardnadze again addressed the issue of balance, which appeared to concern him quite a bit. He stressed the fact that the Soviet Union must have time to think about what was supposed to happen now. "Give us time to convince our people. Germany can unite—that is a natural process. But balance must be maintained. Developing European structures takes time, so that internal processes can run their course. That is most important, after all." I replied, "The internal and external aspects are equally important to us, and they must not be separated." My colleague replied that if that were the case, the Soviet Union would have to wait and see. The Potsdam Agreement remained in force, and Moscow wanted to make certain that we remembered as much. He spoke with great firmness, the remark even seemed harsh. I therefore replied in a similar tone: "I hope that we will not continue our conversation in this manner. We met to look for solutions. The united Germany will consist of the Federal Republic and the Democratic Republic. The Soviet Union must receive an equivalent for the security factor that previously was provided by its connection with East Germany; therefore Soviet military forces can remain for a transition period. I feel that we have moved closer on many issues. Perhaps I am wrong, perhaps we tend to overestimate the CSCE, the negotiations in Vienna, the new relationship between the alliances. But I do have to say very clearly that we cannot agree to separating the two aspects. Perhaps it would now be prudent to continue our conversation in private."

As we resumed in confidence, Shevardnadze asked the question that to him evidently represented the crux of the problem: "How strong are the German armed forces projected to be?" I was prepared: "Far above the numbers mentioned in Geneva. What do you think of three hundred and fifty to four hundred thousand troops?" I stressed that this estimate was my personal proposal. If for Shevardnadze the main problem was merely the strength of the united Germany's army, we were out of the woods.

A strong intuition urged me to hurry. Helmut Kohl and I were worried that some unforeseen circumstance might hinder our plans. I had frequent occasion to warn my associates, "We cannot even imagine the imponderables that might crop up." Many incidents still might interfere with, delay, bring to a halt, or reverse the unification process, such as an assassination or a putsch. Domestic Soviet events might deprive Gorbachev of authority and power, and the day might come when he was unable to accomplish those changes that he was willing and able to accomplish now. His critics had become louder. In Europe and elsewhere crises could develop, wars could break out; any of these eventualities would affect the unification process. Thus a sword of Damocles, suspended by a silken thread, hung over our heads. All too often world history has proven that great events do not happen with the regularity of a train. More often they move forward in spurts, but when they do, they move with irresistible force.

These ruminations were again running through my mind when the Moscow putsch of August 1991 started the decline in Gorbachev's power. And when Iraq's attack on Kuwait in August 1990 unleashed the Gulf War, it became even more evident that our fears of the early summer of 1990 were not unfounded. Fortunately the full effect of these events did not become clear until after the Two-Plus-Four Treaty was signed. Had they occurred a mere few months or weeks earlier, or had we unduly prolonged the unification process, much could have been different.

Acting in our mutual interest—but for different reasons and from different perspectives—Shevardnadze and I agreed in Brest to keep the contents of our conversation from the press. The journalists saw only my utterly satisfied face but did not learn the reason for my elation.

The message of Turnberry had not failed to have its effect on the Soviet leadership. For the cautiously deliberating Shevardnadze, this change was so important that he could afford to give a hint at the concluding press conference: "Progress in solving other issues would facilitate the future status of a united Germany." This remark referred to a ceiling for a united Germany's armed forces and to the relationship between the two alliances. I, who understood what he was referring to, found his message clear and encouraging.

Shevardnadze and I agreed on another meeting only a week later, where I would play host. We needed to seize the momentum of our negotiations.

Among the events that impressed me most deeply in Brest was the visit to the grave of Shevardnadze's brother. It added a special, personal touch to the diplomatic meeting. Soviet soldiers marched in front of us as we walked up to the Eternal Flame to lay down the flowers the soldiers carried. Shevardnadze and I looked at each other while the loudspeakers resounded with Schumann's "Reverie." Then we placed the flowers one by one on the long, approximately chest-high, wall that was inscribed with the names of those who had been killed in action, among them the name of Shevardnadze's brother Akaky. We looked firmly into each other's eyes and shook each other's hands. "Never again"—for me the words were a pledge. Never before had I felt so close to a representative of the Soviet Union. Did so many millions have to die before we could come to this point? So much misery had befallen our nations since that first day of the war in Brest in 1941. For every single person, soldier or civilian, man, woman, or child, in his or her last hour, it no longer mattered how it had begun; they lost their lives. But the survivors must not forget. Not the dead, and not what had led to their deaths, and who was responsible, and what needed to be done to prevent any repetition.

For me personally the negotiations in Brest were difficult. I was troubled by arrhythmia, standing was a problem. Once I asked for an intermission, so as to consult with my associates. The delegation and I retreated to the apartment we had been assigned. While the delegation remained in the little parlor, in the adjacent bedroom the army doctor and the medical orderly with her worked to bring me back to a state where I could go on. Half an hour later we continued our session. None of the numerous members of the delegation leaked a word to the press.

Back in Bonn on the morning of June 12, I reported to the Chancellor. My summary was as follows: "It is important to Shevardnadze that at its London summit NATO issue a statement of similar significance as the Moscow statement made by the Warsaw Pact nations. It is my impression that along with a ceiling for German armed forces of 350,000 to 400,000 troops, the issue of commitment can be resolved in accordance with our wishes. We should aim to establish a ceiling within the disarmament negotiations in Vienna."

On June 15, 1990, the second CSCE Conference on the Human Dimension took place in Copenhagen. I first spoke with Secretary Baker and next with Shevardnadze, who steered our conversation to the American-Soviet summit in Washington. He noted that an impressive package of bilateral agreements had been achieved. Of course other issues had been raised as well, among them the question of Germany. Neither side had wanted to commit to definitive conditions, since both were very well aware that, though they were among the decision-making governments, they could not take ultimate steps alone. Nevertheless, they had considered publishing such agreements as had been reached. In the end they had refrained from doing so; there were still some differences of opinion. When I asked what the agreement consisted of, Shevardnadze remarked that it was the direction they had taken that was important: It concerned the transformation of the alliances. To regulate relations between them, it was possible to arrive at agreements, concur on basic principles, and conclude accords. That concept was the most promising path. Much, he said, would depend on the degree to which the alliances were genuinely prepared to change. A common basis in international law would certainly be a new, highly political event.

The term *transformation of the alliances* seemed open to misunderstanding, not free of danger. It was hard to imagine that Bush and Baker had used such words. On the other hand, I did not doubt Shevardnadze's honesty. Even with the best interpreters, misunderstandings can occur, especially in matters that are new to the discussions.

Neither President Bush nor Secretary Baker, the Soviet foreign minister continued, had objected to his approach. When I asked whether the crux was to define the relationship between the alliances and to arrive at formal agreement on the matter, Shevardnadze replied in the affirmative. Now that this matter was clear, I remarked that it was indeed important to redefine the future relationship between NATO and the Warsaw Pact.

Shevardnadze continued by noting that they had avoided discussing Germany's status. If the relationship between the two alliances was going to change, we would be dealing with an entirely different situation. It was now necessary to move ahead more quickly in shaping Europe's security structure; settling the external aspects of German unity would not be particularly difficult thereafter. What really mattered was the transition period. I heard in these statements that my remarks in Geneva—to the effect that the situation in Europe must be radically changed—had certainly fallen on fertile ground in Moscow. Apparently the Soviets were now looking for the solution to the German problem under such new conditions.

I said that the Soviet statement at the Washington press conference to the effect that it was up to the Germans themselves whether or not they wanted to belong to an alliance had received a good deal of attention—favorable attention at that, I could not help but add—in Germany, as I had called for in Geneva. In his reply Shevardnadze used the words I had used at the time: The Germans' right to belong to an alliance was established in the Helsinki Final Act. In order to make certain that no ambiguities remained, I interrupted to add: Not merely *an* alliance but a particular one. It was well known that we meant NATO. Shevardnadze replied that obviously the Potsdam Agreement remained, and it conferred on the Four Powers the right to determine Germany's fate. But at this time, he argued, we should not focus on the most difficult problems but should look at the background, and in this connection he was eager to stress once more the great importance of new relations between the Warsaw Pact and NATO and their agreement on a transition period, so that they could face the future more confidently.

I remarked that public opinion frequently focused on certain aspects of a complex problem without seeing the whole, as I had pointed out in Geneva. However, we believed that the preparations for the CSCE summit in Paris as well as a new relationship between the alliances and our right to make a decision in favor of one of them were part of the whole. It was necessary to find a solution that would serve the balance of interests without assigning inferior legal status to the united Germany.

The time had come, I added, to concentrate on creating the proper framework for long-term German-Soviet relations. I reminded the group that, as I had pointed out, the Washington summit had improved the prospects for unification. I asked whether Shevardnadze agreed, and he replied that I was absolutely correct: Coming closer to an agreement on the transformation of the alliances was a very important step forward, with huge potential benefits. Shevardnadze's agreement with me signaled that Moscow would accede to the new requirements we had proposed for Germany's NATO membership.

We now broached the subject of conventional disarmament. In Washington there had been talk that consensus on this issue was possible. Should this be reached within the existing framework or outside it? Shevardnadze declared that the existing mandate should be used for the negotiations, so that they could be concluded before the summit, when the next phase could be set. Would it not be possible, he asked, for the Chancellor or me to issue an official statement regarding the ceiling for the Bundeswehr? Such an announcement was needed before the conclusion of the negotiations—Shevardnadze meant the Two-Plus-Four talks—because it would not be a good step if the Soviet Union, the Four, or even the Six were first to make the appropriate proposal. Germany should be the nation to do so; the proposals had to come from us. Apparently the Soviet foreign minister wished to avoid any impression that unacceptable conditions were imposed on Germany. I replied to the effect that issues of conventional disarmament—including German disarmament—should be resolved in Vienna. In this matter we required a context that did not focus exclusively on Germany. I assured him that we had no ambitions to be alone in disposing over a huge arms potential if others were disarming, but we would not want to be singled out in the opposite direction. It was necessary to find a middle way.

In Copenhagen, Shevardnadze also had a meeting with Baker. In their conversation he responded favorably to his American counterpart's nine-point list. His reaction was in accordance with what we had discussed, and the fact that Shevardnadze now confirmed this accord to Baker was a sign for the progress we had made. Later that evening Baker asked to see me so that he could brief me on our Soviet colleague's response. We concurred: Moscow had made its decision, the die had been cast.

Back in my hotel room, I immediately telephoned Helmut Kohl, who was in New York. In coded language, but clear enough for him, I signaled: Moscow is coming around.

During our return flight my mind was already at my next meeting with Shevardnadze, which had been scheduled for a week after our encounter in Brest. For that occasion I had looked for a site pregnant with history and found it in Münster in Westphalia, where the Thirty Years' War was concluded with the Peace of Westphalia in October 1648; the current goal was to bring a more than forty-year-old Cold War to a conclusion.

The Meeting in Münster: Progress

We met at the Münster airport like good friends. As we drove into town, I explained to Shevardnadze that 90 percent of the inner city had been destroyed in the Second World War. Seeing the handsome downtown area, Shevardnadze kept asking incredulously, "All that was destroyed? There are no signs of it now." He seemed deeply impressed, preoccupied with the symbolic meaning of ruins and renewal. Evidently he had been unaware of the amount of damage done to Germany. "Münster was not the only city to have been destroyed; I could just as easily have taken you to Dresden, Hamburg, Magdeburg, or Cologne, to Pforzheim or Nuremberg." He was impressed by the reconstruction undertaken in West Germany; all traces of the war had been removed. The university town of Münster, where commerce and industry flourish, harbors an eminent past. "Here in Münster," I explained to my guest, "the great European peace of 1648 became a possibility. This thought should characterize today's deliberations."

When we arrived at the city hall, we were enthusiastically welcomed by a crowd of thousands. We left the car and approached the people standing behind the police barricades. They tried to grasp Shevardnadze's hand, to thank him for supporting reform and peace in Europe. The Foreign Minister was visibly moved by the warmth and affection with which he was received. "They mean it from the bottom of their hearts," he remarked to me. It did not matter that the people were unaware of the decisive turn our talks had taken by now. They sensed that the new Soviet leaders had abandoned their old course and were seeking an understanding and balance with Germany and Europe. The crowd spoke to Shevardnadze with such intensity and speed that the interpreters were unable to translate quickly enough. As Georgia's former party secretary, Shevardnadze knew perfectly well that enthusiasm can be stage-managed, but in Münster he realized that Germans were well-intentioned toward their Eastern neighbor, that they wanted only to live in peace with the people of the Soviet Union.

On a political level this overwhelming reception was extraordinarily important for my negotiations with Shevardnadze. Again and again I had reassured Gorbachev and the government in Moscow that they enjoyed the trust of the Germans. Now my words were confirmed. To this day I do not know how truthfully the new Soviet leadership was kept informed about the mood in the Federal Republic. Even if Shevardnadze had been favorably impressed by the friendly reception he and Mikhail Gorbachev had been given when they visited in June 1989, that day in Münster he was bound to feel that he and his policies were reaffirmed.

When we stepped out on the terrace of the city hall, deafening cheers rose once again, and again Shevardnadze seemed overwhelmed by this spontaneous outburst. The mayor welcomed us and Shevardnadze signed the city's Golden Book. In the so-called Peace Hall we drank from the "Golden Rooster," the symbolic peace goblet. A picture of this event was broadcast around the world at the time.

Our visit to Münster was of significance mainly for the atmosphere between us; it was no longer necessary, as it had been in Brest, to reach a breakthrough. When, after lunch, we sat together in the city hall, I remarked that we would not advance our cause by delaying. "We must take care of the essentials now. It has become clear that the strength of the united Germany's military force is of crucial importance to the Soviet Union. We respect your concerns." Again my guest inquired whether the federal government was working to speed up the process of unification even more. "It is not we who are speeding up events, events are speeding up on their own momentum," I replied. I continued, "It would be helpful to all of us if the elapsed time between the economic and the political unification of Germany were kept as short as possible." The key date for economic unification was July 1, 1990, but the final date for political unification had not yet been set.

I interpreted Shevardnadze's suggestion to put the issue of the alliance aside for the present as an indication that he considered it settled to all intents and purposes. Evidently he assumed that we would reach an agreement that would satisfy our expectations as well. The Soviet Union seemed to have accepted what I had explained to the Soviet foreign minister from the start: "German unification will fundamentally change the situation in Europe, a new relationship will develop between West and East as well as between the alliances. Therefore Germany's membership in NATO offers many more advantages to the Soviet Union than does a nonaligned Germany."

Again Shevardnadze expressed ideas on a transition period. As I listened, I gained the impression that occasionally his thoughts strayed far afield. What worries were weighing on him? He spoke in a monotone, free of his usual zeal. Was he merely reciting his arguments as an exercise in fulfilling an obligation, so that he could assure the people back home that he had tried one more time but had met with rejection? With this possibility in mind, I made certain to produce counterarguments when I reiterated to him the reasons why a transition period such as he had in mind was not tenable.

Our meeting in Münster was marked by two important notes. The meeting had run a cordial course, and Shevardnadze pointed out to the press the significance of the upcoming NATO Council meeting: "Should NATO at its London summit decide on a similarly important declaration as the Warsaw Pact did in Moscow, the issue of Germany's military status could be discussed in a new atmosphere and on new terms, and we might make great progress." That statement affirmed and corroborated my assessment of Brest.

This assessment had already been corroborated earlier. Before our luncheon Shevardnadze's head of planning, Sergei Tarasenko, had taken Frank Elbe aside and handed him a memorandum that made no mention of the transition period Shevardnadze had publicly insisted on. "Don't worry, matters will work out just like this note specifies," Tarasenko told Elbe. No doubt Shevardnadze had authorized Tarasenko to pass these jottings on to Elbe. This act was another indication that the Soviets were ready to move.

All in all, therefore, Münster was an exceptionally positive event. The Soviet Union would no longer oppose Germany's full membership in NATO on principle; only the particulars and details were left to be elaborated. Beyond sending a signal at Turnberry, the West needed to reaffirm its willingness to structure a relationship of mutual trust between the alliances. Further, it was crucial that the number of German armed forces be limited. The elements of the framework for German unification, however, were in accord with our basic concept, which I had repeatedly outlined to Shevardnadze.

The atmosphere in which we concluded the meeting was hopeful and warm. It was a sensation not easily conveyed to the press; but in the service of our cause, we had no wish to completely initiate the reporters. It was important that the burden publicly placed on Shevardnadze and Gorbachev before the party convention not be too heavy; after all, they were still obligated to steer their concepts and ideas past the cliffs of the CPSU party convention.

At the end of this long, eventful day Shevardnadze and I returned to the airport. He, too, seemed rather sanguine about the further course of the negotiations. As we parted, he placed his hand on mine: "We will arrive at a good outcome."

I flew from Münster directly to Luxembourg to attend the ministerial meeting of the European Community to inform my counterparts at once on the results of my talks with Shevardnadze. I wanted all of my colleagues to realize that Germany was fully aware of its responsibility within Europe and within the alliance.

The morning after my return to Bonn the government coalition met; after the meeting I briefed the Chancellor at length on my impressions of the meetings in Münster and Luxembourg. "Now the Soviet leaders must concentrate mainly on evading the dogmatists' barrage at the CPSU party convention. The Soviet leaders are interested in bringing everything to a prompt conclusion after the party convention, they are not interested in long drawn-out talks.

The Two-Plus-Four meeting in Moscow will therefore be the crucial one." Helmut Kohl nodded in agreement. Then I elucidated a possible problem: "We will have held Two-Plus-Four meetings in Bonn, East Berlin, Paris, and Moscow, but none in London or Washington. At the appropriate time I therefore want to ask Hurd and Baker if they believe additional meetings to be absolutely necessary. If they do, these two meetings would have to be held immediately after the one in Moscow. Progress has been more swift than we originally expected. That is why we do not really need the meetings in London and Washington—not merely to save time. In this time of upheaval the Soviet Union may suddenly find itself in a precarious situation, or crises might arise elsewhere. We cannot delay the Two-Plus-Four process! We should bring it to a swift conclusion."

It is indicative of Hurd's and Baker's professionalism that they judged it unnecessary to hold a round of Two-Plus-Four talks in their capitals. Once more these two men proved to be good friends.

Two-Plus-Four in Berlin: A Reversal or Shevardnadze's Caution?

On June 22, 1990, precisely forty-nine years after Hitler's invasion of the Soviet Union, the second round of Two-Plus-Four talks began in East Berlin. Before the meeting opened, the six foreign ministers participated in the dismantling of the Allied Checkpoint Charlie. Also present was Willy Brandt, who as mayor of Berlin, as foreign minister, and as chancellor had contributed materially to West Berlin's self-determination and to the end of the division of Europe, Germany, and Berlin. Representatives of two sectors of the city attended as well. A huge crane lifted the checkpoint and deposited it in a nearby courtyard: That is how simple it was to get rid of this shack and its purpose, which had won worldwide notoriety during times of crisis. After the erection of the Wall in August 1961, American and Soviet tanks faced each other at that very place, a mutual threat only a few feet apart.

But that was in the past; now we were negotiating German unification during the second round of talks. While my mind was still focused on these happy dynamics, an astonishing setback suddenly seemed to be overshadowing the beginning of the conference—*seemed* to be. Shevardnadze presented a proposal for a treaty on a unified Germany's position under international law that took no account of what had been discussed and, in part, what had already been decided upon in our bilateral meetings and at American-Soviet talks. It also diverged widely from the unofficial text Elbe had been given in Münster.

We rejected the draft. Baker emphatically criticized it for singling out and discriminating against the unified Germany: "Any infringement of Germany's sovereignty is out of the question!" Douglas Hurd, too, rejected Shevardnadze's proposal. I declared, "At the time of its unity Germany must have full sovereignty and must not be restricted by unresolved questions."

When Shevardnadze finished speaking, Baker passed me a note; it read, "What is this all about?" I responded, in English, "Window dressing." Baker nodded his agreement. Both of us were certain that the Soviet leaders delicate domestic situation before the party convention forced Shevardnadze to take this stand, though it had long since been overtaken by events.

His behavior could hardly come as a surprise. In our negotiations my Soviet counterpart had always wielded a number of options, a method that allowed him to work toward his elected goal without forcing him to give it his formal endorsement. In that respect my task was easier—within the West German government and within the Alliance there was no conflict. In the West, particularly in West Germany, two quite different groups opposed each other. One witnessed the course of events almost in disbelief. Those who for years had never concealed their contempt for NATO, the United States, and the Bundeswehr, or had simply pursued some delusionary politics, now were compelled to realize that the Soviet Union's approval of the united Germany's membership in NATO was becoming increasingly likely. This attitude explains the German left's intellectual disorientation during the unification process, with effects that can still be felt. The other side consisted of those who, in 1988, had viewed the double-zero option and relinquishing the Pershing II as the decline of Western civilization, and the modernization of short-range nuclear missiles as a top priority of Germany's security and foreign policy. They could not read the signs of the times and had remained mired in the Old Thinking. Now these groups were competing in declaring most vociferously how necessary German membership in NATO was—which made it only more difficult for the Soviets to agree to our wishes.

To be absolutely certain that Shevardnadze had not in fact changed course, I approached him after the morning session. First I inquired about Gorbachev's health—we had received news that the President was suffering some cardiac trouble. I was interested as a human being, a politican, and a fellow invalid; mentioning my own history, I offered any medical help we could give. Shevardnadze replied, however, that Gorbachev was feeling very well. I went on to say jokingly that the process of democratization in the Soviet Union seemed to have moved to a stage that allowed the Soviet Foreign Minister to speak harshly before the party convened, just as sometimes happened in the West before such events. Shevardnadze laughed—but he did not comment or contradict. He had understood me, and now I was certain that I had interpreted his behavior correctly. My impression was confirmed during the ministers' luncheon.

Those present at the subsequent press conference noticed that despite our rough exchange during the previous negotiation, Shevardnadze and I were whispering together, even laughing. Though that image was in marked contrast to the official version, it also served to correct it. Such a correction was important to me, and evidently to Shevardnadze as well. Accordingly, he enhanced that impression for the journalists: The Soviet proposal, he stated, was not the last word. His government was willing to continue searching for compromises. Much, he argued, would depend on the response of the North Atlantic Alliance at its London meeting. The strategy of changing the environmental setting was beginning to work.

The London NATO summit took place on July 5 and 6, entirely dominated by the new situation in Europe and the impending unification of the two Germanys. "The Cold War is history," NATO General Secretary Manfred Wörner declared, meaning that NATO was responding to the upheavals in Europe with actions of its own. One aspect, however, Wörner continued, must never be forgotten: NATO could accomplish its tasks only if it respected its original obligation to preserve peace.

Given the turnaround in Europe, Wörner, the former West German minister of defense, began to pursue a course that was much closer to my ideas than the road he had taken in years past. Especially when preparing NATO for its future tasks, he displayed his great skill at developing programs. It seemed as if in fighting the horrible cancer that was devastating him, he was gaining new strength, which he applied to meeting his grave responsibilities. When I attended his memorial services in Brussels and the West German Parliament, I knew that I was taking leave of a long-time colleague who had become one of NATO's most significant secretaries general.

Because Helmut Kohl was intent on speaking directly to the Soviet security concerns in London, he said that he welcomed a joint NATO and Warsaw Pact declaration that would establish "that we no longer look on each other as enemies and that, in accordance with the United Nations Charter and the Helsinki Final Act, we reaffirm our commitment to renounce resolutely the use of force throughout Europe." In addition, the Chancellor repeated his resolve to ensure membership in NATO for the future Germany. But in order to complement the Alliance, he argued, CSCE must also become a supporting pillar of the pan-European security structure. Together both of us urged the other summit participants to include the Soviet Union in European cooperation.

The foreign ministers held one round of talks to discuss the draft of the summit declaration. Jim Baker and I—who, because of our constant contact with Moscow, were in the best position to estimate what the Soviet Union required before it could agree to Germany's membership in NATO—were closely allied as we joined in the debate. The previous year we had led the discussion when I was so deeply concerned with preventing a vote on the modernization of short-range nuclear missiles; at the time, however, we had not fought on the same side until near the end of the debate. NATO's London summit declaration finally turned into a document that led the way into the future, marking the beginning of new relations with yesterday's enemies.

Meeting in Moscow and the Caucasus

Only two weeks later the unforgettable German-Soviet meeting in Moscow and the Caucasus would begin, immediately after the CPSU party convention. Gorbachev and Shevardnadze had weathered the storm—but how? In any case, it was impossible to ratify and formalize the decisions drafted during the long talks with Shevardnadze until the convention was over.

First, however, on Sunday, July 8, 1990, I flew to Houston, Texas, for the world economic summit. When the date had been set, it was impossible to know that the timing was perfect to prepare for the German-Soviet meeting in Moscow and the Caucasus. The sequence of events was ideal: After the agreement reached at the EC summit in Dublin on June 25 and 26, 1990, and even more important, the agreement of the NATO summit on July 5 and 6, as well as accords at the G7 meeting in Houston from July 8 to 11, successful talks in Moscow could be hoped for.

The first night we were invited by President Bush to a barbecue and country music. Everyone was relaxed. "What will you achieve in Moscow?" was the question the summit participants who had already arrived asked over and over again. No hint of mistrust could be felt—a mood that was to last through the entire summit. The foreign ministers talked about the status of the Two-Plus-Four meetings, particularly since four of the seven foreign ministers present in Houston were also among the Six.

After the American-Soviet meeting had gone so well and after my impressions during the encounters with Shevardnadze in Brest and Münster, we were fairly certain that Moscow would be a success. That may explain why over dinner, the seven foreign ministers not only spoke to each other like statesmen, but also had a great time together. We told jokes and laughed easily. Had the Moscow party convention loosened a knot? But perhaps the reason for our good mood was a quite different one: In the course of the dramatic year and a half since the beginning of 1989, as we had worked ever more closely and were now seeing the end of the Cold War and of the division of Europe and Germany, collaboration had turned into friendship. The way we talked about Shevardnadze showed that at heart we thought of him as one of us. Again and again the talk returned to him. A Soviet Union that was treading such a path belonged among us. I left Houston firmly resolved to do all I could to include Gorbachev and Shevardnadze in the next world economic summit, to be held in London in 1991.

On the whole the Houston meeting was not quite as successful as we had hoped. The German delegation tried to procure joint financial aid for Gorbachev, and France and Italy were especially supportive of our attempt. When he met with President Bush, Helmut Kohl pointed out that the Soviet Union had already been granted a loan of 5 billion deutsche marks, guaranteed by West Germany. We had reached the limits of our ability as the sole aid provider; our estimate was that 15 billion deutsche marks, raised jointly, was needed. However, the other summit participants' response was disappointing: Some demanded more drastic reforms in the Soviet Union, while others criticized that the funds were oozing away. Japanese Prime Minister Toshiki Kaifu made financial aid dependent on the return of the Kurile Islands, a demand I found difficult to understand. In my opinion, such a move would not help Gorbachev and would not bring Japan any closer to solving the problem of the Kurile Islands. And yet it is impossible to know whether there might not have been a "window of opportunity" to resolve Japanese concerns; if such an opportunity had existed, a loan would certainly have made it easier to address it.

In the end Houston resulted in a political resolution that, patting Gorbachev on the back, as it were, encouraged him to continue on his reform course. In response to the question of joint financial aid, IMF, the World Bank, the OECD, and the Eastern European Bank were asked to draft a paper. The nations "already in a position to do so" were generously granted the option of initiating steps even before the draft was issued—wording that put the spotlight on West Germany, since it was likely that a substantial part of the burden of aiding Moscow would fall to us.

Considering that before the summit Gorbachev himself had written a letter asking the participants for aid, this response was disappointing. We felt particularly frustrated, not only because we were more active than the others, but also because, with a view to German unification, we had direct experience of the courage the Soviet leaders exhibited in replacing old thinking with policies that were shaping the future. Of course this new political course could not be bought, but supporting the reforms was surely in the West's best interests.

On the evening of July 14, 1990, the Chancellor and I arrived in Moscow. We were well equipped: The framework necessary for concluding the Two-Plus-Four talks had been erected. Issues that remained to be settled were the strength of the German military forces—between 350,000 and 400,000 troops—the extent of German financial aid, the legal foundation for the Soviet forces' temporary continuation on German soil, the date of final withdrawal, and the issue of deployment and status of German troops in the former East Germany until the last Soviet soldier was withdrawn.

The following morning, shortly after ten o'clock, I met with Foreign Minister Shevardnadze for a talk in the guest house. He described the party convention, which had gone exactly as we had feared and as we had learned from our embassy in Moscow. Two questions had been predominant: "Why did you allow the loss of Eastern Europe?" and "Why are you acceding to the unification of a country that will be fully integrated into NATO?" Questions had also been asked to determine who bore the responsibility for this course of events. Shevardnadze had twice taken the floor during the plenary session and in turn had asked rhetorically whether the Soviet Union had not gone into the countries of Central and Eastern Europe as a liberation army. Were these nations now to be considered as the spoils of war? If that was the case, he would have to apologize, but not otherwise. As for Germany, he had explained to the delegates that the Soviet Union had been faced with a choice. On the one hand there had been the Germans' right to self-determination and the protection of Soviet interests by creating different security structures as well as an attempt to establish a new kind of mutual relations. The alternative had been to set in motion an army consisting of 500,000 troops and many tanks in order to fight the Germans, who were exercising their right to self-determination. The consequences of the latter course could be imagined. I thanked Shevardnadze for his bold position.

We discussed not only events that had occurred since our last meeting but also the question of future relations between our two nations. I explained the steadiness with which the Western Alliance and other Western organizations had adapted to the new situation; this circumstance was demonstrated by the ministerial statement in Turnberry and the resolutions of the NATO London summit and the economic summit in Houston. I further thanked my Soviet counterpart for his encouraging discussion with NATO Secretary General Wörner. Once again I communicated our ideas concerning future developments in Europe. I mentioned that I was old enough to be aware of the horrors Germany had caused—horrible not only for ourselves but for all of Europe. I was all the more satisfied that the impending unification of Germany would prove beneficial for the entire Continent. I was willing to say this much: The Chancellor would specify to the President the maximum force of the German army that we were aiming for, an issue Shevardnadze had proclaimed of particular importance.

He also appreciated my part in gaining some understanding for perestroika. He remarked that I had played a significant role—starting as early as 1985—in shaping favorable public opinion in the West. He had noted all my statements on this matter. But now the most crucial moment had arrived: We had the responsibility both to determine Germany's destiny according to the will of the German people and to invest all our strength and experience and seize every possible opportunity to guarantee genuine security and stability in Europe. To this end European institutions must be created. The process of German unification, he said, was taking an irrevocable course forward; lagging behind in such a situation would lead to a failure to grasp a great chance. Relations between our two countries were of paramount importance in every aspect.

Shevardnadze next suggested that we discuss the Two-Plus-Four document. It was with trepidation that I heard him say that the thought of our next ministerial conference in Moscow being scheduled for as early as September was causing him anxiety. He was concerned about whether a treaty could really be drafted by that date. That explanation took care of my principal fear; if Shevardnadze was worried only about the contents of the treaty, all serious problems had indeed been settled according to our wishes.

Of course, I replied, a lot of work remained. Nevertheless, I would consider it a huge mistake to reschedule the meeting. We must keep the date, but we should make every effort to put the intervening time to better use. As I had repeatedly stated from the outset, the unified Germany needed to be free and unfettered by unresolved questions; because the new country required independence in every respect, we could not consider provisional solutions. The presence and strength of Soviet military units, and particularly the time to be allowed for their withdrawal, were part and parcel of a procedure that must be firmly established from the very start, rather than resolved gradually. I reminded him that we had agreed on the importance of expanding the CSCE process and of nurturing relations between the members of the two alliances in order to establish a foundation for a unified Germany. Acknowledging the Chancellor's and my contribution to the London resolution, Shevardnadze affirmed its significance. Above all, he said, it must be recognized that this resolution called for a joint statement by NATO and the Warsaw Pact to the effect that both alliances renounced an antagonistic stance. That move—especially that move—was the crux of the matter. Shevardnadze and I were eager to begin talks on a comprehensive German-Soviet treaty. He suggested Ambassador Vladislav Terekhov as chief negotiator, I chose Dieter Kastrup.

On the flight to the Caucasus I sat with Shevardnadze. We reviewed the long road that had brought us to this moment, from our first meeting in Helsinki in 1985 through the acrimonious meeting in Vienna in 1986 to Brest and Münster.

We made a stopover in Stavropol. Even though this area had been occupied only briefly by the German army during the Second World War—from August 1942 to January 1943—the city's memories of the war are deeply rooted. Mikhail Gorbachev and the Chancellor placed wreaths at the Monument for the Fallen of the Second World War. Numerous veterans were present. They must have been thinking about the past, but when they spoke with us it also became clear that they were looking to the future—with us. We visited the office Gorbachev occupied during his time as regional party secretary. Standing on an elevation with a chest-high stone wall, we waved to the people. They waved back and applauded; their applause was enthusiastic.

Most of the way from the cars to the war memorial, the town hall, and the stone wall I walked with Raissa Gorbachev. She wanted to talk, and we discussed the meaning of the agreements and their possible effect on the future. I detected a trace of fear in her words. She knew only too well what this step might mean for Mikhail Gorbachev's life and career.

We continued our trip by helicopter, with another stopover in a wheatfield. The crowd of farmers, men and women awaiting us next to their combines, received us with great cordiality. They offered bread and salt. As in Stavropol, here, too, I felt that our presence lifted a burden from the people. Of course they were not aware of the far-reaching decisions being made at this time. And yet, they felt that a gate to the future was opening. All of them were aware of what the war had meant. They had had to wage and win that war, at the cost of great sacrifice, against a Germany that had attacked the Soviet Union. Yet they also possessed a natural sense of the fact that peace and a future cannot be won in conflict but only in collaboration with one another, including the people of Germany.

The negotiations with Shevardnadze and the American-Soviet preparatory talks had given us a clear point of departure for the talks in Moscow and the Caucasus. The NATO declarations of Turnberry and London had freed relations between NATO and the Warsaw Pact from the traditional image of friend and foe. Germany's freedom to choose its alliance needed to be regulated in accordance with the Helsinki Final Act. We had also agreed on holding a CSCE summit in Paris in November, and we were in accord on stipulating that the unified Germany would renounce atomic, biological, and chemical weapons, just as the old West Germany had done. The size of the unified country's armed forces was set at well under that of the West German army's 500,000 troops—somewhere between 350,000 and 400,000. Finally, as a member of NATO, a unified Germany's security interests must be safeguarded; NATO's protection clause would have to include all of Germany. The formulation "No expansion of NATO structures to former GDR territory" meant that German troops would be stationed immediately in the former East Germany, that NATO-integrated German forces would be stationed in this area no later than after the withdrawal of the Soviet forces, and that no Allied armed forces would ever be stationed in the new German states. Given the total withdrawal of Soviet forces, Moscow could hardly watch the arrival of Allied forces. Of course the correct procedure was to avoid connecting NATO's Allied forces with the withdrawal of Soviet forces. But for the purpose of the negotiations, and probably even more so for the well-being of Gorbachev and Shevardnadze, it was important that they could announce that the traditional NATO military structures had not advanced eastward. Tipping the balance of power in favor of the West and moving back the Soviet Union's military operating space must not be followed by the Western Alliance's simultaneous and structurally unchanged expansion eastward. For us, on the other hand, it was absolutely mandatory to make certain that no zone of decreased security would be created in the new German states.

425

During our flight to the Caucasus and the following night I frequently asked myself if the Soviet leadership really believed that NATO and the Warsaw Pact would coexist permanently. In conversations with my new colleagues from the smaller Warsaw Pact nations, at any rate, I had learned that they did not believe that the Eastern Alliance could remain in force much longer. Shevardnadze's doubts expressed at our bilateral encounters also came to mind. Perhaps he had not merely harbored doubts but had already known the outcome.

Having arrived in Arkhits, we were shown to our quarters. I was given accommodations in a comfortable old Russian wooden building, where medical services, both Soviet and German, had also been set up. Without the good care of my doctors I could hardly have withstood the rigors of 1990. Late that evening, too, I had to seek medical help; my circulation was dropping, and a severe attack of arrythmia was beginning. These troubles would continue until our return the following evening. An important day would prove physically challenging for me.

The famous walk, which was so widely publicized on television and in numerous photographs, began at the main building and ended at the riverbank. Helmut Kohl and Mikhail Gorbachev sat on two tree trunks before a solid wooden table. A third trunk remained. The other members of the two delegations—Ministers Shevardnadze and Stepan Sitaryan, Theo Waigel, Hans Klein, and I—surrounded the two in a wide circle. Gorbachev asked me to sit. I gestured to Shevardnadze to sit instead, but he declined. We exchanged a glance, and I took the seat.

My thoughts were far, far away—with my parents and grandparents, at our home near Halle. Less than two years ago my mother had died; she could not witness the advent of what she had always wished for. I also thought of the time immediately after the war, when my grandfather had predicted that fifty years would pass before the Red Army left Germany and we would be one again.

On the walk to this table one event had made me confident even as it indicated the great seriousness of the situation. When we started out—according to the laws of our modern media society, we were embarked on a joint publicity stroll—Gorbachev, Kohl, Shevardnadze, and I formed a foursome that walked in front, the interpreters between us. Abruptly a hand on my forearm held me back. I turned around to see Raissa Gorbachev. She wanted to talk with me again; did we know, she inquired, the full meaning of all that was discussed and decided here? Did we realize the responsibility her husband was assuming, the risks he was taking? I nodded. She continued, "Herr Genscher, Germany is making concessions too, Germany too must give something, Herr Genscher, you must keep your promises—everything." She sounded almost entreating. I stopped for a moment and took her hand. "You can depend on it. We have learned our lessons from history in every respect. I know exactly what your husband is doing. Everything will turn out well."

Her fearful questions confirmed my belief that Gorbachev and Shevardnadze were walking a tightrope. Despite the ill feeling the party congress seemed to have caused between them, they appeared very close again. This reconciliation was also hinted at.

All of us felt relaxed as we met for the evening meal. Gorbachev told us about a walk he had taken with Shevardnadze just after the Soviets invaded Afghanistan. At the time Gorbachev had risen from party secretary in the Caucasus to secretary of the Central Committee in Moscow. In the spring after the invasion he had traveled to Tiflis, and it was then that he and Eduard Shevardnadze went for a walk, as they had occasionally done in the past. Abruptly Shevardnadze asked, "Were you told about the attack on Afghanistan beforehand?"

"No."

"But you are the secretary of the Central Committee."

"Not even all the members of the Politburo were informed ahead of time."

Shevardnadze stopped short: "Our system—we have to change it from the ground up."

"That," Gorbachev concluded, "is what we determined to do together."

Was the story intended to appease Shevardnadze, who was obviously disappointed by Gorbachev's behavior at the party congress? In this version Gorbachev gave Shevardnadze the role of initiator on the road to the New Thinking. Now I understood completely why in 1985 he gave the foreign ministry to the Georgian, who was inexperienced in international politics. The verdict on the "system," uttered as an immediate reaction to the attack on Afghanistan, which broke international law, corroborated my ini-

427

tial assessment of these two men. Perestroika and glasnost—these were not tactical variants, they were not an attempt to reach old goals by new methods. They constituted a fundamental change of direction. And in this case *fundamental* meant based in morality as well.

On July 16, 1990, our second day in Arkhits, the delegations met together for talks. Our side was represented by the Chancellor, Ministers Waigel, Klein, and myself, as well as our ambassador to Moscow, Klaus Blech, Undersecretary Kastrup, and several other officials. On the Soviet side were Gorbachev, Eduard Shevardnadze, Deputy Prime Minister Sitaryan (Shevardnadze's equivalent in terms of responsibility), Deputy Foreign Minister Kvitsinksy (the former Soviet ambassador to Bonn), and the new ambassador to Bonn, Vladislav Terekhov.

We began with a detailed discussion of our relationship's long-range prospects. We agreed both on the negotiation and the signing of a long-term treaty, which was obviously important to Gorbachev both in terms of content and psychologically. He could use it to demonstrate to the Soviet public that in the long run resolving the German question was advantageous to their country. Two months later, therefore, Moscow insisted that I sign this document in close conjunction, in time and place, with the signing of the Two-Plus-Four Treaty in Moscow on September 13, 1990. Helmut Kohl was right in choosing this topic for his introduction. It served to demonstrate to the Soviet leaders that we too were interested in wider and deeper cooperation and that we were perfectly aware of our partners' concerns. It was quite obvious that for Gorbachev it was important for us to begin with this topic.

Next we discussed the Two-Plus-Four document, which defined the units to become unified: The Federal Republic of Germany, German Democratic Republic, and Berlin. For Gorbachev, the united Germany's renunciation of atomic, biological, and chemical weapons held an added significance. He stated that he would approve Germany's membership in NATO only on condition that "NATO's military structures" be kept to outside the territory of the former East Germany. As for Soviet troops in that area, he urged a separate treaty. The Chancellor remarked that the core goal of the Two-Plus-Four talks was unqualified independence for the united Germany. I added that we needed to agree unanimously that this stipulation included the united Germany's right to belong to an alliance—in our case, to NATO. After the Chancellor had summarized the entire document, Gorbachev voted in the affirmative. In order to avoid misunderstandings as to the Secretary General's precise meaning when he specified that NATO's structures must not be extended, I considered it my task at this point as well as in the further course of the discussion to clarify all questions that had already arisen in the Two-Plus-Four talks or that might still arise. Keeping constant eye contact, Helmut Kohl and I led the discussion at this stage and signaled to each other as to the other's role. Because it was important that Articles Five and Six of the NATO Treaty apply to all of Germany, I remarked that there must be no zones of different degrees of security in Germany—that is, NATO's security guarantees would have to apply to East Germany as well. This concern was finally established by a general consensus on the applicability of Articles Five and Six.

I noted that as far as the status of the new federal states was concerned, the former East Germany would house units of the Bundeswehr until 1994, after which date, with the withdrawal of Soviet forces, NATO-integrated units would be stationed in these areas as well. To avoid any misunderstanding, I summarized all paragraphs in the same vein. Gorbachev gave his approval, but not before remarking that no foreign troops could ever be deployed in these territories. The Chancellor accepted that restriction.

Thus we achieved clarity on difficult issues, and Germany's status as regards security policy was established. For our part, everything necessary for security was done, including the stationing of NATO-integrated German units. On the other hand, the form of the NATO structures as they existed in the Federal Republic of Germany was not extended to the East. In my view we had succeeded in avoiding zones of different degrees of security.

Gorbachev categorically insisted that foreign forces must not be stationed on the territory of the former East Germany after the withdrawal of Soviet forces. In order to make certain that the situation was crystal clear, I repeated my statement that after the Soviet military forces' withdrawal, NATO-integrated German military forces could be stationed in that part of Germany. The Chancellor once more reaffirmed this position, because of its special importance.

Those who, in the spring of 1989, had believed in the necessity of deploying short-range nuclear missiles and who only a year later, in the spring of 1990, considered the expansion of the existing NATO structures to the Eastern border of the united Germany a distinct possibility, lacked both perspicacity and sound judgment; in 1989 they had not understood that a transformation of historic dimensions was under way. In 1990 they failed to realize that as a result of these upheavals, the new federal states gained a degree of security that surpassed the security enjoyed even by the old West Germany. In the past we had been confronted by 300,000 troops of the Red Army at the border that ran right through Germany. By the end of 1994, however, the united Germany would be a neighbor of such nations as Poland and Czechoslovakia, where no more Soviet units were stationed, and the 300,000 troops in the former East Germany would also be withdrawn.

Every step in the direction of democratization increased our security. It seemed all the more anachronistic when on September 11, 1990, the eve of the signing of the Two-Plus-Four Treaty, the British tried to interpret the term *not station,* which had been taken over from the wording used in Arkhits, to mean that allied NATO-integrated military forces could go on maneuvers in the new federal states. As if that were what mattered.

The ceiling for German military forces was also established in our Arkhits negotiations. As I had estimated from the start, the figure was ultimately set at anywhere from 350,000 to 400,000. The final number was 370,000; after the talk between the Chancellor and Gorbachev the previous night, we had used that number as a starting point. It was also important to notify the CFE conference in Vienna about our conclusion.

Regarding the ceiling for armed forces, we found a way to preserve our goal—using a statement at the CFE conference in Vienna as the basis for the ceiling—while at the same time doing justice to the concerns of the Soviet Union, which was intent on having these figures specified in the treaty. On August 30, 1990—in other words, before the Two-Plus-Four Treaty was signed—the two German states made a relevant statement, to which Article Three of the treaty refers. But what was decisive was the statement in Vienna.

It was extremely important for Helmut Kohl and myself to obtain resolutions on all questions relating to Germany in Arkhits. It was clear that there was agreement on the facts, and it was becoming clear that we agreed on a human level as well. The road we had traveled together culminated in shared success.

I had to clarify one final matter with the Soviet leaders—especially with Shevardnadze, since he would be among the negotiators at the next Two-Plus-Four meeting, to take place in Paris. This concerned Poland's wish to withhold full sovereignty from Germany until the border treaty was concluded; further, I intended to make it quite clear in Paris that the issues of Germany's eastern and Poland's western border constituted a bilateral matter and not one that involved Europe as a whole—at least not in terms of law. I was certain that Skubiszewski and I would arrive at an agreement in Paris. Poland could not be interested in mingling the border issue with other controversies, thus hampering rather than facilitating its resolution. Besides, Skubiszewski knew that I was equally interested in clarifying matters rather than complicating them.

I felt grateful to Mikhail Gorbachev and Eduard Shevardnadze. "We will never forget what you did," I assured them when we parted. I spoke on my own behalf as well as our country's. And that sentiment will not fade.

Two-Plus-Four in Paris: Accord with Poland

The following day, in Paris, I made haste to brief Secretary Baker on the talks in the Caucasus; Baker, who had done so much to bring this meeting about, was very pleased with the outcome. After a consultation among the four Western foreign ministers—Dumas, Baker, Hurd, and myself—we moved to the Centre Kleber, the site of the third round of the Two-Plus-Four talks.

Roland Dumas, as host and chairman, opened the meeting. He placed it within the context of the changes that had already occurred, referring principally to the London NATO summit, the world economic summit in Houston, and the Caucasus talks. He noted the participation of a Polish delegation, to begin that same afternoon, as an indication that the border issue would occupy a prominent place at this round.

Shevardnadze remarked on the political courage required to view the unification of Germany as a step in a new direction. Now it was necessary to create the requisite conditions for new security structures. He, too, appreciated the signals sent by the meeting of the Warsaw Pact in Moscow, the EC summit in Dublin, and the NATO summit in London. All three meetings had signaled a turn away from confrontation and toward cooperation; and, Shevardnadze continued, it must be said frankly that progress in the unification process had become possible only because so much had been achieved within the two alliances and CSCE. Thus Shevardnadze reaffirmed the plan we had pursued from the outset—making the core issues of unification and NATO membership accessible to resolution by changing the external conditions.

At the talks in the Caucasus, Shevardnadze continued, we had had an opportunity to examine four problem areas: Germany's independence, the rights and responsibilities of the Four Powers, Germany's military-political status, and the issue of Soviet forces in the territory of today's East Germany. Though not all problems had been resolved, the essential ones had been adequately dealt with, allowing other matters to be addressed more easily now. Wording for the definitive regulation should be drafted before the meeting in Moscow, which he proposed for September 12. Should that wording not be available by that date, we could meet again during the general assembly of the United Nations in late September, or at a possible additional meeting in London. Shevardnadze concluded by again pointing to the enormous difficulties and fears rampant in the Soviet Union.

In my address I emphasized that we were aware of the fundamental changes that had occurred since the last Two-Plus-Four round. Now we were in a position to discuss the external aspects of German unification from a different perspective. We felt confirmed in our opinion that the German question could be resolved within a pan-European context. Further, it was now evident that the dynamics of the German unification process not only failed to hinder developments in Europe but exerted a favorable effect. The entire Continent was in the process of undergoing a general transformation. I went on to explain that the talks with the Soviet leaders had been conducted with these facts in mind. Further, I welcomed the fact that everyone at the table clearly understood that the results produced at our talks would benefit all of Europe—they sacrificed no nation but aided all. "We Germans," I continued, "feel that what is happening now is advantageous to all of Europe. And since it is an advantage to Europe, it is also a boon to our people. That thought may confirm you and your nation in the conviction that Germany's decision to place her fate within the fate of Europe is definitive and final. We are convinced that German unification constitutes a contribution to the creation of a single Europe. That Europe, which will be built by all those nations that have appended their signatures to the Helsinki Final Act, includes the United States and Canada." Particularly in the present situation, I considered such a statement important.

I went on to say that the Polish Foreign Minister's participation lent special significance to the second section of the Paris meeting. We were aware that reaffirming the definitive character of the German borders was an essential contribution to the foundation of a European peace. "We Germans," I concluded, "want nothing more than to live with our neighbors in unity, liberty, and peace. In that spirit the two German parliaments and the two German governments have submitted their statements to the Polish government."

I went to the Polish ambassador's quarters for preliminary discussions with the Polish foreign minister. We wanted to consult with each other on the signing of the German-Polish border treaty, which was scheduled to take place after the unification of Germany but before the parliamentary elections on December 2, 1990. However, the plan was that it would not be ratified until Germany had gained full sovereignty—that is, after full ratification of the Two-Plus-Four document. We also needed to discuss the comprehensive agreement between Bonn and Warsaw that was to be settled soon afterward, to establish the basis for our future relations.

The schedule provided that on November 14 we would meet in Warsaw where, in the presence of Prime Minister Mazowiecki, Foreign Minister Skubiszewski and I would sign the treaty between the Federal Republic of Germany and the Republic of Poland on the confirmation of the existing shared border. Finally, the treaty on good neighborly relations and friendly cooperation was signed on June 17, 1991, in Bonn by Chancellor Helmut Kohl and myself and Prime Minister Mazowiecki and Foreign Minister Skubiszewski.

□   □   □   □

On the afternoon of July 17 the second part of the negotiating round began, this time with Skubiszewski's participation. In my introductory remarks I said, "We are pleased that, like ourselves, after a treaty on the unalterability of the German-Polish border, Poland will pursue the goal of another treaty, concerning the future of German-Polish relations. . . . At this meeting, and in the presence of the Polish foreign minister and his delegation, we are mindful of the painful German-Polish history in all its phases, above all its darkest chapter." I then reported that in its resolution, which the federal government had adopted as well—and the same held true for the Volkskammer and the East German government—the Bundestag expressed a desire to bestow permanence on the border between the united Germany and the Republic of Poland through an internationally binding treaty. I remarked that these decisions had been formally submitted by the two German governments, so that they would be as binding as possible before unification. "We have acted in the desire to make German unity a contribution to building a foundation for peace in Europe in which borders no longer separate."

A not entirely smooth discussion on a statement by the Four Powers concerning the border followed. Foreign Minister Skubiszewski's extraordinary knowledgeability on the subject proved extremely helpful. He was also the only one of the seven foreign ministers who could follow the debate without headphones, since in addition to Polish he spoke German, Russian, English, and French.

Skubiszewski noted that he would welcome a separate discussion of the German-Polish border by the Four Powers, particularly if the two German states might also join in. Eventually this kind of procedure would put the issue of a peace treaty or a similar arrangement permanently to rest. But he wanted to go on record to say that Poland did not consider this statement to be a guarantee; it had never been thought of in that way. I was relieved; I had been worried about just this possibility in Arkhits. He thanked me for my statement on the future of German-Polish relations.

Jim Baker then suggested the following wording: "The Four Powers declare that the frontiers of the united Germany will have permanent character and cannot be questioned on account of external circumstances or events."

Skubiszewski's clarifying remark on the character of a Four

Power Declaration had also expressed our concerns. The German-Polish border was a bilateral matter. Poland knew the importance of Germany's signature on the border treaty, while the value of guarantees always depends on the relevant concerns and constellations. Besides, we would be unable to accept it if the impression were left that an agreement reached by the Federal Republic of Germany and the German Democratic Republic, which was now democratically legitimized, on the issue of the border must be vouchsafed by others. Not least, third parties could have derived rights from this accord in future, thus infringing on our sovereignty.

Germany's and Poland's shared fears led to a somewhat lengthy discussion. Poland wanted to make certain that a treaty on the finality of the border would not subsequently be annulled, with the argument that at the time the border treaty was signed, no peace treaty or a similar arrangement was in effect. However, we were not eager to construct either one, since both had long since become obsolete. If we accepted the timeliness of a peace treaty with Poland, we would have had to make a treaty with the whole world, and anyone could have presented us with their bills. Thus, for different reasons, Poland and Germany were working in the same direction.

I took advantage of this debate, which I did not find unwelcome, by putting into words the tacit agreement of the four that there would be no peace treaty or similar arrangement: "The West German government agrees with the Four Powers and wishes to add that the events and circumstances mentioned in the Four Powers' statement will not take place; that is, no peace treaty or similar arrangement is intended."

To satisfy the demands of the minutes, the French foreign minister, as chairman, stated, "I notice general consent." Thus we had unanimously established that neither the Potsdam Agreement nor the Paris Treaty between the old Federal Republic and the three Western Powers could serve as the basis for a demand for a future peace treaty. It therefore became impossible to demand a peace treaty now or in future—and thus the fear of incalculable requests for reparations was lifted from our shoulders. This act finalized the decision Kastrup had already enforced in the various governmental levels.

On July 27, 1990, Krzysztof Skubiszewski addressed the Sejm, the Polish parliament. He praised the outcome of the Paris meeting, particularly emphasizing the great significance of the resolutions of both German parliaments, which, he said, had been a "harmonious prelude" to the negotiations. He had told the press even earlier that after the "final" resolutions of the Paris conference a "peace treaty" was "no longer necessary."

Witnesses at the Paris meeting to the Four Powers' commitment to recognizing the German-Polish border were able to realize how many obstacles, beginning with my statement at the United Nations in 1989, had been removed one by one. At the same time it became evident how much harm had been done whenever Germany hesitated. That circumstance was all the more regrettable when it was taken into account that it was clear from the start that recognition of Poland's western border was essential to gaining approval of German unification from both the East and the West.

Paris represented a great deal of progress. In terms of substance, we had covered the most difficult part of the road. Realizing that borders must be finalized was one thing; acting on that realization was another. That fact had always been in my mind during the many years when I had supported such an agreement. But awareness of the necessity for such a treaty meant not merely acknowledging its inevitability, a price, so to speak, to be paid for German unity; the crux was an essential moral category as a basis for a new relationship between Poles and Germans. I never stopped asserting that the vicious circle of injustice and repeated injustice, which had burdened Europe's history and particularly German-Polish relations, must be broken. After the disasters unleashed on Poland from 1939 to 1944 by Germans and in the name of Germany, it was up to Germany to take this step. I have often wondered how much psychological repression it takes to claim that the particularity of the Polish-German relationship is based solely on the fact that Poland had been the first nation to be attacked—especially since this is an historical untruth, the first victim having been Czechoslovakia; after that, the attack on Poland started the Second World War. But within the "Greater German Empire" the Polish people were forced to serve as slave labor. The plan was to eliminate the Polish intelligentsia—and the plan was carried out. What happened in Poland was selective genocide and enslavement of the survivors. Historical truth thus commands us to remember that even if Germany had not been divided after the Second World War, the border issue would have been settled along the same lines. The Germans living in the territory now incorporated into Poland were made to bear the harsh sacrifice of paying the price for all that had occurred—and the price was high, with the loss of their homes and, for many, their lives or health, with severe abuse and humiliation. That these effects did not result in a new revanchism or extremism is an historic accomplishment on the part of the expellees.

At the end of July, Douglas Hurd and I called on Margaret Thatcher. We talked about the status of the Two-Plus-Four talks, and the Prime Minister's principal concern seemed to center on the question of what would happen to the British troops stationed in Berlin during the transition period, until 1994. She was worried about discipline, wondering what should keep the troops busy. "The same as before," I replied laconically.

In early August I telephoned Shevardnadze in Moscow to describe to him domestic developments in Germany, in particular the relationship between the Federal Republic and the German Democratic Republic. Statements by Prime Minister De Maizière concerning the date for the first all-German elections had caused some confusion. Because I wanted to prevent Moscow from believing that we intended to present the Soviet Union with a fait accompli, I specified that the date for unification would fall somewhere between September 15 and October 14—certainly no later. At any rate, I was certain that we would be able to conclude our talks at the Two-Plus-Four meeting in Moscow on September 12. The date for unification would therefore not present a problem.

All promises made in the Caucasus, I continued, would be honored unconditionally. Foreign Minister Meckel and I had already agreed that later in the month we would deliver in Vienna the statement in which we committed ourselves to the future ceiling for Germany's military forces. And should there be resolutions in the Volkskammer for an earlier unification date according to Article 23 of the Basic Law, I would inform Shevardnadze immediately. He was immensely grateful for my call. Events in East Germany were occurring at breakneck speed, he said, and the Two-Plus-Four talks must not lag behind. He was therefore placing particular importance on our meeting in Moscow on August 16 and 17, as well as on the joint declaration of the two Germanys concerning future German troop strength.

The Unity of the Liberals

August 10, 1990, was a special day of an entirely different sort: It was the day of the FDP's unification party congress in Hannover.

By joining together, the Free Democratic Party, the Liberal Democratic Party, and the FDP East succeeded in the unification of Germany's Liberal parties. We became the first pan-German party. For me, too, the day marked the closing of a circle: On January 30, 1946, I had joined the Liberal Democratic Party in the then-Soviet Zone of Occupation, and I had remained a member until I left Halle on August 20, 1952. I had barely arrived in Bremen when I joined the FDP in October of that same year. To me that enrollment had always signified a continuation of my LDPD membership, even though the latter had long since abandoned—or rather, been forced to abandon—Liberal principles. Whenever I was asked how long I had been a member of the FDP, I answered, "Since January 30, 1946."

In Hannover we once again committed ourselves to the political unity of German Liberalism: It was the great achievement of West Germany's Liberals after the Second World War that they overcame the historic split in German Liberalism. They had found the strength to unite highly different Liberal parties of the postwar era under the umbrella of the FDP and to offer all of them a political and organizational home. The Liberal party always attempted to cover the entire Liberal spectrum. Its call for liberty is a comprehensive one; it does not allow for restriction to specific political areas or of the social spectrum. The same is true for its commitment to responsibility, which is connected with the Liberal commitment to liberty. Any attempt to narrow the party down to certain areas of politics, therefore, damages its spiritual claim as a party of liberty. Even if it could preserve its organizational unity under such conditions, a split from below can still occur—and a split among its constituency may be more dangerous than an organizational schism. Standing up courageously and confidently for the comprehensive Liberal claim to liberty therefore represents a chance as well as a challenge—but it is not the same as fence-straddling, as some have claimed. For Liberals there is no split between two different liberties.

As a Liberal party, the FDP by definition cannot be a party of the rich but only a party for liberty, populism, progress, and reform. As soon as it becomes the defender of one group of constituents it enters on the path of intellectual self-restriction, even self-strangulation. What alone must determine its actions is responsibility for the future, based on Article One of the West German Basic Law, which states that "the dignity of the person is inviolable."

Last Round: The Two-Plus-Four Meeting in Moscow

On August 16 I flew to Moscow. Foreign Minister Shevardnadze and I went to the guest house together, so as to have a first opportunity for an extensive conversation—an exchange that had recently become almost habitual.

Along with our ambassador to Moscow, Klaus Blech, and Undersecretary Kastrup, a number of top-ranking officials from the Foreign Office and other ministries made up our negotiating team. Shevardnadze opened the official session by noting that 50 percent of all questions had already been settled at our private discussion. However, it was important to remember that the next few days and weeks would be crucial to future relations between the Federal Republic of Germany and the Soviet Union. We must remove the last obstacles in the Two-Plus-Four talks. First, the Two-Plus-Four meetings must be completed by September 12; second, by that time we must have clarified all aspects of bilateral relations; third, we must think about our possible contributions to the CSCE process to create new security structures in Europe. This process must not lag behind German unification. Shevardnadze's words indicated that we agreed on the program for our negotiations.

I too stressed the importance of completing the treaty by the set date. But the document must confine itself to related topics; I believed that the Soviet draft contained provisions that more properly belonged in the realm of bilateral relations.

Next I broached a subject of particular importance to Germany. Since the final document of the Two-Plus-Four talks required ratification by all participants, I said, some time would necessarily elapse between signing and ratification. Because ratification ended the Four Power privileges, I saw a necessity to suspend these rights from the moment of signing, preferably through unilateral declarations by the former victorious powers. Shevardnadze was fearful: Such a move could hamper the ratification process in Moscow. I insisted, and I produced solid reasons. Uncurtailed continuation of these rights must not be held out as an incentive for delaying ratification. Shevardnadze replied that he thought finalization could come in two to three months. (In fact another six months—from September 12 to March 15—would elapse before full ratification.) If the time was so brief, I retorted, it was surely all the easier to suspend these rights.

We next debated all unresolved questions of the treaty one by one, in particular the German statement on the limitation of our armed forces. Again I insisted on delivering this statement not only to the Four Powers but also to our negotiation partners in Vienna. When Shevardnadze replied that our text proposal was drafted in such a way as to imply stipulations that made the ceiling dependent on the result of the Vienna II negotiations, I explained that we were presenting neither a package deal nor a prerequisite but were formulating an expectation. My Soviet counterpart laughed and commented that we could debate the point for hours. Trying to restate my remark in different words, I stated that our declaration should be seen in relation to the other negotiations in Vienna. This was a view he could finally agree to. I also informed him that I planned to deliver the declaration personally, along with Foreign Minister Meckel, in Vienna, before September 12, most probably in late August. It could certainly be incorporated in the concluding internationally binding legal arrangement within the framework of the Two-Plus-Four Treaty, but it was really addressed to all twenty-three participants in the Vienna disarmament negotiations.

When we began to discuss the relationship between the Soviet troops and the East German population, I suggested an all-out effort at cordial relations. It was obviously Moscow's choice, I said, to decide on the kind of contact its troops would have with the Germans. I had toured the Western Allies' forces in West Germany, and I would be happy to visit Soviet units on the territory of the present East Germany as well. Besides, West Germany offered many opportunities for friendship, including social clubs where the foreign troops and the locals could meet. Perhaps the Foreign Office and the Soviet Foreign Ministry could consider steps along the same lines. After all, half a million Soviet citizens were currently living in East Germany, and we would prefer for them to return to the Soviet Union with positive feelings and pleasant memories. Shevardnadze thanked me. When Soviet troops withdrew from Hungary and Czechoslovakia, there had been risky moments. He was also deeply troubled about the housing situation of the soldiers' families returning to the Soviet Union: Some were still living in tented compounds, even though winter was approaching. Many able young officers wanted to leave the army.

Next we returned to a particularly thorny topic: The expropriation measures taken before 1949 in the territory of the formerly Soviet-occupied zone. I pointed out that West Germany had made total restitution of all property Hitler had expropriated, mainly through so-called Aryanizations. No comparable action had been taken in the Soviet-occupied zone after 1945; on the contrary, property had been expropriated without a search for former Jewish owners or other owners persecuted by the Nazis. The former property of persecuted persons must definitely be returned, even if it had been expropriated a second time. When Deputy Foreign Minister Kvitsinsky suggested that individual cases could be investigated, I pointed out that a very large number was involved. Everyone must be entitled to restitution, even if expropriation had occurred according to valid laws of the occupied zones.

I wanted to preserve for the united Germany's lawmakers the freedom to decide on the how and when, and on the amount, of restitution payments and to keep open the possibility for persecuted persons of bringing legal action. Shevardnadze did not disagree, but he emphasized that the measures could not be revoked.

Ultimately the Two-Plus-Four talks made no changes in the previously agreed-upon provisions of the German-German Declaration and the Unification Treaty between the Federal Republic and the German Democratic Republic. The freedom of the unified Germany's lawmakers regarding this issue was preserved. Conversely, what was crucially important for the Soviet Union was our acknowledgment that the measures it had taken in its zone of occupation were legal; taking a different view of this aspect would have been to ignore the Soviets' way of negotiating and this particular negotiating position. As best I could tell, this aspect also played a large role in Shevardnadze's fears for the ratification process of the Two-Plus-Four Treaty in the Supreme Soviet. Our focus during the negotiations was to leave the decision on the issue of compensation entirely up to Germany. The decision as to how and when, and how much compensation should be given must be left to the courts and the constitutional offices of the united Germany.

During my visit to Moscow on August 16 and 17, 1990, it became clear that the Soviet Union was eager to get results by September 12. We had also been able to agree on how the other topics should be treated: On August 24 separate talks would be held with the German ministers of the treasury and of commerce. But Shevardnadze returned to the peace treaty: Since more and more concessions were made, the concept of a peace treaty should not perhaps be dropped altogether. I rejected that suggestion and called it unacceptable, particularly since our agreement in Ottawa on the structure of Two Plus Four had already explicitly decided this issue and all participants in the Two-Plus-Four meetings had decided against a peace treaty, most recently on July 17, 1990, in Paris.

On Thursday, August 30, I traveled to Vienna to deliver the statement on the limitations of German troops. East Germany was represented, not by Foreign Minister Meckel, as planned—the Social Democrats had left the East German government—but by Prime Minister De Maizière; for the transitional period before unification he had also assumed the office of foreign minister. After a brief conversation in one of our delegation rooms, we entered the conference room together—a symbolic gesture that warmed the atmosphere. We took adjoining seats as prescribed by protocol. The chairmen of the other delegations took their places at the tables, which were arranged in a square. It was our turn to speak.

In my address I recalled Foreign Minister Shevardnadze's statement at the beginning of the negotiations early in 1989, when he remarked that we were setting out to overcome the division of Europe. His words, I added, had proven dramatically correct. Europe was on the threshold of a new phase in its history. It was about to recover its unity and its identity; liberty, human and civil rights, constitutionality, and pluralistic democracy were becoming the unifying credo. Once again I explained the basic philosophy of the changes in Europe that we had done so much to bring about, seeing the German question as part of the developments in Europe. That view was the reason why the Atlantic Alliance's heads of state and government had suggested that our new identity be expressed in a joint declaration by NATO and Warsaw Pact member nations.

The imminent unification of Germany, I continued, marked a break of historic magnitude, not only for Germany but for the entire Continent. Overcoming the division of Europe and the unification of the two Germanys were inseparably intertwined. I quoted the French poet and diplomat Paul Claudel, who in 1945 had said that Germany did not exist to divide nations "but to make all those different nations that surround it sense that they cannot live without each other." Our Basic Law, I continued, obligated us to serve world peace in a unified Europe; we were therefore committed to the politics of responsibility, rather than to power politics. Finally I read our statement on the limitation of armed forces: "The government of the Federal Republic of Germany commits itself to the reduction of the armed forces of the unified Germany within three to four years to a manpower of 370,000 [land, air, and sea forces]. This reduction shall begin with the enforcement of the first CSCE treaty. Within the framework of this total ceiling, no more than 345,000 troops will belong to the land and air forces which, according to the agreed-upon mandate, are the sole subject of the negotiations on conventional armed forces in Europe." I added, "The federal government views its obligation to reducing land and air forces as a significant German contribution to the reduction of conventional armed forces in Europe." And now came the crucial sentence, which placed our step in the larger European context: "[The government] assumes that at follow-up meetings the other participants to these negotiations will make their contributions to increased security and stability in Europe, including measures to limiting manpower." Thus we had delivered our statement of commitment—not as part of the CFE negotiations in Vienna, as I had originally planned, but within the framework of this conference—and it was accepted as an important step toward the general reduction of armed forces in Europe. On the one hand this action stimulated disarmament in all of

Europe; on the other, it allowed us to avoid the appearance of an arrangement that discriminated against and singled out Germany.

But that was not the only issue that concerned me here. As I spoke, I was also intent on explaining our thoughts on continuing the Vienna negotiations. I therefore called for a program for military stability in Europe, emphasizing confidence- and security-building measures. I continued by appealing in favor of CSCE, which I characterized as a "framework of stability"; I suggested that the right time had come to expand and strengthen this framework by institutional means. New CSCE institutions were needed, I noted, for open discussion and resolution of conflicts between member nations, for periodic CSCE summits, for regular ministerial meetings, and for a permanent CSCE center for conflict prevention, as well as additional viable institutions. All these proposals would be on the agenda of the CSCE summit in November. After the members had listened to my declaration with great approval, Prime Minister De Maizière delivered East Germany's statement. Yet another crucial step toward Germany's and Europe's unity had been taken.

At the end of August a letter from Eduard Shevardnadze arrived, documenting the Soviet leaders' difficulties once the orthodox section of the leadership had understood the full extent of the changes that had been agreed to. All in all, the missive was a catalogue of requests for emendations. The letter seemed to corroborate our belief that Gorbachev and Shevardnadze were walking a tightrope.

The West frequently overlooked an important fact: Even before the Two-Plus-Four document was signed, the Soviet leaders were being asked for additional proof of their New Thinking by their Western counterparts. For example, it was expected that in the Persian Gulf conflict Moscow would join the West and turn against its old partner, Saddam Hussein—and Gorbachev and Shevardnadze, acting on their own conviction, fulfilled this expectation. They were determined to abolish the power politics of the past.

As early as the beginning of August 1990, speaking on the telephone, I had supported Shevardnadze's stand. I told him that I considered it an important moment for the United States and the Soviet Union to have reached the same conclusion concerning events in the Persian Gulf; their joint resolute response in the Security Council promoted global stability. Again, I said, their behavior proved that eliminating differences in Europe made it possible to assume shared responsibility on a global basis as well. We were interested in acting in concert with Moscow in this matter as well, in accordance with the new German-Soviet relations. Shevardnadze had welcomed European support of the Security Council's position, particularly since—he stressed his wish to speak frankly—the traditionally good relations with Iraq had made it harder for the leadership in Moscow to adopt the position it took. The Soviet Union had worked very closely with Iraq for decades, especially in the area of economics but on other levels as well. Nevertheless, any other decision would have been a mistake: Moscow had had no right to act differently. I assured him that Germany fully appreciated the solidarity the Soviet Union had shown with the other nations in the Security Council and its cooperation with the United States.

I noticed with increasing concern that the general population in the West as well as some influential voices in Germany did not realize that both the conclusion of Two-Plus-Four and Moscow's stand on the conflict in the Persian Gulf meant that the Soviet Union was abandoning significant positions. The ability to see through the eyes of another—enemy, rival, or associate—is invaluable in arriving at the proper conclusions.

The requests for emendations Shevardnadze had listed in his letter referred primarily to the time frame for the withdrawal of Soviet forces; the Soviets claimed that five to seven years, rather than the proposed three to four years, would be more realistic. Further, the treaty must specify additional arrangements in the area of security. It was also necessary to discuss the proper time to sign and ratify the document.

I understood that, because of their domestic problems, the Soviets were looking for certain assurances on the actual enforcement of the border agreement before they would sign the Two-Plus-Four Treaty. Concerns in Germany about proceeding in a different order seemed unfounded, particularly since the Polish government would also prefer that the agreement be signed before the conclusion of the Two-Plus-Four talks. That suggestion, however, met with resistance in Germany.

I was therefore eager to do all I could to prevent disagreements from weakening the historical value of the German-Polish border treaty. It was more than the price we paid for German unity: Though unification could not have been won without an acknowledgment of the border, the moral-historical dimension of these events must not be allowed to be lost. That effort was important both for the Poles and for our own people. In 1990 we did not barter unity for abandonment of the eastern territories; a criminal government and its criminal policies had gambled these away forty-five years earlier.

During the weeks that followed, the required work was again placed chiefly in Dieter Kastrup's hands. Once again he could wield his outstanding skills as well as the tremendous amount of trust he had earned among his associates. The negotiations he conducted were discussed again and again within a very small group at internal conferences and meetings. We were coming closer and closer to the great day, the trip to Moscow that was expected to culminate in the completion of the Two-Plus-Four process.

Friends from all over the world wished us well for the final stage. On Sunday, September 9, near noon, while I was at my desk at home, I received a telephone call from India's foreign minister, Inder Kumar Gujral, to extend his best wishes.

On September 10, James Baker briefed the NATO allies in Brussels on the American-Soviet summit, which had taken place in Helsinki the previous day. The principal topic had been the superpowers' cooperation in the conflict in the Persian Gulf, but Baker and Shevardnadze had also discussed the upcoming Moscow meeting. The fact that an air of goodwill had marked the conference in Helsinki, as Baker emphasized, made me feel confident about the final meeting. As Baker delivered his report at NATO headquarters, my thoughts strayed repeatedly. Saddam Hussein's attack on Kuwait proved that the negotiating process could be jeopardized by events over which we had no control. We had been right to press for speed from the outset.

On the evening of September 10 I was on the telephone with Shevardnadze, who had returned to Moscow. We discussed the few remaining questions, and even though our talk did not resolve them (we had not expected that it would), there was every indication that we were moving closer, and the certainty of an agreement in Moscow was beginning to emerge.

A Last-Minute Stumbling Block

On the morning of September 11, 1990, I flew to the Soviet capital. When we arrived at three o'clock in the afternoon Moscow time, I was surprised to see the depressed looks on the faces of Dieter Kastrup and Frank Elbe, who had come to meet me at the airport. They briefed me on last-minute difficulties concerning the wording of the treaty. At issue was Clause Three of Article Five, the question of whether after the withdrawal of Soviet forces allied military units could move into former East German territory. That unresolved question would play a major role in my scheduled talk with Shevardnadze.

Shevardnadze, who welcomed me warmly, asked me to forgive the delay in starting our scheduled talk. He explained that he had had to address the Supreme Soviet and then stay to answer delegates' questions. The meetings between Kastrup, Kvitsinksky, and Alexander Bondarenko had resolved most problems. As recently as six months earlier, it would have been hard to imagine the natural growth—as Shevardnadze called it—of current events, though the German question had always been in the air and the Soviets had always realized that at some point it would have to be addressed. It was fortunate, he emphasized, that our political endeavors did not lag behind the process.

These events had hardly been imposed on the Soviet Union from outside, I commented. His country had made its own contribution to the situation, as was proven, for example, by his own speech at the Vienna CSCE conference in early 1989. At that time he had stated that the Iron Curtain was growing rusty, and only a few months later Hungary had opened its borders. Tomorrow, I said, would not mark an end to the dynamics of events; what mattered now was to make sure that the onrush of coming events pursued a positive course. It was therefore crucial that Germany and the Soviet Union initial the treaty on mutual relations on the day after September 12, as a signal that matters were moving on. Shevardnadze nodded and remarked that it was a great honor for everyone present—including the two of us—to participate in this process, particularly since we had found solutions. The Soviet Union would enjoy a new relationship with the unified Germany, the one nation, as he put it. The external aspects of unification would be settled, and he was hoping that no controversial issues were lying in wait for the foreign ministers, even though his associates were complicated people, not as docile as mine. He must have meant to indicate that his advisers had not made it easy for him to agree to compromises and concessions, while he had evidently noticed—and correctly so—that Kastrup and I were entirely in agreement. He asked Kvitsinsky to speak.

The Soviet deputy foreign minister stated that the United Kingdom, as well as United States and France, insisted on their right to go on maneuvers and execute military exercises on the territory of the former East Germany. The Soviet Union, he remarked, was certainly prepared to cooperate in arriving at the proper wording. However, Great Britain was requesting a ministerial statement to the effect that the allies were free to perform maneuvers using fewer than 13,000 troops. Since such a provision was not in accordance with the agreement made between the Chancellor and Gorbachev in Arkhits, the foreign ministers had to settle the issue. As for Article Five, Clause Three, Kvitsinsky noted that Secretary Baker had informed me about his talk with Shevardnadze. According to their meeting, it was clearly important to the Soviet Union to have it laid down that large maneuvers be prohibited; the idea had therefore apparently arisen in Washington that military exercises with fewer than 13,000 troops could be permitted. President Gorbachev's and the Chancellor's statements in the Caucasus were not entirely identical; nevertheless, it had to be possible to find a solution. The question remained of who would decide the admissibility of such maneuvers with the participation of allied units after 1994—that is, after the withdrawal of all Soviet forces and long after Germany had gained full sovereignty. Neither the United Kingdom nor France, and certainly not the United States, had that authority, nor did the Soviet Union. Only the united Germany was in that position. I reminded the gathering that the preamble of the final document expressly stated that each nation's security concerns must be respected. The new German government would arrive at a sensible and responsible decision, and I would be happy to explain how our side would interpret such a regulation.

Shevardnadze and Kvitsinsky next discussed several different formulations. Finally the Foreign Minister suggested that the term *maneuvers* be avoided altogether; it would only lead to dissension.

Instead, the wording would mention only that troops would not be stationed in or moved through the debated territories.

I declared that Germany would decide whether small-scale maneuvers would be allowed, and Germany would act within the parameters of the preamble. Shevardnadze and I argued back and forth for a long time, as I pointed out that we should place some trust in the future: In as little as five years' time today's discussion might already seem obsolete. But Shevardnadze once again referred to the Chancellor's statement. I pointed out, however, that the Chancellor had said that foreign military units could not be moved into the territory in question.

Because I thought it dangerous to enter into yet another discussion of the wording of the treaty at this time, I said very firmly that the text of Article Five, Clause Three, must not be revised and that we certainly could make an official statement at the negotiating table to the effect that in interpreting this provision, the German government would take into consideration the security concerns of all nations involved, in accordance with the preamble, and would act sensibly and responsibly in reaching a decision. That proposal seemed to make sense to Shevardnadze. I was also prepared, I persisted, to state as much the following day at the ministerial meeting. Such a procedure put the decision squarely into our hands while avoiding an explicit ban of all maneuvers.

In order to conclude the discussion, which had arrived at a concrete result with my suggested wording, I pointed out that I had an appointment to meet with Douglas Hurd and asked if we could move toward a close. I did in fact want to meet Hurd for dinner in the German ambassador's quarters; however, I was also concerned that continuing this argument might complicate matters.

"We trust that you will make responsible and sensible decisions," Shevardnadze finally said. "But how long will you remain in office?"

"A long time," I replied. "How about you?"

Then I turned the discussion to the major bilateral treaty that Shevardnadze and I were scheduled to initial on Thursday, September 13. The actual signing was planned to be done by the Chancellor and President Gorbachev. I asked what should be done about the three other treaties, dealing with the transition, economic matters, and the accord on military units. Kvitsinsky reported that the last of these treaties required more negotiations; Shevardnadze suggested that we initial these treaties in New York. I objected. The foreign ministers were initialing the major treaty only because of its special significance; the particular negotiators could initial the other accords. Shevardnadze concurred.

I next addressed the suspension of the rights of the Four Powers, reminding the group that on August 17 Shevardnadze had elucidated the problem at the Supreme Soviet. Where did we stand now? Shevardnadze asked to postpone a decision until our meeting in New York. At that time, he said, all treaties would be ready, and enough time remained before the official day of German unification, October 3. After the bilateral agreement was finalized, it would be easier for him to endorse the suspension of the privileges until the Two-Plus-Four Treaty was enacted. In other words: Within the Soviet leadership, all decisions had been taken.

During our discussion Shevardnadze had gone to the telephone to discuss various proposals with Gorbachev. The question of possible maneuvers by allied military forces in the new German states was apparently too important for him to decide by himself. However, my suggestion, which placed the decision into the hands of the German government, appeared acceptable. I did not think that it would cause any problems in the West.

As we approached the end of our meeting, I said that the following day the historic significance of the results we had reached would be discussed, but even tonight I felt the need to emphasize that we recognized the significance of the treaty as well as of the contribution he, Shevardnadze, and Gorbachev had made. I wanted to thank him and express my gratitude as well as for the personal relationship that had developed between us. In view of my background, particularly my departure from the German Democratic Republic, I was especially moved by our friendship. Tomorrow, I said, the final regulations within the provisions of international law would be signed. But because we must never forget those who had lost their lives in that terrible war, Prime Minister de Maizière and I intended to honor the fallen Soviets at the Grave of the Unknown Soldier on September 13, and to pay our respects as well at the graves of those buried in the German soldiers' cemetery in Lublino. Though it was not common to lay a wreath on such an occasion, I did not want to leave Moscow without remembering the dead. Those who were setting out on a new and better future must not forget the past.

Shevardnadze replied that he too would have a few words to say on the momentous occasion, but that he did not wish to elaborate before addressing the Supreme Soviet a few days from now. He promised to try to find the appropriate words, for both the conclusion of the Two-Plus-Four process and the accomplishment of the treaty on bilateral relations and for their significance to Europe, the world, and the future. He wished for a final meeting without debates and without unresolved questions—such a meeting had symbolic significance as well. My words, Shevardnadze assured us, were important to him, since he was firmly convinced that he and I had done the right thing in Brest. It was also good that the document contained a passage concerning respect for monuments and for the past. Both sides, he noted, had dealt with dignity with this historical period, which was one of the most important ones in the history not only of our nations but of all of Europe. This policy was not a mistake, no matter if it met with criticism, and Gorbachev, who was planning to address me with regard to this, thought so as well.

As for the schedule for the following day, Shevardnadze explained that he would open the session and then give me the floor, to be followed by de Maizière, Baker, Hurd, and Dumas. He believed that we would meet for no more than an hour and a half to two hours at most; then Gorbachev would join us for the signing. Afterward a luncheon with the President was planned, the "family photograph" would be taken, and finally a meeting between Gorbachev and myself was scheduled. The treaty could be initialed on the morning of September 13. Though there would be no speeches at tomorrow's signing, they could occur at the initialing ceremony.

The ministerial meeting was scheduled for eleven o'clock in the morning of the following day. After my talk with Shevardnadze I sent word to Douglas Hurd that I could meet him now and went to the German delegation's quarters. Accompanied by one associate each, we sat down to dinner. The atmosphere was relaxed. I told Hurd that an agreement had been reached with Shevardnadze, showed him the text, and summarized our conversation. Hurd nodded. He complied with my request that he inform his political director that he agreed with the solution we had found. Our meal ended at a late hour on a very cordial note. It was nearly midnight when, after meeting with some German journalists, I returned to my hotel.

Once again Dieter Kastrup came to meet me looking downcast. We retired to my suite, where he told me that the British political director—supported by the Americans, with the French abstaining—had rejected the solution we had found. In fact, the British negotiator had insisted on including a clause expressly allowing maneuvers with fewer than 13,000 troops. That move was an unpleasant surprise. The Soviets had truly gone as far as they could go; they had placed the decision about maneuvers fully into German hands, without any guarantee as to what that individual decision would be in five years. It was impossible to predict the future course of events, even though one could assume that the issue would play a less weighty role in five years than it did at the moment. While our group was discussing what should be done, Frank Elbe was called to the telephone. His Soviet counterpart informed him that Shevardnadze had briefed Gorbachev on the outcome of the day's negotiations, as well as of the discussion held between the political directors while I was at dinner with Douglas Hurd. As a consequence, the Secretary General had decided to cancel the scheduled signing of the Two-Plus-Four Treaty. Shevardnadze asked Elbe to let me know that I could reach him by phone all night.

It became essential to act at once, particularly since I was afraid that when the public learned what Gorbachev had decided, they would believe that negotiations had failed at the last minute. In view of international occurrences, including events in the Persian Gulf, the topic in question—maneuvers—was not really very important. Nor was it an urgent issue. Five years from now Germany would be free to decide responsibly and in the spirit of the preamble to the Two-Plus-Four Treaty. Besides, the solution we had found meant that the North Atlantic Treaty Organization unreservedly protected the new German states. In view of that inclusion, whether or not maneuvers of the size intended could be held was not important. Considering how far the Soviet leadership had come, it could not be asked to go further at the last moment. I asked Elbe to call the hotel where the American delegation was lodged and to leave word for Baker that despite the late hour, I needed to see him immediately to discuss an important and complicated issue that was crucial for the following morning. The American response was understandable but not acceptable: Baker was already asleep, and he had taken a sleeping pill. Despite this, I left word that I was coming over immediately. If necessary, I would personally wake up my friend.

Baker received us in his suite, with only his closest associates present. Our group consisted of Dieter Kastrup, Frank Elbe, and myself. Baker and his associates were dressed in pajamas under grayish-brown robes, all the same, furnished by the hotel. That is why later, when the pressure was over, I would refer to this meeting as the bathrobe conference. The great work must not founder at the last moment, I entreated James Baker, especially not over an issue that was neither essential nor comprehensible. On no account must we risk the talks breaking off at this time. I was convinced that Gorbachev's and Shevardnadze's threat should be taken very seriously, and I urged Baker to support our position, particularly since the United States had been firmly with us every step of the way. It was essential that the signing ceremony take place in the morning at the specified time. I would be quite frank: I was certain that besides myself, de Maizière would participate, as would the Soviets, and I asked the American secretary of state to sit next to me. Each minister must now decide if he was willing to allow the negotiations to fail because of one minor issue. The public would then be able to see who was absent from the ceremony.

James Baker replied that the United States had always been on our side. Though it had supported Britain's position, he promised to come to my aid in this matter. In that case, I suggested, we should tell Shevardnadze immediately that the signing could take place. We could finish our conversation the following morning at the meetings of the four Western foreign ministers—France, the United Kingdom, the United States, and the Federal Republic of Germany—scheduled for half past eight in the French quarters. Baker agreed. We returned to our quarters, briefed de Maizière, and informed Shevardnadze that we were convinced that the signing would take place the following morning.

I was deeply agitated. It was not surprising that during this night and on September 12 I was troubled by arrhythmia. My signatures on the documents give evidence of my condition.

In the early morning hours of September 12, upon returning from my meeting with Baker, I sat by the open window and looked out into the Moscow night. Since 1969, on my first visit to Moscow as a member of the Bundestag, I had spent a lot of time in the city. My visits had taken place under very different circumstances; frequently I came alone as foreign minister, at other times I accompanied Chancellors Helmut Schmidt and Helmut Kohl, and on still other occasions, I was traveling with Presidents Walter Scheel, Karl Carstens, and Richard von Weizsäcker.

Of all these experiences, the one that had made the deepest impression on me was my first meeting with Mikhail Gorbachev in 1986. We had come a long way since then. Tomorrow, I was absolutely certain, the Two-Plus-Four Treaty would be signed, finally making German unity possible. The next big challenge would be internal unification, which had already started from below. Our constitutional obligation to aid in the unification of Europe and in bringing about peace in the world would remain, as would our obligation to stay committed to the basic values of our constitution and the policies of responsibility rather than power politics.

A long time ago, I thought to myself, especially during the long days and nights of recovery from tuberculosis and my stay at the sanatorium, I had often wished that I could have a part in bringing about German unity. Now these dreams had become reality. I was filled with enormous gratitude.

Consummatum Est: The Treaty Is Signed

I went early to the French quarters so as to be able to talk with Roland Dumas in private. "Roland, I have never asked for any special favors. Today I'm asking you to chair the meeting and to declare that France will sign the agreements in their present form." Without hesitation Roland Dumas promised to do so. At the meeting Jim Baker also confirmed that the United States would come to the table and sign the document. Douglas Hurd agreed as well.

It was my impression from the start that Hurd was unconditionally in favor of unification. On the eve of the signing he had not been troubled by the solution we had agreed upon with the Soviet Union. But evidently his associate took his instructions not only from Hurd but also from London, which may explain why, after Hurd had announced his approval during dinner, the British negotiator adopted a position that differed from that of his Foreign Secretary. The verbal agreement we had reached with the Soviet Union had been written down during the night. As a text signed by the six of us, it was eventually incorporated in the treaty.

The signing was delayed because there was a problem with the French translation. We provided some technical aid, lending our secretaries and interpreters—a small repayment for Roland Dumas's help earlier in the morning. Finally, we could take our places at the table. The Two-Plus-Four Treaty was ready, as was the communiqué. Eduard Shevardnadze made certain that the formal statement concerning the regulation of expropriations in the former Soviet-occupied zone, signed by Prime Minister de Maizière and myself, was at hand. Then we signed the document. The work was done.

Afterward Mikhail Gorbachev, with Eduard Shevardnadze by his side, received me. He opened our talk by noting that destiny had arranged for the Soviets and the Germans to be the leading actors in the process. All the events leading up to this day could not have happened without profound changes in the Federal Republic, the German Democratic Republic, and the Soviet Union; now we must be careful to navigate an extremely complicated stage of history with dignity. Such a process was very difficult within the Soviet community, he remarked, especially if, once Germany's political unification was finalized, all other treaties still seemed unresolved. That sense could lead to an explosive situation. This remark alluded to the significance of the bilateral major treaty and the necessity for further aid—not only from Germany but from the West as a whole. Gorbachev reminded me of the Chancellor's promise to support the Soviet Union now and in the future.

He then began to speak in personal terms; his tone was warm. The Secretary General thanked me for my personal conduct toward him and assured me that I could continue to count on him as a partner; he hoped that the reverse was true as well.

I could only return his sentiments, I replied. I explained that a lifelong dream of mine was coming true: From now on I would be living in the nation of my ancestral home. After fifty-seven years, all Germans were again united in *one democratic* state. I would be very pleased if Gorbachev could see his way to visiting Halle, so that I could thank him again there. Three years later, under entirely different circumstances, he reminded me of my invitation, and the visit came about in December 1993.

At the end of our conversation we shook hands wordlessly. We looked at each other and nodded. It was as if we were swearing an oath: Yes, we wanted to continue to work toward a better future for our nations, for a better Europe.

The day ended with a gala dinner in the guest house of the Soviet Foreign Ministry, to which Mikhail Gorbachev had invited the six foreign ministers. Now, after all the work was done, the conversations became personal and relaxed. Politics was placed in the background.

On September 13 Shevardnadze and I initialed the Treaty on Good Neighborly Relations, Partnership, and Cooperation. It had been the Soviets who had suggested the ministerial action, on the day following the signing of the Two-Plus-Four Treaty. They wanted to demonstrate that after the multilateral treaty was signed, new perspectives opened for the German-Soviet relationship; such a signal was also in our best interest, both in regard to bilateral relations and to stability in Europe. The speedy ratification of the Two-Plus-Four Treaty obviously played a role as well—it could be helped along by both the content and the date of the German-Soviet treaty. Shevardnadze therefore explicitly made the connection between September 12 and 13, 1990: "Wide horizons and comprehensive possibilities are opening up for Soviet-German cooperation."

After the signing and a subsequent conversation with the Soviet foreign minister, I flew back to Bonn. In our talk Shevardnadze again emphasized the importance of the "Big Treaty." It was evident that it was of great importance for the Soviet leaders not only to demonstrate, with the help of this agreement, concrete long-range possibilities, but also to do so only a day after the signing of the Two-Plus-Four Treaty. Shevardnadze noted that we must give a realistic demonstration to every nation that we were truly going about building a new relationship.

Finally I invited Shevardnadze to visit Halle. I reminded him that our numerous conversations had shown him how deeply the division of Germany touched me personally, and now it would give me great pleasure to visit my native city in his company. The local people should be able to see for themselves that these two men—Shevardnadze and Genscher—get along well with each other. In any case, I would tell them how much he had contributed to fulfilling their wish for unity and democracy.

On September 15 James Baker came to Bonn, if only for a few hours. This visit gave me another opportunity to thank him for his and his president's support. Now, however, we must look to the future: Since mid-1990 Baker and I had discussed ways to shape NATO and transatlantic relations in the post–Cold War world. "The Atlantic Ocean must not grow wider," was my key phrase. We agreed that the CSCE process should be intensified; new initiatives were necessary. We must move ahead, step by step, toward a foundation for a permanent and just peace in all of Europe— NATO's great objective.

I thought it equally necessary to strengthen relations with the United States and Canada on the one hand and with their European allies on the other. Originally I had planned to draft a transatlantic treaty to be signed in Paris, immediately before the CSCE summit, to strengthen and deepen our cooperation beyond the indispensable NATO Alliance. However, it proved impossible to draft an actual treaty in the time available; further, its ratification in the United States appeared problematic. Baker and I therefore decided to propose a transatlantic resolution, which did not require ratification even though it would be heard as a clear political message.

Referring to the transatlantic treaty, I told my associates, "To be resubmitted in five years." There is no doubt in my mind that Europe and North America bear a joint responsibility that demands new responses now that the Cold War is over. NATO alone will not be adequate to this task; we will need global cooperation in politics, trade, economy, ecology, and security. Global challenges categorically require no less. Similar instruments are called for in Europe; here too stability requires closer cooperation within the European Community—renamed the European Union.

The United States—which withdrew from Europe after the First World War, leaving the Continent to its own devices, with all the well-known consequences—remained in place after the Second World War, as the Marshall Plan, NATO, and participation in the

CSCE attest. Without the United States, the events of 1990 would not have been possible—at least not in the same way. But how will the United States behave now that the Cold War is over? And at this time, is Europe so very important? Is it not rather global cooperation that is needed?

I am firmly convinced that this partnership, which is not directed against others but geared toward freedom and stability, is an historical necessity, significant for all of Europe. Yet the nations thus united bear the shared responsibility of bringing together all of Europe, of establishing the foundation for peace in Europe defined in the Harmel Report, and to include Russia in a comprehensive cooperative effort. Russia is part of the G7, which must become the G8.

Jim Baker was followed to Bonn by Roland Dumas, who arrived later that same day. The next morning, I took him to Halle. One item on the agenda was a visit to the Market Church, where a crowd was waiting. In this public place I thanked Dumas and President Mitterand for their friendship in a difficult time, for their support, which had been crucial to the last moment before the Two-Plus-Four Treaty was signed. I had brought a copy of the treaty to give to Halle's mayor at the subsequent reception at the town hall. I held up the document: "This treaty opened the road to unity. It bears the names of my friend Roland Dumas, of Prime Minister de Maizière, of James Baker, of Douglas Hurd, of Eduard Shevardnadze, and of myself." In my hometown—as well as my homeland in a larger sense—my good and reliable friend in hard times was welcomed with deep gratitude and friendship. The following summer Jim Baker was to have a very similar experience when he attended the first meeting of the CSCE foreign ministerial Council. I took him to Halle as well, and the crowds expressed their great fondness for him. The people of Halle had not forgotten the enormity of his contribution to unification.

On September 22, at the invitation of my friend Uffe Ellemann-Jensen, I addressed the party congress of the Danish Liberals, who bestowed honorary membership on me. I took the opportunity to thank the Danish Foreign Minister for supporting German unity. The recognition I received from the Danish Liberals meant a great deal to me personally: By honoring me, they accepted the German

Liberals into their community at the time of our unification. They knew that they had nothing to fear from a German Europe, because a European Germany was being shaped.

On September 25, my flight to New York for the General Assembly of the United Nations started my international routine anew. And yet this time the entire trip took on a different tone. For the first time I no longer had to remind the assembled delegates that the Germanys must unite—they were about to do precisely that. Only a year had passed since I spoke in this same hall and negotiated opening our Prague embassy.

I began my address this year by expressing our feelings and our responsibility: "What determines the feelings of the Germans on this historic day is a pondering of the past and of our responsibility, not nationalist enthusiasm. We will not forget the endless misery that befell the nations of Europe and the world in Germany's name. We remember all the victims of the war and of the tyranny in Germany. We particularly remember the ineffable sufferings of the Jewish people. We recognize our responsibility, and we accept it."

I delivered the following message to the General Assembly of the United Nations:

> We Germans are uniting in the desire that none of these horrors must ever happen again. Our people live in a democratic state once more, united. Our common state will be founded on respect for the inviolable human rights. Only peace will originate from the soil of the united Germany.
>
> The fundamental principles of our constitution—human rights and dignity, democracy and constitutionality, social justice and respect for creation, peace and good neighborly relations—will determine our thoughts and actions forever.
>
> As an equal member in a united Europe, we are eager to serve world peace. This obligation from our Basic Law's preamble determines our policy. It is a rejection of power politics; it means a policy of responsibility.
>
> Ever since we joined the United Nations, the Federal Republic of Germany has demanded the national unification of our indivisible country before the forum of the United Nations. Since 1974 I personally have affirmed before the General Assembly of the United Nations

our will to work toward a state of peace in Europe, in which the German people would regain its unity in free self-determination.

Whenever I expressed these sentiments, I always also thought of the Germans in my native country—the German Democratic Republic— the people who live where I was born and grew up. I knew that they were longing for German unity just as fervently as we in the Federal Republic of Germany were. But living where they did, they could not express their feelings and beliefs. Now they have made their commitment to freedom and unity. Together we are now looking forward to German unity. We know that it will also bring unity for Europe.

Thus today, united in our hearts and in our desire, we greet the people of the world. . . . The Germans who are about to unite with us have, by their peaceful revolution, proven in the eyes of the whole world that they are committed to freedom, unity, and democracy, and therefore to Europe. . . . We Germans want only to live in liberty and democracy, in unity and in peace with all our neighbors. . . . Our politics is meant to be a politics of setting a good example. . . . On the eve of its unification Germany declares before the community of nations: We will do justice to our responsibility in Europe and in the world.

When in the night of October 2 to 3, 1990, the Germans unite, they will be motivated by gratitude and joy, by reason and responsibility. That connects us with the peoples of Europe and the world. The united Germany will make its contribution to peace and unity, in Europe and in the world.

The talk on the fringes of the United Nations assembly was also different this time; our unity and its significance was on everyone's lips. Saddam Hussein's war of conquest was also the subject of many discussions, and in that area it became evident that we had taken the correct course when, fearful of unforeseen international events, we had insisted on speed in the Two-Plus-Four talks.

On October 1 and 2 the CSCE's ministerial conference was held on American soil for the first time. Twenty-four years had passed since I had told Soviet Prime Minister Kosygin, "We are in favor of such a conference, but only if the United States and Canada participate as well." That was in the summer of 1969, and I was still a member of the opposition. It was the German Eastern treaties that first cleared the way; the Soviet Union realized that any attempt to drive a wedge between Europe and North America would fail. The United States, though holding no high opinion of CSCE but believing that it posed no threat to American interests, agreed to participate. As early as the 1980s it had begun to take a more favorable view of CSCE's potential and to use the organization primarily for human-rights issues. During the Bush administration the United States also realized how right Germany was in believing that CSCE was changing the situation in the Communist countries, since it offered a stable framework for advancing a transformation from above and encouraging it from below. We believed that CSCE was thus in the best position to give structure and weight to a new Europe. These were the goals which the Paris Charter, which was scheduled to be signed on November 19, 1990, was to serve. The New York conference was intended as a preparation for Paris. For us, the timing was ideal: On October 3 Germany would be reunited, and even earlier, on October 1, I could brief the CSCE ministerial conference on the outcome of the Two-Plus-Four talks. Thus we adhered to our earlier promise that we would present the result of the Two-Plus-Four process to CSCE.

Even earlier, the foreign ministers of France, the United Kingdom, the Soviet Union, and the United States signed the document suspending their rights over Germany as a whole as well as over Berlin. On October 3, 1990, therefore the united Germany would be free from any threat of outside interference. However, it would gain full sovereignty only with the ratification of the Two-Plus-Four Treaty by the Four Powers and by Germany itself. Now the Four Powers declared that the effectiveness of their rights and responsibilities in regard to Berlin and Germany as a whole, effective from the time of Germany's unification until the taking effect of the treaty on the final arrangement in regard to Germany, was suspended.

In my twenty-three years as minister of the interior and of foreign affairs I was forced to accept much that did not cause me unalloyed joy. But the Four Powers resolution was one event I acknowledged with satisfaction and gratitude. I was fully aware of its historic significance.

It meant most of all that the obligation to understand German politics as a politics of responsibility grew stronger as we achieved unity; even this suspension of rights served to deepen it. To assert as much in the face of those Germans who saw their country as a powerhouse serving their selfish interests once more would be of particular importance. Never again must nationalism be allowed to gain a foothold in Germany.

Only a year had passed since I had declared, on the balcony of our embassy in Prague, that the road was clear. On October 1, 1990, it was the American president who submitted comprehensive proposals for institutionalizing CSCE—a significant change as well. We now held identical opinions in still another new area, the evaluation of CSCE. President Bush openly stated that together we could forge a new transatlantic partnership in CSCE—a league of free nations, as he called it, that spans the ocean. This assertion was more than we had ever asked for: We had always limited the term *transatlantic partnership* to the relationship between the European and the North American allies. President Bush, it was clear, was thinking in terms of the Harmel Report, with its objective of a permanent and just foundation for peace in all of Europe. In that respect, too, George Bush proved himself a politician of high caliber.

As Bush spoke, I was reminded of the many difficulties we had encountered in dealing with United States officials on the lower and middle rungs of the hierarchy and even with some aides at the United States embassy in Bonn, whenever the topic was the significance and potential of CSCE. Bush and Baker, as well as their close associates, had recognized the potential of CSCE sooner. Others accused us of trying to replace NATO with CSCE. They understood neither the process of CSCE nor NATO's political function as defined in the Harmel Report. At the time I could not have known that their narrowness would have an effect even in reviews of the Two-Plus-Four talks.

In New York, I, too, advocated further expansion of CSCE, pointing to the need for regular meetings of the heads of state and government, for a ministerial council for security and cooperation in Europe, a conflict-prevention center, and a center for conflict resolution. I also called for the effective protection of human and civil rights and the rights of minorities.

On the night of October 1, 1990, I left New York so that I could be with my family in Berlin the following day. It was the eve of unification; outside the Reichstag we experienced the unforgettable midnight hour of German unification. Unity had not come about on its own. Was it a gift, as people often say? Yes, if the term is meant as a gift after everything done in Germany and done by Germans to other peoples between 1933 and 1945. But since then, the Germans in West and East had also earned this new unity, by peacefully reconstructing and creating a free democracy in the West and by the peaceful revolution for freedom in the East. Trust was established step by step along a long road.

Speaking outside the Reichstag in Berlin, the President remarked: "We are determined to complete Germany's unity and liberty in free self-determination. As for our task, we are aware of our responsibility before God and man. We are eager to serve world peace in a united Europe."

It is important to remember always that regaining unity was not a matter of course, that it was not inevitable. Our awareness of our own history must continue to guide us, as Richard von Weizsäcker had noted on May 8, 1985. A list of the milestones on the road to German unity must include that speech. The historic address sharpened Germans' awareness of their responsibility and built worldwide trust, which was especially necessary for us in the years 1989–90. Now, however, we found ourselves on the dais outside the Reichstag: Richard von Weizsäcker and Helmut Kohl, with whom I was connected by eight years, almost to the day, of joint political work, as his deputy and foreign minister in the government coalition of CDU/CSU and FDP, which he headed.

Kohl and I had shared difficult times, and some disappointments, in our professional and personal relationship. However, there had been great moments in recent months, and the present hour crowned our collaboration. Such an event brings people closer than is thought possible by many who are in the harsh business of politics.

Willy Brandt was with us as well. He too probably experienced this day as the zenith of a long and frequently difficult political life.

The End of a Long Road: The German-Polish Border Treaty

In late 1990 a final diplomatic move remained, one of great impact. The German-Polish border treaty marked a new beginning in German-Polish relations. On the morning of November 14 I left for Warsaw.

Poland was naturally eager to invest the signing of the treaty with a festive character. The Poles had hoped that I could arrive a day earlier, and they assumed that I would stay for two days. When I telephoned Foreign Minister Skubiszewski about the schedule during my visit, I asked him to remember what the treaty meant to many Germans; I wanted no festivities and no official dinner with speeches. Further, I planned to arrive in the morning and leave Warsaw that same night.

When I parted from my wife the morning I flew to Poland's capital, the farewell was more difficult than usual for both of us. What would she feel as her husband signed a treaty that absolutely acknowledged that her home, Silesia, from where she had been forced to flee with her mother and brother at the end of the Second World War, had ceased to belong to Germany? My wife had understood my position on the border issue from the outset, she had always supported it without reservation. Like me, she was convinced that new misery must never be allowed to set in. Yet she remained—and remains to this day—a Silesian who loves her home.

In Warsaw, Foreign Minister Skubiszewski met me at the airport. In the car I explained to him once more why I had rejected any festivities connected with my visit. My signature on the treaty served as a link between the burden of our past and the Germans' moral insight and the responsibility for peace that grew out of this burden. I also asked that the traditional drinks not be served after the signing. The occasion did not allow for champagne glasses.

We had a detailed discussion of the order of events. Earlier, there had been a long debate on which ambassadors should be invited; the Polish government wanted to include the ambassadors of the Four Powers. Why the representatives of the Four Powers? I had asked. We were here to attend to a strictly German-Polish matter, even though it had been discussed within the framework of the Two-Plus-Four negotiations. Skubiszewski, a highly educated man whom I held in great esteem for personal and professional reasons, understood my concerns perfectly. The ceremony at the signing was therefore as simple as it was dignified. I chose to speak last, after Prime Minister Mazowiecki and the Polish Foreign Minister.

On that November 14, 1990, I did not want to keep silent about the aspect of the day that was painful to Germans. Part of the new relationship between Germany and Poland was that our Polish partners understood what the treaty meant to us, and it was important that these circumstances were addressed by someone the Poles knew to be trying sincerely and with all his strength to achieve a new relationship between Germans and Poles. It was crucial to point out that no sacrifice had been forced on us. We were acting in accordance with our own historical and moral responsibility, and we were taking this step in full awareness of the crimes that had been committed in the name of Germany and by Germans against the Polish people. We also realized that questioning the existing German-Polish border would lead Europe into a new disaster and plunge Germans into the abyss—this time irrevocably: "Confirming the existing border is Germany's voluntary decision. No one has compelled us to do so." In Warsaw I also remembered, as I had done repeatedly on other occasions, the expellees. I expressly honored their moral contribution to reconciliation and their contribution to creating a free social order in the Federal Republic of Germany. The decision we were making by signing the treaty, I said, was not an easy one for Germans— for none of us, not even for me. Yet for those, I continued, who had lost their homes and suffered the anguish of expulsion, this step was particularly painful. At this moment their feelings and their committment to peace earned our special respect, since losing one's *home* is a heavy sacrifice. And our thoughts were also with those who lost their lives in the course of expulsion. "Our feelings do not diminish the significance of our decisions as a contribution to peace in Europe. They do not diminish the significance for a new European future. They only make clearer the profound awareness of our responsibility to peace in Europe."

When I spoke these words, I thought especially of my wife. The treaty did justice to my profound conviction. And yet, signing it was a difficult act for me. I signed in the full awareness that we were moving in the right direction and that morally we were doing the right thing.

Over the years a deep personal relationship had developed between Foreign Minister Skubiszewski and myself. It was therefore possible in 1991 to arrange a meeting in Weimar between Dumas, Skubiszewski, and myself, at which we jointly delivered a French-

Polish-German statement on the future of Europe. It was the first meeting among these three countries' foreign ministers, and at the end of it we jointly committed ourselves to the unity of Europe. Thus was formed the Weimar Triangle or Weimar Arc, as it has been called: France, Poland, and Germany sharing responsibility for the unity of Europe. This signal originated in Weimar, the city of Goethe and Schiller.

History frequently surprises us with events that go beyond the imagination of even the most audacious novelist. As a conclusion to our meeting, I had invited both my counterparts to go sightseeing not only in Weimar, but in another town as well. Skubiszewski suggested Naumburg, which, like Weimar, had been part of East Germany. He wanted to see Naumburg Cathedral because his brother, an art historian, had told him a great deal about its architecture.

Dumas had to return to Paris, but Skubiszewski and I flew to Naumburg by helicopter. We proceeded by car to the marketplace, where we were welcomed by the mayor and representatives of the city council. A large crowd had gathered outside the city hall. We heard military music—was it a police band or an orchestra of the Bundeswehr? As we got out of the helicopter, we saw that we were being serenaded by a Soviet army band that was still stationed in the eastern part of Germany. The mayor later explained to us that it had been impossible to find a Bundeswehr orchestra in time, and that he had therefore asked the Soviet army to help out; they had instantly agreed to provide the musical accompaniment to the event. Skubiszewski and I looked at each other, and when we had a few minutes alone, we commented: "Who would have thought possible a Europe where a Soviet army band can serenade the Polish and German foreign ministers at a visit in a united Germany! Truly, a new future has begun."

At every stage on the road leading to this day nothing had been given us as a gift. We earned every detail by taking responsibility for the past and for the future, by dealing honestly with our own history and sincerely with our neighbors. An attitude was needed that broke with the Old Thinking's categories of national egotism and power; we were compelled to acknowledge responsibility and to act responsibly.

The relationships between Germany and France and between Germany and Poland are without a doubt a deciding factor for the future of the entire Continent. If the Germans, French, and Poles act jointly as Europeans and do not allow nationalism to arise again, they will exert a confidence- and peace-building effect on all of Europe. Our commonality in favor of Europe can and will result in a new way of thinking, a new culture of coexistence. Such is the moral and historical dimension of the Weimar Arc. An encounter and a collaboration associated with the name of a city that in the course of its history led us to the heights of European intellect and European culture and yet never lets us forget the horrible abysses—with the memory of all the horrors that, only a few miles away, occurred at the concentration camp called Buchenwald. We would do well to perceive this Weimar Arc as symbolizing a constant German-French-Polish obligation toward Europe.

Part Five

New Crises and New Developments

12

Germany and the War
in the Persian Gulf

The Invasion of Kuwait: The Community of Nations Responds

In the early morning of August 2, 1990, Iraqi forces invaded Kuwait with tanks and airplanes. Following the attack on Iran, this incursion marked the second attack by Iraq of a neighboring country in a decade.

President Bush condemned Iraq's aggression the same day and called on the international community to take a clear and unyielding stand against Baghdad. After meeting with Bush in Aspen, Colorado, British Prime Minister Thatcher called Iraq's invasion absolutely unacceptable; if such behavior were tolerated, she remarked, no nation in the region could feel safe. At the instigation of the United States, the United Nations Security Council convened in New York that same August 2. A resolution was issued—with fourteen in favor and Yemen abstaining—which asserted that Iraq's invasion of Kuwait signified a disturbance of world peace and international security, which the United Nations condemned in all respects. Further, the Security Council demanded that Iraq withdraw all its armed forces immediately and unconditionally to the positions they had held on August 1, 1990; it also called on Iraq and Kuwait to begin immediate negotiations to settle their differences. The resolution declared that the United Nations was prepared to support all efforts in that direction, particularly those of the Arab League and would reconvene whenever necessary to consider further steps to assure that the resolution was observed.

The following day, after consulting at the Moscow airport, the foreign ministers of the Soviet Union and the United States issued a joint statement in which they called on the world community to stop shipping weapons and military material to Iraq and to follow the condemnation of Iraq's aggression with concrete steps. On August 4 the European Community voted to impose sanctions, among them a complete ban on the import of crude oil from Iraq and Kuwait; the confiscation of Iraqi property; the ban on exporting weapons and other military material; the suspension of military, scientific, and technical cooperation with Baghdad; and the freezing of trade preferences. In Paris, Roland Dumas raised the possibility of a naval blockade of Iraq. In the name of the movement of the nonaligned nations, whose acting president he was, Budomir Loncar, the Yugoslav foreign minister, condemned the invasion and demanded the unconditional withdrawal of Iraqi forces and recognition of the constitutional government and the sovereignty of Kuwait.

The German government condemned the attack on Kuwait. On the very day of the Iraqi attack we made contact with friendly and allied governments in order to cooperate in a concerted, united action. No doubt our most important allies were more surprised than we were. For us, this new aggression fit in with the image of the Iraqi government's policies, which strive for hegemony in the region. Some of our important allies, however, had supported Saddam Hussein's regime for years with arms shipments, because they saw it as a bulwark against the Ayatollah's regime in Tehran, which they regarded as more dangerous. When I called Iraq the aggressor at the time that country attacked Iran, my verdict met with reservation, even with criticism, in some Western nations. Israel, however, shared our view that Saddam Hussein was a threat not only to his own country but to the entire region.

We were extremely concerned about the fate of Germans and

other foreigners in Iraq and Kuwait. Saddam Hussein prevented thousands of foreign citizens who lived and worked in Iraq from leaving the country. They were held as hostages, whenever possible close to war-related installations. In Kuwait, which held approximately 400 Germans, close to ten thousand Westerners were ordered to gather at certain hotels; otherwise, they were told, they and their governments would have to bear full responsibility for all negative consequences resulting from actions by hostile forces. Saddam Hussein further announced that the Westerners would be released as soon as President Bush gave written assurance that United States forces would be withdrawn from Saudi Arabia, that the economic blockade against Iraq would be called off, and that the country would not be attacked.

On August 20 Iraq even went so far as to demand that the diplomats who had remained in Kuwait close down their embassies. German concerns centered on the unification process, which had entered its crucial phase in the summer of 1990. When the Gulf crisis erupted, we were approaching the end of the Two-Plus-Four talks among the United States, the Soviet Union, the United Kingdom, France, and the two Germanys; only a few weeks remained for drafting the accord, suspending the Four Powers' privileges, and negotiating the bilateral German-Soviet treaty.

My first thought after Iraq's attack was therefore directed to the possible effects of this event on the relationship between the West and the Soviet Union, which was crucial to German unification. How could the Federal Republic support the interests of the international community of nations in the Persian Gulf? Like the other friendly and allied governments, we were worried about possible consequences for the Middle East.

When, mindful of the Iraqi troops' threat to Saudi Arabia and other countries, the United States decided to station troops in Saudi Arabia, Germany unconditionally endorsed the plan to use American military installations in Germany for these purposes. That step was an important element in confidence building, particularly since earlier, under different circumstances, the Federal Republic would have been much more restrained—and for good reasons.

As early as August 16, 1990, a fleet of German minesweepers sailed out of German ports for the Adriatic. On August 20 I met with the Chancellor and Defense Minister Gerhard Stoltenberg.

We confirmed our belief that our constitutional law precluded the possibility of sending German troops to the Gulf to participate in the use of force. The state of the Two-Plus-Four talks also suggested a reserved attitude.

On August 23, 1990, I rendered an accounting to the Bundestag: "Our Basic Law does not permit us to send troops into territory beyond the borders of our alliance. We have informed our allies that the federal government has taken up discussions with the Social Democratic opposition on an amendment to the Basic Law. It is our objective to enable the German forces to participate in military actions that have been voted in by the Security Council in accordance with the provisions of the United Nations Charter. The Federal Republic of Germany thus expresses its preparedness, once the division of Germany has been overcome and the East-West conflict has been allayed, to assume its responsibility for securing world peace within the framework of the United Nations and on the basis of its charter."

This issue sharply divided public opinion. The West German government announced that it was prepared to make tracker tanks available. The speed with which some were ready to abandon their former reserve, based on their interpretation of the Basic Law and of our particular German history, was astonishing, as was the support certain circles gave to military action on the part of West Germany, without any consideration of the fragile Two-Plus-Four process and the relationship between Moscow and Baghdad, which had been close in the past. These people entirely ignored the fact that the Bundeswehr was not prepared for action in the Gulf, either psychologically or in terms of training, equipment, and logistics.

On August 25, 1990, the United Nations Security Council passed Resolution No. 665, which empowered the member nations' naval forces to take appropriate measures for enforcing the embargo of Iraq. There was talk of a significant exception in the history of the world organization, since to this time the Security Council had only twice approved the use of force to compel the realization of its resolutions—in 1950, in the Korean conflict, and in 1965, regarding Rhodesia. Since even the Soviet Union and China, despite their traditionally close relations with Iraq, endorsed the resolution, the Iraqi dictator found himself isolated to a degree the world had never known. The end of the Cold War, it seemed, gave rise to new forms of cooperation outside of Europe as well.

The direction German foreign policy would take was clearly drawn. The salient point was to stand up to Iraq resolutely even while availing ourselves of every diplomatic opportunity to move the Baghdad dictator to retreat. The principal objective was to end Iraq's occupation and annexation of Kuwait and to safeguard the security of the nations in the region. The embargo the United Nations Security Council had imposed, which was in effect from August on, was intended to restore Kuwait's territorial integrity and sovereignty. The essential requirement was not only the consistent enforcement of the resolution but also solidarity with those nations particularly affected by the crisis, since the embargo could be successful only if the nations with close economic ties to Iraq received aid in shouldering the burden of the embargo and that of the resulting flood of refugees that was to be expected. That situation applied first of all to the Kingdom of Jordan, which found itself in a vulnerable position and with which we had enjoyed very cordial relations for years. Egypt was also deeply affected economically by the return of hundreds of thousands of its citizens from Iraq, as was Turkey, which up until that time had not only received a large part of its crude oil supply from Iraq but had close economic ties with Iraq in general.

In all these considerations I mainly counted on the position taken by the Security Council. That its resolutions were so unequivocal proved that overcoming the East-West conflict had also enhanced the United Nations' ability to act in new ways; now the United States and the Soviet Union could agree on and implement concerted action. That was a crucial difference, since it was only the unity and resolve of the community of nations that could limit Saddam Hussein's expansionist policies and possibly compel him to retreat.

On September 14, after Iraqi troops in Kuwait had forced their way into the French and Dutch embassies, the EC issued a statement condemning this action as a serious violation of international agreements. Four days later the foreign and defense ministers of the WEU (Western European Union), meeting in Paris, followed France's suggestion to coordinate the use of all WEU members' naval forces in the Persian Gulf, though without a joint supreme command. With the exception of Luxembourg and Germany, all WEU members participated in the naval action.

Speaking to the Bundestag, I emphatically condemned the fact that citizens of the Federal Republic and other countries were detained against their will in Iraq and Kuwait. I called attention to the particularly reprehensible fact that they were kept close to military bases, which violated international law and the norms of civilized conduct. I made it clear that the Federal Republic and the European Community were in agreement on ignoring Iraq's demand to close foreign embassies in Kuwait, since Iraq had no right to make such a demand. Compliance with the demand would be tantamount to accepting Iraq's annexation of Kuwait. Further, our diplomats were needed to look after our nationals trapped in Kuwait. I expressed my thanks and appreciation to the members of our embassies in Kuwait and Baghdad for their willingness to continue their work; they were performing their duties under the worst possible conditions.

All of us realized that Iraq's aggression had plunged the world into a serious crisis, which must be resolved by energy, solidarity, and prudence. It was not the United Nations countermeasures that posed a threat to world peace but Iraq's aggression—a fact that must not be forgotten. Particularly in view of anti-American protests in West Germany that came to the surface in those months, I was resolute in pointing out the true state of affairs: "Resist the first step," was my motto. The conclusion of the great European peace that was to find its visible expression in the CSCE conference of November 1990 must not open opportunities for aggression elsewhere in the world. Europe's responsibility for peace extended to these regions.

In response to the U.S. government's August 30 query as to whether Bonn was prepared to assume a share of the cost of the necessary measures in the Gulf, Chancellor Kohl declared on September 13 that the Federal Republic was willing to do so within its limitations; he repeated his earlier statement that after the November elections to the Bundestag he would introduce a constitutional amendment allowing Germany to deploy the Bundeswehr in areas of crisis within the framework of the United Nations. On September 15 Secretary Baker came to Bonn to consult on the details of the measures and support we had pledged. Helmut Kohl and I were in agreement with the administration, the parliamentary opposition, and the majority of our population that we should make a significant contribution to the liberation of Kuwait and the pacification of the Middle East—but not by sending German troops into action.

The Soviet Union was willing to act in concert with the West, particularly the United States, in this crisis, but it was unwilling to participate in military deployments. For Gorbachev and Shevardnadze to join Washington and the European Community in this matter was not an easy decision from the outset. Iraq had been close to Moscow for decades. Large segments of the Iraqi army had been equipped and trained by the Soviet Union; at the time of the invasion some 8,000 Soviet advisers were stationed in Iraq.

My respect for the efforts of these two politicians, who were attempting to comply with the Security Council's Resolution No. 660 diplomatically and to avoid a military conflict, was all the greater. I supported their efforts at mediation—which, however, were to no avail. Saddam Hussein could not be moved.

On September 26, at the United Nations General Assembly, I stated: "We condemn Iraq's aggression against its Arabic and Islamic neighbors, against Kuwait, a United Nations member nation. This community of nations must not permit a country to be attacked and annexed. Aggression must be treated as aggression, blackmail as blackmail, violation of human rights as violation of human rights, lest the spirit of international law be compromised." In my address I further assured the United Nations of our unqualified support of its demands: complete and unconditional withdrawal from Kuwait, reinstitution of the country's full sovereignty, and immediate release of all hostages.

On November 18 Saddam Hussein announced that all foreign nationals would be allowed to leave Iraq by Christmas. That statement gave us reason to hope. By this time several heads of government and high-ranking statesmen from all over the world, among them Willy Brandt, working through bilateral talks and negotiations in Baghdad, had gradually achieved the release of more and more foreign nationals.

But the situation in Iraq continued to escalate. Saddam Hussein was clearly unwilling to withdraw from Kuwait voluntarily. The trade embargo was scheduled to be in effect until January 15,

1991. The Security Council had made it unmistakably clear to Saddam Hussein that the United Nations resolutions—which were unconditionally supported by Germany's government—would be enforced with military power unless he complied by that date. This ultimatum demonstrated a new quality in international crisis management: Thanks to the participation of Egypt, Syria, and Morocco, the United Nations' mustering of forces was a concerted action by Western and Arab countries.

In December 1990, the Turkish government requested the deployment of units of the AMF (Allied Mobile Force). Since these batallions included air and land units of the Bundeswehr, the proposal triggered a vehement controversy, both in the German populace and within the nation's political parties, in view of the NATO Treaty.

NATO was eager to demonstrate its determination to defend Turkey against outside attack. In this context Germany committed itself to sending German air units to Turkey to deter Saddam Hussein from attacking our ally.

By now the public increasingly demanded our actual military participation in the Gulf coalition. Yet even aside from constitutional qualms, we had to bear in mind the fact that the Two-Plus-Four Treaty had not yet been ratified by Moscow, and we were therefore well advised to take the Soviet Union's domestic situation into account. We must in no way supply the forces that opposed Mikhail Gorbachev's policy in regard to Germany with valid arguments; if the Soviet parliament refused to ratify the Two-Plus-Four Treaty, the decision would have catastrophic consequences for Germany and Europe. Shevardnadze's decision, on December 20, to resign from his post as foreign minister had disconcerted me greatly.

Shevardnadze justified his resignation in the following words: "This is my protest against the impending dictatorship. The democrats are quitting the scene, and a dictatorship is approaching—I am not speaking lightly. No one knows what the dictatorship will look like, what kind of dictator there will be, or what things will be like. I will always support the ideas of renewal and of democracy." And he continued, "If you create a dictatorship, no one can say who will be the dictator. When you push the button, you decide not only on Gorbachev's fate but on that of perestroika and democracy." Though he did not say so explicitly, I thought that his concluding sentence could only mean that the end of perestroika would also jeopardize ratification of the Two-Plus-Four Treaty in the Supreme Soviet. Given this particular situation, therefore, I opposed the use of Bundeswehr troops in the Gulf for reasons not only of constitutionality but also of foreign policy. As matters turned out, several more months would pass before the Soviet ambassador handed me the ratification document at the German Foreign Office on March 15, 1991; not until then did Germany regain its full sovereignty.

On January 14, three days before war was declared, all German parliamentary parties issued a joint resolution appealing to the Iraqi dictator to save his people from war by withdrawing from Kuwait. Helmut Kohl declared that it was Saddam Hussein who held the key to war or peace and urged him to let reason prevail. These reflections resulted in the following principles for Germany's policy in the Iraq crisis:

- Extremely close cooperation with the United States in the spirit of partnership in order to solve this conflict was central to Germany's position.
- Concerted actions to reestablish peace and Kuwait's independence precluded unilateral action on the part of Germany, since we must make our contribution within the framework of the community of nations.
- Since the use of Bundeswehr troops was not a possibility, it was important for us to make relatively high nonmilitary contributions to support the defensive alliance.
- The Persian Gulf crisis must not jeopardize the process of German unification or, above all, cooperation with the Soviet Union.
- In the course of the unification process, the Federal Republic must once again demonstrate its trustworthiness in matters of foreign policy and its loyalty to the other Western democracies.
- We must put particular effort into Germany's historically founded responsibility to securing the existence of Israel.

In my official address to the German Bundestag of February 22, 1991—when the war had gone on for more than a month and Iraq was forced to retreat farther and farther—I once again clarified our position. We were on the side of international law, I remarked, on the side of the United Nations, and on the side of the liberation coalition: No other stand would have done justice to the lessons from our history or to our constitutional values. We were aware that our allies' soldiers in the Gulf—principally the American, French, and British troops—were wearing the same uniforms as those who had stood by us here in Europe, some even in West Germany. At the hour of a significant threat to West Berlin, they had not hesitated to create the airlift, and along with us they had guaranteed peace in Europe at a time when it was imminently threatened by Soviet intervention in Hungary and, subsequently, in Czechoslovakia. I also expressed appreciation to the Arab forces within the coalition. Their participation made it impossible for Saddam Hussein to present himself as the protector of Arab interests. Hussein was waging war even on his own people.

This last point was particularly important. In negotiations with my friends in the West I had repeatedly warned against equating Saddam's regime with the Iraqi people. Public statements and resolutions tended to speak merely of Iraq. Yet it was Saddam's regime that was responsible; the Iraqi people had not been consulted. They were themselves victims of the policy of aggression.

Talks in Israel

Germans who were watching television on January 18 and witnessed Iraqi missiles hitting Israel for the first time must have experienced a profound shock. Germany bore a special responsibility for Israel's security. In Israel voices were raised calling for counterstrikes to destroy Iraqi missile installations. But the government in Jerusalem refused to be provoked. The responsible, extraordinarily restrained conduct of the Israeli government and the nation's people deserved all our respect and support.

Two days later, a Sunday, I telephoned the Chancellor at home to say that I thought it necessary for us to visit Israel and follow the visit with a trip through its neighboring nations. Though Helmut Kohl agreed in principle, he did not believe that an immediate decision was required. I was none too pleased at his response. I also advised the Chancellor to make a contribution to the speedy repair of incurred damage. We finally agreed that a decision should be taken early the following week. The Chancellor endorsed financial aid but not until the matter had been discussed with the minister of finance. That discussion took place three days later, on January 23; Waigel immediately agreed to financial support. Only then did the Chancellor propose sending a delegation to the area, so that the entire coalition could express its concern and solidarity. Unfortunately the spontaneity of the gesture was lost, but when I talked with Prime Minister Yitzhak Shamir, who treated me with exceptional cordiality, I realized that he had understood our action correctly. He and I had known each other for a long time, and he knew where I stood in regard to Israel.

In light of the missile attacks I wanted to assure Israel of the German people's solidarity, respect, and active support. Israel needed to know that after the unification Germany continued to stand by its side. Together with the minister for economic cooperation and development, Carl-Dieter Spranger, I visited some of the sites that had been severely damaged by the Iraqis' Scud missiles.

In our conversation Foreign Minister David Levy remarked, "Saddam Hussein's chemical weapons, as well as his nuclear technology, came from Germany and enable him not only to threaten Israel but to destroy it. The Israelis still bear the scars of their sad past. Today the people are trapped in airtight rooms, wearing gas masks. We never would have believed that such a state of affairs would recur." I expressed my understanding of his outrage and his disgust with those Germans who, ignoring our laws, were complicit in constructing poison-gas factories in Iraq. I was all the more angry at that unconscionable conduct given the fact that I had been the one who had insisted on toughening export regulations, increasing the penalties for violations. I had had differences of opinion with a number of finance ministers when it came to arms-export policy and export legislation. In that area, too, Germany's policy of responsibility had to prove itself; the country must not lose its direction because of power politics or economic concerns.

Our reservations regarding the export of weapons did us no harm on the whole; particularly in the Arab countries we were highly regarded nonetheless, and our principles did not cause us to restrict nonmilitary exports. In view of the various forms of subordination that may result from large-scale weapons exports in the long run, I still believe that concern for foreign and economic policy compel us to exercise extreme caution.

While Foreign Minister Levy seized the opportunity of our visit to voice harsh criticism of Germany—primarily for reasons of domestic policy, it seemed to me—President Chaim Herzog and Prime Minister Shamir were exceedingly cordial to us. Shamir, a hard man who knew exactly what he wanted and who did not mince words, was nevertheless experienced enough to understand the significance of Germany's stand on Israel; he realized that it would be imprudent to hurt a tried-and-true friend. In fact, in our talks we decided to establish a German-Israel economic committee.

Germany was aware of its special responsibility to Israel and its ties with the Israeli people. Carl Dieter Spranger handed Shlomo Lahat, the mayor of Tel Aviv, a check for 5 million deutsche marks for immediate aid to the victims of missile attacks.

On January 29, after my return from Israel, the administration approved my proposal to assemble an immediate aid package for the security of Israel and its population. It was our intention to procure for Israel equipment to protect against chemical weapons as well as medical supplies; to guarantee financing for a long-planned purchase of two submarines built in Germany, which were particularly suitable for protecting Israel's coastal zone; and to offer Israel Patriot missiles. In addition Germany offered Israel 250 million deutsche marks to repair war damage.

Leading Israeli politicians thanked us for our visit and our aid at this difficult time. At home and elsewhere, however, we had to endure heavy criticism, since the weapons shipments in part violated the guidelines for weapons exports to non-NATO nations. The circumstances, however, made this an emergency.

Germany's Contribution to the Liberation of Kuwait

On February 23 the final phase of the Gulf War began. We were all relieved that, despite some predictions to the contrary, the war could be ended so quickly. Never before had an aggressor been given as many chancess to concede as had Saddam Hussein. But he had refused to seize even a single one of these opportunities.

Within its limits Germany had proved a reliable partner of the war alliance: It was one of the first nations to transform the

United Nations embargo of Iraq and occupied Kuwait into binding national law; we also subjected our government to the United Nations Security Council resolutions on the Iraq crisis as well as all further resolutions passed by other international organizations. Since we were not represented in the Security Council, our participation in other international associations—such as the EC and the European Political Cooperation, the WEU, and NATO, as well as institutions for economic cooperation—was all the more important. In March 1991, after the suspension of hostilities was announced but before the official truce, Bonn also met the United States' request to send naval units to the Gulf to sweep for Iraqi mines.

Germany made an important contribution to Kuwait's liberation by facilitating the Soviet Union's political cooperation with the West; we advocated opening the West's financial institutions to Soviet interests and needs.

In this crisis situation we significantly stabilized the situation in Europe through our Eastern policy and contributed to the balance of interests and cooperation with the Soviet Union. Germany's willingness to support the Soviet Union's economy facilitated its withdrawal from Central Europe. That move in turn improved the Alliance's strategic position in regard to security.

A stable position of security for Europe at a time of fundamental change was a precondition and basis for the actions in the Persian Gulf. Without the peaceful political developments in Central Europe that had resulted from the London NATO summit of July 1990 and the agreements made shortly thereafter between the Federal Republic and the Soviet leaders, it is doubtful whether Moscow would have helped to implement the United Nations' measures against Iraq and the presence of American units in the Gulf. And on September 17, 1990, Eduard Shevardnadze, speaking in Tokyo, had stated, "If the crisis [the Gulf War] had erupted before the end of the Cold War, we would have prepared our missiles for firing, unleashing the Third World War."

Prudence in foreign policy and a clear endorsement of the policy of the Western Alliance, with consideration of the Soviet Union's basic needs—these were our guidelines. Our American, British, and French allies were entitled to solidarity from us. At the same time we supported the final French as well as Soviet attempts at mediating the conflict. Because I viewed it as our primary task to

483

avoid war without abandoning our objectives, I regarded Mitterand's and Gorbachev's efforts as an expression not of weakness but of responsibility.

As the most important transfer point for American and British troops, Germany was far more involved in the war against Iraq than was generally realized. We had allowed the United States to use its installations on our territory for their military actions, and Germany allowed U.S. planes to fly over and land in our territory. We further supported the transport of U.S. and British units stationed in Germany to the Persian Gulf. Particularly during the second phase of deployment of allied forces beginning in November 1990, almost 900 German freight trains, 450 Rhine boats, and land vehicles transported the bulk of the U.S. and the British Rhine forces' equipment to the ports of Bremerhaven, Nordenham, Emden, Rotterdam, and Antwerp within a few weeks. The German air force also served as an important tool in transportation, not only as part of several humanitarian missions but in more than 250 military actions by American, British, and Dutch forces.

Germany's financial aid to the alliance in 1990–91 amounted to approximately 18 billion deutsche marks; of that, 10.3 billion deutsche marks—more than half the total amount—went to the United States. Unlike many other nations, Germany delivered the full amount on the promised date. Included in part of the total sum were contributions of 800 million deutsche marks to Great Britain and 300 million deutsche marks to France. By 1993 Turkey, in addition to Germany's regular contribution to that nation's defense forces within NATO, received additional aid from German arms reserves worth 1.5 billion deutsche marks.

On February 28 I flew to Washington for talks with U.S. officials. I met with several congressmen and of course with President Bush, Secretary of State Baker, and Secretary of Defense Richard Cheney. We now had the task of fashioning a foundation for a peace in the Middle East that would make it impossible for Iraq to own weapons of mass destruction and the appropriate delivery systems. President Bush and I discussed the prospects for postwar arrangements in the Middle East.

It was necessary for us to remember that efforts for peace in the Middle East were marked by two conflicting concepts: Israel was advocating bilateral negotiations between Jerusalem and the individual parties to the conflict, while the Arabs supported one inclusive set of negotiations. I explained to Bush the road we had taken in Europe in the early 1970s. At the time West Germany, in accordance with its policy of responsibility, had arrived at separate arrangements with the Soviet Union, with Poland, with East Germany, and with Czechoslovakia; this process made possible a comprehensive solution within the framework of the CSCE process. President Bush and I also agreed on continuing to support Soviet President Gorbachev, despite his domestic difficulties, because he had been extraordinarily constructive during the Gulf crisis.

On April 2 I met in Bonn with Jordan's King Hussein to discuss Jordan's economic problems and its involvement in the peace process. Both of us favored a local security arrangement that would have to be worked out in bilateral talks or at a local conference. Simultaneously with Israeli-Arab talks, talks should be held between Israel and the Palestinians, so that substantial progress could finally be made. It would take another three years, however, before this vision became a reality. In my talk with Hussein I recommended some interregional mediation between the oil countries and the other Arab nations, including Jordan. I further suggested that cooperation between the EC and the Gulf Cooperation Council be expanded from economic issues to include political matters.

German contributions to overcoming the crisis in the Persian Gulf amounted to a total of approximately 25 billion deutsche marks. These funds also aided the "frontline nations" of Egypt, Turkey, and Jordan.

In April 1991 Germany offered 470 million deutsche marks in humanitarian aid to Iraqi refugees, domestically and within the European Community; that sum represented approximately 30 percent of the humanitarian aid advanced by all nations. After the cease-fire the federal government also issued several initiatives to promote ecological measures in the Gulf region.

The fact that, in general, the German people showed no "enthusiasm" for the Gulf War, regarding it merely as unavoidable in order to establish international law, was not a circumstance I viewed as negative. In an interview I gave at the time I remarked that I preferred German thoughtfulness to German thoughtlessness, and I still hold the same view in retrospect. The government's policy was also characterized, for reasons outlined earlier, by reservations.

Even at the time I considered it a dangerous belief that Germany should have participated, directly or indirectly, in military actions in the Gulf. Such demands as "Germany must finally assume responsibility again" suggested—erroneously—that we had not done so in the past. Yet Germany's contribution to the unification of Europe and to the European Community was tremendous; Bonn had assumed an historic responsibility by offering the Bundeswehr as an essential guarantor of the West's security in Europe and a harbinger of CSCE policy. All these moves had brought about the unique constellation that was obtained early in the summer of 1989, when both superpowers called Germany their principal partner in Europe.

The accusation that Germany had bought its way out of the Gulf War with money is just as unfounded. Because of Germany's great economic and political weight, it was a matter of course for the Federal Republic to make an appropriately large contribution to the effort to reinstitute peace, justice, and order in the Gulf.

13

War in Yugoslavia

A Vote for Europe

Origins of the Crisis

Germany's policy toward Yugoslavia after the Second World War was determined by Germany's desire to shed the burdens of the past. When our nation entered into diplomatic relations with Yugoslavia in 1951, the early date was set partly to improve our relationship with the Yugoslav people, who endured extreme suffering under German occupation in the Second World War. The Germans had been especially harsh and brutal in fighting the Yugoslav resistance, just as the offensive war of conquest against Yugoslavia was criminal through and through: Under the Croat fascist leader Ante Pavelić the Serbs were systematically persecuted, taking the lives of hundreds of thousands—not to mention the Third Reich's policy of exterminating the Jewish population.

The Yugoslav struggle against the German occupation was marked in part by ethnic and ideological animosities within and among the resistance forces. Marshal Josep Broz Tito's successful guerrilla warfare caused the German Army great losses. At the end of the war German POWs were badly mistreated, and the German minority in Yugoslavia was eliminated to all intents and purposes—typically through expulsion but frequently by killing.

The beginning of new German-Yugoslav relations in 1951 was propitious. West Germany's first ambassador to Yugoslavia was Karl-Georg Pfleiderer, who had become an FDP delegate to the Bundestag in 1949. He was opposed to breaking off diplomatic relations with Yugoslavia after that nation entered into diplomatic relations with East Germany. Pfleiderer and the FDP recognized the paralyzing effect of the Hallstein Doctrine on German foreign policy.

Once diplomatic relations were resumed, they evolved quickly, taking a positive turn. At the same time the people of the two countries cultivated ever closer contact with each other. Numerous Yugoslavs came to Germany as guest workers, and there they were welcome fellow citizens of Europe; conversely, Yugoslavia became a favorite vacation spot for West Germans. Thus the relationship between the two countries grew increasingly stronger during the 1960s, 1970s, and 1980s, particularly since Germany was the one country within the European Community that made a special effort to achieve closer cooperation between Belgrade and the EC—and did so successfully.

When I took office, still another aspect of German-Yugoslav relations was important to me; contrary to most Western government officials, I viewed the movement of nonaligned nations as an important stabilizing factor, which could contribute to keeping the effects of the West-East conflict on the Third World in check. What was more, the influence of the nonaligned nations on freeing international relations from ideology was not to be underestimated: the movement included the most diverse political units, different in their political arrangements, different in their religious beliefs, and different in their economic systems. One of the movement's most influential personalities was President Tito, whose nation took on an important independent role among the nonaligned countries and later in CSCE. This involvement was particularly significant in regard to pan-European development. Clearly Europe was not eager for the movement of the nonaligned nations to continue viewing itself as an anti-European movement. For that reason alone, this important European nation's cooperation was a gain from which the whole Continent would profit.

Yugoslavia's status also resulted from the fact that Tito had removed himself from Stalin's suffocating grip and was pursuing his own foreign policy. He was searching for a third way somewhere between communism and capitalism.

I first met Tito in the summer of 1974 on one of the first official visits early in the Schmidt-Genscher administration. The following year Chancellor Schmidt and I met Tito and his foreign minister in Helsinki on the occasion of the signing of the Final Act. On both occasions, Tito seemed the dominant figure in Yugoslav politics.

Using his authority, Tito enforced a number of constitutional regulations that established a balanced relationship among the various republics and nations within the Yugoslav confederacy. He had realized that the dominance of one people—in this case, the Serbs—must lead to what would amount to an increase in centrifugal force. After his death this insight proved prophetic: Without Tito's personal authority the Serbian struggle for hegemony intensified, as, consequently, did the centrifugal tendencies among the other peoples in the country.

In late 1980s two decisions were made in the Republic of Serbia that proved explosive to Yugoslavia's cohesiveness: In 1989, Vojvodina, the province with a strong Hungarian population, was stripped of its autonomy; in 1990 the same occurred to Kosovo-Metohija and its Albanians. Yet it had been precisely these two autonomous provinces that had defused the issue of nationalities within the Serbian republic. Consequently the abolition of their autonomous status could only have an adverse outcome. Given the large number of Albanians resident in Serbia, removing Kosovo's autonomy was even more dangerous than had been the case in Vojvodina. Both events should have shaken up the people of Europe, even the world; in fact, a fuse had been lit under the Yugoslav peoples' peaceful coexistence—thus jeopardizing the unity of the nation. Nevertheless, it is understandable that the international response was so minimal, since 1989 was the year of peaceful revolutions, not only in East Germany, but in all of Central and Southeastern Europe, and 1990 was entirely devoted to the breakup of the Warsaw Pact, the reestablishment of German unity, and the events in what was still the Soviet Union.

Slobodan Milošević, president of Serbia, used that time to establish facts in his favor. His efforts, however, affected not only those directly concerned, but, inevitably, all the other republics within the Yugoslav confederation as well. These republics were fearful that Milošević was unleashing a policy that corresponded to the objective raised in a memorandum issued by Serbia's Academy of Science several years before, which outlined the ideological basis for a greater-Serbian policy. This move was exacerbated by the Serbian leaders' demand that Serbs in the other republics be granted the right to join Serbia if the greater nation—Yugoslavia—should be dissolved. At the same time, in the spring of 1991, Yugoslavia's Serb-dominated Collective Presidency refused to cede the chair to the Croatian member of the committee, Stipe Mesič, leading to an escalation of the existing tensions and winning more support for the statesmen in the non-Serbian republics who sought independence. That circumstance held particularly true for Slovenia and Croatia, where the call for exercising the constitutional right to secede from the confederacy grew louder and louder.

Established after the First World War, the greater Yugoslav nation was stabilized principally by two foreign policy factors that appeared to have been rendered obsolete by the end of the Cold War. The first was fear of German expansion to Southeastern Europe, which appeared as a threat should Germany and Austria unite. The realistic nature of this expectation was soon revealed when Austria's Anschluss to the Third Reich in 1938 was followed by Hitler's attack on Yugoslavia in 1941. Germany's capitulation in 1945, its subsequent partition and the Allies' continued military presence, the re-creation of the Republic of Austria, and not least, Yugoslavia's excellent relations with the new Federal Republic of Germany—all made this concern seem unfounded. Fear of Germany could no longer serve as a unifying bond for Yugoslavia. Instead, a new danger was emerging: Worries arose that once Yugoslavia left the Soviet sphere of power, Moscow might look for an opportunity to reestablish its influence and re-annex the strategically important country into its sphere of power. This new concern—in no way less weighty than earlier fears—combined with Tito's authority and the nation's constitutional obligation to seek a balance between the various republics had contributed to the cohesiveness of multinational Yugoslavia.

But after the East-West conflict was resolved and the Soviet Union had undergone a fundamental change of direction under

Gorbachev, fears of Soviet intervention lessened considerably, and the situation was reversed: Serbia's new method of dealing with the issue of nationalities and greater Serbia's strife for hegemony jeopardized the cohesiveness of the nation from inside. Like the entire international community of nations, the West vigorously supported the preservation of the confederacy in 1990 and well into 1991. The same is true for German foreign policy, which consequently was made to endure increasing criticism from all sides of the domestic political spectrum. As late as May 9, 1991, the European Community publicly endorsed a democratically united Yugoslavia. On June 8, 1991, it called for restitution of the nation's constitutional rule, which had been violated by the refusal to honor the rotation of the presidency. In the early summer of 1991 Secretary Baker, on a visit to Belgrade, also strongly advocated the unity of the Yugoslav nation.

During the first half of 1991 I was in frequent touch with Yugoslav statesmen. During a stay in Davos, Switzerland, on February 3, for instance, I met with Janez Drnovšek, a Slovenian member of Yugoslavia's Collective Presidency, who explained his fears. On Wednesday, March 20, I received Slovenia's president, Milan Kučan and Foreign Minister Dimitrij Rupel; they also spoke of their concerns and of Slovenia's increasing move to independence. I urged them to proceed slowly and above all to take no unilateral steps but to be alert to opportunities to hold the confederation together in some other constitutional form.

Especially in view of our delicate, historically burdened relationship with the region, two aspects were of particular importance to German foreign policy: one, not to encourage centrifugal tendencies, and two, to make no unilateral changes in our policy toward Yugoslavia. Neither the public nor the political parties in Germany—including the FDP—were always fully aware of these issues. But unity within the European Community was of paramount importance, and the old fronts of the First and Second World Wars must not be revived to jeopardize the new Europe. It was important to adopt a joint position within both the EC and CSCE.

From the beginning of the crisis until I left office, it was important to me to keep in touch with *all* parties to the conflict. I therefore repeatedly met with the foreign ministers, as well as with other high-ranking officials of the six republics; these included

Serbia, whose foreign minister, Vladislav Jovanović, I received twice in Bonn. During our encounter on October 7, 1991, he explained Serbia's stand in a monologue that lasted almost three-quarters of an hour. During the second half of 1991 Chancellor Kohl and I also met with Croatia's president Franjo Tudjman; Slovenia's and Croatia's foreign ministers, Dimitrij Rupel and Zvonimir Šeparović; Macedonia's president, Kiro Gligorov; President Kučan of Slovenia; and finally, Stipe Mesič, the Croatian member of Yugoslavia's Collective Presidency. At that time Mesič was Yugoslavia's legitimate head of state, although his power had been severely limited by Serbia's president and the leaders of Yugoslavia's so-called People's Army.

Of particular significance was a visit by Alija Izetbegović, the president of Bosnia-Herzegovina, on November 22. The tension in his republic was extreme, since the area was Yugoslavia in miniature, with Muslim Bosnians living in close proximity to Serbs and Croats.

On October 15, 1991, the Republic of Bosnia-Herzegovina, following Slovenia and Croatia, also declared its independence, but the act went against the wishes of its strong Serbian minority. There was much to recommend a policy of wait and see toward the rest of Yugoslavia, even though events were escalating dramatically at the time.

When Slovenia's and Croatia's presidents returned to Bonn on December 3 and December 5 respectively, the war in and against Croatia was still raging wildly. In addition, mass expulsions of Croats from Serb-occupied areas had begun. Serbia's policy of "ethnic cleansing" was under way.

To return to the situation in mid-1991: From June 19 to 20 the first conference of the CSCE Council of Foreign Ministers was held in Berlin. As the host nation, Germany chaired the meeting.

Before the conference, I received a few foreign ministers for bilateral talks. Among them was Yugoslavia's foreign minister, Budomir Loncar, because I wanted to discuss with him first of all the question of how to deal with the issue of Yugoslavia—as might be expected, one of the core topics at the conference. Once again we were impelled to emphasize our interest in maintaining a unified but democratic and federated nation; the conference must remain true to the principles that had been established by the Paris

Charter a few months earlier. Besides Loncar, before the conference I also met with Baker; with Alois Mock, the foreign minister of Austria; and with my Soviet counterpart, Alexander Bessmertnykh. I always firmly believed that it was necessary to include the Soviet Union in all phases of our Yugoslav policy. The CSCE framework offered particularly good conditions for such inclusiveness.

I succeeded in keeping the discussion on the declaration of the CSCE ministerial conference out of the public plenary session, placing it instead within the group of the foreign ministers and section heads over lunch. The coincidence of the "CSCE alphabet" saw to it that Germany, the United States, the Soviet Union, and Yugoslavia were seated next to one another, so that we were able to communicate directly in the course of the discussion. Even before we sat down to eat, I had reached a general agreement with Loncar, Bessmertnykh, and Baker. In this context it was of special importance to link support for unity and territorial integrity with the demand for respect for democracy; this position aimed at acknowledging the rights of minorities and the ability of democratic institutions to function, all of which were threatened by the Serbian policies. It was also important for us to establish that the Yugoslav peoples alone had the right to freely determine the future of their nation. In holding this view, the community of CSCE nations did justice to the right to self-determination—and, incidentally, to an individual nation's "right to secede" from the larger polity, which was codified in the constitution of the Socialist Federal Republic of Yugoslavia of February 21, 1974.

Our joint balanced statement represented the lowest common denominator—but it was not all that low. Yugoslavia's foreign minister's approval of this statement was astonishing in itself.

On Monday, June 24, the President of Germany and I departed for an official visit to Italy. On our second day I met with Foreign Minister Gianni De Michelis. Even as we were discussing the worrisome events in Yugoslavia, we learned that the parliaments of Croatia and Slovenia had been called into session for that same evening to vote on independence for their nations. There were increasing indications that the Yugoslav People's Army would intervene in Slovenia—with the imminent danger of a serious military conflict. I therefore suggested to De Michelis that we immediately telephone Loncar to urge him to do everything in his power to prevent military intervention.

Eventually we made contact with him, and both of us spoke with him. I noted that according to what we had learned—he had the same information—Slovenia and Croatia would probably declare their independence that same evening. That, I remarked, was a political issue on which disagreement was certainly possible; the right of the Yugoslav people to determine their own future, however, had just been supported in Berlin. Therefore, whatever position was taken on the issue, military intervention was not permissible on any account. One of the established elements of European postwar policy was that the use of force to resolve political issues was not acceptable. The renunciation of force, I stated, was a basic element of peace in Europe; it was established in the Helsinki Final Act, just as it was in the Paris Charter. Loncar listened to my statements very seriously; he probably shared our fears, without being in a position to say so openly. De Michelis urged Loncar to speak with all the leading figures in Belgrade to prevent the use of military force. Soon after, events got completely out of hand.

The War On Slovenia and Croatia

On Wednesday, June 26, I received Vernon Walters, the U.S. ambassador. Later that same day I met with the Yugoslav ambassador, on whom I once again seriously impressed our position on the use of military force. I also spoke by telephone with Foreign Minister Mock of Austria and with De Michelis to discuss the dramatic course of events.

I finally decided that early the following week I would pay a short visit to Yugoslavia in my capacity as chairman of the CSCE's Council of Ministers. Just before leaving, on July 1, I went to the Bundestag's committee on foreign relations; I was planning to leave for Belgrade directly afterward. At that time I received a telephone call from Slovenia's foreign minister, urging me to visit Slovenia as well. First, however, I traveled to Belgrade, where Foreign Minister Loncar, a Croatian, received me. We had known each other for many years, both from our collaboration as foreign ministers and from Loncar's tenure as Yugoslavia's ambassador to Bonn. A worldly, multilingual man, Loncar was a tough representative of Yugoslavia's interests and not always an easy partner for the German foreign minister. He was personally acquainted with many of the leading players in international politics and possessed great insight into the Soviet Union's domestic and foreign policy. I therefore valued him as an interesting, informative, and serious counterpart.

I spoke with the prime minister, the foreign minister, and representatives of the individual republics. Wherever I went, I explained our firm conviction that there was absolutely nothing that could justify the use of military force and that all issues would have to be resolved politically. I also stressed that in the Helsinki Final Act and the Paris Charter the community of nations had guaranteed to each country the right to self-determination; in the CSCE's ministerial resolution issued in Berlin on June 20, this principle had been reaffirmed. I also met with Serbian Prime Minister Milošević; I urged everyone I spoke with to end the bloodshed in Slovenia and to enter on the path of negotiation.

My scheduled flight from Belgrade to Ljubljana was canceled because of low-level flights over the city by Yugoslavia's People's Army. There were reports of attacks on ground targets and of bombing. Quite clearly the chairman of the CSCE Council of Ministers was to be prevented from visiting embattled Slovenia. In order to avoid any provocation, I decided not to use the airport in Ljubljana, which in any case had already been closed. On July 2, 1991, I therefore landed in Klagenfurt, Austria, near the Slovenian border, to continue on by car to Slovenia's capital. At the airport in Klagenfurt I was received by President Kučan and Foreign Minister Rupel, who for security reasons were reluctant to proceed to Ljubljana by automobile. They explained that an armed train was waiting at the station instead, which could take us to a station midway between Klagenfurt and Ljubljana. Having seen the train, which was safeguarded by two armed cars in front and back, both of which were provided with four-barreled antiaircraft guns, and because the Slovenian leaders themselves did not believe a trip to Ljubljana possible, I suggested that we conduct our talks in Klagenfurt.

President Kučan accepted: He was pleased to show the whole world that the CSCE chairman was kept from visiting Slovenia's capital by military force. Nor did the Austrian government object to our meeting on its soil. I told President Kučan, who impressed upon me his country's difficult situation, that as CSCE chairman and foreign minister of Germany, I was interested in a political solution. Under no circumstances could we accept the use of force.

The demonstration of military strength convinced me that the leaders of Yugoslavia's People's Army and the political powers behind them would use all means possible to attain their objectives. I had received the same impression during my talk with Milošević in Belgrade the previous day. Though the conversation had been unemotional, Milošević left no doubt about his determination to realize his plans regarding Yugoslavia's future as he saw it.

After my return from Yugoslavia I first made a telephone call to a confidant of Yugoslavia's President Mesič, who explained his president's delicate situation. Next I spoke briefly with President Kučan and Foreign Secretaries Hurd and Baker. The same evening I explained to the Chancellor my view of events in Belgrade, which were growing increasingly frightening. The following day I continued my discussions with Mesič, Hurd, Dumas, the Dutch foreign minister Hans van den Broek, De Michelis, and Mock. I had recieved a dramatic phone call from Mesič himself that I could only interpret as a plea for help: Apparently he feared for his own safety and that of Yugoslavia's prime minister. I immediately informed the Chancellor, FDP chairman Count Lambsdorff, and the Social Democrat Hans-Jochen Vogel; early that afternoon I also briefed several foreign ministers of European Community and NATO nations. The following day the agenda was similar: talks with van den Broek, who headed the European Community; with Slovenia's foreign minister; with Drnovšek, a member of the Collective Presidency; and with Loncar. It was important to me that Belgrade understand the alarm felt throughout Europe.

Yugoslavia's People's Army had begun its attack on Slovenia on June 27, 1991. The European Community's troika—until June 30 under the chairmanship of Luxembourg's foreign minister, Jacques Poos, and thereafter under van den Broek—made energetic and successful attempts to stop the fighting. On July 5, 1991, the European Community also imposed an arms embargo against all of Yugoslavia; on September 4 CSCE adopted the same measure, as did the United Nations Security Council on September 25, 1991. After three troika missions, a meeting between the European Community and all parties to the conflict in Yugoslavia held in Brioni issued the following resolutions on July 7, 1991.

1. Yugoslavia's People's Army will retreat to its barracks. There will be a cease-fire.
2. Implementation of Slovenia's and Croatia's declarations of independence will be suspended for three months.
3. As planned, the Croatian Mesič will assume the leadership of the Collective Presidency.
4. No later than August 1, 1991, negotiations on the future of Yugoslavia's domestic affairs will resume.

However, fighting between armed Serbs and Croatia's National Guard increasingly hampered this process. After losing to Slovenia's resistance—the well-trained and well-equipped armed territorial forces had refused to return heavy arms to the center in Belgrade—the Serbs and the Yugoslavia's People's Army seemed to have moved their activities closer to Croatia.

On June 29 the Council of Europe, meeting in Luxembourg, also dealt with the situation in Yugoslavia. Subsequently the Chancellor publicly stated our position, which we had defended at the Council session. Yugoslavia's unity, he remarked, could not be maintained by the use of force; this declaration was yet another clear rejection of the use of military force as a means to political ends. When the EC's foreign ministers convened in The Hague on July 5, they agreed on a statement to the effect that the EC would reexamine its position after each new violation of the truce.

CSCE also went beyond the June 20 resolution. Early in July, Germany, as the nation holding the chairmanship, activated CSCE's crisis management. Shortly thereafter the Committee of High Authority convened in Prague.

In order to clarify what actions we could take, I asked my EC colleagues what part the European Community was looking to play in the negotiation process for Yugoslavia's domestic affairs. Even though the EC must not appear to preempt Yugoslavia's final decision, I noted, we could not help but consider the outcome. I particularly welcomed the fact that Italy's foreign minister categorically rejected a change of Yugoslavia's internal borders; instead, he argued, a system of rights for minorities, firmly based on international law, must be established. We agreed that a close connection existed between the two issues: without a guarantee of rights for minorities, a change of borders could hardly be avoided. The Committee of High Authority, CSCE's highest committee below the ministerial level, had expressly welcomed the planned EC mission to monitor the stipulated truce. This fact supported my desire to fully include the Soviet Union, by way of CSCE, in the EC's resolutions on the conflict in Yugoslavia; fortunately that inclusion could also be achieved during the EC's following proceedings.

As chairman of the European Community, the Dutch foreign minister, without mentioning the names of those with whom he had spoken, confirmed Yugoslavia's clear indication that it was willing to cooperate with the EC, although it could not state this intention officially. Therefore he suggested that Germany, as the current holder of the CSCE chairmanship, should so inform those members who wished to participate in the mission. We also decided on a brief statement in which we called on all the parties in Yugoslavia to support the Brioni agreement in all its aspects. On July 19, 1991, the Collective Presidency in Belgrade announced its decision to withdraw Yugoslavia's People's Army from Slovenia.

Six days later, the European Community's General Council convened in Brussels. Naturally this meeting was also dominated by events in Yugoslavia. Trying for accord with France, I spoke with Dumas and Poos before the session, and we went into the talks with a joint position. This harmony was all the more important because representatives from Yugoslavia had been invited to our luncheon.

As CSCE chairman, I once again placed the main emphasis on insisting that the EC's endeavors be incorporated in CSCE, so as to prevent the belief that the European Community was acting without including the Soviet Union or any other European nation. The EC always kept in close touch with the United States and Canada.

During the subsequent luncheon I raised the question of how Yugoslavia's representatives would respond to the expansion of the monitoring mission. The question was intended to put the idea to the others. They approved the expansion, with the understanding that none of Yugoslavia's immediate neighbors would participate. Dumas suggested three to four hundred observers, a number that was generally accepted. We were also pleased to learn that other CSCE nations, among them Sweden, Canada, and Czecho-slovakia, were willing to be included.

I left no doubt as to the fact that we would have preferred representatives from all the Yugoslav republics, including Slovenia, Croatia, and Serbia, to be present at our luncheon. Apparently there had been confusion within the Collective Presidency as to whether or not all members had been invited; why the confusion had arisen, and who was responsible for it, was not clear. In the subsequent extensive discussion limited to the group of conference participants, the continuing bloodshed was unanimously condemned; again we voiced our support of a peaceful solution to the conflict and appealed to the Collective Presidency in Belgrade to encourage an immediate truce and to begin negotiations on the future of Yugoslavia's peoples. The EC offered its services for the planned conference. Recalling the removal of the autonomous status of Vojvodina and Kosovo, we reaffirmed our earlier statement that any change of internal and external borders of the country achieved by force was unacceptable; an acceptable solution must guarantee the rights of ethnic groups and nationalities in all parts of Yugoslavia. Finally those responsible for the present deadlock were given a sharp warning, although consensus to explicitly name Serbia could not be reached among the conference's participants.

In evaluating the EC troika, I declared firmly that, in my opinion, the mission had not failed; however, we were forced to admit that it had been Serbia that had prevented a concrete outcome. It was still necessary to go on with our efforts at peace and mediation. What was interesting was the analysis rendered by the members of the troika of their talks with Serbian President Miloševic; disappointed with Serbia's stance, they warned against any support of Miloševic personally, since such a decision would inevitably result in Yugoslavia's dissolution. One of the troika members went so far as to state that Serbia was planning a war of annexation against Croatia and other republics to create a closed Serbian territory.

I also expressed my concerns about the attitude of the leaders in Belgrade. Germany, I explained, would under no circumstances grant retrospective recognition to borders changed by force. We had always supported a truce, and we therefore felt that equal importance needed to be attached to our appeal to the Yugoslav

Collective Presidency to enter into negotiations on the country's future.

Agreement on sanctions against Serbia could not be reached because several members rejected such a move. However, we did agree on establishing a commission to determine possible economic and financial measures against any parties unwilling to observe a truce or cooperate on national economic improvements or to negotiate about Yugoslavia's future.

In case a republic—and at that stage this provision could only apply to Serbia—were to prevent negotiations, thus permitting hostilities to continue beyond the month that had been established in the accord on the monitoring mission of July 10, 1991, Germany would propose that the EC reexamine the issue of recognizing the republics of Croatia and Slovenia. The political solution, which all participants wanted, must not be blocked, either by military action or by a refusal to negotiate. The Federal Republic, I pointed out, would only act within the framework of and in agreement with the EC. If negotiations were blocked and warfare continued, it would be necessary to investigate whether, as a last political resort to end the bloodshed and the expulsions, it might be advisable to internationalize the conflict by recognizing both republics.

Asking for support for the latest EC initiatives on establishing a truce and advancing a peaceful dialogue, we turned to CSCE, which as part of the "crisis management," had been summoned to Prague for August 8. We also suggested examining the possibility of dispatching peacekeeping forces within the framework of the EC or CSCE.

French Foreign Minister Dumas also suggested that we inform the United Nations Security Council about the European Community's efforts. But a number of members, especially Great Britain, expressed reservations. Eager to keep Germany acting in concert with France, and because I agreed with Dumas, I strongly supported the French initiative; after all, the United Nations Security Council is the only international committee whose resolutions are universally binding. Further, involving the Security Council as well as CSCE was important in regard to the Soviet Union. In the end we agreed that France, the United Kingdom, and Belgium— which at that time was a nonpermanent member of the Security

Council—brief the Council on the EC's actions regarding Yugoslavia.

At Germany's insistence, another extraordinary ministerial conference of the EPC (European Political Cooperation) took place on August 27, 1991. This time those EC members who until then had been reserved joined Germany in its position on Serbia's conduct. Harsh criticism was expressed of "the completely misguided politics of the Serbian guerrillas"; the EC further determined that support for Serbian troops indisputably came from segments of Yugoslavia's People's Army. The Collective Presidency was immediately told to end the illegal activities of the troops under its command. What was particularly significant was the statement that the EC and its members would never accept a policy of faits accomplis, since they were determined to refuse recognition to border changes brought about by force. The EC criticized Serbia's opposition to the expansion of the EC monitoring commission in Croatia; the EC, for its part, would not stand idly by as the bloodshed grew worse day by day.

At long last the European Community had arrived at an unmistakable position and a new agreement on determining responsibility for the situation. For Germany, with its interest in a united stand among EC nations, this last move was of particular importance.

The August 27 session further demonstrated the closeness between France and Germany. Even before the session I had spoken with Dumas by telephone to suggest that we join in giving new momentum to the European Community's endeavors. We scheduled a meeting in Brussels preceding the EPC conference. In a private conversation we confirmed our determination to work through this difficult issue in close collaboration between France and Germany.

Everything possible must be done to arrive at a negotiated resolution. I therefore proposed a conference on Yugoslavia, to be held under the auspices of the European Community. This method, I suggested, was the only way to get all parties to the conflict to sit down at the negotiating table. Dumas developed the idea of an independent commission of jurists that could function as a kind of arbitration committee to deal with the legal problems that could be expected to arise in the course of resolving the conflict. I immediately agreed to the proposal. Dumas, in turn, supported mine. We proceded to introduce the project to the group of ministers as a German-French initiative. Dumas had not worked out the composition of the committee, though he proposed that it be headed by the president of the French constitutional court, Robert Badinter. I knew Badinter well and valued him as a highly qualified jurist and political thinker. He also enjoyed the confidence of President Mitterand. In order to obtain clear criteria for selecting committee members, I suggested to Dumas that additional high-court presidents of member nations besides Badinter be involved, among them Germany's Roman Herzog (who succeeded to the German presidency in 1994). Our proposal met with approval, and high-ranking judges from Italy, Spain, and Belgium, along with the two previously named judges, eventually formed the Badinter-Herzog Commission. Our proposal also met with approval in the group of EC's foreign ministers. For me this joint initiative and its acceptance by our other colleagues had a meaning beyond Yugoslavia: Once again Germany and France had given significant impetus to the policies of the European Community.

Even before the next ministerial meeting in The Hague, I received a telephone call from Hans van den Broek, who wanted my opinion on the idea of appointing Lord Carrington, Britain's former foreign secretary, to chair the Yugoslavia Conference. I immediately agreed. I knew Lord Carrington, with whom I had worked closely and confidentially as a foreign minister, to be a knowledgeable and experienced politician. During the meeting of EC's foreign ministers in The Hague on September 3, the other members also accepted the proposal.

Representation at the Yugoslavia Conference in The Hague was intended to include CSCE—through Germany's chairmanship—as well as Yugoslavia's Collective Presidency, the government of Yugoslavia, and the six republics. Further, it was planned that each national community that did *not* feel represented by a republic would be given the opportunity to follow the conference proceedings and to respond. Adherence to the truce, however, was a prerequisite set by its leaders for the peace conference to open.

A tough struggle ensued concerning the relationship between the conference and the arbitration commission. Dumas and I were primarily interested in allowing all Yugoslav parties to call on the arbitration commission. In the end we agreed that the chairman should define the commission's sphere of concern, and the commission should report to the conference through the chairman. The commission should also retain absolute freedom on methods and structure. The suggestion by the Netherlands that the commission collaborate closely with the World Court in The Hague, was rejected; it was important that the commission retain absolute independence.

On the evening of September 19 we met again in The Hague within the framework of an extraordinary EPC meeting. Lord Carrington, who by this time had visited the crisis area, reported on his observations as well as on the working session of the Yugoslavia Conference in The Hague. Each Yugoslav group was interested in the conference, but several republics considered it useless as long as the fighting continued. There was unanimity, however, on the desire that the EC monitoring commission continue its work, in particular in Bosnia-Herzegovina and Macedonia. In these two areas it seemed advisable to initiate preventive actions on the part of the observers before hostilities broke out. Compared to the republics, Yugoslavia's national government had ceased playing a role in the negotiations. The next session was scheduled for September 26; at that time a final determination should be made as to whether the truce had hopelessly failed. In summing up, Carrington pleaded that the opportunity offered by the conference be kept alive—though such a continuation required all parties' willingness to negotiate. Basically the success of the conference depended on the participants' political will to resolve the fundamental problems—and the European Community had no viable substitute for such a desire.

What could we do to help the truce prevail? I asked Lord Carrington whether he advocated a larger number of observers or the use of a peacekeeping force, and whether we could count on the approval of all the Yugoslavian participants. Dumas urged us to lose no more time. Given the pressure on the EC from general expectations, he noted, it was essential to show a firm resolve and, unless Europe was willing to withdraw from the conflict altogether, the EC must provide the appropriate means to enable the monitoring commission to do its work again. France further believed that the time had come to involve the Security Council. I expressly supported that motion. We referred to statements by Chancellor Kohl and President Mitterand issued in Berlin that same day. We believed that the following principles in particular continued to be indispensable to a just resolution:

1. rejection of all force;
2. no recognition of borders changed by force;
3. protection of the rights of national groups and communities, as well as protection of the legitimate interests of Yugoslavia's peoples.

Since CSCE had commissioned the European Community to seek a peace, responsibility must continue to be borne by the EC.

As CSCE chairman, I was charged with apprising all CSCE participants—through the channel of the "urgency mechanism," created in Berlin on June 20, 1991—of the EC's actions. This mechanism was to make certain that the Soviet Union, the other European nations, the United States, and Canada would also be informed. CSCE thus won additional responsibility. I was particularly pleased to inform the other EC members that two CSCE participants—Poland and Czechoslovakia—had expressed an interest in cooperating in potential actions within the framework of the WEU. The EC observers, I noted, had already given their approval, and should WEU come to a decision, I would be in favor of such a participation. On the one hand, Poland's and Czechoslovakia's offer supported us politically; and it also disproved the argument of some Serbian leaders, that the EC was pursuing anti-Slavic policies.

Once again I examined France's request to involve the United Nations Security Council. It seemed important to me that we assure ourselves of international support and that, in particular, all permanent members of the Security Council be granted their appropriate role. My Italian counterpart warned against involving this highest authority, the Security Council, before we were absolutely certain what we wanted and would be able to achieve. In spite of all setbacks, Italy believed that the European Community still had the best chance of success.

The British Foreign Secretary also spoke out emphatically against even beginning to entertain the thought of peacekeeping forces. Speaking from his own experience—he must have been thinking of Northern Ireland—he could only caution against starting military action, since history had repeatedly shown that it was far easier to start such actions than to end them later. As soon as a situation worsened, he argued, the predicament arose of either breaking off all endeavors or escalating all efforts. Great Britain was, however, unwilling to oppose general consensus on requesting the WEU to examine such a possibility.

Douglas Hurd argued in favor of continuing to utilize the opportunities available to exert increased political and economic pressure, especially monitoring the arms embargo. De Michelis requested that the monitoring commission be expanded significantly, a move that would be especially useful in places where hostilities had not yet broken out—in other words, outside of Croatia. I supported Hungary's suggestion to employ monitoring forces in the region near the Yugoslav border as well; this proposal was unanimously endorsed. We further voted to send EC monitoring forces to Yugoslavia's outer borders, with particular attention to guaranteeing enforcement of the arms embargo. Since the Netherlands and Greece objected to the preventive expansion of the mission to the republics of Bosnia-Herzegovina and Macedonia, where fighting had not yet erupted, we agreed merely to continue to study the issue. This was a regrettable solution: Those familiar with the history of the peoples of Yugoslavia were aware of the problems dormant in Bosnia-Herzegovina and Macedonia. But nothing could be done if even one nation objected.

The following day I emphatically pleaded in the German Bundestag for a joint stand of the European Community, once again stressing our collaboration with France: "The widest possible support will make every step we take more efficient. The same holds true for the issue of whether Croatia and Slovenia should be recognized, a matter that can be decided in accordance with the Chancellor's and the French President's statements. We consider it crucial to take a joint stand with France." That declaration meant a rejection of unilateral steps by Germany.

My appeal referred to the statement by President Mitterand and Chancellor Kohl of September 19, which, drawing on the CSCE ministerial resolution of June 20, 1991, among other things, requested respect for the right to self-determination and the recognition that the individual peoples were entitled to exercise this right peacefully and democratically if they so desired. At the same time, the statement noted, the rights of minorities must be safeguarded.

Hans van den Broek had sent out the invitations to the informal ministerial gathering customary during each country's presidency of the EC. Not unexpectedly, the talks in Haarzuilens in the Netherlands on October 5 and 6, centered entirely around the conflict in Yugoslavia. Because I was eager to demonstrate our unity with France again, I scheduled a breakfast with Dumas for the morning of the second day; we shared our thoughts on the resolutions the EC needed to issue. On the first day the EC's foreign ministers published a statement that dealt with Yugoslavia's Collective Presidency's position—or, to be more precise, with the position of Serbia's and Montenegro's representatives in the Collective Presidency. These men had announced that in future they wished resolutions to be passed merely by representatives' votes. Further, they intended to assume certain functions that constitutionally were under the jurisdiction of the parliament. Montenegro's and Serbia's seizure of control of the Collective Presidency had already been condemned by the other republics. Now the European Community and its members also criticized this illegal act, which violated both Yugoslavia's constitution and the Paris Charter. In addition, the statement asserted that the nations joined in the European Community were not willing to recognize the decisions taken by a legislature that could no longer claim to represent the entire nation. Thus the European Community took an unequivocal stand on constitutional power struggles within Yugoslavia; it was emboldened to do so by the CSCE conference which had taken place in Moscow in September, shortly after the failed putsch in the Soviet Union.

In Moscow I had emphatically advocated condemning violations of the constitutions of CSCE member nations as violations of the democratic principles established by the Paris Charter. I suggested that CSCE be placed in a position to arrive at such decisions without the agreement of the nation in question and that therefore the new formula should be unanimity minus one. To my great pleasure, my stand was supported by the Soviet representative, who—still influenced by the failure of the putsch—took the floor. Not much later, on January 31, 1992, the so-called "consensus minus one" principle was adopted by the next session of the CSCE Council of Foreign Ministers.

This vote was an important confirmation of the position I had adopted in connection with the putsch. On the Monday of the coup, August 18, 1991, when Soviet ambassador Terekhov called on me and handed me the declaration of the junta, I told him that the principles elaborated in the Charter of Paris, guaranteed by CSCE and therefore binding on all members, included the principle of democratic procedures, which must never be violated. Thus I made the Charter of Paris the yardstick by which to measure the events in Moscow; since the Soviet Union had also expressly accepted the Charter, Germany could use it as a basis for partisanship according to CSCE principles. Thus we were the first Western government to take a clear stand in regard to the attempted putsch.

On the second day of the negotiations in Haarzuilens we endorsed a statement regarding Yugoslavia. Explicitly affirming the position Germany had adopted from the outset, it declared that the ministers were particularly concerned about reports to the effect that the Yugoslav Army had resorted to disproportionate and random violence, proving that this armed force had ceased acting as a neutral, disciplined institution. However, we were determined to apply the standards of international law to hold accountable those responsible for the unprecedented violence in Yugoslavia, which was taking more and more human lives. For the first time, personal responsibility for acts of violence was mentioned, as I had advocated for a long time. The statement further read, "In reference to a relevant agreement at the fourth plenary session of the Yugoslavia Conference on October 4, a political solution in regard to recognition was . . . considered." Recognition was intended to crown a negotiating process conducted in good faith and including all parties.

Thus the full body of the European Community endorsed the right to independence for those republics that desired it. As I had proposed before, this document made the connection between the right to self-determination, to which all the peoples of Yugoslavia were entitled, and the rights of ethnic groups and communities living in the various republics. We confirmed our determination never to recognize border changes established by force. We again condemned the Serbian and Montenegran representatives' control of the Collective Presidency, and we announced restrictive measures—that is, sanctions—against any group that failed to respect the accord to end hostilities. We urged the Secretary General of the United Nations to expedite the report the Security Council's Resolution No. 713 of September 21, 1991, required him to submit and immediately to send a special envoy to Yugoslavia to that purpose.

That agreement on the wording of this resolution could be reached was principally due to the fact that Roland Dumas and I had chosen to cooperate. To display our solidarity publicly, we decided to pool our press conferences, which we usually held separately after meetings.

For an End of the War on Slovenia and Croatia

The most important results of the meeting in Haarzuilens were, above all, that a political solution was accepted to recognize those republics who so desired it.

On October 10 the CSCE's Committee of High Authority—its highest organization below the ministerial level—affirmed the Haarzuilens resolution. Recognition of those republics that asked to be recognized was generally approved by CSCE, and thus by the two superpowers, the United States and Soviet Union. That step was crucial, since this policy now constituted the platform for the actions not only of the European Community but of the Soviet Union and the United States as well. Clearly with every step we took within the framework of the EC, we were considering its potential consequences for the situation in the Soviet Union.

To me, acknowledging the inviolability of borders was of preeminent importance; the refusal to recognize borders changed by force on the one hand and the protection of the rights of nationalities and minorities on the other were both essential to stability in the entire CSCE territory.

Exercising his EC presidency, van den Broek began to implement the resolutions passed at Haarzuilens. On October 10, 1991, after meeting with the presidents of Serbia and Croatia, Milošević and Tudjman, he issued a press release that read in part: "At the conclusion of the political process in, we hope, one or no later than two months, the time will have come for the Twelve to vote on recognizing those republics that, in a democratic process, have expressed a desire to become independent." In an interview with the Austrian newspaper *Die Presse* on October 18, 1991, van den Broek was more specific on dates: "Should we have failed to find a political solution by December 10, 1991, and should the Yugoslav Army not have entirely withdrawn from Croatia, the time will have come for the Community to vote on recognition of Slovenia and Croatia. At that time we can no longer deny them the right to independence." He added, "We are not trying to force on the republics a united Yugoslavia that has ceased being a reality." The Council's president thus informed the whole world that the European Community considered the dissolution of Yugoslavia inevitable.

The schedule van den Broek had set—two months from October 10, 1991—coincided with Germany's ideas: The target date did not go beyond 1991. Thus the European Community demonstrated its unwillingness to postpone a decision on independence indefinitely. However, we had no wish to burden the Maastricht summit with this decision; the Chancellor in particular was eager to keep this topic away from that conference. The negotiations would be difficult enough, he remarked, and the time available hardly sufficient to bring up such a complex topic as recognition in the meeting of all the heads of state and government as well as the foreign ministers. The declaration the German government finally issued—that we considered it advisable to come to a decision on the question of recognition before Christmas—went even beyond the point in time specified by the Dutch foreign minister as leader of the EC Council.

On October 27, 1991, the EC's foreign ministers condemned the Yugoslav Army's continued attacks on Croatian cities. We stated in part: "The Yugoslav People's Army's latest attacks have no relation to Croatia's breaking of agreements. The repeated attacks on Dubrovnik have put the lie to the claim that the YPA intervenes only in order to liberate military bases under siege or to protect Serbian communities."

The following day, the Twelve's foreign ministers convened for an extraordinary meeting in Brussels. These negotiations were conducted in a sober atmosphere, and the result was unambiguous: The European Community made a distinction between cooperating and noncooperating republics. Five were ready to cooperate on the basis of the draft Lord Carrington had submitted while one republic—Serbia—continued to withhold a decision. Once again we stressed our principles: no unilateral changes of borders, protection of the rights of minorities and of ethnic and national communities. The latter phrasing was important, because increasingly one of the pivotal questions centered on what constituted a minority and what an ethnic and national group or community— for example, the Albanians in Kosovo in no way regarded themselves as a minority but always as a national community. The EC expressed its great distress over the continued violations of these principles, going so far as to name those responsible: "In this context they pointed out Serbia's stance at the conference, to the coup d'état by four members of the Collective Presidency, and to the announcement of a plan for the creation of a Greater Serbia. The statements concerning the actions by the Yugoslav national army, condemned in the Dubrovnik Resolution of October 27, 1991, must therefore be seen in this light." We further called on CSCE and the United Nations Security Council to continue to support the EC's efforts and to condemn the role of the national army and the coup d'état by the four members of the Collective Presidency. The opinions that crystallized within the European Community proved that even those countries that initially granted Serbia's leadership some credence were forced to realize that Germany's assessment of Serbia's leadership had been correct from the start. What, I asked myself over and over, can end the bloodshed? More and more it seemed as if recognizing Slovenia and Croatia and thus turning the conflict into an international matter was the only remaining political means.

Because of Serbia's failure to cooperate Lord Carrington suspended his work on the conference for the present. In the October 23, 1991, version, the convention paper the conference had drafted contained the clause declaring that the republics should reapply the 1990 regulations concerning autonomous provinces; this demand referred to the reinstitution of Vojvodina and Kosovo's independence, which Serbia had abolished. But the convention draft of November 4 omitted this regulation—much to the disappointment of the Albanians in Kosovo and the Hungarian minority in Vojvodina. As was to be expected, Serbia's leaders took the suspension of the conference and the about-face regarding the issue of autonomy as encouragement. We had never approved omission of the clause on independence, and it sent the wrong signal.

On November 4 the EC's foreign ministers convened in Brussels once again to decide on the immediate suspension and cancellation of the cooperation agreement with Yugoslavia. Yugoslavia was not invited to the G24's ministerial meeting scheduled for November 11.

The issue of an oil embargo was linked with possible future measures taken by the United Nations Security Council. Additional measures against Serbia—for example, freezing the foreign accounts of Yugoslav banks, suspension of bilateral traffic agreements, suspension of export licenses for sensitive goods and of guaranteed export loans, preventing international financing organizations from making loans to Yugoslavia, as well as a general trade embargo—remained on the daily agenda and continued to be examined. Yugoslavia's neighbors and the Soviet Union indicated their support of EC measures, and conversely, we assured Greece, which feared harmful repressions on Serbia's part, of our solidarity and support.

During the subsequent press conference I expressed my belief that Serbia would be persuaded by the seriousness of the EC resolutions: The vote for sanctions was only a first step; we were hoping to implement it with further measures. Most important, an oil embargo could be effective even without a United Nations resolution if Yugoslavia's neighbors and the Soviet Union were to act in concert with us, as they had indicated they would. I characterized the resolution we had just issued as overdue. The following principles, I said, should determine our actions:

- independence for the republics that so desired, with the option of voluntarily forming an association or a closer form of national union;
- inviolability of internal and external borders.

I stressed the importance of the inviolability of external borders to prevent Macedonia from making territorial claims on Greece.

Further, I called for equal rights for the minorities and nationalities in all republics by emphasizing that the sanctions must be activated as well if the war machine of Yugoslavia's People's Army began to advance in Croatia. For the rest, negotiations in The Hague would have to be continued, with a view toward possible recognition.

Four days later, when the EC's foreign ministers met again, we were forced to note that not all the parties in Yugoslavia supported the basic elements of our proposals. That state of affairs jeopardized the negotiation process; we therefore decided to impose sanctions on Serbia and Montenegro. We further requested the United Nations Security Council to impose an oil embargo. Formally these resolutions were passed in the fringes of the NATO summit in Rome: The foreign ministers of the European Community gathered in a room set aside in the conference hotel even before the start of the NATO discussions, and we succeeded remarkably quickly in reaching a consensus on these weighty resolutions.

As on several previous occasions, I found it extraordinarily helpful that all parties in the German Bundestag supported our policy. At heart we were even considered too cautious—an attitude that became evident especially in response to the request for the recognition of Croatia and Slovenia.

The Chancellor, with whom I had discussed our Yugoslavia policy many times and in great detail, on November 27, 1991, spoke to the Bundestag on the situation in the crisis area. He laid special emphasis on the fact that formal international recognition of those republics who requested it must not be delayed by blocking efforts to achieve peace. He also mentioned a date for a decision on recognition: It should take place before the Christmas holidays—which would begin two weeks after December 10, the date set by van den Broek.

No country had raised objections to the Dutch foreign minister's suggestion. Furthermore, the trend toward recognition of Slovenia and Croatia was gaining strength. That state of affairs also proved the case when the foreign ministers of the Hexagon Group—Poland, Czechoslovakia, Austria, Italy, Yugoslavia, and Greece—convened in Venice on December 1, 1991. Two of these nations belonged to the European Community while four did not; the consensus among them, too, was that Yugoslavia no longer existed in its previous form. This agreement did not result in a suspension of Belgrade's membership, but two far-reaching resolutions were taken: Yugoslavia, which was scheduled to hold the chair in 1992, was stripped of that right and, most importantly, Slovenia and Croatia were granted observer status. That step was a signal indicating subsequent recognition.

After the European Council summit in Maastricht the EC membership agreed that on December 16 we would make the necessary decisions regarding the recognition of Croatia and Slovenia. But before we had a chance to do so, the Badinter-Herzog Commission submitted its evaluation. This document, issued on December 7, had a profound impact on the EC's Yugoslavia policy. The commission composed of high-court presiding judges determined that "The Socialist Federal Republic of Yugoslavia is in the process of dissolution. It is left to the republics to resolve problems regarding successor states resulting from this process, in accordance with the principles and regulations of international law and with respect in particular for human rights and the rights of peoples and minorities. It is up to the republics that so desire to cooperate and to form a new association, with democratic institutions of their choice." The Badinter-Herzog Commission presupposed the dissolution of Yugoslavia. The sole important issue was a choice between recognition of the republics that wanted independence and a new association of those striving in that direction.

A decision had become even more urgent than before. As I explained in my letter of December 13, 1991, to the United Nation's Secretary General, Javier Pérez de Cuéllar, the assumption was inevitable that delaying recognition would lead to further escalation of violence by Yugoslavia's People's Army, since the troops would necessarily regard our refusal to recognize the republics as an encouragement for their policy of conquest toward Croatia. At the same time Roland Dumas proposed a new German-French initiative for the preparation of the EC ministerial conference on December 16, 1991. Subsequently Jürgen Chrobog, a high official in the Foreign Office, worked with his French counterpart on a joint draft establishing criteria for recognition; he and I were communicating by telephone, discussing every word of the draft. The European Community foreign ministers subsequently accepted the document—which also had been endorsed by President Mitterand and Chancellor Kohl—with only minimal changes. The paper listed objective criteria for the recognition of new states in Eastern Europe and in the Soviet Union, as well as additional stipulations concerning the recognition of independence for the Yugoslav republics. The Community had now adapted to this resolution and established neutral guidelines for it.

On December 16 we convened as planned. When I arrived in Brussels in the afternoon, the public did not expect a vote for recognition that day. Radio and television reports—not only in

Germany but everywhere in Europe, above all in Croatia and Slovenia—indicated that the topic would be tabled once more.

While the debate, which went on until long past midnight, increased the number of members who supported recognition, others still expressed doubt. Greece, for instance, was not opposed to recognition as a matter of principle, but Foreign Minister Antonis Samaras was fearful that recognition of Slovenia and Croatia might cause Macedonia to consider a similar step and lay claim to Greek territory, including Saloniki. I did not hesitate to assure him of Germany's support on the border issue to protect Greek land and Greek interests in the event of such a territorial demand, though I did not believe it would occur.

The discussion among the ministers was very objective. That such a complicated debate could be conducted for hours without harshness testified to the spirit of the EC. The meeting went on and on; pros and cons were thoroughly deliberated. I explained repeatedly that the European Community's credibility was at stake. We had the Badinter-Herzog Commission report and the announcement that a decision would be made after the two-month period, and it was evident that only the Serbs were attempting to prevent an agreement. Any further delay would merely encourage them to continue the war of conquest against Croatia. And we must never reward the use of force. What, I asked, could possibly end the war in Croatia if not recognition and thus internationalization? What else remained for us to do if we consistently withheld recognition?

In the course of the discussion I telephoned the Chancellor twice in order to brief him on the state of affairs and to make certain that he and I were in agreement. He too believed that the Serbs would inevitably interpret adjournment as encouragement to continue the fighting. In the end the twelve foreign ministers issued the following resolution:

> The Community and its members agree to recognize the independence of all those Yugoslav republics that meet all the requirements listed below. This resolution will go into effect on January 15, 1992. Therefore they call on all Yugoslav republics to declare by December 23 whether they wish to be recognized as independent states; whether they accept the obligation contained in the above-mentioned guidelines; whether they accept the regulations contained in the draft of the

agreement submitted to the Yugoslavia Conference, in particular the regulations in Chapter Two on human rights and the rights of national or ethnic groups; whether they will continue to support the efforts of the Secretary General of the United Nations Security Council and the continuation of the Yugoslavia Conference. The conference chair will submit the applications of those republics that reply in the affirmative to the Arbitration Commission, so that it may evaluate them before the effective date.

To be fully knowledgeable in that area as well, the German government had commissioned Christian Tomuschat, a widely recognized expert on international law, to prepare an evaluation of methods to deal with minorities in Croatia. After a stay of several days in Zagreb, Tomuschat announced in late November that Croatia's constitutionally established protection of minorities was "of exemplary significance to the further development of the protection of minorities in Europe; Serbia will have to be evaluated by the same standard."

After all the foreign ministers had arrived at basic agreement, I stated to the group that the German government intended to make a decision on recognition before Christmas. But even a vote for recognition would not be implemented with the opening of diplomatic relations until the end of the time specified by the European Community—January 15, 1992. Regarding this schedule, I was again eager to be in harmony with our resolution and my counterparts' opinions. Based on the Tomuschat report, as well as our own knowledge of the status of minorities in Croatia, I noted, we were able to make a decision now, and the Badinter-Herzog Commission would certainly reach the same conclusion. The others agreed: Our decision could indeed be made before Christmas. I nevertheless repeated my question at our discussion, since it was important to me that the German government be able to follow the schedule it had laid down without violating any agreement among the Twelve. Yet even when I raised the question a second time, none of the foreign ministers spoke in disagreement. The accusation, leveled by misinformed voices, that our decision had seized the initiative by force is therefore entirely unwarranted.

I made certain that the Foreign Office prepared the German government's resolution with extreme care. It read:

515

The federal administration agreed on December 19 to recognize, in accordance with international law, those Yugoslav republics that declare by December 23, 1991, that they wish to be recognized as independent states and that they will meet the requirements set forth in the December 16 declaration on Yugoslavia of the European Community's foreign ministers. Immediately after December 23 the minister of foreign affairs will begin discussions regarding the preparation of entering into diplomatic relations as of January 1992 with those republics that fulfill the above-mentioned requirements for recognition.

This statement was followed by the remark that this decision of the German government was in accordance with the resolutions of the European Community's foreign ministers taken in Brussels on December 16. We wanted our position to clearly reflect the fact that several Yugoslav republics had exercised free self-determination and had acted democratically and on a constitutional basis in choosing independence. As announced by Chancellor Helmut Kohl on November 27, as soon as the listed requirements were met, we would be able to grant formal recognition to Croatia and Slovenia. At the same time, the resolution stated, the German government would actively support the continuation and successful conclusion of the peace conference on Yugoslavia. However, we were ready to recognize any new republics that so desired and met the requirements. Thus the German resolution fully respected the criteria established by the European Community. On January 11, 1992, the Badinter-Herzog Commission submitted its report; as we had expected, it recommended recognition of Croatia and Slovenia and came out in favor of recognizing Macedonia. Croatia's president promised the commission that its Serbian inhabitants would be granted special autonomic status, in accordance with Lord Carrington's convention paper. We considered the Badinter-Herzog Commission's report an impressive corroboration of our own earlier evaluation.

On January 15, 1992, the EC presidency—held by Portugal since the beginning of the year—announced the decision of the Twelve: Croatia and Slovenia were to be recognized. Then—and not before—we assumed diplomatic relations, as promised in Brussels. With respect to the recognition of Macedonia, the German government kept its promise to protect Greece's interests; the debate, however, went on until the spring of 1993. Subsequently the discussion focused mainly on a change in Macedonia's official name.

Recognition of Croatia and Slovenia did not result in escalation of the war in Croatia, as some of my colleagues and some other nations had feared. On the contrary, on January 9, 1992, President Slobodan Milošević of Serbia pronounced the war in and against Croatia at an end, and hostilities ceased gradually. That Milošević could unilaterally declare the war finished, and that indeed it was finished with this declaration, demonstrates where the responsibility for the war lay. Hostilities had originated entirely in Serbia, and therefore that republic was the only party that could end them; at that time Serbia occupied one-third of Croatia's territory, not the reverse.

Subsequently, at the instigation of France, the EC's foreign ministers declared on February 2, "The Community and its members recognize Serbia's constructive attitude." I did not find it easy to characterize the Serbian attitude in those terms, since the continued occupation of one-third of Croatian territory seemed to me anything but "constructive." On the other hand, I had no wish to jeopardize our unity with France at that time, especially since the declaration contained two statements of particular importance to us:

1. That hostilities had originated in Serbia (though this fact was expressed only indirectly).
2. As soon as Belgrade adopted a "constructive attitude," hostilities ended, confirming our expectation that an unequivocal stance on the issue of recognition would have a pacifying effect, rather than increasing the violence.

Since the Badinter-Herzog Commission proposed a referendum for Bosnia-Herzegovina, a decision on that proposal was tabled.

Acceptance of the United Nations peace plan also contributed to the pacification of Croatia, of course. On December 11, 1991, President Tudjman had unconditionally accepted the Vance Plan concerning the stationing of United Nations forces in Croatian-occupied territories with a predominantly Serbian minority. It had been difficult for Tudjman to reach this decision, since it meant primarily that after the occupation ended, Croatia would have to accept Serbian administrative offices in its districts. On the other hand, the Vance Plan also provided for disarmament of Serbian troops in that area, allowing for the return of expelled Croatians and structuring new police forces according to the population's ethnic composition before the eruption of hostilities.

In a number of telephone calls I had convinced President Tudjman that Croatia would have to make its contribution to the pacification and accept the Vance Plan. Initially Tudjman made a statement that was somewhat ambiguous, whereupon I spoke with him again, at Cyrus Vance's request. Finally he consented unconditionally. Vance subsequently thanked me for my efforts. On February 6, 1992 he wrote to tell me that he had received a second letter from President Tudjman, which accepted all the terms. He thanked me again for my efforts and expressed his desire to remain in close touch.

In retrospect it is clear that the United Nations did insist that Croatia accept the plan but that the organization failed to meet all the obligations to Croatia contained in that plan. In particular, the dissolution of Serbian associations never came about, nor was the police restructured according to the original ethnic composition. For that reason alone Croatia's expelled population was unable to return. The United Nations owes a great debt to Croatia and has assumed a serious responsibility for future events in that area because it failed to insure the implementation of the plan in Croatia's Serb-occupied territories.

In March 1992 I learned of a speech Lord Carrington had delivered at Chatham House on March 10. A member of the audience observed that recognizing Croatia had been a mistake, or at least precipitate; Lord Carrington replied that his own position was no longer so unequivocal because the outcome had revised his former advocacy of recognition. There was no denying that after the recognition of Croatia violence had decreased. He had had different expectations but had been set right. Recognition of Slovenia and Croatia had been unavoidable; the decision, he insisted, had been inevitable. Knowing what he knew today, he understood as much.

Douglas Hurd also commented on the matter very firmly, at a time when the futility of efforts at achieving peace in Bosnia-Herzegovina gave rise to occasional attempts in the Western camp to link the recognition of Bosnia-Herzegovina with that of Slovenia and Croatia and to hold Germany responsible for the situation in Bosnia-Herzegovina. In a radio interview on July 14, 1993,

Hurd was asked whether one of the lessons of these past events was that by and large doing what Germany wanted—recognizing first Croatia and then Bosnia—was simply one mistake after another. He replied that he did not consider the question justified. He wondered if the interviewer was really saying that Great Britain should not have recognized Croatia, that Croatia did not exist. He went on to say that by the time recognition was granted Croatia, it had existed for a long time, and people like Margaret Thatcher were strongly critical of the support given to the idea that Yugoslavia—in its entirety—might be preserved. He admitted that the timing was arguable, but he rejected the thought that recognition created the war in Bosnia. My successor, Klaus Kinkel, has told me about conversations within the group of EC ministers in which the participants were astonished by the criticism of Germany's stand, which they called absolutely unfair. That, incidentally, was also the opinion of Hans van den Broek, who has since moved to the EC Commission and most certainly was not among the strongest supporters of recognition; his fairness was never in doubt.

In retrospect it can be claimed that recognizing Croatia and Slovenia brought peace to the people in those republics. That the decision of December 16, 1991, brought an end to the hostilities in Croatia and an end to the continued threat to Slovenia was a great accomplishment. Critics of the EC's declaration of recognition therefore, owe us an answer to the question of whether they were truly willing to risk continuation of the war in Croatia. Halting aggression in and against Croatia, putting an end to the threat of renewed aggression against Slovenia—that was our main goal, and we achieved it. What is there to criticize? Recognizing Slovenia and Croatia triggered no violence but ended the first war for which Belgrade was responsible. Germany took no unilateral action; the decision was made by the Twelve, and the CSCE nations and the whole community of nations joined in agreement.

The war in Bosnia-Herzegovina—the second Yugoslav war—began later, and it was not Germany who initiated the recognition of Bosnia-Herzegovina. Quite the contrary. In early March 1992 Washington suggested that the United States and the European Community act in concert. Washington not only recognized Slovenia and Croatia but also wanted to extend recognition to Bosnia-Herzegovina. Recognition was declared on April 6, 1992, and went into effect on April 7, 1992, simultaneously by the United States and the EC. On that occasion, as previously, consensus within the European Community and unity with France were important to us.

In the debates within the EC, as well as in public statements, I repeatedly advocated a European response to the problems of the former Yugoslavia. In practical terms this move meant that the offer of forming an association, which had previously been made to the countries of Central and Southeastern Europe, should also be extended to those successor states of the former Yugoslavia that accepted the suggestions of the European Community and its mediators for a solution to the conflict. This offer was designed to make the suggestions much more attractive, because such a European offer held a promise of extraordinary improvement for all well-intentioned parties. It is in this area where the European Union's true potential lies, and even now it is not too late for such an offer. In that respect the EU has options unavailable to any other power or any other organization. The EU's offer to enter into treaties with any successor state of the former Yugoslavia that is ready for peace—that is the European response to the nationalism that fueled fighting in the area. The states that are ready for peace in the former Yugoslavia would be supported by such treaties.

Nonetheless, it is a popular view to see the European Union's stand on the events in Yugoslavia as a sign of failure. Is such a view really justified? On the positive side, German-French cooperation proved its viability during that phase. As did Paris, Bonn did everything possible to keep events in Yugoslavia from placing a strain on German-French relations, particularly since public opinion in the two nations, at least during the early months, varied in its response to the situation. The EC, too, upheld its principle of acting only in concert: Germany delayed its recognition of Slovenia and Croatia until it had gathered the consent of all twelve members. On this issue German-French unity should not be disregarded, nor should the European Community's struggle for shared positions; the Balkans did not divide the EC nations.

Nevertheless, the individual governments and the European institutions—the European Community as well as CSCE—were not sufficiently prepared for occurrences in Yugoslavia. Of course, after the dramatic events in Central and Eastern Europe during

1989 and 1990, anything else could hardly be expected. From the very beginning German policy set the prohibition of the use of armed force to solve political issues as an important criterion.

The possibility of ending the war by way of a comprehensive embargo on oil and other energy carriers was not implemented to the extent that it should have been. An effective energy embargo would at least have crippled the supply of heavy weapons, such as tanks and artillery, and the air force, which initially only the Serbs deployed, and it therefore would have compelled the Serbs to come to the negotiating table, a method the other participants to the conflict were prepared to use from the start. And in this respect the United Nations Security Council in particular failed to take full advantage of all its options. Germany, on the other hand, by trying to involve the Security Council and CSCE, was intent on countering the impression that a solution without or even against the Soviet Union was considered.

One of the essential lessons to be learned from the course of events in the former Yugoslavia must be the continued renunciation of force: It is the only way to preserve or create the culture of coexistence implicit in the Paris Charter. The authority and effectiveness of the institutions of CSCE—now OSCE—must be strengthened; anyone eager to resolve conflicts in opposition to OSCE, or without it, by the use of force, must not expect leniency or even approval after the fact by the community of nations. Because the debate on justifiable and unjustifiable aggression results in old patterns of behavior, renunciation of force must remain the unalterable basis for peaceful coexistence in Europe. Aggression can never be justified, just as victims and aggressor must never be placed on the same plane and ethnic cleansing must never be accepted. No matter who is responsible for initiating such extermination, there can never be retrospective approbation.

However, it is equally important to support the desire to resolve conflicts peacefully by concluding European treaties with those of the former Yugoslavia's successor states that want them. That is where the European Union's special responsibility lies—and its special opportunity.

14

Developments After the Great Changes in Europe

The New Treaties with Our Eastern Neighbors

The historic changes in Central and Eastern Europe resulted in the dissolution of the Warsaw Pact and in liberty, democracy, and national self-determination for its former members. The Federal Republic's entire Eastern policy, as well as bilateral relations with our neighbors, were placed on a completely new basis. If the treaties of our former Eastern policy had been structured on the model of the 1970 Moscow Treaty, the united Germany now had an opportunity to both reach back to old historic connections and to explore radically new approaches. This process began immediately after the conclusion of the Two-Plus-Four Treaty, with a treaty with the Soviet Union.

In March 1991 the Supreme Soviet, the last of the signators' parliaments, approved the Two-Plus-Four Treaty, as well as the treaty on good neighborly relations and the treaty on comprehensive economic cooperation between Germany and the Soviet Union. The Bundestag followed immediately and ratified the treaty on good neighborly relations. "After much suspicion," I noted at the time, "even pessimistic predictions that Soviet foreign policy would change if it had not already done so, we have learned that Gorbachev does not change course, he stands behind his promises and the basic principles of his policies. That is, he is steadfastly continuing the policy of democratization in Eastern Europe, the policy of overcoming the division of Europe. That policy is good news for Germany, as well as for Europe and the world." On March 15, 1991, Ambassador Terekhov delivered the ratification document to the Foreign Office. Thus the Two-Plus-Four Treaty was enacted.

Now the road was finally clear for the formation of relations with the Soviet Union that would no longer be strained by Moscow's insistence on the division of Germany. Gone, too, was the burden of the East-West conflict, particularly since the process of the two Germanys' unification had proved that Germany's incorporation in the Western communities was irrevocable and irreversible. Restructuring our bilateral contacts was in our interest as well as that of the Soviet Union. In order to avoid competition, I tried to pursue our Eastern policy in concert with our partners in the European Community; primarily I sought close ties with France. The nations of the European Union should respect this need for unity in future as well, for competition in the West in regard to Central and Eastern Europe policies would necessarily create new instabilities in those territories. The European Union's policy of making European treaties and partnership treaties, which Germany was instrumental in structuring, plus the offer by the Partnership for Peace made through NATO are therefore the correct programmatic approaches. Full utilization of CSCE and further growth of its institutions are similarly indispensable for stability in all of Europe. The West must not lose sight of the larger objective of a foundation of a pan-European peace that is accepted throughout Europe as such.

I believed that the Soviet Union was an important partner in the process of creating Europe's future and securing global stability; developing that partnership was therefore of vital interest to us. Even today, given the country's size and importance, any attempt to isolate Russia would be bound to fail, but isolating it by ignoring it would be equally wrong and dangerous. Within the European Community, therefore, I supported intensive relations based on treaties; this program eventually became a reality in the cooperation treaty with Russia. It seemed particularly important to me that Gorbachev participate in the 1991 world economic summit in London. I incorporated my request that the Soviet President be invited in the larger plan of enlarging the group of G7 to G8—in other words, to accept the new Soviet Union as an equal member. The new opportunities such a change offered should be seized.

But matters ran a different course, and the hesitation and coolness with which the West treated Gorbachev at the world economic summit—against the advice of the German and French delegations—certainly did not help his position in the crucial summer of 1991. An opportunity was missed; even worse, the consequences of the London summit may have been graver and more far-reaching than we could realize at the time. How would Moscow have reacted to a Gorbachev who was ostentatiously supported in London?

The Two-Plus-Four Treaty had reaffirmed Germany's obligation to give permanence to its border with Poland, which was drawn at the end of the Second World War; the German government met this obligation by concluding the German-Polish border treaty along international-law terms. On November 14, 1990, Foreign Minister Skubiszewski and I both signed it in Warsaw.

If the border treaty redressed a situation created in the past, the treaty on good-neighbor relations and cooperation, signed subsequently in Bonn, was aimed at the future. The popular peaceful revolutions in Poland, East Germany, and Czechoslovakia, as well as the courageous stand of Gyula Horn's Hungarian government and of the entire Hungarian people, had unlocked the borders in the formerly Communist part of Europe. It was now our task to work together to make certain that this border did not become a line dividing rich from poor. Germany, acting on its convictions, therefore supported Poland's wish for incorporation in the European Community; we believed that the advantages Western Europe can offer through the Common Market should also be available to the peoples of Central and Eastern Europe who had regained their freedom. Their long liberation process, therefore, should culminate in the prospect of joining the European Community. The closer Poland got to the EC, the more effectively we would be able to fulfill the bilateral framework of German-Polish cooperation.

From the outset the unified Germany had combined its bilateral Eastern policy with the struggle for an active Eastern policy in the European Union. It was important to me that the set of new bilateral treaties with the countries of Central and Eastern Europe not be interpreted—or misunderstood—as a relapse into national power politics. I wanted them to be clearly seen for what they were intended to be: reinforcement of the multilateral, cooperative, and in some cases integrative efforts at treaties the German government undertook on an all-European level. Building Europe with these bilateral accords and agreements beyond the framework of the EC meant creating a new community of all of the Continent's peoples and nations. The burden of their past made Germany and Poland the most clearly chosen to achieve that end.

On June 17, 1991, after six lengthy rounds of negotiations, the treaty on good-neighbor relations and cooperation was signed by Germany and Poland. Poland's Prime Minister Jan Krzysztof Bielecki and Foreign Minister Skubiszewski came to Bonn for the occasion, and we asked Willy Brandt to join us. We also signed the accord on creating a German-Polish youth welfare agency and of a joint environmental council; we further exchanged notes on establishing a German-Polish government commission for regional and border cooperation.

A Putsch and Its Aftermath

On August 19, 1991, I was awakened early in the morning by a telephone call: the war room of Foreign Office informed me that a putsch had occurred in Moscow. I discussed the situation with the Chancellor, who called the heads of the parties and parliamentary factions to the Chancellor's Office. Even with all the imponderables of such a situation, I never found it credible that Gorbachev was ill or that, as was subsequently claimed, he permitted the coup d'état.

Early in the evening the Soviet ambassador, Vladislav Terekhov, called on me to pass on a statement by the new rulers, but his behavior made it very clear that he was not siding with the insurgents. We were waiting for a statement by Gorbachev, I replied, who was still the Soviet Union's elected president. Besides, I remarked, respect for another nation's laws was among the principles of CSCE, in particular the Paris Charter. It was my impression that Ambassador Terekhov was not unhappy at my disapproval of the coup—when he had briefed me on the provisional government's statement, he had been noticeably distant and had shown an almost pointed lack of enthusiasm. When I visited Moscow soon after, to attend the CSCE human-rights conference, respect for other nations' laws was a central topic of my address—which, incidentally, the Soviet delegation supported.

But that day had not yet come. The insurgents were still in the saddle. The opposition to the insurgents by Russia's president, Boris Yeltsin, was impressive; he made history in the best sense of the word. In this crisis Yeltsin—whom I had met only once—displayed not only courage but also a willingness to accept responsibility. When I was unable to reach him by telephone, I directed our ambassador in Moscow, Klaus Blech, to assure Yeltsin or his associates of our solidarity.

Because of the attempted putsch, Russia, Kazakhstan, and Uzbekistan did not sign the new union treaty as scheduled: The dissolution of the Soviet Union began. More and more openly the Baltic states demanded independence. On Yeltsin's initiative, they were released from the Soviet Union on September 6, 1991.

As early as August, shortly after the putsch, members of the EU conferred on a joint position with regard to the Baltic states. They must not be abandoned once again; the Federal Republic of Germany had never recognized their incorporation into the Soviet Union. For that reason I had always refused to visit the Baltic states or, as the Soviet officals would word it, the Baltic republics. It was not, therefore, a matter of recognition but of reestablishing diplomatic relations.

In interviews I advocated that step, combining it with the suggestion that the EC prepare for negotiations on association treaties with the Baltic states. On August 28 the foreign ministers of Lithuania, Latvia, and Estonia visited Bonn in order to sign letters reestablishing diplomatic relations.

On September 8—a Sunday—I flew to Moscow to participate in the CSCE conference on the human dimension, which was slated to begin on September 10. I had long since advocated in the West that the conference be held in Moscow. Now the time had come: It was taking place, but under entirely unforeseen circumstances.

Moscow as well as the conference were under the impact of the shock occasioned by the putsch.

On Monday morning I first met with my friend Eduard Shevardnadze over breakfast. He briefed me on the power shifts that had taken place between the Central Committee and the republics. Subsequently the picture he sketched turned out to be wholly realistic. This meeting was followed by talks with Yakovlev and Gorbachev, who seemed depressed. He spoke openly about his fears. Next I met with Vadim Bakatin, the new KGB chief, in our ambassador's quarters; it was an unusual encounter in every respect. Ambassador Blech and I considered it phenomenal that the talk took place at all, but it was even more phenomenal for Bakatin to come to our residence to explain to us that he wanted to place the KGB under democratic control. He himself seemed aware of the enormity of the task he had assumed.

Speaking from my experience as minister of the interior, I told him that in the Federal Republic of Germany, sensitized by the lessons from our history, we had reached a stage at which the intelligence services considered themselves part of a democratic state, respected the constitution, and considered democratic control a natural state of affairs.

After talks with Baker, Hurd, and Foreign Minister Boris Pankin of the Soviet Union, I attended an evening meeting with Leningrad's chief mayor, Anatoli Sobchak, whose clear ideas about reform impressed me deeply. In my address to the conference I made several recommendations for reforming CSCE: that we declare insistence on meeting CSCE's obligation as different from interference with another nation's internal affairs; that the usurpation of power through violations of CSCE obligations should not be recognized and that regimes in serious violation of the Paris Charter should not expect recognition; and that—of the greatest importance, even a revolutionary change in CSCE—we should be able to demand, without the consent of those involved, reinstitution of the values of the Paris Charter and the dispatch of CSCE monitors. The Soviet delegation was my most fervent supporter.

From Moscow I traveled to the three Baltic states. The visits to Tallinn, Riga, and Vilnius will remain unforgettable. Lithuanians, Latvians, and Estonians were determined to take advantage of their newly won independence by instituting democratic processes and a market economy. During talks with foreign ministers Lennart Meri, Yanis Yurkans, and Algirdas Saudargas we recalled the very different circumstances of our previous meetings—in Berlin at the conclusion of the first CSCE ministerial conference and in Bonn when we agreed to reestablish diplomatic relations.

Meanwhile the internal struggle to hold the Soviet Union together continued. Without interfering with domestic events, the world nevertheless indicated that it had an interest in a continuance of the Soviet Union, though not necessarily under that name. The same held true for the German government, which was well-disposed toward Gorbachev's efforts to contain the nation within a new structure and with a new union treaty. The German stance was not only an expression of loyalty; it was also a sign of our fears about the political, military, and economic consequences a dissolution of the Soviet Union might bring. Naturally in that context we were particularly concerned with the issue of atomic weapons; there must be no proliferation.

On November 15, 1991, the seven republics of the Soviet Union—Russia, Kazakhstan, Azerbaijan, Kyrgyzstan, Tajikistan, Turkmenistan, and Belarus—reached an agreement with President Gorbachev concerning the establishment of a Confederation of Independent States. It was the last attempt to preserve the old Soviet Union as a democratic confederacy. I literally felt power and institutions being wrenched from Gorbachev's hands, twist by twist.

But November 19, 1991, brought good news: Gorbachev reappointed Eduard Shevardnadze to the post of foreign minister. After Shevardnadze's resignation, Alexander Bessmertnykh, a career diplomat, had assumed the position, using his own experience and good instincts to continue his predecessor's policies. It was my impression that Yuli Kvitsinksy, the Soviet ambassador to the Federal Republic, who, early in 1991, might have had hopes of becoming Shevardnadze's successor himself, was extremely loyal to the new minister; and I will always be grateful to him for the skill and commitment with which he supported the ratification of the Two-Plus-Four Treaty in the Foreign Commission, even though, at least initially, he had seemed less than delighted with the new course Gorbachev and Shevardnadze were taking regarding the German question. However, in the end both of them—

Bessmertnykh and Kvitsinsky—were forced to give up their offices in the context of the coup d'état. I had, and still have, my doubts whether they had really given cause for dismissal.

Pankin became the next foreign minister of the Soviet Union; he had most recently been ambassador to Prague, where he had openly opposed the insurgents. Working with him was also easy. However, it became increasingly apparent, especially after the putsch failed, that the foreign ministry of Russia, which had been a mere formality for decades, was becoming the center for management and decision-making in the area of foreign policy. Andrei Kosyrev had long since assumed that post, exercising his function with great commitment, the knowledgeability of a young but experienced diplomat, and apparently with the backing of Russian President Yeltsin.

Shevardnadze's reappointment as the Soviet foreign minister was universally welcomed. Over the telephone I told him how happy we were in Germany with Gorbachev's decision. However, the tracks had already been shunted to lead to the dissolution of the Soviet Union.

On December 21, 1991, the time had come: The Community of Independent States was established, marking the end of the Soviet Union. Four days later, Gorbachev resigned. The whole world honored his accomplishments; Helmut Kohl stated, "No one will deny him his place in the history of our century." At the time I wondered whether all those affected were aware of the consequences of the Soviet Union's dissolution—in politics, on security, and economically.

On December 25, 1991, Gorbachev made his last public appearance as president of the Soviet Union. In a television address he bid farewell to his fellow citizens. All that Christmas Day I tried to reach by telephone the man to whom the world, Europe, and Germany owed so much. In the afternoon I was finally connected. It would be the last conversation Gorbachev conducted from the Kremlin. "After I hang up, I am leaving the Kremlin," Gorbachev said.

I thanked him for all he had done for us, and we reminisced about the long road we had walked together since our first meeting in 1986. The extent to which the world had changed in these five and a half years was hard to believe. "I could have given my television address yesterday, but I didn't want to spoil your

Christmas Eve goose dinner," he joked. We both laughed, although neither of us were really in a merry mood. I had telephoned Gorbachev to tell him on that difficult day that no matter what the future would bring, he could count on me. He could be sure of the Germans' gratitude, I promised him, not only because of German unity, but also because he had been instrumental in ending the disastrous East-West conflict. Friends, I wanted him to realize, would never forget.

An epoch had come to an end. The post-Gorbachev era was beginning, as was the post–Soviet Union era. Now it was important to secure political and economic stability in the successor states. This task was all the more urgent since some of them held huge arsenals of nuclear weapons, an incalculable potential for danger. The Western community advocated recognition of Russia as the Soviet Union's legitimate successor. The decision was vital on two counts: It determined who would occupy the permanent seat in the United Nations Security Council, and it affected obligations the Soviet Union had entered into regarding the limitation and reduction of nuclear capability.

On December 20, 1991, the first session of the North Atlantic Cooperation Council was held, gathering together the members of NATO and the former members of the Warsaw Pact. The suggestion to create such a commission had come from the United States secretary of state, James Baker, and from me; we were concerned with making certain that the dissolution of the Warsaw Pact would not result in a security vacuum; we preferred developing cooperative security structures.

The session in Brussels witnessed one of the sensational acts we had almost come to expect: The Soviet flag was lowered, and the Russian delegate announced that he had received instructions to represent only Russia from this point on. It is nearly unimaginable what it meant for us to be conferring with the representatives of the former Warsaw Pact nations in the same NATO rooms where we had in the past held highly confidential discussions. The world had really changed.

Only a few months earlier, on October 9, I had gone to Sofia to sign the German-Bulgarian Treaty on Friendly Cooperation and Partnership in Europe with my Bulgarian counterpart Victor Valkov. Article One dealt with the expansion of bilateral relations and the creation of a common Europe "in which human rights and basic liberties are respected on the basis of democracy and constitutionality and in which borders lose their divisive character in part by decreasing economic and social differences." In Article Two, referring to the Helsinki Final Act and the Paris Charter, both sides endorsed the principle of resolving conflicts without the use of force, and in Article Three they accepted the obligation to consult within the framework of CSCE and the United Nations. A peculiarity was embedded in Article Fifteen because it explicitly regulated cooperation in the area of environmental protection, specifically reduction of pollution in the Danube and an increase in safety measures for nuclear reactors.

At the signing ceremony, in which Bulgaria's president, Zhelyu Zhelev, participated, I paid tribute to the historically close relations between Germany and Bulgaria, also emphasizing the opportunity offered for a new beginning and new prospects. In fact no problems of the past remained to be settled by the treaty. In addition it expressed the German government's efforts to support the new European democracies and to smooth their way into the European Community.

Kazakhstan and the Ukraine: Two Visits with New Partners in the East

In October 1991 I thought the time was ripe for me to form my own view of the current situation in some important republics of the Soviet Union. I decided to go to Kazakhstan and follow that trip with a visit to the Ukraine. I had chosen that sequence deliberately, since I was concerned that my trip might contribute to the strengthening of the Soviet Union's centrifugal forces; nor did I wish to put a strain on our relationship with Moscow. As had been true for Yugoslavia, we had no intention of promoting the dissolution of structures that had united different peoples and nationalities. We acted on the principle of allowing all peoples, including those of the Soviet Union, to decide on their own future, and we respected their decision. Kazakhstan's president, Nursultan Nazarbayev, was among the political leaders who, together with Gorbachev, was working to find new rules for the republics' coexistence within the Soviet Union. In Kiev, however, the process of separating from the union was already far advanced.

Very soon Nazarbayev began to speak of the present situation in Kazakhstan, expounding his thoughts on his country's future. Above all, he remarked, the economy would need to grow quickly. To achieve that end, he needed the resident Germans, and he would allow them to realize their national identity to the fullest. The huge country with a small population is rich in mineral resources, and Germany could become an interesting partner for Kazakhstan.

I was particularly anxious to hear his assessment of Gorbachev's position and equally eager to learn his opinion of Yeltsin. Evidently Nazarbayev did not favor dissolution of the Soviet Union, preferring a strengthening of the individual republics and their presidents. Gorbachev could therefore count on his support to a degree.

The following day I had another meeting with the President. Again he welcomed me very warmly and emphasized my contribution to the development of good relations between Germany and the Soviet Union in general and to Kazakhstan in particular. Then he addressed our efforts in transforming a planned economy into the structures of a market economy. He also described the parliament's work on Kazakhstan's laws concerning the adaptation of a market economy.

Nazarbayev expressed his satisfaction at Germany's lively interest in the course of events in Kazakhstan. By honoring Germany's position within the European Community and our accomplishments in the unification of Europe, he was expressing his hope that, with Germany's help, Kazakhstan would also be able to build a good relationship with the European Community. He stated that he was an advocate of modernization for his country. Though in fact the country had a wealth of raw materials and energy, he was unwilling to go on with the present colonial economy—as he called dependency on the export of raw materials. In the long run he would like to maximize domestic production. That plan coincided precisely with our own ideas about pan-European economic cooperation. The European Community must of necessity be pleased with economic partners who developed their own economic independence rather than restricting their efforts to supplying raw materials and energy. At the same time these nations would also have to continue exporting, not only because, as suppliers of foreign currency, we were indispensable to them, but also because we wanted diversification in the import of raw materials and energy, which during the years of West-East conflict had unilaterally favored the south.

I replied that in regard to cooperation with other nations, it would be important to define as soon as possible the responsibilities of the union as opposed to those of the individual republics; I added that I hoped the men in charge would keep this element in mind when arriving at decisions in the next few days. It was not up to Germany, I continued, to advise Kazakhstan or other republics on whether they should become independent or remain in the union. However, clarity regarding future conditions and relations was necessary, as our own experiences had taught us. For our part, I noted, our efforts at integration within the European Union were intended to lead to the Common Market by January 1, 1993, and we hoped decisions could be made about the political union before the end of the current year. Events on the whole appeared to tend, not toward new frontiers, but toward overcoming existing ones. That state of affairs favored remaining together in a new structure.

I assured Nazarbayev that our relations with Kazakhstan mattered a great deal to us. Mentioning the increasing number of Germans emigrating from the Soviet Union, I remarked that all of them must be free to choose where they wanted to live, a choice surely determined to a large degree by the opportunities a country offered them to realize their skills and needs. Therefore, President's Nazarbayev's idea of steering investments to the areas in which Germans had settled, among others, was a step in the right direction, which would probably enable him to influence German investors favorably, and these could then serve as a bridge. I also remarked that I understood Nazarbayev's interest in cooperating with the EC and with Germany to be a nod in the direction of cooperation with Europe. It was important for us to know as much—such responsible politics would bear abundant fruit.

Picking up where he had left off the previous day, Nazarbayev noted that, since Kazakhstan was a multinational state, he cared about keeping the union together. He was afraid that dissolving the Soviet Union would lead to territorial demands, with incalculable consequences. The resulting situation might turn out to be even more terrible than that in Yugoslavia, and such an outcome would have a disastrous global fallout. That prospect was another

533

reason why he wanted to continue his policies and be a model for guaranteeing human rights.

In reply I pointed out that history had taught us that borders must never be changed by force, and this realization included respect for the rights of minorities, respect for all principles of the Helsinki Final Act. The current situation in Yugoslavia was the result of numerous mistakes, the primary one being one nation's claim to hegemony in a multinational state. Throughout history Europe's borders had been changed again and again, with dire consequences, but discussion of historic borders led nowhere. We must look to the future together; we were offering to cooperate with the Soviet Union and its republics in whatever way the peoples of the Soviet Union thought right.

Nazarbayev agreed. He was eager to accelerate negotiations on the economic treaty between the republics, so that he could begin work on the political treaty. He believed that the republics would confederate. Once they sensed that the totalitarian center had disappeared—and that realization was important mainly for psychological reasons—they would be impelled to resume the natural striving for cooperation. As soon as the current political struggle was ended, the republics would have to improve their populations' general living conditions, and such a step could succeed only through close cooperation. Now they must support Gorbachev: He was the only integrating figure in the country's political affairs.

The conversation left me with the distinct impression that Nazarbayev was sincere in his preference for a loose confederation within the Soviet Union. He clearly realized the enormous problems total dissolution of the Soviet Union would entail. His remarks about Gorbachev seemed to have been equally sincere; conversely, Gorbachev had given me a similar evaluation of Nazarbayev.

Nazarbayev was among the Soviet Union's strongest political figures in this final phase of its existence. He was also one of the most farsighted representatives of the independent states that came into being in the territory of the former Soviet Union. Only time will tell whether his pragmatic concept of political, social, and economic transformation will be more successful in the long run than other models. In the transition period Nazarbayev managed to safeguard the stability of his multinational state. And that alone is a great deal.

My visit to the Ukraine was also very important because I realized that that country would play a large role in Eastern Europe's future stability. If, as the West hoped, the foundation for a permanent and just peace was to be created, the Ukraine would play a major part in it. Whether the Soviet Union continued to exist in a new form or whether a number of independent and autonomous states came into being, the relationship between Russia and the Ukraine would be crucial. Considering the history of the Ukraine, current developments must seem like a dream come true—the dream of a Ukraine finally able to realize its own identity, develop its own culture, speak its own language, and determine its own future. During the Second World War, the Ukraine was the part of the Soviet Union that had suffered the most—except for Belarus— and Kiev was branded as a battlefield and the site of horrible German massacres of the Jewish population.

At the outset of our meeting Foreign Minister Slenko explained the Ukraine's foreign policy goals and expressed his interest in working within the United Nations, where his country had always been represented, as well as within CSCE. The Ukraine was also eager to make use of the process of European unification to safeguard Ukrainian concerns and to assure it a place within Europe's cooperative network.

I assured him that we were very interested in contacts with the Ukraine. In recent times, I noted, we had witnessed a dangerous amount of instability, as the case of Yugoslavia illustrated. We must therefore be extremely prudent in dealing with the future structure of the Soviet Union and the Ukraine's role within the Soviet Union, deliberations for which each individual peoples carried great responsibility. As for nuclear weapons, the separate entities must assume all the obligations the Soviet Union had agreed to.

I explained that the European Community was in the process of taking further steps toward integration. On January 1, 1993, the Common Market would be in place, and we were close to concluding the government conferences on economic and currency union as well as political union. We were convinced, I stated, that close cooperation with transnational structures would both serve

535

European stability and be advantageous to each individual state. Now that Germany was united, our policies were determined by our intention to make a crucial contribution to the unification of Europe. We therefore wanted to do whatever we could to prevent a new division between East and West through an economic and social dividing line that would replace the former military-ideological confrontation. I affirmed that we favored European structures within the framework of CSCE and that EC and NATO were pivotal to Europe's future. Further, it was essential that we all work toward creating pan-European infrastructures in transportation, energy, and telecommunication.

Foreign Minister Slenko spoke of the Ukraine as a successor state of the former Soviet Union. He assured me that it would adhere to the START agreements and was prepared to enter into negotiations with the Soviet Union's republics and with the union itself to discuss the demolition of strategic weapons in accordance with START. He was also interested in a form of economic cooperation that would be to universal advantage. The Ukraine, he stated, understood the principles underlying European integration very well, but it also realized the length of the road that had been covered so far. At the same time he shared our fears concerning recent events in Europe, above all in Yugoslavia. A united Europe and an independent Ukraine should speak the same language.

On the subject of arms control, I explained that, especially since Germany was not a nuclear power, we had a vital interest in and a right to insist that the number of nuclear powers be kept at current levels. The single nuclear power, the Soviet Union must not be transformed into several nuclear powers, since such a measure was simply another form of proliferation, a state of affairs we could not permit. Therefore, the fact that the presidents of the United States and the Soviet Union, in separate statements, had made clear their intention of totally eliminating short-range nuclear missiles and nuclear artillery ammunition was important; we could only welcome such a program. However, this action alone did not address the question of strategic weapons. In that area we were expecting further steps, independent of the issue of proliferation.

After this meeting I called on President Leonid Kravchuk. He expressed an expectation that my visit would open up possibilities of cooperation. My visit, I replied, was important because of the particular time it was occurring, a time full of great changes in Europe as well as in the Soviet Union. For that reason, too, I appreciated the opportunity of a talk with him. Since German unification had been achieved, we were interested in bringing about European unification; the immediate reason for our objective lay in our geography and our history. We were concerned with the entire Continent, not merely its western sector. I reminded Kravchuk that we were members of the European Community, but the West's industrialized nations were fully aware of their responsibility for what was occurring in Central and Eastern Europe. After I had stressed the significance of CSCE, I spoke of the opportunities of future cooperation. In order to contribute to preserving the Soviet Union's market, we needed to know the Ukraine's position. Even as we were meeting here, I pointed out, an important meeting was taking place in Moscow. We respected the peoples' right to self-determination and whatever decision they chose to make. But it was important to take account of where the new road would lead—and it must not lead back to nationalism; instead, all of us must make an effort to move toward closer supranational cooperation. We fully understood that, after decades of Communism, which stifled the republics' identity, the desire for realizing that identity was particularly strong. But we also felt it of paramount importance that this evolution be structured with a sense of responsibility. New borders, I noted, generated not new opportunities but new risks.

Kravchuk assured me that he shared my belief that no country could separate itself from the overall integration processes. However, if these procedures deprived groups of their own nationality, people would not accept them. The situation was different in the European Community, where nations kept their identity and independence; the positions of Germany, France, and the Netherlands illustrated his point. In the Soviet Union there were attempts to make the republics members of a new union. However, Kravchuk remarked, such a solution would deprive the republics of their national identity and independence. The population as a whole was eager to build a nation of its own that would enter into relations with other nations and with the previous Soviet Union's republics as an equal partner. Kravchuk was in favor of preserving the territory of the former Soviet Union as a viable market, but such a future must be based on equal rights—a concern not universally understood. Besides, as this new union was being established, elementary rules were violated. For example, a treaty was scheduled to be signed in Moscow this very day whose text he had never even seen; under the new leadership in Moscow that kind of procedure had become the norm. The Ukraine could not possibly sign a document sight unseen—its signature could only be appended to an examined text. His country's most critical concern at the moment was the question of survival as a nation and relations with the other states.

Further Steps in Treaty Diplomacy

Completing the network of treaties with the nations of Central and Eastern Europe remained a major concern of mine. In February 1992 Helmut Kohl and I traveled to Budapest to sign the treaty with Hungary. Not only were Germany's relations with that country free of problems, against the backdrop of the events of 1989 they were also characterized by a special friendship and extraordinary gratitude on our part. We will always feel indebted to the Hungarians for opening their own borders to thousands of refugees from East Germany in the fall of 1989. This bilateral treaty, signed on February 6, 1992, not only determined general principles but fully expressed our will to friendship and good neighborly relations. Its preamble resembles those of the treaties with the Soviet Union, Poland, and Bulgaria. Further, in Article Three Germany declares its willingness to endorse Hungary's membership in the EC; Article Nine provides for the promotion of contacts between the German and the Hungarian parliaments; Article Ten is intended to facilitate contact between regions, cities, and communities.

The treaty was signed by the two heads of government, Helmut Kohl and József Antall, as well as by myself and my counterpart, Ferenc Madel. I first met Antall before the West German coalition of CDU/CSU and FDP was elected, in Budapest, along with representatives of other oppositional groups; he was already clearly marked by illness. It was with great respect and deep sympathy that we witnessed this brave man's struggle against his fatal illness, sacrificing himself to his last breath for the new democratic Hungary. I will remember him with admiration. Although I did not agree with him on certain issues of domestic and foreign policy, I recognized him as one of Hungary's great figures. It was this small, courageous nation's good fortune that at a time of cataclysmic change great men appeared on every level to shape the country's destiny.

Our excellent bilateral relations, for which Gyula Horn, among others, is crucially responsible, helped to accelerate Hungary's march toward Europe. The European treaty with the European Union offers a good basis for progress in that direction.

We concluded a treaty on good neighborly relations and friendly cooperation with Czechoslovakia as well. On February 27 and 28, 1992, Chancellor Kohl and I traveled to Prague for the signing, and from there we proceeded to Slovakia. With the aid of this treaty, forty-seven years after the end of the Second World War, we were eager to make a new beginning. President Havel expressed our hope: "This treaty represents the beginning of a new era in the relations of our two nations, an era of understanding, mutual trust, and fruitful cooperation, an era that will build on all that is good in our thousand-year-old history of coexistence and that will bury for all time all the evil that has shadowed the history of our coexistence. I believe that this treaty will inaugurate an era of joint construction of a united, democratic Europe. I believe that the relations we are working to shape today and of which this treaty is a part, will be for the benefit of future generations. I believe that when we signed this treaty, we contributed to peace between our peoples and to a peaceful and creative future of our Continent."

President von Weizsäcker had visited Czechoslovakia in October 1991. It was fortunate indeed for German-Czech relations that in those decisive years two such eminent presidents as Václav Havel and Richard von Weizsäcker headed the two nations. Havel had sent out a courageous and clear signal of reconciliation when he admitted that expulsion of the German minority following the Second World War had been unjust. Conversely, President von Weizsäcker delivered one of his most impressive speeches at the Czech parliament, acknowledging the unspeakable injustice and suffering Germans had caused in Czechoslovakia in the 1930s and 1940s.

During that visit Foreign Minister Jiři Dienstbier and I had initialed the treaty on good neighborly relations and friendly cooperation, a document pointing to the future that we signed "in commemoration of the many victims sacrificed to the reign of terror, to war, and to expulsion, and of the great suffering imposed on many of the innocent." This document also listed the rights of the German minority and reaffirmed them.

More extensive arrangements are required to consolidate the relationship between Germany and Czechoslovakia—for example, dealing with the issue of restitution for Czech victims of National Socialist persecution. It must be a priority of German relations with Prague to resolve this issue by establishing a foundation.

A new treaty with Romania established, among other issues, a basis of international law for the rights of the German minority in that nation. The treaty specifically secured the protection of minorities along the lines established by CSCE, so that the approximately seventy thousand Germans resident in Romania were given a binding guarantee to preserve their ethnic, cultural, linguistic, and religious identity. That treaty also certifies Germany's promise to support Romania's application for associate status in the EC. As I noted at the signing ceremony on April 21, 1992, in Bucharest, that clause initiated Romania's future full membership in the European Community.

Only a little more than two years after the dictator Ceausescu was toppled, Romania had evolved irreversibly in the direction of democracy, although difficult problems remained. Romania's foreign minister, Adrian Nastase, stressed Bucharest's desire for close ties to NATO; after all, he noted, Romania was a Central European nation. He suggested bilateral agreements between members of the North Atlantic Cooperation Council.

The treaty on friendship, partnership, and cooperation with Romania was the cornerstone of a number of bilateral treaties with countries of the former Eastern bloc. Aside from their basic significance, these treaties were also intended to secure the structure for peace in Europe. It will remain our task to pave the way into the EU for those countries. It is imperative that we set dates for the onset of negotiations on joining the European Union.

On April 22, 1992, I left Bucharest for a brief visit to Albania, where President Sali Berisha welcomed me as the bearer of friendship and hope. In Tirana I announced Germany's support for Albania's efforts to gain closer ties to international institutions. I also spoke in favor of the country's association with the European Community and the North Atlantic Cooperation Council. Albania had been the first nation to leave the Warsaw Pact, and for that reason, I argued, it seemed absurd for the pact's former members to be in the Cooperation Council while Albania was excluded. My counterpart, Alfred Serrequi, and I also signed an accord on work and social policy as well as a general agreement on air traffic.

Speaking to the parliament in Tirana, I addressed CSCE's obligations, which, I noted, should also apply to the Albanian population in Kosovo. Albania's concerns regarding Serbia's policies in Kosovo were only too understandable. At the conclusion of my visit, after talks with the party chairmen and with Prime Minister Meksi, I visited the industrial city of Elbasan, where the main square had been renamed Genscher Place. Thousands of Albanians responded to the speeches President Berisha and I gave with thunderous applause.

Visiting a Friend

Another aspect of our Eastern policy since the upheaval was the establishment of diplomatic relations with the new nations that appeared or reappeared after the dissolution of the Soviet Union.

Thus I visited Georgia's capital, Tiflis, from April 12 to 13, 1992, to explore ways of bringing Georgia closer to the European Community and of increasing German economic aid. My principal personal motive for the visit was to to thank my friend Eduard Shevardnadze one more time before my resignation as foreign minister. As chairman of the State Council, he had become the head of government in his homeland.

My former colleague described the difficult road he envisioned for himself as well as for Georgia. But he assured me that he was determined to continue pursuing democratic goals in his homeland and to preserve human rights and the rights of minorities in a country that was seriously debilitated by economic problems, political instability, and ethnic conflicts. Shevardnadze was grateful for Germany's offer of aid in these troubled times. We talked about a comprehensive German-Georgian treaty and a cultural agreement. Further, we anticipated a proposed academic exchange; Georgian students would be admitted to German universities.

Shevardnadze, ruling in Tiflis, appeared to be a president in charge, literally, of everything. He was the only integrating figure who could hold the country together. It was that insight that had made him leave Moscow—where he lived in effect as a foreigner after the dissolution of the Soviet Union—and return to Tiflis. He was willing to serve; he considered it his duty. Although, as usual, he radiated determination and clearheadedness, I sensed the heavy burden this responsibility laid on him. He spoke of our earlier collaboration with a touch of nostalgia; and I, too, felt transported back to that past, which was not so long ago. I must admit that the way we worked together and the way our personal relationship evolved were proof to me of the power of shared convictions, which are stronger than ideologies and political oppositions. Eduard Shevardnadze, who had opposed the war against Afghanistan; who had endorsed the peoples' right to self-determination, to human rights, to pluralistic democracy; and who had backed a market economy—this man had long ago ceased being my opponent. It was these shared basic convictions that enabled him to clear the way for Germany unity and to affirm the Paris Charter. We should therefore always remember what we owe him and his country, Georgia, what the president of this independent and sovereign republic accomplished, when he was the foreign minister of the Soviet Union, for a better Europe and for Germany's unification.

The diplomacy of visits and treaties concluded another stage in our European politics of responsibility. It was especially important during this time of revolutionary changes to build trust and contribute to stability.

15

The Resignation

A Personal Decision

I had held the post of foreign minister for eighteen years and had served as a member of the administration for almost twenty-three. These are very long terms given the fact that democracy means the regular transfer of responsibility. The German president, for example, may remain in office for no more than ten years. Elections and other events had seen to it that I did not have to leave office against my will. I therefore had an even greater responsibility to decide for myself the right time to resign. In the summer of 1991, after many discussions, my wife and I came to the conclusion that I should leave office before the following year's parliamentary hiatus—in the spring of 1992. That date would give my successor sufficient time to familiarize himself with his job before the national elections of 1994. The next foreign minister must be given an opportunity to develop a personal style, a personal profile, and a personal signature in Germany's foreign policy. I fully realized that my resignation might lead to speculations about whether I was trying to position myself more favorably for the elections to the federal presidency. Of course, I considered running for our country's highest office. But I have always been a parliamentarian and a cabinet member, and I could make my experience affect German politics in other ways. It would have been inconsistent for me to resign voluntarily after twenty-three years while angling for another office. I therefore decided to take advantage of the next opportunity to state publicly, even before my official announcement of resignation, that I had no interest in assuming the federal presidency. When the debate on the presidency began as early as November 1991—much too soon, in my opinion—I criticized the move in a newspaper opinion piece on November 10 and added that "at no time and under no circumstances" did I plan to run for the office of federal president.

My decision to resign before the summer break of 1992 did not prey on my mind in the following months; the die had been cast. But as always when weighty decisions were waiting to be made, my wife and I planned to discuss the matter again in the week between Christmas and the New Year. It turned out that we were even more firmly convinced than before that I had made the right decision. May 18, 1992, seemed the best date for my announcement, since that day marked the eighteenth anniversary of my assuming the post of foreign minister.

In January 1992 I told Helmut Kohl about my decision and gave him my reasons. He asked why I had scheduled my resignation for May; after all, there were a number of important international conferences set for June and July: an EC summit, the world economic summit in Munich, the CSCE summit in Helsinki, and the NATO summit. Kohl requested that I reconsider; perhaps it was better for me to postpone my resignation until the fall, if only so that there would be opportunities for proper farewells at these gatherings. I replied that though conferences offered good opportunities to say good-bye, there were also other opportunities. I thought it much more important for my successor to meet all the important people in the EC, the Western Alliance, CSCE, and among our world economic partners at these conferences—an opportunity not to be missed under any circumstances.

Our conversation was very calm and the mood was cordial, as was characteristic of the relationship we had developed over the years. We will always be connected, beyond the personal level, by having walked the road to German unity together, as well as by the struggle to get the FDP to agree to the courageous decision to form a government with the CDU/CSU.

Finally I also admitted that I was reluctant to retire from politics altogether. However, though I was retaining my seat in parliament, I planned to keep my own counsel for some time so as to avoid any possible rivalry with my successor and so as not to interfere in his work. I intended to run in the next parliamentary elections as well. This was a plan I mentioned in order to preempt the Chancellor's question as to whether my resignation was related to a run for the presidency. He had put that question to me a year earlier, and I had told him then that I had no such plans.

We agreed that we would not mention this conversation to anyone in our parties. It was not always easy for me, when I was with close confidants and friends, to keep silent about my decision.

I had also asked for an appointment with the President for later that same morning. I briefed him on the foreign policy situation and expressed my concerns about certain domestic developments. As I had promised the Chancellor, I did not mention the talk I had had with him. The silence weighed heavily on me, since over the years Von Weizsäcker and I had developed a close and trusting relationship. In many difficult situations he had stood by my side; his international reputation was a significant support for German foreign policy.

The Chancellor and I had agreed that the public announcement would be made in the second half of April, so as to give me time before the actual resignation to say good-bye, to wrap up my affairs, and to prepare my resignation properly without having to act surreptitiously.

At nine o'clock on the morning of April 27, 1992, my announcement was given to the press as planned. At the same time I made an announcement to the FDP's executive committee, and subsequently I informed my associates in the Foreign Office.

It had been extraordinarily difficult for me to keep my plans secret from my friends Roland Dumas and Krzysztof Skubiszewski when the three of us met on April 24, 1992, in Périgueux—Dumas's district. In continuing the discussion begun in Weimar, we concerned ourselves with future relations among our three nations. The Weimar Arc—comprising France, Germany, and Poland—was intended to initiate new prospects for Europe. Sitting outside in the sunshine, all three of us, I am certain, were aware of the closeness in our personal relationship. Talking with my two friends, I was repeatedly tempted to tell them about my plan to resign. But I could imagine the conflict of loyalty my revelation would cause them, since their superiors had no idea, and I refrained from acting on my natural impulse. I was keenly aware, to my great pleasure, of the close friendship Roland Dumas and I had forged, and I realized how close Skubiszewski was to both of us. It is my wish that the spirit that had come to link us will always reign among our three peoples. When I left France in the early evening, I knew that this had been my last encounter—of that nature, at any rate—with my two friends.

A talk had been scheduled in Prague with Jiři Dienstbier for Tuesday morning, the day after I announced my resignation. Our Czech friends were depressed: Saying good-bye was extremely difficult for them, and for me as well. We had gone through and achieved too much together, and had become close personally. I assured them that German policy would not change in any respect and that they could continue to count on me in future.

That evening the President and I left for an official visit to Washington; during the night of April 30 to May 1, 1992, I flew back to Europe to attend an informal ministerial meeting of the EPC in Porto. In the evening Deus Pinheiro hosted a dinner for us in Guimaraes, where the atmosphere and the conversations with my colleagues were dominated by my impending departure. I had always realized how closely we were connected, but that evening a further fact became clear: Europe lived here, represented by its foreign ministers, in a way we could not have dared to hope in our boldest dreams after the Second World War. Deus Pinheiro made my resignation the only topic of the dinner. He sang a Portuguese song, a traditional fado with lyrics he had written himself and dedicated to me. My other colleagues were equally cordial, so that I left Guimaraes knowing that, together with friends, I had created a new sense of fellowship in Europe, an atmosphere of humaneness that would also prove its mettle in difficult times because it was based on friendship.

On May 5 the European Council convened in Strasbourg. I am particularly pleased that I was still present for the admission of Estonia, Latvia, and Lithuania into the European Council, which occurred at this session. I had emphatically supported their admission against some political opposition in Germany. On the same day we also decided on the admission of Bulgaria and made the public announcement.

The following day I addressed the Bundestag in my capacity as minister of foreign affairs for the last time. The agenda included the first reading of the treaty between the Federal Republic and the Czech and Slovak Federal Republic on good and friendly relations and cooperation and of the treaty on friendly cooperation and partnership in Europe with the Hungarian Republic. We had already concluded similar treaties with Poland and Bulgaria. Step by step the unified Germany tightened its bonds with the pan-European course of events. "Thus they are elements of the pan-European architecture, which open up for our Continent the chance of a better, a more peaceful future," I remarked. "This architecture will last only if it is founded on respect for human rights, human dignity, and the peoples' right to self-determination." I went on to pay tribute to the historical dimension of the two treaties: in Prague, Václav Havel was now president. He, the great European, the man whose forceful words and exemplary political credibility had shown his people the road to freedom, had made a gesture of reconciliation to Germany by condemning what had been done to the Sudeten Germans as unjust. Would both sides find the strength to take advantage of the unique opportunity now available?

Once again I seized the chance to thank Hungary for its courageous stand in 1989; Germany would never forget. To remember always, with gratitude and respect, I noted, was an absolute necessity for the reputation, the reliability, and the credibility of German politics.

Balance Sheet and Outlook

At the end of my speech I took my leave of the Bundestag as minister of foreign affairs. I defined my resignation as a contribution to the credibility of our democracy, which fortunately conferred responsibility only for a limited time. I emphasized the values of our constitution and stressed our constitutional task to unify Europe and to serve world peace as the basis of and guideline for German foreign policy; thinking and acting in a European way, I stated, must oppose all forms of the new nationalism. I concluded my speech with the words: "Fraternity and solidarity, they are the only way the new Europe can come about, that is the only way we can do justice to the people of the Third World. Fraternity and solidarity, humaneness and understanding—we will need them if after national unification we Germans want to find our internal unity. The delegate Hans-Dietrich Genscher is determined to go on working toward that goal in future." The Bundestag thanked me with sustained applause, the delegates giving me a standing ovation. The demonstration filled me with gratitude—and with a little bit of pride.

As early as September 25, 1991, addressing the General Assembly of the United Nations, I had explained the unified Germany's politics of responsibility, reliability, and credibility with its partners and neighbors:

> Today I speak for the first time as foreign minister of the united Germany. Germany is taking its place in the family of the United Nations on the basis of the charter of our community of nations. As a nation in Europe we are committed to the Charter of Paris. Our people, united in one state, carry increased weight, which we see as an obligation to increase our sense of responsibility regarding freedom, democracy, and human dignity in a European Germany that has left behind the nation-state thinking of the past. . . . Germans want this Europe to evolve with close transatlantic ties. The North Atlantic Alliance and the United States' and Canada's participation in CSCE express that sentiment. . . . Germany is formulating the following goals for its policies: One, we want to turn the European Community, of which we are a founding member, into the European Union and finally into the United States of Europe. . . . Two, we want all democratic nations in Europe to be free to join that community. For the new democracies in Europe which are introducing a market economy, association with our community must pave the way to full membership. Three, we want to link all of Europe ever more closely on the basis of the Paris Charter. The peoples of the Soviet Union who are choosing a new form of coexistence as independent republics must have a place in that Europe as well. Europe will receive its new order in confederated structures. These will find their expression in diverse forms. They will do justice to structures that have evolved over time,

and they will grant the different regions new opportunities. With greater unity, Europe will also gain greater diversity. . . . Four, as a nation in the heart of Europe, we want to work with all our energies toward our continent's unity. The unique connection between Germany and France highlights that aim. To reach the goal, close cooperation with our Eastern neighbors is also important. I expressed as much in the Weimar Declaration of August 29, 1991, with my French colleague Roland Dumas and my Polish colleague Professor Krzysztof Skubiszewski. . . . The German-Czech treaty on good-neighbor relations and friendly cooperation is about to be signed as well. . . . Five, we wish to see the Western Alliance working toward stability in all of Europe under the new conditions. The contacts that have already been established with the former members of the Warsaw Pact, including the Soviet Union, must evolve into a comprehensive partnership in security. . . . We want the unremitting continuation of conventional disarmament according to the first CFE treaty; we want a worldwide ban on chemical weapons. The elimination of short-range nuclear missiles and nuclear artillery ammunition is paramount. These weapons always have a destabilizing effect, and the threat of their spread is increasing. We expect the nuclear powers to continue the reduction of strategic nuclear weapons. Six, we want to see CSCE enabled to take genuine action. After creating the Council of CSCE's Foreign Ministers and CSCE's urgency mechanism, on September 10 of this year I submitted concrete suggestions at the CSCE Conference on the Human Dimension in Moscow with the goal of a more efficient protection of the respect of human rights, of democracy, and of constitutionality; this protection must be possible even without the particular nation's consent. The right to self-determination and, in an immediate connection, the rights of minorities must be respected everywhere. Europe is developing toward greater identity and greater plurality. That evolution must not result in renewed nationalism. European structures must embrace these developments, we have to have European answers to all questions at hand. . . . Seven, we want the new Europe to realize its global responsibility. It must and will not deal only with itself. The development toward a Euro-Atlantic cooperative sphere extending from Vancouver to Vladivostok opens up an historic opportunity for the southern developing countries as well. . . . Eight, we want the United Nations to become an active center of the new world order. The actual implementation of the Security Council's resolutions, fully and unconditionally, is an absolute prerequisite to that end. Nine, for the sake of better coordinating the United Nations' auxiliary measures during disasters we are requesting the appointment of a high-ranking commissioner who is accountable only to the secretary general. . . . Ten, we want to strengthen the instruments that help justice and law prevail throughout the world. Our own history has obligated us in a special way to the constitutional state of liberty and to human rights. . . . We are demanding a court to which anyone can turn who feels that his or her human rights have been violated. We are demanding a ban on torture and on the death penalty. We need efficient international environmental laws and the establishment of an international control system. It must be possible to impose sanctions against nations that deliberately destroy the environment. Part of this effort is an effective fight against the waging of wars by methods that destroy the environment. . . . Eleven, as we want civil human rights to triumph; we also want a victory for economic and social human rights. The united Germany will continue to make a significant contribution to the development of Third World nations. . . . Twelve, we want the nations of the Third World to be equal participants in the dialogue on the future of humanity in all areas: politics, the economy, ecology, and culture. . . .

In my statement of resignation of April 27, 1992, I also drew up a balance sheet:

I am leaving office at a time when the lines of Germany's foreign policy are clearly drawn. Given the dramatic developments in Europe and in the world, such firmness is important both to us and to all our neighbors and partners. On March 15, 1991, Germany, which was unified on October 3, 1990, regained its full sovereignty. On September 25, 1991, I explained to the United Nations the unified Germany's position and foreign policy. Germany's foreign political road is clearly drawn, our foreign policy's focus on Europe is irreversible. We are pitting a European mentality against a new nationalism. We are staking our future on the values embodied in our constitution and on a politics of responsibility as opposed to power politics. We know that in the long run Western Europe would not fare well if Eastern Europe were faring badly. After amending our constitution, we are eager to assume all the rights and obligations of membership in the United Nations. After the national parliamentary elections of 1990, important European initiatives could be taken with the critical support of German diplomacy and, in most cases, at our instigation. The European Council in Maastricht; the Alliance's resolutions taken at the NATO ministerial conference in Copenhagen and at the NATO summit in Rome; the first convention of the CSCE Council of Ministers in Berlin; important steps toward the institutionalization of the CSCE process, and new tasks for our Alliance set by the establishment of the North Atlantic Cooperation Council, which encompasses a sphere of security from Vancouver to Vladivostok; and the decision in favor of the European Union and the new role of WEU. All these are the pillars upholding a pan-European architecture in which predictable as well as unpredictable events—above all in Eastern and Southeastern Europe—can occur within a pan-European framework of stability. In these crucial years since 1989 German-French friendship has again proved itself in the service of Europe; our joint cooperation with Poland takes our pan-European responsibility into account. I am pleased that the United States, with which we are linked by a degree of consensus hardly ever before achieved, will continue to honor its responsibility in Europe through its commitment to the Alliance, to the North Atlantic Cooperation Council, and to CSCE. The European Community's policies of association with the new democracies in Central and Southeastern Europe, which we have vigorously pursued, and the new models of cooperation for relations with the successor states of the former Soviet Union will gradually fill this architecture. The united Germany is linked to its immediate neighbors in the East, to Poland and Czechoslovakia, to the great Russian people, and to the other nations of Central, Southeastern, and Eastern Europe, by close ties of friendship and trust. Ratification of the contracts with Poland and the signing of the treaties with Czechoslovakia, Hungary, Bulgaria, and most recently, on April 21, 1992, with Romania have provided our relations with our immediate and more distant neighbors in the East with new perspectives. These pan-European policies are allowing us to keep the promise we made in the year of our unification, the promise to create a European Germany. The resolute steps toward conventional disarmament and the removal of short-range nuclear missiles and nuclear artillery ammunition that we had suggested, as well as the forthcoming accord on the worldwide elimination of chemical weapons, will increasingly demilitarize international and European relations and establish an ever stronger political, economic, social, and ecological understanding of stability. We are assuming our responsibility in meeting global challenges, overcoming the North-South contrast, as we are also doing in the global protection of the natural resources essential to life and in the prevention of the proliferation of weapons of mass destruction.

Partly in response to German initiatives, partly with Germany's crucial support, European and global structures had been generated over a period of time; now it was our task to utilize and develop them. Integrating Germany in the European and the transatlantic organizations (EU, WEU, European Council, NATO, North Atlantic Cooperation Council, CSCE, and United Nations); participating in G7; becoming part of the EU's global cooperation policies as they are explicated in the Lomé Treaty, in the EU-ASEAN cooperation, in the Euro-Arabic dialogue; as well as in the contacts of EU and Central America and EU and Contadora—these established the framework for Germany's policies in a fundamentally different situation in Europe and in the world. It is a situation characterized by overcoming the ideologically determined contrasts between Moscow and Washington as well as by the development of economic, political, and religious connections. This change, which also includes the increasing global expansion of international relations, affects not only Germany but all participants in international diplomacy as well; the other Western democracies must also meet the new European and global challenges. Their responsibilities include creating a lasting and just foundation for peace which, although laid down as early as the Harmel Report, did not become tangible until the East-West conflict was overcome. Germany's weight has, of course, increased since unification, not least because the nation has overcome the previous limits placed on independence and activism as a result of the division. Nevertheless, the new extent of responsibility in diplomacy receives its impact not so much from German unification as from the changes that have taken place in Europe and the world: The concept of German foreign policy as a politics of responsibility rather than of power has remained unchanged since unification. Only the continuation of these basic principles will provide the European Germany with opportunities to exert influence such as West Germany had gained before the reunification.

In early May 1992 Roland Dumas invited me to Paris. President Mitterand received me as well and thanked me for all I had done to promote German-French cooperation. We recalled our many

talks and joint efforts, and we agreed that German-French friendship must be permanent, independent of the individuals in power.

On May 11 I attended the meeting of the Council of Ministers
in Brussels, where I was given a formal farewell. Besides the president of the Commission, Council Chairman Deus de Pinheiro and,
as our senior colleague, my good friend Uffe Ellemann-Jensen
gave official speeches. I will always remember his words and the
tone in which he spoke.

On the afternoon of the following day, my wife, Barbara, and I
flew to London. Prime Minister John Major, who had briefly been
my counterpart as foreign secretary, received me at 10 Downing
Street. He thanked me and stressed the importance of German-
British friendship. In Carlton Gardens, the residence of the British
foreign secretary, Douglas Hurd held a dinner for Barbara and
me. He had also invited my former colleagues and their wives:
Francis Pym, Geoffrey Howe, David Owen, and Jim Callaghan;
only Peter Carrington and John Major were unable to attend. The
mood of the evening was cordial and relaxed and demonstrated
the wealth of trust that can be accumulated in many years of
cooperation. Such trust was extremely significant to German-
British relations, which did not always run smoothly but which
were so very important. At the conclusion of the evening Douglas
Hurd presented me with an etching of the House of Commons,
signed by all those with whom I had traveled part of the road.
Only the signature of Tony Crosland, Jim Callaghan's immediate
successor, who had since passed away, was missing from this
beautiful memento.

Much has been written and conjectured about German-British
relations, and frequently these relations were hampered by
presuppositions, by the detection of seeming conflicts and misunderstandings. And yet, the truth revealed on this occasion made it
clear that over a period of eighteen years not only a solid political
relationship but personal relations between men had developed in
a way that would have been impossible if all those stories about
mutual mistrust had had any basis in reality. It is possible that the
relationship among the foreign ministers is easier than are relations between the heads of government, but this may be simply
because we meet more frequently and have more opportunities for
discussion. Whatever the case, I left London with the certainty

553

that England and Germany had grown extraordinarily close since the end of the Second World War.

The years to come proved that Douglas Hurd and I had developed a close understanding as more than professional colleagues. Hurd had expressed an interest in attending the Wagner Festival in Bayreuth; when I invited him in 1991, last-minute political obligations forced him to decline. Immediately after the public announcement of my resignation I let him know that I considered it inappropriate for myself, the foreign minister who had just stepped down, to extend an invitation for 1992; I begged him to wait another year. When I discussed the matter with my successor, Klaus Kinkel, at the appropriate time, he was fully cooperative with my plan that I—now a private citizen—invite my former colleague and friend Douglas Hurd to Bayreuth for the opening of the 1993 Festival. As always, Roland Dumas came to Bayreuth as well; as frequently happened, we all stayed at the same hotel in Bischofsgrün. Thus we all joined together, even on opening night and again after the opening performance, a cheerful group at the familiar hotel. It was somewhat of a family reunion, the kind of informal party such as those who think of politics only as the calculated display of power and pursuit of personal interests may not imagine possible. Barbara and I are grateful for having had the privilege of meeting a man such as Douglas Hurd and his charming wife, Judy.

Ties of friendship also connected me to Jim Callaghan, my first British counterpart, who had received me with great cordiality; he was like a fatherly friend. His great experience opened many doors for an understanding of England, of the Labour Party, and of the relationship between party and unions, as well as an understanding of the conflict in Northern Ireland.

Peter Carrington and I also had a close personal relationship. He, the modern, enlightened conservative, once told me how Franz Josef Strauss, seated next to him during a dinner, had explained his view of the world as defense minister, assuming—as Carrington put it with his particular sense of irony—that an English lord must surely be at least as conservative as the Prime Minister of Bavaria.

My collaboration with Francis Pym was brief and for that reason could not grow as intimate as my relations with my other counterparts; the same holds true for Tony Crosland and John

Major, who was foreign secretary for less than a year. Yet the criticism subsequently leveled at him as prime minister seemed to me patently unfair. He is a committed European and a man who knows very well the appropriate place for England within the European family or in the European Community. It must always be borne in mind that in domestic as well as foreign policy but most important, in economic policy, the government he inherited was never easy or simple.

Geoffrey Howe and I understood each other exceptionally well. Since he distinguished himself by his deep loyalty to Margaret Thatcher, it cannot have been easy for him subsequently to have been among the group that opposed the Prime Minister. Once, when I was his guest at the British foreign secretary's country estate, we openly discussed our work and our positions within our administrations. Being foreign secretary in a Thatcher administration cannot have been easy, I realized. As an aside he mentioned that in the past he could not have imagined executing his office in a coalition headed by someone who belonged to a different party. More and more, however, he was coming to the conclusion that it might be an advantage to the foreign secretary to belong to a different party. My reply was short: "I know what you mean," I said, and we merely exchanged a glance. Nothing more needed to be said, and more would have transcended the boundaries of this honest and well-mannered diplomat's loyalty.

On May 13 in a restauant in Bonn I said good-bye to the press corps with whom the Foreign Office had worked particularly closely. Over the years we had developed a conversational relationship that mattered a great deal to the public interpretation and the general understanding of Germany's foreign policy. Nevertheless, the charge of cronyism between the Bonn journalists and Bonn politicians, which has frequently been leveled, is entirely unfounded. I always placed great emphasis on laying all my cards on the table, even in dealings with the press. Thus a relationship of trust was established, in which journalists were able to describe and explain our foreign policy with great clarity, even though it by no means prevented them from taking critical stands.

After receiving the papal nuncio on May 14, I flew to Bologna to attend the Gerold von Braunmühl Memorial Lecture. I myself had delivered the first lecture in the series; this time the speaker was Turkey's prime minister Suleyman Demirel, with whom I met before the lecture for a pressing reason. Turkey's dealings with its Kurdish population had been publicly criticized in Germany, and I too had taken a clear stand on the issue. NATO is a community based on the recognition of basic values, and the obligation to respect them must be discussed openly even among friends. For that reason our talk met with tremendous public interest. Fortunately, once again the stability of German-Turkish relations stood the test of time. Because of the significance of the relationship between Germany and Turkey, which is important to me, and because of the many Turkish citizens living in Germany, I placed great importance on reaffirming the quality of these relations at the end of my tenure. Most important, we learned that it was possible to express dispassionate criticism, even in public, on the issue of human rights—it is my belief that good friends are especially able to do so. No doubt having known and worked with Demirel for many years contributed to the sense of harmony. I had called on him when he was under house arrest during the military regime, and he knew that I had fought for continuing German aid to Turkey even at a difficult time. Our talk assured me that relations between Germany and Turkey had not worsened, even if differences of opinion were unavoidable, especially with regard to several statements by President Turgut Özal. Turkey's treatment of the Kurds forced Germany to openly voice its opinion, which was based on its constitutional values and the goals of the NATO Treaty.

On May 15 I hosted a farewell reception for the diplomatic corps. This occasion gave me another good and important opportunity to present my views on foreign policy by allowing me to make a concluding statement of my guiding principles. Just before the dinner the Danish ambassador, Knud-Erik Tygesen, presented me with a personal gift from our mutual friend Uffe Ellemann-Jensen: a standing desk. It has found a place in my study—a memento of a long-standing close friendship.

On Sunday, May 17, 1992, I flew to Berlin to attend a meeting of my party's executive committee, which was convening at the Villa Borsig. When I returned to Bonn the following morning, the ground crew at Wahn airport gave me a unique farewell reception: Several fire engines spewed water up into the air, creating impromptu fountains. Almost all the members of the ground crew had come to say good-bye to a notoriously frequent flier.

I lunched with the head of the Ministry, my personal press representative, all my other associates in the office, and the under-secretaries and ministers of state. In the afternoon of May 18 I went to the Villa Hammerschmidt, the residence of the Federal President, to accept the certificate of discharge he handed me in the Chancellor's presence. Afterward Richard von Weizsäcker, Helmut Kohl, and I sat on the terrace. After such a long term in office, I found myself disquieted after all. But not once did I question my decision.

On May 21 I assembled the personnel of the Foreign Office to say good-bye. When my wife, Barbara, and I went back to the Ministry a second time the same morning, we were greeted by my successor, Klaus Kinkel, who had been sworn in during the previous day's Bundestag session, and his wife.

I had gone in and out of this Ministry for eighteen years. A deep sense of gratitude toward my associates swept through me. Memories of painful and uplifting times, times of success and of defeat and struggle, passed through my mind. My team and I met in the World Hall, whose long wall is decorated with symbolic depictions of the continents.

What feelings predominate on such a day? Deep inside I had already departed, an important chapter of my life was closed. I could look back at it with a sense of unqualified satisfaction. It seemed to me an act of grace that I had been granted the privilege of holding such an office, and even more, of having been allowed to achieve everything I had set as my political goal and had fervently longed for. When I looked back at my twenty-three years as a member of the government, eighteen of them as foreign minister, I did so with a light heart and a clear conscience. I had been allowed to determine when to end my tenure; I was not leaving office as a consequence of political defeat, a change of administration, a loss of confidence, or even a mistake. That circumstance meant a great deal to me—it was reason enough for gratitude. My wife and I therefore left the Foreign Ministry without nostalgia, and above all, with our best wishes for Klaus Kinkel. It was good to know that, after we had walked such a long road together, he was in that chair.

Retrospection and Thanks in Halle

Long afterward, in late 1993, I had another reason for looking back and drawing up a balance sheet. On the morning of December 5 Mikhail Gorbachev, Henry Kissinger, and I discussed the prospects for a federated Europe during a live television broadcast. But important as the debate with these two great men was, what occurred afterward meant more to me: All three of us flew to Halle. How did this trip come about, and what did it mean?

When Mikhail Gorbachev was secretary general of the CPSU and president of the Soviet Union, and I was foreign minister of the Federal Republic of Germany, I had repeatedly told him, "I would love to welcome you as my guest in Halle one day." That invitation was extended long before unification. Repeatedly I used the fact that I came from Halle as a hook to address the problems of the division of Germany and our will to unification. My audience was meant to understand that we would never become resigned to the division of our country. I had said as much to my friends Roland Dumas, Jim Baker, Douglas Hurd, and Eduard Shevardnadze, all of whom I had been able to welcome in Halle. When I appeared with Mikhail Gorbachev at an event in Geneva in 1993, he said to me at lunch, "You've brought so many people to Halle—everyone except me." I replied, "My invitation to you still stands. If you wish, you can come this year." We agreed on December 5.

I had often spoken with Henry Kissinger about Halle as well. He was familiar with the central German landscape in part through his close associate Helmut Sonnenfeldt, who was from a small town in Altmark and thus is a son of Saxony-Anhalt, like myself. Now I asked Kissinger if he would like to visit Halle along with us in December. He agreed at once.

So it came about that our three planes landed at the Leipzig-Halle airport. From there we proceeded to Halle in two cars; Gorbachev, Kissinger, and I rode in the first one, while Raissa Gorbachev and my wife followed in the second. At the Halle-East ramp we exited the autobahn. On our way we passed Halle's Reideburg section, which at the time of my birth was a separate village of five thousand people. When I said, "The house where I was born is nearby," Gorbachev and Kissinger insisted that we go see it. We made a detour and stopped in front of the house where I had first seen the light of day. Then we proceeded to the city center.

On our first evening in Halle I played host as a private person and as an honorary citizen of Halle. I gave a dinner in the old courtroom in the Moritzburg, at which representatives of the city and the state of Saxony-Anhalt participated.

Now they were both here, the two men with whom I had worked so closely and to whom I owed so much. Henry Kissinger who, because of his Jewish background and the Nazi persecution, had emigrated to America, understood Germans even at the most complicated times, and he had been an important mentor to me when I was first in office. With his courageous policies, Mikhail Gorbachev, former secretary general of the CPSU and former president of the Soviet Union, had made the unification of Germany and of Europe possible. The United States and the Soviet Union were meeting in Halle—the United States whose army had conquered and liberated Halle in 1945, and the Soviet Union, whose army had occupied Halle on July 1, 1945, in accordance with the Allied agreements and whose occupation policies had dashed our hopes for a new democratic beginning for many decades. But on that night the former Soviet Union was represented by a man whose policies had opened the door to unity and to democracy in my homeland.

I owed a great deal to both men, Gorbachev and Kissinger, and I thanked them for what they had brought about after all that had been done by Hitler's fascism; these men had finally given Germany a new beginning. To me, this meeting also marked the conclusion of a course of events I had personally lived and suffered through with absolute commitment.

This visit to Halle is one of a number of encounters in that city whose symbolic value cannot be surpassed for me. In 1990, in the Market Church, standing with Dumas, I had held up the document of the Two-Plus-Four Treaty and had been able to say, "Roland Dumas has helped to create this treaty. His signature, like mine, is appended to this document to testify for all time that France and Germany are united as never before in their history." With Douglas Hurd I had listened to the *Messiah* during the Handel Festival. "I have returned to Halle," I had stated at the Market Church in December 1989. But I had not come alone; Eduard

Shevardnadze and I sat at the desks in my schoolroom, and we laughed as if we had been spirited back to childhood. And Jim Baker, the faithful friend and persistent supporter of German unification, who visited Halle in June 1991, was given a rousing welcome by the crowd. And now Mikhail Gorbachev and Henry Kissinger had come. All these visits clearly demonstrated to me that German unification was anything but a whim of history.

The circle closes. All our hopes and longings were fulfilled in Halle. In Halle I could thank all those who, in their different ways and at different times, had contributed to that moment. In a way that December weekend in 1993 was the culmination of my political work; the fact that I have been allowed to experience the completion of my task will always fill me with deep gratitude.

Glossary

Bold-faced terms within glossary definitions are defined elsewhere in the glossary.

ABM (Anti-Ballistic Missiles) Treaty: The ABM treaty was part of the 1972 **SALT** I Treaty concluded by the United States and the Soviet Union on the limitation of strategic-defense missiles. According to the Treaty, the development, testing, and installation of a comprehensive system of defense against ballistic missiles are prohibited. The treaty was intended to limit the arms race by allowing both superpowers to develop only a locally limited defense system. The ABM Treaty was an important initial step toward arms control and disarmament. The United States and the Soviet Union became embroiled in a controversy over whether United States' work on **SDI** is a violation of the Treaty.

ASEAN (Association of Southeast Asian Nations): ASEAN, established in 1967, includes Indonesia, Malaysia, Singapore, Thailand, the Philippines, and, most recently, Vietnam. The association exists to promote peace and economic prosperity in the region.

Basic Treaty: Its full name is Treaty on the Basis of Relations between the Federal Republic of Germany and the German Democratic Republic, and it was concluded on December 21, 1972. It regulated relations between the two countries with regard to equality and independence. Sections of the Treaty also dealt with the differences in interpretation of nationality and the national question. The regulations regarding humanitarian relief were of immediate practical significance.

BND (Bundesnachrichtendienst) [Federal Information Service]: The BND officially became active as the international branch of the secret services of the Federal Republic of Germany in 1956, collecting information from all over the world, especially from socialist countries.

Glossary

Bundesrat [Federal Council]: The Bundesrat represents the sixteen German states on a federal level and participates in the legislative process and administration of the Federation.

Bundestag [Federal Assembly]: The Bundestag is the parliamentary assembly representing the people of the Federal Republic of Germany. Its members are elected by the people every four years.

CCSE (Conference on Conventional Security in Europe): Held in Vienna from March 1989 to November 1990. The NATO alliance and the Warsaw Pact nations managed to agree on deliberations for actual disarmament of conventional weapons.

CDU/CSU (Christliche Demokratische Union/Christliche Soziale Union) [Christian Democratic Union/Christian Social Union]: Conservative party in the FRG, Federal Republic of Germany. It has been the ruling party since 1982, in coalition with the **FDP**. The CSU is the Bavarian sister party of the CDU.

CSCE (Conference on Security and Cooperation in Europe): The CSCE was opened on July 3, 1973, in Helsinki, the participants being the foreign ministers of thirty-three European nations as well as of Canada and the United States. The Helsinki Final Act, signed in August 1973, evolved into a process of cooperation in matters of security, trade, and culture between the two political blocs. Within the framework of the so-called CSCE follow-up meetings, which were usually held at two-year intervals, the CSCE process developed with its newly created CSCE institutions. Since January 1, 1995, the CSCE has been renamed Organization for Security and Cooperation in Europe (OSCE).

Contadora Group: Term applied to the group of nations made up of Colombia, Panama, Mexico, and Venezuela, whose foreign ministers met in 1983 on the Pacific island of Contadora to ease tensions between Nicaragua and the nations bordering it.

COMECON (Council for Mutual Economic Assistance): Economic association of the socialist countries, founded in 1949. COMECON was intended to be the socialist counterpart to the European Union. Members included Albania (until 1962), Bulgaria, CSSR, Cuba, GDR, Hungary, Mongolia, Poland, Rumania, USSR, and Vietnam.

Conference on CSBMs (Confidence- and Security-Building Measures): The conference on CSBMs took place from January 17, 1984, until September 19, 1986, in Stockholm and was based upon the second Madrid follow-up meeting of the **CSCE**.

CPSU (Communist Party of the Soviet Union): Dominant party in the former Soviet Union.

DNVP (Deutsche Nationale Volkspartei) [German National People's Party]: A conservative, monarchist party, the DNVP participated in some governments during the Weimar Republic until its new chairman, Alfred Hugenberg, led the party into a right-winged, anti-Weimar position.

EC (European Community): Collective term for the European Economic Community (EEC), the European Atomic Energy Community (Euratom), and the European Coal and Steel Community (ECSC). Founding members of the three communities are Belgium, the Federal Republic of Germany, France, Italy, Luxembourg, and the Netherlands. Subsequently the United Kingdom, Ireland, Denmark, Greece, Spain, Portugal, and finally Finland, Austria, and Sweden joined. The first step toward European unification was represented by the ECSC, founded in 1951, which was followed by the establishment of the EEC in 1957 and of Euratom through the so-called Rome Treaties. The community was further consolidated by the Single European Act (SEA) of 1985, which aimed at establishing the European single market by 1992 and economic and currency unification. This organization laid the foundation for the further development of the EC toward the **European Union** (EU). The European Economic Area (EEA), ratified by the Council of Europe, represented the most significant step toward the Maastricht Treaty, which at present marks the acme of European unification. The organs of the EC are the Council of Europe, the European Council of Ministers, the **European Commission**, the **European Parliament**, and the Court of Justice.

EPC (European Political Cooperation): The EPC was established in 1969 by the heads of state and government of the European Community (EC) member nations as a coordinating and consulting institution for matters of foreign and security policy. With the ratification of the Maastricht Treaty it was renamed Common Foreign and Security Policy (CFSP).

EURECA (European Research Coordination Agency): EURECA, founded in 1985, is a European initiative toward increased cooperation in research and technology. The aim is to improve Europe's competitive standing through enhanced industrial, technological, and scientific cooperation in key areas. The members, aside from the twelve member nations of the EC, are the European Commission, the EFTA nations, Turkey, and Hungary. The exclusively nonmilitary projects are determined by industry, the scientific community, and the governments of the member nations. They are organized through private initiative's and up to 50 percent of their costs may be subsidized.

European Commission: An organization within the EC that consists of seventeen commission members who are appointed by their governments for a four-year period. The Commission was established as a sort of planning group with the task of elaborating suggestions on the basis of the Treaty of Rome to accomplish their goals. According to this original concept, the Commission is solely dedicated to the common welfare, and thus it is unlike the European Council of Ministers, which represents the member nations. The Commission has developed into a highly differentiated administrative institution, where all data and activities of the EC converge and where most of them also originate. The Commission is obligated to present an annual report on all EC activities. Independent of the member nations and the Council of Ministers, it can be forced to step down only through a vote of no confidence by the **European Parliament.**

European Parliament (EP): Assembly of the EC (European Community), headquartered in Strasbourg. Direct elections send 518 delegates for a five-year term, proportional representation being accorded to reflect member nations' population. Party caucuses are formed on both supranational and national levels. The powers of the European Parliament are limited to control and counseling, and do not extend to legislating. The parliament has the right to determine its own budget and to put questions to the **European Commission** and the Council of Ministers; with a two-thirds majority it has the power to cast a vote of no confidence in the European Commission and force it to step down.

European Union (EU): Ratified in December 1991 at the summit of Maastricht, the Union Treaty—or **Maastricht Treaty**—intended the transformation of the **European Community** into a European Union with the long-term goal of a European federation. The uppermost decision-making organ of the European Union is the Council of Europe, which is charged with determining policy directives. To the earlier EC is added the Common Foreign and Security Policy (CFSP), which is intended eventually to lead to the development of a common defense.

EMU (European Monetary Unit): EMU is used to determine the value of international loans.

FDP (Freie Demokratische Partei [Free Democratic Party]): Center party in the Federal Republic of Germany. From 1969 to 1982 the FDP formed the government in coalition with the **SPD,** and since 1982 with the **CDU/CSU.** The Free Democrats are typically referred to as the Liberals, to express the fact that the party espouses political liberalism.

GATT (General Agreement on Tariffs and Trade): GATT was established in 1947 with the objective of achieving global free trade. GATT also functioned as a forum where problems in international trade could be discussed and multilateral negotiations could occur. In future the World Trade Organization (WTO) will assume this function. At the present time GATT membership stands at 123.

Harmel Report: Popular name given to the "Report on the Future Tasks of the Alliance," presented by Pierre Harmel on December 14, 1967, to NATO. The report codifies NATO's security strategy, based firmly in defense and détente, which is still in force.

Helsinki Final Act: See CSCE.

INF (Intermediate-Range Nuclear Forces) Negotiations: Negotiations between the United States and the Soviet Union on intermediate-range nuclear forces ended with the INF agreement of December 8, 1987, which called for the complete elimination of both nations' land-based intermediate-range nuclear weapons with a range of 300 to 3,500 miles.

Jungvolk [Young People]: The junior division of the Hitlerjugend [Hitler Youth]. The Jungvolk consisted of boys from ten to fourteen years of age.

KPD (Kommunistische Partei Deutschlands) [Communist Party of Germany]: The KPD was founded at the end of 1918 and played a major political role during the Weimar Republic until it was outlawed in 1933. Reestablished after the war in West Germany, the KPD was outlawed again in August 1956. Renamed the DKP the party was legalized again in 1968 with new statūtes and statements of purpose carefully crafted to be compatible with the Basic Law of the Federal Republic.

Lance: Mobile missile-firing system first stationed in 1972 by the U.S. forces, 1976 in several European NATO member nations.

564

LDPD (Liberaldemokratische Partei Deutschlands) [Liberal Democratic Party of Germany]: Founded in Berlin (East) in 1945 by Wilhelm Kuelz. The LDPD as East Germany's liberal party became one of the "bloc parties" that had to cooperate with the **SED** during GDR-times. Merged with the **FDP** on August 10, 1990 to create a liberal party for all of Germany.

Lomé Convention (Lomé Agreement): Comprehensive economic agreement, named for the capital of Togo, between the **European Community** (EC) and the developing nations of Africa, the Caribbean, and the Pacific. The agreement, covering a period of five years, was first concluded on February 25, 1975, and, with some modifications, has been renewed regularly.

LRTNF (Long-Range Tactical Nuclear Forces): Tactical nuclear forces with a range of 600 to 3,500 miles.

Maghreb Nations: Nations in the western section of the Arabic-Islamic world.

Mashrek Countries: Nations of the eastern section of the Arabic-Islamic world.

Maastricht Treaty: The heads of state and government of the European Community agreed at their meeting in Maastricht, Holland, in early December 1991 on a Treaty on the European Union (TEU), which signified thoroughgoing reform of all EC treaties and defined new areas of cooperation. The **European Union** is characterized by three so-called pillars: The principal one is the European Community Treaty, which succeeded the former EEC Treaty; it contains regulations for the European Economic and Monetary Union (EMU), which outline the establishment of a European central banking system and introduction of a common currency. In addition, there is the Common Foreign and Security Policy (CFSP), an expansion of the **EPC** (European Political Cooperation). All issues pertaining to security are handled by CFSP. The objective is the "eventual framing of a common defense policy," which "might in time lead to a common defense." Initially the institutions of the **Western European Union** are to be employed to that purpose. Finally there is cooperation in law and domestic policies, especially in regard to asylum and immigration policy and the war against drugs and terrorism. The Maastricht Treaty was signed by the foreign and finance ministers on February 7, 1992. After complicated ratification procedures in the various nations it finally went into effect on November 1, 1993. An Intergovernmental Conference (IBC) is scheduled for 1996 "to examine those provisions of the Treaty for which revision is provided, in accordance with (the TEU's) objectives."

MBFR (Mutual and Balanced Force Reductions) Negotiations: Negotiations on mutual and balanced reductions of military forces in Europe.

NATO (North Atlantic Treaty Organization): The North Atlantic Alliance was established on April 4, 1949, as a Western defense league. Its founding members pledged to provide mutual military assistance and to increase political, economic, and cultural cooperation. The North Atlantic Council, in which all member nations have a seat and a vote, is NATO's highest administrative organ. It convenes twice a year as a conference of foreign ministers or, as a defense planning committee (DPC), of defense ministers under the chairmanship of NATO's secretary general. The Council issues resolutions on NATO's common goals and activities. First signatories of the security treaty were Belgium, Canada, Denmark, France, Iceland, Italy, Luxembourg, the Nether-

Glossary

lands, Norway, Portugal, the United Kingdom, and the United States. Subsequently Greece, Turkey, the Federal Republic of Germany, and Spain joined as well, while France and Greece left in 1966 and 1974 respectively.

NATO Double-Track Resolution: Resolution of the North Atlantic Council, NATO's highest administrative organ, issued on December 12, 1979, on the modernization of INF (nuclear intermediate-range missiles). Parallel to planned modernization, the Soviet Union was offered negotiations on arms control, the topic of which were to be nuclear medium-range defense missiles on both sides. The NATO Double-Track Resolution led to the INF Treaty, sometimes referred to as the "dual-track" decision.

Nonproliferation Treaty: Name given to the Treaty on the Nonproliferation of Nuclear Weapons, signed by the United States, the United Kingdom, and the Soviet Union on July 1, 1968. A number of additional countries, among them the Federal Republic of Germany, joined in the agreement. The nuclear powers of France and China, however, have not joined.

OSCE: See **CSCE.**

PLO (Palestine Liberation Organization): Founded by the first Palestinian national council in Jerusalem June 1, 1964, PLO claimed as its official goal the liberation of Palestine. The PLO, led by Yasir Arafat since 1967, is the head organization of all Palestinian liberation movements.

perestroika: Literally: *rebuilding, restructuring.* After Gorbachev took office as General Secretary of the Central Committee of the CPSU in March 1985, the term became synonymous with overall modernization of the social, political, and economic system of the Soviet Union.

Pershing 1 and 2: U.S. nuclear surface-to-surface missiles. The P.1-A, developed in 1962, had a range of approximately 460 miles; the following Version P.2, developed in 1985, had a range of approximately 1,100 miles. Both systems were abolished under the **INF**-treaty.

Politburo: The leading party and governing body in the Eastern European socialist systems.

SALT (Strategic Arms Limitation Talks): Terms for negotiations between the United States and the Soviet Union, conducted since 1969, that resulted in SALT I in 1972 and SALT II in 1979. SALT II, however, was never ratified, especially as the result of the war in Afghanistan.

SDI (Strategic Defense Initiative): A United States research program for the development of modern strategic defense systems against ballistic missiles. The project, introduced by President Ronald Reagan on March 28, 1983, has also been called the Star Wars program because the combat against intercontinental missiles was to take place predominantly in outer space and in part over enemy territory.

SED (Sozialistische Einheitspartei Deutschlands [Socialist Unity Party of Germany]): Dominant party in the former German Democratic Republic.

SNF: Short-range Nuclear Forces.

SPD (Sozialdemokratische Partei Deutschlands) [Social Democratic Party of Germany]): Traditional left-of-center party in the Federal Republic of Germany. During the so-called great coalition with the **CDU/CSU,** the SPD formed the government from 1969 to 1972; in coalition with the FDP, the SPD ruled from 1972 to 1984.

SRINF: Short-Range Intermediate Nuclear Forces.

SS 20: Soviet surface-to-surface and ship-to-ship missiles. The mobile, highly accurate SS 20 (Saber) was first stationed 1977 and had a range of approximately 3,000 miles.

START (Strategic Arms Reductions Talks): The negotiations on the reduction of strategic nuclear weapons began on June 29, 1982, as a continuation of the SALT process. No concrete preliminary result was achieved until the signing of the treaty between the United States and the Soviet Union on the reduction of strategic nuclear weapons in 1991. The negotiations, continued with nations of the former Soviet Union, led to the START II treaty of January 3, 1993, which scheduled the reduction of existing nuclear weapons potential by two-thirds.

SWAPO (South West African People's Organization): Resistance movement in Namibia, founded in 1958.

Two-Plus-Four Treaty: The signing of the treaty on the final settlement with respect to Germany in Moscow on September 12, 1990, marked the end of the postwar era for Germany. The accord confirmed that Germany, after the restoration of its unity on October 3, 1990, had regained its full sovereignity.

WEU (Western European Union): WEU was established in 1954 as a Western European regional pact within **NATO.** The alliance has the following members: Belgium, Federal Republic of Germany, France, Greece, Italy, Luxembourg, the Netherlands, Spain, Portugal, and the United Kingdom; Iceland, Norway, and Turkey are associates.

Vance Plan: Cyrus Vance (Secretary of State 1991–1993) was chairman of the Conference on Yugoslavia in Geneva. The Vance Plan to station armed UN-forces in certain parts of Croatia was accepted by President Tudjman on December 11, 1991.

Volkskammer [People's Chamber]: On October 7, 1949, the Volkskammer declared itself as the parliamentary body of the GDR and put the constitution into force. Article 50 declared the Volkskammer to be the highest legislative organ of the German Democratic Republic.

Waffen-SS (Waffen-Schutzstaffel) [Armed Elite Guard]: The military arm and the largest branch of the SS. Originally the black-shirted personal guard of Hitler but later transformed by its leader, Heinrich Himmler, into a major armed force on which was to rest the ultimate exercise of Nazi power.

Index

Index

Index

Index

Mischnick, Wolfgang, 40, 44, 46
Missiles: ABM treaty, 216–217, 561; definitions, 561, 564, 565; double-track resolution (see NATO, double-track resolution); double-zero option (see Double-zero option); INF Treaty, 217, 220, 228–229, 230, 564; Lance, 59, 68, 232–259, 359; Mitterand-Gorbachev talks and, 177; modernization of short-range, 232–259, 296, 298, 300, 334, 359–360, 384, 393, 398, 417, 429–430, 551; NATO Reykjavík conference and, 207; nonproliferation treaty, 145–146, 565; Pershing (see Pershing missile); SALT, 154, 176, 181, 217, 220, 561, 565; Soviet Union dissolution and, 530; START, 536, 565–566; zero options (see Zero options). See also Arms control; Defense; Disarmament; Strategic Defense Initiative (SDI)
Mitterand, François, 50, 51, 108, 133–134, 136, 140–141, 163–164, 169, 176–177, 185, 189, 190, 191, 206–207, 222, 267, 275, 295–296, 307–310, 321, 323, 324, 330, 333, 337, 365–366, 395, 458, 484, 502, 503–504, 505, 513, 552
Mladenov, Petar, 396
Mock, Alois, 1, 359, 493, 494, 496
Modrow, Hans, 302, 312, 330, 331
Mondale, Walter, 148
Montenegro, 506, 507, 512
Montfort, Norbert, 152
Morocco, 478
Moscow. See Soviet Union
Moscow Declaration, 398, 403
Moscow Treaty, 48–49, 71, 95–96, 179, 181, 183, 289, 293, 314, 318, 522
Moscow Two-Plus-Four meeting, 439–457
Mozambique, 120
Mubarak, Hosni, 176
Mudge, Dick, 120
Mulroney, Brian, 349
Munich Olympic Games, 25–37
Münster meeting, 412–416, 420
Muskie, Edmund, 151, 152–153
Mutually balanced force reductions (MBFR), 218–219, 564

Namibia, 119–124, 126, 133, 352–353, 357–359
Nastase, Adrian, 540
Nationalism, 138, 140, 236, 282, 294, 321, 459, 461–462, 467, 537, 548, 549, 550
Nationalities: rights of, 504, 508, 509–510, 511, 513, 515
National Socialism. See Socialism
NATO (North Atlantic Treaty Organization), 56, 59, 61, 65–66, 68, 72, 95, 97, 101, 107–108, 126, 134, 135, 136, 137, 138–139, 147, 149, 156, 158, 188, 191, 207, 216, 219, 224, 236–237, 240, 241–243, 244–247, 250–251, 253–259, 267, 274, 297, 298, 301, 304, 306, 307, 308, 310–311, 315, 319, 325–326, 333–342, 344–345, 347–350, 355, 356, 358–359, 360, 361, 365, 367, 368, 371, 374–376, 382, 384–394, 395–399, 402–407, 409–411, 414–415, 418–420, 422–424, 425–426, 428–432, 443, 452, 457–458, 462, 478, 482, 483, 484, 496, 512, 523, 530, 536, 540, 544, 551, 552, 556, 563–565, 566; double-track resolution, 59, 134, 154–156, 157, 160–168, 177, 180–181, 188–189, 191, 203, 214–215, 218, 227, 231, 246, 305, 565. See also Double-zero option; Harmel Report; Missiles; Zero options
Nazarbayev, Nursultan, 531–535
Németh, Miklos, 277, 279, 300
Netherlands, the, 139, 156, 237, 244, 348, 484, 496, 498, 502–503, 505–506, 508–509, 512, 537, 562, 565, 566
Neubauer, Representative, 9–10, 11, 285
Neutrality, 236, 274, 294, 333, 334, 337, 342, 356, 388–389, 402, 405
Neutron bomb, 146–150
Niezabitowska, Malgorzata, 289
Niklas, Ambassador, 8
Ninth Army, 19, 20
Nitze, Paul, 160, 226, 254, 281, 282
Nixon, Richard, 59, 61–63, 105, 186
Nollau, Günter, 40–41, 42–44, 45–46
Nonalignment, 127
North Atlantic Alliance, 61, 233, 247, 250, 255, 282, 418, 443, 548, 551, 564
North Atlantic Cooperation Council, 335, 358, 530, 540, 541, 551, 552, 564–565
North Atlantic Treaty Organization. See NATO
Norway, 158, 244, 565, 566
Nuclear Nonproliferation Treaty, 145–146, 565
Nuclear weapons: West Germany's renunciation of, 342, 384, 392, 425, 428. See also Arms control; Disarmament; Missiles
Nujoma, Sam, 120, 122, 352–353
Nunn, Sam, 254
Nyerere, Julius, 170

Obminski, Ernest, 391
Oder-Neisse Line, 3, 76, 85, 96, 181, 273–274, 289–290, 306, 320, 321, 365
Oder offensive, 18
Ogarkov, Nikolai, 159
Olszowski, Stephan, 77–78, 84, 85
Olympic Games, 25–37, 157–158
Open Skies Conference, 338–339, 344–350, 360, 442
Ordóñez, Francisco Fernández, 256, 351–352
Organization for Security and Cooperation in Europe (OSCE). See Conference on Security and Cooperation in Europe (CSCE)
Orlov, Yuri, 103
Ottawa conference. See Open Skies Conference
Owen, David, 121, 553
Ozal, Turgut, 556

Pacific countries, 133, 564
Pakistan, 173
Palestine Liberation Organization (PLO), 54

576

Index

Index

East and, 53, 54, 150–154; Namibian conflict and, 121–122, 123; NATO and, 65–66, 126, 207, 368, 565; NATO double-track resolution and, 134, 154–156, 157, 160–162, 180–181; Persian Gulf War and, 471, 472, 473, 476–477, 479, 480, 483, 484–485; Russia and, 358–359, 530; Soviet Union and, 24, 52, 58, 60–62, 63, 68, 103, 104–105, 109, 180, 181, 182, 183, 186, 187, 189, 190–191, 196, 202, 203, 214, 215–222, 223, 224–226, 228, 230, 268, 269, 297, 311–312, 324, 338, 402, 406, 409–410, 411, 446, 448, 460–461, 475, 477; united Germany and, 296–300, 311, 312, 338–341, 349, 356, 359–361, 376, 379, 384–385, 395, 396, 397, 433, 448, 452–453, 454, 457–458, 461, 548, 551, 552, 559; United Nations and, 114, 352; West Germany and, 52–54, 56–66, 116, 118, 122, 137, 145–150, 154, 155, 171–172, 177, 178, 182, 203, 217–224, 228, 229, 236, 240–251, 253–259, 263–265, 266–267, 268, 285–286, 296–300, 312, 322–326, 338–341, 344, 349, 356, 359–361, 384–385, 411, 416, 419, 420–421, 431, 433, 457–458, 473, 476; World War II and, 18–19, 20, 21; Yugoslavia and, 491, 493, 496, 504, 508, 519–520. *See also* Defense; Four Powers; G7; Western Alliance
United States of Europe, 548
Ustinov, Dmitri, 74, 159
Uzbekistan, 526

Vance, Cyrus, 121, 145, 146, 147, 148, 149, 156, 517–518
Varkonyi, Peter, 176
Vatican, 90–92. *See also* Catholic Church
Versailles Peace Treaty, 338, 390
Vienna review conference, 107–109, 195–196, 230, 239, 243, 267, 340, 361, 362, 409, 411, 440, 444
Violence, 37, 120, 194, 507, 518, 519. *See also* Terrorism
Vogel, Hans-Jochen, 25, 27, 34, 163, 496
Vogel, Wolfgang, 2, 285
Volkskammer, 22, 336, 351, 356, 368, 434, 437

Walesa, Lech, 81, 86, 87–89, 278–279, 288
Walters, Vernon, 249–250, 322, 323, 324, 494
War: graves of, 82–83. *See also* Afghanistan; Persian Gulf War; World War II; Yugoslavia
Warsaw: East German refugees in, 5, 6. *See also* Poland
Warsaw Pact, 59, 68, 73, 74–75, 80–81, 87, 90, 95, 97, 99, 100–101, 103, 107–108, 110, 129, 158, 159, 166, 202, 221, 228,

239, 255, 258, 259, 264, 269, 273, 277–278, 282, 293, 306, 323, 334–336, 338, 341, 355, 358, 387–388, 393, 396–399, 402–403, 405, 409, 410, 414, 419, 424, 425–426, 443, 522, 530, 541, 549
Warsaw Treaty, 48, 71, 75–76, 95–96, 289, 293, 314
Watergate Affair, 52, 59
Wechmar, Rdiger von, 55
Wehner, Herbert, 38, 39, 43, 46
Weimar Arc, 465–467, 545–546, 549
Weinberger, Caspar, 205
Weizman, Ezer, 56
Weizsäcker, Richard von, 138, 208–209, 210, 225, 246–248, 263, 361, 367, 370, 463, 539, 545, 546, 557
Well, Günther van, 61, 96
Wellhausen, Hans, 39
Wenck, Walter, 18, 19, 20
West Berlin. *See* Berlin
Western Alliance, 49, 53–54, 61, 65–66, 68, 76, 81, 95, 105, 134, 155–156, 161, 167, 183, 191, 203, 216, 219, 222, 229–230, 232, 235, 236, 239, 243, 244, 245–246, 248, 251, 254, 257, 259, 265, 282, 289, 291, 298, 307–308, 315, 334, 336–337, 358–359, 371, 393, 402, 405–406, 419, 422, 483–484, 544, 549, 551. *See also* North Atlantic Alliance
Western European Union (WEU), 475–476, 504–505, 551, 552, 564, 566
West Germany. *See* Federal Republic of Germany
Weston, John, 369
Winzer, Otto, 96, 102
Wischnewski, Hans-Jürgen, 133
World War II, 4, 12, 16–20, 60, 68, 76
Wörner, Manfred, 220, 221, 243, 418–419, 422
Wyszynski, Stefan, Cardinal, 87

Yakovlev, Alexander, 265, 527
Yalta, 202
Yeltsin, Boris, 526, 529, 532
Young, Andrew, 121, 122
Yugoslavia, 91, 100, 109, 110, 141, 166, 170, 472, 487–521, 533–534, 536
Yurkans, Yanis, 528

Zagladin, Vadim, 313
Zero options, 154, 158, 161–162, 163, 177, 214, 216, 217, 218, 220, 233, 238, 245, 257
Zero-zero option, 59, 68, 165, 214–231, 417
Zhelev, Zhelyu, 531
Zhivkov, Todor, 74–75
Zhou Enlai, 173